NELSON BALANCED SCIENCE

THE material WORLD

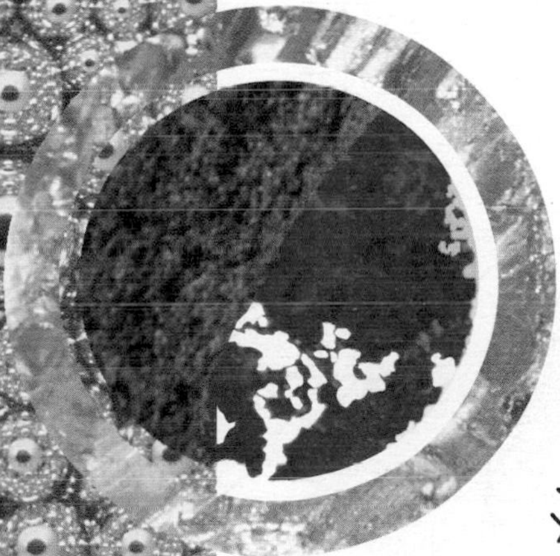

John Holman

Nelson

To Thomas, Alice and William

Thomas Nelson and Sons Ltd
Nelson House   Mayfield Road
Walton-on-Thames   Surrey
KT12 5PL UK

51 York Place
Edinburgh
EH1 3JD UK

Thomas Nelson (Hong Kong) Ltd
Toppan Building 10/F
22A Westlands Road
Quarry Bay   Hong Kong

Thomas Nelson Australia
102 Dodds Street
South Melbourne
Victoria 3205   Australia

Nelson Canada
1120 Birchmont Road
Scarborough   Ontario
M1K 5G4 Canada

First published by Thomas Nelson and Sons Ltd 1991

ISBN 0–17–438406–8
NPN 9 8 7 6 5 4 3 2 1

Printed in Hong Kong.

To the reader

The Material World is about chemistry. It's about the materials the world is made from and the way new materials can be produced. Studying chemistry helps you understand how materials behave, whether they are in the kitchen, in your clothes or in a builder's yard. It helps us understand how to make better materials, how to get the energy we need and how to protect the environment.

The book is split up into short topics. Each topic includes Activities (with a blue background) — things to do in the lab and at home — and Questions (mauve background). There are also case studies and extension exercises (with a green background) which take some of the ideas a bit further.

You'll notice that there are references to the two other books in the **Nelson Balanced Science** series. Michael Roberts' book **The Living World** is mainly about biology and Ken Dobson's **The Physical World** is mainly about physics. By using our books together we hope you will enjoy finding out about science — and that you'll want to study it further.

John Holman, January 1991

Many people have helped me write this book, particularly Michael Roberts, Ken Dobson and Judith Ramsden. I would like to thank the following for helping me with particular topics:

Eileen Barrett, Mineral Industries Manpower and Careers Unit
Tony Travis, Hebrew University of Jerusalem
Carole Lee, University of Hong Kong
Neil Hart, Watford Grammar School
Tony Williams, ICI Fertilisers
William Stanton, Somerset
Dick Garbett, ICI Petrochemicals
David Bott, Courtaulds Research
David Knight, University of Durham
Peter Borrows, ASE Laboratory Safeguards Committee
Bernard Aylett, Queen Mary and Westfield College, London
Peter Sunderland, Ind Coope Burton Brewery
David Fielding, Radley College
MJ Keavney, ICI Chemicals and Polymers

Contents

A1 Changing substances

Chemistry is about what things are made of, and how we can change them.

Picture 1 The stages in making a clay pot: (1) shaping

Picture 2 (2) drying

Picture 3 (3) firing

Think about the stages in making a clay pot. You take a lump of wet clay, then you change its shape so it's pot-like. If you don't like the result, you can easily reshape it. Once you have the shape you want, you let the wet clay dry. As it dries, it becomes hard, but quite crumbly. Even now you *could* reshape it: you would have to soak the dry clay in water to make it soft again.

When the clay is dry, you 'fire' the pot by heating it in a kiln. Now the clay changes a lot. Its colour changes, and it becomes much harder and no longer crumbly. However long you soak it in water, it stays hard. In other words, *it has changed permanently*. Fired clay is a different substance from unfired clay. Try activity A if you haven't done pottery for a while.

Pottery is chemistry

Making a pot involves changing one substance into another. This is what chemistry is all about. Notice these things about chemical changes:

- They involve making new substances
- They usually involve energy transfers
- They can usually be explained if we know the **chemical formulas** of the substances involved — the atoms it contains, and the way the atoms are arranged.

This last point is an important feature of chemistry, and we will come back to it many times in the book. You can find out in topic C7 about the changes that happen to the arrangement of atoms in clay when it is fired.

Who uses chemistry?

You do, I do — everyone does. Living things are constantly changing one substance to another, so life is all about chemistry.

Many people use chemistry as part of their work.

Cooks use chemistry all the time. They may not have studied chemistry like you, but they learn by experience how to control the changes that happen when food is cooked.

Farmers use chemistry, when they decide how to neutralise acid soil, or how much fertiliser to use.

Doctors use chemistry, because everything that goes on in the human body involves chemistry.

Engineers use chemistry, when they decide what materials to make things from.

People who have trained as chemists work in hospital laboratories, in breweries, in oil refineries, in food laboratories and in factories making

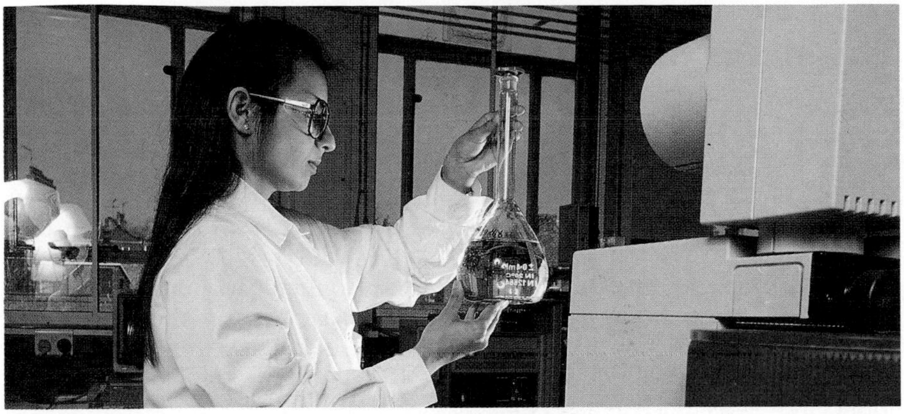

Picture 4 This chemist is checking the purity of a water sample

everything from plastics to poppadums. Chemists do a particularly important job in protecting the environment from the effects of human activities (pictures 4 and 5).

Matter and substances

'Matter' is the name that scientists give to anything that has mass. You and I are made of matter; so is this book and so is the air you are breathing.

Scientists also use the word 'substance'. This means a particular type of matter, which you can put a name to. Salt is a substance, and so is water. Light is not a substance, because it isn't matter and it has no mass.

Chemistry involves studying the properties of substances. If you know the properties of a substance, you can say what it could be used for — and how it might be changed.

In a chemical change, one substance changes to another. Take charcoal for example, which is nearly pure carbon. When this sustance burns, it joins with oxygen in the air to form a new substance, carbon dioxide. We can summarise this change as

carbon + oxygen → carbon dioxide

This summary is called a **word equation**. You can also write a summary using the formulas of the substances involved. This is called a **balanced equation**, and in this case it would be

$$C + O_2 \rightarrow CO_2$$

There is more about equations in topic C4.

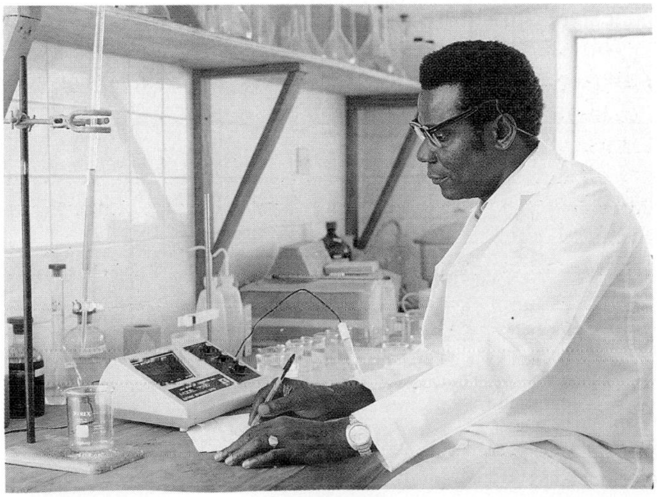

Picture 5 Chemists analyse substances, to find out what is in them, helping to protect our health and our environment

Activities

A Changing clay

Try these activities using ordinary clay from your school pottery.

1 Take some wet clay and divide it into two equal pieces. Mould each piece into a pot or other shape.
2 Leave the clay to dry. This will take a few days.
3 Examine the dry clay. How has it changed?
4 Fire *one* of the dry pots in a kiln. You will have to come to an agreement with the pottery teacher!
5 When the pot has been fired, compare it with the unfired one. How has it changed?
6 Put both the clay pots (the fired and the unfired one) into a container and cover them with water. Leave for a day.
7 After one day, carefully pour off the water and examine the clay. What do you conclude?

B Changing Plaster of Paris

Plan an experiment, similar to the one with clay, to see whether Plaster of Paris changes chemically when you mix it with water. Before you carry out any experiment, get your plans checked by your teacher.

Questions

1 Which of the following are *substances*?
(a) Water (b) Sugar (c) Electricity
(d) Alcohol (e) Sound (f) Oxygen.

2 Which of the following involve chemical changes? Remember — in a chemical change a new substance is formed.
(a) Burning wood (b) Drying wet wood
(c) Turning wood to charcoal (d) Slicing bread (e) Turning bread to toast
(f) Burning gas (g) Boiling water.

3 When magnesium burns, it gives out a bright white light and gets very hot. The magnesium turns into a white powder. Give *two* pieces of evidence that this is a chemical change.

A2
Matter and materials

Matter is what the world is made of. This topic is about matter and how we can make use of it.

Picture 1 Serving drinks at the fast food restaurant involves all three states of water — ice, water and steam from hot drinks

The states of matter

There are three states of matter: solid, liquid and gas (picture 2). **Solids** have a fixed shape — think of an ice cube. **Liquids** have no fixed shape, but they take up the shape of their container and their volume is fixed — think of a litre of water. **Gases** have no fixed shape or volume. They spread out (**diffuse**) to fill all the available space — think of steam coming out of a kettle.

Gases are usually invisible, which makes it difficult to think of them as matter at all. But we know gases are a form of matter because they have mass. You can weigh gases — though their density is low, so they don't weigh much. A balloonful of air weighs about 10 g. A bedroomful of air weighs about 75 kg — as much as a person!

Most substances can exist in all three states, depending on the temperature. Water is a solid (ice) below 0°C, a gas (steam) above 100°C and a liquid between these temperatures.

When we say 'water is a liquid', we mean that the substance scientists know as H_2O is a liquid at normal temperatures. 'Normal' temperature is around 20°C in Britain. But if you live in the Arctic it might be more sensible to say 'water is a solid', because it certainly is that most of the time.

You can decide the normal state of a substance if you know its melting point and boiling point. For example, the element bromine has a melting point of −7°C and a boiling point of 59°C. So at the 'normal' temperature of 20°C, bromine will be melted but not boiled. In other words it will be a liquid.

Changes of state

The state of a substance can be changed by heating or cooling (picture 3). Notice the words used to describe the changes of state shown in the picture.

You will see that liquids can be turned to gases by *boiling* and by *evaporating*. Liquids can evaporate even when they are cold. This is just as well, because we rely on water evaporating from wet clothes to get them dry.

Subliming means turning directly from a solid to a gas, without melting to a liquid first. It is less common than other changes of state. Carbon dioxide sublimes. If you cool carbon dioxide gas to about −55°C, it turns directly to a solid. If you allow the solid to warm up, it turns straight back to carbon dioxide gas, without melting. This makes it useful for keeping things like ice creams cool, and it is sometimes called 'dry ice'.

Air is a gas at normal temperature, but you can condense it into a liquid by cooling it to −194°C. You can even freeze it to make solid air if you cool it a bit further.

There is more about changes of state in topic C1 on the kinetic theory.

Look around you. What state of matter is the most common where you are at the moment? Unless you are reading this in the bath, it is likely to be the solid state. Admittedly there is a lot of invisible gas in the air around you, but

SOLID
LIQUID
GAS
Solids have a fixed volume and shape
Liquids have a fixed volume, but they take the shape of the container
Gases don't have a fixed volume – they spread out to occupy all the space available

Picture 2 The three states of matter

the furniture, the building, your clothes and even you yourself are all in the solid state.

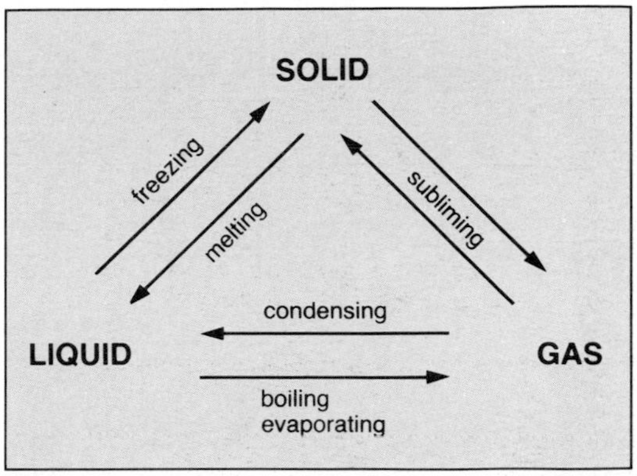

Picture 3 Changes of state

Materials — matter for making things

The word 'material' has several meanings. We often use it to describe the fabrics used to make clothes. But to a scientist or an engineer, a material is a form of matter, normally solid, which is used to make things.

Materials for packaging food

Have a look inside a food cupboard. You will see containers made from all sorts of materials. There are cans made from **metal**. Drinks and some foods come in bottles and jars made from **glass**. There are boxes and bags made from **plastic** or **paper**. There may be pots made from **china**. There might even be some boxes made from **wood**.

These different materials have different properties that make them suitable for packaging different foods. Metals are tough and malleable, so a can doesn't break when you drop it. Glass is transparent, so you can see what's inside. Plastic is waterproof and flexible, and paper is cheap and easily printed on. China is hard and easy to clean. For a particular type of food a material is chosen that is best suited to the food concerned.

One of the many useful things that chemistry can do is help you to explain the properties of different materials. Chemists can find out the **structure** of materials — the way their atoms and molecules are joined together. Once the structure is known, it's quite easy to explain properties — why plastics are flexible and metals tough, why glass is transparent and china hard. There is more about structure and properties in topic C6.

Once you can explain properties, you can change them to suit your needs, and then make the material you want. This is what **materials scientists** do — they can design materials to suit almost any need. You want a soft, transparent material for contact lenses? You can have it, made from a special plastic. You want a material that will withstand the high temperatures of a supersonic plane? You can have it, made from a nickel or titanium alloy.

Picture 4 Food containers can be made from many different materials

Classifying materials

Materials can be classified in several ways.

Natural or human-made?

Wood is a natural material, but metal, glass and plastic are made by humans. Paper is a bit of both: it's made by humans, starting with a natural material (wood).

Making materials is an important human activity, and it has been going on for thousands of years. Metals are obtained from ores, and china is obtained from clay. Glass is made from sand and limestone, and paper is made from wood. These are the **raw materials** from which they are manufactured. You take a raw material that is worth very little, like iron ore, and you turn it into a material that is much more valuable, like china pottery.

Picture 5 For years, people used buckets made from wood. Today, metal and plastic have replaced this traditional natural material

What kind of properties?

Another way of classifying materials is by their properties. Metals are a group of materials with similar properties, and these properties make metals very different from plastics.

When you classify materials according to properties, they fall into five major groups: metals, ceramics, glass, plastics and fibres. Think of the food containers again.

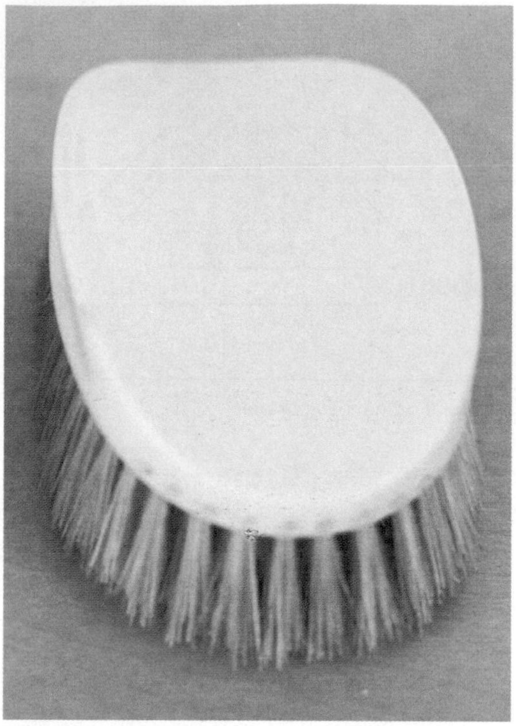

Picture 6 What modern materials are used to replace ivory? Why is it important to do this?

Cans are made from steel or aluminium, both **metals.**

China jars are made from a **ceramic**. The word ceramic comes from a Greek word meaning pottery, but ceramics include a whole range of materials made from clay, including bricks and concrete as well as pottery.

Bottles are made from **glass**. There are many different kinds of glasses with different properties.

Bags and boxes are made from **plastics**. Plastic materials are flexible and easily moulded, and today there are thousands of different types.

Bags and boxes may also be made from paper or cardboard. These materials are made of cellulose **fibres** obtained from wood. Fibres are materials that form long, thin, strong strands. Fibres such as cotton, wool and polyester are used to make clothes.

We will meet all these different types of materials again later in this book. For now, you can see a summary of their typical properties in table 1.

Notice the following points about table 1.

- The properties given include *physical* properties such as strength, hardness and melting point and *chemical* properties such as reaction with air. Both of these are important when deciding which materials to use for a job.
- The raw materials for manufacturing materials mainly come out of the ground: ores, clay and crude oil, for example.
- Ceramics and glasses have quite similar properties (hardness, brittleness, etc.) and both contain the elements silicon and oxygen.
- Plastics and fibres have similar properties (flexibility, etc.) and both contain the elements carbon and hydrogen. Both belong to a larger group of materials called **polymers** (topic H3).

Try questions 2, 4 and 5 at the end of this topic to help you get familiar with the information in table 1.

Table 1

Type of material	Examples	Typical properties	Manufactured from	What chemical element do they contain?	Where can you find out more about them?
METALS	Iron, copper	• Strong • Hard • Malleable — can be bent • High density • Conduct heat and electricity well • May react with air, water and acids	Ores dug out of the ground	Metallic elements	Topic E1
CERAMICS	China, bricks	• Hard • Strong when compressed, weak when stretched • Brittle • High melting points • Heat resistant • Chemically unreactive	Clay and other minerals dug out of the ground	Mainly silicon, oxygen, aluminium, hydrogen	Topic C7
GLASSES	Bottle glass, lead crystal glass	As for ceramics, but also • transparent	Sand, limestone and other minerals dug from the ground	Silicon, oxygen and various metallic elements	Topic C7
PLASTICS	Polythene, polystyrene	• Flexible • Easily melted and moulded • A wide range of properties depending on the particular plastic • May burn when heated in air	Crude oil	Carbon, hydrogen and various other non-metals	Topic H3
FIBRES	Cotton, polyester	• Form long, strong hair-like strands • Flexible • May burn when heated in air	Natural fibres: plants and animals Human-made fibres: crude oil	Carbon, hydrogen and various other non-metals	Topic H3

Picture 7 Pyrex (borosilicate) glass is particularly strong and heat-resistant

Activities

A Changing the state of iodine

CARE Iodine has irritating vapour and it is harmful if it contacts your skin. You *must* work in a fume cupboard for this experiment.

Wear eye protection. Put one very small crystal of iodine in a test-tube. Heat the crystal *very, very gently* — you should do no more than gently wave the tube from side to side well above the bunsen flame. Observe carefully to see what happens to the solid iodine as it is heated. What change of state has occurred?

Repeat the experiment using a new test-tube and a new crystal of iodine. This time heat the iodine a little less gently — hold the tube in the tip of the flame. Again observe to see what change of state occurs.

Discuss your results with other groups of students. Do you all agree what happened? Try to explain any differences.

B A survey of materials

Make a list of a least 20 different objects and the material each is made from. The objects might be around your home, your school or any other place where a wide variety of different objects are to be found. Try to choose objects that are made from a single material, rather than complex objects like a radio that are made from lots of different materials.

Put your results in a table like the one below (two examples have been entered in the table to help you).

Object	Material it is made from
cup	china
paper clip	steel

Once you have collected your list, try to classify the materials in each of the following ways:

1 Natural or human-made materials.

2 Metal, ceramic, glass, plastic or fibre materials.

3 Materials that would or would not have been used a hundred years ago.

C Identifying materials

Suppose you are given a piece of a material that is painted black so you cannot tell its normal appearance. Plan the tests you would do on the material to decide whether it is metal, ceramic, glass, plastic or fibre. Remember, your tests must be safe.

Your teacher may give you some samples of materials to try out your tests on.

Questions

1 a What are the three states of matter?

b What words are used to describe the following processes? (For example, the answer to (i) is 'melting'.)

i) Turning a solid to a liquid.
ii) Turning a liquid to a gas.
iii) Turning a gas to a liquid.
iv) Turning a liquid to a solid.
v) Turning a solid to a gas.

c What do you get when you carry out each of the following processes?

i) Condensing steam.
ii) Subliming ice.

2 What will be the state of each of the substances A — D at 20°C?
Substance A, melting point 1064°C, boiling point 3080°C.
Substance B, melting point 29°C, boiling point 669°C.
Substance C, melting point −112°C, boiling point −117°C
Substance D, melting point −39°C, boiling point 357°C.

3 Classify each of the following materials as metal (M), ceramic (C), glass (G), plastic (P) or fibre (F):

concrete brass polystyrene Pyrex Perspex silk solder brick hair nylon leather earthenware raffia granite rope glaze (the shiny surface coating on pottery)

4 Classify the materials listed in question 3 as natural or human-made.

5 Classify each of the materials described in (a) — (f) as metal, ceramic, glass, plastic or fibre.

a A hard, brown material which melts at over 1000°C.

b A shiny material which can be bent without breaking.

c A transparent material which melts at 130°C.

d A transparent material which melts above 800°C.

e A grey material which conducts electricity.

f A white material which melts and catches fire when heated.

A3 Choosing materials

Choosing the right material means suiting the properties of the material to the job it has to do.

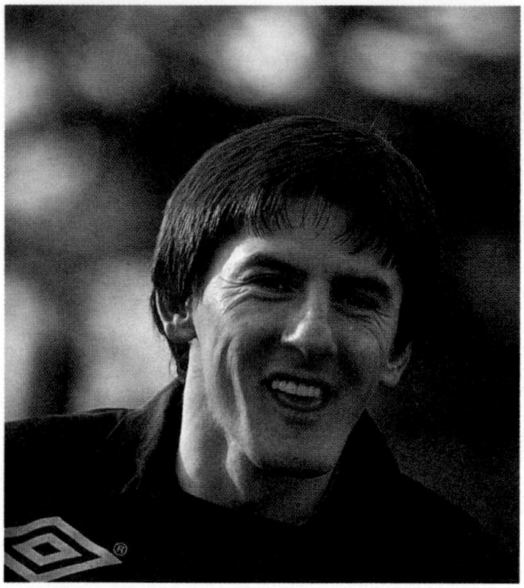

Picture 1 Peter Beardsley has false teeth, though you wouldn't know it. They are made from a material that looks and behaves just like the real thing

What kinds of materials are used to make false teeth?

You will probably think first of plastics — a white acrylic plastic is often used. Sometimes a ceramic, a kind of porcelain, is used instead of plastic. Metals are less common, although gold teeth are still popular with some people, and metals are often used for fillings. Fillings are also made using a special type of glass. As far as I know, fibres are not used for false teeth — although George Washington is said to have had teeth made out of wood.

When you choose materials for a job, you have to make sure their properties are right. False teeth have a demanding job to do. They are constantly bathed in saliva, which is quite corrosive. The material chosen has to be hard, waterproof and unreactive, and preferably tooth-like in appearance. What's more, it has to be reasonably priced, which is why you don't see many gold teeth. Acrylic plastic is fine in all these ways, but Washington's wooden teeth must have given him all sorts of problems.

The right properties for the job

When you are considering a material for a particular purpose, you have to ask some basic questions.

Are the physical properties right?
Physical properties mean things like hardness, strength, density (The Physical World, topic A2), and melting point. If these properties are wrong, there is no chance of the material doing the job.

Are the chemical properties right?
Chemical properties are to do with the chemical reactions of the material. Does it burn or corrode in air? Is it attacked by water or acid? These considerations are important if the material is to last and be safe.

Is the price right?
It's no use getting the properties of the material right if it costs a fortune.

Let's look at an example. Suppose it is the 50th anniversary of your school and you want to produce a commemorative drinking vessel. Think about the properties it will need. These will be the **criteria** for deciding the material to use.

First the physical properties. It should be hard and strong so that it lasts a long time. It should not conduct heat well, so it will keep drinks warm. It must have a reasonably high melting point so that it can stand hot liquids.

What about the chemical properties? It should be chemically unreactive so that it will last a long time without corroding. It must not react with drinks that are acidic.

And the cost? Naturally it must be as low as possible, so that everyone will buy it.

With these criteria in mind you will probably decide against metal because of corrosion problems. A fibre isn't really on, because the vessel needs to be completely waterproof. Glass would be all right, but it's not very easy to decorate. That leaves ceramic or plastic, and which you go for will probably depend on the price. In the end you may well go for a ceramic mug made of china because that will last well — but remember it is more likely than plastic to break if dropped.

Picture 2 Early airplanes were made from wood and even paper, but now we use stronger materials like aluminium

Composite materials — the best of both worlds

Sometimes you want a material that combines the properties of two different materials.

Glass-reinforced plastic is an example. It's used to make the body of things like boats and caravans which need to be light but strong. Plastic resin is light and quite strong, but it cracks easily. Glass fibres are also strong, and flexible. Glass reinforced plastic has a plastic **matrix** with glass fibres embedded in it (picture 3). The glass fibres give the plastic extra strength so that it does not crack when it is bent or hit.

Glass-reinforced plastic is an example of a **composite material** — it contains two or more materials working together. Concrete is another composite, and you can read about it in *The Physical World*, topic A2. Table 1 gives some more examples of composite materials.

Nature uses composite materials a lot. Bone is a composite: it is made of protein with calcium phosphate added. Calcium phosphate is hard and without it the bones would be soft and flexible.

Many of the most useful modern materials are composites. More and more, we are turning to these combinations of materials to get the exact properties needed for a particular job.

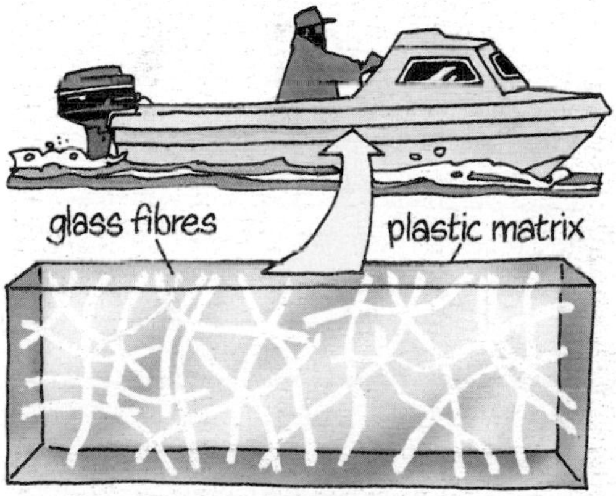

Picture 3 Glass-reinforced plastic

Table 1 Some composite materials

Material	Made from	Advantages	Uses
Bone	Calcium phosphate matrix reinforced with protein fibres	Harder than protein, more flexible than calcium phosphate	Skeletons
Reinforced concrete	Concrete matrix with steel reinforcing rods	Stronger than concrete, cheaper and lighter than steel	Construction
Glass-fibre reinforced plastic	Plastic matrix (often polyester) reinforced with glass fibres	Stronger than plastic, less brittle than glass	Boats, lightweight vehicles
Carbon-fibre reinforced plastic	Plastic matrix reinforced with carbon fibres, which are very strong	Much stronger than plastic, cheaper than carbon fibre alone	Golf clubs, fishing rods, tennis racquets, aircraft parts
Tyre rubber	Rubber reinforced with rayon fibres or steel wires	Stronger than rubber, but still elastic and flexible	Tyres for cars, bikes, etc.

Picture 4 The ancient Egyptians used clay and straw when they made bricks — an early example of a composite material

Activities

A A survey of materials and uses

Choose 10 different objects from around your home and decide what material they are made from. (If you have done activity B in topic A2, you could choose your objects from the list you made then.)

For each object, answer each of these questions to decide why that particular material was used.

1 What *physical* properties of the material make it suitable?

2 What *chemical* properties of the material make it suitable?

3 Is the *cost* of this material suitable? If it wasn't for cost, could another, better material have been used?

B Looking for composites

Look around your home to try and find at least 10 examples of composite materials. If possible, try to decide what separate materials each composite is made from, and why these are used.

C Finding out about special materials

Use a library or some other source of information to find out about the following new or unusual materials:

1 car engines made from ceramics instead of metal — what are the advantages, and what kind of ceramics are used?

2 'Kevlar' (also called aramid), a fibre that is so strong it is used to make bullet-proof vests;

3 'Teflon' (also called ptfe), the most slippery material known. What is it used for, and why is it so slippery?

4 heat-resistant materials that are used in fire blankets and heatproof mats;

5 superconducting materials, which have zero electrical resistance when they are cooled in liquid nitrogen.

Questions

1 What are composite materials? Why are they often used instead of single materials?

2 Here is a list of materials:

steel earthenware pottery polythene cotton glass concrete wood aluminium Bakelite (a hard, brown plastic which is difficult to melt)

Which material or materials would be suitable for each of the following uses? If you think none of the materials is suitable, suggest a different one. In each case, give the reason for your choice.

a The casing for an electric plug.

b A container for concentrated sulphuric acid.

c The lining for a furnace.

d A dustbin.

e The barrel of a pen.

f An air filter.

3 Suppose you are planning a journey to the centre of the Earth in a self-propelled tunnelling machine. What special materials would be needed to build the machine?

4 During the Battle of the Atlantic in World War II it was suggested that icebergs should be towed into the middle of the ocean and turned into floating landing strips for aeroplanes. Unfortunately, ice tends to crack easily so the idea was never used. What modifications could be made to ice to get over this problem?

5 Here are some words that can be used to describe the properties of materials:

strong
electrical conductor
high melting point
transparent
brittle
dense
hard
malleable
low melting point
flexible
flammable

Which of the words describe the *typical* properties of each of the following materials?

a metals,

b ceramics,

c glasses,

d plastics,

e fibres.

Choosing materials

Table 1 gives some properties of different materials. Use the table to answer 1 to 4 below.

1 Tennis racquets

The frame of a tennis racquet needs to be strong and stiff, yet light. Traditionally, tennis racquet frames were made from wood, but to get a strong and stiff enough frame you have to use a lot of wood. This gives a thick, heavy frame. Nowadays racquets come in a number of different materials.

For each of the possible materials a) to d) below, list what you think are the advantages and disadvantages of the material for making tennis racquet frames:

a) steel
b) aluminium
c) nylon
d) carbon-fibre reinforced plastic.

2 Canoes

At one time canoes were made of wood. Modern canoes are usually made from glass-fibre reinforced plastic.

Explain why glass-fibre reinforced plastic has largely replaced wood. Suggest *one* other material that might be used instead. Remember to bear cost in mind as well as properties.

3 School chairs

List the criteria that must be considered when choosing a material for making school chairs.

Now use these criteria to select the best material in the table for this purpose.

4 Car bodies

Most cars have bodies made from steel. What other materials in the table *could* be used instead? Are any of them ever used in fact? Why do you think steel continues to be much the most popular material for car bodies?

5 Classifying the materials

Classify each of the materials in the table as **metal, ceramic, glass, plastic, fibre** or **composite.**

Table 1 Some properties of selected materials

Material	Description	Density/ (kg/m^3)	Strength/ GPa	Stiffness/ GPa	Cost
Steel	Grey metal which rusts readily unless protected	7800	1	210	Low
Aluminium	Silvery metal	2700	0.2	70	Low
Wood (spruce)	Brown fibrous material which rots unless protected	500	0.1	20	Low
Polythene	Plastic which can be given any colour	960	0.02	0.6	Low
Nylon	Plastic which can be given any colour	1100	0.08	3	Medium
Kevlar	Plastic or fibre which can be given any colour	1450	3	190	High
Glass-fibre reinforced plastic	Plastic matrix containing glass fibres. Can be given any colour	1900	1.5	21	Medium
Carbon-fibre reinforced plastic	Plastic matrix containing black fibres	1600	1.8	200	High

Picture 5 This golf club is made from a composite material: plastic reinforced with carbon fibre

A4 Elements — the building blocks for materials

Every substance on Earth is made from the same building blocks — the 92 elements.

Picture 2 When wood is heated, it decomposes to form carbon

Picture 1 These materials all look very different. Despite their variety, they are all made from some of the same 92 elements

Have you ever felt spoilt for choice? You go shopping and you can't decide what to buy from the enormous choice available? It's the same with clothes, food — and materials for that matter. There is an almost infinite selection of materials available, both natural and human-made.

Yet all this choice is built from less than a hundred chemical elements.

What is an element?

Iron and wood are both materials. Iron is an element, but wood is not. The difference is that wood can be turned into simpler substances, but iron cannot. If wood gets hot, it chars — it turns black on its surface. The wood has broken down (**decomposed**) and formed carbon, which is the black solid. But no matter what you do to the carbon, you cannot break it down any more. It is an element.

An element is a substance that cannot be broken down into any simpler substance.

Obviously, wood is not an element, because it can be broken down to give carbon (and other substances as well). On the other hand, iron *is* an element, because whatever you do to iron you cannot turn it into anything simpler.

There are 92 elements occurring in nature. Another 12 or so have been made artificially by scientists. Each element is given a **symbol** of one or two letters. For example, oxygen is O and chlorine is Cl. There is a full list of all the elements and their symbols in the Data Section.

The 92 elements range from reactive gases like chlorine to unreactive metals like gold. All these different elements can be classified according to their various properties. One simple way is to classify them as metals or non-metals (page 116). A very important classification system is the Periodic Table (topic F1).

What is a compound?

Consider water. For centuries scientists believed this familiar substance to be an element. We now know that water can be decomposed to form hydrogen and oxygen, which means it isn't an element. On the other hand, hydrogen and oxygen cannot be decomposed any further, so they *are* elements. Hydrogen and oxygen are **combined** together in water, and water is a **compound** of hydrogen and oxygen.

A compound is a substance made by chemically combining two or more elements.

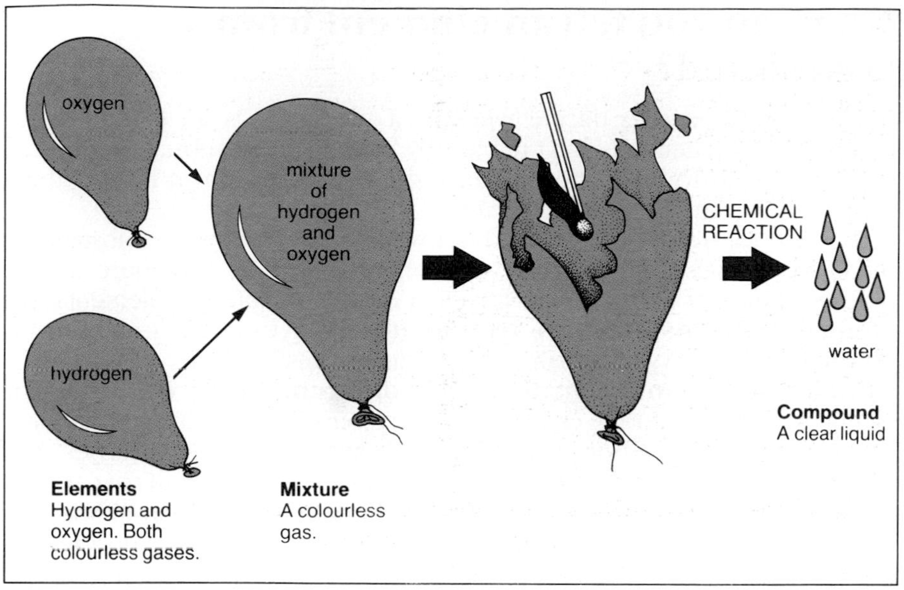

Picture 3 A mixture of elements is different from a compound made by combining them

Combining elements to form a compound is different from simply mixing them together (picture 3). When you make a mixture you get something that still looks like the starting substances, just mixed together. But a compound usually has *completely different* properties from the elements it is made from.

Salt is a good example. If you melt salt, then pass electricity through it, the salt decomposes. You get a green gas called chlorine and a soft metal called sodium. Both these substances are elements because you cannot break them down any further. But you can easily make them combine together again by warming the sodium with the chlorine, when you get salt again. Salt is a compound of sodium and chlorine; its chemical name is sodium chloride.

As you can see from picture 4, the compound sodium chloride has very different properties from the elements sodium and chlorine. You would be very unwise to eat either of these elements, but sodium chloride is an essential part of your diet.

Combining sodium and chlorine to form sodium chloride is an example of **synthesis** — building up simple substances into more complicated ones. Synthesis is the opposite of decomposition.

Names and formulas of compounds

The chemical name of a compound often tells you which elements it contains. The name sodium chloride tells you the compound contains the elements sodium and chlorine. The ending **-ide** shows the elements are combined together, not just mixed. A chemical name like 'sodium chloride' is more useful to a scientist than a common name like 'salt' because it tells you what elements are present.

Some compounds have names ending in **-ate**. This usually means that oxygen is present as well as the other two elements. For example, copper sulphate contains copper, sulphur and oxygen.

Every compound has a **formula** which tells you the elements that it is made from. The formula of sodium chloride is NaCl — Na and Cl are the symbols for sodium and chlorine. The formula of water is H_2O, which tells you it contains the elements hydrogen (H) and oxygen (O). The number 2 tells you there is twice as much hydrogen as oxygen.

You can find out more about formulas in topic C3.

Picture 4 Sodium chloride (salt) is very different from the elements it is made from

How can you tell an element from a compound?

It isn't always easy to decide whether a substance is an element or a compound. You certainly can't tell just by looking at the substance. You can do experiments to see if the substance can be broken down into anything simpler, but even this isn't always easy.

The sure way to decide is to find out what kind of atoms the substance is made from. Everything is made of atoms (topic C3), and there are 92 different kinds of atom — one for each of the 92 different elements. **An element contains only one type of atom.** For example, iron contains only iron atoms, oxygen contains only oxygen atoms.

Compounds contain at least two different kinds of atom. For example, sodium chloride contains sodium atoms and chlorine atoms. Sugar is a compound of carbon, hydrogen and oxygen (formula $C_{12}H_{22}O_{11}$). It contains three different kinds of atoms — carbon, hydrogen and oxygen.

If you know the formula of a substance, you can tell straight away whether it is an element or a compound. You just look at the formula and decide how many different elements are present.

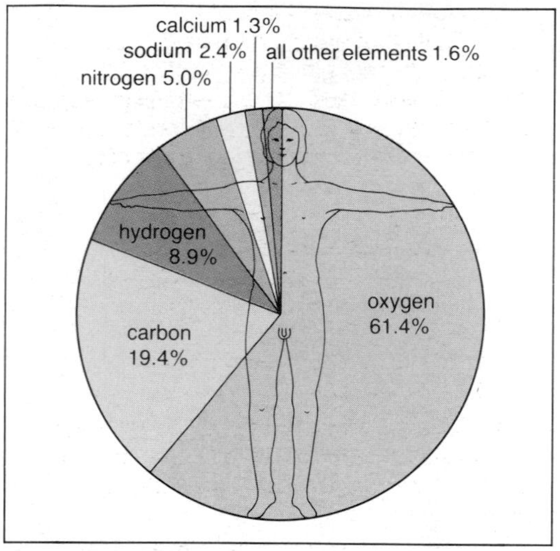

Picture 5 The main elements in the human body

Elements in your body

Everything is made of elements, and your body is no exception. Picture 5 shows the proportions of different elements in the human body. These elements do not occur on their own in the body. They are combined together as compounds — thousands of different ones.

You can see that 95% of the mass of the body is made up of just four elements — oxygen, carbon, hydrogen and nitrogen. More than half the mass of the human body is water, so it's not surprising that there is so much hydrogen and oxygen. Apart from water, the main compounds in the body are proteins, fats and carbohydrates (topic H3).

Fats and carbohydrates are made from carbon, hydrogen and oxygen, while proteins also contain nitrogen. So you can see why these four elements are so abundant in the body.

We get the elements our bodies need from the food we eat. That's why it is important to eat a balanced diet that will provide all the elements you need in roughly the right proportions. Elements like iron, copper and zinc are only present in tiny amounts, but they are still vital for good health. These are known as trace elements.

There is more about food and diet in *The Living World*, topics C1 to C4.

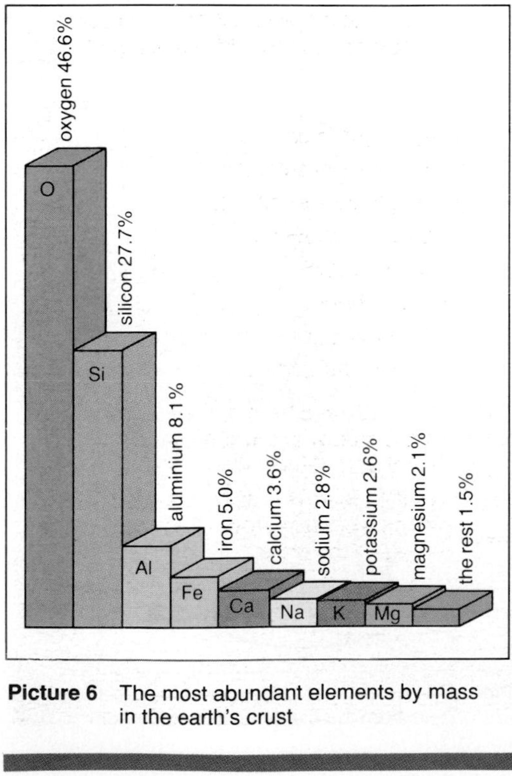

Picture 6 The most abundant elements by mass in the earth's crust

Elements in the Earth

The elements we need for our diet start off in the Earth and in its atmosphere — and eventually end up there again. The same is true for every one of the elements we use for making houses, clothes, furniture, fuels, medicines and other necessities. All the raw materials we need to keep life going come from the Earth. To be more exact, they come from the Earth's atmosphere, oceans and crust. The Earth's crust is the thin layer of rock, about 50 km deep, on the surface.

Picture 6 shows the eight commonest elements in the Earth's crust. There are 92 elements to be found on Earth altogether, but these eight account for more than 98% by mass of the Earth's crust. The remaining 84 make up only 1.5%. What is more, the two most abundant elements, oxygen and silicon, make up almost three-quarters of the mass of the Earth's crust.

Picture 7 These strata get their colours from elements like Iron, which are abundant in the earth's crust

Very few of the elements in the Earth are uncombined. Most occur combined with one another as compounds. Most of the oxygen and silicon in the Earth are combined together in rocks. Sand is almost pure silicon oxide. Clays also contain silicon and oxygen, together with aluminium, which is the third most abundant element after silicon and oxygen.

Iron is the fourth most abundant element, and most of it is combined with oxygen as iron oxide, also called iron ore. Calcium, the fifth most abundant element, is mostly combined with carbon and oxygen as calcium carbonate, the compound in chalk and limestone.

Topic D2 has more about the storehouse of raw materials to be found in the Earth.

Activities

A Elements in your food

Look at the tables of ingredients on a range of foods and drinks. Tables of ingredients are found on the label or package.

Use these tables of ingredients to make a list of elements present in the foods.

In some cases elements may be mentioned by name. Most of the ingredients that are mentioned will be compounds, though. Try to work out what elements are present in as many of these compounds as you can. Use information given in this topic and in other parts of the book.

Compare your list of elements with the elements shown in picture 5. Which elements from picture 5 do not appear on your list? Suggest reasons why.

B Explaining about elements

The idea of elements and compounds is quite difficult to understand. Often the best way to see if you understand something is often to try and explain it to another person.

Find someone who does not know much science. It might be a neighbour or a relative. Try to explain to them the difference between an element and a compound.

Afterwards, get them to tell you how well you did. Try to find out how much they really understand. You could test their understanding by getting them to do some of the questions at the end of this topic!

Questions

When answering these questions, you can get information about elements from table 1 in this topic, and from page 00 of the Data Section.

1 The formulas of several substances are listed below:
(a) CH_4, (b) $CuSO_4$, (c) Zn, (d) $CaCO_3$, (e) Fe, (f) Cu, (g) MgS, (h) $AlCl_3$, (i) $NaNO_3$, (j) H_2, (k) HBr, (l) S_8, (m) $C_6H_{12}O_6$, (n) He, (o) V_2O_5, (p) $BaCl_2$, (q) Ag.

For each substance:

i) say whether it is an element or a compound;

ii) name the elements that it contains.

2a Explain what is meant by the terms i) synthesis and ii) decomposition.

b Each of the word equations below describes a chemical reaction. For each reaction, say whether it is an example of i) synthesis or ii) decomposition.

1. mercury oxide → mercury + oxygen
2. carbon + oxygen → carbon dioxide
3. aluminium + sulphur → aluminium sulphide
4. calcium carbonate → calcium oxide + carbon dioxide
5. potassium chlorate → potassium chloride + oxygen
6. iron + chlorine → iron chloride

3 What elements are present in each of the following compounds? In each case, give the name and symbol of each element present:

a hydrogen bromide,
b magnesium sulphide,
c magnesium sulphate,
d aluminium iodide,
e potassium nitrate,
f zinc fluoride,
g tin chromate,
h gallium arsenide.

4a Use picture 5 to list the elements in the human body in order of abundance, most abundant first.

b Use picture 6 to list the elements in the Earth's crust in order of abundance, most abundant first.

c Would you expect the two lists in (a) and (b) to match up in any way? Do they in fact?

Lavoisier's Elements

Antoine Lavoisier was a great French scientist. He was born in 1743 and became a civil servant. But he also developed an interest in science and he was especially good at very accurate experimental work. This helped him to make discoveries which other scientists missed because their results were not accurate enough.

Lavoisier was executed in 1794 by French revolutionaries because he had been a tax-collector. After his death a colleague said, 'It only took them an instant to cut off his head, and a hundred years may not produce another like it.'

In 1789 Lavoisier published a book called *Traité Elementaire de Chimie*. It explained his ideas about burning and the air and it changed people's thinking about chemical reactions. In fact, many people say this book marked the beginning of chemistry as a subject in its own right.

One of the important ideas Lavoisier put forward in this book was the idea of elements, which he called in French *substances simples*. He listed 33 things that he thought were elements. The list as it appeared in his book is shown in table 1.

Use table 1 to answer question 1.

1 Use your knowledge of French, plus guesswork, plus (as a last resort) a French dictionary, to translate into English all the names in the middle column (the one headed 'Noms nouveaux').

Check and correct your answer to question 1 using table 2 on page 17. Use the corrected table to answer the remaining questions.

2 Two of the things in Lavoisier's table of elements are not even substances. Which two?

3 Of the remaining substances, five are not in fact elements, but compounds. Which five? Use the table of elements in the Data Section to help you if necessary.

4 For each of the five substances you have mentioned in your answer to 3, find out the proper chemical name. For example, the proper chemical name for *lime* is calcium oxide. You may have to use an encyclopaedia or an advanced chemistry book to find them all.

5 Why do you think Lavoisier thought that these five compounds were elements?

192 DES SUBSTANCES SIMPLES.

TABLEAU DES SUBSTANCES SIMPLES.

	Noms nouveaux.	*Noms anciens correſpondans.*
Subſtances ſimples qui appartiennent aux trois règnes & qu'on peut regarder comme les élémens des corps.	Lumière	Lumière.
	Calorique	Chaleur. Principe de la chaleur. Fluide igné. Feu. Matière du feu & de la chaleur.
	Oxygène	Air déphlogiſtiqué. Air empiréal. Air vital. Baſe de l'air vital.
	Azote	Gaz phlogiſtiqué. Mofete. Baſe de la mofete.
	Hydrogène	Gaz inflammable. Baſe du gaz inflammable.
Subſtances ſimples non métalliques oxidables & acidifiables.	Soufre	Soufre.
	Phoſphore	Phoſphore.
	Carbone	Charbon pur.
	Radical muriatique.	Inconnu.
	Radical fluorique	Inconnu.
	Radical boracique	Inconnu.
Subſtances ſimples métalliques oxidables & acidifiables.	Antimoine	Antimoine.
	Argent	Argent.
	Arſenic	Arſenic.
	Biſmuth	Biſmuth.
	Cobolt	Cobolt.
	Cuivre	Cuivre.
	Etain	Etain.
	Fer	Fer.
	Manganèſe	Manganèſe.
	Mercure	Mercure.
	Molybdène	Molybdène.
	Nickel	Nickel.
	Or	Or.
	Platine	Platine.
	Plomb	Plomb.
	Tungſtène	Tungſtène.
	Zinc	Zinc.
Subſtances ſimples ſalifiables terreuſes.	Chaux	Terre calcaire, chaux.
	Magnéſie	Magnéſie, baſe du ſel d'Epſom.
	Baryte	Barote, terre peſante.
	Alumine	Argile, terre de l'alun, baſe de l'alun.
	Silice	Terre ſiliceuſe, terre vitrifiable.

Table 1 Lavoisier's table of elements

Picture 1 Antoine Lavoisier

6 Suppose you could go back in time and talk to Lavoisier. Write down what you would say to him to explain that lime is not an element. What might his reply be? You can write your answers in English if you like.

7 Give five elements that are not included in Lavoisier's table. Why do you think he failed to list them?

Table 2 Translations into English of Lavoisier's list of 'Noms nouveaux' (new names) are shown here.

Light	Tin
Heat	Iron
Oxygen	Manganese
Nitrogen	Mercury
Hydrogen	Molybdenum
Sulphur	Nickel
Phosphorus	Gold
Carbon	Platinum
Chlorine*	Lead
Fluorine*	Tungsten
Boron	Zinc
Antimony	Lime
Silver	Magnesia
Arsenic	Barytes
Bismuth	Alumina
Cobalt	Silica
Copper	

*Lavoisier actually confused chlorine and fluorine with their oxides, but this can be ignored as far as this exercise is concerned.

When were the elements discovered?

Find the list of elements in the Data Section (table 1). The list includes the dates when each element was discovered. Use these dates to carry out this exercise.

1 Count the *total* number of elements that had been discovered by each of the following dates: (a) 1700, (b) 1750, (c) 1800, (d) 1850, (e) 1900, (f) 1950, (g) the present.

2 Using your results from 1, plot a graph showing the total number of elements discovered (vertical axis) against date.

3 Why were relatively few elements discovered after 1900?

4 Why were relatively few elements discovered before 1700?

5 What was the peak time for discovering elements? Suggest a reason why this was such an active time.

6 In the second half of the nineteenth century, scientists became very interested in classifying elements by grouping them together.

a Why do you think they became so interested in it at that particular time?

b What is the name of the grouping system that they eventually came up with?

A5 Different kinds of mixtures

Most of the materials around us are not pure elements or compounds, but mixtures. In this topic we look at the different kinds.

Picture 1 Is it really pure ?

Is it pure?

We like our food to be pure, but if it was really pure in the way that chemists understand the word, food would actually be rather boring.

When people use the word 'pure', they usually mean 'not mixed with anything else'. 'Pure orange juice' contains only the juice of oranges, with no additives. But in chemistry the word 'pure' means more than this. **A pure substance is a single substance on its own.**

Elements and compounds are pure substances, but mixtures are not. To a chemist, orange juice isn't really pure because it is a mixture of many different substances such as water, sugars, vitamins and acids. That's why it tastes so nice. Any one of these pure substances on its own would taste much less interesting.

Practically all the things we eat are mixtures. Usually they contain many different compounds mixed together.

The last topic looked at elements and compounds. We saw that compounds are very different from the elements they contain. But a mixture resembles the substances it contains. The properties of a mixture are a kind of average of the properties of the substances in it. So a mixture of sugar and water is both sweet and wet.

Table 1 sums up the differences between compounds and mixtures. Notice that an important property of mixtures is that they can be *separated* into their component parts. The separation of mixtures is covered in the next topic, topic A6.

Table 1 Comparing compounds and mixtures

Compounds	Mixtures
Consist of a single substance	Consist of two or more substances
Properties are very different from the elements in them	Properties are similar to the substances making up the mixture
Can only be separated into elements by a chemical reaction	Often quite easily separated
The amounts of the elements in the compound are fixed	The amounts of the different substances in the mixture can vary

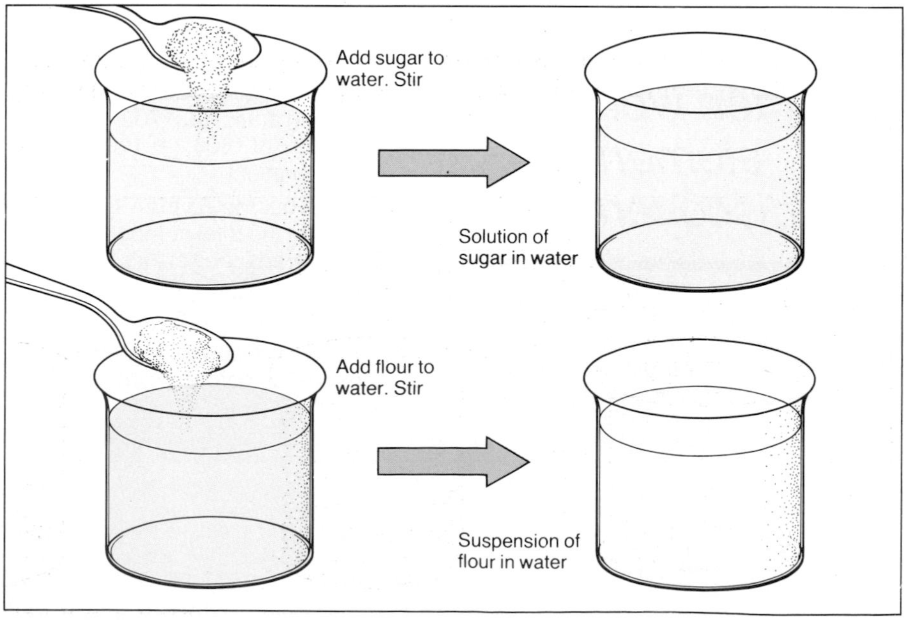

Picture 2 The difference between a solution and a suspension

Mixtures of solids and liquids

When you shake a solid with a liquid, the solid sometimes disappears into the liquid. The solid has **dissolved**, and the result is a **solution**. Sugar forms a solution in water and many drinks contain sugar dissolved in water. (There is more about solutions in topic B5.)

Not all solids form solutions in liquids. If you add flour to water, the flour does not dissolve, no matter how much you stir. The flour stays suspended in the water, and eventually it settles out. The flour forms a **suspension** in water. Picture 2 shows the difference between a solution and a suspension.

Sometimes you get a **gel** when you mix a solid with a liquid. The solid makes a kind of network which traps the liquid so it cannot flow freely. The result is a semi-solid which can move around, but not as freely as a liquid.

The jelly you sometimes eat for pudding is a gel made from water and a protein called gelatine. The kind of gel you put on your hair is made from water and an oil. Starch forms a gel when you heat it with water. You can investigate this in activity A.

Picture 3 This tasty gel is a mixture of protein and water

Mixtures of liquids

When you add one liquid to another, the two liquids sometimes dissolve in each other so they form a single layer. The liquids are **miscible**. Alcohol and water are miscible — if they were not, alcoholic drinks like whisky would separate into two different layers.

But some pairs of liquids are **immiscible**. When you add them together, they form two different layers. Oil and water are like this. If you have ever mixed a 'French dressing' for salad from oil and vinegar, you will know that the oil floats on top of the watery vinegar. These liquids are **immiscible**. Picture 4 shows the difference between miscible and immiscible liquids.

Immiscible liquids will mix together better if you can break down one of the liquids into tiny droplets. The droplets of one liquid float suspended in the other liquid, so they do not separate out into different layers. This kind of mixture is called an **emulsion**. Picture 5 shows the idea. Unlike pure liquids, emulsions are cloudy (opaque) so you cannot see through them. To make an emulsion, an **emulsifier** is used to stop the droplets joining together to form a separate layer.

Mayonnaise and salad cream are emulsions of oil and vinegar. In mayonnaise the oil is broken up into tiny droplets which float suspended in the watery vinegar. The emulsifier used in traditional mayonnaise is egg yolk.

Cream is an emulsion. It has tiny droplets of butterfat floating in water. If you churn the cream around a lot, the drops of fat join together and you get butter.

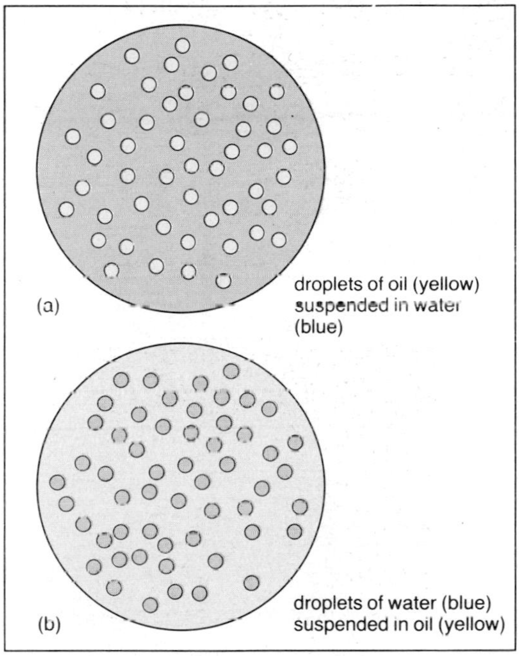
(a)
droplets of oil (yellow) suspended in water (blue)
(b)
droplets of water (blue) suspended in oil (yellow)

Picture 5 In an emulsion, droplets of one liquid are suspended in another liquid

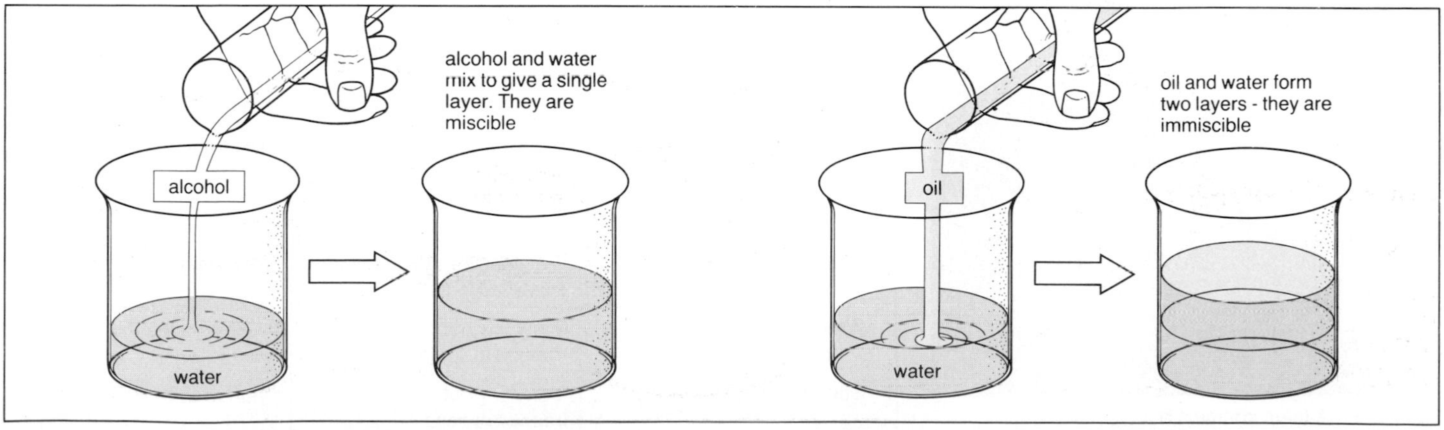
alcohol and water mix to give a single layer. They are miscible
alcohol
water
oil and water form two layers - they are immiscible
oil
water

Picture 4 Miscible and immiscible liquids

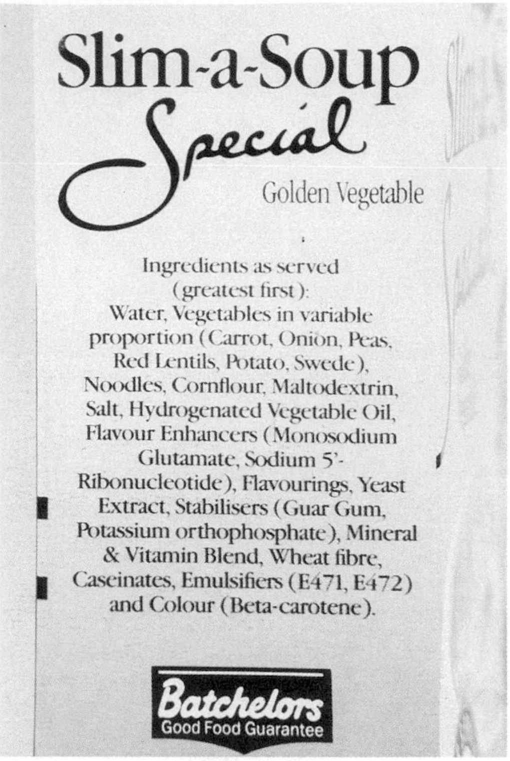

Picture 6 Food products often contain an emulsifier to make oil and water mix

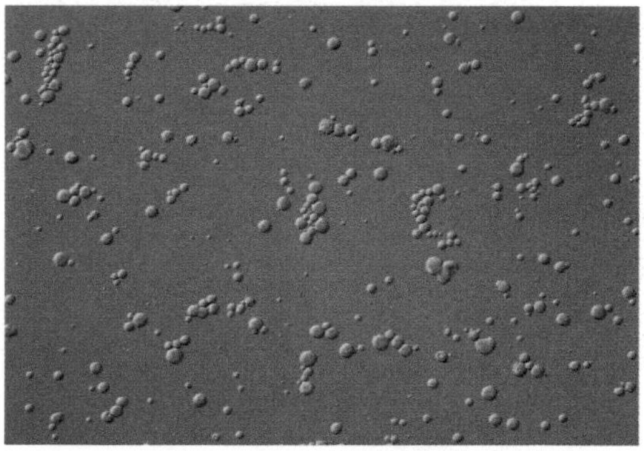

Picture 7 Cream under the microscope. Notice the droplets of fat suspended in the water

Picture 8 A foam contains bubbles of gas suspended in a liquid

Many cosmetics are emulsions too. Hand creams and foundation creams are usually emulsions of oil in water. Oil helps prevent skin from getting dry, but if you use oil on its own it makes the skin feel greasy. An emulsion of oil in water feels much nicer.

Some cosmetics are an emulsion of water-in-oil, rather than oil-in-water — picture 5 on the previous page shows the difference. Cold cream and cleansing cream are water-in-oil emulsions. If you feel their texture you will notice they feel oilier than oil-in-water emulsions like hand cream.

Mixtures of gases and liquids

What happens when you add a gas to a liquid? You do this every time you shake or stir some water — a little air always gets added to the water. When you blow into a drink through a straw you are adding air to the drink.

It may seem that the gas just bubbles through the liquid and comes out again. But in fact, some of the gas actually dissolves in the liquid. It disappears into the liquid and forms a solution. Fizzy drinks are solutions of carbon dioxide in water, with a bit of sugar and flavouring also dissolved to make them taste interesting.

Fizzy drinks like cola and beer often have a frothy 'head' on top. This is a different kind of gas-liquid mixture, called a **foam**. The gas is not dissolved in the liquid, but has formed tiny bubbles in it (picture 8). Unlike pure liquids, foams are usually opaque because the bubbles of gas scatter the light. This is why the water in a waterfall looks white instead of transparent.

Eventually, the tiny bubbles in a foam join together to form bigger bubbles, and these escape from the foam. The foam collapses. Some foams last for a very long time — they are stable. If you whip egg white with air you get a stable white foam. If you then heat the foam in an oven, the liquid egg white dries out and solidifies. You now have a **solid foam:** meringue.

Bread is a solid foam, with bubbles of carbon dioxide gas trapped in the solidified dough. Plastics are often made as solid foams: sponge and foam rubber, for example.

Table 2 Important types of mixtures

Name	Description	Example
Solution of solid in liquid	Transparent solution of solid dissolved in liquid	Sea water, sugar in water
Suspension of solid in liquid	Cloudy mixture of solid particles suspended in liquid	Muddy river water, flour in water
Gel	Jelly-like mixture of solid and liquid	Fruit jelly, cold custard
Solution of two miscible liquids	Single transparent liquid layer	Vodka (alcohol and water), two-stroke mixture (petrol and oil)
Emulsion of two immiscible liquids	Cloudy mixture containing tiny drops of one liquid suspended in the other liquid	Milk, skin cream
Solution of gas in liquid	Transparent solution of gas dissolved in liquid	Soda water
Foam of gas in liquid	Many tiny bubbles of gas trapped in liquid	Washing lather, shaving foam
Solid foam of gas in solid	Many tiny bubbles of gas trapped in solid	Sponge cake, foam rubber

A summary of different kinds of mixtures

Table 2 summarises the important kinds of mixtures that have been mentioned here. Notice that each mixture has two parts, or **phases**, which may be solid, liquid or gas.

Notice too that there are several kinds of solutions: solid-in-liquid, liquid-in-liquid and gas-in-liquid. In a solution, the two phases are *completely* mixed, so that they become a single liquid phase. In other types of mixtures, such as suspensions, emulsions and foams, the two phases are separate. But one phase may be broken up into such tiny particles, bubbles or droplets that you can only see them with a microscope.

Activities

A Making a gel with flour and water

When flour and water are heated together, they form a gel. The flour contains tiny grains of starch, and these burst open when they are heated in water. The long molecules of starch make a network which traps water, forming a gel.

This process is very important in cookery. It is used to thicken sauces and soups. Custard is a gel made from cornflour and milk.

Try this basic experiment first. You could do it at home or in the school laboratory. If you do it in the lab, use a beaker instead of a saucepan to heat the mixture in. You will not be able to taste the product as beakers and laboratory benches may not be clean enough.

1 Put two heaped teaspoonfuls of flour in a small saucepan. Add 50 cm^3 of *cold* water. Stir so the flour gets evenly spread through the water, with no lumps.

2 Heat the mixture *very, very gently*, stirring all the time with a spoon. The mixture will thicken. You can test how thick it is by seeing how easily it runs off the spoon.

3 As soon as the mixture starts to bubble, turn off the heat.

4 Examine your gel. Allow it to cool, then examine it again.

You can modify the basic experiment to carry out the investigations below. Plan your investigation carefully and then get your plan checked by your teacher before you start.

Investigation A: At what temperature does the mixture start to form a gel?

Investigation B: Try varying the proportions of flour and water. What difference does changing the proportions make to the gel you get?

Investigation C: Try making gels with cornflour and/or arrowroot instead of flour. (Cornflour and arrowroot are purer forms of starch than flour.) Are these gels different from the one you made using flour?

B Making meringues

Find a recipe for meringues. Write a summary of the recipe using diagrams, with as few words as possible. If possible, use the recipe to make some meringues at home, or in the Home Economics room.

1 Why are only egg *whites* used to make meringues, not the whole egg?

2 Why is sugar added to the egg whites *after* beating them, and not before?

3 Why is the meringue cooked in a very cool oven?

C Looking for emulsions

Many food products are emulsions. They contain emulsifiers to make oil and water mix. You can often spot emulsifiers in the ingredients lists on the food package. Emulsifiers have E numbers beginning with 4.

Have a look in your food cupboard for food products that are emulsions. List at least 10. For each one, list the emulsifier(s) it contains.

Questions

1 Explain, in your own words, the difference between a compound and a mixture. Use as examples i) the compound iron sulphide (FeS), and ii) a mixture of iron filings and powdered sulphur.

2 David and Susan were looking at a jar of honey. The label said 'Pure Honey'. David said, 'That means it's natural honey, with nothing else added.' Susan said, 'It isn't really pure. It's a mixture of lots of different substances.'

Who was right? Explain your answer.

3 Look at the following list of substances. Classify each one as a pure substance or a mixture:
salt, sugar, tap water, distilled water, coal, carbon, soil, copper, brass, oxygen, air, sodium hydroxide, sodium hydroxide solution.

4 Use table 2 to decide what type of mixture each of the following contains. In some cases there may be more than one type of mixture present:
expanded polystyrene, margarine, bubble bath, golden syrup, whipped cream, mud, marshmallow, ice cream, dilute sulphuric acid (hint: pure sulphuric acid is a liquid).

5 'Instant whip' desserts are sold as a powder in a packet. You add the powder to milk. Then you beat the mixture with a food mixer, and leave it to set for a few minutes. It becomes a kind of frothy milk jelly.

a Name three types of mixture that are present in the dessert when it is ready to eat.

b Name two ingredients the powder is likely to contain.

A6 Separating mixtures

In the kitchen and in the laboratory, we often need to separate mixtures.

To separate mixtures, a cook might use a sieve, a tea strainer or simply a jug. Scientists need to separate mixtures too, and they often use similar apparatus to cooks. The equipment used depends on the type of mixture being separated.

Separating solids from liquids

The method that you use depends on whether or not the solid dissolves in the liquid.

Separating an insoluble solid from a liquid

Tea leaves don't dissolve in tea. You use a tea strainer to separate them. This is a kind of **filtration**. But if you can't be bothered to use a tea strainer, you just drink the tea and the leaves stay behind in the bottom of the cup. This is a kind of **decantation** — pouring the liquid off from the solid.

When you carry out filtration in the laboratory, you use the apparatus shown in picture 2. The filter paper has tiny holes that let the liquid through, but these holes are too small for the solid particles. The clear liquid that runs out of the filter is called the **filtrate**. The solid that is left behind is called the **residue**.

Sometimes **centrifugation** is used instead of filtration. The suspension of solid in liquid is poured into a tube, then spun round very fast in a centrifuge. This forces the solid to the bottom of the tube. The liquid can then be easily poured off (decanted) from the solid.

Centrifugation is used in dairies to separate milk from cream. This is possible because milk is denser than cream.

Separating a soluble solid from a liquid

Suppose you are marooned on a desert island. You need fresh water to drink. How will you get it?

To get pure water from a salty solution, you need to use **distillation**. You boil the solution, and water comes off as steam. The steam is then cooled in a **condenser**, to give liquid water again. The liquid water is collected as the distillate. Picture 4 shows the equipment that you would use in the laboratory. What kind of equipment might you use on a desert island? (See question 2.)

Picture 1 A filter is used to separate the grounds from coffee. Coffee grains are smaller than tea leaves so a filter is used instead of a simple strainer

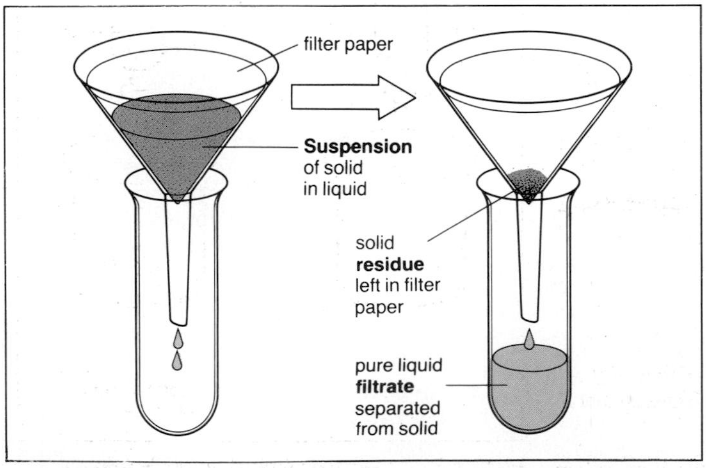

Picture 2 Filtration

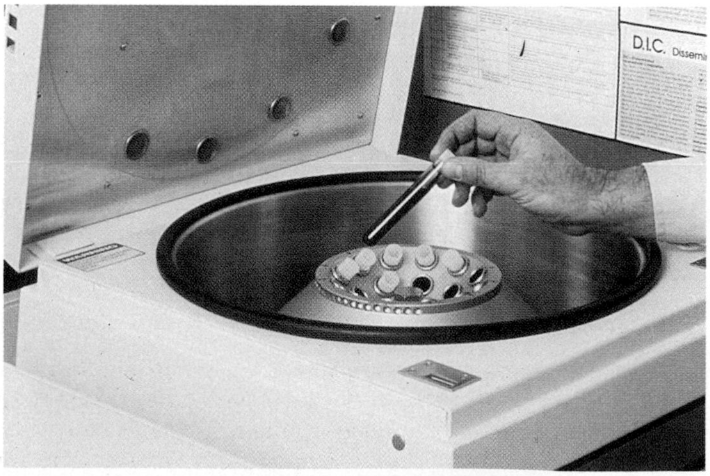

Picture 3 A centrifuge is used to separate blood cells from blood plasma

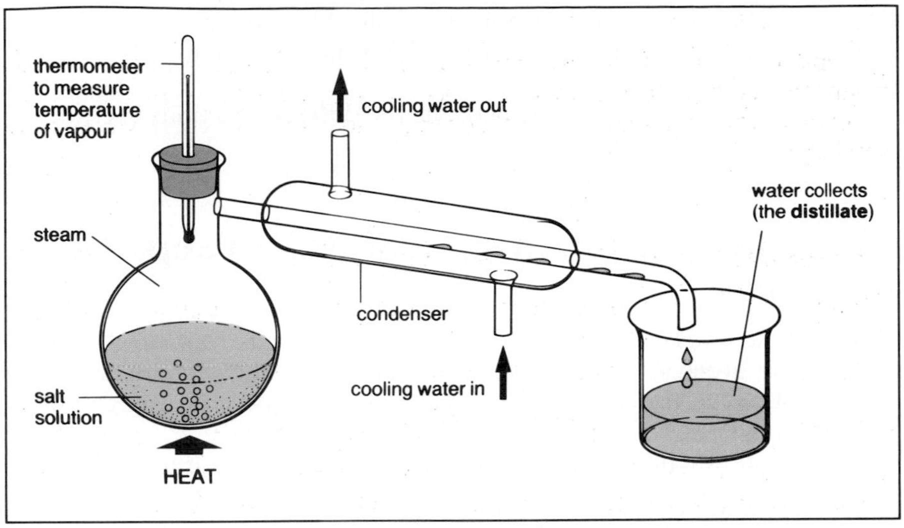

Picture 4 Distillation

Distillation can be used whenever you want to separate and collect the liquid part (the solvent) from a solution.

Sometimes the part of the solution you want is the solute, not the solvent. For example, suppose your desert island already had a supply of fresh water. Then you would only need the salt from the sea water, not the water itself. There would be no need to collect the steam and condense it — you could just let the steam escape into the air. This is called **evaporation** (picture 5).

During evaporation, you boil the solution and let the solvent vapour escape into the air. The solid part (the solute) is left behind, usually in the form of small crystals. It has **crystallised**. If you want larger crystals, you don't boil all the solvent off. You leave some of it behind, and let it evaporate slowly. This allows the crystals to grow gradually, so they grow bigger in the end.

Making toffee involves evaporation. You make a solution of sugar in water, plus a bit of butter and other things to make it taste interesting, then you evaporate off the water. If you evaporate *all* the water away, you get a hard, brittle toffee. If you leave some of the water, you get a softer toffee, more like fudge.

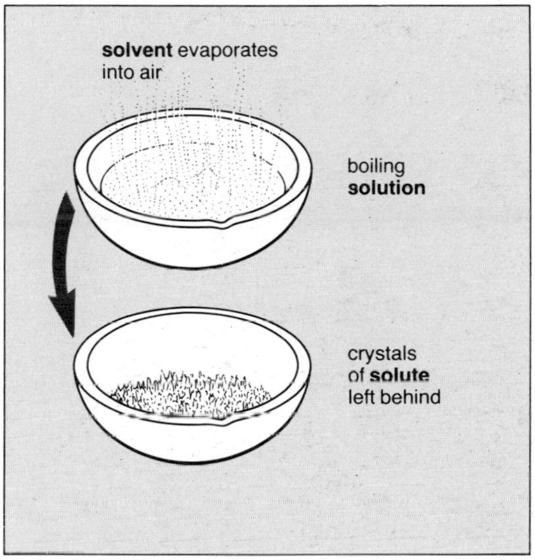

Picture 5 Evaporation

Separating liquids from one another

The method that you use depends on whether or not the two liquids mix.

Separating immiscible liquids

When you roast a joint of meat, a watery gravy oozes out of the meat. Fat also melts and runs out of the meat. The fat floats on the watery gravy, because fat and water are immiscible. This makes the two quite easy to separate. You can spoon the melted fat off the gravy.

In the laboratory, immmiscible liquids are separated using a **separating funnel**, as shown in picture 6.

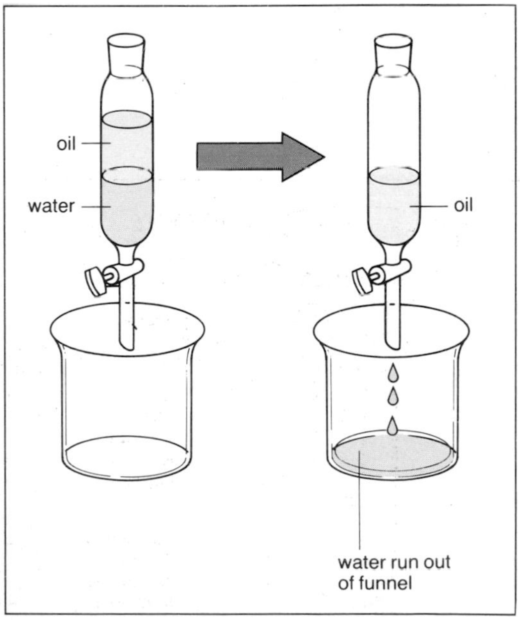

Picture 6 Separating immiscible liquids using a separating funnel

Separating miscible liquids

Alcohol and water mix completely with one another. You cannot use a separating funnel on them, because they form a single layer. To separate these two liquids, you must use distillation.

Simple distillation is shown in picture 4. To separate miscible liquids, a special form of distillation is often used, called **fractional distillation**. The

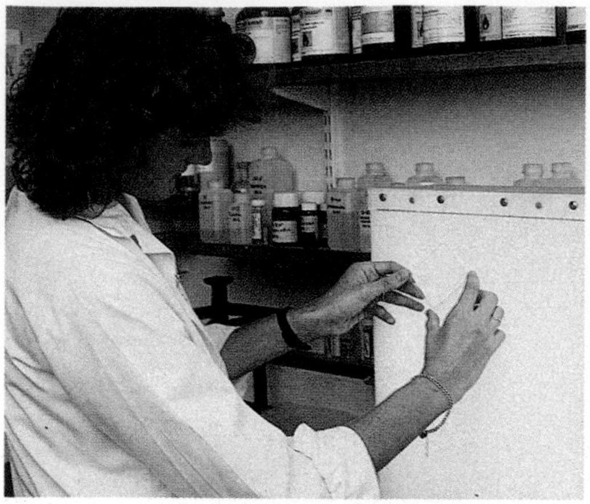

Picture 8 Chromatography is used to check the urine of a patient to see if they have a rare disease

different liquids have different boiling points. When the mixture is boiled, the vapours of the two liquids boil off at different temperatures. They can be condensed separately.

Fractional distillation is used to separate the different fractions in crude oil. Details of the process are given on page 155.

Chromatography: a special way of separating mixtures

Suppose you have bought a green food colouring to make coloured icing for a cake. The green colouring might be made of a single green dye, or a mixture of a blue dye and a yellow dye. You could use chromatography to find out which it is.

Picture 7 shows the simplest type of chromatography — **paper chromatography**. The dyes separate because some dyes prefer to stick to the paper, but others prefer to dissolve in the solvent. The dyes that prefer the solvent travel further up the paper.

Chromatography is very useful for separating small amounts of substances in a mixture, to find out what these substances are. It is often used in hospitals. For example, chromatography might be used to find out whether sugar is present in a person's urine. This would help the doctor to know whether the person has diabetes.

The substances being separated by chromatography do not necessarily have to be coloured. Colourless substances can be made to show up by spraying the paper with a **locating agent**. The locating agent reacts with each of the colourless substances to form a coloured product.

Testing the purity of a substance

Chemists often need to know if a substance is pure. For example, medicines must be tested for purity before they are sold. Impurities might harm the patient.

Chromatography can be used to see if a substance is pure. If it's pure, a single spot will show up on the chromatogram. But if it is impure, there will be several spots.

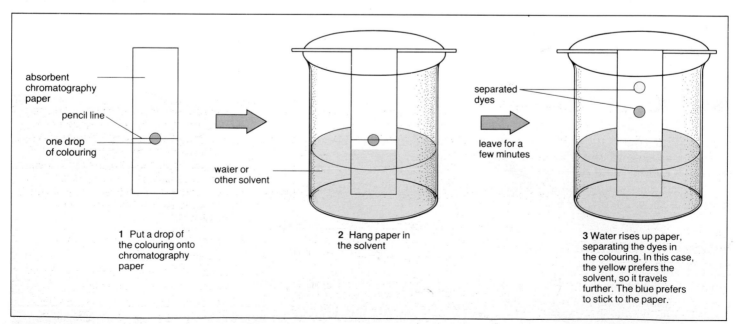

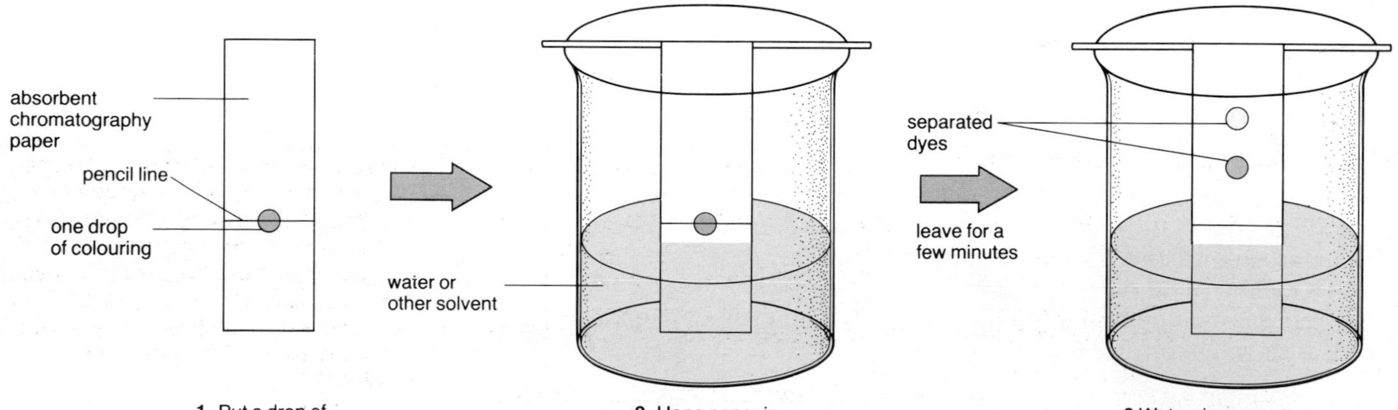
absorbent chromatography paper
pencil line
one drop of colouring
water or other solvent
separated dyes
leave for a few minutes
1 Put a drop of the colouring onto chromatography paper
2 Hang paper in the solvent
3 Water rises up paper, separating the dyes in the colouring. In this case, the yellow prefers the solvent, so it travels further. The blue prefers to stick to the paper.

Picture 7 Paper chromatography

Another way of testing a substance's purity is to measure its **melting point** or **boiling point**. The melting points and boiling points of most elements and compounds are known accurately. They can be found in data books. If a substance is not pure, its melting point or boiling point will be different from the known, accurate value. For example, pure water boils at 100°C. But if the water contains impurities, such as salt, the boiling point is higher.

Activities

A Using chromatography to investigate inks

Suppose you are a detective investigating forged signatures on cheques. If you know the type of ink that has been used in a signature, it might help you decide if the signature is genuine or a forgery.

1 Investigate water-based inks, the types of inks used in fountain pens and in most felt-tip pens. Use the method shown in picture 7, with water as the solvent.

Get a selection of different inks, of different makes but all of the same colour. Black is best. Make a chromatogram for each different ink. You will find that different inks separate into different colours, because they contain different dyes. Try to control the conditions so the chromatograms can be easily compared.

Now ask someone to make a mark on a piece of chromatography paper using one of the inks, secretly so that you do not know which ink was used. Run the chromatogram as before. Now use your collection of chromatograms to decide which ink was used.

2 Try repeating the investigation using 'permanent' inks — inks which do not dissolve in water. These are the inks in ball-point pens and permanent marker pens. Most permanent inks dissolve in alcohol, so you can use the same method as before, but with alcohol as the solvent instead of water.

B Growing crystals

Try this basic method for growing crystals of alum. Alum is the common name for potassium aluminium sulphate.

Wear eye protection.

1 Put 150 cm^3 of water in a 250 cm^3 beaker. Warm the water until it is nearly boiling.

2 Add alum to the warm water. Stir. Go on adding alum until no more will dissolve.

3 Let the solution cool. You now have a saturated solution of alum — a solution that has dissolved as much alum as possible. You will notice that there are crystals of alum at the bottom of the beaker.

4 Hang a thread in the solution, as shown in picture 9.

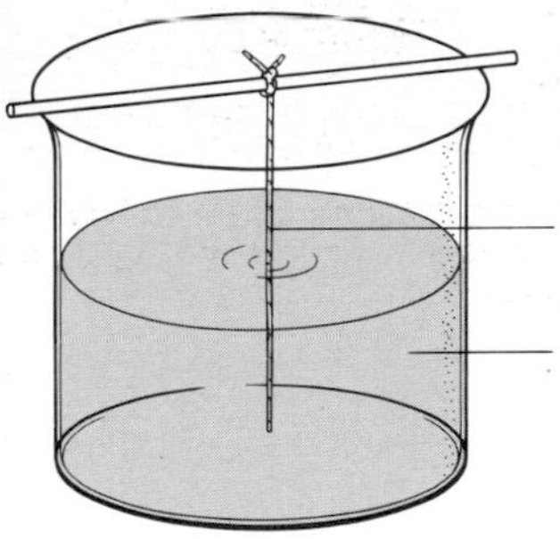

Picture 9 Growing crystals of alum

5 Leave the solution to stand for several days. Water will evaporate and crystals will grow. Examine the thread from time to time. You should notice small crystals of alum growing on the thread, and these small crystals will gradually grow larger. With patience you can get quite big crystals.

You could adapt this experiment to grow crystals of other substances. Sugar, salt and copper sulphate are good ones to try.

Questions

1 For (a), (b) and (c), write a sentence containing each of the words, to make the meaning of the words clear:

a Filtration, filtrate, residue.

b Distillation, distillate, residue.

c Evaporate, crystallise.

2 You are cast away on a desert island. There is a stream with fresh water, but it is very muddy. There is sea all round. You hunt around and manage to find the following: some newspaper, a saucepan, a kettle, several tumblers, a knife, some wire, an empty plastic lemonade bottle and a short piece of copper piping.

Draw diagrams to show how you would obtain:

a clean water from the muddy river water,

b fresh water from the sea water,

c salt from the sea water.

3 In 'dry cleaning', a special solvent is used to dissolve grease and dirt from clothes. A dry-cleaning machine is basically a washing machine that uses this solvent instead of water. After use, the solvent is dirty. The dirty solvent cannot be thrown away: it is expensive and it would cause pollution.

What method could be used to recover pure, clean solvent from the dirty solvent? How could this method be built into the working of a dry-cleaning machine?

4 What method would you use to get

a pure water from ink?

b copper sulphate crystals from a solution of copper sulphate in water?

c petrol from a mixture of petrol and oil?

d salt from a mixture of salt and sand?

B1
What's in the air?

Air is a vital resource — a mixture of very useful gases. And it's free!

If you rest all day today, you will breathe in about 15 000 litres of air. If you take exercise you'll need quite a lot more.

Air isn't just vital for humans. It is needed by most living things, and for other everyday happenings such as burning and rusting. And it's an important raw material for manufacturing industrial gases.

The composition of air

The Earth is very unusual among planets, because it has an atmosphere containing oxygen. Until about 2000 million years ago, the atmosphere was mainly nitrogen, with virtually no oxygen at all. It was the first primitive plants that released oxygen. Gradually the amount of oxygen increased until there was enough to support more advanced living things — like us humans.

The activity shows an experiment to find the percentage of oxygen in air. Accurate experiments show that air is 21% oxygen. The rest is mainly nitrogen (picture 2). Table 1 gives the most important gases in dry air.

Table 1 The composition of dry air. In practice, air also contains water vapour, but the amount varies according to the weather

Gas	Percentage by volume
Nitrogen	78.03
Oxygen	20.99
Argon	0.93
Other noble gases (neon, helium, krypton, xenon)	0.002
Carbon dioxide	0.03
Hydrogen	0.001

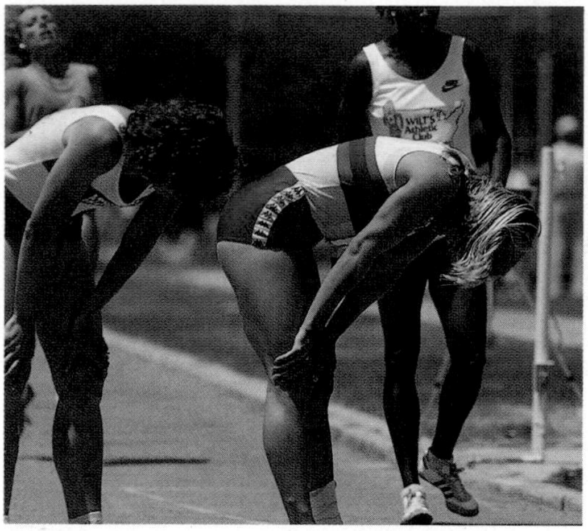

Picture 1 When you breathe, 79% of the air goes in and out of your lungs unchanged

Nitrogen is a very unreactive gas.
Oxygen is the most reactive gas in the air. When you breathe, it passes from the air in your lungs into your bloodstream, and is carried to the cells of your body. There is more about oxygen in topic B2.
Argon and the other noble gases are almost completely unreactive.
Carbon dioxide is only present in small amounts, but it is very important to plants, which use it in photosynthesis (see *The Living World*, topic C13).

Some of the important uses of these gases are described in *Industrial gases from air* on page 31.

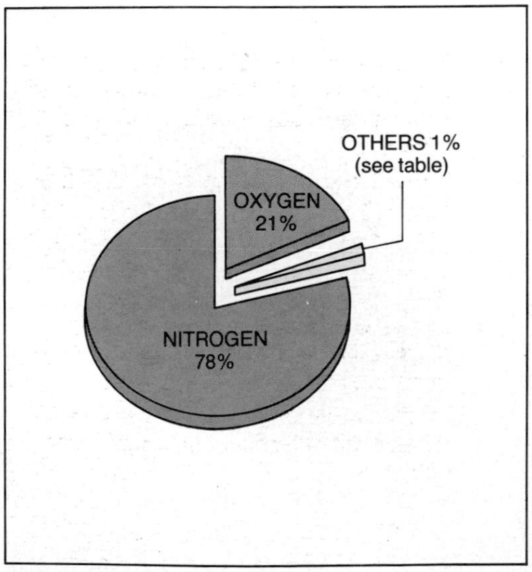

Picture 2 The composition of air

Separating air

Many of the gases in air are very useful. Separating the gases from one

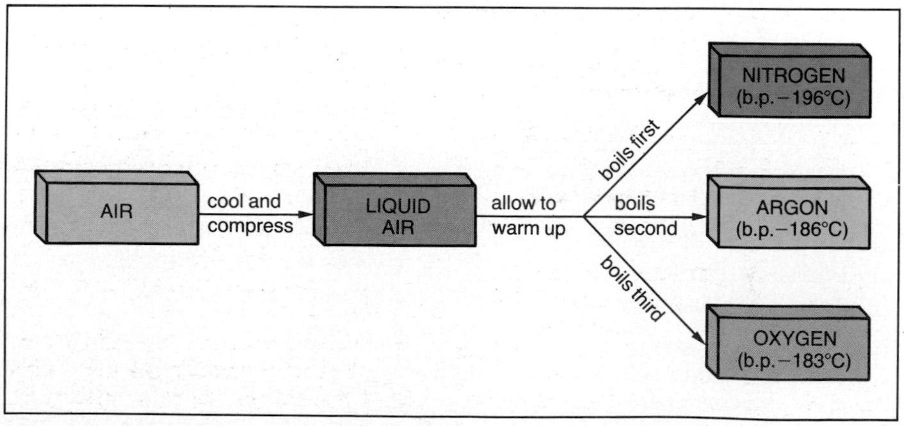

Picture 3 Separation of air by fractional distillation

Picture 4 An air separation plant. Notice the tower used for fractional distillation

another is an important industrial process, called the **fractional distillation** of liquid air.

Air is liquefied by cooling it and compressing it. The liquid air is then allowed to warm up. At a temperature of −194°C it begins to boil. The different gases of the air boil at different temperatures (picture 3). They can be collected separately as they boil off. *Industrial gases from air* on page 31 gives more information about what the gases are used for.

Activity

How much of the air is oxygen?

When air is passed over heated copper, the oxygen reacts with the copper forming black copper oxide. This removes the oxygen from the air, and the volume of the air decreases. If you measure the volume change, you can find the proportion of oxygen in the air. Picture 5 shows the apparatus that you can use.

Care Eye protection must be worn.

1 Start with one syringe empty and the other containing 100 cm^3 of air.

2 Heat the copper turnings strongly.

3 Use the syringes to pass air back and forth over the heated copper. Do this several times.

4 Allow the apparatus to cool. Read off the new volume of air.

5 Repeat steps 2 to 4 to check that all the oxygen in the air has reacted. There should be no further change in the volume. If there is a change, repeat steps 2 to 4 again.

Question 2 below gives some typical results.

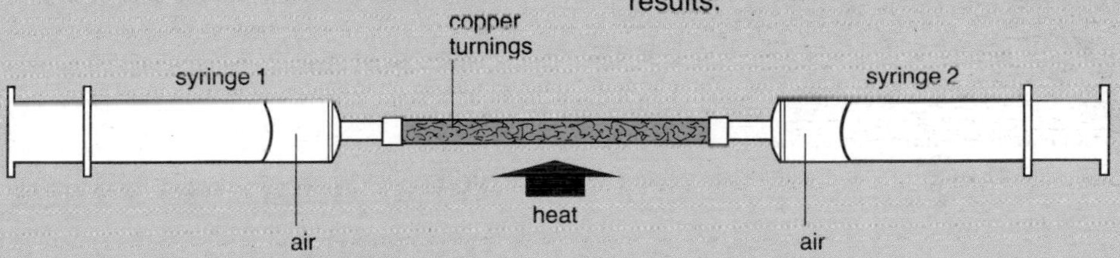

Picture 5 Finding the proportion of oxygen in air

Questions

1 List the five most abundant gases in the air, in order of abundance.

2 Here are some typical results for the activity above.

Volume of air before heating = 100 cm^3
Volume after first heating and cooling = 83 cm^3
Volume after second heating and cooling = 80 cm^3
Volume after third heating and cooling = 80 cm^3

During the experiment the copper turned black.

a Why is the tube allowed to cool before reading the new volume?

b Was all the oxygen used up after the first heating?

c Was all the oxgen used up after the second heating? How do you know?

d What volume of oxygen was removed by the copper?

e What is the percentage by volume of oxygen in the air?

f Why did the copper turn black during the experiment?

g Would you expect the copper to weigh more or less after this experiment? Give a reason for your answer.

3a Suppose air was 78% oxygen and 21% nitrogen instead of the other way round. What differences would this make to the world?

b Table 1 shows only the most abundant gases in air. But other gases are present in tiny amounts. Suggest four gases you might expect to be present apart from the ones in the table.

4 Liquid air is separated by fractional distillation. This method is also used to separate crude oil into fractions.

In what ways is the fractional distillation of liquid air *different* from that of crude oil?

B2
Oxygen, oxides and oxidation

Oxygen is the reactive part of the air.

Picture 1 Oxygen is used to remove impurities in steel by oxidising them

Have you flown in an airliner? If so, you will probably have heard the cabin crew explaining the emergency oxygen masks. These are used for breathing if the plane accidentally becomes depressurised. Passengers are always reminded to put out cigarettes before using the masks. A wise precaution, because like all fuels, tobacco burns much more fiercely in pure oxygen than in air!

Some of the properties of oxygen are shown in picture 2. One of the most important things about oxygen is the way it helps things to burn. Unlike air, oxygen has no unreactive nitrogen to 'thin it out'. If a substance burns in air, it will burn much better in oxygen.

What happens when elements burn in oxygen?

In the activity on the next page you can see how various elements burn in oxygen, and you can investigate the products. Picture 3 shows the method, and table 1 gives the results for some elements.

Here are some key points about the reaction of elements with oxygen. Check them against the results in table 1.

- When elements burn in oxygen, they form *oxides*. Oxides contain the element combined with oxygen. For example

  magnesium + oxygen → magnesium oxide
  carbon + oxygen → carbon dioxide

- *Metals* form solid oxides. These oxides give alkaline solutions when they dissolve in water.

- *Non-metals* form oxides which are solid, liquid or gaseous. These oxides give acidic solutions when they dissolve in water.

Oxygen encourages many substances to burn — not just elements. This can be very useful, for example in the oxy-acetylene torches used to cut and weld metals. Some of the major uses of oxygen are described in *Industrial gases from the air* on page 31.

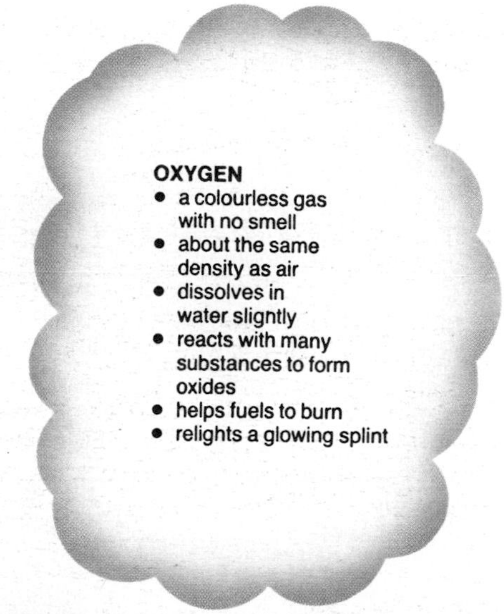

OXYGEN
• a colourless gas with no smell
• about the same density as air
• dissolves in water slightly
• reacts with many substances to form oxides
• helps fuels to burn
• relights a glowing splint

Picture 2 Some properties of oxygen

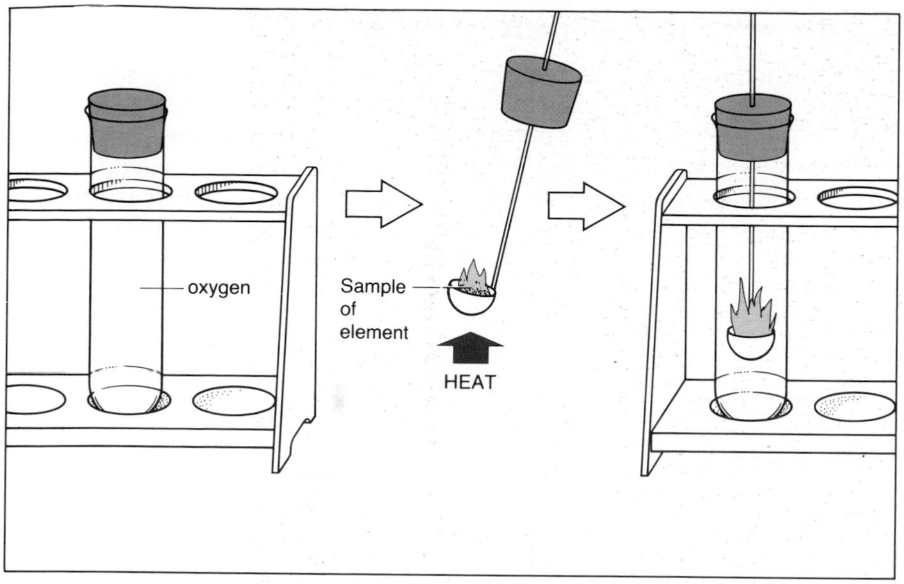

Picture 3 Investigating the reaction of elements with oxygen

Table 1 How different elements react with oxygen

Element	How it reacts	Product	Effect of adding product to water, then testing with indicator
Sodium	Burns vigorously with yellow flame	White solid (sodium oxide, Na_2O)	Dissolves, alkaline solution
Magnesium	Burns vigorously with bright white flame	White solid (magnesium oxide, MgO)	Dissolves slightly, weakly alkaline solution
Sulphur	Burns with bright blue flame	Colourless gas (sulphur dioxide, SO_2)	Dissolves, acidic solution
Carbon	Burns with bright red glow	Colourless gas (carbon dioxide, CO_2)	Dissolves slightly, weakly acidic solution

Oxygen and oxidation

When a substance combines with oxygen, we say it has been **oxidised**. Oxidation reactions are very common.

Burning (topic I2) is rapid oxidation. For example, natural gas is mainly methane, CH_4. When methane burns, it is oxidised to carbon dioxide and water.

$$\text{methane} + \text{oxygen} \rightarrow \text{carbon dioxide} + \text{water}$$
$$CH_4 + 2O_2 \rightarrow CO_2 + 2H_2O$$

Respiration (*The Living World* topic C4) is a slower, more controlled kind of oxidation. Living organisms use it to get energy from foods like glucose.

$$\text{glucose} + \text{oxygen} \rightarrow \text{carbon dioxide} + \text{water}$$
$$C_6H_{12}O_6 + 6O_2 \rightarrow 6CO_2 + 6H_2O$$

Sometimes food oxidises when you don't want it to. Fats turn rancid because they are oxidised to nasty-tasting substances. Antioxidants are added to fatty foods to stop this happening (picture 4).

Rusting (topic B3) is the slow oxidation of iron.

$$\text{iron} + \text{oxygen} \rightarrow \text{iron oxide}$$
$$2Fe + 3O_2 \rightarrow 2Fe_2O_3$$

Notice that in all these reactions, oxides are formed.

Picture 4 Crisps contain an anti-oxidant to prevent the fat in them oxidising and going rancid

Reduction — the opposite of oxidation

In some chemical reactions, oxygen is *removed* instead of being added. This is called reduction. For example, iron is manufactured from iron oxide, Fe_2O_3. To turn Fe_2O_3 to Fe, you need to take away the oxygen. This is done by heating the iron oxide in a blast furnace with carbon monoxide (topic E3). The carbon monoxide, CO, takes away the oxygen and gets oxidised to carbon dioxide, CO_2. The iron oxide is reduced to iron (picture 5).

Whenever oxidation happens, reduction must also happen. If something is gaining oxygen, something else must be losing it. The two processes together are called **redox.**

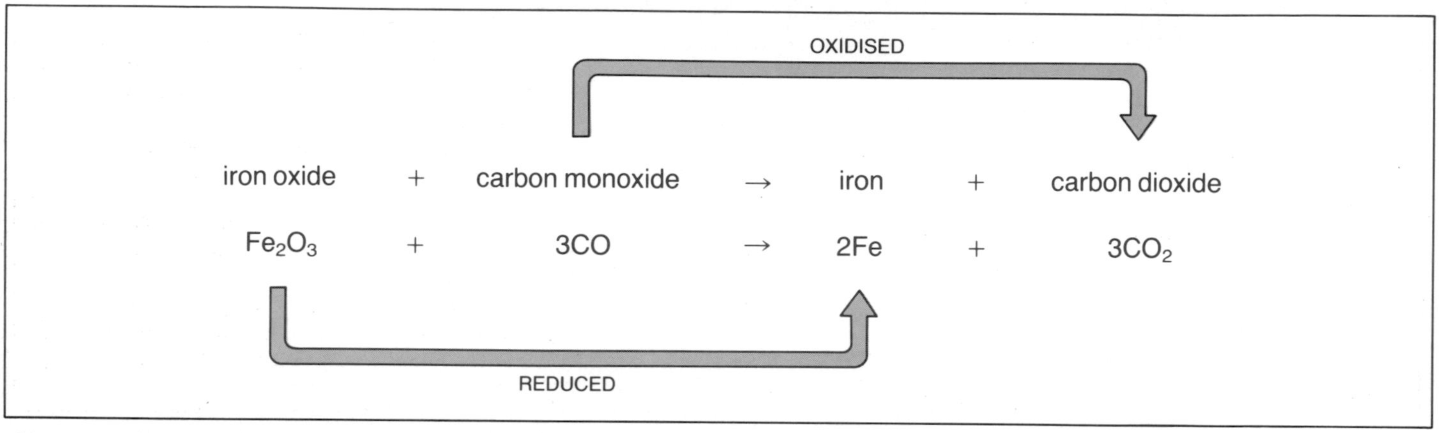

Picture 5 Oxidation and reduction both take place when iron oxide is converted to iron

Activity

What happens when elements burn in oxygen?

You will need the apparatus shown in picture 3. **Eye protection must be worn.**

Elements you could test include carbon, iron and copper.

1. Put a small amount of the element in the burning spoon.
2. Heat it in a bunsen flame until it starts burning.
3. Quickly put the spoon into the tube of oxygen. Observe the reaction.
4. When the reaction has finished, remove the burning spoon. Add a little distilled water to the tube. Replace the bung and shake to make the oxide dissolve. If the oxide dissolves, test the solution with universal indicator paper.
5. Record your results in a suitable table.

Questions

1 Consider the elements aluminium, phosphorus (a yellow waxy solid) and zinc.

a Which would burn more readily in oxygen than in air?

b Which would form an oxide when heated in oxygen?

c Which would form an oxide which gives an acidic solution in water?

2 Look at the following reactions. In each case, say whether the element that is underlined has been oxidised or reduced.

a sulphur + oxygen → sulphur dioxide

b magnesium + carbon dioxide → magnesium oxide + carbon

c iron + copper oxide → iron oxide + copper

d $NO_2 + SO_2 \rightarrow NO + SO_3$

3 Space rockets carry liquid oxygen.

a What is it used for?

b Why is liquid oxygen carried, rather than oxygen gas?

c What are the safety hazards involved in using liquid oxygen?

4 The test for oxygen is to see if it relights a glowing splint. *Why* does a splint relight in oxygen?

Industrial gases from air

Table 1 gives information about three important gases manufactured from air: oxygen, nitrogen and argon.

Gas	Approximate cost of the gas bought in cylinders	Amount of gas used in UK in 1984/tonnes per day	Major uses of the gas
Oxygen	£0.80 per cubic metre (volume measured at atmospheric pressure)	11 000	In steel making — used to remove impurities from iron by oxidising them In hospitals — for patients with breathing difficulties For divers and high altitude climbers — as a breathing gas For welding — an 'oxy-acetylene' flame is hot enough to melt metal For treating sewage — oxygen helps micro-organisms to break down harmful materials
Nitrogen	£1.00 per cubic metre	4000	For freezing — liquid nitrogen is so cold (−196°C) it can be used to freeze food and biological material in order to preserve them As an unreactive atmosphere — nitrogen is used as a cheap, unreactive gas 'blanket' to stop things reacting with air (for example, in petrol storage tanks and food packaging)
Argon	£3 per cubic metre	300	As an unreactive atmosphere — an inert gas 'blanket' to stop reaction with air (for example, inside light bulbs and in welding)

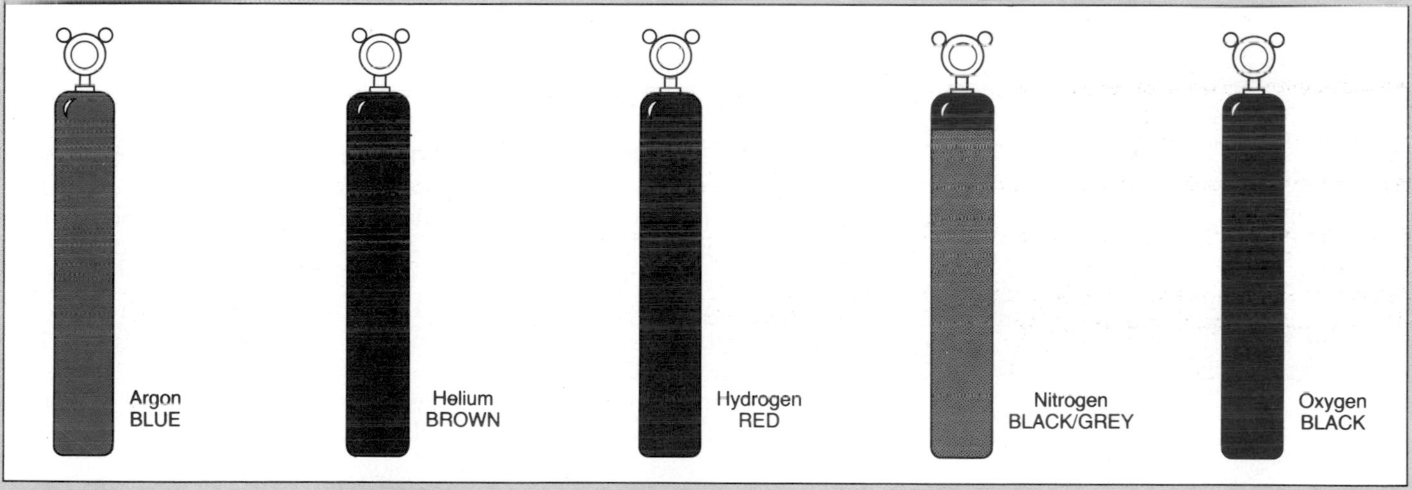

Picture 1 Gas cylinders are colour coded according to their contents

Use the information in table 1, and any other things you know, to answer these questions.

1 Which of the uses of oxygen depend on the fact that it is needed by living things?

2 Which of the uses of oxygen depend on the fact that it is needed for fuels to burn in?

3 Nitrogen and argon can both be used to provide an unreactive atmosphere. For what kind of uses might argon be more suitable than nitrogen? For what kind of uses might nitrogen be more suitable than argon?

4 Liquid nitrogen is used to freeze food, but liquid oxygen and liquid air are never used for this purpose. Why?

5 Compare the *costs* of nitrogen, oxygen and argon. Try to account for any differences and similarities.

6 Compare the *amounts* of nitrogen, oxygen and argon used each day. Try to acount for the differences.

7 Industrial gases have to be transported from the manufacturing plant to the user. Small quantities are transported in cylinders, carried in lorries. Larger quantities are transported in the liquid form, in tankers. What *safety problems* do you think there might be in transporting the gases? How might these problems be overcome?

B3 Corrosion and rusting

Rusting costs Britain about £6000 million a year. What causes rusting, and how can it be prevented?

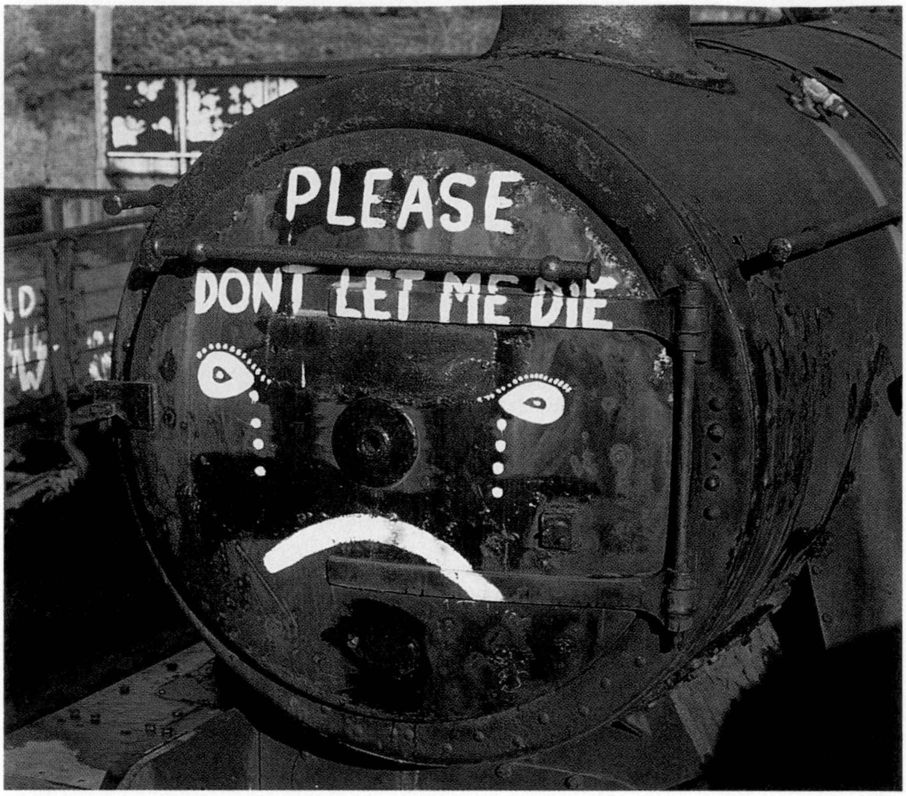

Picture 1 Rusting steam engines in a scrapyard

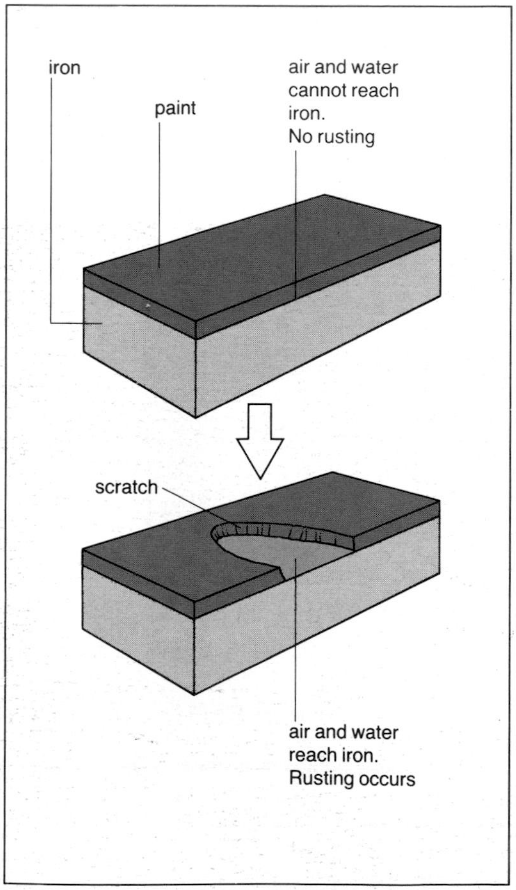

Picture 2 Paint protects iron from rusting, but only until it is scratched

In the 3 or 4 seconds it takes you to read this sentence, Britain will have lost about 40 kg of iron and steel. It will have turned to rust. Forty kilograms is enough to make four bicycles!

Rusting is a form of **corrosion**. Corrosion is the reaction of metals with air, usually forming an oxide. Metals usually corrode faster if they are wet. If the air contains acid pollutants, such as sulphur dioxide, corrosion happens much faster.

Corrosion is a **chemical reaction**. When a metal corrodes, it changes into a new substance, and it is very difficult to change it back.

When a metal corrodes it loses its shine. If the corrosion is bad the metal may break. Sometimes corrosion causes a layer of oxide to form on the surface of the metal which protects it from further corrosion. This is why aluminium stays bright and shiny for a long time, even though it's a fairly reactive metal. Unreactive metals generally corrode slowly. Gold is so unreactive it doesn't corrode at all.

When iron or steel corrode, it is called rusting. Under the right conditions, iron corrodes fast, even though it is a relatively unreactive metal.

What happens when iron rusts?

In activity A you can look at the conditions which make iron rust.

For rusting to occur, two things must be present: air and water. The iron is oxidised by the air, forming iron oxide:

$$\text{iron} + \text{oxygen} \rightarrow \text{iron oxide}$$
$$2Fe + 3O_2 \rightarrow 2Fe_2O_3$$

The iron oxide then reacts with water to form *hydrated* iron oxide — which is rust. ('Hydrated' means the iron oxide has water combined with it.) The rust is brittle and it swells up and flakes off as it is formed. The surface of the iron is then exposed to more air and water, and so the rusting goes on. The rusting occurs even faster if the water contains impurities like salt.

How can you stop iron rusting?

Iron and steel are used more than any other metals, because they are strong and cheap. But they have to be protected from rusting somehow. There are several methods.

Stop air and water reaching the surface of the iron

This is most commonly done by covering the surface with paint (picture 2). But if the paint gets scratched, the iron starts to rust. The iron may also be **plated** with another metal, such as tin or chromium. The trimmings on bicycles and cars are sometimes chromium-plated, to stop them rusting and to make them look nice.

Coat the iron with a more reactive metal

(See picture 3) Zinc is most commonly used. Zinc is more reactive than iron, so the oxygen in the air reacts with the zinc instead of the iron. The zinc is 'sacrificed' to protect the iron. Zinc-plating is often used to protect things like dustbins that are kept outdoors. The iron is said to be **galvanised**.

Mix the iron with another metal to make an alloy

Mixing iron with chromium or nickel makes an alloy which does not rust. It is called stainless steel, and it is used to make cutlery among other things. Unfortunately, these metals are expensive, so stainless steel costs quite a lot more than iron or ordinary steel.

Some rust-protection methods are cheaper than others. The method that is chosen depends on the value of the item being protected. More is given about this in the exercises on page 35.

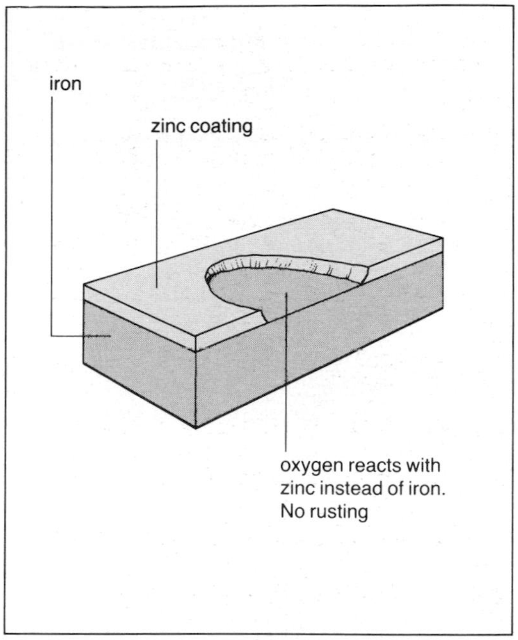
iron
zinc coating
oxygen reacts with
zinc instead of iron.
No rusting

Picture 3 Zinc protects iron from rusting — even if the zinc layer is scratched

Picture 4 Coating steel helps prevent rust. Paint is being used on the ship on the left. The lorry on the right is being zinc plated

Activities

A What conditions favour rusting?

You will need the apparatus shown in picture 5. Set up seven tubes containing ordinary iron nails, as shown in the picture. Carefully examine the nail in each tube after 2 or 3 days. Examine them again after 1 week. Make a suitable table to record the results in.

Try to explain the different results for each tube.

B How much of the air gets used up during rusting?

Set up a test tube as shown in picture 6. You could do the experiment at home, using a drinking glass instead of a test-tube.

Observe the tube over the next few days. What happens? Why?

C A rusting survey

Do a survey to see what things are affected by rust. You could look around your home and garden, your local streets and/or your school. Make a note of:

1 The object that has rusted.
2 Its situation (outdoors/indoors, wet/dry, etc.).
3 Any rust protection it has been given.
4 Any parts that have rusted particularly badly.

In each case, try to decide why rusting has occurred.

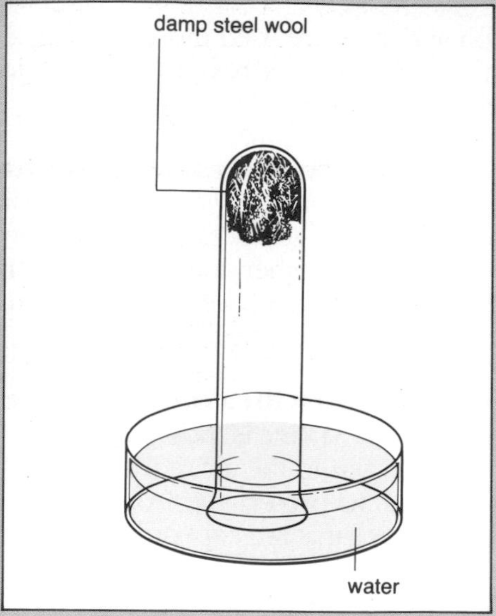

Picture 6 How much of the air is used up during rusting?

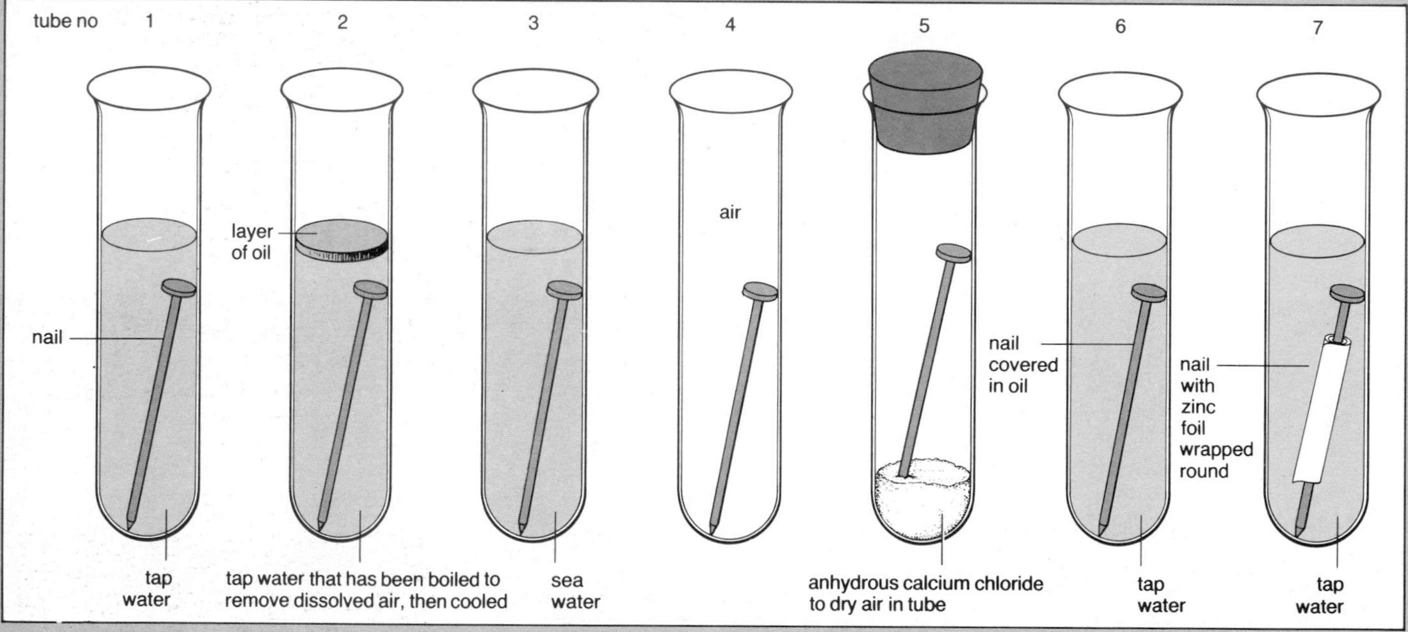

Picture 5 Investigating the conditions needed for rusting

Questions

1 Look again at the experiment shown in activity A (picture 5).

a Why is the water in tube 2 covered in a layer of oil?

b Why does tube 5 have a stopper in?

c What form of rust-protection is represented by tube 7?

d In tube 6 the nail is protected by oil. This is a cheap form of protection, but it doesn't last long. Why not?

2 Suppose each of the metal articles in the following list were left outside: an iron nail, a galvanized iron dustbin, a bright new penny, aluminium foil, a stainless steel knife.

a Which would corrode quickly?

b Which would corrode slowly?

c Which would not corrode at all?

3a Why is the steel hull of an ocean-going ship especially likely to rust?

b Blocks of zinc are often bolted to a ship's hull. Why do you think this is?

c A small child dropped an iron nail into a kettle. The nail was only discovered weeks later by the child's parent, but it had hardly rusted at all. A similar nail dropped in the garden pond rusted badly in 2 days. Explain the difference.

4 Which methods are normally used to protect the following from rusting: (a) wheelbarrows, (b) bicycle handlebars, (c) pins and needles, (d) car bodies, (e) a surgeon's scalpel, (f) food cans?

Which kind of rust protection?

Table 1 compares some different methods of rust protection.

1 Why does zinc plating give better protection than chromium plating? (Look at table 2, which lists some metals in order of reactivity.)

Table 2 Some metals listed in order of decreasing reactivity

aluminium, Al
zinc, Zn
chromium, Cr
iron, Fe
tin, Sn
gold, Au

2 What metal in table 2 might give even better protection than zinc?

3 Why does painting on top of rust give only poor protection?

4 What method would be suitable for each of the following situations? Give your reason in each case. If you can think of a different method, not in the table, then say so.

a To protect a steel pencil sharpener.

b To protect steel railings on a cross-channel ferry.

c To protect steel scissor blades.

d To protect iron gutters on a house. They were painted once, but they are starting to get rusty.

e To protect a steel bridge over a motorway.

f To protect a secondhand car whose doors have started rusting.

Table 1

Method	Protection given	Finished appearance	Relative cost
Zinc plating	Very good	Dull silvery	Medium
Chromium plating	Good	Bright, shiny	High
Painting (after sandblast cleaning)	Fairly good	Colour of paint	Medium
Painting (after ordinary cleaning)	Fair	Colour of paint	Medium/low
Painting on top of rust	Poor	Colour of paint	Low

Picture 1 Iron is galvanised (coated with zinc) to prevent it from rusting

Car exhaust systems

Your car exhaust has rusted badly. It has a large hole in it and is making a terrible noise. You have to buy a replacement system, and you have a choice of two types.

An ordinary steel system. This is guaranteed to last 2 years before it is rusted through again. It costs £100.

A stainless steel system. This is guaranteed to last the lifetime of the car. It costs £240.

1 Which system is cheaper in the long run?

2 What factors will you consider before you decide which system to buy?

3 Only about 10% of car owners in Britain buy stainless steel exhausts. Why do you think this is?

4 Exhaust systems rust faster than any other part of a car. Why is this, do you think?

5 Exhaust systems cannot be protected from rusting by painting. Why?

6 What is stainless steel? Why does it rust slower than ordinary steel?

Picture 2 A stainless steel exhaust lasts the lifetime of the car

B4
Getting water supplies

Water supplies are vital to all our lives. In this topic we look at where water comes from and how it is purified.

Picture 1 The water works at Hampton near London

Today you will use about 180 litres of water — about two bathfuls. That's the average amount used per person in Britain every day. Picture 2 shows how we use it.

Industry also uses huge amounts of water. About 50 000 litres are used in the manufacture of one car, and it takes about 350 litres of water to make 1 litre of beer! The water is used for cooling, washing out bottles and vats, and so on.

Some of the water needed by industry doesn't have to be very pure. A large power station uses around 200 000 litres of cooling water an hour (picture 3). It is usually taken straight from rivers or the sea.

But when we turn on our taps, we expect something purer than river or sea water to come out.

Picture 3 Cooling towers in a power station. Cooling water does not have to be as pure as tap water

Supplying clean water

In Britain, most of our water comes from rivers and lakes, and from underground wells called **aquifers**. Before the water can be used, it must be purified. Picture 4 shows the main stages in the purification of river water.

In the reservoir, some of the impurities sink to the bottom. The water then goes through filters made of sand and gravel. This traps more clay and dirt. In activity A you can try making a model sand filter.

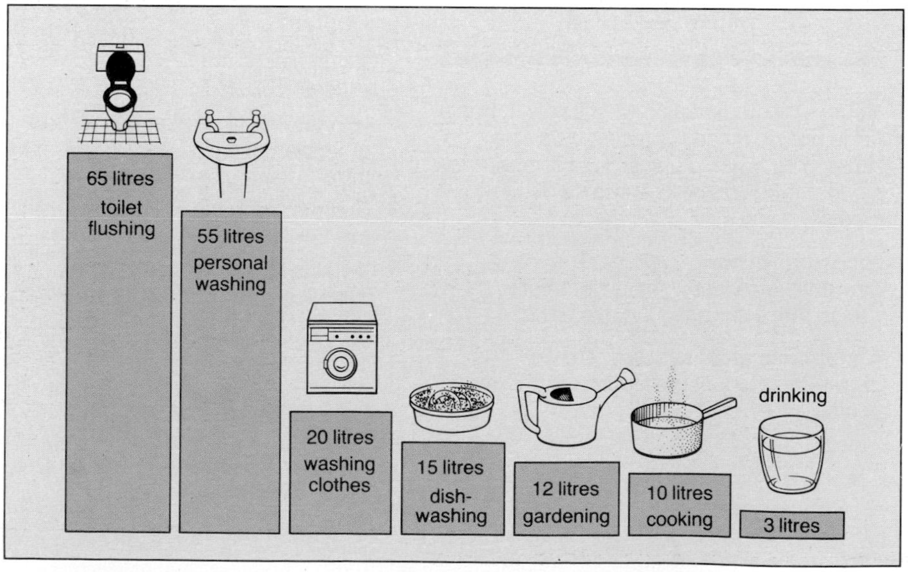

Picture 2 How we use water

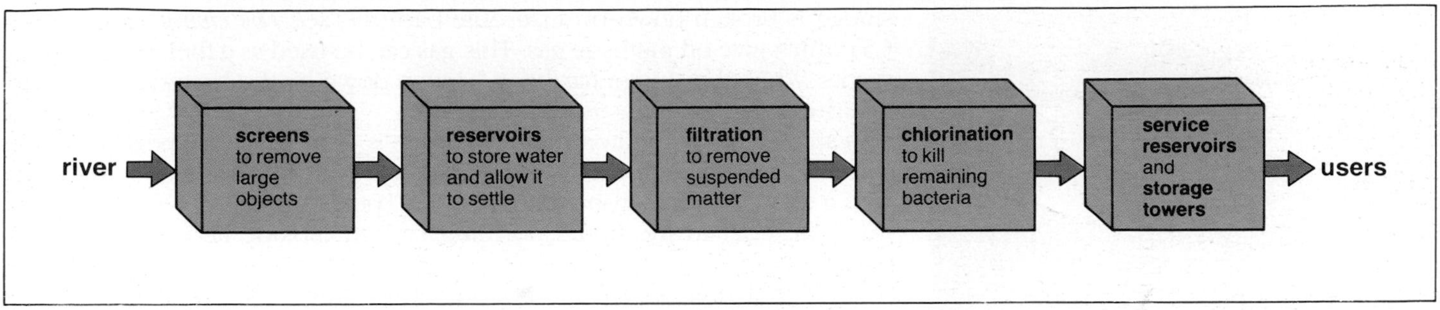

Picture 4 The main stages in the purification of water

Next, a small amount of chlorine is added to the water to kill any bacteria left in it. This is important, because bacteria carried in water can cause epidemics of diseases like typhoid and cholera (see *The Living World*, topic B16). Fluoride may also be added to the water if there is not enough naturally present. Fluoride in the water helps prevent tooth decay.

The purified water is finally pumped to storage reservoirs. From here it flows by gravity to the homes and factories where it is used.

To a scientist, the word 'pure' has a special meaning. A pure substance is a single substance, with nothing else at all mixed with it. Although tap water looks pure, it is really a solution. It has gases like carbon dioxide and oxygen dissolved in it. It also contains dissolved solids, which may make the water 'hard' (topic B5).

And in spite of purification, the water may still contain impurities like nitrates and aluminium which could be harmful to health. There is more about this in topic B6.

What happens to the water afterwards?

After it has been used, water becomes sewage. Sewage is water mixed with waste material such as faeces and urine. Without purification, it would be a serious health risk. It goes along sewers to a treatment works where it gets purified.

What happens in the sewage works?

Sewage treatment uses bacteria to break down the waste material into harmless products. Picture 5 shows how it is done.

The sewage contains both solid and liquid material. First, it is pumped into a large tank. Here the solid matter sinks to the bottom, forming a sludge. The

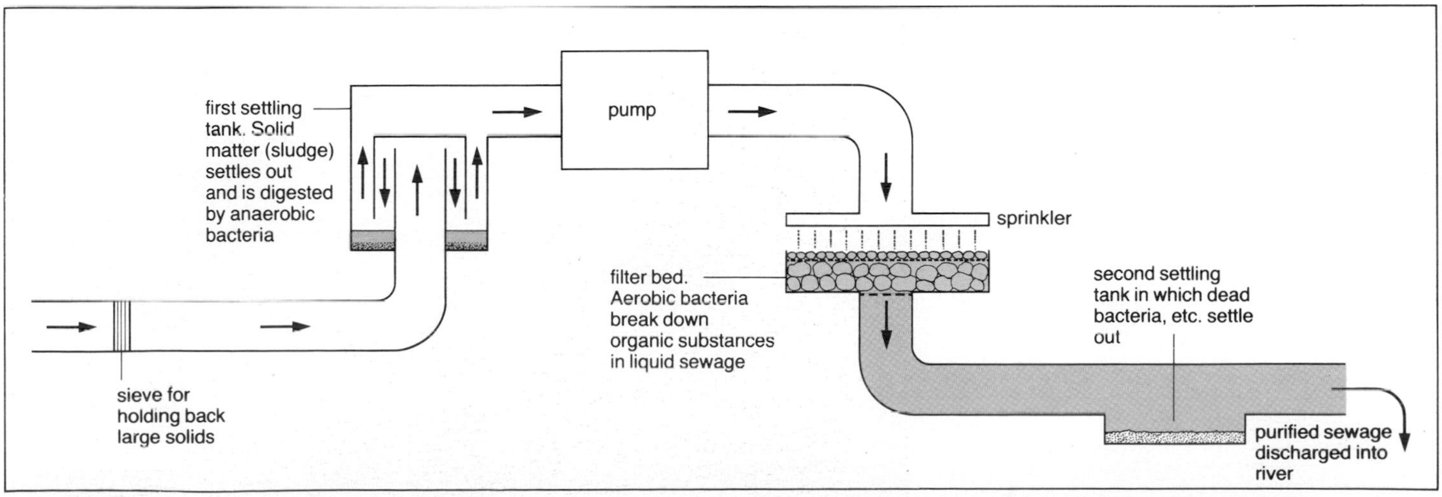

Picture 5 A simplified diagram of a sewage works

Picture 6 The sprinklers and filter beds at a sewage works

sludge is broken down by anaerobic bacteria (see *The Living World*, topic C5) which give off methane gas. This gas can be used as a fuel in the sewage works. When the sludge has been broken down by the bacteria, it is dried. The dried sludge can be used as a fertiliser.

Meanwhile, the liquid part of the sewage is pumped to the next stage. It is sprinkled onto a bed of stones, called a filter bed. These stones are covered with a slimy film of aerobic bacteria. The bacteria break down any organic waste material in the liquid, forming carbon dioxide and nitrogen compounds.

The liquid runs out of the bottom of the filter beds. It is treated with chlorine to kill any harmful bacteria that may remain in it. The liquid is now reasonably pure water again, and it can be discharged into a nearby river. The water may well be collected, purified and used again for household supplies. In fact, the water drunk by people in London has already been through three other people on average! Sewage works are an important way of saving water by recycling.

The water cycle

This recycling is part of a much bigger cycle called the water cycle. Without the water cycle we would soon run out of the fresh water we need.

Picture 7 summarises the water cycle. About 97% of the world's water is in the oceans. The sun keeps evaporating water from the oceans, and this goes

Picture 7 The water cycle

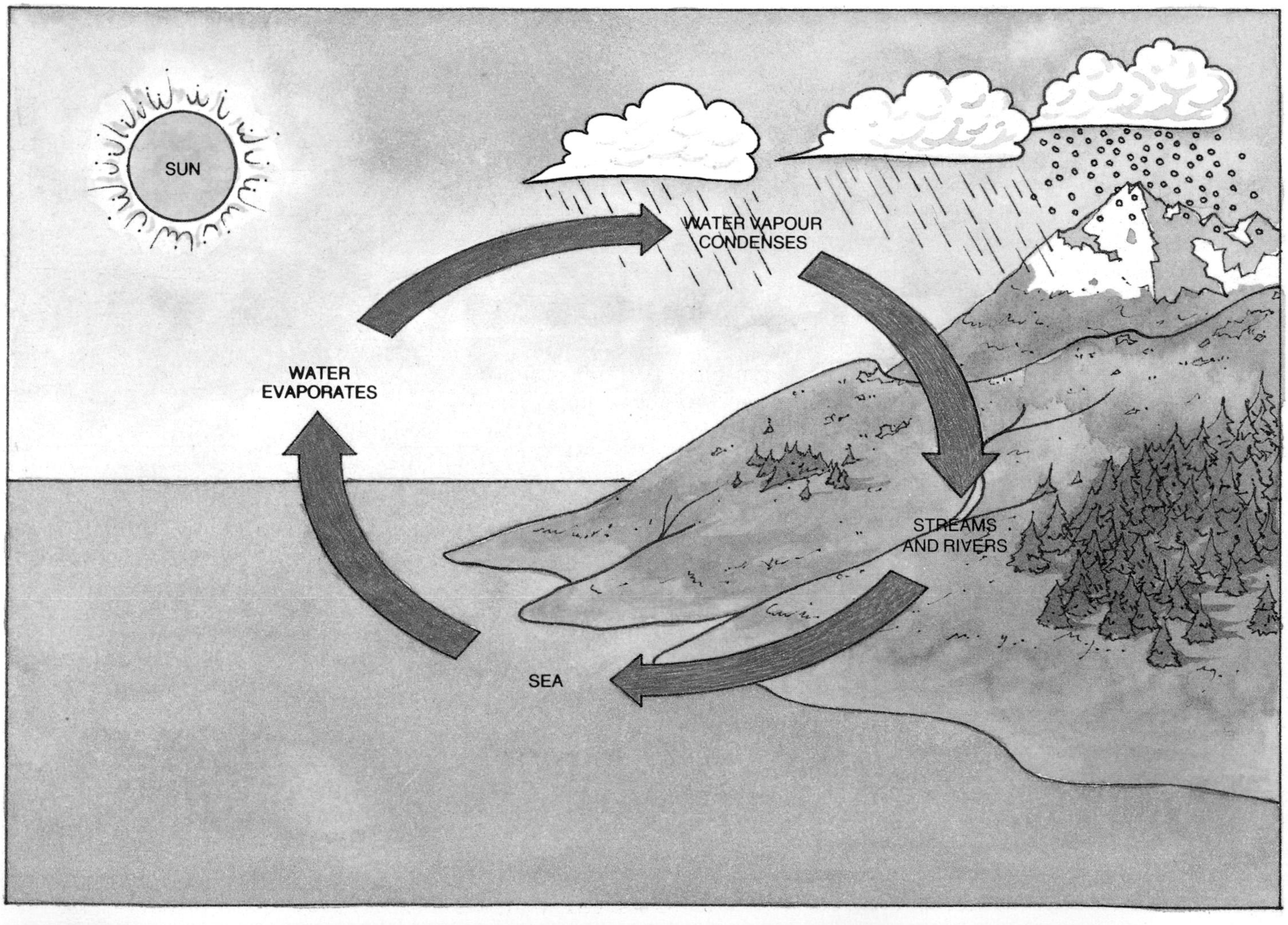

into the atmosphere. Water vapour condenses into drops, which collect in clouds. Eventually the water falls back to earth as rain or snow.

We rely on this cycle to keep us supplied with fresh water. But the cycle is affected by changes in climate. Scientists believe the world's climate is getting warmer because of the 'greenhouse effect' (page 189).

If the climate gets warmer, more water vapour will stay in the atmosphere instead of falling to earth as rain. This could lead to droughts. And a warmer climate would make the sea expand and some of the polar ice-caps might melt. This would make the sea level rise, and it could cause flooding in low-lying countries.

Activities

A Make a model sand filter

You can use an old yoghurt pot to make a model of the filter used in water works. Picture 8 shows the idea. Get some dirty water from a pond or puddle and pour it through the filter. How well does it work? Would the water be safe to drink after going through your filter? How could you test its purity? (Not by drinking it!)

B Where does your water come from?

Try to find out the answers to these questions.

1 What is the name of your local water company? (Try the phone book.)
2 Where is your local water supply taken from?
3 Where is the water purified and treated?
4 How is water paid for? Try to have a look at some water supply bills. What are you really paying for?
5 Do you have a water meter, like an electricity meter or a gas meter? If not, why not?

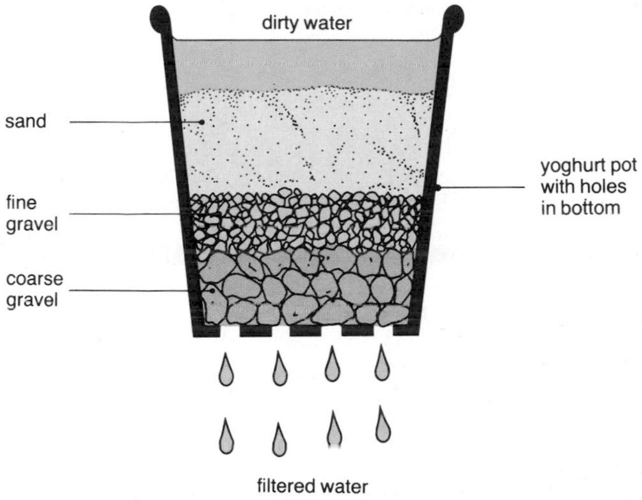

Picture 8 A model sand filter

C Stop that drip!

If you have a dripping tap in your home, try to find out how much water it wastes each day. Put a measuring jug under the tap. Measure the volume of water collected in 10 minutes. From this, work out the volume you would collect in (a) an hour and (b) a day.

Questions

1 Look at the water purification process in picture 4.

a At which stage is each of the following removed?

bacteria, fish, suspended clay particles

b Even after the purification process, the water is still not completely pure. Why?

c Water can be made very pure by distillation. Why don't the water companies distil the water supply?

2 Describe the water cycle. Begin your description 'The sun evaporates water from the sea . . .'

3 Assume each person in your family uses 180 litres of water a day.

a i) How much water is used by the whole family per day?

ii) How much water is used by the whole family per year?

b Find out how much your family pays for its water supply each year. To do this you will need to look at some water bills.

c Use parts a and b to work out the cost per litre of the water used by your family. How does it compare with the cost per litre of (i) milk and (ii) petrol?

4 In a sewage works, waste materials are broken down by bacteria. What type of waste materials are broken down by (a) aerobic bacteria and (b) anaerobic bacteria?

B5 Water, solutions and washing

Water is an excellent solvent. In this topic we look at solutions, solubility, and how water is used for cleaning.

Picture 1 The Dead Sea in Isreal is a concentrated solution of salt. It quickly crystallises in the hot sun

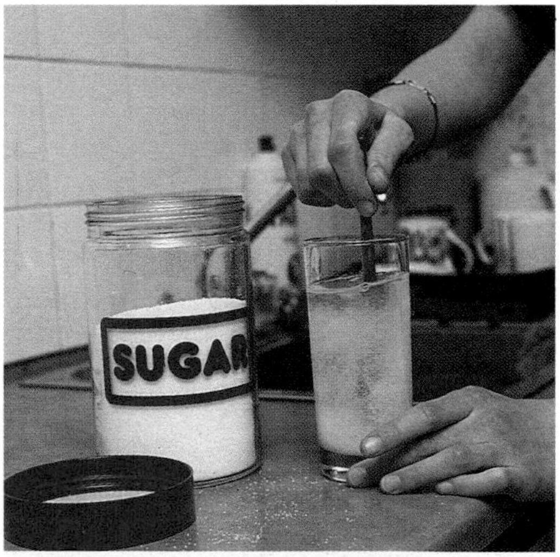
SUGAR

Picture 2 A solution of sugar in water is often used in cooking

How often do you drink a glass of plain water? Most people prefer to take their water in a flavoured form — as tea, lemonade, beer or whatever. All these drinks are over 95% water, but they get their taste from substances that are dissolved in the water.

What are solutions?

When you add sugar to water and stir, the sugar disappears. It has **dissolved** in the water. We say that sugar is **soluble** in water. The mixture of sugar and water is called a **solution**. In this solution, the water is the **solvent** — the liquid part. The sugar is the **solute** — the substance dissolved in the solvent (picture 3). A solution that has a lot of solute in a certain volume of solvent is **concentrated**. A **dilute** solution has only a little solute in a certain volume.

If you go on adding sugar to water, the solution gets more and more concentrated. Eventually no more will dissolve, and the solution is **saturated**.

Suppose you leave a saturated solution in an open container such as an evaporating basin. The water slowly evaporates. When there isn't enough water left to dissolve the solute, the solute comes out of solution, forming crystals. It **crystallises**.

If you add flour to water and stir, the flour *doesn't* disappear. You can still see it, suspended in the water. We say that flour is **insoluble.**

Have a go at question 1 to check that you understand the meaning of these key words to do with solutions.

Sometimes, when you mix two solutions together, a chemical reaction takes place and a new substance is formed. If this new substance is insoluble, it comes out of solution as a **precipitate**. Picture 4 shows an example. There is more about precipitation in topic G4.

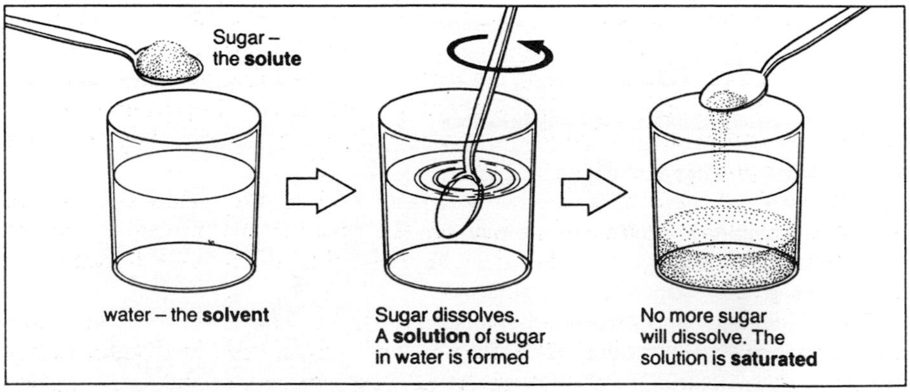
Sugar – the **solute**
water – the **solvent**
Sugar dissolves. A **solution** of sugar in water is formed
No more sugar will dissolve. The solution is **saturated**

Picture 3 Dissolving sugar in water

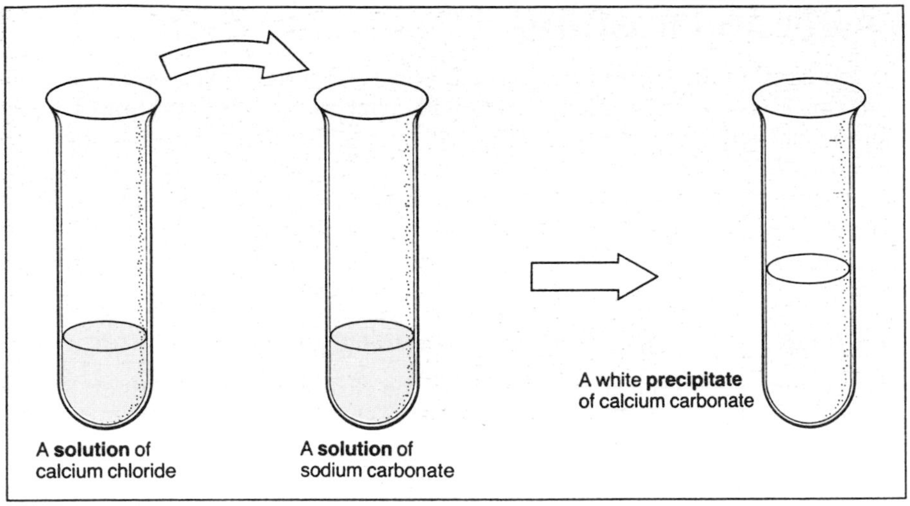

Picture 4 An example of precipitation

Looking at solubility

Water is an excellent solvent, and many different substances will dissolve in it. We rely on water as a solvent whenever we eat, drink or wash. All living things need water in which to dissolve their supplies of food, oxygen and other essentials.

Sometimes, water's solvent properties can be a nuisance. As water runs over the rocks and soil it dissolves substances which may make the water **hard**. These dissolved substances are usually compounds of calcium — hard water is particularly common in areas with rocks made of limestone (calcium carbonate). Hard water prevents soap lathering well, and it forms solid deposits called **fur** in kettles and pipes. There is more about hard water in topics D3 and G4.

Harmful waste substances from industry and agriculture may get dissolved in waterways, making them **polluted**. You can read more about this in topic B6.

Table 1 The solubility of some substances in water. The figures show the mass of the substance that will dissolve in 100 g of water at 25°C

Substance	Solubility
Salt (sodium chloride)	36
Sand	0
Sugar	211
Alcohol (ethanol)	Infinite
Oxygen	0.0041
Carbon dioxide	0.144

Some substances dissolve in water better than others. Table 1 compares the solubility of a few common substances. Notice that the table includes two gases, carbon dioxide and oxygen. Gases can be soluble in water, just like solids can. Indeed, the solubility of gases in water is very important to living things, particularly those that live in water. Fish get the oxygen they need out of the water around them.

Notice too that the table includes alcohol which, like water, is a liquid. Alcohol and water always mix, whatever the proportions of each. They are completely **miscible**. That is why the solubility of alcohol in water is described as 'infinite'.

The solubility of a substance depends on the temperature. Solids are usually more soluble at higher temperatures — sugar dissolves better in hot water than in cold. On the other hand, gases are *less* soluble at higher temperatures, which is why fizzy drinks quickly go 'flat' when they get warm.

Measuring the concentration of solutions

The concentration of a solution shows how much of the solute is dissolved in a certain volume of solvent. In chemistry we usually measure concentration in **moles per litre**, shortened to mol/L. (Topic C5 explains what we mean by 'moles'.) For example, the solution of hydrochloric acid, HCl(aq), which you use in the laboratory probably has concentration 2 mol/L. This means there are 2 moles of HCl dissolved in each litre of solution.

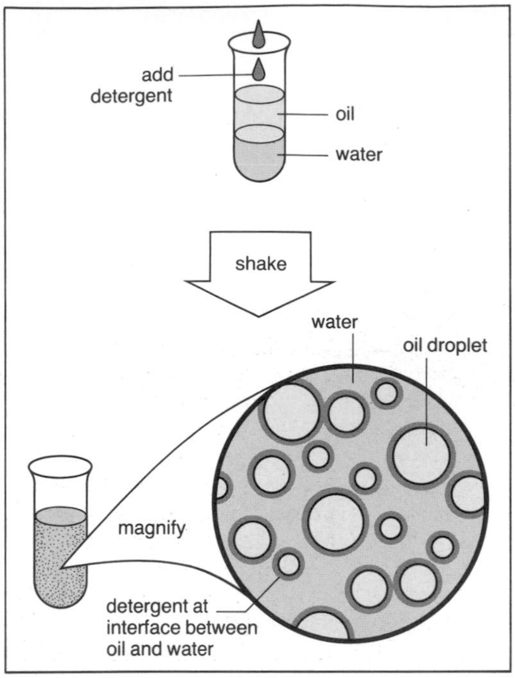

Picture 5 How a detergent works

Picture 6 Soapless detergents are relatively new. Until the 1950s, people always used soap to do the washing and without washing machines it was really hard work

Picture 7 In a dry cleaning machine, the dirty solvent is distilled and re-used. The residue has to be removed every so often

Water and washing

If you work in the garden and get soil on your hands, you can easily wash it off. But if you've been eating chips with your fingers, no amount of water alone will shift the grease. Water and grease just don't mix — they are immiscible.

Unfortunately, most dirt on skin and clothes contains some grease. This binds the dirt on, and makes it difficult to remove with water alone. This is where detergents are needed.

Detergents — boosting the cleaning power of water

Detergents are substances that improve the cleaning power of water. Soap is a detergent, so are washing powders and washing-up liquid.

Detergents help water to mix with grease and oil. If you shake up oil and water together, they form an **emulsion**, containing droplets of one liquid suspended in the other (topic A5). But oil and water repel each other, so the emulsion separates if you leave it to stand. You're left with separate layers of water and oil again. Detergents do the same job as the emulsifying agents mentioned in topic A5. They act as a go-between for oil and water to help them mix and stop them separating.

Picture 5 shows what happens. The key thing about detergents is that *they are able to mix with both water and oil*. When you shake up oil and water with a detergent present, the detergent moves to the interface between the water and the oil. It's able to do this because it can mix with both. With the detergent between them, the water and oil no longer repel each other. The droplets of oil stay suspended in the water.

This is what happens when you use a detergent such as soap to wash your greasy skin. The soap gets between the grease and the water, so they can mix. Rubbing your hands helps, because it shifts the emulsion of grease and water off your hands and into the sink. Rinsing with clean water gets rid of the rest.

A similar thing happens when you wash clothes in a washing machine. The machine does its bit by heating the water and churning the clothes around, but it's the detergent that really does the work — by helping the water to mix with grease.

Your body produces a kind of detergent — called **bile salts** — to help fat mix with water during digestion (see *The Living World*, topic C8).

Different kinds of detergent

Soap (picture 6) is the oldest detergent — it was used by the Romans (some of them, anyway). We still use soap a lot, particularly for washing skin. But there is a serious problem with soap: it does not lather well in hard water.

Most of the detergents we use today are **soapless**. Soapless detergents are usually more effective than soap. They lather well in hard water, and they can be made to suit all sorts of different uses. Some, like washing powders, are solid. Liquid detergents are used in shampoos and washing-up liquid. You can investigate detergents in household products in activity C.

Water isn't the only solvent

We use water plus detergents to do most of our washing, because water is so cheap and abundant.

But sometimes you send clothes to be 'dry cleaned' instead of washed. Dry cleaning uses solvents without any water in them — **non-aqueous** solvents. You may have used a non-aqueous solvent such as alcohol or white spirit to remove ball-pen stains or to get paint off brushes. Non-aqueous solvents generally dissolve grease and oil better than water does. But they are less good at dissolving substances, such as sugar and salt, that dissolve well in water.

A dry cleaning machine is like a washing machine, but it uses a non-aqueous solvent instead of water. Because the solvent is expensive, it is distilled and reused instead of being thrown away like the water from a washing machine (picture 7). Dry cleaning solvents can often remove stains that won't dissolve in water — and they are less likely to make the clothes shrink.

Activities

A Testing solubility

Testing a substance to see if it dissolves isn't always as easy as you might think. The important thing to remember is that a solution is **clear**. When a substance dissolves, it makes a clear solution that you can see through.

Test the solubility of a number of substances by shaking a *small amount* of the substance (about as much as you can get on the end of a wooden splint) with a third of a test-tube of distilled water.

Substances to test could include: chalk, citric acid, potassium manganate(VII), carbon, glucose, copper sulphate.

B Looking for precipitates

Some of the following liquids give a precipitate when they are mixed. Some don't. In each case, mix the solutions, then decide whether a precipitate has formed. It isn't always as easy as you may think!

(**CARE** Eye protection must be worn for all these experiments).

1 Sodium chloride solution and sugar solution.
2 Sodium carbonate solution and calcium chloride solution.
3 Silver nitrate solution and tap water.
4 Sodium thiosulphate solution and dilute hydrochloric acid.
5 Alcohol and water.

(You can investigate precipitates further in topic G4.)

C Looking for detergents

You'll be surprised how many products around the home contain detergents. List as many as you can. Some will be obvious, but it's worth testing less obvious things like toothpaste and cosmetics to see if they contain detergents.

You can test them by putting a little of the product in a test tube or small bottle which is about a quarter-full of water. Shake and look to see if a frothy lather is formed. If so, the product contains a detergent.

D Watching a detergent at work

Detergents help water to mix with things that normally repel water, like grease and oil.

Get a piece of waterproof paper. Waxed paper, baking paper or 'greaseproof' paper would do nicely. Lay the paper flat and put a drop of water on it (picture 8).

Get two pins. Dip the tip of one of them in liquid detergent, and leave the other one clean. *Very gently* touch the drop of water with the tip of the *clean* pin and see what happens. Now repeat, using the pin with detergent on it. What effect does the detergent seem to have?

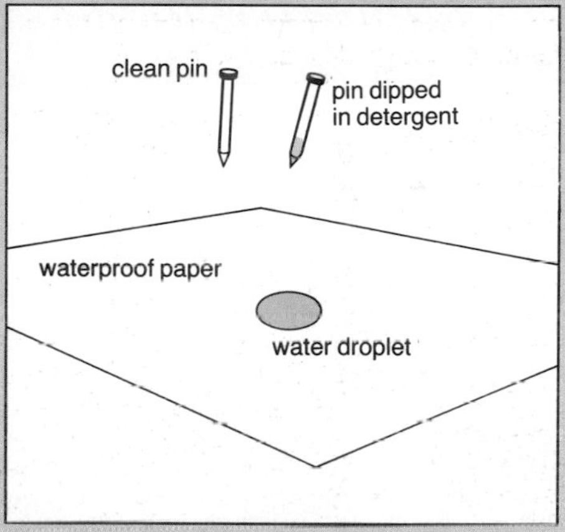

Picture 8

Questions

1 Answer these questions to check that you understand the key words about solutions and solubility.

a Sea water is a solution.
 i) What is the solvent in sea water?
 ii) Name one solute in sea water.

b Soda water (fizzy water) is a solution. What is the solute in soda water?

c What happens to a saturated solution when some of the solvent evaporates?

d Which of the following are soluble in water: sand, salt, alcohol?

2 Try to explain the following observations.

a Ordinary fountain pen ink 'runs' if you spill water on the page. But ball-pen ink doesn't run with water.

b Water alone will not remove a greasy stain from clothing, but alcohol will.

c If you catch a fish in a stream and put it in a jar of water, it survives for quite a long time if the jar is kept cool. But if you let the jar get warm, the fish soon dies.

d The sea is salty, but inland lakes are not.

3a What does the word 'detergent' mean?

b What advantages do soapless detergents have compared with soap?

4a Explain how detergents help water to wash away grease and oil.

b Explain why each of the following is important when you are washing something.
 i) Churning the washing around.
 ii) Rinsing.
 iii) Using hot water.

5 The following questions are about dry-cleaning.

a What happens in a dry-cleaning machine?

b Is dry-cleaning really 'dry'? Explain.

c Petrol dissolves grease and oil, but it is never used in dry-cleaning. Suggest a reason why.

d When you take clothes home from the dry-cleaner in a car, you are advised to have a window open. Why do you think this is?

B6 How pure is the water?

In this topic we look at some of the ways water can become polluted and dangerous to life.

Picture 1 The water *looks* pure, but is it?

On 6 July 1988 a lorry load of aluminium sulphate was accidentally tipped into the water supply in the Cornish town of Camelford. Before the mistake had been discovered, people were complaining of sickness and some people's hair had turned green (see page 48).

A safe, unpolluted water supply is essential to good health. Unpolluted water is even more important to aquatic organisms which spend all their life surrounded by the liquid.

What's the problem?

There are two general ways that water can become harmful through pollution.

1 The oxygen dissolved in it gets used up

This happens when algae and bacteria grow in the water so fast that they use up most of the oxygen. This is usually because the water has become polluted with sewage or other substances such as fertilisers from fields, that encourage bacteria to grow. This is called **eutrophication** (see *The Living World*, topic B13).

2 Harmful substances get into the water

These may poison organisms which live in the water or drink it. These substances may come from industries, farms or homes. Some of them may be **biodegradable** — they can be broken down by living organisms. This is good, because it means that the harmful substances do not stay around too long.

What are the major water pollutants?

Let's look at some of the most serious pollutants of rivers, lakes and oceans.

Sewage

This is produced wherever humans live and work. Sewage is rich in organic substances which can act as fertilisers. They encourage algae and bacteria to grow and cause eutrophication. In 1950, the River Thames at London was so polluted with sewage that there were no fish left in it. Since then, the

Picture 2 The polluted water of the River Seine near Paris

Picture 4 The "Thames Bubbler" bubbles oxygen into polluted river water

dumping of sewage has been controlled, and fish have returned (picture 3). There is more about this on page 48.

Nowadays in Britain, most sewage is purified before it is allowed into waterways. But in some places raw, untreated sewage is still pumped into the sea.

Fertilisers are used in large amounts on modern farms. They can get washed down through the soil by rain, and they end up in streams and rivers. Like sewage, fertilisers cause eutrophication and encourage algae and bacteria to grow.

Fertilisers which contain nitrates are particularly bad, because nitrates are very soluble in water. They also get into drinking water supplies (see below).

Pesticides are used on farms and can also end up in water supplies. Pesticides are designed to kill pests, particularly insects, which eat the crops. Unfortunately they are often poisonous to other organisms as well — including humans.

The best way to control pollution by pesticides is to use less of them, or control pests in some other way. Another approach is to develop pesticides that are relatively harmless to innocent organisms. More is given about pesticide problems in *The Living World*, topic B14.

Detergents get into the water from homes and factories. Most detergents are biodegradable, so they get broken down reasonably quickly. But if a lot of detergent gets into a river, it may cause foaming and it may poison aquatic organisms.

Industrial waste is sometimes pumped into waterways from factories. There are many different kinds of waste, but what matters is whether it is harmful to life. Common industrial pollutants include acids and alkalis and compounds of poisonous metals.

There are laws about how much harmful waste can be pumped into rivers in Britain, but they are sometimes broken. Accidental leakages also sometimes happen.

Oil may get spilt into the sea from refineries or leaking oil tankers. Oil floats on water, so the oil may end up on beaches. It may get on the feathers of sea birds, so they can't fly.

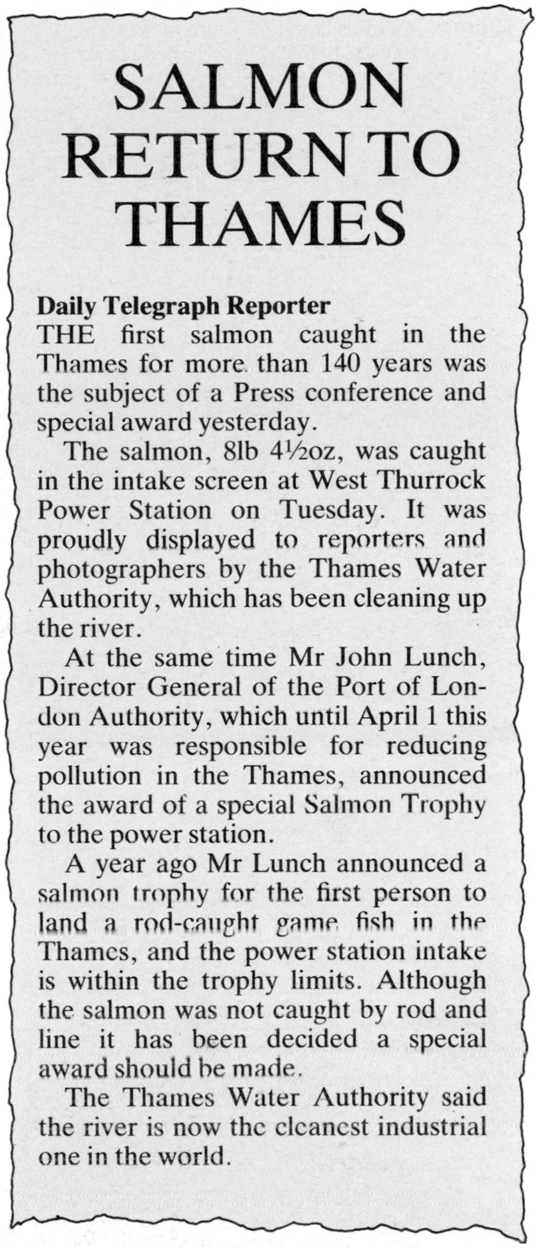
SALMON RETURN TO THAMES

Daily Telegraph Reporter

THE first salmon caught in the Thames for more than 140 years was the subject of a Press conference and special award yesterday.

The salmon, 8lb 4½oz, was caught in the intake screen at West Thurrock Power Station on Tuesday. It was proudly displayed to reporters and photographers by the Thames Water Authority, which has been cleaning up the river.

At the same time Mr John Lunch, Director General of the Port of London Authority, which until April 1 this year was responsible for reducing pollution in the Thames, announced the award of a special Salmon Trophy to the power station.

A year ago Mr Lunch announced a salmon trophy for the first person to land a rod-caught game fish in the Thames, and the power station intake is within the trophy limits. Although the salmon was not caught by rod and line it has been decided a special award should be made.

The Thames Water Authority said the river is now the cleanest industrial one in the world.

Picture 3 The opening of the new sewage works at Crossness in 1974 was a turning point for the purity of the River Thames

Picture 5 To get big wheat crops a lot of fertiliser has to be used, and this can pollute water supplies

Picture 6 Oil spills from tankers are a pollution hazard, particularly on bathing beaches

When these kind of spillages happen, detergents have to be used to try and make the oil mix with the sea water so it is dispersed. Unfortunately, the detergents themselves may also be harmful to life.

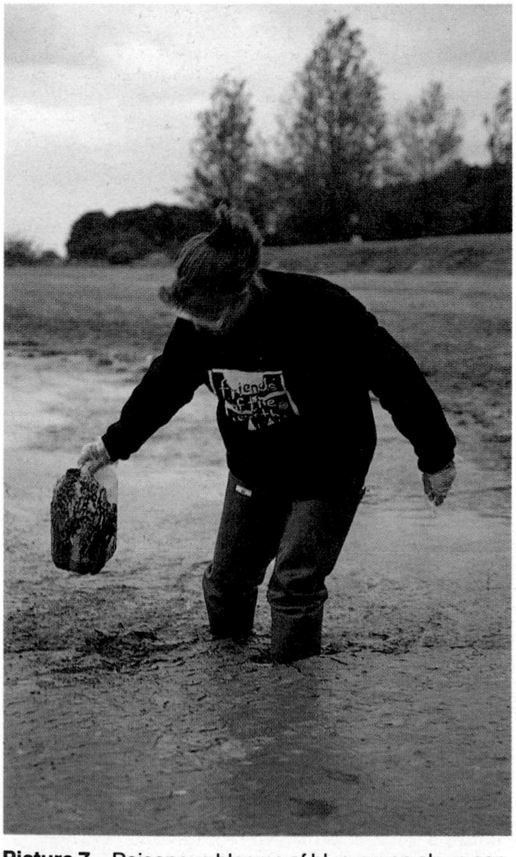

Picture 7 Poisonous blooms of blue-green algae can be a consequence of nitrate pollution

How safe is the drinking water?

Topic B4 describes how water is purified to make it safe for drinking. It is impossible, though, to get *all* the impurities out of the water. In any case, some impurities, like calcium compounds, are useful because they make the water taste better and they may even be good for your health.

But there are some impurities left in the water that may be harmful to health.

Nitrates get into the water from the fertilisers used on farmland. Nitrates contain the NO_3^- ion, and they are very soluble in water. This makes it difficult to remove them.

The trouble is that nitrate takes a long time to reach the water supply after it has been put on the fields as fertiliser. It can take up to 40 years for the nitrate to work its way down through the soil and into the aquifers — the underground reservoirs which feed the water supply. So even if farmers cut down on the use of nitrate fertilisers now, the problem will still be with us for several decades.

There is more about nitrate pollution in *The Living World*, topic B13.

Aluminium gets into water from several sources. Soil is full of aluminium compounds, and these may dissolve in rain water, particularly if the rain is acidic.

Aluminium sulphate is sometimes added at the water treatment works, to help make cloudy water clear. Some excess aluminium sulphate is often left over, dissolved in the water.

Aluminium ions may also get into water in tiny amounts from aluminium kettles and saucepans, especially when they are used to cook acidic foods like fruit.

So what's the problem with aluminium? Until recently it was considered to be fairly harmless, but doctors now believe that aluminium ions are harmful in a number of ways.

Aluminium has been linked with Alzheimer's disease, which results in loss of memory and odd behaviour in some old people. People with Alzheimer's disease have abnormally large amounts of aluminium compounds in their brains. This doesn't prove that aluminium causes the disease, but it is enough to make us suspicious.

Picture 8 Tiny amounts of aluminium get into food from cooking utensils

Cleaning up the water

Stopping pollution always costs something. As consumers, we want all our drinking water to have safe levels of aluminium ions and nitrate ions. This means that in some areas the water companies will have to spend more on purifying the water. Or they may have to find new, purer sources of water.

All this costs money, and in the end we, the consumers, pay. And it's not easy to decide what is a 'safe' amount of an impurity, whether it's aluminium, nitrate or other harmful substances like pesticides. It's impossible to get the water completely pure. We have to decide what we can afford, and what we are prepared to put up with.

Activities

A Examining samples of water

Collect samples of water from two or three local sources — rivers, ponds or streams. Do tests on each sample to see how pure it is. Try the following tests.

1 *pH*. Test a sample of the water with 'narrow range' pH paper. What is its pH? Most fish prefer water with a pH between 7 and 8. If the pH is outside the range 5 to 8.5, the water is seriously polluted with acid or alkali.

2 *Suspended solids*. Pour 100 cm^3 of the water sample through a filter funnel containing a folded filter paper. Do this for each water sample in turn.

Keep the filter paper from each sample. Compare the amount of solid collected from each sample. In general, the more suspended solids, the more polluted the water.

Try to think of other tests you could do to compare the purity of the water samples, bearing in mind the pollutants they are likely to contain. Before you do any more tests, get your plans checked by your teacher.

B Looking at local water

Choose a river near to your home. Find out whether any industries use the river, either as a source of water or for discharging waste.

Try to find out what the water is used for, and what kind of waste is discharged.

C Looking at mineral water

Collect the labels from bottles of mineral water. If all the class collect labels, you will get a good selection.

Use the labels to compare what substances are dissolved in the different brands of mineral water. Are all the dissolved substances good for health?

Questions

1 Here are three sources of water pollution: (a) homes, (b) farms, (c) industries. For each one of these, list two pollutants that it might produce.

2a Why is it important to living things that oxygen dissolves in water?

b What is the effect of sewage on the concentration of oxygen dissolved in the water? Explain why this effect occurs.

3 Three neighbours are having a conversation about the purity of drinking water.

Mr Jenkins says, 'I want my drinking water to be completely pure. I'm not prepared to put up with *any* impurities in it'.

Mrs Johnson says, 'It's impossible to remove *all* the impurities from the water'.

Mr Ahmed says, 'Water is like everything else. You get what you pay for'.

Which of these people do you agree with? Why? What further points would you want to make yourself?

4 **Thermal pollution** may occur when warm water is pumped into a river or other body of water. This sometimes happens near power stations.

a Why do power stations produce warm water?

b What problems might be caused by thermal pollution?

Trouble with aluminium

Lowermoor water works in Cornwall treats drinking water for the nearby town of Camelford. The water coming into the works is rather acidic, so lime (calcium hydroxide) is added. The water is also quite cloudy due to suspended clay particles. Aluminium sulphate is added to make the particles clump together so they can be filtered off.

The aluminium sulphate is normally kept as a solution in a special storage tank. On 6 July 1988 a driver delivered fresh supplies of aluminium sulphate solution. Instead of putting the solution in the storage tank, he pumped it straight into the water supply by mistake.

Picture 1 shows what happened to the concentration of aluminium ions in the water over the next few days. As a result of this accident, the water also became much more acidic. This made copper from pipes and boilers dissolve in the water. Most of the symptoms people suffered were probably caused by copper ions rather than by aluminium ions.

People were soon complaining of sickness, curdling milk and nasty tasting water. Some people noticed that the water coming out of the taps was blue, and some people's hair went green.

When they discovered the problem, the water engineers flushed out the mains into nearby rivers. As a result, 30 000 fish were killed.

Fortunately, the level of aluminium returned to normal before long (see picture 1). Doctors are unsure whether there will be long-term health problems for local people.

1 Why are the following added to the water at the treatment works?
   (a) Lime.
   (b) Aluminium sulphate.
2 Explain in your own words how the excess aluminium ions got into the drinking water.
3 Aluminium compounds are colourless. Why, then, did the water turn blue and some people's hair turn green?
4 Aluminium sulphate is added to water as part of its normal treatment, but normally very little of this aluminium ends up in the drinking water. Suggest a reason why.
5 Apart from water treatment, how else can aluminium ions get into the water supplies?
6 No people were killed as a result of this accident, but it killed thousands of fish. Why were the fish more vulnerable?

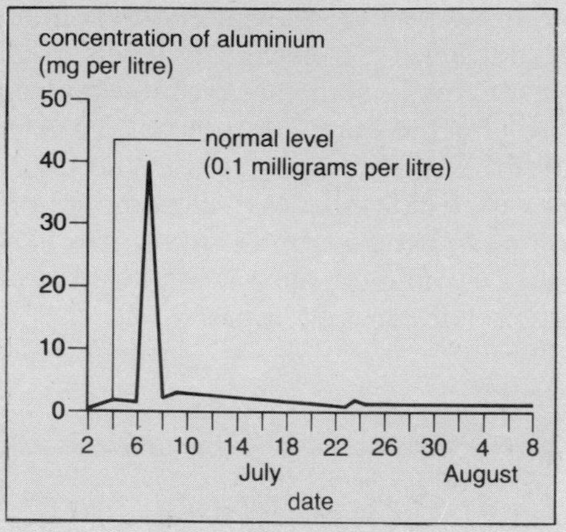

Picture 1 The variation in the concentration of aluminium ions in the Camelford water supply in July and August 1986. The recommended maximum is 0.2 milligrams per litre

Cleaning up the Thames

Picture 2 shows the concentration of dissolved oxygen in different parts of the River Thames. The three graphs show how the concentration has changed during the last hundred years.

1 In which of the three periods was the oxygen concentration at its lowest? Suggest a reason why.
2 Look at the graph for 1981. Whereabouts in the Thames was the oxygen concentration lowest? Explain why the concentration was higher (i) upstream and (ii) downstream of this point.
3 The figures for the concentration of dissolved oxygen are given as '% saturation'. What do you think this means?
4 Between 1835 and 1974 no salmon were caught in the River Thames near London. Today salmon is one of 70 species of fish that can be caught. Explain.

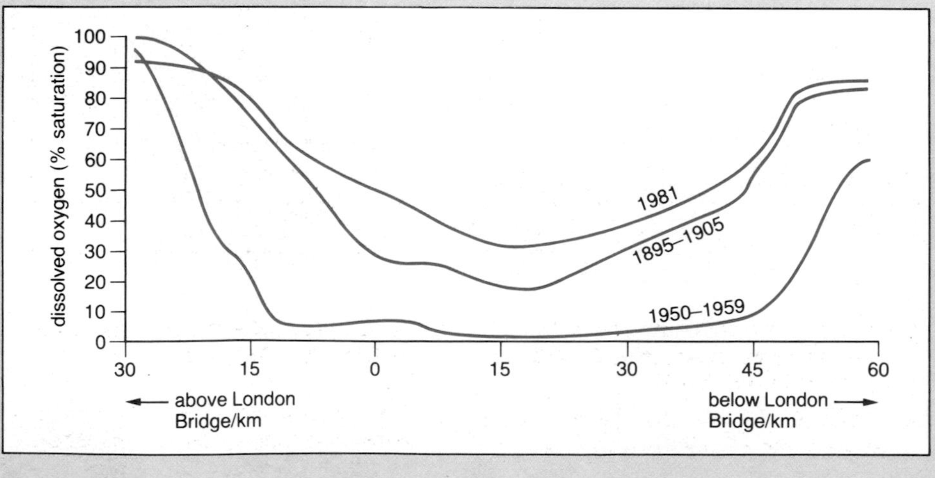

Picture 3 The River Thames is now clean enough to catch fish in, even in the heart of London

Picture 2 The concentration of dissolved oxygen in different parts of the River Thames, at different times during the last hundred years

Examining the water

Table 1 shows the results of an examination of water supplies carried out by the Anytown Water Company.

Table 1

ANYTOWN WATER COMPANY Water Analysis Report

Location **High Street Anytown** ***Date*** **20 May 1990**

Bacteriological

Colony Count per ml, 37°C, 24 h	3

Physical

Appearance	Clear	Conductivity at 20°C (μS/cm)	536
Taste	Normal	Temperature °C	14°C
pH Value	7.13	Odour	Nil

Chemical (concentration in mg/litre)

Total Hardness ($CaCO_3$)	282	Total Residual Chlorine	0.15
Carbonate Hardness ($CaCO_3$)	255	Free Residual Chlorine	0.12
Non-Carbonate Hardness ($CaCO_3$)	27	Carbonate (CO_3)	153
Calcium (Ca)	108	Sulphate (SO_4)	12
Magnesium (Mg)	3.1	Chloride (Cl)	16
Sodium (Na)	8.2	Nitrate (NO_3)	21
Potassium (K)	1.1	Fluoride (F)	0.1
Iron (Fe)	0.02	Phosphate (PO_4)	0.13
Aluminium (Al)	0.01	Silica (SiO_2)	—
Copper (Cu)	0.02	Free Carbon Dioxide (CO_2)	33
Lead (Pb)	0.03		
Zinc (Zn)	0.01		

Table 2 shows the European Community's guidelines for water purity. **Guide level** means the recommended safe concentration. **Maximum admissible concentration** means the highest concentration allowed.

Use the analysis report in table 1, together with the guidelines in table 2, to answer these questions.

1 An easy question to start you off! How many milligrams of magnesium are present in each litre of Anytown water?

2 The tables give figures for the concentrations in water of metals like magnesium, iron and aluminium. Yet none of these metals dissolve in water. Explain.

3 Which metallic element is present in the Anytown water in greatest concentration?

4 Use the water analysis report to decide whether the water is acidic, alkaline or neutral.

5 What do you think is meant by the 'colony count'? (Topic B18 in *The Living World* may help you here.)

6 Why might the *conductivity* of the water tell you something about its purity?

Table 2 Water purity guidelines of the European Community (EC)

Substance present in the water	Guide level/(mg/litre)	Max. admissable conc/ (mg/litre)
Calcium (Ca)	100	
Magnesium (Mg)	30	50
Sodium (Na)	20	150
Potassium (K)	10	12
Iron (Fe)	0.05	0.2
Aluminium (Al)	0.05	0.2
Copper	0.1	
Lead (Pb)		0.05
Zinc (Zn)	0.1	
Sulphate (SO_4)	25	250
Chloride (Cl)	25	
Nitrate (NO_3)	25	50
Fluoride (F)		1.5
Phosphate (PO_4)	0.2	5
acid	pH 6.5—8.5	

7 Compare the concentrations in the water analysis report (table 1) with the EC guidelines (table 2).

a Which substance in the Anytown water exceeds the EC guide level?

b Do you think it matters that the guide level is exceeded for this substance? Explain.

8 What other substances, not mentioned in the water analysis report, might be present in the water?

C1 Particles on the move

We can use the kinetic theory to explain many of the things that happen around us.

If you warm up an ice cube, it melts.

If bread is being baked in the kitchen, you can soon smell it all round the house.

When you get out of a swimming pool you feel cold, even on a sunny day.

The **kinetic theory** is one of the most useful theories in science. We can use it to explain these and many more of the familiar things that happen in the world.

What is the kinetic theory?

The kinetic theory says that matter is made of tiny particles that move all the time. Let's look at the main points of the theory.

- All matter is made up of tiny, invisible, moving particles. (These particles are actually atoms, molecules and ions, as we shall see in topic C3.)
- The particles move all the time. The higher the temperature, the faster they move.
- Heavier particles move more slowly than light ones at a given temperature.

Picture 1 How does the smell reach your nose?

Using the theory to explain the states of matter

A good scientific theory can be used to explain things. It can be used as a model — a mental model, rather than the kind of model you build. The kinetic theory is a good model because it explains lots of things — particularly concerning the states of matter. Also, very usefully, it helps us *predict* things.

Gases, liquids and solids

The kinetic theory explains the difference between gases, liquids and solids.

In a **gas**, the particles are widely spaced. They are free to move anywhere. They move very fast, colliding with each other and with the walls of the container (picture 2(a)).

In a **solid**, the particles are strongly attracted to each other. There are **bonds** between the particles. This holds them close together (picture 2b). The particles are arranged in a regular way, which explains why many solids form regular crystals. The particles in a solid have very little freedom of

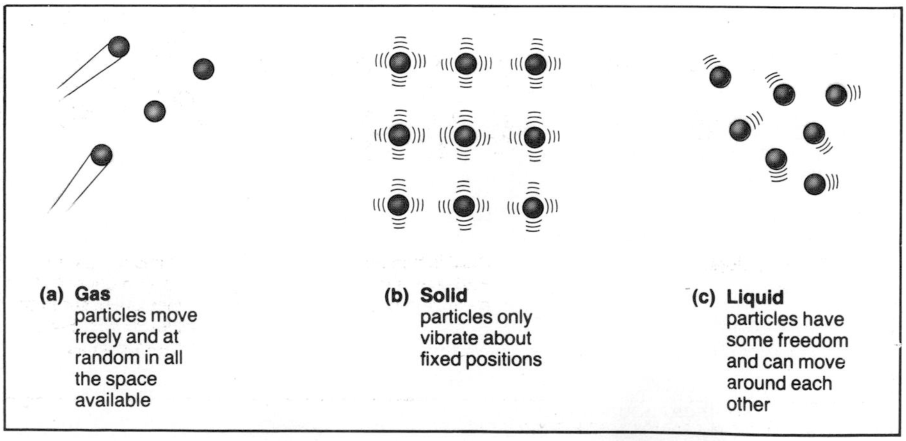

(a) Gas
particles move freely and at random in all the space available
(b) Solid
particles only vibrate about fixed positions
(c) Liquid
particles have some freedom and can move around each other

Picture 2 The states of matter

movement. They are in fixed positions, and all they can do is vibrate. They can't move all over the place like the particles in a gas.

In a **liquid**, the situation is somewhere between a solid and a gas. The particles are quite close together, but they attract each other more weakly than in a solid. The particles have more freedom of movement than in a solid (picture 2(c)).

You can get a feeling for the states of matter using marbles in a tray (picture 3).

Changes of state

Why do substances change state when they are heated or cooled?

We can use the kinetic theory to explain these changes (picture 4). When a solid is heated, the particles vibrate faster and faster until they break away from their fixed positions. The solid has melted to a liquid. Melting a solid needs energy. The energy is needed to break the bonds holding the particles together, and pull the particles apart. We give the solid energy by heating it.

If you go on heating the liquid, the particles are given more energy and move faster and faster still. Eventually the faster ones break away completely from each other. The liquid is becoming a gas. Turning a liquid to a gas needs energy to break bonds between particles. You can feel the energy change as you stand wet and shivering beside a swimming pool. As the liquid water on your body evaporates, it takes the energy it needs from your skin and you feel cold. This is also why sweating keeps you cool. Sweat evaporates from the skin, taking energy away from it.

Liquids evaporate slowly when they are cool. But when you heat the liquid, more and more of the particles get enough energy to break away. Eventually so many particles are escaping that bubbles of gas form in the liquid. The liquid is *boiling*.

The opposite happens when a gas turns to a liquid and a liquid turns to a solid. In these changes, energy is *given out*.

Refrigerators use the energy changes involved in changes of state. A special fluid called a refrigerant circulates around the fridge (picture 5).

When the inside of the fridge starts getting warm, a thermostat makes the pump switch on — you can hear the pump as a humming or whirring sound. The pump compresses the refrigerant so it condenses to a liquid. This gives out energy, and the refrigerant gets hot. There are special cooling fins at the back of the fridge to let it cool down again. The liquid refrigerant circulates in pipes inside the fridge, where it turns back to a gas. This takes in energy, so the inside of the fridge gets cool.

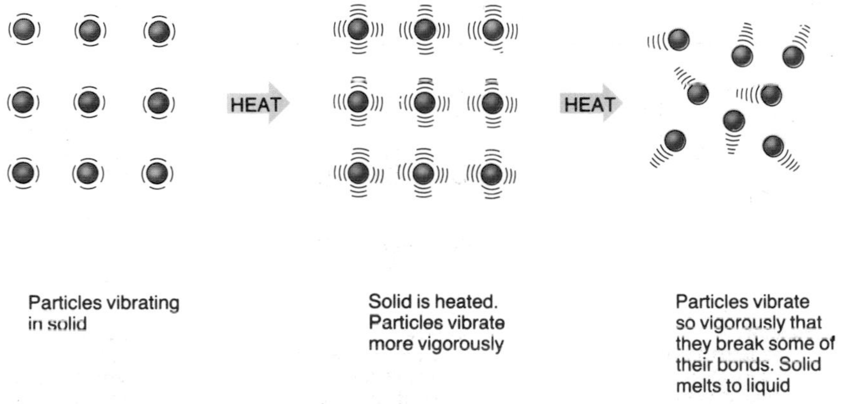
HEAT
HEAT
Particles vibrating in solid
Solid is heated. Particles vibrate more vigorously
Particles vibrate so vigorously that they break some of their bonds. Solid melts to liquid

Picture 4 What happens when a solid melts

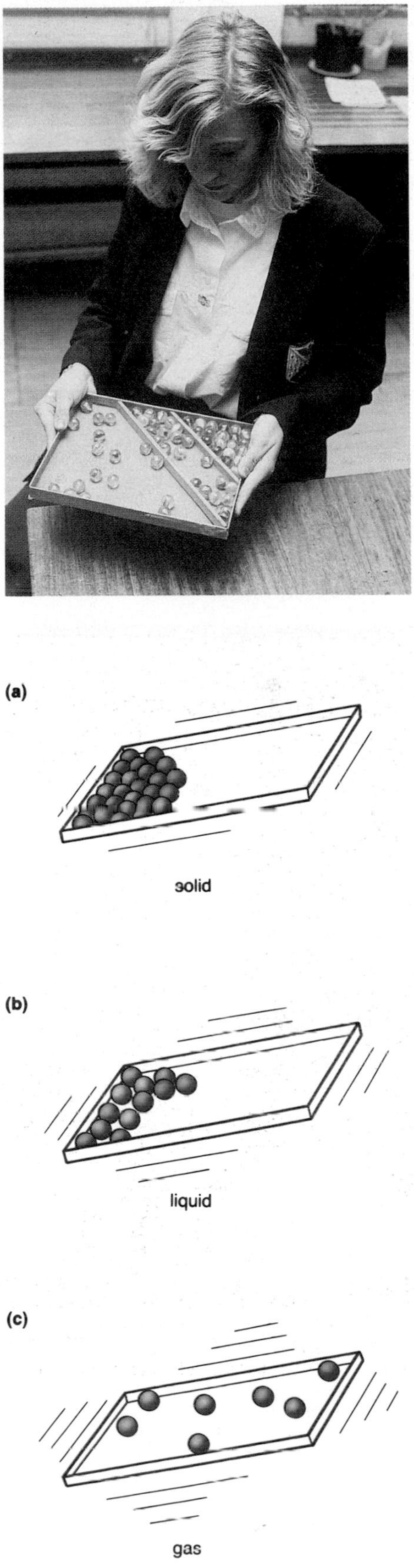
(a)
solid
(b)
liquid
(c)
gas

Picture 3 This experiment with marbles illustrates the three states of matter

Picture 7 When a gas dissolves in a liquid it seems to disappear — but it reappears when the pressure is released

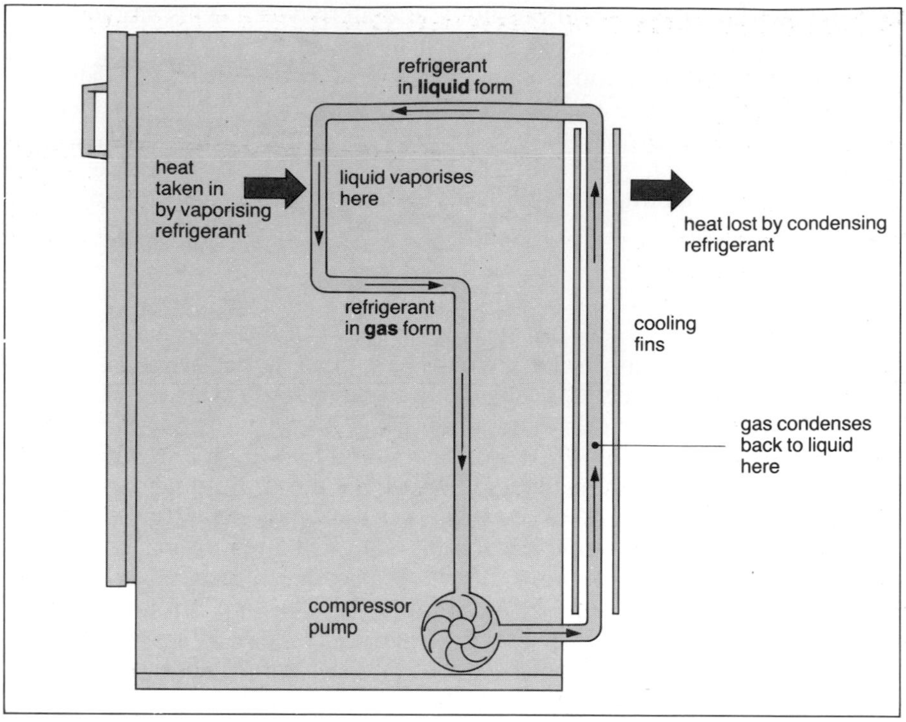

Picture 5 How a refrigerator works. The overall effect is to move heat from the fridge compartment and out of the back

Table 1 sums up the energy changes involved in different changes of state.

Table 1 Energy changes and changes of state

Change of state	Energy change involved	Why the energy change occurs
Solid → liquid (melting)	Heat taken in	Energy needed to break bonds between particles in solid
Liquid → gas (boiling, evaporating)	Heat taken in	Energy needed to break bonds between particles in liquid
Liquid → solid (freezing)	Heat given out	Energy given out as particles bond together in solid
Gas → liquid (condensing)	Heat given out	Energy given out as particles bond together in liquid

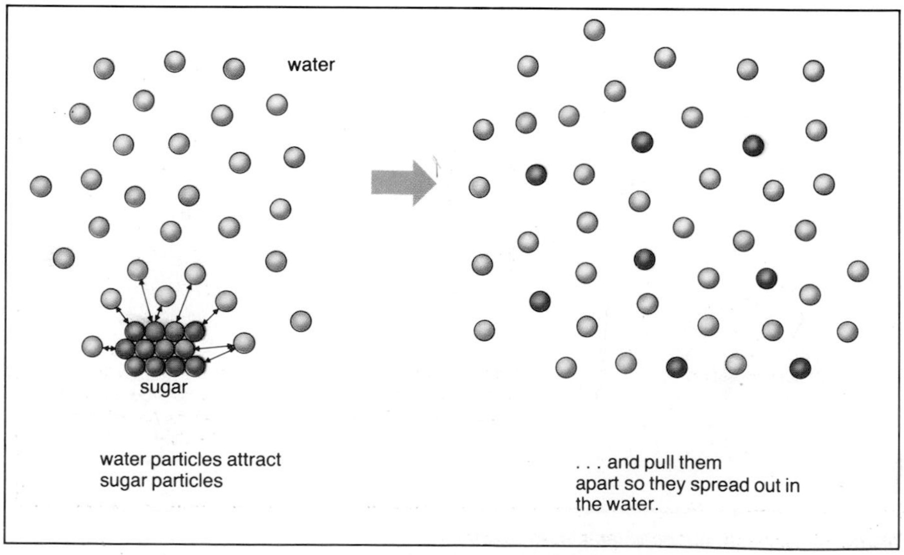

Picture 6 What happens when sugar dissolves in water

What else can the kinetic theory explain?

Dissolving

When you stir sugar into water, the sugar dissolves and seems to disappear. But it's still there, because you can taste its sweetness when you drink the water. Picture 6 shows how we can explain this using the kinetic theory. When a solid dissolves, it seems to disappear because its particles get spread out between the particles of the liquid. The same sort of thing happens when a gas dissolves in a liquid (picture 7).

Diffusion

Baking bread has a delicious smell. If bread is being baked in the kitchen, you can soon smell it all round the house. Particles of gas are released from the bread and they spread or **diffuse** around the house. All gases diffuse to fill the space available to them — even dense gases like bromine (picture 8).

The kinetic theory says that gases contain particles that are free to move anywhere. So it's not surprising that gases diffuse. The particles do not care where they go, so sooner or later they are bound to fill up all the space available.

Dense gases like bromine and carbon dioxide diffuse more slowly than lighter gases like hydrogen. The denser gases have heavier particles which move more slowly. Have you noticed that a balloon filled with a light gas such as hydrogen or helium goes down quicker than a balloon filled with air? The balloon rubber has tiny holes through which the gas particles slowly diffuse. The lighter hydrogen particles move faster, so they get through the holes quicker.

It's not only gases that can diffuse. Diffusion occurs in liquids too. You are using diffusion every time you make a cup of tea (picture 9).

Look at the experiment shown in picture 10. When water is added, the copper sulphate starts to dissolve. Particles of blue copper sulphate diffuse into the water. At first the copper sulphate is more concentrated at the bottom of the jar. But gradually the particles spread throughout the water, until the concentration is the same everywhere. This illustrates an important point about diffusion: **diffusion involves the movement of particles from a region of higher concentration towards a region of lower concentration**.

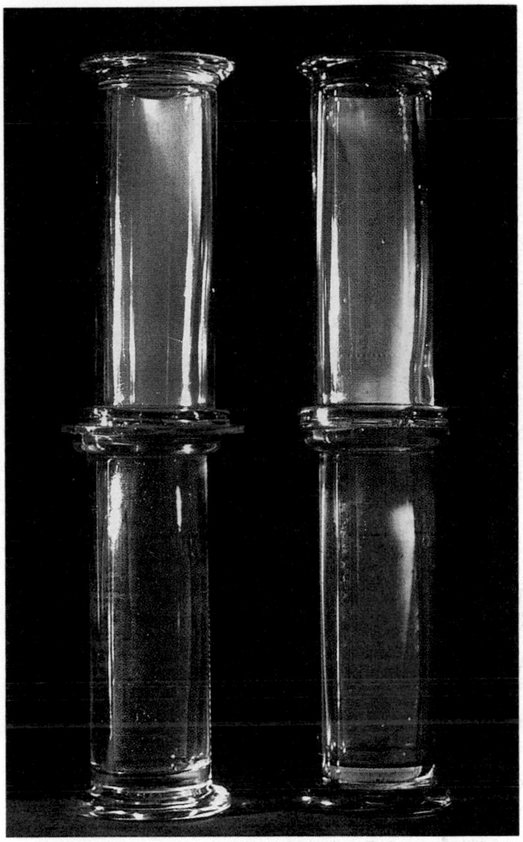

Picture 8 Bromine vapour diffuses to fill a gas jar

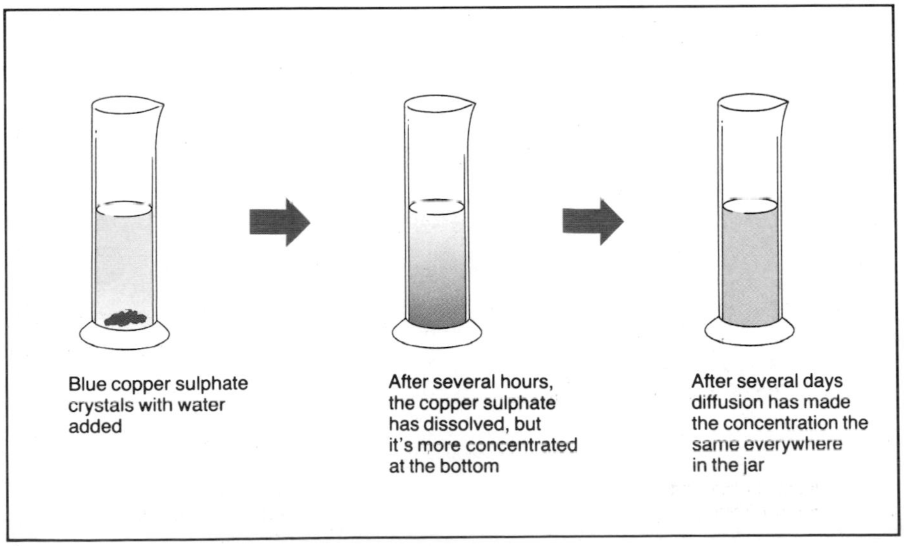

Blue copper sulphate crystals with water added
After several hours, the copper sulphate has dissolved, but it's more concentrated at the bottom
After several days diffusion has made the concentration the same everywhere in the jar

Picture 10 Diffusion of copper sulphate in water

Picture 9 Diffusion makes the colour and flavour of the tea spread through the hot water

Picture 11 This gap allows the bridge to expand in hot weather

Diffusion is very important in all living things. Diffusion makes it possible for oxygen to get into your blood from your lungs. A special kind of diffusion, called osmosis, helps water move in and out of the cells of plants and animals. More is given about this in *The Living World*, topic A4.

Gas pressure

This is covered in the next topic.

Brownian motion

This is covered in the exercise *Dr Brown and Dr Einstein* on page 60.

Expansion

When you heat things, they get bigger. In other words, they **expand**. Solids don't expand very much. Even so, bridge builders have to take precautions against the expansion that occurs on a hot summer's day (picture 11). Liquids expand a bit more than solids, and we use this in thermometers (picture 12). Gases expand a lot when heated — more is given about this in the next topic.

Why do things expand? Think of what happens to a solid when it is heated. The particles stay in the same fixed positions, but vibrate faster. This makes them nudge their neighbouring particles so they move over a bit (picture 13). The more the solid is heated, the more the particles nudge each other, and the more the solid expands.

Many other properties of matter can be explained using the kinetic theory. You can try explaining some in the questions at the end of the topic.

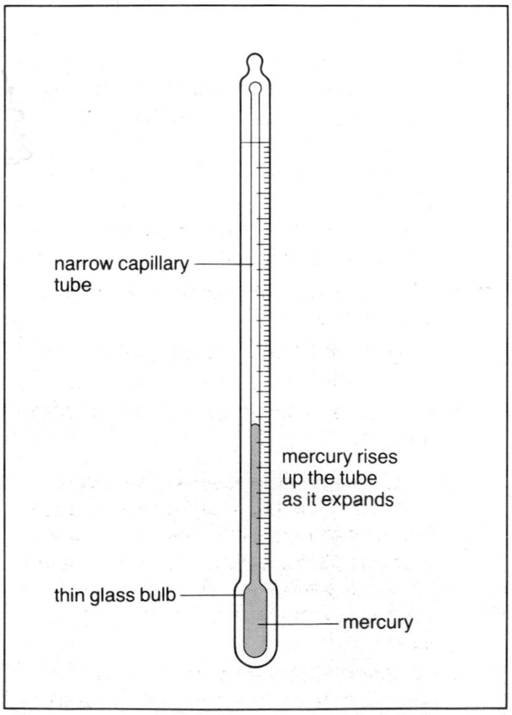

Picture 12 A thermometer uses the expansion of a liquid to measure the temperature. Why is the capillary tube narrow? Why is the glass bulb thin?

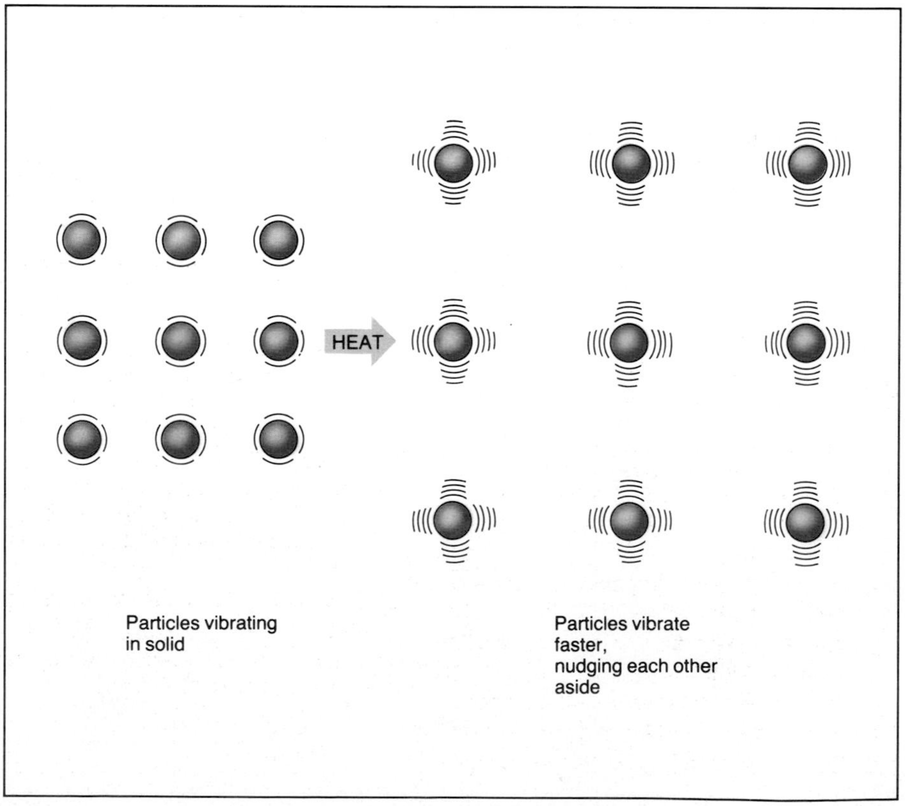

Picture 13 Why a solid expands when it is heated. (The expansion is exaggerated quite a lot)

Activities

A Do all liquids make your skin feel cool?

You will need three liquids: water, olive oil and alcohol. (**CARE** Alcohol is flammable. Make sure there are no flames around when you do this experiment.)

Dip the index finger of one hand into the water. Dip the same finger of the other hand into oil. Gently wave each finger in the air. Does the finger feel cool? How quickly does the liquid evaporate from the finger?

Now repeat the experiment using water on one finger and alcohol on the other.

Answer these questions.

1 Which liquid evaporates most quickly? Which evaporates most slowly?
2 Which liquid cools your skin most? Which cools it least?
3 Use the kinetic theory to explain your results.

B Dissolving and diffusing

Wear eye protection. Use tweezers to put *one* tiny crystal of potassium permanganate in the bottom of a beaker. Stand the beaker somewhere where it will not be disturbed. *Very gently* pour cold water into the beaker until it is half full. Observe the beaker closely for the next 5 minutes.

Answer these questions.

1 What do you observe?
2 Explain your observations using the kinetic theory.

Now plan an experiment to investigate what happens when this experiment is done using water at different temperatures. Think carefully about the observations and measurements you will make. Before you start the experiment, discuss your plan with your teacher.

C The temperature change when a solution crystallises

Wear eye protection. Put crystals of sodium thiosulphate in a boiling tube. There should be about 2 cm depth of crystals.

Gently heat the crystals. They will give off water and form a solution.

Allow the solution to cool without being disturbed.

When it is cool, add *one crystal* of sodium thiosulphate. It is a 'supersaturated' solution, and crystallises very easily. Crystals will form almost at once.

Feel the outside of the tube where the crystals have formed. What do you notice about the temperature?

Try to explain your observations using the kinetic theory.

Questions

1a State the main points of the kinetic theory.

b Use the kinetic theory to explain each of the following. Use diagrams to illustrate your answers.

i) Liquids turn to gases when they are heated.
ii) Gases diffuse to fill all the space available.
iii) When a solid dissolves in a liquid, the solid seems to disappear.
iv) When a solid is heated it expands.

2 The kinetic theory can be used to explain many of the properties of matter. Try to explain each of the following. Use diagrams to illustrate your answers.

a Washing dries better on a warm day than on a cold one.
b Washing dries better if it is spread out than if it is squashed up.
c Gases remain gases, no matter how much they are heated.
d Solids are usually hard, but liquids are soft.
e An air-filled balloon slowly goes down over the course of a week or two, even if the neck is securely tied.
f A balloon goes down faster on a warm day than on a cold one.
g Gases can easily be compressed, but solids and liquids are very difficult to compress.

3 Here are some more things to try and explain using the kinetic theory. Some of them are quite hard.

a Some solids, such as sugar, dissolve in water. Others, such as sand, do not dissolve.
b 1 g of liquid water occupies a volume of 1 cm^3. But 1 g of water vapour, which contains the same number of particles, occupies about 1700 cm^3.
c If a piece of gold and a piece of silver are pressed together for several years, a few atoms of silver pass into the gold, and a few atoms of gold pass into the silver.
d Gases expand more than solids when they are heated.
e Washing dries better on a windy day than on a still day.

4 Look at picture 7. It shows a bottle of fizzy drink before and after opening. Use diagrams to show how the particles of carbon dioxide ('fizz gas') and water are arranged before and after.

5 Look at picture 9. It shows tea being made. Use the kinetic theory to explain some of the following questions about tea making. Use the terms 'water particles' and 'tea flavour particles' in your answer.

a How does the tea flavour get out of the tea leaves and into the water?
b Why does tea get stronger the longer it is left in the pot?
c Why is it important that the water is as hot as possible?
d Why does it help to give the tea a stir in the pot?

6a When onions are being cooked, you can soon smell them around the house. It has been estimated that the particles responsible for onion-smell travel at the speed of a jet plane. Why, then, does it take some minutes for the smell to spread?

b Why don't the gases in the Earth's atmosphere diffuse away into space?

C2 Gases and pressure

The pressure, temperature and volume of a gas are all linked together.

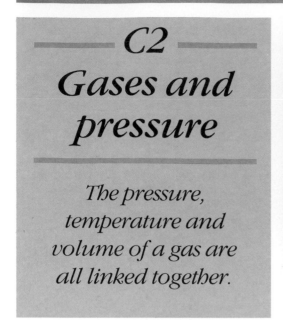

Picture 1 'An experiment on a bird in the air pump', by Joseph Wright of Derby, painted in 1768

Gas pressure is useful. It inflates balloons and it holds up tyres. Gas pressure can be gentle and almost unnoticeable — we hardly notice the changes in atmospheric pressure that happen when the weather changes. But high pressure gases make their presence felt — think how hard an inflated tyre feels.

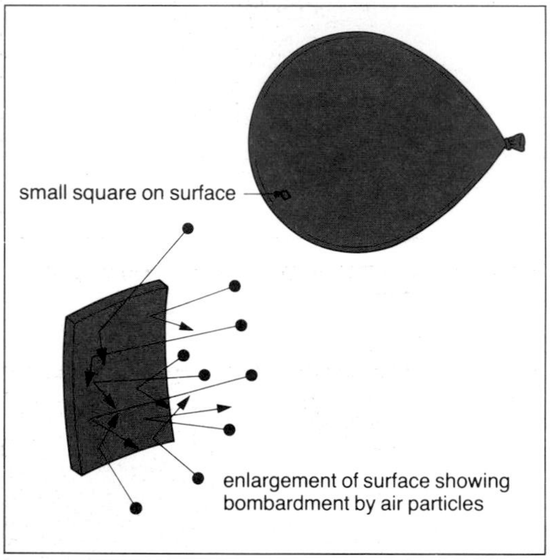

Picture 2 How a gas exerts pressure

What causes pressure in gases?

We can use the kinetic theory (topic C1) to explain gas pressure. Think of gas inside a balloon. The gas particles move around at random. They constantly collide with each other, and with the walls of the balloon. Every square millimetre of the balloon is battered by millions and millions of tiny particles every second (picture 2).

Each particle is too small to have much of an effect on the balloon wall by itself. But the constant battering by millions of particles adds up to a steady force on each square millimetre, and this is what we call pressure. (If you don't remember the definition of pressure, look at *The Physical World*, topic H2.)

In fact the balloon has pressure on it from both inside and outside. Outside, it is battered by particles of air from the atmosphere — this is atmospheric pressure. There is also atmospheric pressure inside — plus a bit more, due to the extra air that was blown in. It's this extra pressure that keeps the balloon inflated.

Picture 3 shows a simple experiment that models the way a gas exerts pressure. Activity B at the end of the topic looks more closely at this experiment.

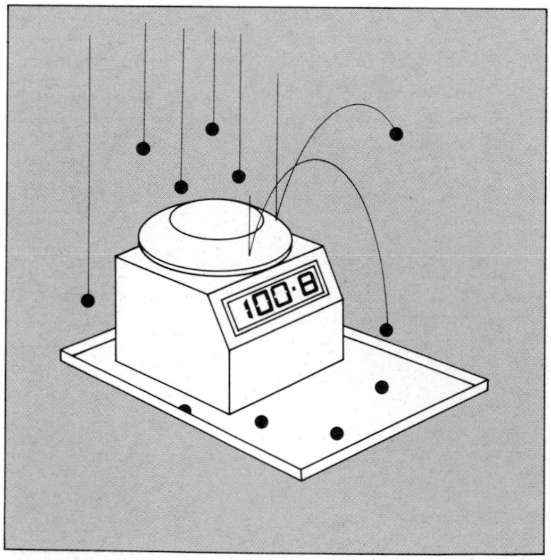

Picture 3 How does this experiment model gas pressure?

What affects the pressure of a gas?

Volume and pressure

Try a simple experiment with a bicycle pump. Hold your finger over the hole and push in the handle of the pump. You can feel the increasing

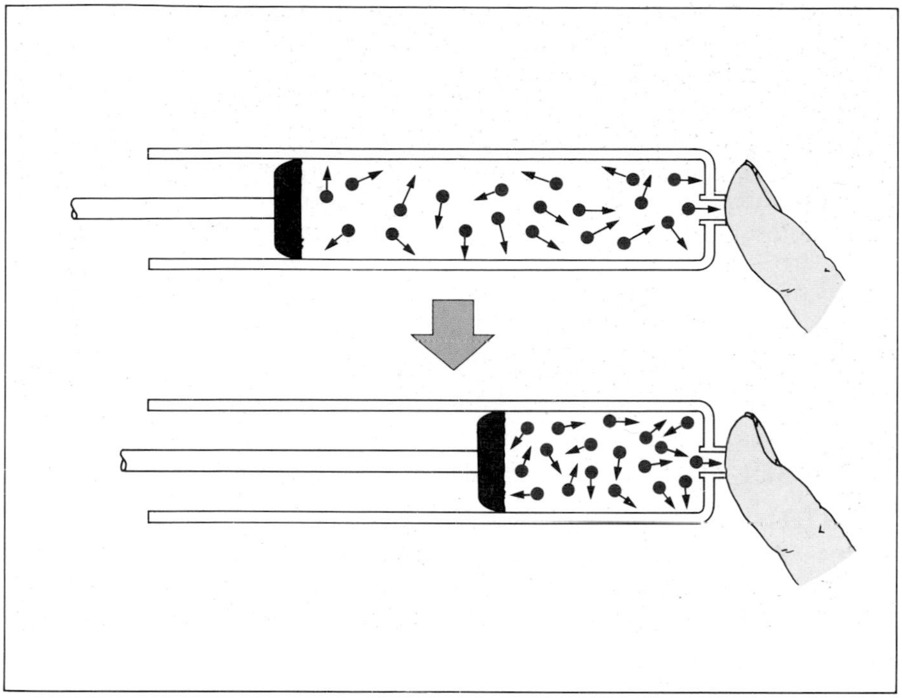

Picture 4 Why the volume of a gas affects its pressure. When the volume is decreased, the particles collide with the walls — and your finger — more often

pressure of gas on your finger. By pushing in the handle you have decreased the volume of the gas inside the pump. This increases its pressure. **When the volume of a gas decreases, its pressure increases.**

We can explain this using the kinetic theory (picture 4). If you halve the volume of the gas, the same number of particles get pushed into half the space. This means that they hit the walls more often. With more particles hitting the walls per second, the pressure increases.

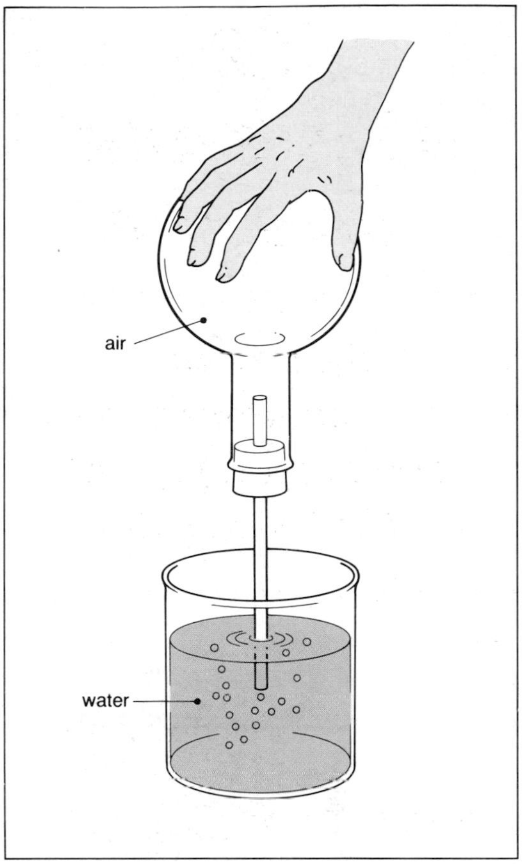

Picture 5 Air expands when it is warmed by your hand

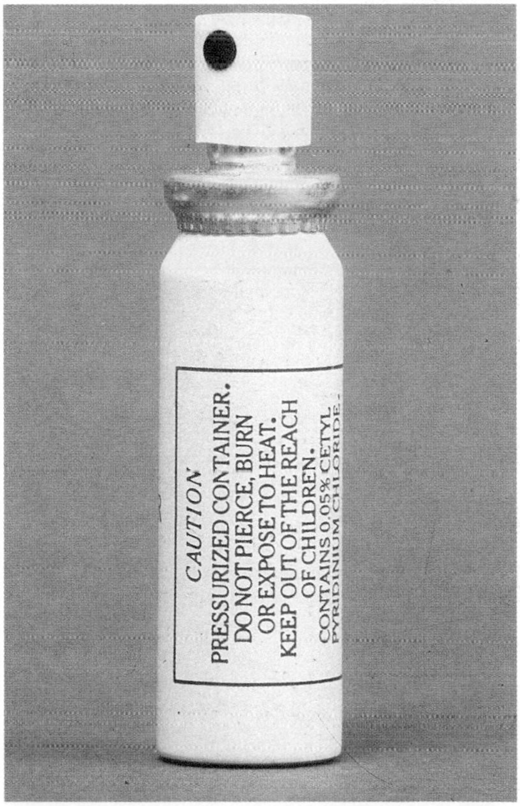

Picture 6 The pressure of a gas can increase spectactularly, when it is heated

Pressure, volume and temperature

Picture 5 shows a simple experiment that you may have done. As you warm the flask with your hands, the air inside it gets warmer. The air expands, and bubbles of it escape from the tube.

What would happen if the end of the tube was blocked? The air would not be able to escape, so the pressure inside would increase. Not by very much in this case, because the temperature rise is only small. But if you heat a gas a lot its pressure can increase dangerously (picture 6).

So temperature can affect both pressure *and* volume. If the volume of the gas is kept constant, its pressure increases. If the pressure is kept constant, the volume increases. In other words, the gas expands. This is what happens in the experiment in picture 5.

When the temperature of a gas increases:
its pressure increases if the volume is constant
its volume increases if the pressure is constant.

Once again, the kinetic theory gives us an explanation. When the temperature is increased, the particles move faster — this is one of the basic ideas of the kinetic theory.

The faster-moving particles collide more often with the walls, and what's more they hit the walls harder. If the walls can't move (in other words, if the volume is constant), the total force on each square millimetere of the wall increases. So the pressure increases (picture 7). But if the walls can move, the extra pressure will push them out a bit. In other words, the volume increases.

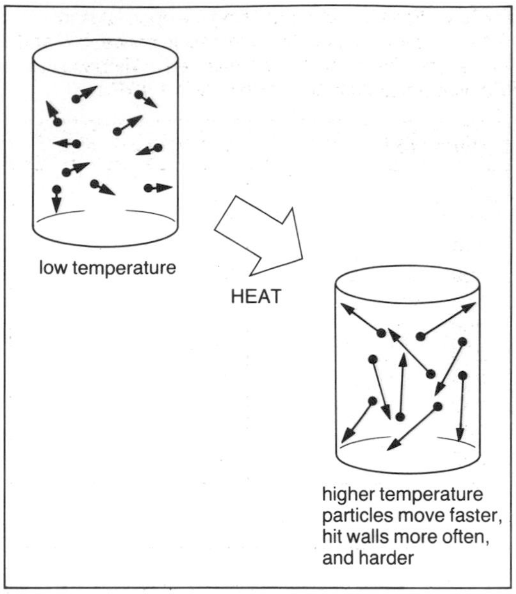

Picture 7 Why the pressure of a gas increases when it is heated

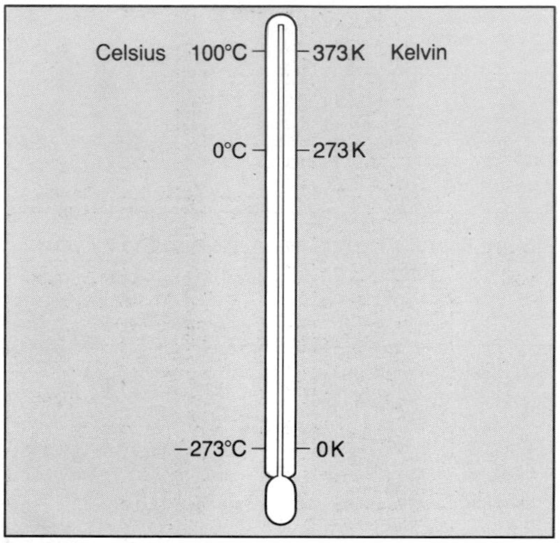

Picture 8 The Celsius and Kelvin temperature scales

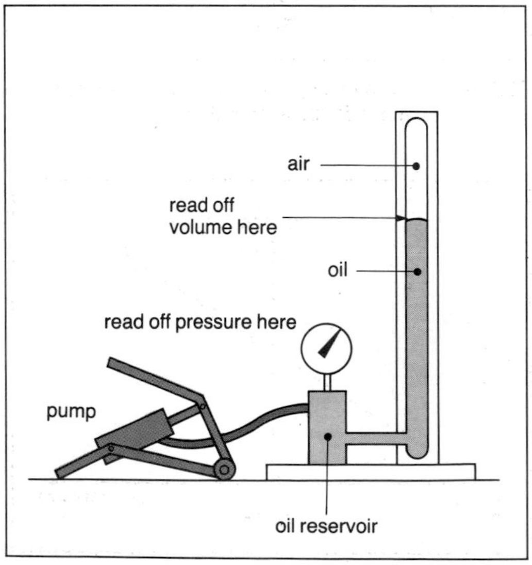

Picture 9 Investigating how the volume of a gas depends on pressure

What happens when you cool a gas, instead of heating it? The particles slow down, so they exert less pressure on the walls. The lower the temperature, the lower the pressure of the gas. But suppose you go on lowering the temperature of the gas. The particles move slower and slower, and eventually they stop moving altogether. The particles of all substances stop moving at the same temperature. This temperature is −273 Celsius, and it is called **absolute zero**. It is impossible to get colder than absolute zero.

Sometimes it is useful to have a temperature scale whose zero is absolute zero. This scale is called the kelvin scale or the absolute temperature scale, and its units are kelvins (K) (picture 8). Kelvins are the same size as degrees on the Celsius scale (°C). To convert a Celsius temperature to a kelvin temperature, you add 273. Thus 27 degrees Celsius is (273 + 27) = 300 K.

A closer look at pressure, temperature and volume

Pressure (***P***) and temperature (***T***) both affect the volume (***V***) of a gas. In this section we will look at equations which show the relation between ***P***, ***V*** and ***T***.

P, ***V*** and ***T*** are three *variables*. We want to know how they affect one another. It's best to investigate the variables two at a time, so you can see how one affects another without the third interfering. So we keep one of the three variables constant, and see what happens when you vary the other two.

Varying pressure and volume, with temperature constant

Picture 9 shows the apparatus we can use to see how the volume of a gas depends on the pressure. The gas being tested is air, trapped in the vertical glass tube. The temperature is kept constant during the experiment.

The pump is used to increase the pressure of the air in the tube. You can read off the pressure from the pressure gauge. The volume of the air is read off from the graduations on the side of the tube.

Table 1 shows some results obtained using this apparatus. What happens when the pressure is *doubled* from 100 kPa to 200 kPa? The volume is *halved*, from 48 cm^3 to 24 cm^3. When the pressure is multiplied by three, from 100 kPa to 300 kPa, the volume goes from 48 to 16 — it's divided by three.

This is an *inverse relationship:* the volume is inversely proportional to the pressure. This can be written mathematically as

$$V \propto \frac{1}{P} \quad \text{or} \quad V = \frac{\text{constant}}{P} \quad \text{or} \quad PV = \text{constant}$$

In Question 4 you can show that the results in table 1 obey these mathematical relationships. Remember, they only work if the temperature is kept constant.

This relationship between ***P*** and ***V*** is known as **Boyle's Law**, after Robert Boyle, the British scientist who first stated the law in 1662. In words, Boyle's Law says **the volume of a fixed mass of gas is inversely proportional to its pressure, if the temperature is kept constant**.

Most gases obey Boyle's Law pretty well, but no gas obeys it perfectly. Life's like that. An imaginary gas which would obey the law perfectly is called a **perfect gas**.

Varying temperature and volume, with pressure constant

Picture 10 shows the apparatus we can use to see how the volume of a gas depends on the temperature. The pressure stays constant during the experiment, because the tube is open at the top.

The gas being tested is air, trapped in the narrow glass capillary tube. The air is trapped by a small amount of concentrated sulphuric acid. This does two jobs. It dries the air so that water vapour does not interfere with the results. It also serves as an 'index' which moves up and down the scale so you can read off the volume of the air.

You increase the temperature by heating the water, and read it off on the thermometer.

Using this apparatus you can get a series of readings for the volume of the gas at different temperatures, with the pressure constant. You can then plot V against T on a graph like the one in picture 11.

Look at the right-hand part of picture 11 first. You can see that the graph is a straight line. V increases steadily as T increases. In other words, pressure is *proportional* to temperature. But the graph does not go through the origin: the volume is not zero at zero degrees Celsius.

Now look at the left-hand part. The graph has been extended back (extrapolated) until it reaches the temperature axis. To do this, we have to assume that the gas will behave in the same general way at all temperatures. The volume of the gas gets less and less as the temperature falls. By the time the line meets the temperature axis, the volume of the gas is zero. You can see that this happens at a temperature of −273 degrees Celsius. This is *absolute zero* — zero kelvin.

At absolute zero, the volume of the gas would be zero. As the temperature is increased, the volume increases in proportion to the absolute temperature. If you double the absolute temperature, the volume doubles. If you halve the absolute temperature, the volume is halved. The volume is *proportional* to the absolute temperature. This can be written mathematically as

$$V \propto T \quad \text{or} \quad V = \text{constant} \times T \quad \text{or} \quad \frac{V}{T} = \textbf{constant}$$

But remember, this assumes that the temperature is kept constant.

This relationship is known as **Charles' Law,** after Jacques Charles, the scientist who first stated the law in 1787. In words, Charles' Law says **the volume of a fixed mass of gas is directly proportional to its absolute temperature (on the kelvin scale) if the pressure is kept constant.**

Like Boyle's Law, Charles' Law is not obeyed perfectly by real gases. In particular, real gases turn to liquids before the temperature reaches absolute zero.

Table 1 Results obtained using the apparatus in picture 9 to investigate the relationship between P and V for a gas. The pressure is measured in kilopascals, kPa. Normal atmospheric pressure is 100kPa

Pressure/kPA	Volume/cm³
100	48
120	40
140	34
160	30
180	26
200	24
220	22
240	20
260	18
280	17
300	16

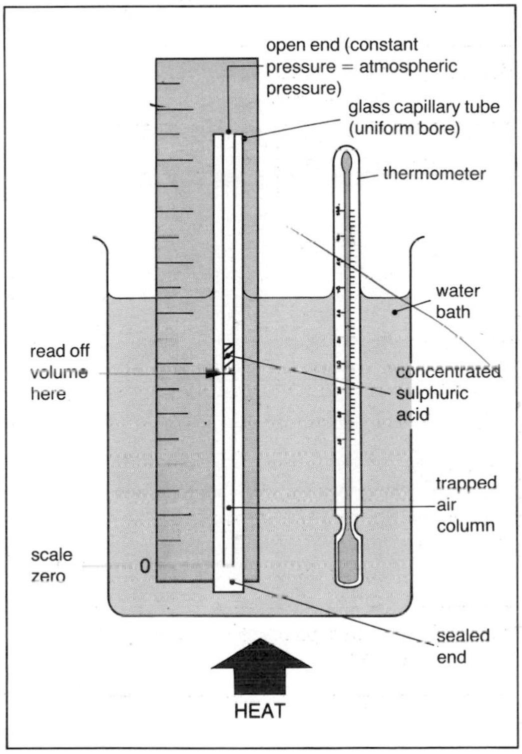

Picture 10 Investigating how the volume of a gas depends on temperature

Combining the laws together

We have two equations involving the volume, temperature and pressure of a gas:

$$\frac{V}{T} = \text{constant (Charles' Law)} \quad \text{and} \quad PV = \text{constant (Boyle's Law)}$$

We can combine these into a single equation, called the **gas equation**:

$$\frac{PV}{T} = \text{constant} \quad \text{or} \quad \frac{P_1V_1}{T_1} = \frac{P_2V_2}{T_2}$$

where P_1, V_1, T_1 and P_2, V_2, T_2 are the pressure, temperature and volume in two different situations. Remember that you must use the *absolute* temperature, in kelvins.

This equation can be used to work out the volume of a gas at different pressures and temperatures.

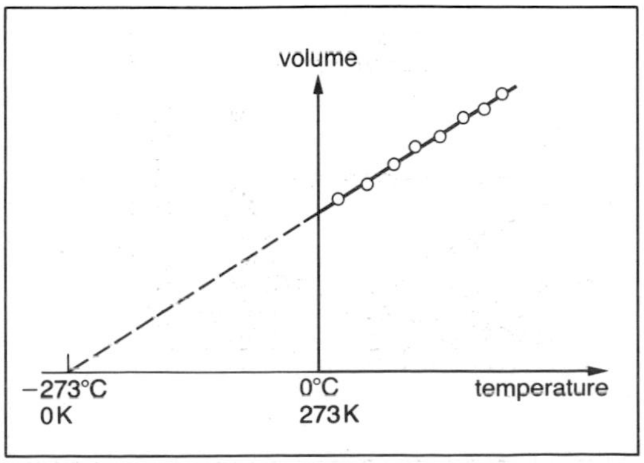

Picture 11 The volume of a gas plotted against its temperature

Questions

1 An inflated car tyre contains air at constant volume.

a Use the kinetic theory to explain why the air inside the tyre exerts pressure on the walls of the tyre.

b What will happen to the pressure in the tyre on a particularly warm day? Use the kinetic theory to explain what happens.

c Suppose you injected some water into the tyre, so that the air was pushed into half the volume it occupied before. What would happen to the pressure of the air?

2 Look at picture 3 on page 56, then answer these questions.

a What would you expect to happen to the reading on the balance as the balls are dropped onto it?

b Explain why this experiment models the way a gas exerts pressure.

c How would you adapt the experiment to model the effect of increasing temperature on the pressure of a gas?

3 Picture 12 shows a thermometer invented by the great Italian scientist Galileo (see *The Physical World*, page 44). He used it to measure room temperatures.

a Explain how the 'thermometer' works.

b Using equipment available in the school laboratory, how would you calibrate the thermometer so its scale reads temperatures from 10°C to 30°C?

c Give two reasons why this might be a rather inaccurate thermometer.

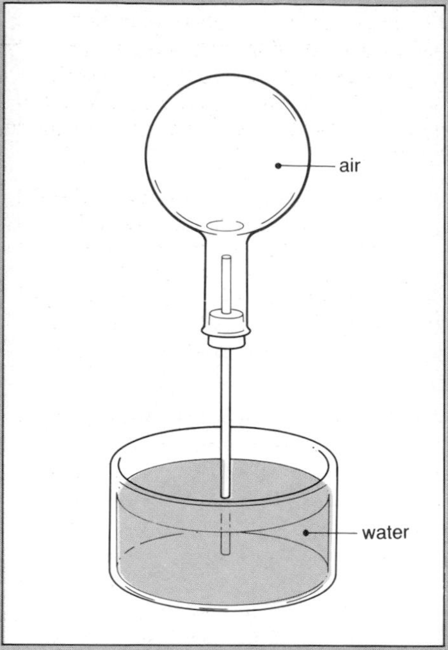

Picture 12 Galileo's thermometer

4 Use the following steps to show that the results in table 1 obey Boyle's Law.

a For each set of results, multiply the pressure (***P***) by the volume (***V***). Does ***PV*** = constant?

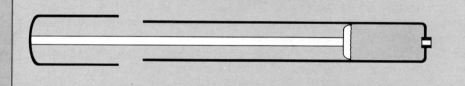

b For each set of results, work out the value of 1/***P***. Now plot a graph of ***V*** (vertical axis) against 1/***P***. Is ***V*** proportional to 1/***P***?

c Use the results to predict the volume of the gas when the pressure is 400 kPa.

5 A bubble is trapped at the bottom of a lake. The volume of the bubble is 0.5 cm^3, and the total pressure at the bottom of the lake is 300 kPa.

a The bubble gets dislodged and rises to the surface where the pressure is 100 kPa. What will its new volume be?

b What assumption have you made in part (a)?

6 Look at the bicycle pump in picture 13. The pump contains 60 cm^3 of air at a temperature of 27°C and a pressure of 100 kPa. Use the gas equation to answer these questions.

a What will the volume of air become if the handle is pushed in so that the pressure rises to 150 kPa? Assume the temperature does not change.

b What will the volume of air become if the temperature rises to 87°C? Assume the handle of the pump is allowed to move freely, so that the pressure does not change.

c What will the volume become if the pressure increases to 120 kPa and the temperature rises to 47°C?

Picture 13

Dr Brown and Dr Einstein

This exercise is about Brownian motion. Before you go any further, you should see Brownian motion for yourself. It was first observed using pollen grains, but you can see it most easily in smoke. You will probably use apparatus like that shown in picture 1. You should see the tiny particles of smoke dancing and jiggling around, as shown in picture 2.

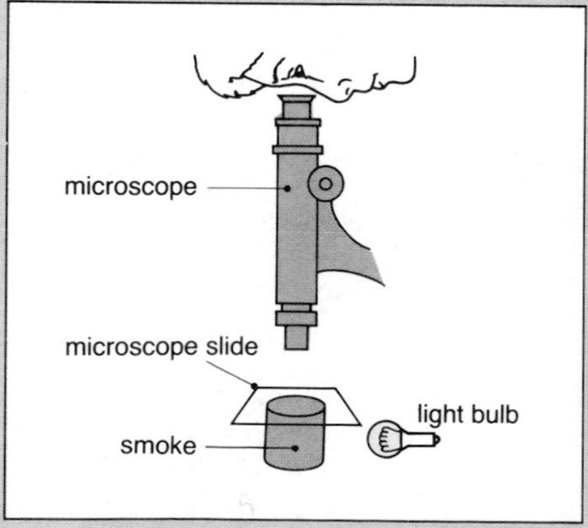

Picture 1 Looking for Brownian motion

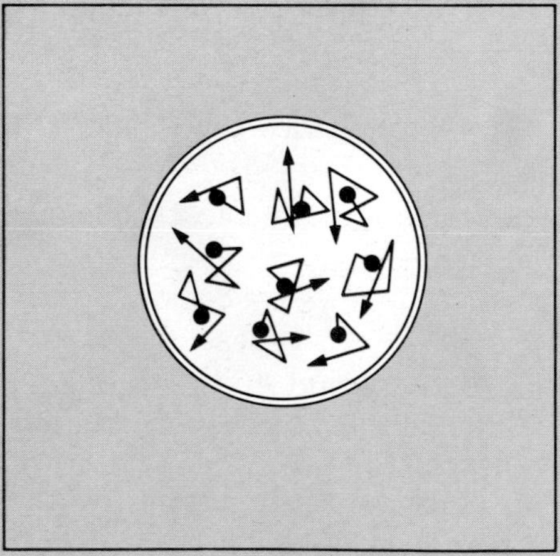

Picture 2 Smoke particles in Brownian motion

Brown discovers, Einstein explains

In 1827, a Scottish biologist called Robert Brown was studying pollen grains. He used a microscope to examine pollen grains suspended in water. To his surprise, he noticed that the tiny grains were constantly jiggling around in a completely random way. He explained what he saw by saying that the pollen grains were alive, and moving of their own accord.

In 1905, the great scientist Albert Einstein was 26 years old. In that year he did three pieces of work, all three of them good enough to win a Nobel Prize. There is more about Einstein in *The Physical World*, topic B9.

One of Einstein's papers gave an explanation of Brownian motion, using the kinetic theory. Einstein suggested that the motion happens because the grains of pollen are bombarded by tiny, fast-moving molecules of water. He even worked out how fast the motion should be, and his calculations matched what was actually observed.

Picture 3 Robert Brown discovered Brownian motion

Picture 4 Albert Einstein

At that time there were still some scientists who did not believe that atoms and molecules actually existed. Einstein's work on Brownian motion was a real breakthrough because it convinced even the doubters that atoms and molecules exist.

Imagine Brown met Einstein . . .

In this exercise you are going to act an imaginary discussion between Robert Brown and Albert Einstein. (Of course, they never actually met because Brown made his discovery over 50 years before Einstein was even born.)

Brown and Einstein would have had different theories about why Brownian motion occurs. Each would have argued for his theory. When scientists disagree on a theory, there is only one thing they can do. They suggest new experiments to test the theory.

Organising the exercise

There are several ways you could organise this exercise. One is to work in groups of four. Two of you will take the part of Brown, and two will be Einstein. The stages are as follows.

Stage 1. Brown speaks for 2 minutes. He describes what he has seen, and explains his theory that the grains move because they are alive.

Stage 2. Einstein speaks for 2 minutes. He describes *his* theory to explain why the grains move.

Stage 3. Brown speaks for 2 minutes. He gives his reaction to Einstein's theory, and explains why he does not believe it.

Stage 4. Einstein speaks for 2 minutes. He gives his reaction to what Brown has just said.

Stage 5. Brown speaks for 2 minutes. He suggests a new experiment that will test Einstein's theory.

Stage 6. Einstein speaks for 2 minutes. He suggests a new experiment that will test Brown's theory.

Preparing what you will say

You need to decide how you will present your theory. It would be a good idea to use diagrams. You also need to decide what experiment you will suggest in stage 5 or 6.

These notes may help you.

Brown's theory. Brown believes the grains move because they are alive. After all, pollen is produced by living plants. Being a biologist, he has often seen microscopic organisms jiggling around under the microscope.

Try to get yourself into Brown's way of thinking. The idea of atoms and molecules seems strange to Brown. They are so small that it's impossble to see them, and there is no evidence that they actually exist. In his time, the idea of atoms and molecules was much less well known than it is today.

Einstein's theory. Einstein believes that the grains move because they are being bombarded by fast-moving molecules of water. The pollen grains may look small, but they are far bigger than the invisible molecules of water. Nevertheless, the water molecules move so fast that they can jolt the pollen grains when they collide with them. Picture 5 illustrates the theory.

After you have finished your presentation, discuss how it went.

Were the arguments convincing?

Were the ideas for new experiments good? Would they test the two theories conclusively? What results would you expect from the experiments?

Would Brown's theory have explained Brownian motion in *smoke*? Would Einstein's theory?

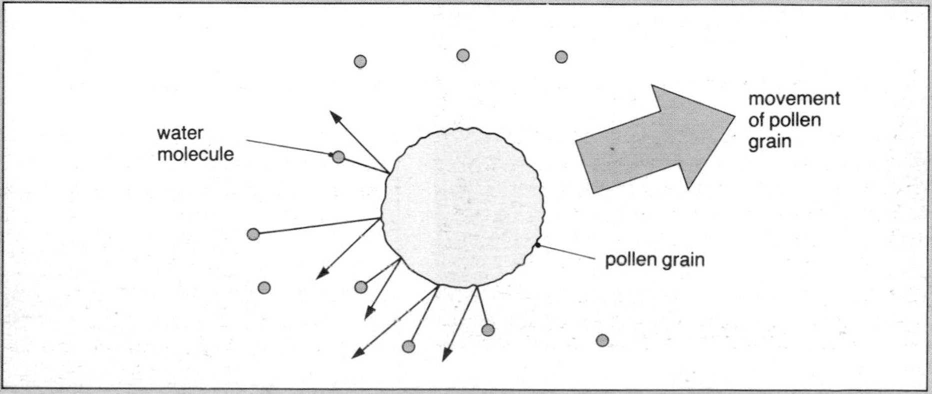

Picture 5 How Einstein explained Brownian motion

C3 Atoms, molecules and ions

The particles of matter come in three types.

Picture 1 The sea, a mixture of many different particles, but mostly water molecules and sodium and chloride ions

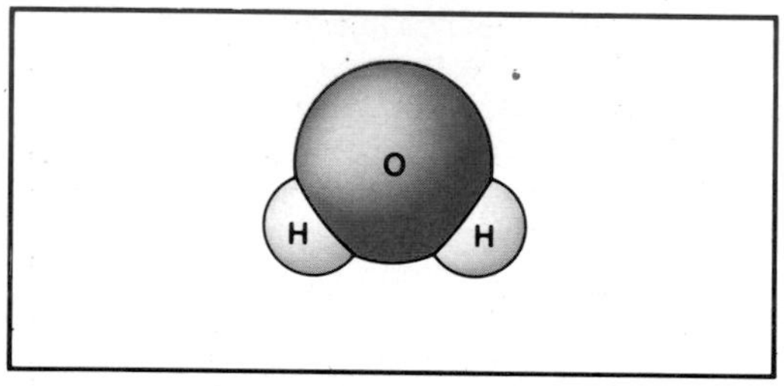

Picture 2 A water molecule

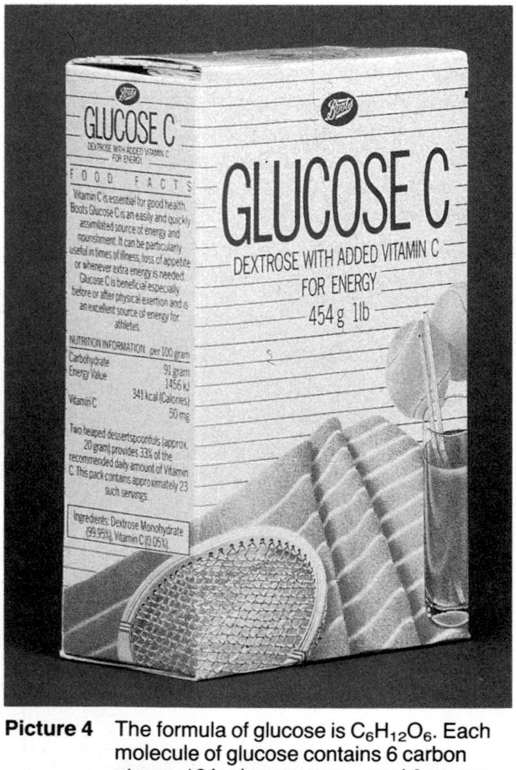

Picture 4 The formula of glucose is $C_6H_{12}O_6$. Each molecule of glucose contains 6 carbon atoms, 12 hydrogen atoms, and 6 oxygen atoms

Ask a person in the street if they have heard of atoms and molecules. They probably will have, and they'll probably be able to give you a rough idea of what atoms are.

The idea of atoms seems obvious to us today. Yet as recently as the beginning of this century there were still some scientists who refused to believe that matter was made of atoms. More is given about this in the exercises on page 61.

In topic C1 we looked at the kinetic theory, which says all matter is made of 'particles'. But what are these particles? There are three types: atoms , molecules and ions.

What are atoms?

The word 'atom' comes from Greek words meaning 'unsplittable'. The idea of an atom is that it is the smallest particle of matter, and cannot be split into anything smaller. We now know that atoms *can* be split (topic J3), but in ordinary life you can think of atoms as the simplest particles.

Elements (topic A4) are made of only one type of atom. Iron contains nothing but iron atoms, and oxygen contains nothing but oxygen atoms. There are 92 different types of atoms which occur naturally, one for each of the 92 naturally occurring elements. Each element has its own symbol. There is a full list of elements and their symbols in the Data Section.

What are molecules?

Atoms can join together in groups. These atoms are held together by **chemical bonds**. These groups, which may be large or small, are called **molecules**. One of the commonest molecules contains two hydrogen atoms and one oxygen atom (picture 2). We can represent this as a **formula**, H_2O. It's a molecule of water, of course.

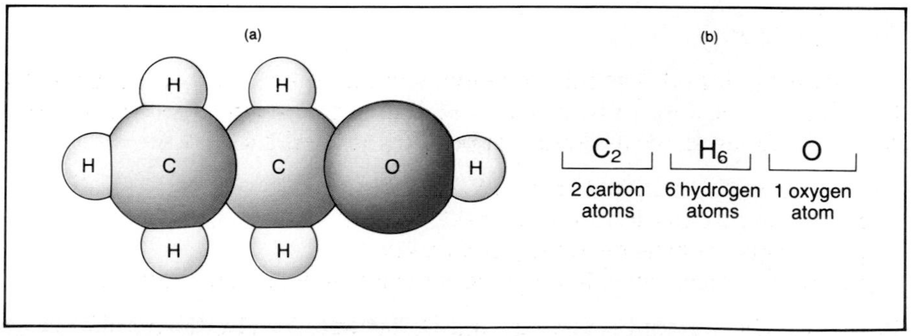

Picture 3 (a) A picture of a molecule of ethanol; (b) the formula of ethanol

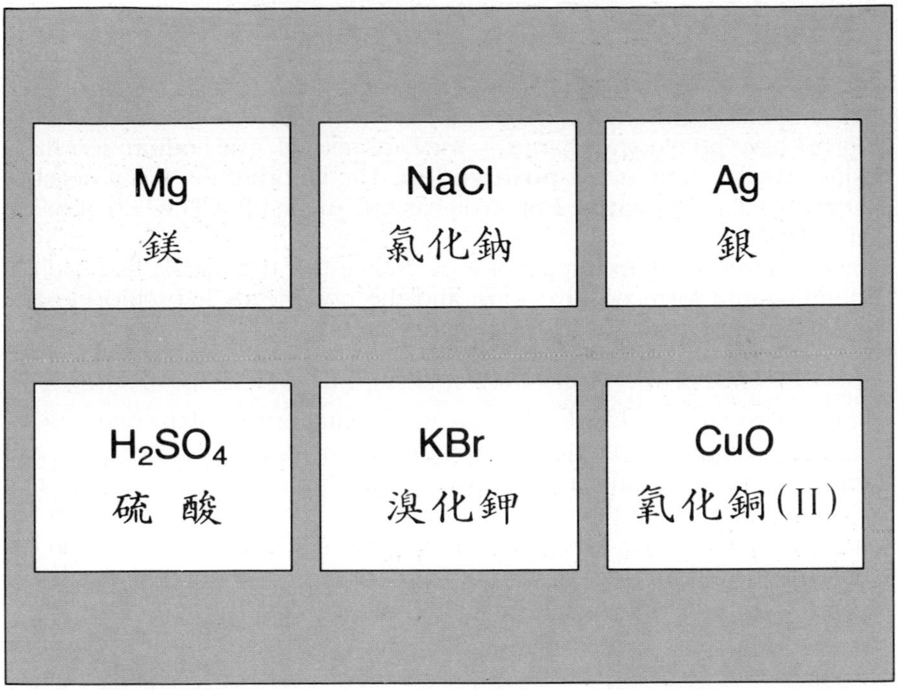

Picture 6 How good is your Chinese? These are labels from bottles of chemicals. Translate the Chinese names into English

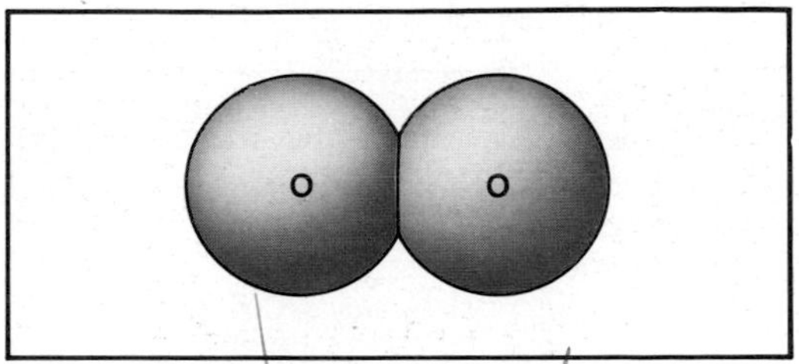

Picture 5 A molecule of oxygen, O_2

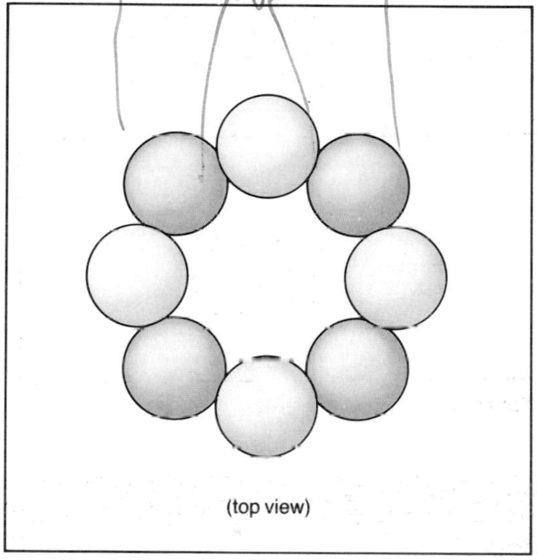

Picture 7 A molecule of sulphur, S_8

A chemical formula shows the types and numbers of atoms in a molecule. The numbers are written after the symbols, as subscripts. Picture 3 shows a molecule of ethanol, also called alcohol, and its formula.

Molecules can be very simple, like water H_2O or carbon dioxide CO_2. They can also be more complex, like octane C_8H_{18} or glucose $C_6H_{12}O_6$. Some biological molecules are very complicated. For example, chlorophyll, which gives leaves their green colour, has the formula $C_{51}H_{72}O_4N_4Mg$!

Molecules of elements

The substances we have mentioned so far contain atoms of at least two different elements. This means they are *compounds* — two or more elements joined together. But molecules are also formed by some elements on their own.

Picture 5 shows a molecule of oxygen. This is the normal form in which oxygen exists, so we write the formula of oxygen as O_2, not O. Several of the gaseous elements form **diatomic** molecules like this. Thus nitrogen is N_2, hydrogen is H_2 and chlorine is Cl_2.

Picture 7 shows a molecule of sulphur. You can see it contains eight sulphur atoms, so the formula of sulphur is S_8.

State symbols

Ice, steam and liquid water are the same substance, but in different states. All three have the same formula, H_2O, which could be confusing. To show the state of a substance, we use state symbols alongside the formula.

(s) means a substance in the solid state
(l) means a substance in the liquid state
(g) means a substance in the gaseous state
(aq) means a substance in the aqueous state — dissolved in water.

So ice is $H_2O(s)$, steam is $H_2O(g)$ and liquid water is $H_2O(l)$. A solution of glucose in water is $C_6H_{12}O_6(aq)$.

Table 1 Some common ions

Name	Formula
Sodium ion	Na^+
Magnesium ion	Mg^{2+}
Aluminium ion	Al^{3+}
Copper ion	Cu^{2+}
Zinc ion	Zn^{2+}
Chloride ion	Cl^-
Bromide ion	Br^-
Oxide ion	O^{2-}
Sulphide ion	S^{2-}
Nitrate ion	NO_3^-
Sulphate ion	SO_4^{2-}
Ammonium ion	NH_4^+

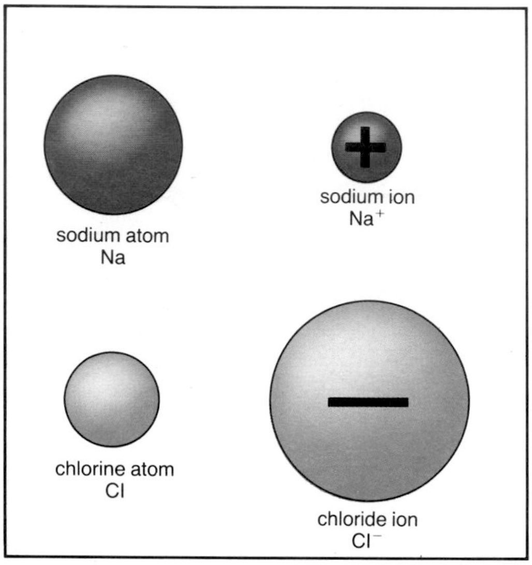

Picture 8 Atoms and ions

What are ions?

An ion is a particle with an electric charge on it. Picture 8 shows atoms and ions of sodium and chlorine. You can see that the *atoms* of sodium and chlorine have no electric charge — they are neutral. The sodium ion has a positive charge on it: it is a **positive ion.** The chloride ion has a negative charge on it: it is a **negative ion**. (You can find out in topic J4 where ions get their charges from.)

Table 1 gives some examples of ions. Notice that the metals like sodium and aluminium form positive ions, and the non-metals like chlorine and oxygen form negative ions. This follows a general rule:

Metals form positive ions and non-metals form negative ions.

You can see from table 1 that ions may contain more than one type of atom. For example the nitrate ion contains a group of one nitrogen atom and three oxygen atoms, with a minus charge on the group. You can also see that an ion may have more than one unit of charge. For example, a sodium ion has one positive charge, a magnesium ion has two and an aluminium ion has three. The formula of an ion shows both the atoms it contains and the charge on the ion. Thus the formula of an aluminium ion is Al^{3+}

Ions in compounds

Look back at picture 8. The sodium ion has a + charge and the chloride ion has a − charge. You would expect these two oppositely charged ions to attract one another. This is what happens in the compound sodium chloride, commonly known as salt. It consists of Na^+ and Cl^- ions holding each other

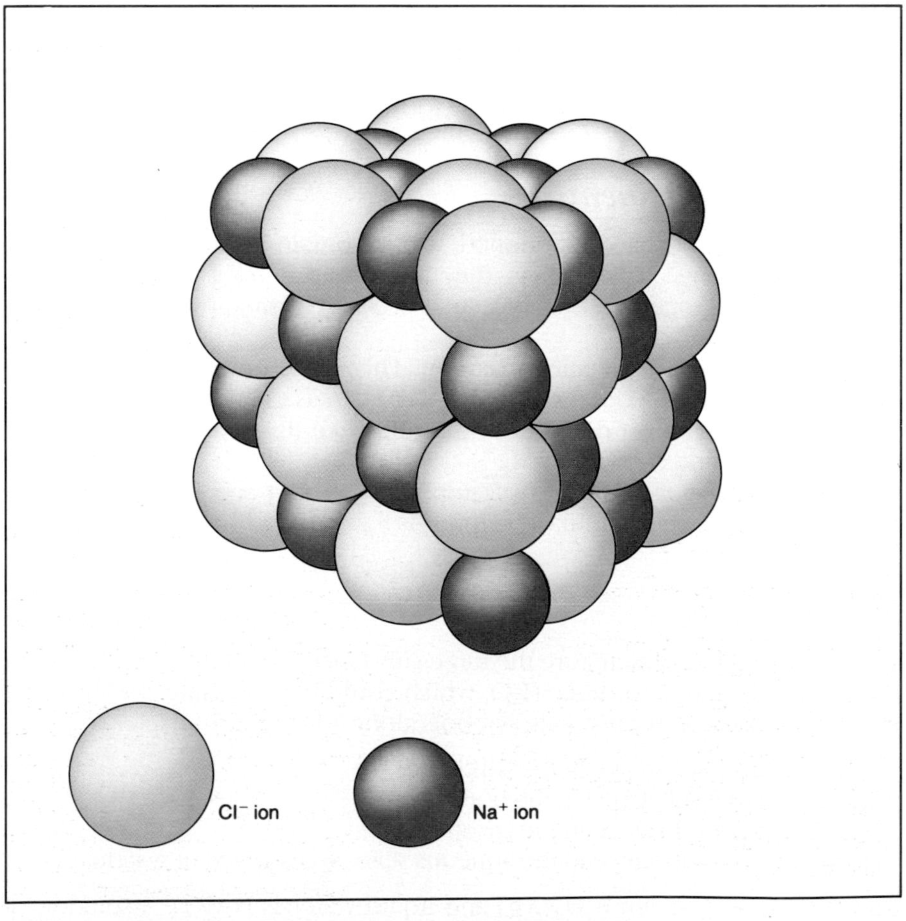

Picture 9 Sodium ions and chloride ions in a crystal lattice

together in a regular arrangement called a lattice (picture 9). More about ionic lattices in topic C7.

Oppositely charged ions pack together in this way because opposite charges attract. But you couldn't pack ions of like charge together — they would repel each other and fly apart. So substances that contain ions are always compounds, with at least two different types of ion — a positive and a negative.

Sometimes the formula of an ionic compound shows the charges on the ions, but sometimes these are left out. For example, the formula of sodium chloride is sometimes written as Na^+Cl^-, but more commonly as just NaCl.

The structure of substances

The formula of a substance shows the types and number of atoms or ions it contains. But the formula doesn't say anything about the way these atoms are joined together: the **structure** of the substance. It's useful to know the structure of a substance because it helps to explain its properties. To see the structure you need diagrams like picture 7 showing the structure of sulphur, and picture 9 showing the structure of sodium chloride.

The structure of substances is covered in detail in topic C6.

How big are atoms, molecules and ions?

Atoms, molecules and ions vary a lot in size, but they are all very, very small.

- The smallest atom is the hydrogen atom. It is about 10^{-10} metres (0.000 000 0001 m) across.

To measure these very small particles, we use a unit called the nanometre (nm).

$$1\,\text{nm} = 10^{-9}\,\text{m} = 1/1000\,000\,000\,\text{m}$$

So a hydrogen atom measures about 0.1 nm.

- Compared to hydrogen atoms, sugar molecules are moderately large — about 1 nm across. But there are still about 10^{19} (10 000 000 000 000 000 000) molecules in one grain of sugar!
- A glass of water contains about 10^{25} molecules. If you could count five molecules a second it would take you 10 million million million years to count them all.

Activities

A Estimating the size of a molecule: the oil drop experiment

When oil gets spilled onto water, it spreads out in a thin layer. It goes on spreading out until the layer is only one molecule thick. We can use this effect to get an idea of the thickness of an oil molecule.

Picture 10 illustrates the method. You will use a solution of olive oil containing 1 cm^3 of oil in 1000 cm^3 of alcohol.

(**CARE** Alcohol is flammable. Make sure there are no naked flames nearby.)

1 Put some clean water in a tray and place it on a level surface. Dust the surface of the water thinly with talcum powder.

2 Put some of the olive oil solution in a dropping pipette with a fine nozzle. Allow *one drop only* to fall in the middle of the dusted water. You will see the solution spread out. The alcohol dissolves in the water, leaving a thin layer of oil. This layer pushes aside the powder leaving a clear patch.

3 Quickly measure the diameter of the patch.

4 Finally, find the volume of one drop of the solution. You can do this by counting how many drops are needed to make 1 cm^3 in a measuring cylinder.

Work out the results by the following stages.

a What is the volume of one drop of solution?

b What volume of olive oil is there in one drop of solution? (Remember the solution contains 1 cm^3 of olive oil in 1000 cm^3 of alcohol.)

c What is the area of the oil patch? Use the diameter you measured, and assume it is a perfect circle.

d If the thickness of the oil patch is t cm, what is its volume?

e You now have two answers for the volume of the oil, from parts (b) and (d). Put them equal to one another and work out the value of t.

f If the oil layer is one molecule thick, then t is the thickness of an oil molecule. Compare your answer with the value given for the size of a sugar molecule on page 65 (sugar molecules and oil molecules are roughly the same size). Comment on your answer.

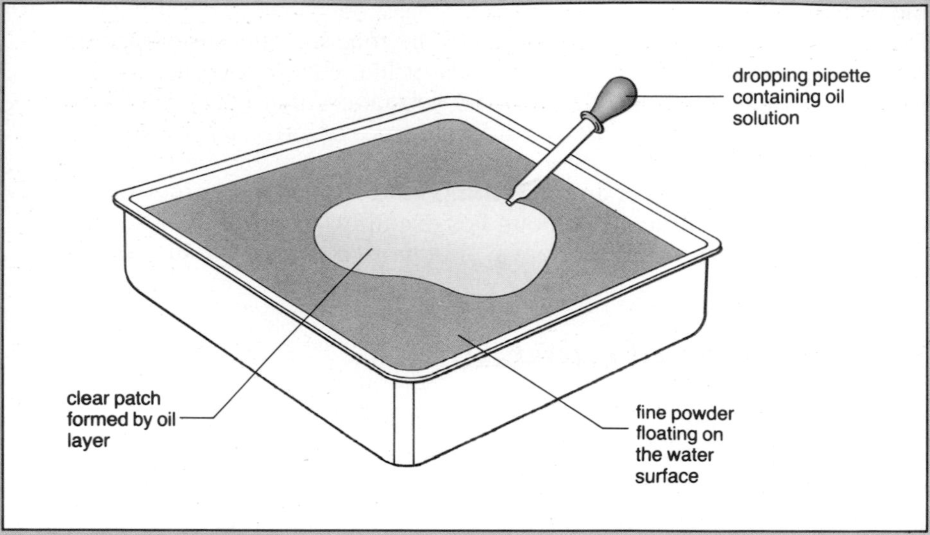

Picture 10 The oil drop experiment

B Do people believe in atoms?

Try asking ordinary people some questions to see if they believe in atoms and understand what atoms are. Try asking parents, relatives, neighbours — anyone as long as they are not expert scientists!

Here are some questions you could ask. Try to think of more.

1 Suppose you had a very powerful microscope. What do you think you would see if you magnified a piece of iron as much as possible?

2 Suppose you take a piece of iron and cut it in half, then in half again and so on. Could you go on doing this for ever (assuming you had a small enough knife!)?

3 Have you heard of atoms? Do you know what they are? What about molecules?

4 How big do you think molecules are? How many molecules do you think there are in a glass of water?

Questions

1 Explain in your own words the difference between:

a an atom and a molecule,

b an atom and an ion.

2 Look at this list of formulas. Classify each as atom, molecule or ion:

a SO_2	e CO_3^{2-}	i C_6H_6
b Fe	f He	j CO
c H^+	g Br^-	k Co
d CH_4	h N_2	l PO_4^{3-}.

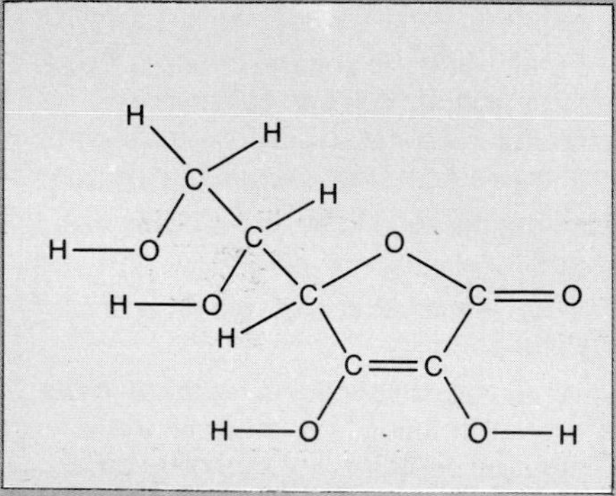

Picture 11 A molecule of vitamin C

3 Vitamin C is an essential part of the human diet. Shortage of vitamin C causes a disease called scurvy. Picture 11 shows how the atoms are joined together in a molecule of vitamin C.

a Which elements does vitamin C contain?

b Write down the formula of vitamin C.

4 In A to D in picture 12, ○ represents an atom of oxygen and ● represents an atom of hydrogen. Choose from A to D the diagram that shows:

i) hydrogen atoms and oxygen atoms;

ii) hydrogen molecules and oxygen molecules;

iii) water molecules;

iv) oxygen molecules and water molecules.

5 Classify each of the substances A to E below as an element, a compound or a mixture.

Substance A contains three different types of molecules.

Substance B contains only one type of atom.

Substance C contains only one type of molecule. Each molecule of C contains two different atoms.

Substance D contains one type of positive ion and one type of negative ion.

Substance E contains molecules. Each molecule has two identical atoms joined together.

6 Write formulas, *including state symbols*, for each of the following. You'll find all the formulas you need somewhere in this topic.

a Gaseous carbon dioxide.

b Solid carbon dioxide.

c Molten iron.

d Oxygen gas.

e A solution of chlorine in water.

f Octane vapour.

g Solid glucose.

h Salty water.

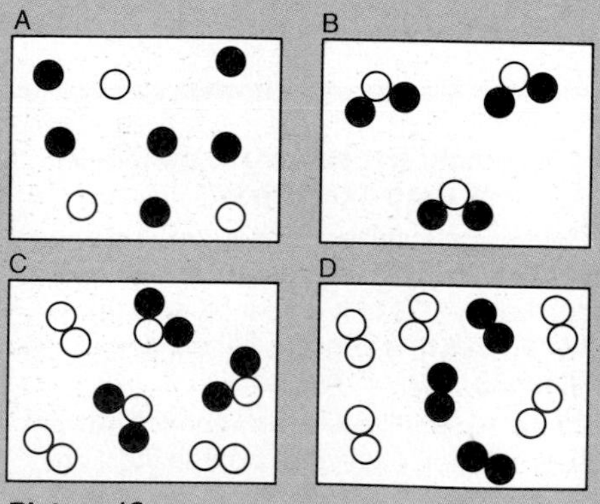

Picture 12

Ideas about atoms

The idea of everything being made of atoms has been around for a long time. But in 1808 John Dalton made a breakthrough.

Going back a bit

The ancient Greeks first thought of the idea of atoms, nearly 2500 years ago. They had no experimental proof for atoms, but they liked the idea because it explained many things about the world.

After the Greeks, the atomic theory was almost forgotten in Europe. But in India, the idea reappeared and was improved. A thousand years ago, Indian scientists suggested that there are four 'elements' and that each of these has its own atoms. Other substances were made by combining these atoms together.

John Dalton's breakthrough

John Dalton was an English schoolteacher who lived near Manchester. He started teaching in the village school when he was 12! He taught himself science and became a professor in a Manchester college.

Like all good scientists, John Dalton observed things closely. He enjoyed walking in the countryside outside Manchester, and he became interested in the gases around him — air, marsh gas, carbon dioxide, water vapour. He began to think about what they are made from.

Picture 1 John Dalton

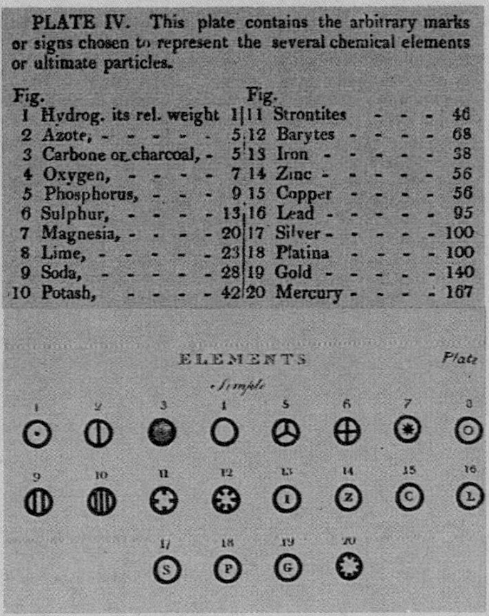

PLATE IV. This plate contains the arbitrary marks or signs chosen to represent the several chemical elements or ultimate particles.

Fig.			Fig.		
1	Hydrog. its rel. weight	1	11	Strontites	46
2	Azote,	5	12	Barytes	68
3	Carbone or charcoal,	5	13	Iron	38
4	Oxygen,	7	14	Zinc	56
5	Phosphorus,	9	15	Copper	56
6	Sulphur,	13	16	Lead	95
7	Magnesia,	20	17	Silver	100
8	Lime,	23	18	Platina	100
9	Soda,	28	19	Gold	140
10	Potash,	42	20	Mercury	167

Picture 2 John Dalton's symbols for the elements

Between 1803 and 1808 John Dalton worked out an Atomic Theory which is the basis of the one we know today. Dalton used the results of his own experiments and those of the French scientist Antoine Lavoisier.

Here are the key points about Dalton's theory.

- Every chemical element is made up of atoms of a unique type.
- All the atoms in a particular element are identical and have the same mass.
- Chemical compounds are made up of molecules. Molecules are made by joining together atoms.
- All the molecules in a particular compound are identical.

John Dalton invented symbols for the atoms of the elements. His symbols are shown in picture 2. He used these symbols to write formulas for compounds, some of which are shown in picture 3.

Dalton was the first person to realise the importance of writing chemical formulas. Today we no longer use his symbols, but chemical formulas are still at the heart of chemistry. The first thing a chemist asks on hearing about a new substance is, 'What's its formula?'

1 In what way was John Dalton's atomic theory more scientific than that of the ancient Greeks?

2 What similarities are there between the ancient Indian atomic theory and John Dalton's theory? What differences are there?

3 Look carefully at Dalton's symbols for the elements in picture 2.

a There are numbers beside each element's name. What do you think they show?

b Are all the substances in the table really elements? If not, name the exceptions.

c Dalton only listed 20 of the 92 elements in his table. Suggest two reasons why he did not list them all. (It will help you to look in the Data Section.)

4 Look at Dalton's compounds in picture 3. For each compound:

a rewrite Dalton's formula using modern symbols for the elements. Note that 'azote' is now called 'nitrogen';

b give the formula we use for the compound today (you may need to look it up in the Data Section).

Which formulas did Dalton get wrong?

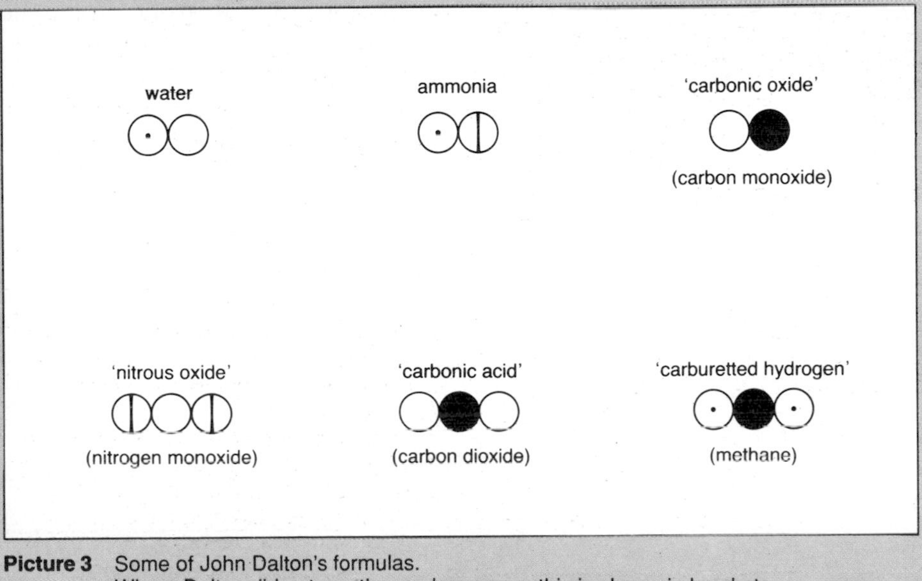

Picture 3 Some of John Dalton's formulas. Where Dalton did not use the modern name, this is shown in brackets

C4 Chemical equations

Equations are part of the language of chemistry.

Picture 1 Methane is a very useful fuel

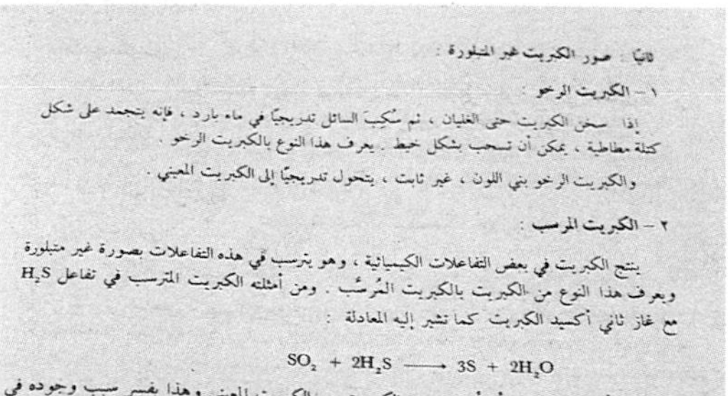

ثانيًا : صور الكبريت غير المتبلورة :

١ – الكبريت الرخو :

إذا سخن الكبريت حتى الغليان ، ثم سُكِبَ السائل تدريجيًا في ماء بارد ، فإنه يتجمد على شكل كتلة مطاطية ، يمكن أن تسحب بشكل خيط . يعرف هذا النوع بالكبريت الرخو .

والكبريت الرخو بني اللون ، غير ثابت ، يتحول تدريجيًا إلى الكبريت المعيني .

٢ – الكبريت المرسب :

ينتج الكبريت في بعض التفاعلات الكيميائية ، وهو يترسب في هذه التفاعلات بصورة غير متبلورة ويعرف هذا النوع من الكبريت بالكبريت المُرسَّب . ومن أمثلته الكبريت المترسب في تفاعل H_2S مع غاز ثاني أكسيد الكبريت كما تشير إليه المعادلة :

$$SO_2 + 2H_2S \longrightarrow 3S + 2H_2O$$

هذا وتُلاحظ مما سبق أن أثبت صور الكبريت هو الكبريت المعيني وهذا يفسر سبب وجوده في الطبيعة . والكبريت في جميع حالاته الصلبة ، يوجد بصورة جزيئية حيث يتكون جزيئه من ثماني ذرات (S_8) ترتبط مع بعضها بروابط تساهمية ، ويتخذ الجزيء شكلاً حلقيًا يشبه التاج (شكل ٥–٨) .

Picture 2 Chemical equations are an international language

Cuando al tener lugar la reacción la entidad representiva de un elemento presenta un balance negativo densidad electrónica, se dice que se ha oxidado; en caso contrario, que se ha reducido.

$$C + O_2 \rightarrow CO_2$$

En esta reacción, el carbono se oxida y el oxigeno se reduce.

Understand? Well, perhaps not all of it. But you probably worked out that this extract (from a Spanish chemistry book) is about the reaction of carbon with oxygen to form carbon dioxide.

Throughout the world, chemists use equations like this to describe reactions. It's a truly international language.

What do chemical equations tell us?

Picture 1 shows a well known reaction. When natural gas burns, it reacts with oxygen to form carbon dioxide and water. We can write a **word equation** to summarise the reaction:

methane + oxygen → carbon dioxide + water

The substances on the left-hand side are the **reactants**, and the **products** are on the right-hand side.

If we use the **formulas** of the substances instead of their names, we get a different kind of equation.

$$CH_4 + O_2 \rightarrow CO_2 + H_2O$$

This equation is an improvement on the word equation because it gives the formulas of the reactants and products. *But there is one thing wrong with it.* The numbers of atoms do not match up. There are four H atoms on the left and only two on the right. Likewise there are two O atoms on the left and three on the right. This is impossible, because atoms can't be created or destroyed in a reaction.

To put this right we need to look at the *amounts* of the different substances involved in the reaction. Experiments show that for every molecule of methane, *two* molecules of oxygen are used up, forming one molecule of carbon dioxide and two molecules of water. So we need to rewrite the equation like this:

$$CH_4 + 2\,O_2 \rightarrow CO_2 + 2\,H_2O$$

The figure 2 in front of O_2 shows there are two molecules of oxygen involved. Now the numbers of atoms are the same on each side. The equation is said to be **balanced**.

A balanced equation like this tells us a lot. We cannot only see what is formed in the reaction, but also the numbers of molecules involved.

Here is another example. You probably know that hydrogen burns in oxygen to form water. The equation for the reaction can be written as:

$$2\,H_2(g) + O_2(g) \rightarrow 2\,H_2O(g)$$

This tells us that two molecules of hydrogen combine with one molecule of oxygen to give two molecules of water. Notice that *state symbols* have been included, so we can tell the state of the reactants and products. What do you notice about the state of the water?

How to write balanced equations

The only way to be sure of the balanced equation for a reaction would be to do experiments. First you need to carry out the reaction to find exactly what the reactants and products are. Then you need to find the numbers of each type of particle reacting.

But chemists write lots of equations, and it isn't possible to do experiments every time. Fortunately, if we know the reactants and products, we can find their formulas and *predict* the equation. Here are the rules for predicting balanced equations.

Rules for predicting balanced equations

STEP 1 Make sure you know what the reactants and products are.
Let's take as an example the burning of magnesium to form magnesium oxide (picture 3).

STEP 2 Write a word equation for the reaction.

magnesium + oxygen → magnesium oxide

STEP 3 Write formulas for elements and compounds.
Remember that gaseous elements like oxygen are diatomic, so we must write O_2, not O. Our example is now:

$$Mg + O_2 \rightarrow MgO$$

STEP 4 Balance the equation.
There must be the same number of each type of atom on both sides. In the equation above there are two O atoms on the left, but only one on the right. To balance the number of O atoms, we need to double the amount of MgO:

$$Mg + O_2 \rightarrow 2\,MgO$$

But now there are two Mg atoms on the right, and only one on the left. So we need to double the amount of Mg on the left:

$$2\,Mg + O_2 \rightarrow 2\,MgO$$

The equation is now balanced, with equal numbers of each type of atom on each side.

Remember that *equations cannot be balanced by altering formulas*. This would create an entirely different substance. You can only balance equations by putting a number *in front* of a formula.

Picture 3 Burning magnesium in a sparkler. What is the equation for the reaction?

Questions

1 Propane, C_3H_8, is used as a portable fuel for homes. The following equation represents the burning of propane:

$C_3H_8(g) + 5\,O_2(g) \rightarrow 3\,CO_2(g) + 4\,H_2O(g)$

a Is propane a solid, a liquid or a gas?

b The normal state of water is liquid. Why is it not liquid in this equation?

c How many molecules of (i) propane, (ii) oxygen, (iii) carbon dioxide and (iv) water are involved in the reaction?

d How many atoms of (i) carbon, (ii) hydrogen and (iii) oxygen are there on (a) the left-hand side and (b) the right-hand side? Can you confirm that the equation is balanced?

2 Butane is present in camping gas. Here are a word equation and a balanced equation representing the burning of butane:

butane + oxygen → carbon dioxide + water

$2\,C_4H_{10}(g) + 13\,O_2(g) \rightarrow 8\,CO_2(g) + 10\,H_2O(g)$

Write down *three* things that the balanced equation tells you which you could not find from the word equation.

3 Write in words everything that the equation below tells you about the reaction of carbon monoxide (CO) with oxygen.

$2\,CO(g) + O_2(g) \rightarrow 2\,CO_2(g)$

Write down two things that the equation does *not* tell you about the reaction.

4 The following equations are not balanced. Write them out and balance them.

a $Zn + HCl \rightarrow ZnCl_2 + H_2$

b $Na + H_2O \rightarrow NaOH + H_2$

c $Fe + Cl_2 \rightarrow FeCl_3$

d $C_5H_{10} + O_2 \rightarrow CO_2 + H_2O$

5 Write balanced equations for the following reactions. If there are any formulas you don't know, look them up in the Data Section.

a carbon + oxygen → carbon dioxide

b nitrogen + hydrogen → ammonia

c aluminium + oxygen → aluminium oxide

d sodium hydroxide + hydrochloric acid → sodium chloride + water

e hydrogen + chlorine → hydrogen chloride

6 Each of the following equations is incomplete. Fill in the blanks to complete them.

a One of the things that happens to iron when it rusts:

______ $+ 3O_2 \rightarrow 2Fe_2O_3$

b An important reaction in making fertilisers:

nitrogen + hydrogen → ammonia

______ $+ 3H_2 \rightarrow 2NH_3$

c What happens when you get energy from glucose:

glucose + oxygen → carbon dioxide + water

$C_6H_{12}O_6 +$ ______ → ______ $+ 6H_2O$

C5 Weighing atoms

In this topic we see how to work out the quantities of substances formed in reactions.

Picture 1 Weighing out the Ingredients for a recipe helps make sure you get the right product

Picture 2 Magnesium atoms are twice as heavy as carbon atoms so the relative atomic mass of magnesium is twice that of carbon

How can we weigh atoms?

When you use a recipe, you have to measure out the amounts of ingredients. You usually *weigh* them out. Getting the quantities right is important: it helps you get the right product, and the right amount of it.

Chemical reactions are similar. Suppose you manufacture lime by heating limestone (topic D3). If you get an order for 1000 tonnes of lime, what mass of limestone should you heat? You need a kind of chemical recipe. The recipe you have to follow is the *balanced equation* for the reaction, which tells you the number of atoms and molecules involved.

Weighing out flour and sugar is easy enough, but how do you weigh atoms?

Finding the mass of atoms is tricky, because it's impossible to weigh such tiny things directly. But scientists have developed a method for finding the mass of atoms, called mass spectrometry. Using this method, we find that the smallest atom, hydrogen, weighs just

$$0.000\,000\,000\,000\,000\,000\,000\,0017\,\text{g or } 1.7 \times 10^{-24}\,\text{g}$$

Or to put it another way, you need getting on for a million million million million hydrogen atoms to make one gram! Even the heaviest atoms are only a hundred times heavier than this.

These numbers are so tiny that a new scale has to be used for measuring the masses of atoms. Instead of working in grams, we say how heavy an atom is compared with other atoms. In other words, we measure the masses of atoms *relative to one another*. This gives numbers that are much easier to handle.

Relative atomic masses

The basis of the **relative atomic mass** scale is the carbon atom, which is given a mass of exactly 12.

Relative atomic mass of C = 12.000

Other atoms are weighed relative to this. For example, the mass spectrometer shows that magnesium atoms are twice as heavy as carbon atoms. This means that the relative atomic mass of magnesium is twice that of carbon, in other words 24 (picture 2).

In this way we can find the relative atomic masses of all the elements. Table 1 gives the relative atomic masses of some of the common ones, and there is a full list for all the elements in the Data Section.

How heavy are molecules?

If you know the formula of a molecule, you can work out its **relative formula mass**. You just add up the relative atomic masses of all the atoms in the formula. For example, what is the relative formula mass of water, H_2O?

relative mass of two hydrogen atoms	$= 2 \times 1$
relative mass of one oxygen atom	$= 16$
$\therefore$ relative formula mass of water	**= 18**

By a similar calculation, the relative formula mass of carbon dioxide, CO_2, is $(12 + 16 + 16) = 44$. Try working out the relative formula mass of methane, CH_4.

Relative masses are very useful when you need to measure the right numbers of atoms for a chemical reaction.

Table 1 Relative atomic masses of some elements

Element	Symbol	Relative atomic mass
aluminium	Al	27
bromine	Br	80
calcium	Ca	40
carbon	C	12
chlorine	Cl	35.5
copper	Cu	63.5
fluorine	F	19
gold	Au	197
hydrogen	H	1
iron	Fe	56
magnesium	Mg	24
nitrogen	N	14
oxygen	O	16
phosphorus	P	31
potassium	K	39
sodium	Na	23
sulphur	S	32
uranium	U	238
zinc	Zn	65

Counting atoms

Let's take an example. Suppose you wanted to make some iron sulphide, FeS. This is easily done by heating iron and sulphur together.

$$\text{iron} + \text{sulphur} \rightarrow \text{iron sulphide}$$
$$Fe + S \rightarrow FeS$$

If you were manufacturing iron sulphide, you would want to do it as cheaply as possible. This means using exactly the right quantities of iron and sulphur, so none is left over and wasted.

The equation shows that one atom of iron combines with one atom of sulphur. To get a decent amount of iron sulphide, you will need very large numbers of atoms, but there must always be equal numbers of iron atoms and sulphur atoms. If you take a trillion atoms of iron, you will need a trillion atoms of sulphur. But how could the atoms be counted out? They are so small that counting them out one by one is clearly out of the question.

The chemist's counting unit

When people count out large numbers of small things, they often use a counting unit. If you buy nails in a hardware shop, you can't buy them singly. They are sold in units of ten, twenty, thirty and so on. And rather than count

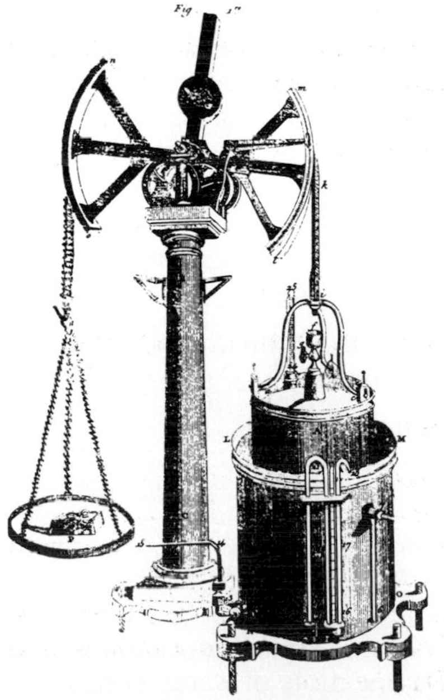

Picture 3 Accurate weighing is a vital part of modern chemistry.

Picture 4 To save counting nails separately, the storekeeper can weigh them out

out the nails singly, the storekeeper might *weigh* them out. If you know the mass of ten nails, you can work out the mass of, say, fifty, and weigh them out instead of counting.

Chemists count atoms by weighing, in the same way that storekeepers count nails by weighing. Atoms are far smaller than nails, so the counting unit is much larger. It is in fact

600 000 000 000 000 000 000 000 (6×10^{23}) atoms

This number is used because it turns out that

6×10^{23} atoms of any element have a mass equal to the relative atomic mass of the element in grams.

Picture 5 This glass contains 18g of water. This means it contains 6×10^{23} molecules

Some examples may help make this clearer. Using the relative atomic masses in table 1,

6×10^{23} atoms of carbon weigh 12 g
6×10^{23} atoms of hydrogen weigh 1 g
6×10^{23} atoms of oxygen weigh 16 g

The number 6×10^{23} is called the **Avogadro Constant**. This is in honour of the Italian scientist Amadeo Avagadro. The amount of substance that contains 6×10^{23} particles is known as one **mole**.

One mole of an element contains 6×10^{23} atoms. It has a mass equal to the relative atomic mass in grams.

Thus,

One mole of magnesium, Mg, weighs 24 g.
24 g of magnesium contains 6×10^{23} Mg atoms.
12 g of Mg is 0.5 mole, and this amount contains 3×10^{23} Mg atoms.
240 g of Mg is 10 moles, containing 60×10^{23} Mg atoms.

If you know the mass of a substance, you can work out the number of moles it contains by dividing the mass by the mass of 1 mole.

$$\text{number of moles} = \frac{\text{mass in grams}}{\text{mass of 1 mole}}$$

Counting molecules

Molecules are counted in just the same way as atoms. For example, the relative formula mass of water, H_2O, is 18. So one mole of water, containing

6×10^{23} H_2O molecules, weighs 18g.

One mole of a compound contains 6×10^{23} molecules. It has a mass equal to the relative formula mass in grams.

Picture 6 Burning carbon

Using moles

The mole is a very useful unit. We can use it to measure out known numbers of atoms just by weighing — we don't have to count them.

Let's go back to the example of iron reacting with sulphur to make iron sulphide.

$$Fe + S \rightarrow FeS$$

To make iron sulphide without any waste, we need to be able to weigh out equal numbers of atoms of iron and sulphur. Using relative atomic masses, we know that

56g of iron contains 6×10^{23} Fe atoms
32g of sulphur contains 6×10^{23} S atoms

So, to make the iron sulphide we would heat together 56g of iron and 32g of sulphur. This would provide equal numbers of iron and sulphur atoms. We would get 56g + 32g = 88g of iron sulphide. If we wanted more or less than 88g, we could scale the quantities up or down. But the mass of iron and the mass of sulphur must always be in the ratio 56:32.

Working out reacting masses

We can use moles to work out the masses involved in chemical reactions, *provided we know the balanced equation for the reaction*.

Look at this example. When you burn charcoal on a barbecue, this reaction takes place

carbon + oxygen → carbon dioxide

$$C + O_2 \rightarrow CO_2$$

This equation tells us that 1 atom of carbon reacts with 1 molecule of oxygen to form 1 molecule of carbon dioxide.

It also means that 1 *mole* of carbon reacts with 1 *mole* of oxygen to form 1 *mole* of carbon dioxide.

We know the mass of 1 mole of each of these substances: C = 12g, O_2 = 32g and CO_2 = 44g. So these are the masses involved in the reaction.

C	+	O_2	→	CO_2
1 mole		1 mole		1 mole
12g		32g		44g

In other words, every 12g of charcoal you burn on the barbecue needs 32g of oxygen — and makes 44g of carbon dioxide (picture 6). Here are two more worked examples.

Worked example 1 — Making lime

Lime is calcium oxide, CaO. It has many uses, including neutralising acid soil. Lime is made by heating limestone, $CaCO_3$. Suppose you heated 100 tonnes of $CaCO_3$. What mass of CaO would you get (picture 7)?

The equation tells us the numbers of moles involved in the reaction. From this we can work out the masses.

calcium carbonate	→	calcium oxide	+	carbon dioxide
$CaCO_3$	→	CaO	+	CO_2
1 mole		1 mole		1 mole

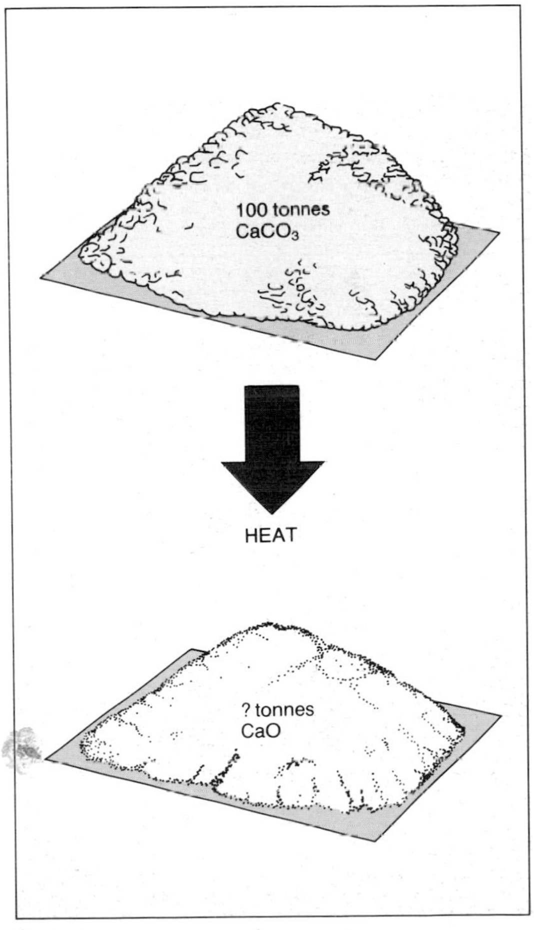

Picture 7 How much calcium oxide can you get from 100 tonnes of calcium carbonate?

Picture 8 Potters use chemical calculations to get the right quantities for the coloured glaze they use on a pot

1 mole of $CaCO_3$ weighs $(40 + 12 + 3 \times 16) = 100$g
1 mole of CaO weighs $(40 + 16) = 56$g. So we can write

$$\begin{array}{ccccc} CaCO_3 & \rightarrow & CaO & + & CO_2 \\ \text{1 mole} & & \text{1 mole} & & \text{1 mole} \\ 100\text{g} & & 56\text{g} & & \end{array}$$

So the equation tells us that 100g of $CaCO_3$ gives 56g of CaO.

→ **100 tonnes of $CaCO_3$ gives 56 tonnes of CaO**

So if you heated 100 tonnes of limestone, you would make 56 tonnes of lime, CaO.

Worked example 2 — Making aluminium

Aluminium has many uses, including making bicycles, saucepans and aeroplanes. It is made from an ore called bauxite. Purified bauxite is aluminium oxide, Al_2O_3. It is split up into aluminium and oxygen by electrolysis.

Here's the problem: what mass of aluminium oxide would you need if you wanted to make 1 kg of aluminium (picture 9)? Once again, the equation tells us the numbers of moles involved in the reaction, and hence the masses.

$$\begin{array}{ccccc} \text{aluminium oxide} & \rightarrow & \text{aluminium} & + & \text{oxygen} \\ 2\,Al_2O_3 & \rightarrow & 4\,Al & + & 3\,O_2 \\ \text{2 moles} & & \text{4 moles} & & \text{3 moles} \end{array}$$

2 moles of Al_2O_3 weigh $2 \times (2 \times 27 + 3 \times 16) = 204$g
4 moles of Al weigh $4 \times 27 = 108$g. So we can write

$$\begin{array}{ccccc} 2\,Al_2O_3 & \rightarrow & 4\,Al & + & 3\,O_2 \\ \text{2 moles} & \rightarrow & \text{4 moles} & & \text{3 moles} \\ 204\text{g} & & 108\text{g} & & \end{array}$$

So the equation tells us that you can get 108g of Al from 204g of Al_2O_3.

→ you can get 1g of Al from $\frac{204}{108}$g = 1.89g of Al

→ **you can get 1kg of Al from 1.89kg of Al_2O_3**

In other words, if you wanted 1kg of aluminium, you would need to start with 1.89kg of aluminium oxide.

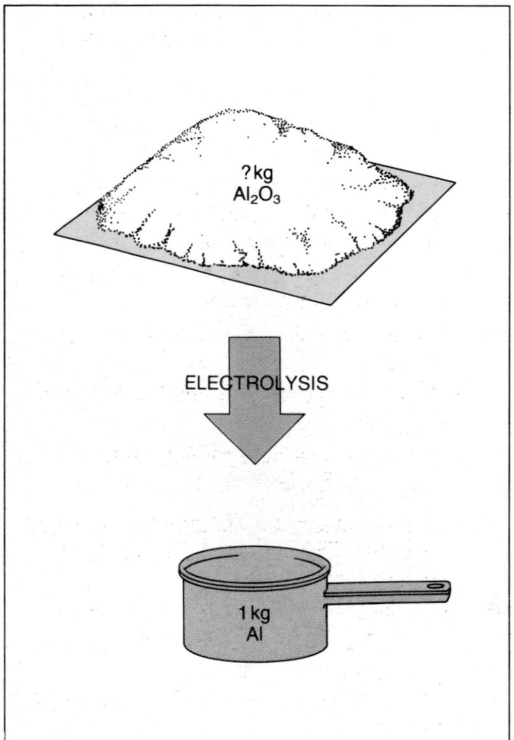

Picture 9 What mass of aluminium oxide do you need to make 1 kg of aluminium?

Activities

A Measuring reacting mass: does theory agree with practice?

In this activity you will burn 0.1 g of magnesium, and find the mass of magnesium oxide that is formed. You will also calculate the mass that should have been formed, and see how well the two agree.

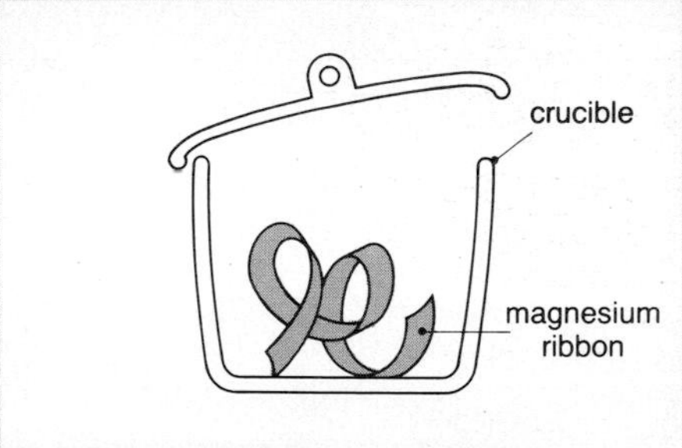

Picture 10 Heating magnesium ribbon

1 Practice

CARE Eye protection must be worn

a Weigh exactly 0.1 g of magnesium ribbon.

b Weigh an empty crucible and its lid.

c Coil the ribbon loosely and put it in the crucible.

d Put the lid on the crucible, leaving a gap so that air can get in (picture 10).

e Stand the crucible on a pipeclay triangle on top of a tripod.

f Heat the crucible strongly for five minutes. The magnesium will burn to form magnesium oxide. **CARE** It will be *very* hot.

g Leave the crucible to cool. Weigh it, including lid and contents.

h Find the mass of magnesium oxide that has been formed by subtracting the mass of the empty crucible from the mass you measured in 7.

2 Theory

The equation for the reaction is

magnesium + oxygen → magnesium oxide

$$2\,Mg + O_2 \rightarrow 2\,MgO$$

Work out the mass of MgO that should be formed from 0.1 g of Mg.
(Mg = 24, O = 16.)

3 Comparing practice and theory

How well do your results to 1 and 2 agree? Try to think of reasons for any disagreement. Compare your results with those of other groups. Discuss any disagreements between practice and theory.

B Find out about the mass spectrometer

The mass spectrometer is used to compare the masses of atoms and molecules. Look at an advanced text to find out what it is and how it works.

Questions

Use table 1 to find the relative atomic masses you need to answer these questions.

1 a i) Which element in table 1 has the lightest atoms?

ii) Which element has the heaviest atoms?

iii) How many times heavier is the heaviest element compared with the lightest element?

b How many times heavier is one sulphur atom compared with one oxygen atom?

c How many hydrogen atoms make up the same mass as one sodium atom?

2 Work out the relative formula mass of each of the following

(a) hydrogen chloride, HCl (b) sulphuric acid, H_2SO_4 (c) carbon monoxide, CO (d) butane, C_4H_{10} (e) glucose, $C_6H_{12}O_6$.

3 What is the mass of 1 mole of each of the following?

(a) magnesium, Mg (b) sulphur dioxide, SO_2 (c) helium, He (d) oxygen, O_2 (e) chlorophyll, $C_{51}H_{72}O_4N_4Mg$.

4 a How many moles of carbon atoms are there in 12g of carbon, C?

b i) How many moles of carbon atoms are there in 3g of carbon?

ii) How many carbon atoms are there in 3g of carbon?

iii) What mass of hydrogen contains the same number of atoms as 3g of carbon?

c i) What is the mass of 3 moles of carbon?

ii) How many carbon atoms are there in 3 moles of carbon?

5 Sulphur burns in air to form sulphur dioxide, SO_2 – one of the main gases responsible for causing acid rain. The object of this question is to find the mass of SO_2 formed when 8g of S is burned.

$$S + O_2 \rightarrow SO_2$$

____ moles ____ moles

____ g ____ g

a Fill in the blanks to show the numbers of moles of S and SO_2 involved in the reaction.

b Fill in the blanks to show the masses involved in the reaction.

c What mass of SO_2 is formed from 1 g of S?

d What mass of SO_2 is formed from 8g of S?

6 Iron is manufactured by reducing iron oxide, Fe_2O_3, in a blast furnace. The reducing agent is carbon monoxide, CO. The object of this question is to find the mass of Fe that could be produced from 16 tonnes of Fe_2O_3.

$$Fe_2O_3 + 3\,CO \rightarrow 2\,Fe + 3\,CO_2$$

____ moles ____ moles

____ g ____ g

a Fill in the blanks to show the numbers of moles of Fe_2O_3 and Fe involved in the reaction shown in the equation.

b Fill in the blanks to show the masses involved in the reaction.

c What mass of Fe is formed from 1 g of Fe_2O_3?

d What mass of Fe is formed from 16g of Fe_2O_3?

e What mass of Fe is formed from 16 tonnes of Fe_2O_3?

7 Ammonia is manufactured by the Haber Process. This involves the reaction of nitrogen with hydrogen.

nitrogen + hydrogen → ammonia

$$N_2 + 3\,H_2 \rightarrow 2\,NH_3$$

What mass of (i) nitrogen (ii) hydrogen is neeeded to make 34g of ammonia?

C6 The structures of substances

Atoms join together to form structures. The properties of a substance depend on its structure

Picture 1 It's hard work sitting on the beach

Picture 2 Like scaffolding, atoms, molecules and ions form structures.

What are structures?

Sand and water are very different substances (Picture 1). Why is the sand a hard and gritty solid, but water a liquid? It's because of their different structures.

Scaffolding is a structure (picture 2). The way it is joined together makes it strong and rigid — which is what you want when you're working 30 metres above the street.

In this topic we shall be looking at much smaller structures, made of atoms, molecules and ions. But the idea is the same. The way the structure is joined together decides the properties of the substance.

Working with models

Models are an essential part of science. Models help us to think about the way things work. The kinetic theory is a model — a mental model that explains a lot about the behaviour of matter.

In this topic we'll be looking at a different kind of model. To represent structures, we use **atomic** and **molecular models**. You can build these models yourself, as shown in pictures 3a and 3b. You can also show the models by drawings, as in pictures 3c and 3d.

Pictures 3a and 3c are the closest to the way we believe a water molecule really is. They are called **space-filling** models, because they show all the space that is occupied by oxygen and hydrogen atoms.

Picture 3b is called a **ball-and-stick** model. This kind of model is sometimes useful, because it shows the **bonds** that hold the atoms together. Picture 3d is a quick and simple way of drawing a ball-and-stick model.

A look at some structures

Picture 3 shows single water molecules. In fact, water is made of vast numbers of these molecules. To understand the structure of water, we need to see how the molecules look when there are many of them together. Today, we know the structures of many substances, even though their atoms are far too small to see. They have been investigated using a method called **X-ray diffraction**. There is more about this method in *Believing without seeing* on page 81.

The structure of water

Picture 4 shows how we think water molecules look in liquid water. Notice these points:

- We have used a space-filling model to represent the water structure.
- The water molecules are arranged in a fairly random way. This is typical of the situation in a liquid.
- *Within* a water molecule, the atoms are bonded strongly together. But *between* the molecules, there are no strong bonds to hold them together. It does not need much energy to separate the molecules completely and turn the liquid water to a gas — steam. Just a little heating is enough. In other words, water has a fairly low boiling point.

Water has a **simple molecular structure**. A simple molecular structure contains small molecules. Within the molecules, the atoms are held together

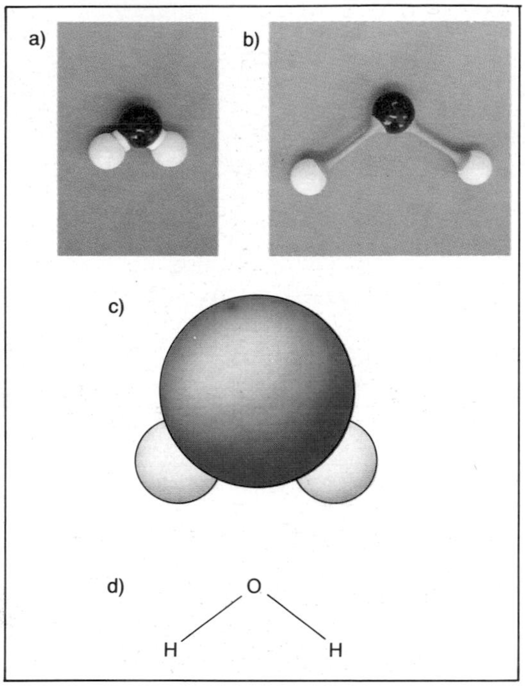

Picture 3 Different ways of showing a water molecule. Oxygen atoms are red, hydrogen atoms are white.
(a) space-filling model built from a kit
(b) ball-and-stick model built from a kit
(c) space-filling drawing (d) simple drawing

Picture 4 The structure of water

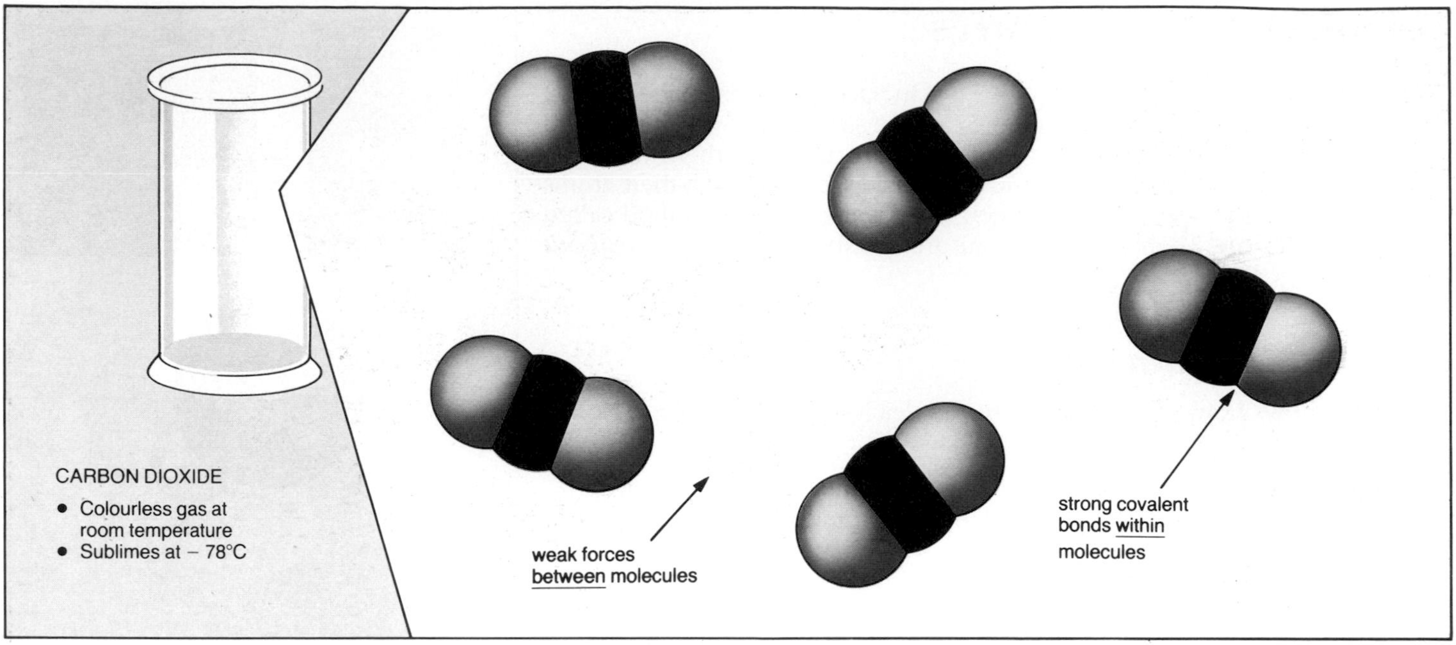

Picture 5 The structure of carbon dioxide

by strong bonds. These are called **covalent** bonds, and there is more about them in topic J5. But between the molecules there are only weak forces holding the molecules together. This is illustrated in picture 5, which shows another substance with a molecular structure: carbon dioxide.

The structure of sand

Sand is not at all like water. It feels hard and gritty and is difficult to melt. Judging from its properties, it has a different structure from water.

Before we can talk about the structure of sand, we need to know what sand is made of. Pure sand is mainly made of a mineral called **quartz**. Quartz is silicon oxide, SiO_2. It sometimes occurs as large crystals with beautifully regular shapes (picture 6). But more often it is found in a powdered state, which is sand.

Picture 7 shows the structure of sand.

Notice these points about the structure.

- We have used a ball-and-stick model rather than a space-filling one. This is so you can see inside the structure clearly.
- The structure is very regular. Every Si atom (grey) is joined to four O atoms (red) by strong covalent bonds. Every O atom is joined to two Si atoms. This arrangement goes on continuously. It holds the Si and O atoms together in a strong, rigid structure — rather like scaffolding. This is why sand is so hard and difficult to melt. It needs a lot of energy to break apart the strongly-bonded Si and O atoms.

The structure of sand, SiO_2, is called a **giant structure**. In a giant structure, the atoms are all strongly bonded together in a vast network that goes on indefinitely. Notice how different the structure of SiO_2 is from the simple molecular structure of CO_2 shown in picture 5. These two substances have a similar formula: the only difference is that one has Si atoms instead of C atoms. But their structures are completely different, and so are their properties. CO_2 is a simple molecular structure, SiO_2 is a giant structure. As a result, CO_2 is a gas, but SiO_2 is a hard solid.

Many of the rocks that the earth is made from are based on the SiO_2 structure in picture 7. These giant silicate structures make rocks hard and strong.

There are several different types of giant structure. Some contain atoms, some contain ions. We look in more detail at the different types in the next topic.

Picture 6 Crystals of quartz

Picture 7 The structure of sand

Comparing simple molecular and giant structures

Both elements and compounds can have either type of structure.

The strength of a structure is decided by the strength of the bonds in it. In a giant structure, the atoms are all bonded together strongly, and the structure is difficult to break up. This gives a strong substance that is difficult to melt or boil. The substance will be a solid, and probably hard, like SiO_2 in sand.

In a simple molecular structure, some of the bonds — the bonds *between* the molecules — are weak. This makes the structure weaker. It tends to fall apart more easily. This gives a substance that is easy to melt or boil — like water. The substance may be a gas or liquid at room temperature. If it is a solid, it is likely to be soft.

Table 1 summarises the main differences between simple molecular and giant structures.

Table 1 The main differences between simple molecular and giant structures

	Description of structure	Typical properties of substances with this structure	Examples of substances with this structure
SIMPLE MOLECULAR	small molecules held together by covalent bonds. Only weak forces between the molecules	• low melting point and boiling point • often liquid or gaseous at room temperature • soft, if solid • do not conduct electricity	oxygen, O_2 chlorine, Cl_2 iodine, I_2 carbon dioxide, CO_2 water, H_2O
GIANT	atoms or ions all strongly bonded together in a giant structure (see topic 00 for more details)	• high melting point and boiling point • hard solids • sometimes conduct electricity	metals sand, SiO_2 diamond, C graphite, C calcium carbonate, $CaCO_3$

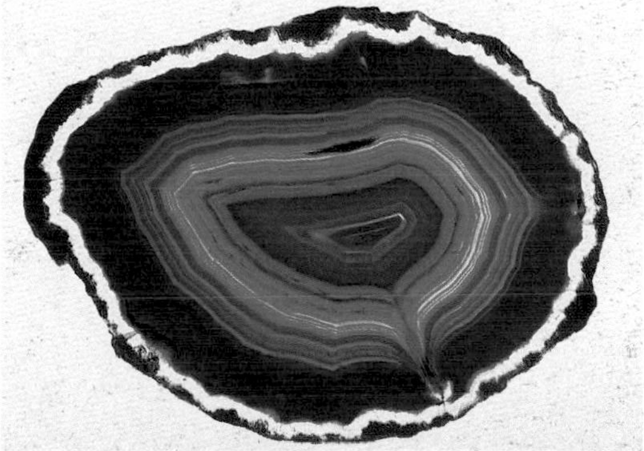

Picture 8 Agate, a form of silicon oxide. Impurities give it the blue colour

Activities

A Building models

The best way to find out about structures is to build models. You will need a model kit for this activity: ball-and-stick models would be best.

1 *Start with carbon atoms only* — as many as possible. If you share your atoms with others, you can make a bigger structure. Notice that the C atoms have four holes: this is because carbon forms four covalent bonds.

Use the 'sticks' to join the carbon atoms together. **Rules**: There should be a stick in every hole, and every atom should be joined to as many other atoms as possible.

What shape is your structure? Is it simple molecular or giant? Would you expect this form of carbon to be solid, liquid or gas? Find out the everyday name of the form of carbon you have built.

2 *Now build another structure using carbon and hydrogen atoms.* Notice that the H atoms have one hole: this is because hydrogen forms only one covalent bond. **Rules:** There should be a stick in every hole. C atoms must *only* be joined to H atoms, and H atoms must only join to C atoms. Go on joining the atoms together until you have used them all up.

What is your structure like? Is it simple molecular or giant? Would you expect this substance to be solid, liquid or gas? Find out the everyday name of the substance you have made.

B Testing substances to find their structure

Suppose you are given a small sample of a solid substance. What tests could you do on it to see which kind of structure it has?

Look at table 1 which compares the properties of giant and simple molecular substances. Plan some simple, safe tests you could do on a substance to find out its structure. Remember some substances burn or give off poisonous gases when they are heated. Discuss your plan with your teacher before you carry out any tests. Try testing the following substances: salt, wax, talcum powder, sulphur.

Questions

1 Fill in the blanks in the passage below. You can use the following words or groups of words:
hardness, giant, low, covalent, melting point, high, continuously, small, weak, boiling point.

The structure of a substance means the way its atoms, molecules or ions are joined together. The structure of a substance decides properties such as ____(1)____, ____(2)____ and ____(3)____.

A simple molecular structure contains ____(4)____ molecules. The atoms in these molecules are held together by strong ____(5)____ bonds. But between the molecules, the bonds are only ____(6)____. This makes the molecules easy to break apart.

In a ____(7)____ structure, all the atoms are bonded together strongly. The structure goes on ____(8)____. The atoms are difficult to break apart, and the structure is strong.

Substances with simple molecular structures tend to have ____(9)____ melting points and boiling points. Substances with giant structures tend to have ____(10)____ ones.

2 Picture 9 shows the structures of substances A to D.

a Classify each structure as giant or simple molecular.

b Which substance(s) would you expect to be hard solid(s)?

c Which substance is most likely to be a gas?

d Which substance or substances are elements?

3 From what you know of their properties, decide whether each of the following substances has a simple molecular or a giant structure.

a iron

b brick

c ice

d glass

e oil

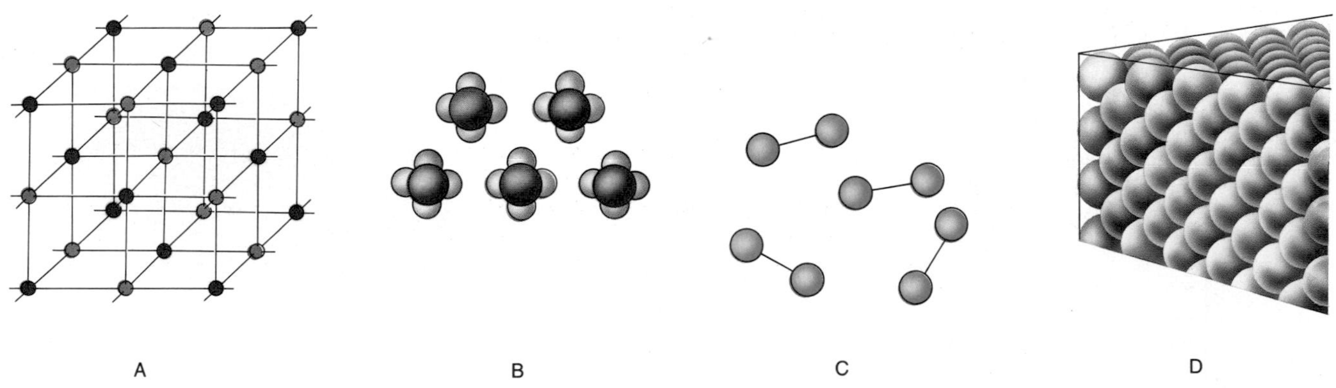

Picture 9

Believing without seeing

How do we know about the structure of materials? Why do we believe that the carbon atoms in diamond are arranged in the way shown in picture 3, page 83? Atoms are far too small to see directly, so structures cannot be found out just by looking!

Most of what we know about structures has been found out by **X-ray crystallography**. X-rays are a form of electromagnetic radiation with a shorter wavelength than ordinary light. Their short wavelength makes it possible to investigate very small structures and find out much more than you can with light.

When you pass X-rays through a crystal, you get a pattern of light and dark spots, called a **diffraction pattern**. You can't see X-rays directly, but the pattern can be recorded on a photographic film. A crystal gives a particular diffraction pattern, depending on its structure. Picture 1 shows the diffraction pattern given by diamond.

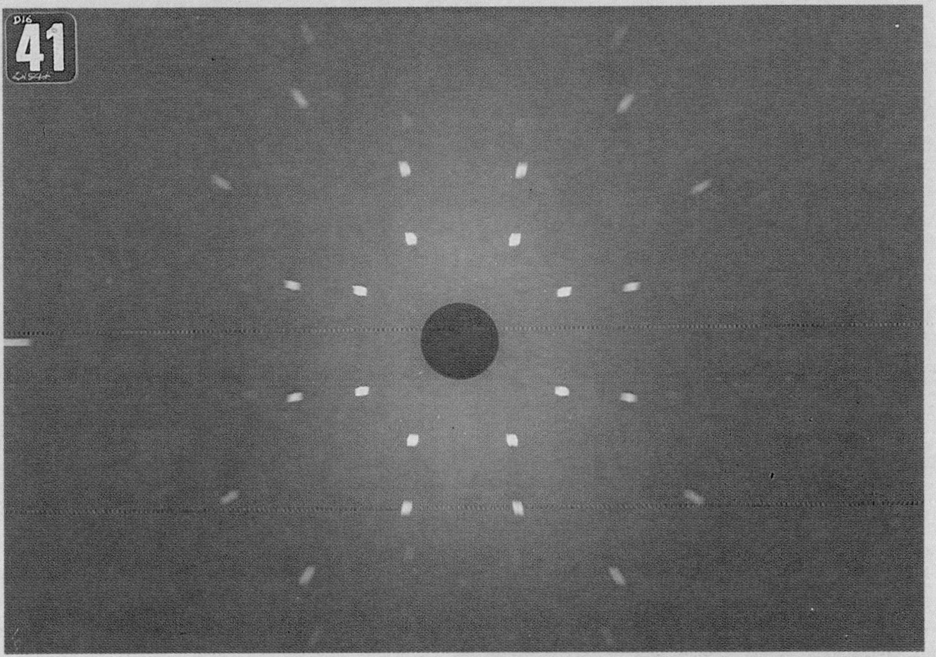

Picture 1 An X-ray diffraction pattern

Plenty to Bragg about

The method of X-ray crystallography was developed in 1912 by a father and son team of scientists, Sir William and Sir Laurence Bragg. Between them, they found a way to record diffraction patterns, then use them to work out how the atoms or ions are arranged in a crystal. They couldn't actually *see* how the atoms are arranged, but they found a way to work out the structure from the diffraction pattern.

Picture 2 Dorothy Hodgkin

The Braggs worked out the structures of many substances, including diamond and sodium chloride. They both received Nobel Prizes for their work.

The method of X-ray crystallography is still used a great deal. It has been used to find the structures of very complex molecules like proteins and DNA (*The Living World*, topic A6).

A very important piece of X-ray crystallography work was done by Dorothy Hodgkin during the Second World War. Penicillin became very important in the war for treating infected wounds. Scientists needed to know the structure of penicillin so they could make it synthetically. Dorothy Hodgkin used X-ray crystallography to find the structure of penicillin. She received the Nobel Prize in 1964 for her work on the structures of biological substances.

1 We cannot see atoms, and we cannot see X-rays. Yet X-rays make it possible to 'see' how the atoms are arranged in diamond. Explain why.

2 Look at these three statements.
'We know the structure of diamond from X-ray crystallography'.
'We know what the surface of Mars is like from photographs taken by spacecraft'.
'I know what I look like because I've seen myself in the mirror'.

For each of these statements, say whether you think it is *certain*. Explain your answers.

Suppose you are Sir Laurence Bragg. You have just worked out the structure of sodium chloride from X-ray crystallography. Another scientist challenges you and says your structure is wrong. What further experiments could you do to show you are right?

C7
Giant structures

Most of the materials we use have one of three types of giant structure.

Picture 1 Crystals grow in a definite, regular shape. The regular shape of the crystal comes from the regular arrangement of the atoms or ions that it's made from

In a substance with a giant structure, the atoms or ions are all joined together strongly in a structure that goes on continuously. There are three different ways they can be joined, and these give three different types of giant structure: giant covalent, giant metallic and giant ionic.

In this topic we'll be looking at details of these different types of structure. We know these details from X-ray analysis experiments (see *Believing without seeing* on page 81).

a)

b)

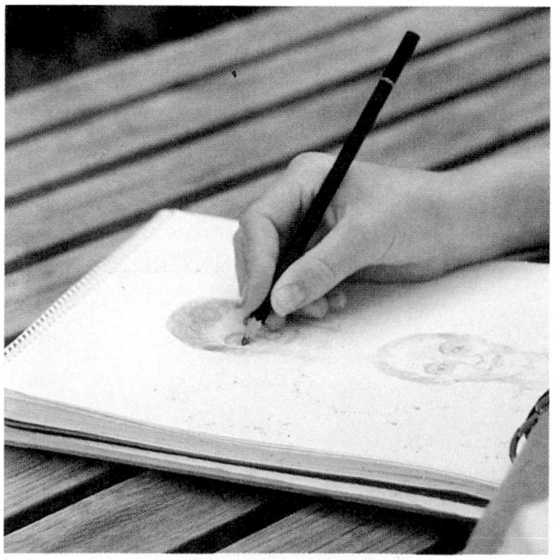

Picture 2 Both of these "pencils" contain a form of carbon. (a) is diamond, (b) is graphite

Giant covalent structures

The structure of sand, shown in the last topic, is a giant covalent structure. The atoms in the structure are joined together by strong covalent bonds.

The structure of diamond

The great strength of giant covalent structures is shown perfectly in diamond. Diamond is a form of carbon, although it looks very different from the more common forms like charcoal and graphite. Apart from making beautiful gemstones, diamond is the hardest of all naturally-occurring substances. This makes it useful for cutting glass and drilling into hard substances (picture 2).

Picture 3 shows the structure of diamond. Of course, this is only a tiny part of the structure. There are over 10^{20} atoms in even a tiny diamond. We've used a ball-and-stick model, so you can see clearly how the atoms are joined together. Every C atom is joined to four others in a regular tetrahedral arrangement. This regular, symmetrical arrangement makes the structure very difficult to break apart. To separate one C atom from the structure, you have to break four strong covalent bonds. No wonder diamond is so hard and so difficult to melt.

Like other giant covalent structures, diamond doesn't dissolve in water, because the atoms cannot be broken apart and spread among water molecules. And it doesn't conduct electricity, because there are no charged particles to carry the current.

The structure of graphite

Graphite is a much commoner form of carbon than diamond. Pencil 'lead' is made from graphite. Like diamond, graphite has a giant covalent structure,

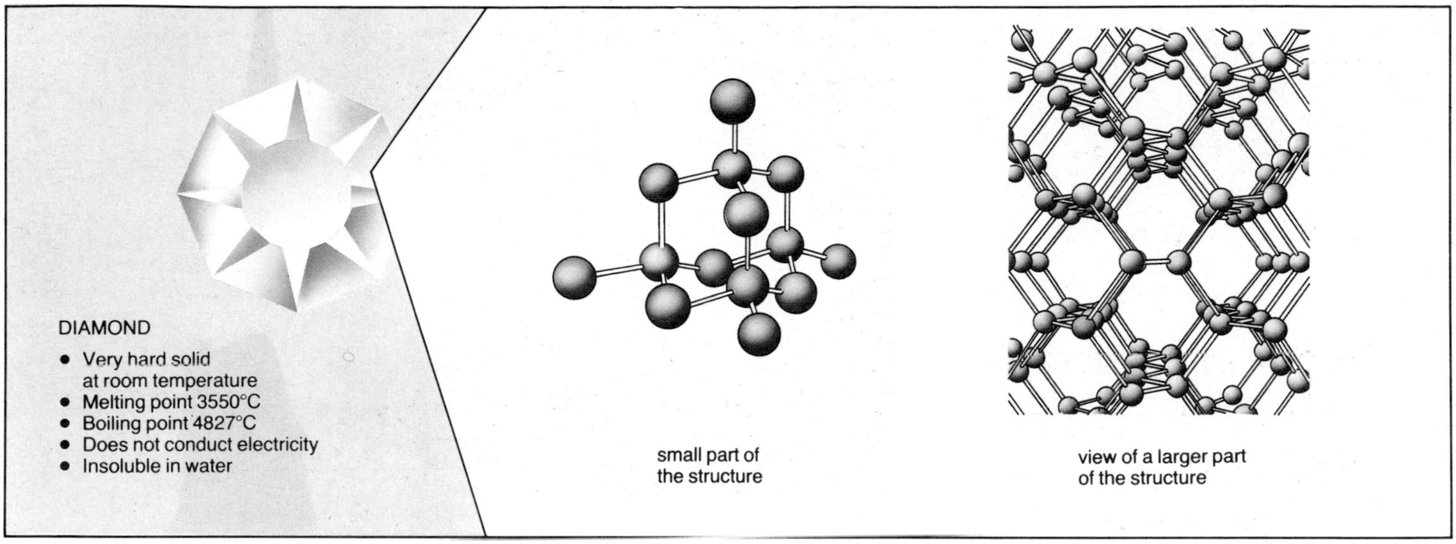

DIAMOND
• Very hard solid at room temperature
• Melting point 3550°C
• Boiling point 4827°C
• Does not conduct electricity
• Insoluble in water
small part of the structure
view of a larger part of the structure

Picture 3 The structure of diamond

but even so its properties are very different. Graphite is soft and slippery, and it conducts electricity.

Picture 4 shows the structure of graphite. You can see it is made up of layers. Within each layer, every carbon atom is joined to three others by strong covalent bonds. This forms a pattern of interlocking hexagonal rings. The carbon atoms are difficult to separate from one another, so graphite, like diamond, has a high melting point.

However, the bonds *between* the layers are weak. The layers are able to slide easily over one another, rather like a pack of cards. This makes graphite soft and slippery. When you write with a pencil, layers of graphite flake off and stick to the paper.

Clay: another giant layer structure

The pictures on page 2 show the changes that happen to clay when it is fired in a kiln. Before firing, it is soft and crumbly. After, it is hard and strong.

Clay has a giant layer structure (picture 5). The layers contain silicon, oxygen, aluminium and hydrogen atoms. When clay is wet, water molecules

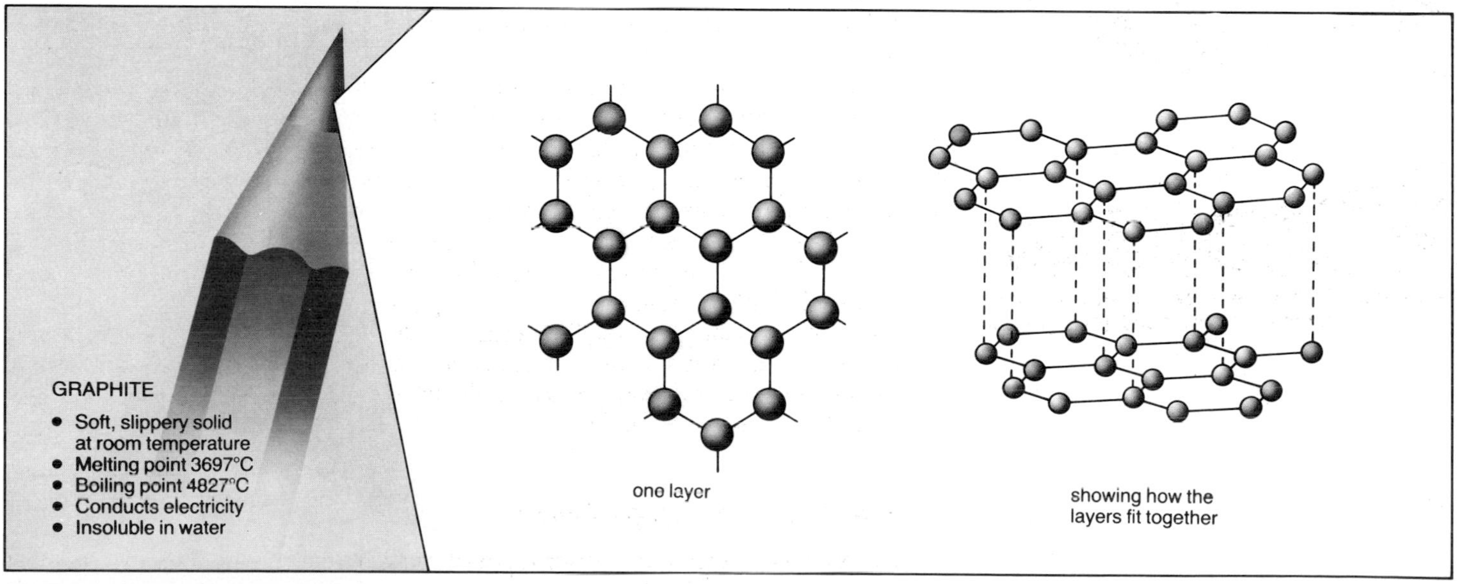

GRAPHITE
• Soft, slippery solid at room temperature
• Melting point 3697°C
• Boiling point 4827°C
• Conducts electricity
• Insoluble in water
one layer
showing how the layers fit together

Picture 4 The structure of graphite

Picture 5 The atomic structure of a form of clay

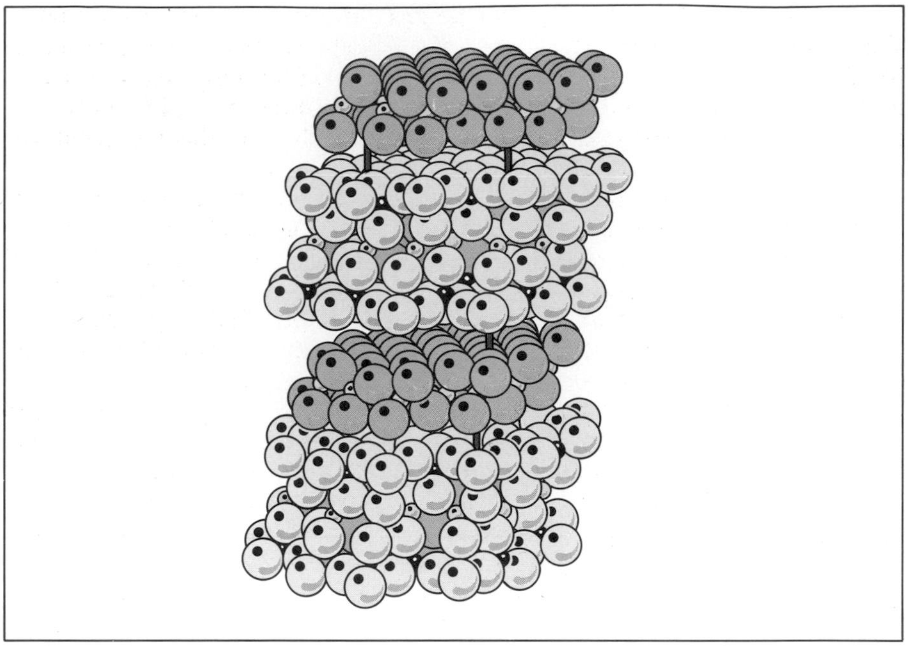

Picture 6 A brass weight, before and after etching in acid

get between the layers and lubricate them so they can slide over one another. The clay is slippery and pliable.

When the clay dries, the water molecules evaporate and the layers can no longer slide over one another. But the layers can break apart, so the dry clay is still crumbly.

When dry clay is *fired* by heating it strongly in a kiln, the structure changes. The atoms in one layer join to atoms in the layers above and below. This locks the layers together, making the clay much harder. This is why a clay pot is so much harder and stronger after it has been fired.

Giant metallic structures

We look at the typical properties of metals in topic E1. Most metals are dense and hard, with high melting points. They conduct electricity and they can be bent into shape without breaking. These are useful properties — in fact, without metals our civilisation would literally collapse. But *why* do metals have these special properties? It's because of their particular kind of giant structure.

Picture 7 The structure of copper

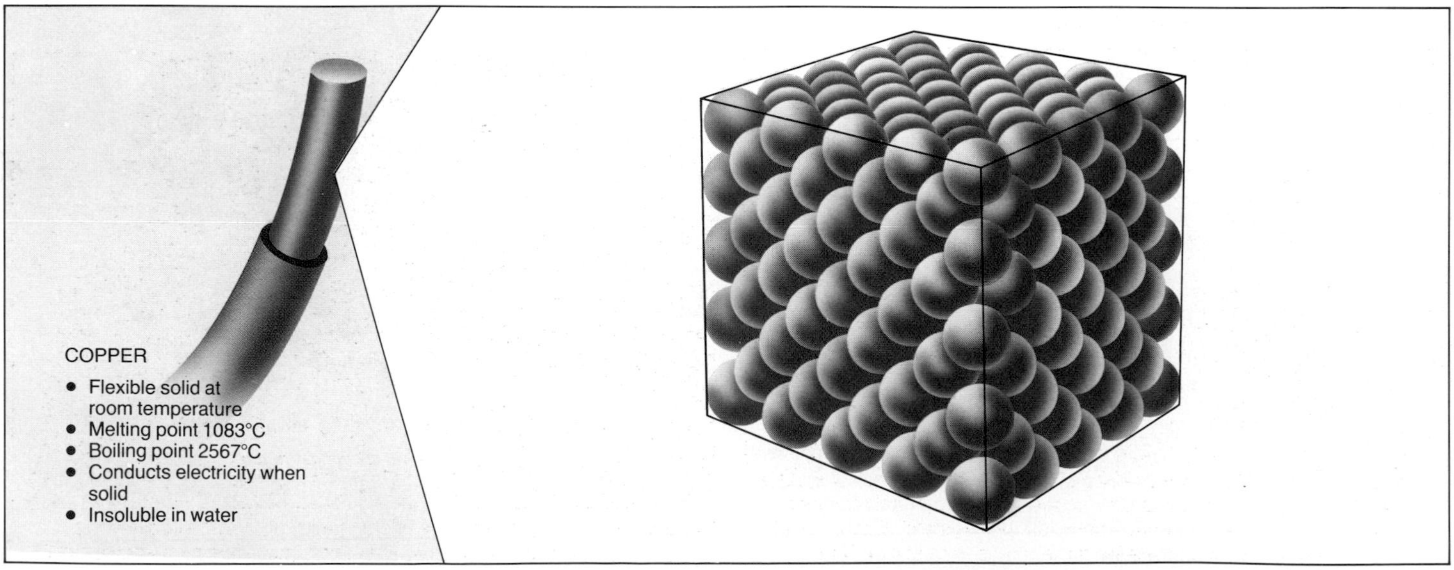

You may not think of metals as being crystalline, but they are. An ordinary, shiny piece of metal doesn't show crystals. This is because the straight, regular edges of the crystals have been rubbed off by polishing. But if you **etch** the metal by dipping it in acid, the crystals show up and you can see them under the microscope (picture 6). The crystals show that the metal has a regular structure — a giant metallic structure.

Picture 7 shows the typical metallic structure of copper. It's a space-filling model, and you can see how closely together the atoms of copper are packed. In fact, they are packed as close together as it is possible to be, and this is called a **close-packed** structure. Every atom has 12 other atoms touching it, and this is the maximum number possible. Try building a close-packed structure with model atoms in activity A. Picture 8 shows an example of a close-packed structure in a greengrocer's shop.

Most metals have a close-packed structure, and this accounts for their high density — lots of atoms are packed into a small space. But what holds them together? In a giant *covalent* structure, the atoms are held together by strong covalent bonds. This makes giant covalent substances hard, but brittle. When you try to bend the substance, it shatters. The covalent bonds have a fixed direction, and if you try to change that direction, they break.

Metals are different. They are malleable, not brittle — when you bend a piece of metal, it stays in its new shape, and does not shatter (picture 9). Metals have a different kind of bond holding their atoms together, called a **metallic** bond. Metallic bonds are strong, but flexible so they don't break when the atoms are moved to a new position.

Picture 8 Greengrocers often stack fruit in a close-packed structure.

Picture 9 Metals are malleable. When you bend a metal, it stays in its new shape

What happens when you bend a piece of metal?

A piece of metal contains many separate crystals. You can see this from the etched brass in picture 6. When a piece of metal is bent, these crystals slide past one another.

What would you see if you enlarged the crystals so you could see the atoms in one layer of the structure? Picture 10 gives you an idea. Each crystal in fact contains many more atoms than are shown here. When the atoms in two crystals slide past each other, the metallic bonds between them do not break, but re-form in their new position. So the metal does not shatter: it just takes its new, bent shape.

Picture 11 represents what happens when you add a small amount of another metal — in other words, make an alloy. The atoms of the second metal are a different size, and they get in the way as the two crystals slide past each other. This makes it more difficult for the crystals to slide. The metal is more difficult to bend — it's harder. This simple model helps explain why alloys are harder than pure metals.

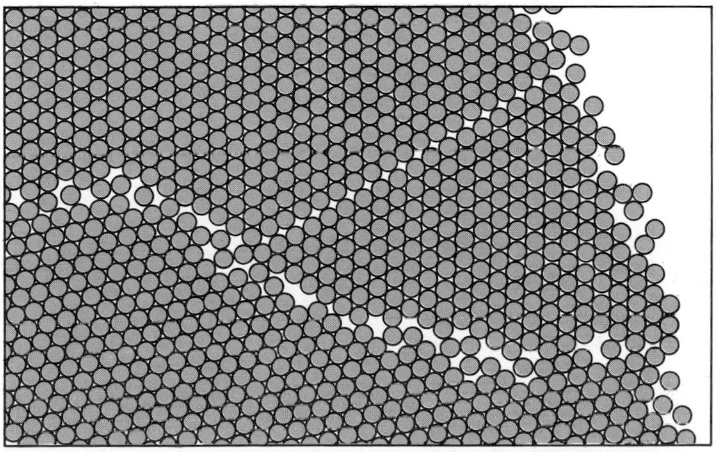

Picture 10 This represents the atoms in one layer of a metal structure. Look for the boundaries between the 'crystals'. Each crystal would actually contain far more atoms than shown here

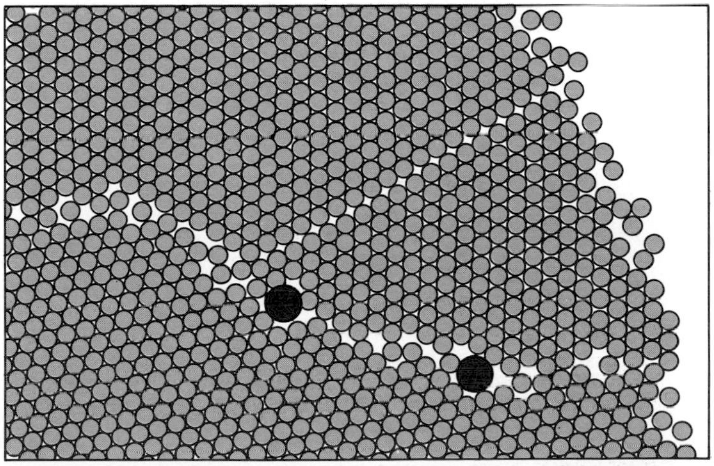

Picture 11 This represents the effect of alloying. What effect will the larger atoms have when the crystals slide past each other?

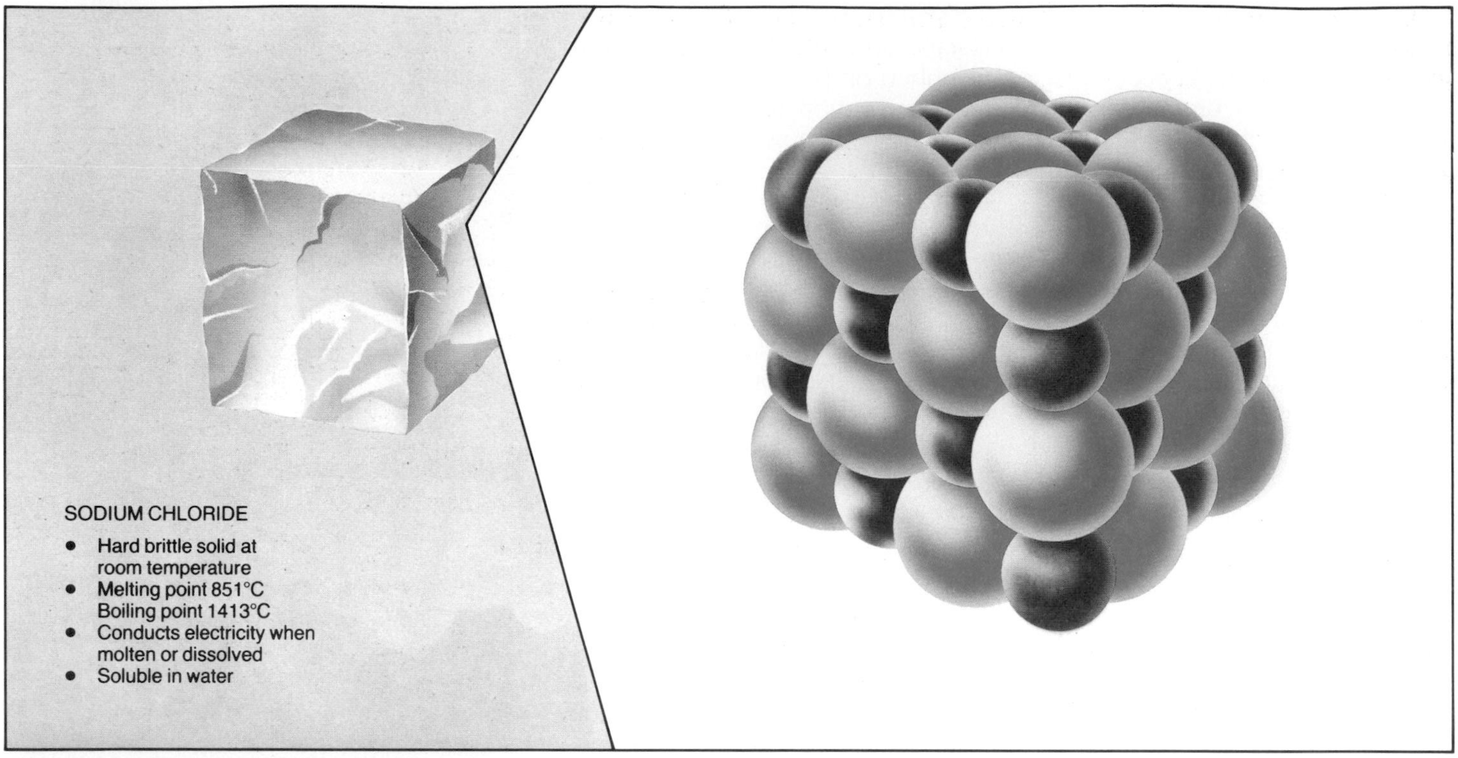

SODIUM CHLORIDE
• Hard brittle solid at room temperature
• Melting point 851°C Boiling point 1413°C
• Conducts electricity when molten or dissolved
• Soluble in water

Picture 12 The structure of sodium chloride

Picture 13 Sapphire. It has a giant structure, made of aluminium ions and oxide ions, coloured by impurities

Giant ionic structures

Giant ionic structures contain positive and negative ions. Every positive ion is next to a negative ion, and vice versa. The oppositely-charged ions attract one another strongly, and this holds the structure together.

Picture 12 shows the structure of sodium chloride, common salt. Notice that the regular arrangement of Na^+ and Cl^- ions builds up into a cubic shape. This is why crystals of sodium chloride are cubic.

Giant ionic substances are difficult to melt, because of the strong bonds holding the ions together. (There is more about ionic bonding in topic J5.) But they often dissolve in water. This is because water molecules have a slight electrical charge on them, and this charge attracts the charged ions.

Giant ionic substances do not conduct electricity when they are solid, because the ions are locked in the structure and cannot move. But when the ions are free to move, they can carry an electric current. So ionic substances conduct electricity when they are molten or dissolved in water. (More about the effect of electricity on ionic substances in topics J1 and J2.)

Table 1 Comparing different giant structures

		TYPICAL PROPERTIES			
	Description of structure	**Melting and boiling point**	**Hardness**	**Solubility in water**	**Electrical conductivity**
GIANT COVALENT	Atoms joined by covalent bonds	High	Hard but brittle	Insoluble	Do not conduct (except graphite)
GIANT METALLIC	Atoms joined by metallic bonds	Usually high	Usually hard, but malleable	Insoluble	Conduct
GIANT IONIC	+ and – ions attracting one another	High	Hard but brittle	Often soluble	Conduct when molten or dissolved

Many of the minerals found in the earth have giant ionic structures. Limestone ($CaCO_3$) is giant ionic. It is made up of Ca^{2+} and CO_3^{2-} ions. Picture 13 shows another example.

Comparing the different types of giant structure

Table 1 compares the three different types of giant structure. Substances with giant structures may be elements (like carbon) or compounds (like sodium chloride). Table 1 in the Data Section gives the structures of the different elements.

The structures of the different types of materials

The main groups of materials are described in topic A2. The particular properties of each group of materials is related to their structure.

Metals have a giant metallic structure (obviously).

Ceramics and glasses have structures which may be giant ionic, giant covalent, or a bit of both. That's why they are hard, but brittle.

Plastics and fibres have a kind of one-dimensional giant covalent structure, called a **polymer** structure. This kind of structure is covered in detail in topic H3.

Activity

Building a close-packed structure

You will need a supply of polystyrene spheres for this activity. The spheres represent atoms.

Use three books flat on the table to form a triangle. This will hold the bottom layer of your structure. Fill the triangular space between the books with 'atoms'. Adjust the books so that the 'atoms' make a regular, close-packed pattern like the 'atoms' in picture 10. You now have one close-packed layer.

Now build further layers on top of the first one. **The object is to fit as many 'atoms' as possible into the structure.**

What arrangement do you end up with? Is it close-packed? Compare it with the arrangements in pictures 7 and 8.

Questions

1 Fill in the blanks in the passage below. You can use the following words or groups of words: **water, covalent, flexible, layer, attract, dissolve, strong, positive, negative, brittle, close-packed.**

A giant covalent structure contains a continuous network of atoms joined together by ____(1)____ bonds. Substances with this kind of structure are hard but ____(2)____, and difficult to melt. Diamond and graphite both have this kind of structure, but they are different because graphite has a ____(3)____ structure.

A giant metallic structure contains atoms held together by metallic bonds. The atoms are usually ____(4)____, with the maximum possible number of atoms fitted into the available space. Metallic bonds are ____(5)____ but ____(6)____, so metals are usually hard, but not brittle.

A giant ionic structure contains ____(7)____ and ____(8)____ ions arranged regularly. The oppositely-charged ions ____(9)____ one another strongly, so giant ionic substances are usually hard, but brittle, and difficult to melt. Unlike other giant structures, they often ____(10)____ in ____(11)____.

2 Using your knowledge of giant structures, explain why

a Diamond is hard and brittle

b Iron is hard and malleable

c Sodium chloride does not conduct electricity when it is solid, but conducts when it is molten

d Crystals of sodium chloride always grow in a cubic shape.

3 Look at table 1 in the Data Section. This gives the melting points of different elements.

a Write down the symbols of all the elements whose melting points are below −200°C.

b Write down the symbols of all the elements whose melting points are above 2000°C.

Now look at the structures of the elements.

c What are the structures of each of the elements you wrote down in (a)?

d What are the structures of each of the elements you wrote down in (b)?

e Comment on your answers to (c) and (d).

4 Look at table 00 in the Data Section, giving the structures of different elements.

a What is the commonest type of structure among the elements?

b i) Write down the symbols of the elements that have *giant covalent* structures.

ii) Now look at the Periodic Table of the elements on page 126. What do you notice about the position of elements with giant covalent structures?

c Why do no elements have giant ionic structures?

5 Sodium chloride (salt) and calcium oxide (lime) both have giant ionic structures. Sodium chloride contains Na^{+} and Cl^{-} ions. Calcium oxide contains Ca^{2+} and O^{2-} ions. The melting points of these substances are: sodium chloride 801°C, calcium oxide 2614°C.

Suggest a reason why calcium oxide's melting point is so much higher than sodium chloride's, even though they both have the same type of structure.

D1 Making things from raw materials

Manufacturing means turning raw materials into valuable things. But there are costs.

Look around you. Can you see anything that has *not* been manufactured?

Tables, walls, clothes, paints, food . . . all have been manufactured in some way from raw materials. And most of the manufacturing processes use chemical reactions to convert raw materials into things that are more useful. We make bleach from salt, glass from limestone, fertilisers from air and computer chips from sand.

Where do we get raw materials from?

Picture 1 shows the major sources of the raw materials used by humans. We get raw materials from:

The Earth, which provides rocks, minerals and fossil fuels.
The air, which provides vital gases.
The sea, which provides water and minerals.
Living things, which provide food, clothing fibres and wood.

The cost of manufacture

Manufacturing involves turning raw materials into products that are more useful — and more valuable.

Take an example. The other day I bought a washing-up bowl which cost £2.50. The bowl is made from polythene. Polythene is manufactured from ethene, and ethene is manufactured from crude oil. The oil was the raw material needed to make the bowl. To make the bowl needed 5 kg of oil, which cost only £0.45. (Mind you, the 5 kg of crude oil produced several other products as well as the polythene for the bowl.)

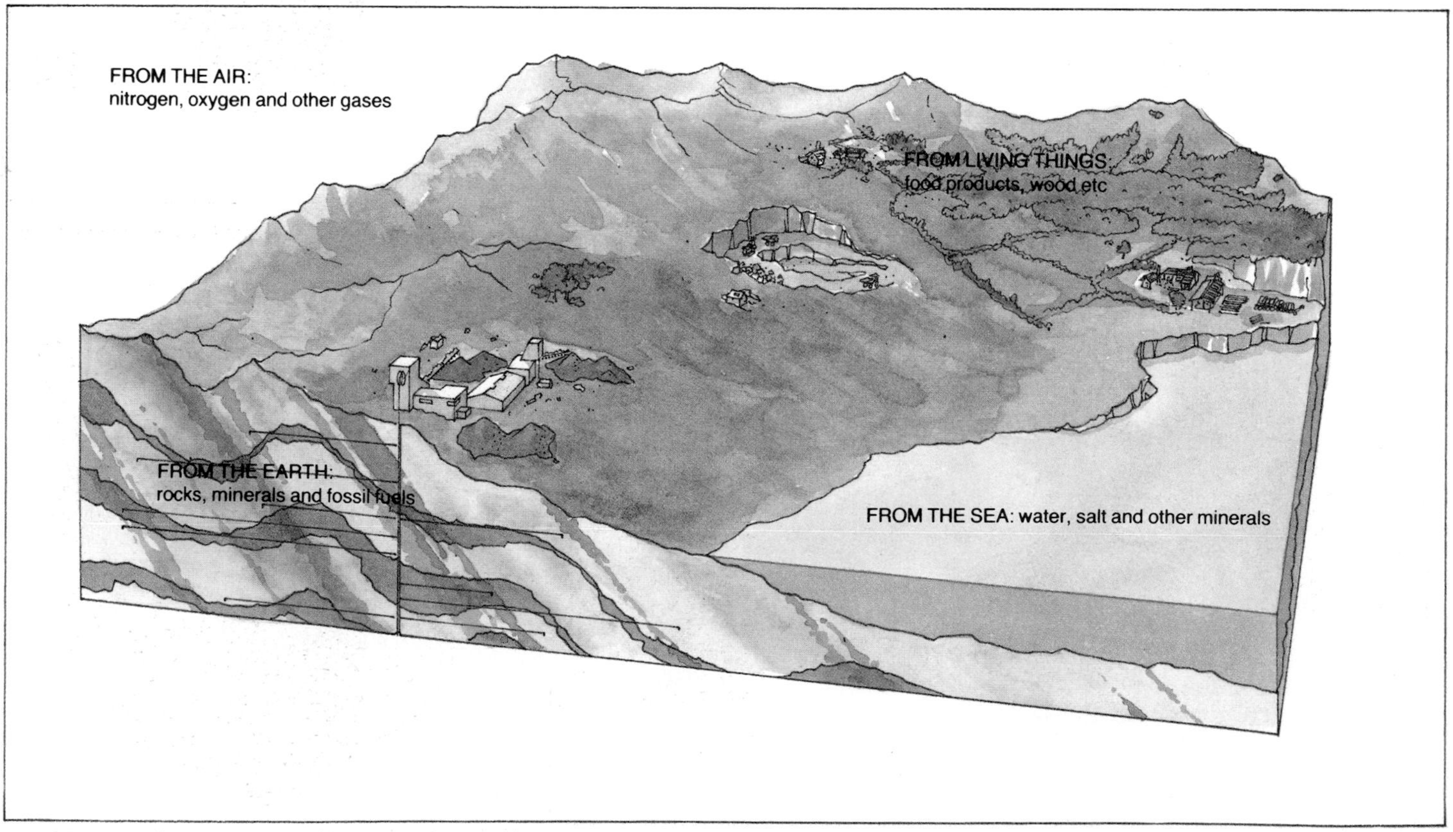

Picture 1 Where do our raw materials come from?

Turning the oil into a bowl has **added value** to the oil, as you can see from picture 2. The bowl is more valuable than the oil it came from — both in terms of its price and its usefulness. Which would you find more useful — a washing-up bowl or 5 kg of crude oil?

But you don't get the extra value without a cost. Picture 3 shows some of the costs that are involved in manufacturing things. All manufacturing processes need **energy** to drive them along. They need **people** to do the work. And they need **machines** and **buildings**. The cost of all these things make up the **economic cost** of the manufacturing process — the cost in money. But there is another cost to be counted.

The environmental cost

All manufacturing processes have some effect on the environment and on people's lives. This is a different kind of cost, but like the economic cost we need to keep it as low as possible. For every process, we have to consider:

People's health and safety, particularly the people who work in the factory or live nearby.
Pollution of the environment by the manufacturing process.
Damage to the landscape and to the habitats of wildlife.
Depletion of resources — using up fossil fuels and raw materials, especially those that are **non-renewable** and cannot be replaced.

These four factors make up the **environmental cost** of a product (picture 4). We will come back to them in other topics in this section.

When you buy a product, you always look to see its cost — its economic cost. Then you decide whether its value is worth the cost.

Try thinking of its environmental cost too. It's much less easy to find out, but it's just as important.

We'll come back to this idea in other topics in this section.

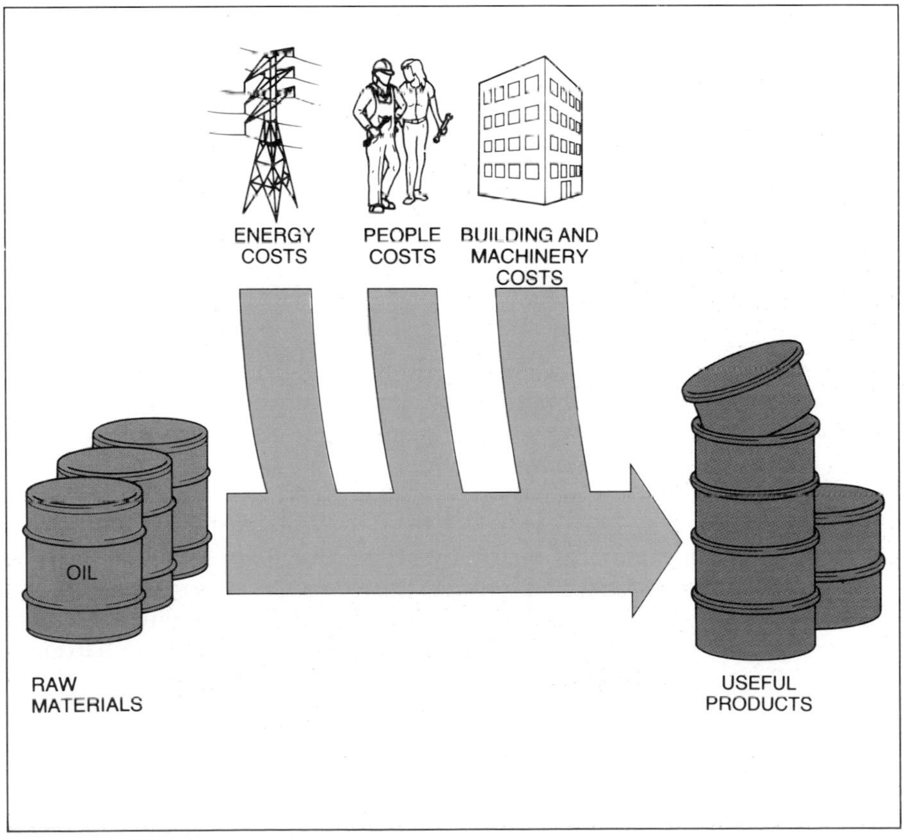

Picture 3 The main costs of manufacture

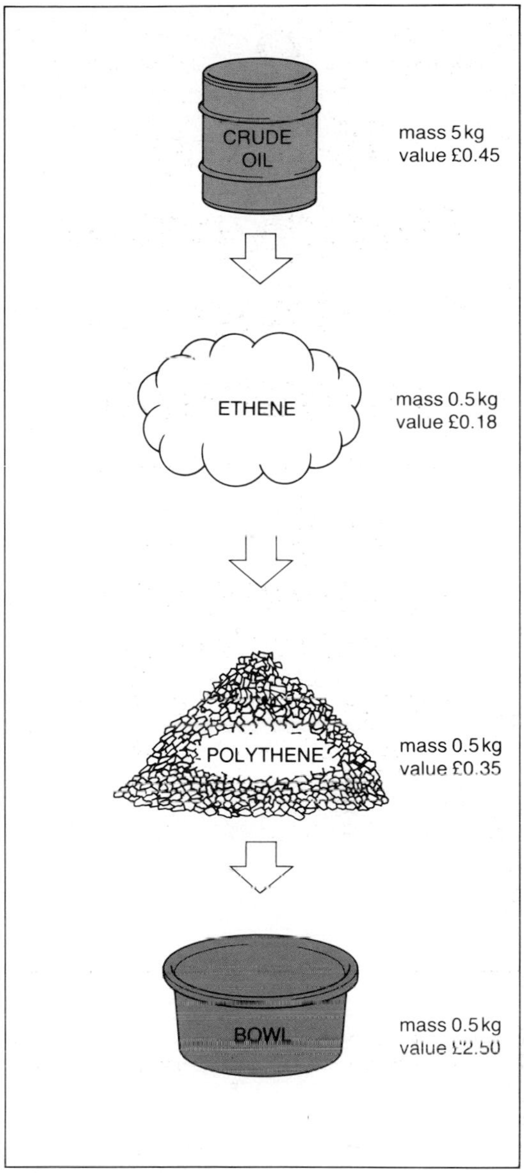

Picture 2 Adding value to crude oil by turning it into washing-up bowls

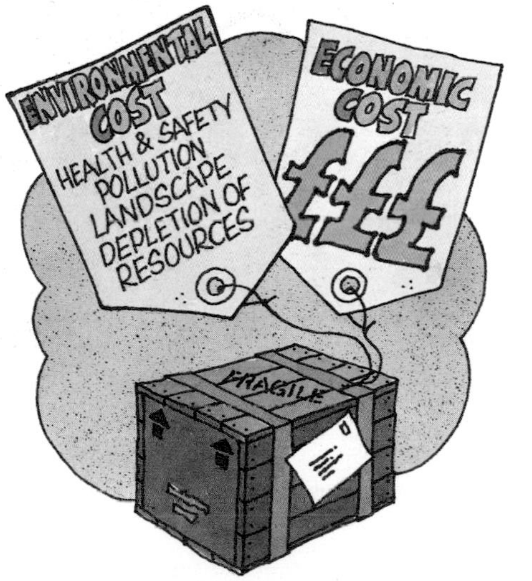

Picture 4 The economic and environmental costs of a product

D2 Useful minerals and rocks

Minerals and rocks provide raw materials for manufacture and building.

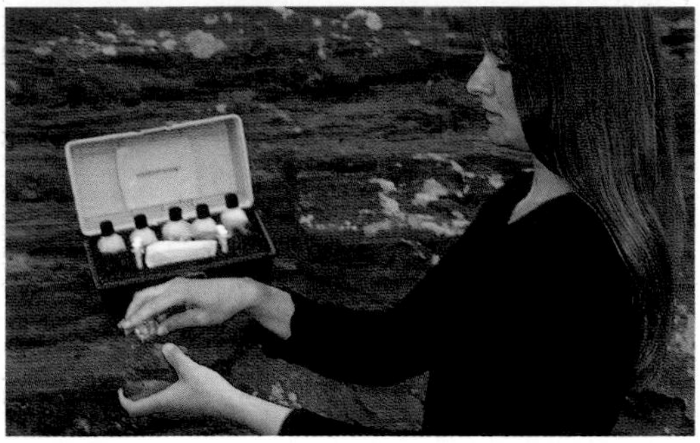

Picture 1 This geologist is testing a rock sample

Name of mineral	Hardness on Mohs' scale	
Diamond	10	VERY HARD
Corundum	9	
Topaz	8	
Quartz	7	
Feldspar	6	
penknife blade (5½)		
Apatite	5	
Fluorite	4	
Calcite	3	
fingernail (2½)		
Gypsum	2	
Talc	1	SOFT

Picture 7 Mohs' scale of hardness

The deepest mine in the world is a gold mine in South Africa. It's so hot at the bottom that a huge refrigeration machine is needed to make it bearable to work there. Yet this mine is only 4km deep. Compare this with the 6 400km from the surface to the centre of the earth.

We get all our minerals from the thin crust just below the surface of the Earth.

What are minerals?

A mineral is a single substance that occurs naturally. Being a single substance, you can write a formula for it and give it a name — just like you can with pure chemicals like copper sulphate. But minerals are often dirty and impure when you first dig them up.

In some places, minerals are found in a fairly pure form. You can dig up limestone which is almost pure calcium carbonate in many parts of Britain. These deposits of minerals became concentrated at some stage in the rock cycle. For example, rock salt became **concentrated** when seas dried up. Some minerals become concentrated by the processes of plate tectonics. For more about the rock cycle and plate tectonics, see *The Physical World*, topics G1 and G3.

Some very useful minerals

Some particularly useful minerals are shown in pictures 2 to 6 . The pictures show very pure samples of the minerals. They wouldn't look as clean as this when you dug them up!

How can minerals be identified?

Suppose you dug up a glittering yellow mineral. It *might* be gold, worth £10 000 per kilogram. Unfortunately, it's more likely to be iron pyrites, worth hardly anything. When you find a mineral, you need to be able to identify it. Like any other substance, a mineral can be identified from its properties. Here are some of the properties that can be particularly useful in identifying a mineral.

Colour and crystal shape
You can tell these by careful observation of the mineral.

Density
The density of a mineral specimen can be measured using one of the methods in *The Physical World*, topic A2. The density of a mineral is usually given as a *relative* density — how many times denser than water it is. This makes the densities easy to compare.

Hardness
The hardness of a mineral is tested by seeing how easy it is to scratch. A harder material will scratch a softer one. There is a special scale of hardness for minerals, called Mohs' scale (picture 7). A mineral with a high number will scratch one with a lower number. It's also useful to know the hardness of a few everyday things like a penknife blade, so that you can easily test any mineral you find.

Reaction with acid
All carbonates react with acid to give carbon dioxide (topic D3). So if a mineral fizzes when you add acid, it's one of the forms of calcium carbonate — probably calcite.

Name of mineral **ROCKSALT**
Chemical name and formula Sodium chloride, NaCl
Occurrence Very plentiful throughout the world
World production per year 150 million tonnes
Uses See topic D5 on salt
Relative density 2.2
Hardness 2.5
Effect of acid Does not fizz

Picture 2 Rocksalt

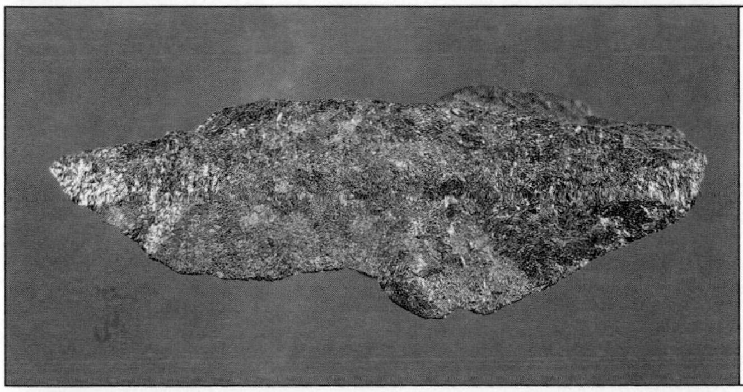

Name of mineral **COPPER PYRITES**
Chemical name and formula Copper iron sulphide, $CuFeS_2$
Occurrence Limited supply and running out
World production per year 20 million tonnes
Uses Making copper
Relative density 4.2
Hardness 3.5
Effect of acid Does not fizz

Picture 3 Copper pyrites

Name of mineral **HAEMATITE**
Chemical name and formula Iron oxide, Fe_2O_3
Occurrence Plentiful
World production per year 900 million tonnes
Uses Making iron (topic E3)
Relative density 5.2
Hardness 6
Effect of acid Does not fizz

Picture 4 Haematite

Name of mineral **CALCITE**
Chemical name and formula Calcium carbonate, $CaCO_3$
Occurrence Calcite is the mineral in limestone, which is very plentiful throughout the world
World production per year Over 1500 million tonnes of limestone
Uses See topic D3 on limestone *Relative density* 2.7
Hardness 3 *Effect of acid* Fizzes

Picture 5 Calcite

Name of mineral **BAUXITE**
Chemical name and formula Bauxite is actually a mixture of several minerals, but you can think of it as aluminium oxide, Al_2O_3
Occurrence Plentiful in several parts of the world
World production per year 80 million tonnes
Uses Making aluminium *Relative density* Varies
Hardness Varies *Effect of acid* Does not fizz

Picture 6 Bauxite

Useful rocks

What's the difference between a rock and a mineral?

Most people think of rocks as great hard lumps. In science the word has a more general meaning than this. **Rocks are made from crystals or grains of minerals.** A rock does not have to be in a hard lump: sand is considered to be rock. A pure mineral is a single substance, but most rocks contain one or more different minerals, so they are mixtures.

In *The Physical World*, topic G3 we look closely at the different types of rock. Here we will look at some rocks that are particularly useful for making things. Some of these rocks are used as raw materials for chemical reactions. More often, rocks are used unchanged to build things with. Different rocks have properties that make them useful for different construction purposes. Pictures 8 to 12 show some of the most important.

Activities

A Testing minerals

You will need a selection of mineral samples.

1 You are going to observe some of the properties of the mineral samples. Decide how you will record your results.

2 Collect a sample of a mineral. Look at it carefully using a hand lens and decide its colour and, if possible, its crystal shape.

3 Test the hardness of the mineral. See if you can scratch the sample with (i) your finger nail, (ii) a copper coin and (iii) a knife blade. To see whether the mineral really has been scratched, wet your finger and rub the scratch mark. Now look at it under a hand lens. Is it a real scratch, cutting into the mineral, or just a mark?

Use these tests to decide roughly where the mineral comes on Mohs' scale of hardness.

4 Test the reaction with acid. (**CARE** Eye protection must be worn.) Put the mineral sample on a tile. Add one or two drops of dilute hydrochloric acid and observe what happens.

B Making a key to identify minerals

We can use keys to identify unknown mineral samples. If you know the properties of a selection of minerals, you can make your own key to identify them. (Look at *The Living World*, topic B1 if you are not sure about keys.)

It's best if you use the results from your own tests in activity A to make the key. But you could use tables of properties like the ones on page 91 instead.

Try to make your key as simple as possible. The shortest keys are the best! Remember that each stage of the key needs to ask a question about the mineral, such as, 'Can it be scratched by a knife?'

When you have made your key, try it out on someone else. Give them an unknown mineral, and see if they can identify it using your key.

C What minerals are extracted in your area?

Find an example of a mineral or rock that is extracted in your area. Include quarries as well as mines. Try to find out:

1 How long the mining or quarrying has been going on.

2 How long supplies are expected to last.

3 The effects on the environment of the operations.

4 What plans there are for restoring the site when mining or quarrying ends.

Questions

1a What is the difference between a mineral and a rock?

b In (i) and (ii) below, say whether you think the sample is a mineral or a rock, and explain your answer.

i) A sample made up of a mixture of light and dark coloured crystals.

ii) A sample made up of pure lead sulphide, PbS.

c Name a rock that contains a single mineral only.

2a What would you expect to happen in each case when A is used to scratch B?

i) A is diamond and B is a penknife blade.

ii) A is a fingernail and B is calcite.

iii) A is calcite and B is a fingernail.

b Your penknife blade is blunt. Suggest a mineral you could use to sharpen it.

c Glass is scratched by feldspar, but not by apatite. Where does glass come in Mohs' scale of hardness?

3 Use the information about rocks given on page 93 to decide which rock would be best for each of the following uses. Explain your choice.

a Building stone for a new office block in an industrial town.

b A kitchen work-surface.

c The base of a fume-cupboard in a school laboratory.

d A plaque to commemorate your valuable service to the school.

e Stone chippings for surfacing a road.

4 Put each of the materials below into one of three groups.

Group A Made directly from a mineral or rock with virtually no processing.

Group B Made by processing a mineral or rock in some way.

Group C Not made from a mineral or rock at all.

a Aluminium,
b Sand,
c Cotton,
d Roadstone,
e Paper,
f Glass,
g Cement,
h Bricks,
i Polythene.

Name of rock **SANDSTONE**
Type Sedimentary
Minerals it contains Mainly quartz, SiO_2
Useful properties Plentiful; abrasive; can be moderately hard, but often crumbles to sand
Uses Building stone. Sand has many uses, including as an abrasive and for making glass

Picture 8 Remains of sandstone columns

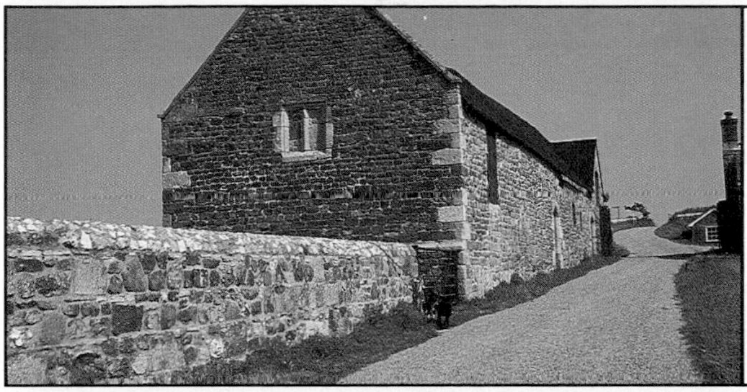

Name of rock **LIMESTONE**
Type Sedimentary
Minerals it contains Calcite
Useful properties Plentiful; often quite hard (but reacts with acid); attractive colour; good source of calcium carbonate
Uses See topic D3 on limestone

Picture 9 Limestone was used to build this house

Name of rock **MARBLE**
Type Metamorphic
Minerals it contains Calcite
Useful properties Hard (but it reacts with acid); very attractive
Uses As a decorative stone for buildings, sculptures, etc.

Picture 10 This statue is made from marble

Name of rock **GRANITE**
Type Igneous
Minerals it contains Several, but mainly feldspar and quartz
Useful properties Plentiful; very hard; attractive, especially when polished
Uses Building and ornamental stone

Picture 11 Gravestone made from polished granite

Name of rock **SLATE**
Type Metamorphic
Minerals it contains Variable
Useful properties Can be split into flat sheets
Uses As a roofing material

Picture 12 A slate roof

D3
Limestone

Limestone is one of the most valuable raw materials of all.

Picture 1 Limestone country in the Pennines

Limestone gives us some of the most beautiful country in Britain. The Derbyshire Peaks, The Mendip Hills, The Sussex Downs, The Yorkshire Dales — all are made of limestone, or chalk, which is a form of limestone.

As well as giving beautiful countryside, limestone is a very useful raw material. And that means there are some difficult decisions to make when it comes to quarrying limestone.

The properties of limestone

Limestone is calcium carbonate, $CaCO_3$. The calcium carbonate you find in the laboratory is a white powder, but limestone comes out of the ground in hard lumps. Some forms of limestone are hard enough to be used for building stone and aggregate.

Aggregate is crushed stone used in construction. Limestone aggregate is popular for making roads (picture 2). Some people feel it is a waste of limestone to use it for aggregate, because other rocks would do just as well.

Picture 2 Limestone aggregate is used as the base for many roads, before the tarmac surface is laid on top

Chemical reactions of calcium carbonate

We might be able to use other rocks as aggregate, but there is no substitute for limestone as a source of calcium carbonate. Calcium carbonate is one of the most important raw materials for the chemical industry. Understanding its chemical reactions helps you to understand its uses — and also why limestone scenery is so spectacular. You can investigate the chemical reactions of calcium carbonate in the activity.

Calcium carbonate reacts with acids

All carbonates react with acid to give carbon dioxide, water and a salt. The carbonate 'fizzes' and dissolves when the acid is added. For example, with hydrochloric acid:

$$\text{calcium carbonate} + \text{hydrochloric acid} \rightarrow \text{calcium chloride} + \text{carbon dioxide} + \text{water}$$

$$CaCO_3(s) + 2\,HCl(aq) \rightarrow CaCl_2(aq) + CO_2(g) + H_2O(l)$$

In this reaction, the calcium carbonate neutralises the acid. Because of this property, the soil in limestone country is neutral or slightly alkaline. This is why such a variety of wild plants grow in limestone country.

Even weak acids will react with calcium carbonate. Ordinary rain water is very slightly acid, due to the carbon dioxide dissolved in it. The acidic rain slowly dissolves limestone:

calcium carbonate	+	carbon dioxide	+	water	→	calcium hydrogencarbonate
$CaCO_3(s)$	+	$CO_2(g)$	+	$H_2O(l)$	→	$Ca(HCO_3)_2(aq)$
		in rain water				

This has two results. One is that limestone gets slowly dissolved away, giving spectacular cliffs, valleys and underground caves (picture 3). This is one reason why limestone scenery is so spectacular.

The other result is that water supplies collected in limestone country contain dissolved calcium hydrogencarbonate, which makes the water 'hard'.

The reaction of calcium carbonate with carbon dioxide and water is reversible — it can go backwards as well as forwards. This means that the dissolved calcium hydrogencarbonate can turn back into solid calcium carbonate:

$$Ca(HCO_3)_2(aq) \rightarrow CaCO_3(s) + CO_2(g) + H_2O(l)$$

This may happen very slowly in limestone caves, forming deposits of calcium carbonate called stalactites and stalagmites. Or it may happen quickly in your kettle, forming a deposit of calcium carbonate called 'fur'.

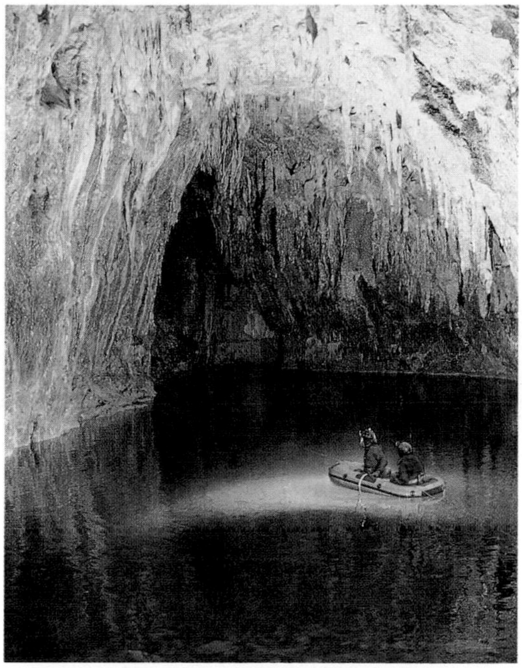

Picture 3 Limestone caves in France

Using limestone as a base

Substances that neutralise acids are called **bases** (topic G2). Calcium carbonate is used as a base a great deal.

- *In agriculture*. Farmers sometimes use powdered limestone to neutralise acid soil.
- *To prevent acid air pollution*. Burning fossil fuels produces acidic gases, especially sulphur dioxide. Limestone can be used to neutralise these gases before they can get into the air and cause acid rain. Power stations are now being fitted with equipment to pass the gases through limestone before they leave the chimney. The reaction forms calcium sulphate, which is used to make plaster for the building industry. A big power station needs 300 000 tonnes of limestone a year to neutralise all its gases.
- *To neutralise acidified lakes*. (see picture 4).

Picture 4 Adding powdered limestone to an acidified lake

Calcium carbonate decomposes when it is heated

Like other carbonates, calcium carbonate decomposes when it is heated strongly. Calcium oxide and carbon dioxide are formed:

calcium carbonate	→	calcium oxide	+	carbon dioxide
$CaCO_3(s)$	→	$CaO(s)$	+	$CO_2(g)$

This is an example of **thermal decomposition** — breaking down by heating.

Calcium oxide is also called 'lime'. It reacts vigorously with water to form calcium hydroxide, 'slaked lime'.

calcium oxide	+	water	→	calcium hydroxide
$CaO(s)$	+	$H_2O(l)$	→	$Ca(OH)_2(s)$

Both calcium oxide and calcium hydroxide are very useful chemicals. Calcium hydroxide is used as a cheap industrial alkali. Water companies use a lot of it to neutralise acid in water supplies. Farmers and gardeners use it to neutralise soil acidity.

Picture 5 The inside of a lime kiln

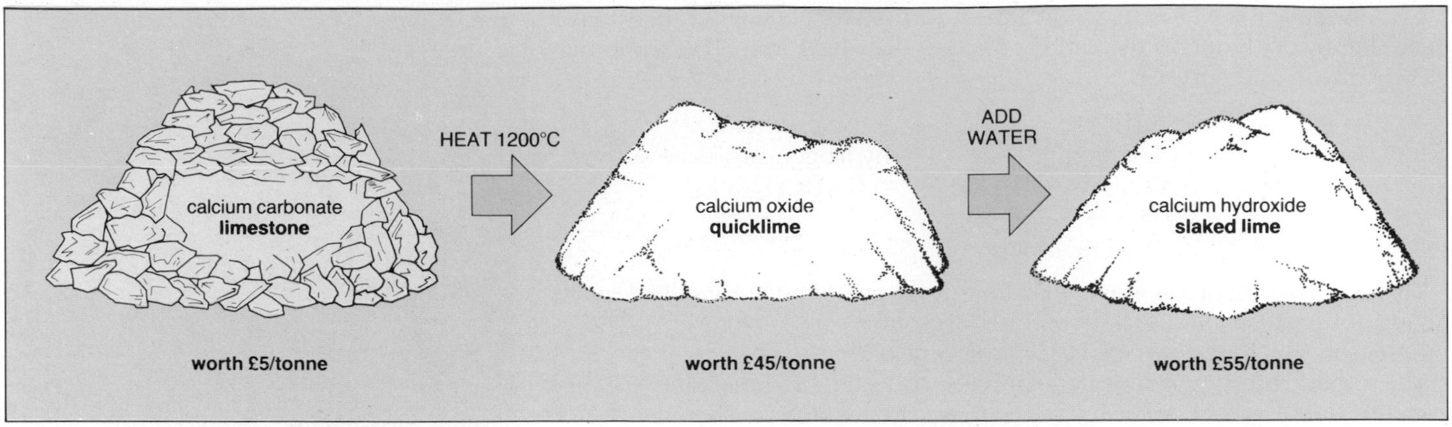

Picture 6 Converting calcium carbonate to calcium oxide and calcium hydroxide adds value. Why does the value increase so much more in the first stage than in the second?

A solution of calcium hydroxide in water is called **lime water**. When carbon dioxide is bubbled into this solution, calcium carbonate is formed as a milky precipitate. This is a common way of testing for carbon dioxide.

$$\text{calcium hydroxide} + \text{carbon dioxide} \rightarrow \text{calcium carbonate} + \text{water}$$
$$Ca(OH)_2(aq) + CO_2(g) \rightarrow CaCO_3(s) + H_2O(l)$$

Adding value to limestone by heating it

You can carry out the thermal decomposition of calcium carbonate in the laboratory (see the activity). Industrially it is done in big **lime kilns** like the one shown in picture 5. The temperature inside is about 1200°C, and the kilns use enormous quantities of energy.

Picture 6 shows how value is added to limestone by turning it to calcium oxide. What do you think are the main economic costs in this process? (See question 3). In *Making money from limestone* on page 98, you can try your hand at making money by making calcium oxide.

Picture 7 summarises the reactions of limestone that have been mentioned here.

The environmental cost of limestone

We couldn't do without limestone. Apart from the uses already mentioned, limestone is used to make cement, steel, glass and sodium carbonate

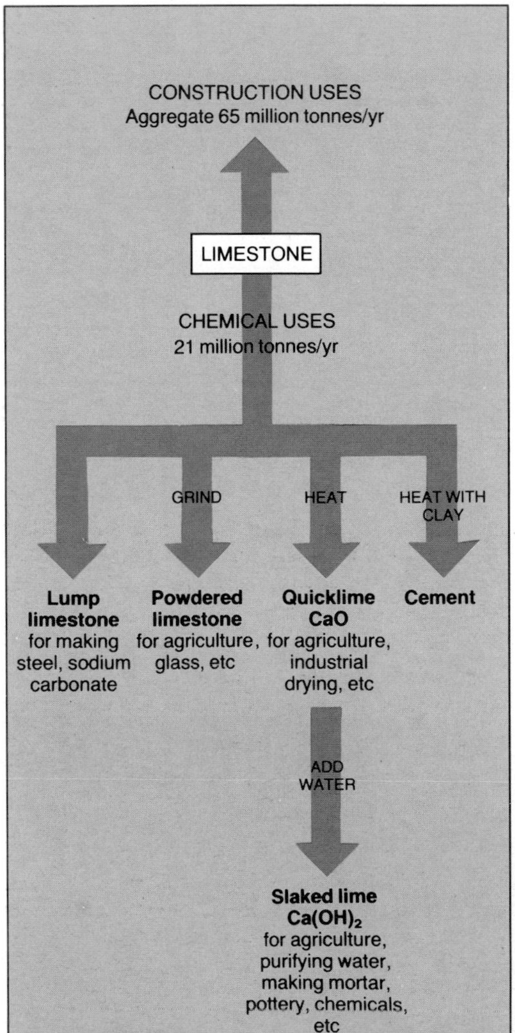

Picture 8 The uses of limestone

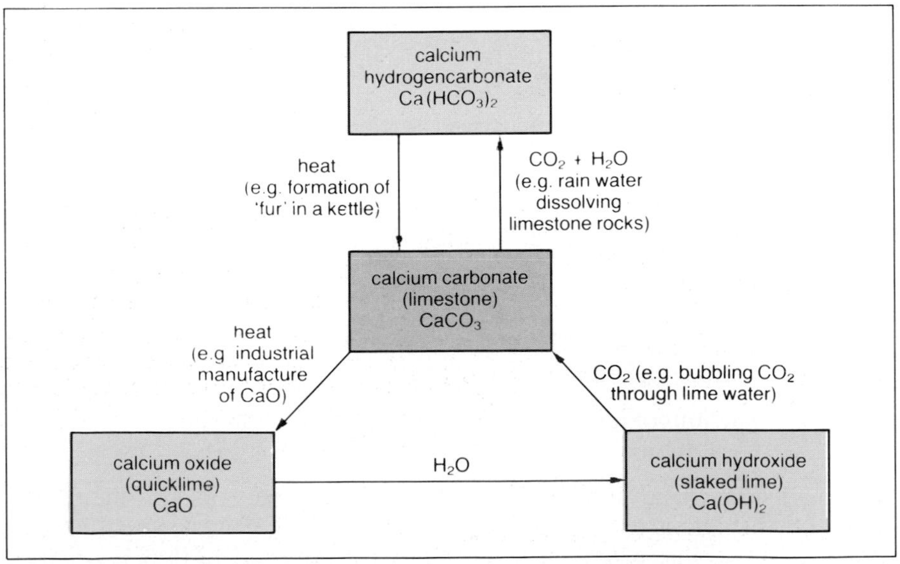

Picture 7 The important reactions of limestone

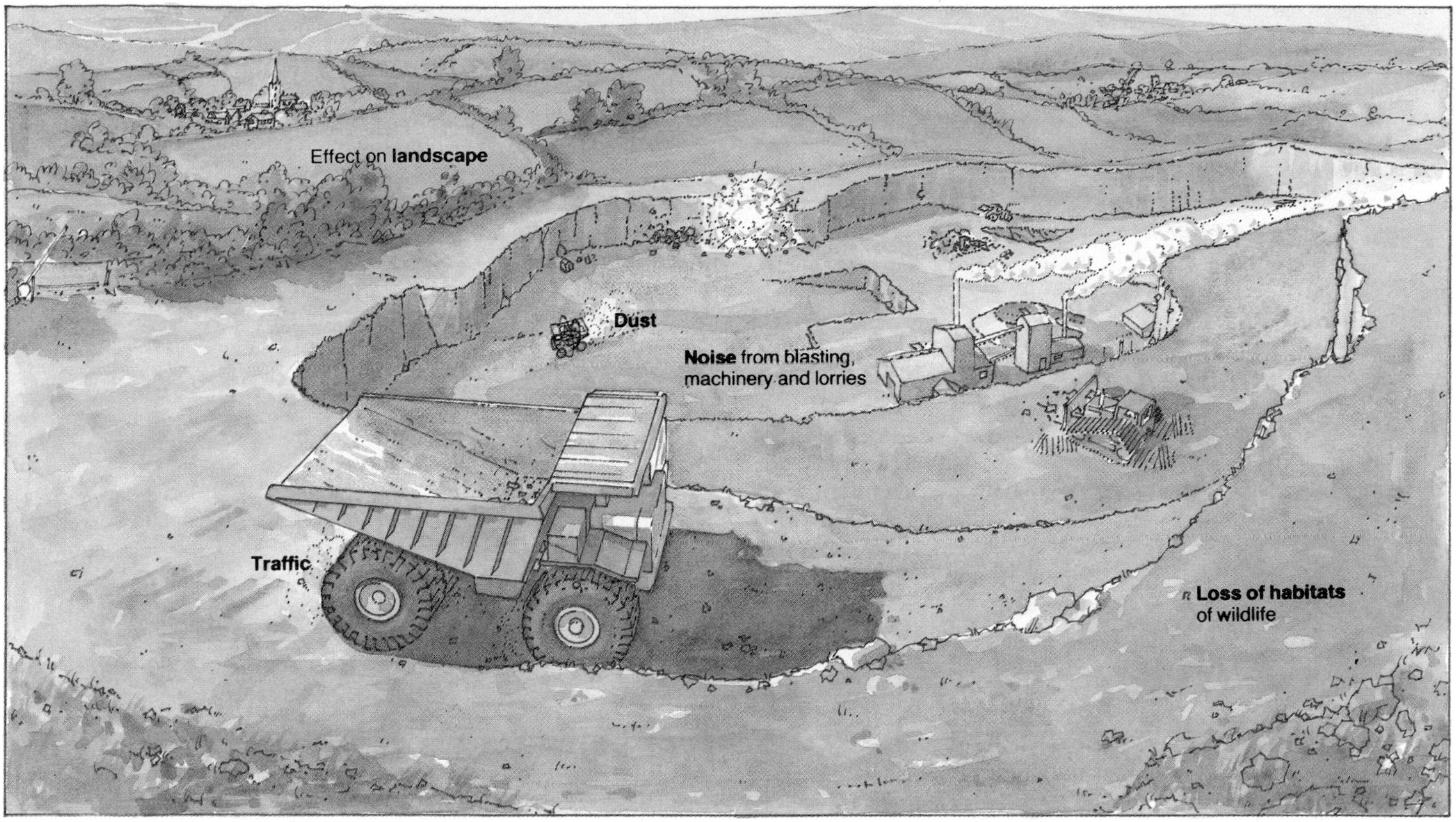

Picture 9 Some of the environmental effects of quarrying

(picture 8). All these things are vital to society. They cannot be made without a supply of pure limestone.

Limestone is very cheap to quarry out of the ground — there's lots of it, and it's near the surface. But there are environmental costs in extracting limestone. Picture 9 summarises the major ones. You can list them under the headings we have used before: people's health and safety; pollution of the environment; damage to the landscape; depletion of resources.

Limestone is one of the most useful of all raw materials. We have to balance its value to us against the cost to the environment of quarrying it. More about this in *What could we use instead of limestone?* on page 99.

Activity

Looking at some reactions of calcium carbonate

You will need: marble chips; test-tubes; tongs; heat proof mat; dropping pipette; dilute hydrochloric acid; lime water. Eye protection MUST be worn.

1 Reaction with acid

Put a small marble chip in a test tube. Add dilute hydrochloric acid to a depth of about 1 cm. Test to confirm that carbon dioxide is given off.

2 The thermal decomposition of calcium carbonate

Calcium carbonate decomposes at about 900°C, which is about as hot as you can get in a bunsen flame. Use tongs to hold a marble chip in the hottest part of the flame. Heat for at least 5 minutes. (Notice the bright white light from the glowing chip. Before electric lights were invented, the light from glowing lime was used to light theatres. Hence the expression 'in the limelight'.)

Let the chip cool completely — it will take several minutes. The calcium oxide is a crumbly powder on the surface, and it will fall off if you don't handle it carefully.

When cool, put the chip on a glass dish. Use a dropping pipette to let *one tiny drop* of water fall on the powdery calcium oxide on the surface of the chip. What do you notice?

3 Answer these questions about the experiments you have just done. What substances are formed

a when the marble chip is heated strongly?

b when water is added to the product?

Write equations for the reactions.

4 Use a good dictionary to look up the meanings of the old-fashioned words 'quick' (it doesn't mean 'fast') and 'slaked'. Decide why calcium oxide is called 'quicklime', and calcium hydroxide is called 'slaked lime'.

If you have time, try dissolving the calcium hydroxide you have made in water. The solution is lime water. Use it to test for carbon dioxide (you'll need to filter your solution first). Does it work?

Questions

1a What are the chemical names for (i) limestone, (ii) chalk, (iii) quicklime and (iv) slaked lime?

b Write equations for the reactions that occur when: (i) calcium carbonate is heated strongly; (ii) hydrochloric acid is added to calcium carbonate; (iii) water is added to calcium oxide; (iv) carbon dioxide is bubbled through lime water.

2 Dolomite is a rock. It is similar to limestone, but contains a mixture of magnesium carbonate and calcium carbonate instead of calcium carbonate alone. Magnesium is in the same family as calcium in the Periodic Table, and has similar properties to calcium.

What products would you expect to be formed when dolomite is: (a) heated strongly; (b) reacted with hydrochloric acid?

3 Look at picture 6, showing how value is added to limestone by converting it to calcium oxide and calcium hydroxide.

a Write down three types of cost that are involved in the first stage, turning calcium carbonate to calcium oxide. (Look back at picture 3, topic D1 if you are not sure).

b Which of these costs do you think adds most to the total cost of turning calcium carbonate to calcium oxide?

c What is the cost of turning: (i) calcium carbonate to calcium oxide; (ii) calcium oxide to calcium hydroxide?

d Why is the answer in (i) so much greater than the answer in (ii)?

4 Picture 9 on page 97 summarises the major environmental costs of quarrying limestone.

a Suggest any other environmental costs, not shown on the picture, that you think are important.

b List each of the costs under one of the four headings: People's health and safety; pollution of the environment; damage to the landscape; depletion of resources.

c For each of the environmental costs, say whether you think it is **A** a very significant cost, **B** a moderately significant cost or **C** a relatively insignificant cost.

5a 50 g of calcium carbonate is heated strongly until it is completely decomposed.

i) Write an equation for the reaction that occurs.

ii) Calculate the mass of calcium oxide that is formed.

b Suppose the calcium oxide formed in (a) is reacted with water.

i) Write an equation for the reaction that occurs.

ii) Calculate the mass of calcium hydroxide that is formed.

(Ca=40; C=12; O=16; H=1)

Making money from limestone

In this activity you will put yourself in the place of an industrial manufacturer. You manufacture calcium oxide from calcium carbonate, and you have to do it as cheaply and efficiently as possible.

Your source of calcium carbonate will be a marble chip. When it is heated strongly, the hard marble chip will glow white hot and turn to powdery calcium oxide.

Here are the rules:

1 You must have a company name. Decide this before you start.

2 You can only use the following equipment: bunsen burner; heating mat; tongs; spatula; stand and clamp; eye protection; glass dish. You can have access to a weighing balance.

3 **Safety rules:** Eye protection must be worn. Do not handle calcium oxide or let it come into contact with your skin. The glass dish should not be heated.

4 Your only source of calcium carbonate is a marble chip. You must weigh it, then scale up from grams into tonnes. (For example if it weighs 2.3 g, call its mass 2.3 tonnes.) You must pay for the chip (see the table for prices).

5 You have to pay for the energy you use. The charge for gas is given below.

6 You have to pay for the depreciation (wear and tear) on the equipment you use. This goes towards eventually replacing it (see table for charge).

7 You have to pay your own wages. The nationally agreed wage rates are given in the table.

8 When you have made your calcium oxide, you must separate it from unreacted calcium carbonate and put it on the glass dish. The glass dish must be weighed beforehand.

You must take the calcium oxide to your teacher, who will weigh it, then test it to see it is genuine. You will be told how much it is worth.

9 You must fill in a balance sheet like the one below.

Outgoings		
Mass of marble chip	tonnes	
Cost of marble chip		£
Time for which gas was used	min	
Cost of gas		£
Total time spent by all workers	hours	
Total wages		£
Time for which equipment was used	min	
Depreciation cost of equipment		£
Total cost		£
Income		
Mass of calcium oxide produced	tonnes	
Value of calcium oxide produced		£
Net profit		£

Table of prices and costs (remember you have scaled up from grams to tonnes):

Marble chips (calcium carbonate)	£5 per tonne
Calcium oxide	£50 per tonne
Gas	£2.00 per minute
Depreciation of equipment	£1.00 per minute
Wages	£5.00 per person per hour

What could we use instead of limestone?

Limestone is a popular raw material because it's cheap and versatile. Unfortunately, quarrying limestone damages some of the most attractive country in Britain. Could we use other rocks instead?

Dr William Stanton, a geologist who is an expert on limestone scenery, has compared the usefulness of limestone with other rocks. He asked geologists, civil engineers and others to award points to limestone and to other types of rocks as a measure of their value.

Table 1 compares the industrial value of limestone with other rocks. Note that the table is concerned with 'hard' limestone. This is the kind in the Mendip Hills, the Peak District and the Yorkshire Dales. This kind of limestone is particularly good for industrial use.

The numbers in the table give the 'score' for each rock, on a 1 to 5 scale.

Table 2 looks at the value of limestone and other rocks *in situ* — left in place instead of being quarried.

1 How scientific is this method for comparing the value of different rocks? Can you think of a more scientific way of doing it?

2 Use table 1 to summarise why there is a big industrial demand for hard limestone.

Picture 1 Limestone scenery in the Pennines

Table 1 The industrial value of limestone and other rocks. The numbers give the score for each rock.

	Hard limestone	Granite	Hard sandstone
Cost of extraction	Low 5	High 2	Very high 1
How much wastage at the quarry?	Low 4	Medium 3	Very high 1
How good for aggregate?	Very good 5	Very good 5	Very good 5
Is it used as building stone?	Yes 2	Yes 3	Yes 2
Is it used as a chemical raw material?	Yes 5	No 0	No 0

Table 2 The value of limestone and other rocks if left in place

	Hard limestone	Granite	Hard sandstone
Quality of landscape	Very varied 5	Good 4	Good 4
Variety of wildlife	Very varied 5	Limited 2	Limited 2
What is the soil like for agriculture?	Good (where 4 present)	Poor 2	Poor 2
Value for recreation: walking, climbing, open spaces	Very good 5	Very good 5	Very good 5
Underground drinking water supplies	Plenty, very pure 4	None 0	Some 2

3 Use table 2 to summarise the arguments for preserving limestone countryside.

4 How far is it possible to satisfy the industrial demand for limestone *and* preserve limestone countryside?

5 Imagine the Minister for the Environment has asked you to report on how limestone countryside can be preserved. You have been told to take account of the country's industrial need for limestone. What recommendations will you make?

Picture 3 Sandstone cliffs in Devon

Picture 2 Granite scenery in Dartmoor

D4 Ammonia and fertilisers

Nitrogenous fertilisers help plants to grow. This topic is about how fertilisers are manufactured.

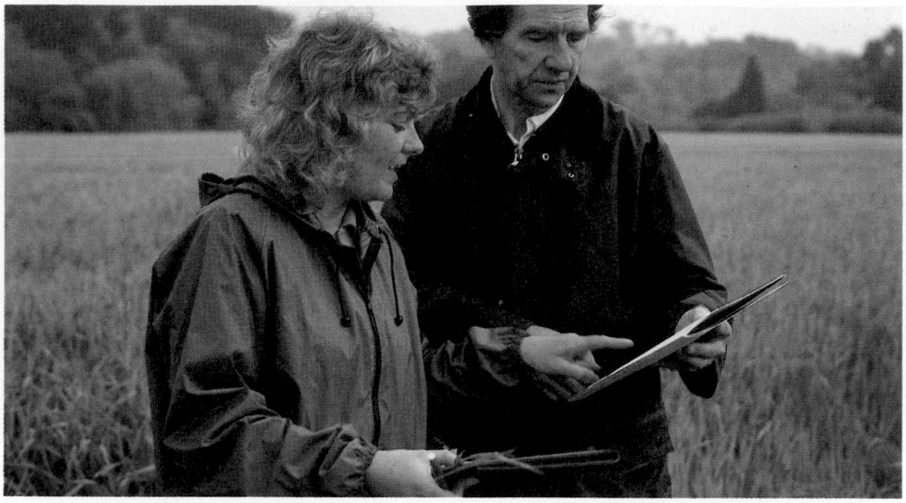

Picture 1 Farmers need to think carefully and take advice on the amount of nitrogenous fertiliser to put on a crop

Here's something rather odd. 80% of the air is nitrogen and yet plants can't use it. On the other hand, carbon dioxide is only 0.03% of the air, and plants *can* use that.

The problem is that the nitrogen in the air is very unreactive. Plants need nitrogen in the form of soluble compounds they can take up through their roots. **Nitrogenous fertilisers** provide nitrogen in this form, and this topic is about the way chemistry can provide them. There's more about plant nutrition and the elements that plants need in topic B13 in *The Living World*.

There are two types of nitrogen compounds that plants can take up through their roots: ammonium compounds and nitrates. Ammonium compounds contain the **ammonium ion, NH_4^+**, and nitrates contain the **nitrate ion, NO_3^-**. *Fertilisers: a story of supply and demand* on page 105 explains how the source of fertilisers has changed since early times.

The modern fertiliser industry is based on one chemical more than any other: ammonia.

What is ammonia?

Ammonia is a smelly gas. You can smell it in some household cleaners and in old nappies and public lavatories. Picture 2 summarises the most important properties of ammonia.

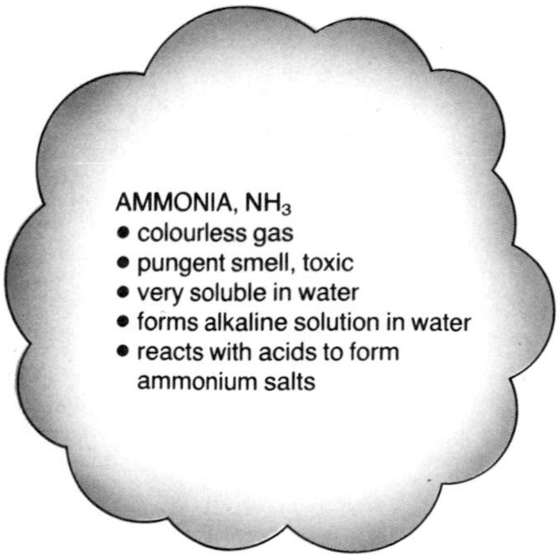
AMMONIA, NH_3
• colourless gas
• pungent smell, toxic
• very soluble in water
• forms alkaline solution in water
• reacts with acids to form ammonium salts

Picture 2 The properties of ammonia

Ammonia or ammonium?

Ammonia is a base — it neutralises acids. When ammonia neutralises an acid, it forms an **ammonium salt**. Ammonium salts contain the **ammonium ion, NH_4^+** (picture 3). For example, when ammonia solution reacts with nitric acid, ammonium nitrate is formed:

$$\text{ammonia} + \text{nitric acid} \rightarrow \text{ammonium nitrate}$$
$$NH_3(aq) + HNO_3(aq) \rightarrow NH_4NO_3(aq)$$

Ammonium nitrate is the most important of all the nitrogenous fertilisers. It's known as 'NITRAM'. Notice the state symbols in the above equation: all the substances are in aqueous solution. Ammonia is very soluble in water, and in laboratory experiments we normally use ammonia solution rather than ammonia gas.

Ammonia reacts with other acids to give other ammonium salts. With sulphuric acid it gives ammonium sulphate, $(NH_4)_2SO_4$. With hydrochloric acid it gives ammonium chloride, NH_4Cl.

Manufacturing ammonia — the Haber Process

All nitrogenous fertilisers are based on ammonia, so it's vital to have a cheap way of making ammonia in bulk. The obvious way to do it is to combine nitrogen and hydrogen together:

$$\text{nitrogen} + \text{hydrogen} \rightarrow \text{ammonia}$$
$$N_2(g) + 3\,H_2(g) \rightarrow 2\,NH_3(g)$$

Unfortunately nitrogen is so unreactive that it doesn't combine with hydrogen under ordinary conditions.

Haber's discovery

In 1908 Fritz Haber, a German scientist, discovered a way to make nitrogen and hydrogen combine. He did the trick by using conditions that often work in chemical reactions: high pressure, high temperature and a catalyst. Even then only 8% of the hydrogen and nitrogen was converted to ammonia: the rest was left unchanged. Nitrogen and hydrogen really are reluctant partners.

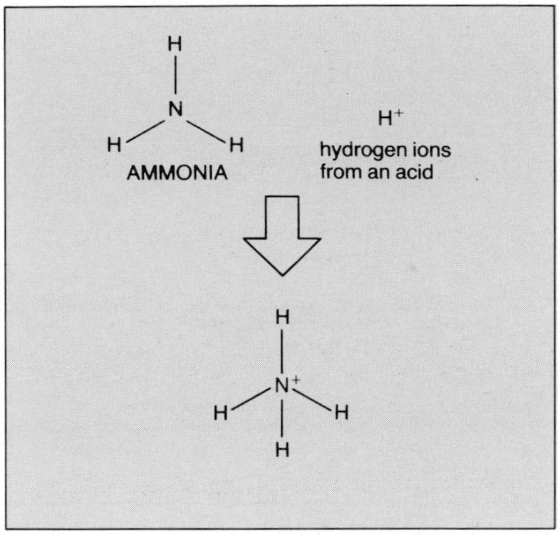

Picture 3 Ammonia and ammonium

Getting the best you can

Look at picture 4. It shows the percentage of ammonia you get by reacting nitrogen with hydrogen under different conditions. Judging from this graph alone, the best conditions would be a temperature of 350°C and a pressure of 400 atmospheres. That would give you a 70% yield of ammonia — much better than Haber got. Indeed, you might do even better if you followed the trend of the graphs and used a higher pressure and a lower temperature.

But it isn't as simple as that. There are two other important things to be considered.

- High pressures are expensive. This is because high pressures need special pumps. The higher the pressure, the more expensive the pump — and the more likely it is to break down.
- All chemical reactions go faster at higher temperatures and slower at lower temperatures. If you have the temperature too low, the **reaction rate** is too slow. You might get a good yield of ammonia, but you have to wait too long for it.

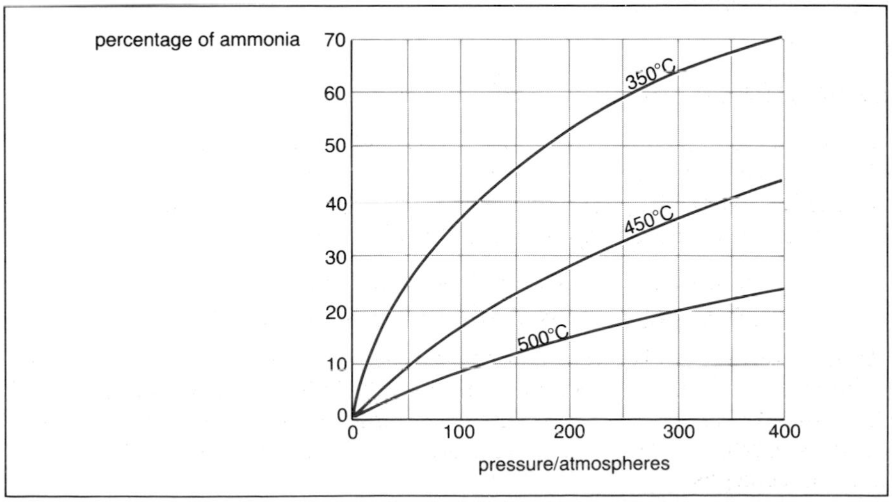

Picture 4 The percentage yield of ammonia under different conditions of temperature and pressure. For example, a percentage yield of 50% means that half of the nitrogen and hydrogen is turned to ammonia. The other half is unchanged

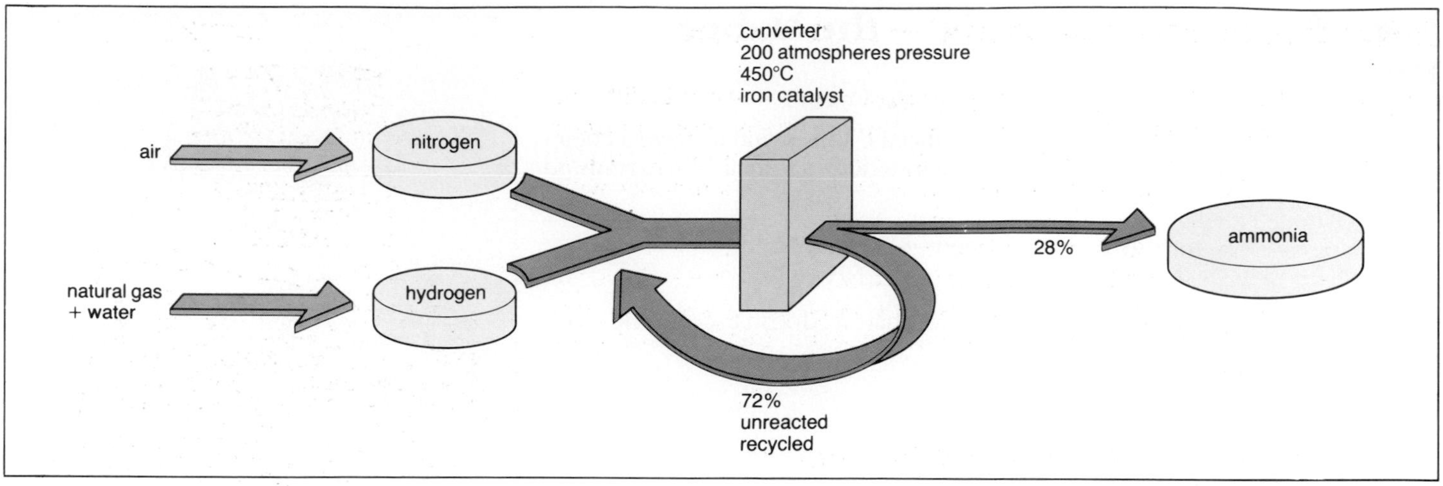

Picture 5 The Haber Process, used to manufacture ammonia

So we have several factors to weigh up in deciding the best conditions for making ammonia. A very high pressure would give a good percentage yield of ammonia — and a good rate too. But it would cost too much because of the pump problem. A low temperature would give a good percentage yield of ammonia, but the rate would be too slow.

The conditions that are actually used are a compromise — a balance between these opposing factors. A medium pressure of 200 atmospheres and a medium temperature of 450°C are usually chosen. This gives a yield of 28% ammonia. Not too bad in the circumstances.

The Haber Process in use today

Picture 5 summarises the Haber process as it is used today in Britain. The actual process is more complicated than this, and involves several stages that are not shown. But the most important stage is the one shown here, in which nitrogen and hydrogen are converted to ammonia.

Notice that 72% of the nitrogen and hydrogen are unreacted and have to be recycled. That means you have to separate the ammonia from the unreacted gases. Table 1 compares some properties of ammonia, nitrogen and hydrogen. It should suggest a way of separating the ammonia (question 4).

Table 1 Some properties of ammonia, nitrogen and hydrogen

Property	Ammonia	Nitrogen	Hydrogen
Appearance	Colourless gas	Colourless gas	Colourless gas
Boiling point	−33°C	−196°C	−253°C
Solubility in water at 20°C (cm^3 of gas dissolved by 100 cm^3 water)	68000	1.5	3.0

The economic costs of the Haber Process

The raw materials for the process are

- Air, which supplies the nitrogen.
- Natural gas (methane) and water, which supply the hydrogen and the energy needed to heat the reactants.
- Iron, which is the catalyst and does not get used up.

All these materials are plentiful, so ammonia can be produced cheaply. Picture 6 shows the main costs involved in making a tonne of ammonia.

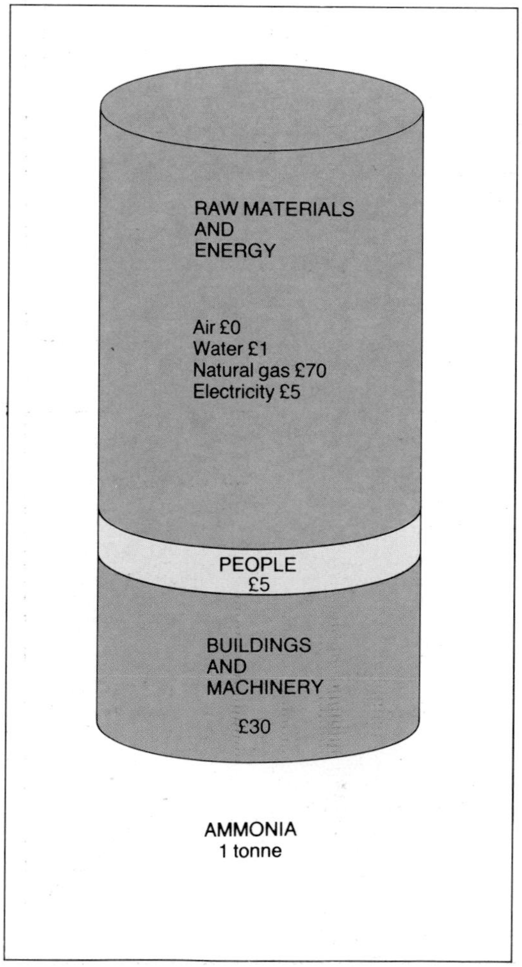

Picture 6 The main costs involved in making 1 tonne of ammonia

Using the ammonia to make fertilisers

Ammonia can be used as a fertiliser on its own, but being a gas it is difficult to apply to the soil. Usually, the ammonia is converted to ammonium salts, which are solids and easier to apply. The most popular is ammonium nitrate, 'NITRAM'. To make ammonium nitrate you need to react ammonia with nitric acid. The nitric acid is made from ammonia itself.

There are many other kinds of fertilisers. Picture 7 summarises the most important ones. Notice 'NPK' fertiliser, which contains the three elements plants need most: nitrogen, phosphorus and potassium. You can get different NPK fertilisers with different proportions of the three elements, to suit the needs of your land.

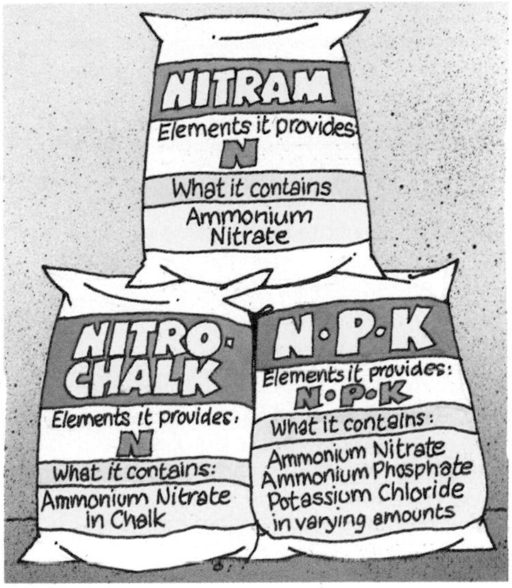

Picture 7 Types of fertilizer

What's the best place to put a fertiliser plant?

Ammonia has many uses, and picture 8 shows some of them. By far the biggest use is in making fertilisers.

To avoid transporting ammonia too far, all the chemical processes for making fertilisers are carried out on the same site. The biggest fertiliser plant in Britain is at Billingham-on-Tees (picture 9). This plant is well placed for all the necessary raw materials, as you can see from the map in picture 10. Question 5 looks more closely at this.

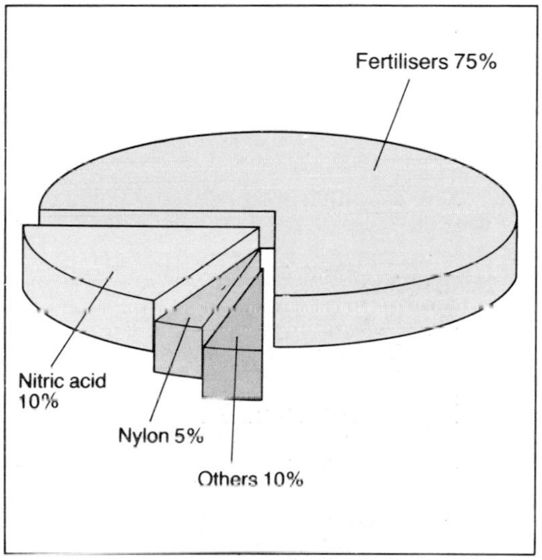

Picture 8 The major uses of ammonia

What are the environmental costs of the Haber Process?

The main environmental problems with ammonia manufacture are

- Accidental escape of toxic ammonia gas from the plant. However, such accidents are rare.
- Emission of nitrogen oxides and ammonia in the waste gases from the plant, causing air pollution. These emissions are normally tightly controlled.
- Effect on the landscape of a large industrial plant.

Against these environmental costs we must balance the value of ammonia and fertilisers to society. But perhaps the most serious environmental problems arise not from the way fertilisers are manufactured, but from the way they are used. The environmental problems of fertiliser use are covered in *The Living World*, topic B13.

Picture 9 The plant at Billingham

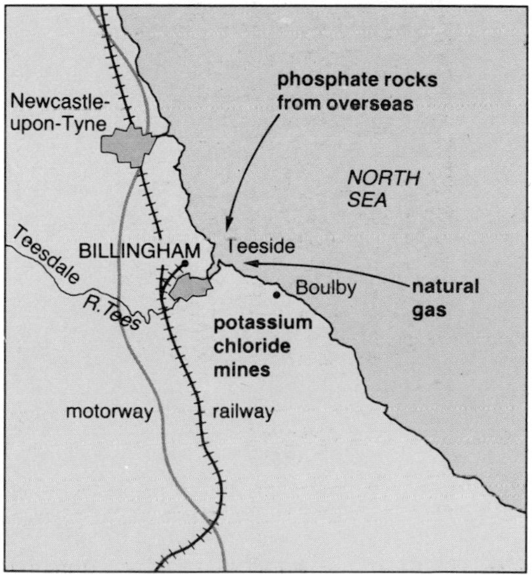

Picture 10 The location of Billingham, Britain's biggest fertiliser plant

Activities

A Making a fertiliser

Ammonium sulphate is sometimes used as a nitrogenous fertiliser. It is formed by reacting ammonia with sulphuric acid:

$$2\,NH_3(aq) + H_2SO_4(aq) \rightarrow (NH_4)_2SO_4$$

ammonia + sulphuric acid → ammonium sulphate

In this activity you have to plan and carry out an experiment to make pure, dry crystals of ammonium sulphate.

You can use the following equipment: glass stirring rod; conical flask (50 cm^3); burette and stand; measuring cylinder (50 cm^3); universal indicator paper; ammonia solution (2M); dilute sulphuric acid (M); eye protection, which **must** be worn throughout the experiment.

Plan your method, then **discuss it with your teacher before you go ahead.** Your plan should include a note of any safety precautions you will take.

Bear the following points in mind.

- Ammonia solution reacts with dilute sulphuric acid to form ammonium sulphate. With the solutions you are using here, approximately equal volumes will react together.
- Your ammonium sulphate fertiliser must be as near neutral as possible, otherwise it will damage the plants.
- You should use between 10 cm^3 and 30 cm^3 of each solution.
- Ammonium sulphate crystals decompose if you heat them too strongly.

B Finding out about a fertiliser

Urea is a nitrogenous fertiliser which is popular in many tropical countries. Try to find out the following things about urea fertiliser. You will need to use advanced books.

1 Its formula.

2 How it is manufactured.

3 The advantages of urea over other nitrogenous fertilisers.

Questions

1 a Write the formula of (i) the ammonia molecule and (ii) the ammonium ion.

b Give two ways that ammonia gas can be detected.

c Name the products that are formed when ammonia solution is added to: (i) hydrochloric acid; (ii) nitric acid; (iii) phosphoric acid.

2 Look at the graphs in picture 4 on page 101.

a What percentage yield of ammonia would you get using each of the following sets of conditions?

i) A temperature of 450°C and a pressure of 400 atmospheres?

ii) A temperature of 450°C and a pressure of 200 atmospheres?

iii) A temperature of 350°C and a pressure of 400 atmospheres?

b Which set of conditions is actually used? Explain why these conditions are used rather than either of the others.

3 The Haber Process combines nitrogen and hydrogen to form ammonia.

a From what raw material is the hydrogen obtained?

b From what raw material is the nitrogen obtained?

c What other raw material does the process need?

d Which of these raw materials is/are non-renewable, and will eventually get used up?

e What might be used instead of any non-renewable raw materials once they are used up?

f What is the biggest single cost in the Haber process?

g Why is the Haber Process so important to society?

4 In the Haber Process, ammonia has to be separated from unreacted nitrogen and hydrogen (picture 5 on page 102 explains this).

Use the data in table 1 on page 102 to suggest a method for separating the ammonia.

5 Look at the map in picture 10, showing the location of the fertiliser plant at Billingham. Explain why Billingham is a particularly good location for a fertiliser plant.

6 What do you think are the main environmental costs of manufacturing ammonia? List them under the four headings: people's health and safety; pollution of the environment; damage to the landscape; depletion of resources.

7 Calculate the percentage by mass of nitrogen in (i) ammonium nitrate, NH_4NO_3 and (ii) ammonium sulphate, $(NH_4)_2SO_4$ (N=14; H=1; S=32; O=16).

What do your answers suggest about these two compounds as nitrogenous fertilisers?

Fertilisers: a story of supply and demand

For almost all of history farmers managed without artificial fertilisers. People knew you could get better crops if you put manure or compost on your fields, and that was enough.

The change came with the Industrial Revolution and the growth of the population. Now farmers began to grow food to sell to other people, not just for themselves. The pressure was on to get as much food as possible from the land.

Picture 1 Fritz Haber

As scientists discovered more about the way plants feed, they realised how important nitrogen is to the growth of crops. They realised too that the nitrogen has to be in a 'fixed' form that can be taken up through the roots. Soluble nitrogen compounds — nitrates and ammonium compounds — are needed, rather than unreactive nitrogen gas.

The trouble with soluble nitrogen compounds is that you don't often find big deposits of them in the ground. Being soluble, they get washed away by the rain. But deposits of sodium nitrate were found — in Chile, South America. For a while it was worth sending ships across the world from Europe to collect this valuable mineral.

An explosive development

By now there was another reason why nitrates were to be prized. The first high explosive, nitroglycerine, was invented by Alfred Nobel in 1867. To make high explosives you need nitrates — another reason for bringing sodium nitrate from the other side of the world.

By the beginning of this century supplies were running out. This worried all the major powers, but particularly Germany. The Germans realised that, if a war came, they would need a reliable supply of nitrogen compounds, for both fertilisers and explosives. The British Navy controlled the seas, so the supply would have to come from home.

The need was clear, and scientists started to do research into the problem. In theory, the solution was obvious: make nitrogen compounds from the nitrogen in the air. That source will never run out. In practice it was much more difficult to make this unreactive gas combine. Many scientists worked on the problem, including Fritz Haber, a talented chemist from Karlsruhe.

Fritz Haber wanted to make nitrogen combine with hydrogen. He used his understanding of chemistry to work out the necessary conditions. He realised that high pressure, high temperature and a catalyst were needed. In 1908 he succeeded in making ammonia from atmospheric nitrogen.

Haber was better at theoretical ideas than making things work on a large scale. It needed a brilliant chemical engineer, Carl Bosch, to 'scale up' the process to make worthwhile amounts of ammonia. By 1913 the process was developed enough for the first industrial ammonia plant to open, at Oppau on the Rhine.

Having found a way to make ammonia, it was relatively easy to convert it to the nitric acid needed to make explosives. Haber's process provided Germany both with fertilisers and with the explosives which were used in such huge quantities in the First World War.

1. Explain why sodium nitrate is no longer used as a raw material for making fertilisers.
2. What raw materials are used for fertilisers today? Are they likely to go on being used in the future?
3. Why was Haber stimulated to do research on nitrogen?
4. Compare the roles of (a) Haber and (b) Bosch in developing the process.
5. The Haber Process has been described as the most important piece of chemistry in the world. Why?
6. Find out more about the life and work of Fritz Haber. Try to find out about:
   a. his work on poison gases;
   b. why his wife committed suicide;
   c. how he tried to get gold from the sea;
   d. what happened to him when the Nazis came to power.

Picture 2 Stacking horse manure. Traditional methods of horticulture take their nitrogen from animal or plant waste

D5 Chemicals from salt

Salt is not just for eating. It's an important raw material.

When you sprinkle salt on your food, you may think it comes from the sea. It's more likely to be from the salt mines of Cheshire — though these salt deposits come from seas of long ago.

The largest of the Cheshire mines produces 2 million tonnes of salt a year. Fortunately, few people have to work down these mines. Most of the salt is extracted by solution mining. Salt is soluble in water, but most of the other stuff in the mine is not. Water is pumped into the mine and the salt dissolves, leaving impurities behind. It is pumped back to the surface as a strong solution (brine), so there's no need for anyone to go down the mine. What a pity coal doesn't dissolve in water.

What's salt used for?

Some of the salt is made very pure and is sold for table salt, but this isn't anything like the biggest use. A lot of salt is used to put on roads in winter to melt the ice.

But the most important use of salt is as a raw material for making other chemicals. Industry uses many sodium compounds. Most of them start life as salt, which chemists know as sodium chloride, NaCl.

Of all the manufacturing processes which use salt as a raw material, the biggest is the manufacture of chlorine and sodium hydroxide by electrolysis. This is called the **chlor-alkali** process. It produces many useful products, as you can see from picture 2.

Picture 1 The scene above the salt mines in Cheshire. The salt is brought out by solution mining, so there are no spoil heaps

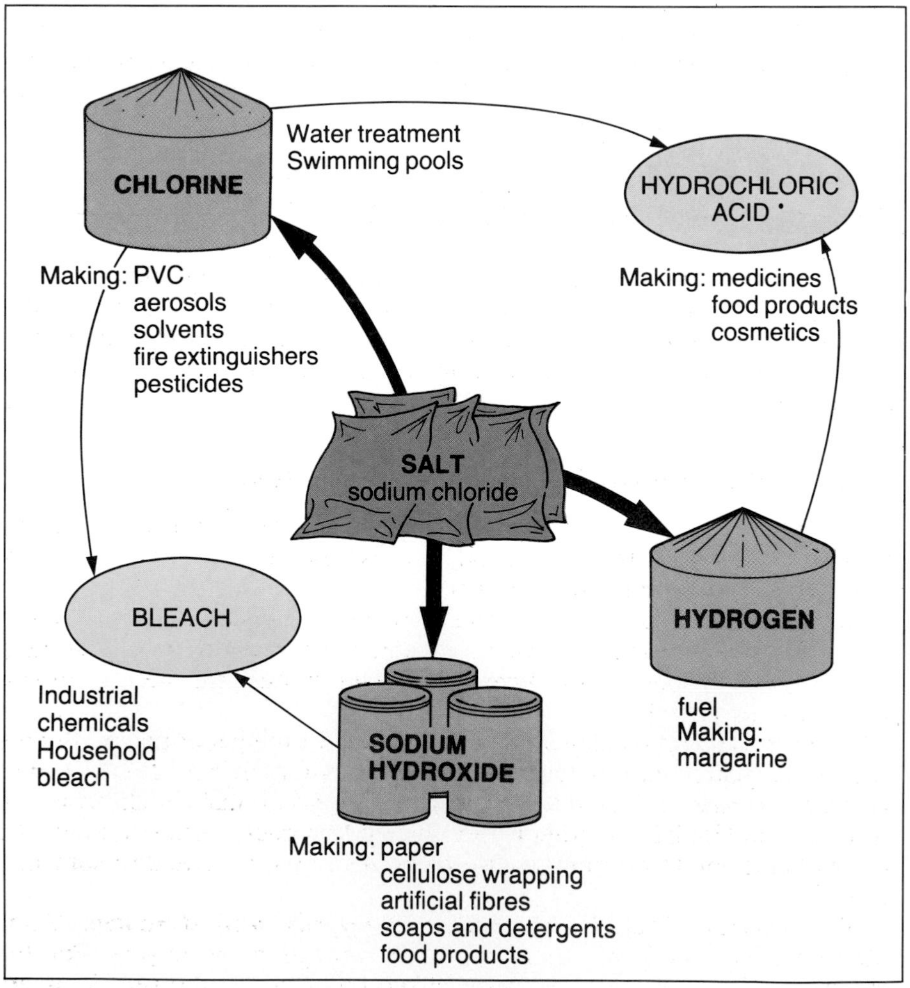

Picture 2 Uses of products of sodium chloride electrolysis

1000 kg		370 kg			607 kg		684 kg		17 kg
SALT	+	**WATER**	ELECTRICITY →		**CHLORINE**	+	**SODIUM HYDROXIDE**	+	**HYDROGEN**
cost: £25		cost: very small		cost: £55	value: £91		value: £125		value: £10

Picture 3 Adding value in the chlor-alkali process

The electrolysis of brine

We look at the basic principles of electrolysis in topic J2.

When electricity is passed through a solution of sodium chloride in water, it decomposes to form sodium hydroxide, chlorine and hydrogen:

sodium chloride + water → sodium hydroxide + chlorine + hydrogen

$$2\ NaCl(aq) + 2H_2O(l) \rightarrow 2\ NaOH(aq) + Cl_2(g) + H_2(g)$$

These three **co-products** are all very useful chemicals.

Chlorine gas comes off at the anode, and hydrogen gas at the cathode. The sodium hydroxide solution is formed around the cathode. The industrial process is carried out in a specially designed cell called a **membrane cell**. Details of this cell are on page 215.

Uses of the products

Picture 2 shows some of the many ways the products are used. Notice that the major products, sodium hydroxide, chlorine and hydrogen, all have major uses in their own right. But they can also be combined together, to make bleach or hydrochloric acid.

The economics of the chlor-alkali process

Picture 3 shows the costs involved in the process. You can see that the value of the products is much more than the value of the salt and water. The electricity used in the process costs much more than the salt. The process involves other costs as well, of course. Think about what they are (see question 3).

Supply and demand: a three-way problem

The three products of the chlor-alkali process are all useful. There are no useless waste products. That's good, because the costs of the process are shared out between the three products.

There is a problem though. Suppose you are in the chlor-alkali business. You sell your chlorine to a water treatment company and your sodium hydroxide to a paper-maker. What happens if the water treatment company goes out of business?

You have to go on making sodium hydroxide for the paper-maker. But the chemical equation tells us that you can't make sodium hydroxide on its own . *You have to make all three products.* You must go on making chlorine and store it — and look for another buyer quickly. You might decide to lower the price of chlorine to encourage customers to buy yours instead of someone else's.

All industries experience problems of **supply and demand.** When demand falls, you lower the price to encourage more buyers. For the chlor-alkali business, with its three linked co-products, the problems are particularly difficult.

Questions

1a Give the names and formulas of the products made by the electrolysis of sodium chloride.

b Give at least two major uses of each of these products.

2a Salt is extracted from underground mines by *solution mining*.

i) Explain how solution mining works.

ii) What property of sodium chloride does this method use?

b The salt that comes straight up from the mines isn't pure enough to use as table salt.

i) What impurities do you think it contains?

ii) What method would you use to purify it?

3 Look at picture 3, which summarises the costs involved in the chlor-alkali process. Apart from electricity, what other costs will be involved in running this process?

4a Write an equation for the reaction that occurs when sodium chloride solution is electrolysed.

b Suppose 117 g of sodium chloride are electrolysed. Calculate the mass of (i) sodium hydroxide, (ii) chlorine and (iii) hydrogen that will be formed (Na=23; Cl=35.5; O=16; H=1).

E1 Metals as materials

Without metals modern civilisation would literally collapse. In this topic we look at the properties of metals that make them so useful.

Picture 1 Metals are at the heart of many modern structures

The properties of metals

There are 92 naturally occurring elements, and 81 of them are metals. The special properties of metals make them excellent construction materials.

Picture 2 shows the characteristic properties of metals. These are physical properties — we look at chemical reactions of metals in topic E2. Notice that the properties of metals are very different from the properties of non-metals like oxygen, chlorine or sulphur. Let's look at some of the properties in more detail.

Metals are strong

There are different meanings of the word 'strength'. Most metals have high *tensile strength*, which means they can support a heavy load. Because of this they can be used to make large structures like buildings and bridges. Iron and steel are the metals normally used in such structures. 'Steel' is the name given to alloys of iron. There are many different types of steel (see below).

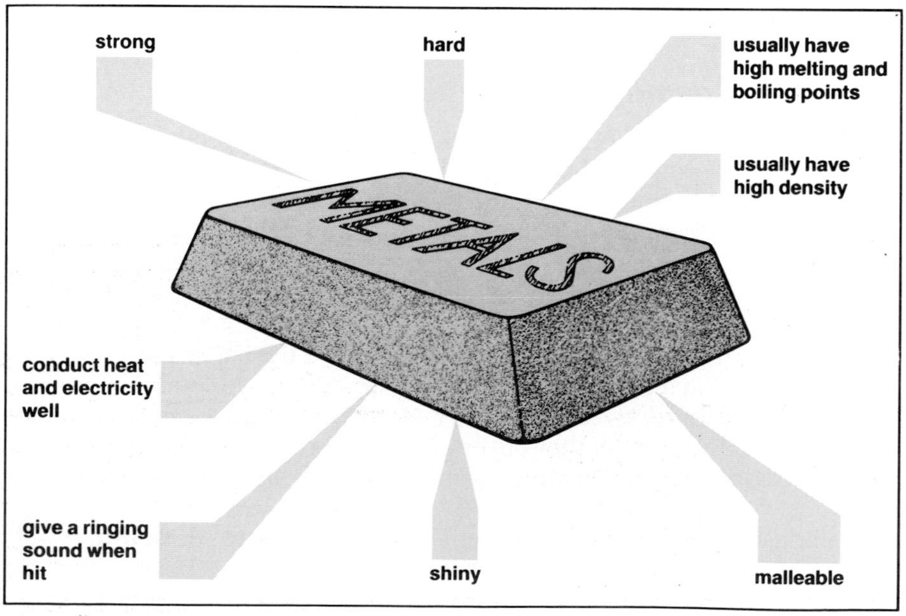

Picture 2 Typical properties of metals

Picture 3 Most metals are hard. The blade of a hacksaw is specially hardened

Metals are hard

For thousands of years metals have been used to make weapons and tools which need to be hard. Knives and saws need to be hard so they don't get blunt. Drills need to be hard to cut through other materials. It's usually some form of steel that is used for tools like this.

Metals usually have high melting and boiling points

There are a few exceptions — for example, mercury is a liquid at room temperature. But the generally high melting points of metals make them useful wherever high temperatures are involved. That's why metals are used to make cooking utensils, car engines and tools which get hot, such as drills.

Metals are malleable

'Malleable' means they can be hammered, bent and changed into different shapes without breaking. This is very different from a non-metallic material like glass, which is brittle and shatters when you try to bend it.

Because metals are malleable, they can be made into all sorts of useful shapes. For example, the door of a car is made by pressing a flat sheet of steel into shape. Aluminium cooking foil is made by rolling sheets of the metal until they are very thin.

Metals become more malleable when they are hot. In a steel mill, the metal is shaped while it is red hot.

Metals are good conductors of electricity

Metals are the only materials which conduct electricity when they are solid. Copper is a particularly good conductor, and most electrical wires are made from copper.

Metals usually have high density

High density is often a disadvantage, because it makes metal objects heavy. Aluminium's low density makes it very useful, for example for making aeroplanes and bicycles.

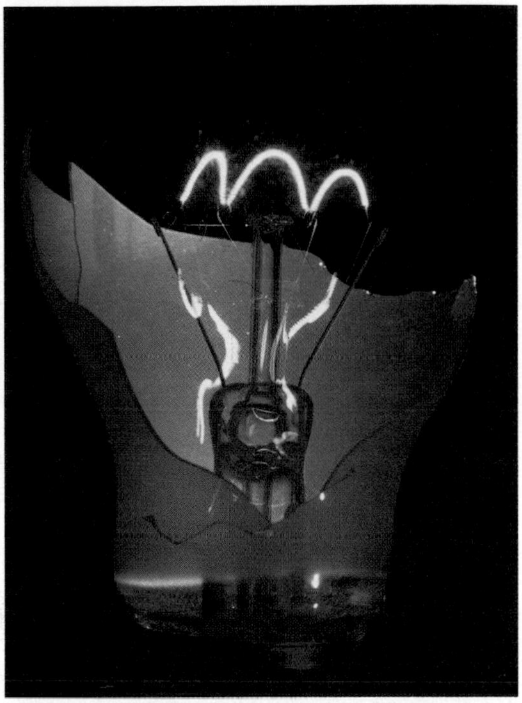

Picture 4 The filament of a lightbulb is made from tungsten, which has a melting point of 3410°C

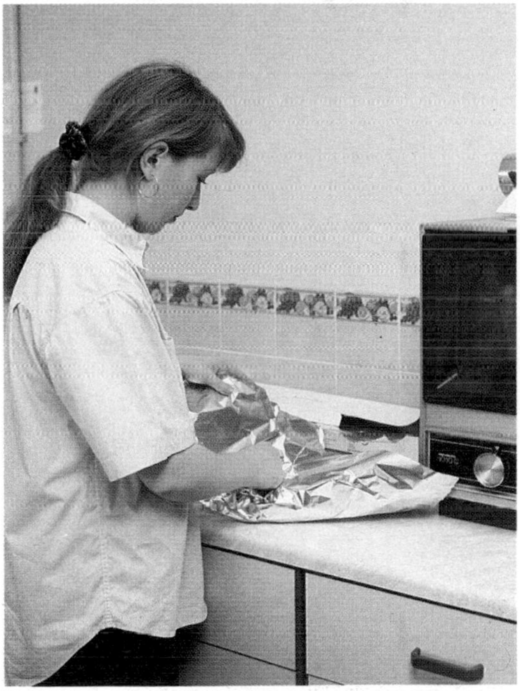

Picture 5 Aluminium is very malleable, so foil can be wrapped into any shape

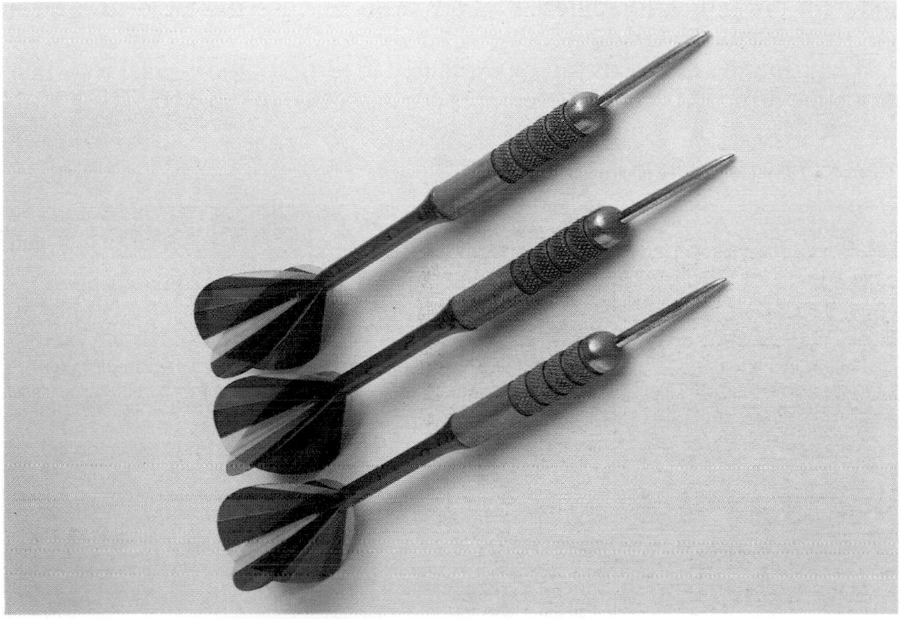

Picture 6 Tungsten darts can be very thin, because tungsten is so dense. This means you can fit more of them into the triple twenty!

Comparing metals

Table 1 compares the properties of some commonly used metals. Use the table to answer questions 2 and 3 at the end of this topic.

In fact the metals in the table are most often used, not on their own, but mixed together as alloys.

Table 1 Properties of some commonly used metals
**** = best, * = worst.

Metal	Density /(g/cm^3)	Melting point/ °C	Tensile strength (relative)	Electrical conductivity (relative)	Corrosion behaviour	Cost per tonne (1985)
Aluminium	2.7	659	**	***	Corrodes very slowly	£750
Copper	9.0	1083	****	****	Corrodes very slowly	£1000
Iron	7.9	1540	****	**	Corrode (rusts) quickly	£130
Lead	11.3	328	*	*	Corrodes very slowly	£290
Silver	10.5	961	***	****	Corrodes slightly (tarnishes on surface)	£150 000
Tin	7.3	232	*	*	Does not corrode	£9100
Zinc	7.1	420	***	**	Corrodes very slowly	£500

Alloys

An alloy is a mixture of two or more metals. Alloys are made by mixing molten metals and then allowing them to solidify. Alloys are used instead of pure metals because they have better properties. For example, brass is an alloy of copper and zinc. Brass is stronger than either of these metals. What is more, alloys can be designed and made with specific properties to match specific needs.

Table 2 gives some important alloys. Note that the compositions given in the table are *typical* ones. In fact the compositions can be varied to give different properties for different needs. You can use the table to answer question 4 at the end of this topic.

The properties of metals can be explained in terms of the special way their atoms are arranged. Metallic structures are described in topic C7.

Picture 7 Coins are made from alloys. "silver" coins are 75% copper and 25% nickel. "Copper" coins are 97% copper, 2.5% zinc, and 0.5% tin

Table 2 Some important alloys

Name of alloy	Typical composition	Special properties
Brass	copper 70%, zinc 30%	Harder than pure copper
Bronze	copper 90%, tin 10%	Harder than pure copper
Duralmin	aluminium 96%, copper 4%	Stronger than pure aluminium
Solder	tin 50%, lead 50%	Low melting point (203°C)
Mild steel	iron 99.7%, carbon 0.3%	Stronger and harder than pure iron
Stainless steel	iron 70%, chromium 20%, nickel 10%	Harder than pure iron, doesn't rust
Manganese steel	iron 86%, manganese 13%, carbon 1%	Very hard
Cast iron	iron 97%, carbon 3%	Hard but brittle

Activities

A Comparing the hardness of metals

You can compare the hardness of metals by using the fact that a harder metal will scratch a softer one.

Get samples of some of the following metals — all of them if possible. It is best if the samples are in the form of foil.

aluminium, copper, iron, lead, nickel, tin, zinc

Plan an experiment to place the metals in order of hardness, with the hardest first. Discuss your plan with your teacher before carrying out the experiment.

B Comparing the malleability of metals

You can compare malleability using the apparatus shown in picture 8.

You will need strips of at least two metals. Aluminium and steel are good ones to start with. The strips must be of the same thickness.

1 Clamp a strip of the metal you are testing firmly in the vice.
2 Bend the strip backwards and forwards as shown. Make sure the strip bends only at the place where it is clamped, next to the vice.
3 Count how many times you bend the strip before it breaks.
4 Repeat for a different metal.
5 From your results, decide which metal is more malleable.

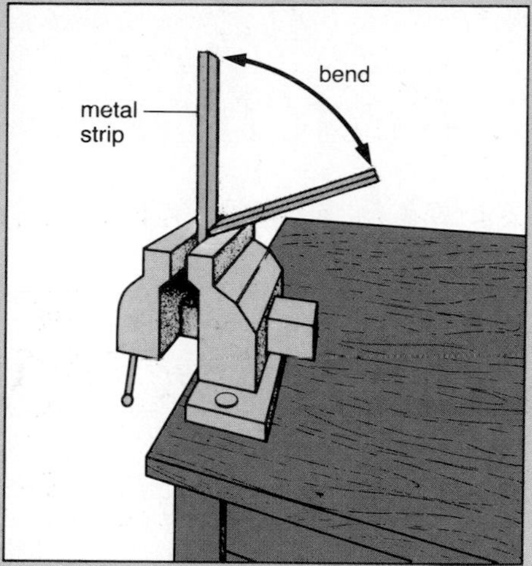

Picture 8 Comparing the malleability of metals

Questions

1 In each of the following examples, which typical metal property is being used? Look at picture 2 on page 108 to remind yourself of typical metal properties. (Note: more than one property may be involved.)

a Saucepans are made from metal.
b Bells are made from metal.
c The heating 'element' of an electric fire is made from metal.
d Car engines are made from metal.

2 Plot bar charts to compare (a) the densities and (b) the melting points of the metals in table 1 on page 110.

3 Use table 1 on page 110 to explain why:

a the chain on a padlock is made from iron, not aluminium;
b tent poles are made from aluminium, not iron;
c the head of a hammer is made from iron, not lead or aluminium;
d deep-sea divers wear boots made of lead;
e 'silver' coins are not made from silver;
f dustbins are made from iron coated with zinc, but not from iron or zinc alone;
g 'tin' cans are not made of solid tin;
h overhead electrical cables are made from aluminium, not copper.

4 Use table 2 on page 110 to answer these questions about alloys.

a Suggest reasons for the following.
i) Aircraft are made from duralmin, not pure aluminium.
ii) Electricians use solder to join wires together, not tin or lead.
iii) Ornamental wrought iron gates are made from pure iron, not steel.
iv) Bridges are made from mild steel, not pure iron.
v) Nails are made from iron, not cast iron.
vi) Doorknockers are made from brass, not copper (give at least two reasons).

b Which of the three kinds of steel given in the table would be best for making each of the following? Give the reason for your answer.
i) The body of a car.
ii) Table cutlery.
iii) Reinforcing wires in concrete.
iv) Crossovers on railway lines.

5 Look again at the typical properties of metals shown in picture 2. Which, if any, of these typical properties are not shown by each of the following metals: (a) iron; (b) copper; (c) lead; (d) aluminium?

E2 Reactions of metals

In this topic we look at the typical reactions of metals, and we see how metals can be placed in order of their reactivity.

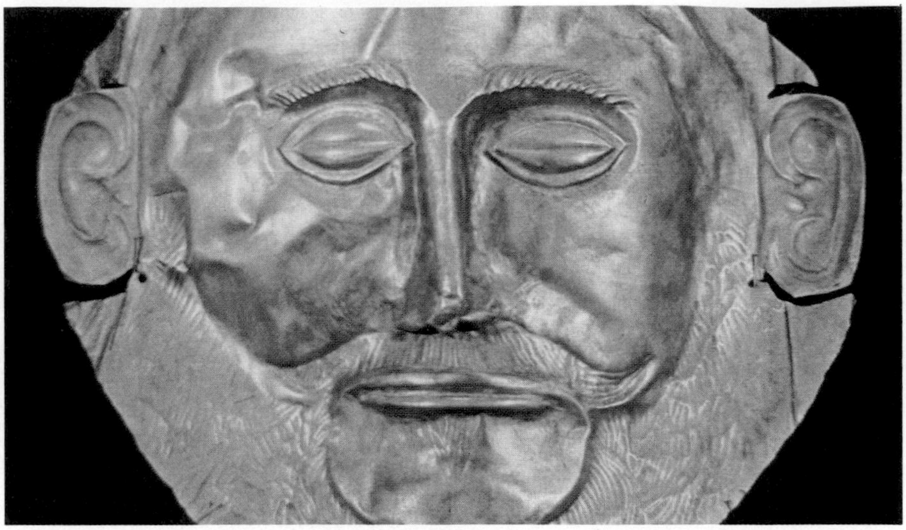

Picture 1 The first metals to be used by humans were the unreactive ones. This gold death mask has stayed untarnished for 3500 years

In many ways it would be useful if all metals were unreactive. Then we would not have to worry about corrosion. But unfortunately many metals are reactive — and some are very reactive indeed.

Picture 2 summarises some of the typical chemical reactions of metals. Not all metals give all these reactions, because some metals are more reactive than others. Let's look at the different reactions in turn.

How do metals react with oxygen?

Oxygen is a reactive non-metal, and it is all around us in the air. Many metals react with the oxygen in the air to form **oxides** (topic B2). For example, with aluminium:

$$\text{aluminium} + \text{oxygen} \rightarrow \text{aluminium oxide}$$
$$4\,Al + 3\,O_2 \rightarrow 2\,Al_2O_3$$

You can investigate the reactivity of metals by heating them in air and seeing how vigorously they react (activity A).

Table 1 shows how some common metals react when they are heated in air. You can see that some metals react better than others. We can use results like these to place metals in order of reactivity. This order is called the **reactivity series**. Picture 4 shows the reactivity series for a number of metals.

Picture 3 Bright sparks from fireworks are often burning metal powders

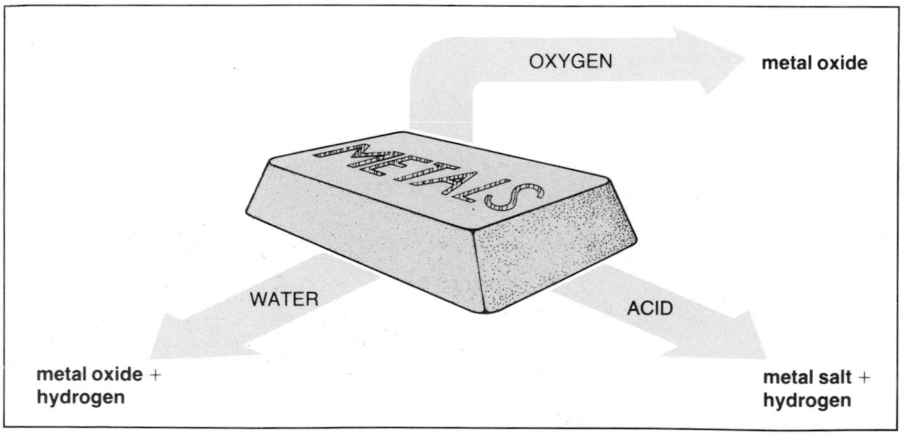

Picture 2 Some of the ways a metal may react

Table 1 The results of heating some metals in air

Metal	How it reacts	Product
Aluminium	Burns slowly, forming a white surface layer	Aluminium oxide, Al_2O_3
Copper	Does not burn. Oxidises, turning black on surface	Copper oxide, CuO
Iron	Only burns when in powder or wool form	Iron oxide, Fe_3O_4
Magnesium	Burns readily with a brilliant white glow, forming white powder	Magnesium oxide, MgO
Sodium	Burns very readily, forming white powder	Sodium oxide, Na_2O

Very reactive metals like sodium react with oxygen as soon as they are exposed to air. Other metals like zinc and iron react when they are heated in air. However, these metals do react with air very slowly even at room temperature, especially if water is present as well as air. This slow reaction with air is called corrosion, or rusting in the case of iron (topic B3).

The very unreactive metals, like gold, don't react with oxygen at all. That's why gold is so popular for jewellery — it doesn't corrode in air, so it keeps its shine.

The reactivity series applies to other reactions of metals, not just their reaction with oxygen. Reactive metals, like sodium and magnesium, have a strong tendency to react with non-metals, like chlorine and oxygen. When they react, they form compounds like sodium chloride and magnesium oxide. Unreactive metals have little tendency to react with non-metals. We can sum up by saying

Reactive metals tend to combine and form compounds
Unreactive metals tend to stay uncombined.

One result of this is that a more reactive metal can take away oxygen from a less reactive metal. This is useful in the extraction of metals from their oxides (see topic E3).

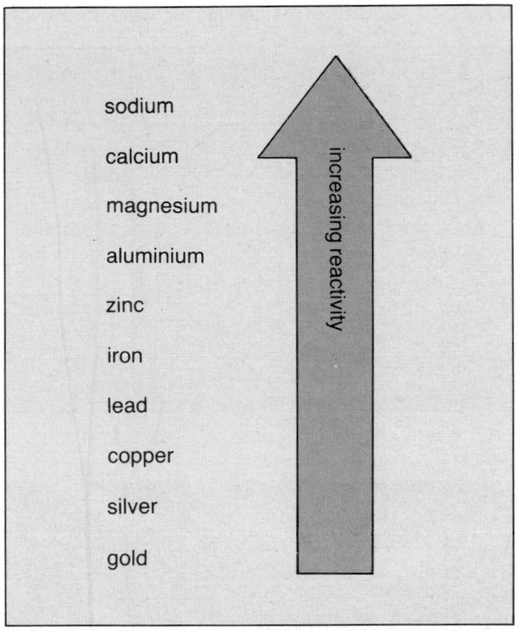

Picture 4 The reactivity series of some metals

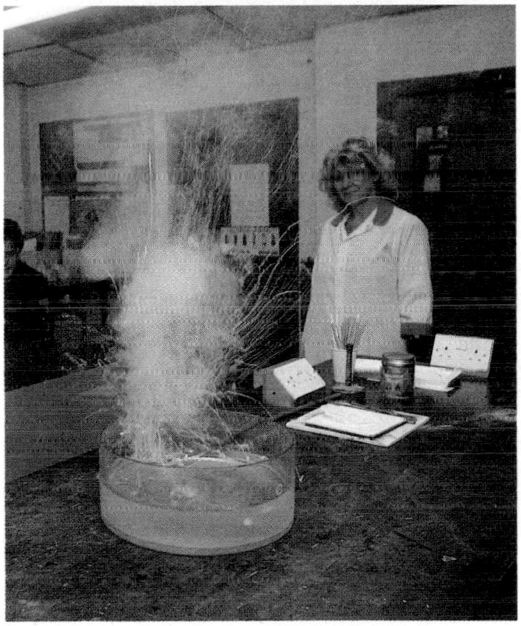

Picture 5 Potassium is so reactive that it bursts into flame when it is put into water

How do metals react with water?

Water is a compound of hydrogen and oxygen, H_2O. As you might expect, reactive metals tend to take the oxygen from water, leaving the hydrogen (picture 6). When this happens, hydrogen gas is formed:

metal + water → metal oxide + hydrogen

For example, with magnesium:

magnesium	+	water	→	magnesium oxide	+	hydrogen
Mg	+	H_2O	→	MgO	+	H_2

Picture 6

Table 2 Reactions of metals with air, water and acids

<table>
<tr><th>Reactivity series of metals</th><th>Reaction with air</th><th>Reaction with water</th><th>Reaction with dilute hydrochloric acid</th></tr>
<tr><td>Sodium, Na</td><td rowspan="6">Burn less and less vigorously</td><td rowspan="3">React with cold water less and less vigorously, giving hydrogen</td><td rowspan="7">React less and less vigorously, giving hydrogen</td></tr>
<tr><td>Calcium, Ca</td></tr>
<tr><td>Magnesium, Mg</td></tr>
<tr><td>Aluminium, Al</td><td rowspan="3">React with steam, giving hydrogen</td></tr>
<tr><td>Zinc, Zn</td></tr>
<tr><td>Iron, Fe</td></tr>
<tr><td>Lead, Pb</td><td rowspan="2">React slowly to form a layer of oxide</td><td rowspan="4">Do not react</td></tr>
<tr><td>Copper, Cu</td><td rowspan="3">Do not react</td></tr>
<tr><td>Silver, Ag</td><td rowspan="2">Do not react</td></tr>
<tr><td>Gold, Au</td></tr>
</table>

Picture 7 These turbine blades are used in a power station. They are turned by high pressure steam at a high temperature. What metal might they be made from?

Table 2 summarises the reactions of metals with air, water and acids. The metals are listed in order of reactivity.

Notice that only the highest metals in the reactivity table react with water. These metals are reactive enough to take the oxygen in water away from the hydrogen. However, metals that do not react in cold water will sometimes react at higher temperatures. Magnesium reacts quickly when it is heated in steam.

How do metals react with acids?

Topic G1 describes the nature of acids. All acids contain two parts. One part is hydrogen. The other part is a non-metal or a group of non-metals. For example, hydrochloric acid contains hydrogen combined with chlorine: its formula is HCl. Reactive metals remove the chlorine from hydrochloric acid, releasing hydrogen:

metal + hydrochloric acid → metal chloride + hydrogen

Picture 8 illustrates this. Notice that the reaction is similar to the reaction of metals with water, but here the metal is competing for chlorine instead of oxygen. For example, with zinc:

$$\text{zinc} + \text{hydrochloric acid} \rightarrow \text{zinc chloride} + \text{hydrogen}$$
$$Zn + 2\,HCl \rightarrow ZnCl_2 + H_2$$

You can see from table 2 how different metals react with dilute hydrochloric acid.

Dilute sulphuric acid and dilute nitric acid react in a similar way. Whereas hydrochloric acid forms chlorides, sulphuric acid forms sulphates and nitric acid forms nitrates. These are all **salts** (topic G2). In general:

metal + acid → metal salt + hydrogen

Picture 8 What happens when metals react with hydrochloric acid

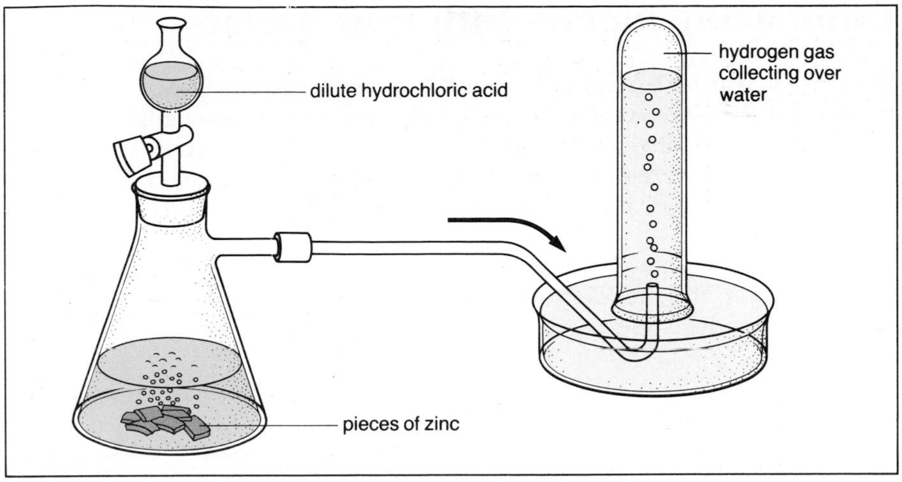

Picture 9 Making and collecting hydrogen in the laboratory

The reaction of a metal with an acid is a useful way of making hydrogen in the laboratory. Usually a moderately reactive metal is chosen, so that the hydrogen comes off neither too quickly nor too slowly. Zinc is often used. Picture 9 shows apparatus that can be used to collect test tubes of hydrogen in the laboratory.

The reactivity of metals with acids can cause corrosion problems when there are acidic gases in the air. Sulphur dioxide is an acidic gas which pollutes the air in industrial areas, causing acid rain. This acidity can make metal objects like bridges, cars and statues corrode faster than they would do in unpolluted air. You can investigate this further in activity D.

How do the uses of metals depend on their reactivity?

The reactivity of metals limits their usefulness. Very reactive metals like sodium would be no use at all for constructing bridges and cars. Imagine what would happen when it rained! Magnesium is less reactive than sodium, and its lightness makes it useful in construction. Magnesium was once used to build racing cars, but not any more because of the safety hazards (see question 5).

On the other hand, very *unreactive* metals like silver and gold are excellent for constructing things. The trouble is, the very unreactive metals are rare, and therefore expensive. For construction purposes, metals must be cheap. The most common construction metals are the abundant, moderately reactive ones — like aluminium, iron and copper.

Making predictions using the reactivity series

If you know the position of a metal in the reactivity series, you can predict how it will react. For example, chromium comes below zinc but above iron in the reactivity series. Using table 2, we might predict these things about chromium:

- it will react with acids to give hydrogen;
- it will not react with cold water, but it will react with steam;
- it will burn with difficulty in air, forming chromium oxide.

Try making these kinds of predictions in questions 3 and 4.

Picture 10 Rhubarb is rather acidic. What kind of saucepan should you cook it in?

Comparing metals with non-metals

From what you have read about metals in this and other topics, you will realise that they have very different properties from non-metallic elements like oxygen, chlorine and sulphur. The differences between metals and non-metals are covered in a number of different topics in this book. Table 3 summarises the most important differences. You can use it to help you to answer question 7.

Some elements show both metal and non-metal properties — particularly elements near the middle of the periodic table. For example, carbon (graphite) conducts electricity even though in other ways it behaves as a non-metal.

Table 3 A comparison of metals and non-metals

Property	Metals	Non-metals
1 Physical properties		
(a) State at room temperature	Usually solids (occasionally liquids)	Solids, liquids or gases
(b) Melting and boiling point	Usually high	Often low
(c) Electrical conductivity	Conduct when solid	Do not conduct
(d) Strength	Strong and malleable	Often weak and brittle if solid
(e) Density	Usually high	Often low
2 Chemical properties		
(a) Reaction with air	Reactive metals form oxides	May react to form oxides
(b) Nature of oxides	Usually solids. Give alkaline solutions when they dissolve in water	Solids, liquids or gases. Give acidic solutions when they dissolve in water
(c) Reaction with water	Very reactive metals give hydrogen	Usually no reaction
(d) Reaction with acids	Reactive metals give hydrogen	Usually no reaction
(e) Type of ions formed	Positively charged	Negatively charged

Activities

A The reaction of metals with air

CARE Eye protection MUST be worn.

You will need samples of the following metals: aluminium (foil), copper (foil), iron (wire), magnesium (ribbon).

Hold the sample in an a blue bunsen flame and observe what happens. **CARE** Do not look directly at the burning metal. Look slightly to the side of it.

Your teacher may demonstrate the reactions of some of the more reactive metals with air.

Try to place the metals in order of reactivity from the results of this experiment.

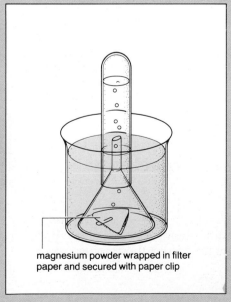

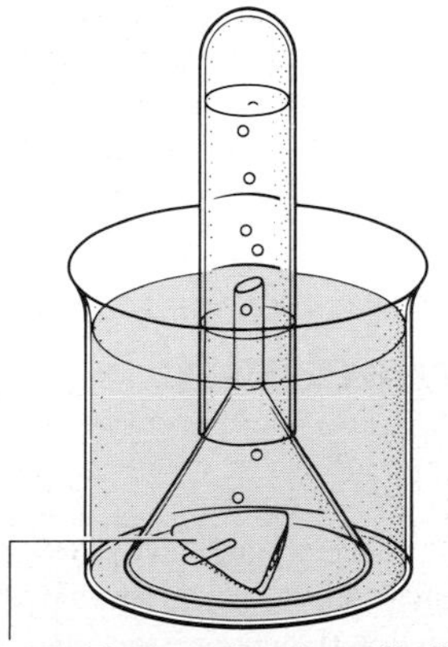

Picture 11 Testing the reaction of magnesium with water

B The reaction of magnesium with water

Investigate the reaction of magnesium using the apparatus in picture 11.

Set up the apparatus and leave it until the next lesson. Test the gas that collects in the test tube with a burning splint.

C The reaction of metals with dilute acid

CARE Eye protection **must** be worn.

You will need samples of the following metals: aluminium (foil), copper (foil), iron (wire), magnesium (ribbon), zinc (granule). Test each sample as follows.

Put 2 cm depth of dilute hydrochloric acid in a boiling tube standing in a rack. Add the sample of metal. Observe. Is a gas given off? If so, test it with a burning splint.

If there is no reaction with the cold acid, warm it carefully in a bunsen flame, then remove the tube from the heat. Is a gas given off? If so, test it as before.

D The effect of sulphur dioxide on metals

Picture 12 shows apparatus that can be used to investigate the effect of sulphur dioxide on the corrosion of metals. Design an investigation using this apparatus to find answers to the following questions.

1 Which metals corrode fastest in the presence of sulphur dioxide?

2 Does it make a difference if the surface of the metal is wet or dry?

3 How can metals be protected from the corrosive effect of sulphur dioxide?

Suitable metals to test would include aluminium, copper, iron and zinc. Bear the following points in mind as you design your investigation.

- The surfaces of the metals must be clean at the start.
- The metals may corrode to a certain extent even without sulphur dioxide present, so you will need some kind of control.
- Corrosion is a slow process, so it may take several days or even weeks to get results.

Discuss your plans with your teacher before you try to carry out any investigation.

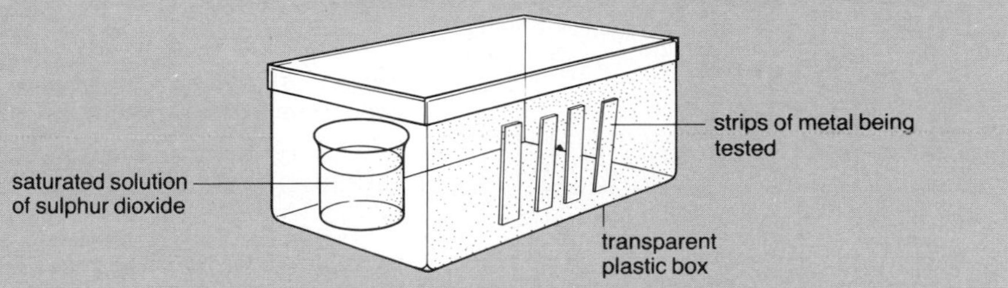

Picture 12 Investigating the corrosive effect of sulphur dioxide on metals

Questions

Use table 2 to help you answer questions 1 and 2.

1 What would you expect to happen in each of the following cases? Say what you would expect to see, and name all the products you would expect to be formed. If you would expect no reaction to occur, say so.

a Calcium is added to water.

b Silver is added to dilute hydrochloric acid.

c Lead oxide is heated with magnesium.

d Calcium is heated in air.

e Aluminium is heated with lead.

f Zinc is heated in steam.

2 For each of the reactions in question 1:

a write a word equation summarising the reaction;

b write a balanced equation using formulas.

3 Potassium comes above sodium in the reactivity series. Predict how you would expect potassium to react in each of the following cases. In each case name the products you would expect to be formed.

a Potassium is heated in air.

b Potassium is added to water.

c Potassium is added to dilute hydrochloric acid.

4 Vanadium is a metal you may not have heard of before. It is used to make special steels for tools such as spanners.

Vanadium comes below aluminium but above zinc in the reactivity series. Predict how you would expect vanadium to react in each of the following cases. In each case name the products you would expect to be formed.

a Vanadium is heated in air

b Vanadium is added to cold water

c Vanadium is heated in steam

d Vanadium is added to dilute hydrochloric acid.

e Vanadium oxide is heated with aluminium.

f Magnesium oxide is heated with vanadium.

5 Magnesium has been used for making cars because it is very light. But it is no longer used because of safety hazards. What would happen if a magnesium car caught fire, then firemen used water to fight the fire?

6 Zirconium is a silvery metal. Suppose you were given a piece of foil made from zirconium. Describe the tests you would do on it to find out where zirconium comes in the reactivity series. Describe how you would use the results of these tests to place zirconium correctly.

7 Below you will find information about 10 elements **A** to **J**.

a For each element, say whether you think it is

i) a metal,

ii) a non-metal,

iii) you cannot tell from the information given.

b For each of elements **A**, **C**, **E** and **F**, give two further properties that you would expect the element to have.

Element **A** is a grey solid which does not conduct electricity.

Element **B** is a colourless gas.

Element **C** is a grey solid which gives off hydrogen when acid is added.

Element **D** is a solid which does not react with air, water or acid.

Element **E** is a yellow solid which shatters when hit with a hammer.

Element **F** is a shiny, dense solid.

Element **G** is a solid which burns in air.

Element **H** is a solid which burns in air to give an acidic gas.

Element **I** is a liquid which conducts electricity.

Element **J** is a solid which floats on water but does not react with it.

E3 Extracting metals

All metals come from the Earth. This topic is about the ways we get metals from their ores.

Picture 1 Panning for gold in the Californian Gold Rush. Gold is one of the few metals which occur in the earth uncombined

Most metals are too reactive to exist on their own in the ground. Instead, they exist combined with other elements as compounds, called **ores**. Table 1 shows the ores of some common metals. You can see that many ores are oxides. This is because oxygen is a reactive element and is very abundant on Earth.

A few metals are so unreactive that they occur in the earth in an uncombined state, as the pure metal. Gold is an example.

Table 1 The ores of some common metals. Most metals have more than one ore. The ores shown here are the especially important ones

Metal	Name of the ore	What's in the ore
Aluminium	Bauxite	Aluminium oxide, Al_2O_3
Copper	Copper pyrites	Copper iron sulphide, $CuFeS_2$
Iron	Haematite	Iron oxide, Fe_2O_3
Sodium	Rock salt	Sodium chloride, NaCl
Tin	Cassiterite	Tin oxide, SnO_2
Zinc	Zinc blende	Zinc sulphide, ZnS

How do you get metals from ores?

Ores are the **raw materials** for making metals. One of the useful things about chemistry is that it gives us ways of turning raw materials into substances we need — like metals.

Getting a metal from its ore is called **extracting** the metal. Take iron as an example. Iron ore is iron oxide, Fe_2O_3. To get iron from iron ore you need to take away the oxygen. Taking away oxygen is called **reduction** (topic B2). To reduce iron oxide to iron you need a **reducing agent** that will grab the oxygen from the iron (picture 2). This 'oxygen grabber' must be more reactive than iron, otherwise the iron will hang on to the oxygen and stay combined as the ore.

What can we use to reduce iron ore? One possibility would be to look at the reactivity series of metals discussed in the last topic. Any metal above iron in the reactivity series will 'grab' the oxygen from iron oxide, leaving iron. For example, aluminium is above iron in the reactivity series, so if we heat iron oxide with aluminium metal, aluminium will take the oxygen from the iron:

$$\text{aluminium} + \text{iron oxide} \rightarrow \text{aluminiumj oxide} + \text{iron}$$
$$2Al + Fe_2O_3 \rightarrow Al_2O_3 + 2Fe$$

In this reaction, aluminium is the reducing agent. It gets oxidised to aluminium oxide. Iron oxide gets reduced to iron.

Picture 2 To turn iron oxide into iron, you need a reducing agent that will 'grab' the oxygen from the iron

But there is a problem with making iron this way. Aluminium actually costs more than iron! So this method would be too expensive for making iron on a large scale. A cheaper reducing agent than aluminium is needed, and the one that is used is carbon.

Carbon, in the form of coke, can be made cheaply from coal. At high temperatures, carbon has a strong tendency to react with oxygen, so it is a good reducing agent. The details of the extraction of iron using carbon are given later in this topic.

Carbon is useful for extracting a number of other metals besides iron. For example, you can use carbon to get zinc from zinc oxide:

$$\text{zinc oxide} + \text{carbon} \rightarrow \text{zinc} + \text{carbon monoxide}$$
$$ZnO + C \rightarrow Zn + CO$$

But some metals are too reactive to be extracted this way. They hang on to the oxygen so strongly that the carbon can't take it away. These are the metals towards the top of the reactivity series, like sodium, magnesium and aluminium. To extract these metals, you have to use **electrolysis**. This is described in more detail in topic J1.

Table 2 summarises the methods used to extract different metals. The metals are listed in order of reactivity, and you can see that the method used depends on the metal's position in the reactivity series.

Table 2 A summary of methods used for extracting metals

Metal	Method
Potassium Sodium Calcium Magnesium Aluminium	Electrolysis of molten ores
Zinc Iron Tin Lead	Reduction of ores using carbon
Copper	Heating copper sulphide in air
Silver Gold	Metals occur uncombined

From ore to metal

Extracting the metal from its ore is just one stage (a very important one) of making things from metal. Picture 3 shows all the stages.

Over millions of years, natural processes in the Earth have formed rich deposits of ores in certain parts of the Earth's crust. But even the richest deposits do not contain pure ore. The ore is mixed with lots of useless dirt and rock, which have to be separated off as much as possible. This is called **concentrating** the ore.

Some ores are already fairly concentrated when they are dug up — iron ore is often over 85% pure Fe_2O_3. But other ores are much less concentrated — copper ore usually contains less than 1% of the pure copper compound.

After concentration, the ore is reduced to the metal using one of the ways you have read about. The metal made in this way is usually quite impure, so it must then be purified.

Now at last the pure metal can be made into whatever products are needed — wires, cars, saucepans, bikes and so on. But it doesn't even end there. When the product is worn out and finished with, the metal can be reclaimed as scrap. This is **recycling**, and there is more about it later in this topic.

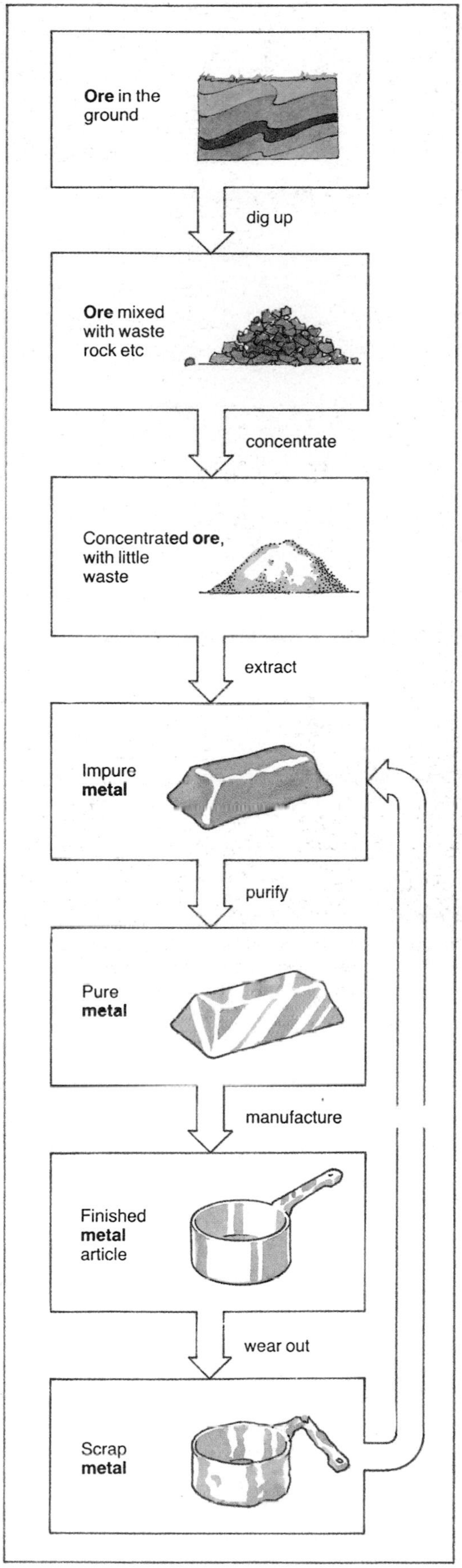

Picture 3 Stages in making a metal article

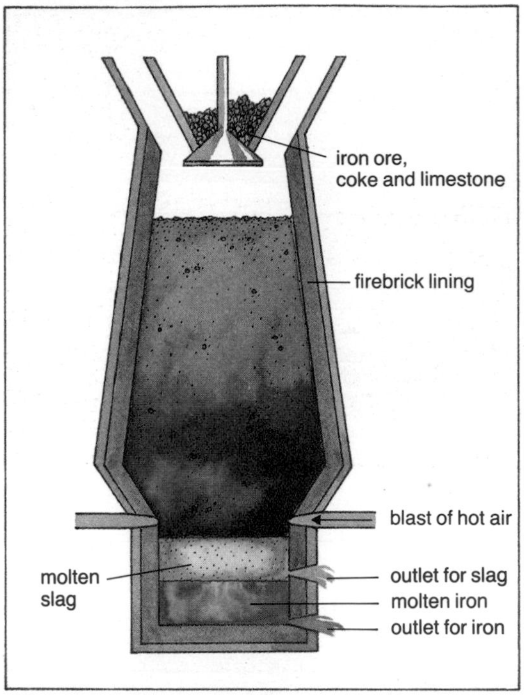

Picture 4 A blast furnace for making iron from iron ore

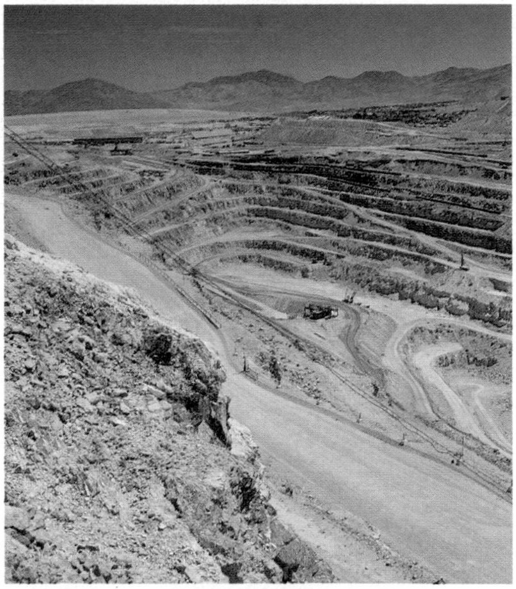

Picture 5 This is an open cast copper mine in Chile

An important example: the extraction of iron

Iron is the cheapest and most important metal available to us, and it is produced in huge amounts in **blast furnaces** (picture 4).

The best quality iron ore comes from places such as Scandinavia, the USA and Australia. It is concentrated enough to use straight away. Iron ore and coke (carbon) are fed in at the top of the furnace. Limestone is added as well, to remove impurities. A blast of hot air is sent in at the bottom of the furnace (this is how the furnace gets its name). The carbon burns in the air blast and the inside of the furnace gets very hot. Two important reactions occur.

- Carbon burns in the air blast to form carbon monoxide:

$$\text{carbon} + \text{oxygen} \rightarrow \text{carbon monoxide}$$
$$2C + O_2 \rightarrow 2CO$$

- Carbon monoxide takes oxygen from iron oxide, reducing it to iron:

$$\text{iron oxide} + \text{carbon monoxide} \rightarrow \text{iron} + \text{carbon dioxide}$$
$$Fe_2O_3 + 3CO \rightarrow 2Fe + 3CO_2$$

At the high temperature of the furnace, the iron is molten. It runs out at the bottom of the furnace. Impurities in the iron ore combine with the limestone to form a molten slag. This floats on the molten iron at the bottom of the furnace and runs out separately. It is used for making roads.

From iron to steel

The iron that comes out of the blast furnace is called **pig iron**. It is impure, because it contains about 4% carbon and smaller amounts of other elements. These impurities make it brittle. Before use, the pig iron is purified. The carbon content is reduced to about 0.15%, which helps make the metal tough and hard. It is then called **steel**. Other metals may be added to improve the quality of the steel.

The steel made in this way is sent to factories which turn it into countless useful products. Eventually these products get worn out and rusty, and they go as scrap iron to be recycled. About a third of all iron and steel gets recycled.

If you have studied rusting in topic B3, you will know that rust is iron oxide — the same compound as iron ore. So iron starts and ends its life as iron oxide.

Mining metals — the benefits and drawbacks

Metals mean mining. If we want metals, there have to be mines where the ores are dug up.

Most of the metals we use in Britain are mined in other countries. There are benefits to be had from mining ores: it gives people jobs, and it helps create wealth for the community and the country.

But there are drawbacks too, because mining affects the environment. Mines are often **open cast**: that means they are on the surface, like quarries. Open-cast mining makes huge holes which are an eyesore and which destroy the habitats of wildlife. Even underground mines can cause environmental problems: sometimes they cause **subsidence**, when the land above sinks into the mine below.

Mines produce enormous amounts of waste. The ore is dug up mixed with useless rock and dirt, and this has to be separated when the ore is concentrated. This is done at the mine itself, because the cost of transporting the ore together with the waste would be far too high. The waste that is separated off has to be dumped somewhere, and often this leads to huge, ugly spoil heaps near to the mine.

Eventually, all mines become exhausted — the ore gets used up. Then the mine has to close, and this can bring serious unemployment to the local community. Sometimes the mine has to close before it is exhausted. If demand for the metal falls, its price falls too. It may no longer be worth keeping the mine open. This is what happened with many of the tin mines in Cornwall.

So mining metals has its problems. The fact that these problems are often in another country than our own doesn't make them any less serious. But remember how much we use metals: if we want these metals, we have to face the problems that come from getting them out of the ground. And it is often possible to reduce these problems. For example, open-cast workings and spoil heaps can be reclaimed and landscaped so that wildlife can return to them.

Picture 6 Mining subsidence

What decides the price of a metal?

Metals vary enormously in price (picture 8). Why? Obviously it has something to do with abundance — if a metal is plentiful, it is likely to be cheap. Look how cheap iron is compared with gold. Iron makes up 5% of the earth's crust, whereas gold is only 0.000 0004%.

But it isn't only abundance that matters. Aluminium is even more abundant than iron, yet it is more expensive. This is because aluminium is fairly reactive, so it is more difficult to get from its ore than iron.

There are three major factors affecting the price of any metal.

1 *Its abundance in the Earth's crust.*
2 *The quality of the ore.* If the deposits of ore are concentrated, the metal is cheaper to produce because the ore does not need so much purifying.
3 *The cost of reduction.* To get the metal, the ore must be reduced. The less reactive the metal, the easier the ore is to reduce. So the cost of reduction of unreactive metals like copper is less than for reactive ones like aluminium.

You can try explaining the relative costs of metals in *The prices of metals* on page 125.

Picture 7 A disused tin mine in Cornwall

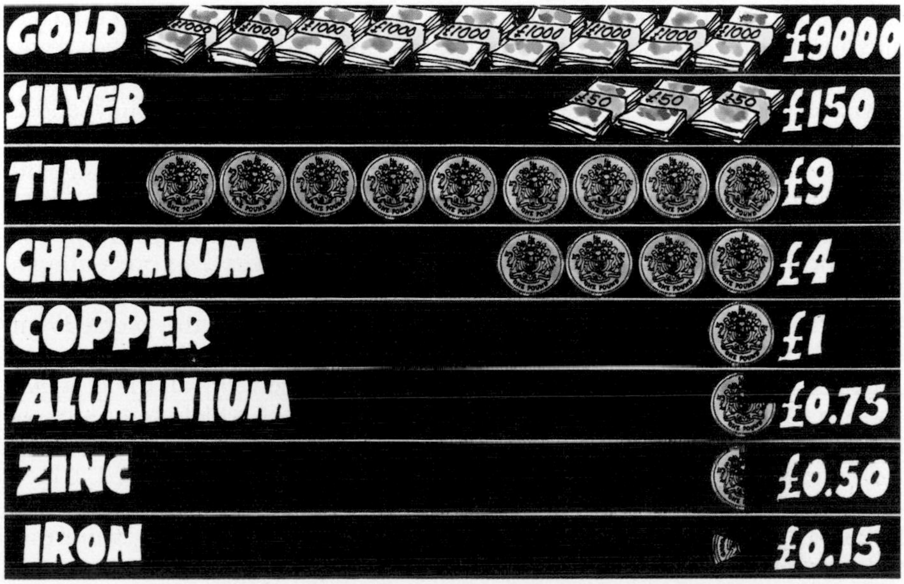

Picture 8 The relative prices of a kilogram of different metals

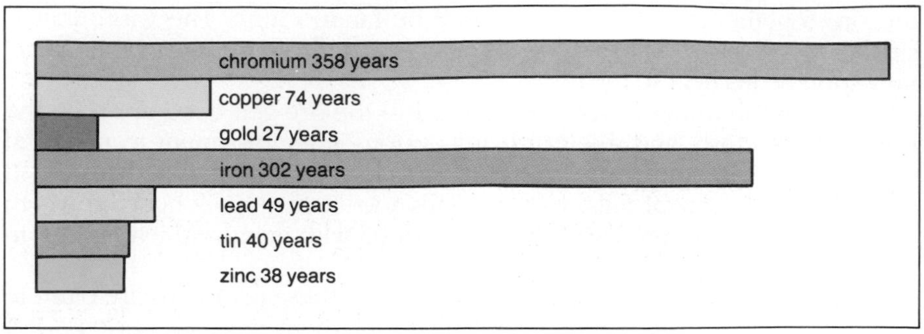

Picture 10 How long reserves of different metals will last

How long will metals last?

Our supplies of metal ores will not last forever. Picture 10 shows how long the known reserves of certain metals will last. 'Known reserves' are the amounts of ore which we know it is worth mining at present prices.

Notice that the reserves of some metals will last much longer than others. Some metals, such as copper, are in very short supply. What should we do as reserves of these metals run out?

- *Try to find new reserves.* As old ore deposits run out, it is very likely that new ones will be discovered. But this cannot go on for ever!
- *Try to find other materials to replace the metals.* For example, copper pipes are being replaced by plastic ones.
- *Use the metals more carefully, and avoid waste.* We can save a lot of metal by recycling scrap material and using it again.

Picture 9 Dealers on the London metal exchange. The price varies constantly according to supply and demand

Recycling metals

Have you recycled any metal lately? You might have put drink cans in a recycling 'bank'. Your family might save aluminium foil milk bottle tops, or maybe you recently sold an old car for scrap. This kind of scrap metal can be melted down and used again — in other words, recycled.

All metals can be recycled. Recycling makes sense because

- it saves money;
- it means we need to dig up less metal ore, so reserves last longer;
- it solves the problem of waste disposal. Recycling metals stops them causing a litter problem and spoiling the environment.

Unfortunately, recycling isn't always easy. The scrap metal has to be collected and transported to the place where it will be processed. Each metal has to be separated from other materials — it's no use trying to recycle aluminium if it is mixed with iron. All this separating and transporting costs money, and if the cost is too high, recycling isn't worthwhile.

Ordinary people like you and me can do a lot to help by separating and transporting the metal ourselves. It's worth saving aluminium milk bottle tops and drink cans: even if you don't earn anything from them yourself, you have the satisfaction of knowing you are saving resources *and* preventing a litter problem!

Picture 11 Recycling an aluminium can

Of course, recycling metals is more worthwhile when the metal is an expensive one. Even millionaires don't throw away gold jewellery when they are tired of it. They have it melted down instead. Practically all the gold we use gets recycled; compare this with aluminium, of which only 40% is recycled.

Of course, metals are not the only materials that can be recycled. Glass, paper, cloth and plastics can all be recycled too. Old glass bottles returned to Bottle Banks can be melted down to make new bottles. Once again, this saves resources and solves a litter problem.

Activities

A Reducing metal ores using carbon

In this experiment you can use carbon to reduce lead oxide to lead. **CAUTION** Eye protection must be worn. The experiment must be done in a well ventilated room.

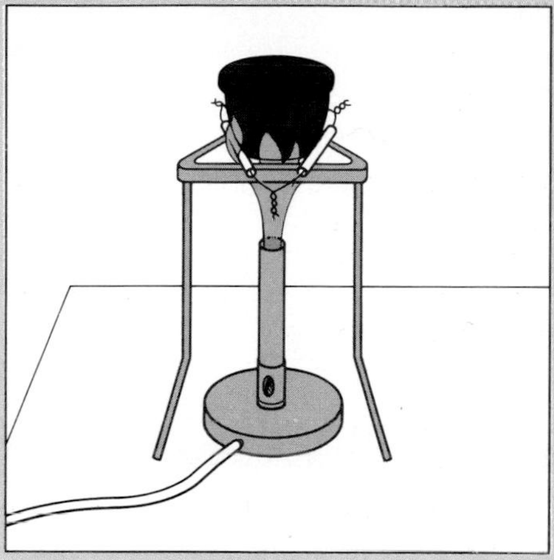

Picture 12 Heating lead oxide and carbon in a crucible

Put three spatula measures of yellow lead oxide on a piece of paper. Add one spatula measure of powdered carbon and mix thoroughly.

Put the mixture in a crucible. Put a few small lumps of charcoal on top.

Put the lid on, then heat the crucible strongly for 5 minutes, as shown in picture 12. Then leave it to cool.

When the crucible is cool, tip the contents onto a heat-resistant mat. Look for evidence that lead has been formed (the lead may be stuck inside the crucible).

You could try repeating the experiment using oxides of other metals. Aluminium oxide and copper oxide would be good ones to try.

B How much do metals cost?

Get a copy of a newspaper which has a lot of financial and business news. You should be able to find a section giving the prices of metals.

Try to work out the current prices of as many different metals as possible.

You will notice that there are often several different prices for the same metal. Try to work out what the various prices refer to, and why they are different.

C A recycling survey

Do a survey in your class to find out how much metals get recycled by the families of people in the class. You could try and find out who recycles aluminium foil, bottle tops and cans. You could ask whether any family has recently sold metal for scrap — for example an old car, or copper piping, or lead from the roof.

D Metal mining in Britain

Britain used to be a major source of metal ores. Today most of the mines are closed because the ores have run out.

Try to find an example of metal mining in Britain, preferably near to your home. It might be an old mine that is now closed, or it might even still be open. Use libraries, newspapers or just ask around to find out about the mine. In particular try to find out:

- What metal ore was mined there?
- When was the mine opened? When did it close?
- Where was the ore processed into metal? Near the mine, or somewhere else?
- What impact has the mine had on the environment? Are there any spoil heaps or quarrying scars? Is there any subsidence?

Questions

1 Explain the meaning of the words that are underlined in the following passage.

Most metals occur in the Earth as ores. First the ore is dug up and then it has to be concentrated. Then the metal is extracted from the ore using a reducing agent.

2 Give an example of a metal that occurs in the Earth: (a) as an oxide; (b) as a chloride; (c) as a sulphide; (d) uncombined, as the metal itself.

3 Chromium metal is manufactured by heating chromium oxide, Cr_2O_3, with aluminium. The products are chromium and aluminium oxide.

a What substance is oxidised in this reaction, and what is reduced?

b Write a balanced equation for the reaction.

c Does chromium come above or below aluminium in the reactivity series? Explain your answer.

d Give two important uses of chromium metal.

4 a Iron is the cheapest of all metals. Give two reasons why.

b Gold occurs uncombined and does not need extracting from an ore. Why, then, is it so expensive?

c The Romans used iron, copper, lead, gold and other metals. Yet they never used aluminium, one of the most versatile of metals. Why not?

d Give one important use of tin. What materials might replace tin for this use when reserves of the metal run out?

e Less than half the iron we use gets recycled, yet practically all gold is recycled. Explain the difference.

5 Zinc is made by reducing zinc oxide, ZnO in a blast furnace similar to the one used to make iron.

a What is the reducing agent in this process?

b Write two equations to show the reactions that occur in the furnace to reduce zinc oxide to zinc.

6 What methods would you expect to be used to extract each of the following metals from their ores?

a Magnesium.

b Lead.

c Nickel (nickel comes between iron and lead in the reactivity series).

d Vanadium (vanadium comes between aluminium and zinc in the reactivity series).

Atmospheric corrosion of zinc

The map in picture 1 is about the corrosion of the metal zinc. It shows how fast zinc corrodes in different parts of England and Wales. Use the map to answer these questions.

1 The rates of corrosion are given in 'g per m^2 of zinc per year'. What do you think this means?

2 Suppose you had the job of producing a map like this one. What experiments would you do?

3 What general rule can you make about the parts of the country where zinc corrodes particularly *fast*?

4 What general rule can you make about the parts of the country where zinc corrodes particularly *slowly*?

5 The rate of corrosion of zinc is affected by air pollution.
   i) What type of air pollutants would tend to make zinc corrode faster?
   ii) Give one example of this type of air pollutant.

6 Would you expect a similar pattern for the corrosion of *iron*? Explain your answer.

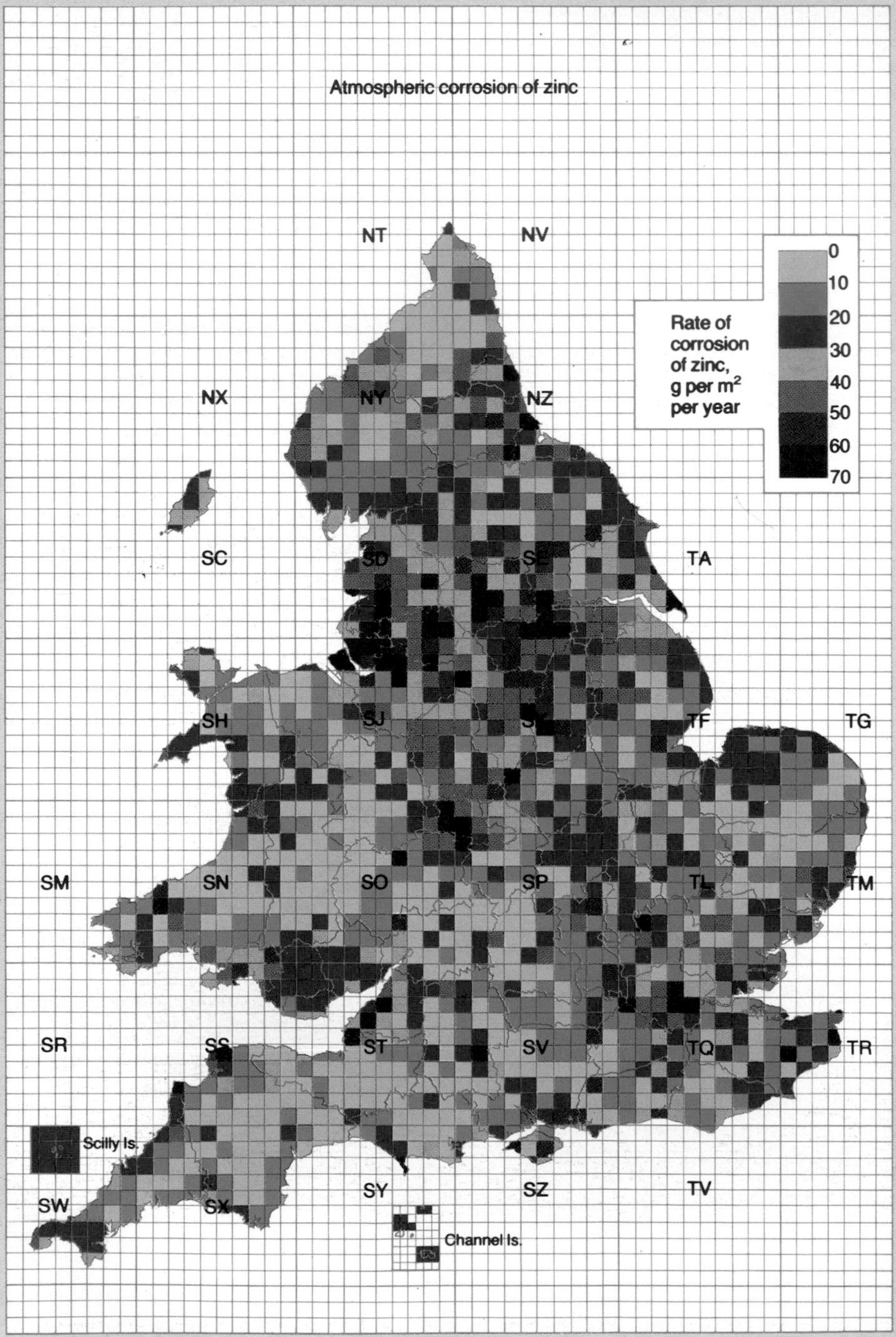

Picture 1 The atmospheric corrosion of zinc

The prices of metals

Table 1 gives the average abundance of a number of metals in the Earth's crust.

1 Make a list of the metals in order of abundance. Put the most abundant first.
2 Use picture 8 on page 121 to list the metals in order of price, cheapest first.
3 If the price of a metal depends on its abundance, you would expect the order to be the same in both your lists. How well do the two lists match up? Mention any exceptions you notice.
4 The order of reactivity of these metals (most reactive first) is

aluminium, zinc, chromium, iron, tin, copper, silver, gold

Use this order of reactivity to try and explain any exceptions you noticed in (3).

5 Table 2 gives the lowest concentration of ore deposits from which four different metals can be economically extracted. For example, the table shows that it is not worth extracting iron from ore deposits that are less than 25% pure iron ore.

Try to give explanations for the relative sizes of the figures for the four metals. For example, why is it worth using copper ore deposits that are only 0.06% pure, but not worth using iron ore unless it is at least 25% pure?

Table 1 The average percentage abundance of some metals in the Earth's crust

Metal	Average percentage abundance
Aluminium	8
Chromium	0.01
Copper	0.0055
Gold	0.000 0004
Iron	5
Silver	0.000 007
Tin	0.0002
Zinc	0.007

Table 2 The lowest concentrations of ore deposits from which metals can be economically extracted (in the case of gold the figure is for the pure metal, not the ore)

Metal	Concentration (% of deposit)
Aluminium	32
Iron	25
Copper	0.5
Gold	0.0014

Mining copper in Papua New Guinea

One of the biggest copper mines in the world is on Bougainville Island in Papua New Guinea, north of Australia. It is an enormous open-cast pit.

Every day, about 100 000 tonnes of ore and rock are mined. From this, just 400 tonnes of pure copper are extracted. The copper ore contains small amounts of silver and gold, and these help pay the cost of extracting the metal.

Picture 2 shows what happens to each tonne of ore and rock after it is dug up. Purification of the ore produces enormous amounts of powdered waste rock. This waste is dumped in the river, and a lot of it ends up in the sea where it is forming a huge delta at the mouth of the river.

1 What percentage of the *ore and rock* that are mined is pure copper?
2 What percentage of the ore and rock that are mined is waste?
3 The percentage of copper in the ore is so low that it is not worth extracting the copper alone. However, there is a special factor about this mine that makes it pay. What is this special factor?
4 This mine produces enormous quantities of waste rock. Explain why.
5 What *advantages* do you think this mine brings to the island of Bougainville?
6 What *disadvantages* do you think this mine brings to the island?

Picture 2 What you get from each tonne of ore and rock

F1
A guided tour of the Periodic Table

The Periodic Table is a classification system for the elements.

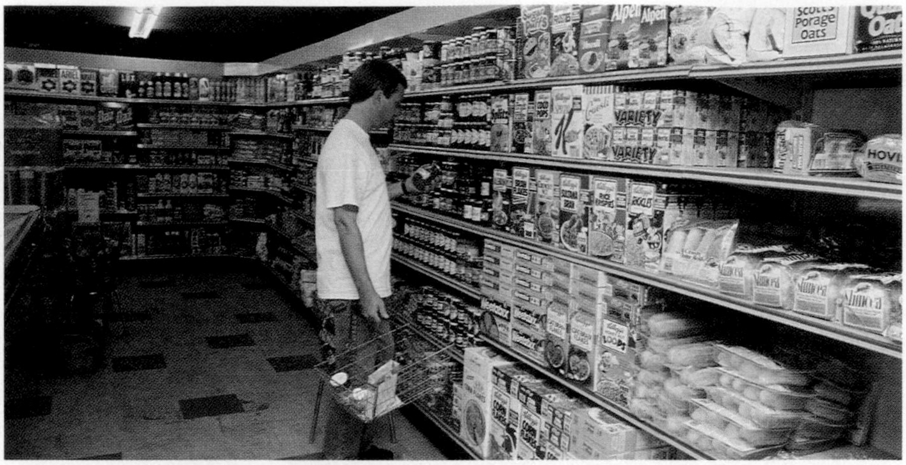

Picture 1 In a supermarket, similar foods are classified together to make it easier to find your way around

If you visit a supermarket regularly, you will know that it uses a classification system. The food products are not all mixed up on the shelves — if they were, it would take ages to find what you want. Instead, similar food products are grouped together (picture 1). If you are an experienced shopper, you know which part of the supermarket to go to for what you want.

There are 92 naturally-occurring elements. This is less than the number of products in your average supermarket, but it is still useful to have a way of classifying elements so that similar ones are grouped together. We have already seen that elements can be classified as metals and non-metals (topic E1), but these are two rather large groups. The Periodic Table provides us with a more precise classification system. The system was developed by a Russian chemist, Dmitri Mendeleev, in 1869 (see topic F2).

Like the supermarket, the Periodic Table groups similar elements together. Like an experienced shopper, a scientist knows what type of elements to expect in different parts of the table. Picture 2 shows the usual form of the Periodic Table. There may be a similar one on the wall of your science laboratory.

Picture 2 The Periodic Table. The elements after 92 are all artificially made

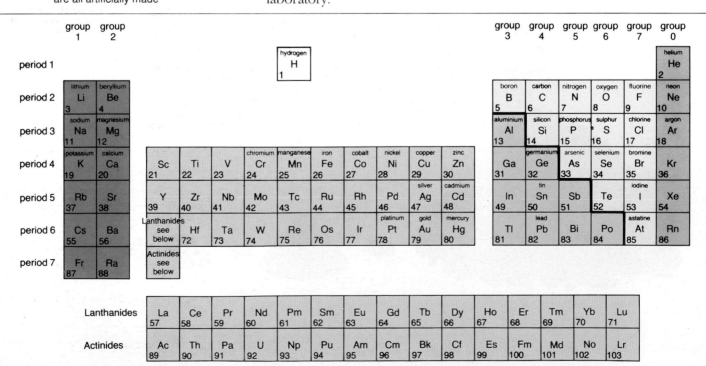

	group 1	group 2											group 3	group 4	group 5	group 6	group 7	group 0
period 1							hydrogen H 1											helium He 2
period 2	lithium Li 3	beryllium Be 4											boron B 5	carbon C 6	nitrogen N 7	oxygen O 8	fluorine F 9	neon Ne 10
period 3	sodium Na 11	magnesium Mg 12											aluminium Al 13	silicon Si 14	phosphorus P 15	sulphur S 16	chlorine Cl 17	argon Ar 18
period 4	potassium K 19	calcium Ca 20	Sc 21	Ti 22	V 23	chromium Cr 24	manganese Mn 25	iron Fe 26	cobalt Co 27	nickel Ni 28	copper Cu 29	zinc Zn 30	Ga 31	germanium Ge 32	arsenic As 33	selenium Se 34	bromine Br 35	Kr 36
period 5	Rb 37	Sr 38	Y 39	Zr 40	Nb 41	Mo 42	Tc 43	Ru 44	Rh 45	Pd 46	silver Ag 47	cadmium Cd 48	In 49	tin Sn 50	Sb 51	Te 52	iodine I 53	Xe 54
period 6	Cs 55	Ba 56	Lanthanides see below	Hf 72	Ta 73	W 74	Re 75	Os 76	Ir 77	platinum Pt 78	gold Au 79	mercury Hg 80	Tl 81	lead Pb 82	Bi 83	Po 84	astatine At 85	Rn 86
period 7	Fr 87	Ra 88	Actinides see below															

Lanthanides	La 57	Ce 58	Pr 59	Nd 60	Pm 61	Sm 62	Eu 63	Gd 64	Tb 65	Dy 66	Ho 67	Er 68	Tm 69	Yb 70	Lu 71
Actinides	Ac 89	Th 90	Pa 91	U 92	Np 93	Pu 94	Am 95	Cm 96	Bk 97	Cf 98	Es 99	Fm 100	Md 101	No 102	Lr 103

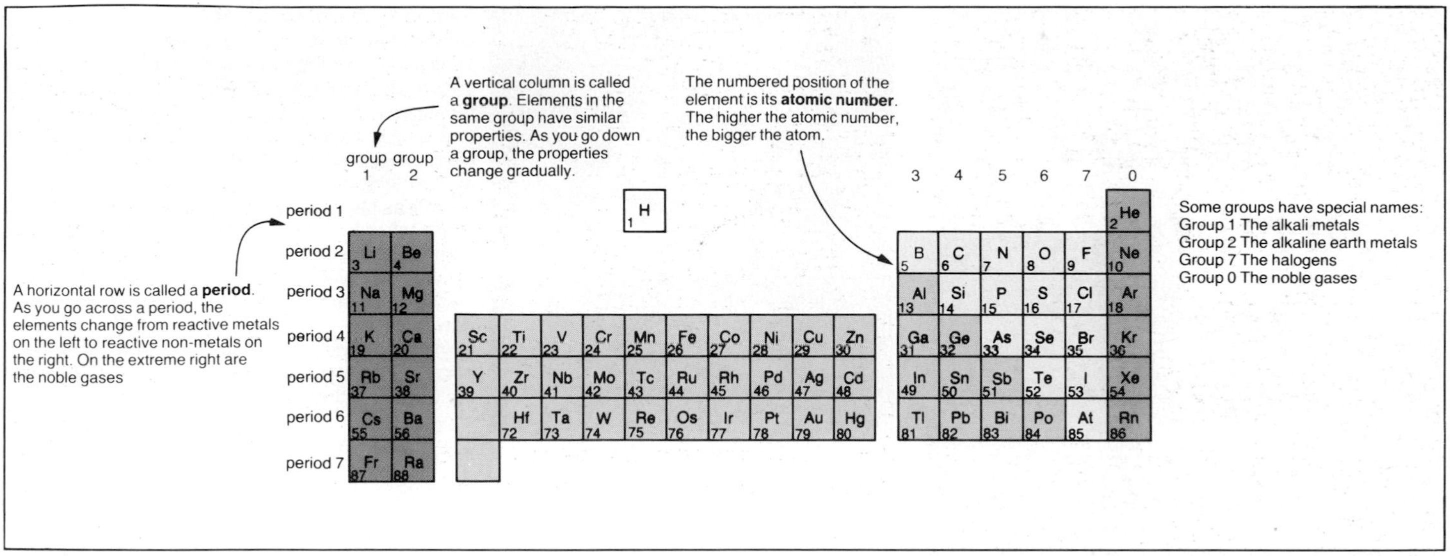

Picture 3 Names used in the Periodic Table

The parts of the Periodic Table

Picture 3 shows the names used to describe the different features of the Periodic Table. You find particular types of elements in particular areas, or **blocks**, of the table, as shown in picture 4.

Why does the Periodic Table classify elements so well?

The arrangement of elements in the Periodic Table is linked to the structure of their atoms. There is more about this in topic J4.

Picture 4 The blocks within the Periodic Table

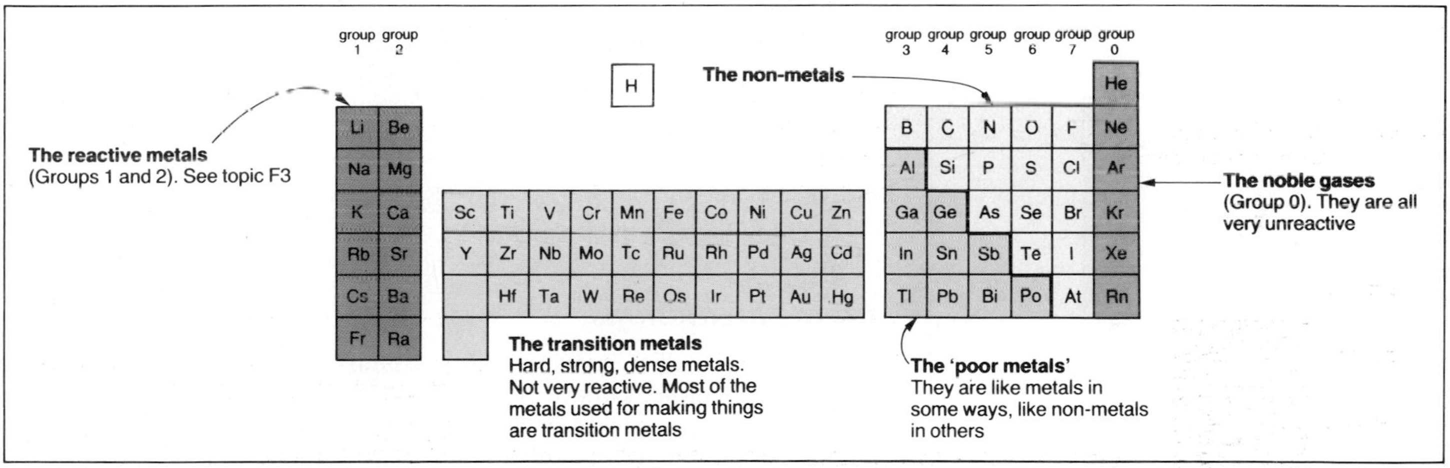

Questions

1 How do the properties of elements change as you go (a) down a group (b) across a period?

2 To which block of the Periodic Table does each of the following elements belong?

a Chromium, Cr
b Argon, Ar
c Calcium, Ca
d Germanium, Ge
e Sulphur, S.

3 Which of the following elements will be most like selenium, Se?
Bromine, Br; arsenic, As; iodine, I; sulphur, S; aluminium, Al.

4a Why is argon, Ar, used to fill light bulbs?
b Would you expect bromine, Br, to conduct electricity?
c Sodium, Na and aluminium, Al are in the same horizontal row (period). Which is more reactive? Explain your answer.

5 Whereabouts in the Periodic Table would you expect to find
a the most reactive metal
b the most reactive non-metal?

F2 Dmitri Mendeléev and the Periodic Table

The Periodic Table was invented by Dmitri Mendeléev in 1869.

Picture 1 Dmitri Mendeléev
Dmitri was born in 1834 in Siberia, the youngest of 15 children. His father went blind when Dmitri was young, and his mother struggled to bring up the family while running the family glass factory. She saved up to send Dmitri to be educated, though she died, exhausted, shortly after he started his studies at St Petersburg.
As well as his famous work in chemistry, Dmitri was a brilliant chemistry teacher. Everyone wanted to come to his lectures. At that time, women were not allowed in university classes, so Dmitri gave extra classes for women in his spare time. He was very down-to-earth — he always travelled third class in trains, along with the peasants, and he swore like a trooper. He cut his hair once a year, in Spring when the warm weather set in

By 1869, over 60 elements had been discovered, and scientists were wondering what to do with them all. The time was right to look for a way to classify elements. By this time, a very important piece of information was known about most elements — their atomic weights. (Nowadays we call 'atomic weight' *relative atomic mass.*)

Dmitri classifies the elements

Dmitri Mendeléev was a chemistry professor in St Petersburg, now called Leningrad, in Russia. He looked for a way to classify the elements, and he started by collecting as much information as he could about all of them. Mendeléev enjoyed playing cards, and one day he tried writing out a card for each element. On each card, he wrote the name of the element, and also its atomic weight (picture 2). The atomic weights were important because they meant he could put the cards in order (picture 3).

Next, Mendeléev tried arranging the card in sets — and he noticed an amazing thing (picture 4). *Cards with similar elements came together*. For example, sodium and potassium, both very reactive metals, came together. Fluorine and chlorine, both reactive non-metals, also came together.

From this discovery, Mendeléev made the first Periodic Table. Picture 5 shows part of it. You will see that it is different in some ways from the modern version shown on page 126. But the basic idea of vertical groups containing similar elements is the same.

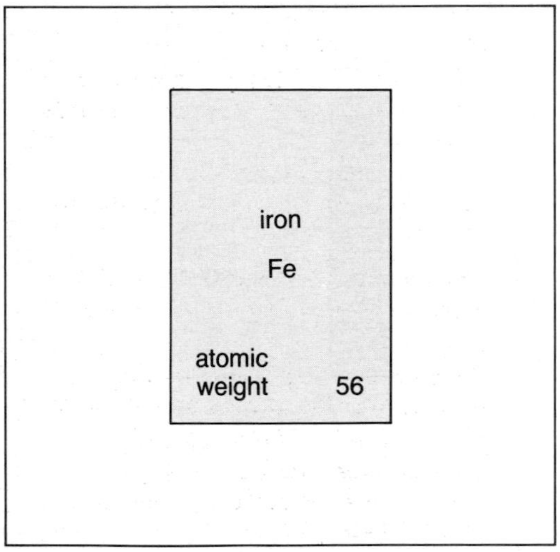

Picture 2 An 'element' card

Making predictions

Mendeléev still had to convince other scientists that his ideas were right. Many of them didn't believe in his classification. The best way to test a scientific idea is to use it to make *predictions*. If the predictions turn out to be right, people are more likely to believe your theory. You haven't *proved* the theory, because your next prediction might turn out to be wrong. But the more correct predictions you make, the more people will believe the theory.

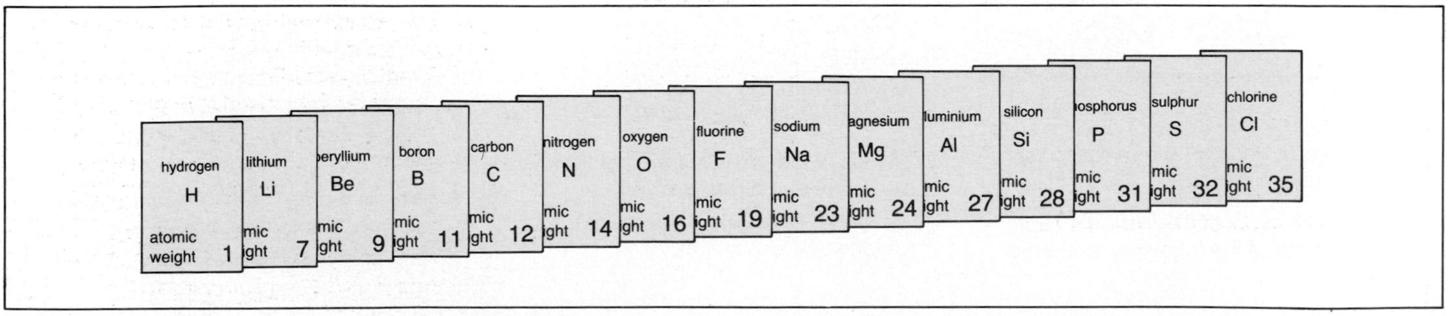

Picture 3 The cards arranged in order of atomic weight

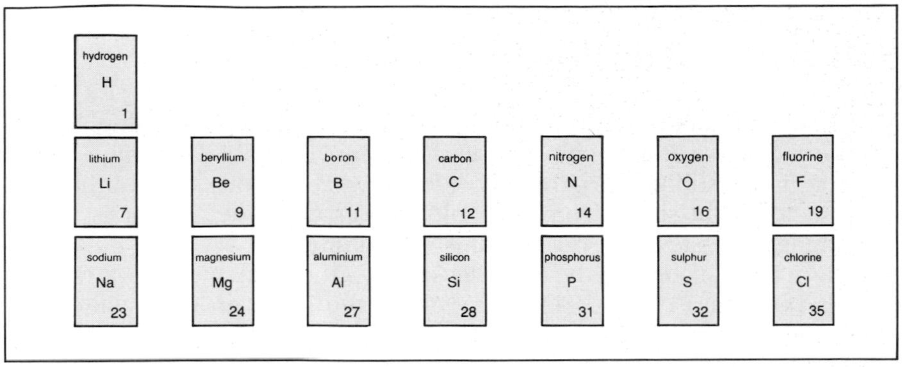

Picture 4 The cards arranged in sets

When Mendeléev drew up his Periodic Table, he found that there were gaps in it (marked ? in picture 5). He decided that these must correspond to missing elements that had not yet been discovered. He realised he could use his Periodic Table to make *predictions* about these missing elements.

For example, you can see there is a missing element between silicon, Si, and tin, Sn, in picture 5. Mendeléev knew the properties of silicon and tin, and he knew that properties change steadily as you move down a group. So he was able to predict the properties of the missing element, which he called 'eka-silicon'. For example, he predicted that the relative atomic mass of 'eka-silicon' would be the average of silicon (28.1) and tin (118.7), which comes to 73.4. He also predicted the colour (grey), density and melting point of 'eka-silicon'.

Well, in 1886 'eka-silicon' was discovered in Germany and named germanium. Sure enough, its properties were almost exactly what Mendeléev predicted. Its relative atomic mass, for instance, was 73.6, compared with the prediction of 73.4! Mendeléev's prediction about other missing elements — gallium and scandium — also turned out to be very accurate. Now everyone had to admit that he was right.

Today, you will find a modified version of Dmitri Mendeléev's Periodic Table on the walls of chemistry laboratories the world over. But remember: it was only by making successful predictions that Mendeléev convinced the world he was right.

	GROUP							
	1	2	3	4	5	6	7	8
Period 1	H							
Period 2	Li	Be	B	C	N	O	F	
Period 3	Na	Mg	Al	Si	P	S	Cl	
Period 4	K Cu	Ca Zn	? ?	Ti ?	V As	Cr Se	Mn Br	Fe Co Ni
Period 5	Rb Ag	Sr Cd	Y In	Zr Sn	Nb Sb	Mo Te	? I	Ru Rh Pd

Picture 5 Mendeléev's Periodic Table

Questions

1 You may need to re-read the topic to answer some of the following.

a Why was 'the time right' in 1869 for Mendeléev to look for a way of classifying elements?

b Mendeléev made his breakthrough by writing the names of elements on cards. Why did this help?

c Many scientists did not believe Mendeléev's ideas at first. How did he convince them?

2 Compare Mendeléev's table, as shown in picture 5, with the modern table on page 126.

a A complete group of elements is missing from Mendeléev's table. What is this group? Why is it missing?

b What is different about the way Mendeléev arranged the elements in periods 4 and 5?

c Give the symbols of the four elements (marked ?) missing from Mendeléev's table.

d Write down the dates of discovery of the four elements you listed in (c). (Use the table in the Data Section showing the dates of discoveries of elements.)

e What is different about the numbers Mendeléev used to order the elements in his Periodic Table?

3 Describe in your own words how Mendeléev predicted the properties of elements that had not yet been discovered.

F3
Sodium and family

The alkali metals are a typical group of reactive metals in the Periodic Table.

Salt without sodium

Most of us put salt on our food, but it's bad for people who have high blood pressure. Salt is sodium chloride, and the part that's bad for high blood pressure is the sodium, not the chloride. So what do you do if you like salt on your food but suffer from high blood pressure? The answer is to use something that tastes salty, but contains no sodium.

Sodium is in Group 1 of the Periodic Table — the alkali metals — and next to it is potassium (picture 1). Elements in the same group usually have similar properties. Potassium is similar to sodium — and potassium chloride is salty like sodium chloride. Elements in the same group also show differences, and unlike sodium, potassium does not cause high blood pressure. 'Low sodium' salt (picture 2) contains potassium chloride, and it's safe to eat if you have high blood pressure.

The other metals in Group 1 are lithium at the top, and rubidium, caesium and francium at the bottom. Rubidium and caesium are rare and extremely reactive, and you never meet them in school laboratories. Francium is radioactive and does not occur naturally. So in this topic we'll be looking mainly at lithium, sodium and potassium.

lithium	Li	3
sodium	Na	11
potassium	K	19
rubidium	Rb	37
caesium	Cs	55
francium	Fr	87

Picture 1 Group 1 — The alkali metals

Picture 2 "Low sodium" salt

Alkali metals are similar

The alkali metals in Group 1

- are all reactive metals. They have to be stored under oil to stop them reacting with the air
- all form ions carrying a single plus charge (e.g. Li^+, Na^+, K^+)
- form compounds with similar formulas (e.g. lithium chloride LiCl, sodium chloride NaCl, potassium chloride KCl). This is handy — if you know the formula of a sodium compound, say, you can quickly work out the formula of a similar potassium compound.
- all react with non-metals to form salts. These salts are all white, crystalline and soluble in water.
- are soft and can be cut with a knife
- all have low density — lithium, sodium and potassium will float on water.

Notice that where physical properties like strength and density are concerned, the alkali metals are pretty feeble compared with transition metals like iron and copper. But when it comes to chemical reactivity, they're much more impressive.

Alkali metals are different

The alkali metals are all very reactive, *but they get more reactive as you go down the group*. Let's look at an example.

The reaction of alkali metals with water

All the alkali metals react with water, forming hydrogen and the metal hydroxide. For example, with sodium:

$$\text{sodium} + \text{water} \rightarrow \text{sodium hydroxide} + \text{hydrogen}$$
$$2Na(s) + 2H_2O(l) \rightarrow 2NaOH(aq) + H_2(g)$$

The sodium hydroxide makes the water become alkaline. That is why these are called the alkali metals. The reaction is highly exothermic — it gives out a lot of heat.

Picture 3 shows what happens when sodium is added to water. The sodium melts and skids around on the surface of the water as hydrogen is given off. Sometimes the hydrogen catches fire — the reaction gives out enough heat to ignite it.

If you move down the group, to potassium, the reaction with water is even more vigorous. Once again hydrogen is given off, but this time it catches fire immediately, and the potassium may explode dangerously. Rubidium and caesium explode as soon as they are put into water.

Table 1 summarises the reactions of lithium, sodium and potassium with water. Notice that lithium, following the trend, reacts relatively quietly. Table 1 also shows the reaction of these three metals with air. Once again, you can see there is a gradual increase in reactivity as you go down the group.

Table 1 Reactions of lithium, sodium and potassium with water and air

Element	Reaction with water	Reaction with air
Lithium	reacts steadily $2Li(s) + 2H_2O(l) \rightarrow 2LiOH(aq) + H_2(g)$	tarnishes slowly to give a layer of oxide
Sodium	reacts vigorously $2Na(s) + 2H_2O(l) \rightarrow 2NaOH(aq) + H_2(g)$	tarnishes quickly to give a layer of oxide
Potassium	reacts violently $2K(s) + 2H_2O(l) \rightarrow 2KOH(aq) + H_2(g)$	tarnishes very quickly to give a layer of oxide

Changes in physical properties

The melting points of the alkali metals decrease gradually as you go down the group. Lithium at the top of the group melts at 180°C, caesium at the bottom melts at 29°C. There is a similar trend in the hardness of the metals. Lithium is the hardest, but it can still be cut with a knife. Sodium is easier to cut — a bit like butter from the fridge. Potassium is easier still — like butter at room temperature.

What are the alkali metals used for?

One familiar use of sodium is in sodium vapour lamps, the yellow street lamps you often see in cities. In general, though, the alkali metals are so reactive that as *elements* they have few uses. But they have many important *compounds*, and these have lots of uses.

Sodium compounds are particularly important: your home probably contains sodium chloride (salt), sodium hydrogencarbonate (bicarbonate) and sodium hydroxide (oven cleaner), to name just three. You will come across compounds of the alkali metals in several other topics in this book.

Picture 3 Sodium reacting with water

Questions

1 List the alkali metals in order of reactivity, with the most reactive first.

2 How do each of the following properties of alkali metals change as you move down the group?

a Relative atomic mass
b Melting point
c Hardness
d Density
e Chemical reactivity

3 Rubidium comes just below potassium in Group 1. Predict the following properties of rubidium.

a What happens when it is exposed to air.
b The equation for the reaction of rubidium with water.
c How readily rubidium can be cut with a knife.

4 Look at the label from 'LoSalt' shown in picture 2. Here is part of the information section of the label:

> It is suggested that people receiving medication for diabetes, heart or kidney disorders should consult their family doctor who will advise on how to use this salt alternative.
> 1 g of LoSalt contains approximately 131 mg of sodium and 346 mg of potassium.

a What is the mass in *grams* of (i) sodium (ii) potassium in 1 g of 'LoSalt'?
b Add together the masses of sodium and potassium which you worked out in (a). Why don't they add up to 1 g?
c Why do you think 'LoSalt' contains sodium chloride as well as potassium chloride? Why not potassium chloride alone, since the point of using this salt is to reduce the amount of sodium in the diet?

F4 Chlorine and family

The halogens are a typical group of non-metals in the Periodic Table.

Picture 1

Fancy a swim?

Everyone knows the smell of chlorine — it's the smell you get in swimming pools. It gets in your hair and your swimming costume, and your skin smells of it even when you are dry. What's more, the chlorine in the swimming pool water can really make your eyes sting.

Why do they put this stuff in swimming pools? The trouble is, you can easily get infected with diseases from swimming pool water. It's full of people, some of them with sore throats, ear infections or worse. And it's usually warm, which encourages the germs to breed.

The chlorine is put in the water to kill the germs. Chlorine is a reactive element, and it combines with many substances — picture 2 shows an example. Chlorine reacts with substances in the cells of living things, killing the cells. In fact, chlorine has been used as a poison gas: See *Chlorine in the First World War* on page 136.

Fortunately, there isn't enough chlorine in swimming pools to do much damage to you — apart from affecting some of the cells on the surface of your eyes. But the people who look after swimming pools do have to be careful about the amount of chlorine they use. There is more about this in activities B and C.

Picture 2 Iron wool burning in chlorine. Notice the brown iron chloride that is formed

fluorine	F	9
chlorine	Cl	17
bromine	Br	35
iodine	I	53
astatine	At	85

Picture 3 Group 7 — the halogens

Household bleach also smells of chlorine. Bleach contains chlorine and chlorine compounds. These reactive substances combine with dyes in cloth, and turn them into colourless compounds. Bleach also kills bacteria, so it's good for pouring down toilets and other places where germs may lurk.

Chlorine — a typical halogen

Chlorine has many of the typical properties of its family, the halogen family. They form Group 7 of the periodic table.

The elements in a group of the periodic table are *similar* to each other — but they also *change* gradually as you go down the group. Group 7 shows this very well (picture 3). In this topic we will concentrate mainly on the first three halogens, chlorine, bromine and iodine (picture 4). The first halogen, fluorine, is so reactive that it is very difficult to handle. The last halogen, astatine, is radioactive and does not occur naturally.

Halogens are similar

The three halogens in picture 4 don't *look* very similar. But a closer look at their properties shows they have a lot in common.

The halogens

- are all poisonous and smelly
- are all non-metals
- all form diatomic molecules (e.g. Cl_2, Br_2, I_2)
- often form compounds with similar formulas (e.g. hydrogen chloride HCl, hydrogen bromide HBr, hydrogen iodide HI)
- all react with metals to form salts
- all form ions carrying a single negative change (e.g. Cl^-, Br^-, I^-).

The best known salt is common salt, sodium chloride NaCl. It contains chlorine in the form of chloride ions, Cl^-. The other halogens form similar salts: sodium bromide and sodium iodide are white solids, very similar to common salt. They contain halide ions: Br^- and I^-.

Halogens are different

Picture 4 shows some of the differences between the halogens. Notice the gradual change in properties, from gas to liquid to solid as you go down the group. The bar chart in picture 5 compares the boiling points of the halogens. There is also a gradual change in the intensity of colour, from pale to dark.

The gradual changes you see are typical of the variation of properties in a group of non-metals. Following the trend, it will not surprise you to learn

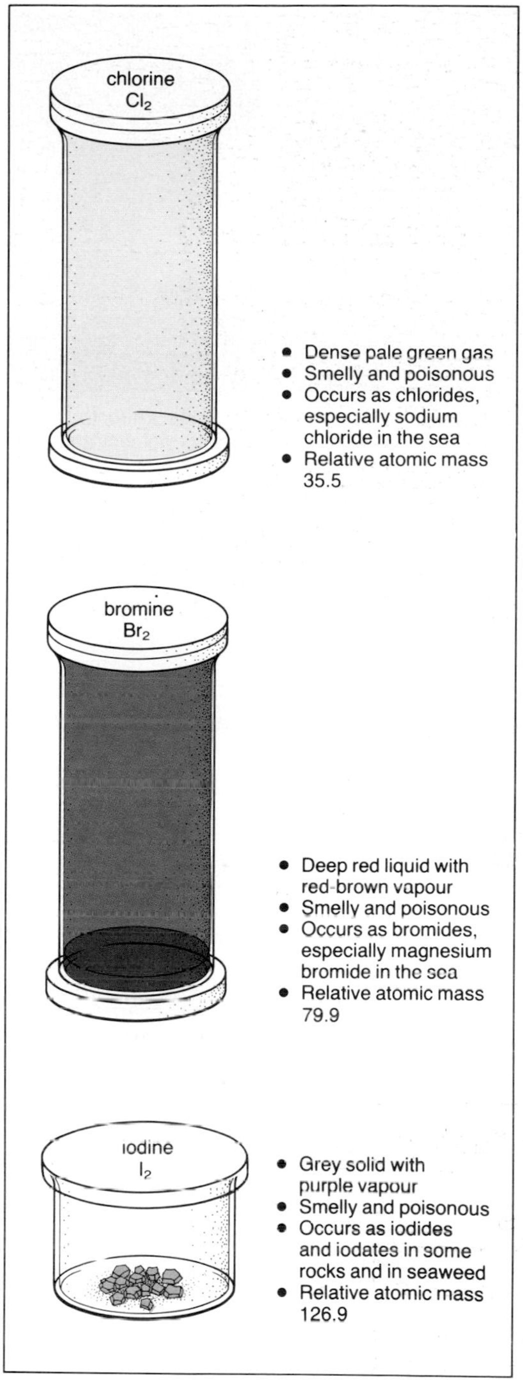

chlorine
Cl₂
• Dense pale green gas
• Smelly and poisonous
• Occurs as chlorides, especially sodium chloride in the sea
• Relative atomic mass 35.5
bromine
Br₂
• Deep red liquid with red-brown vapour
• Smelly and poisonous
• Occurs as bromides, especially magnesium bromide in the sea
• Relative atomic mass 79.9
iodine
I₂
• Grey solid with purple vapour
• Smelly and poisonous
• Occurs as iodides and iodates in some rocks and in seaweed
• Relative atomic mass 126.9

Picture 4 Chlorine, bromine and iodine

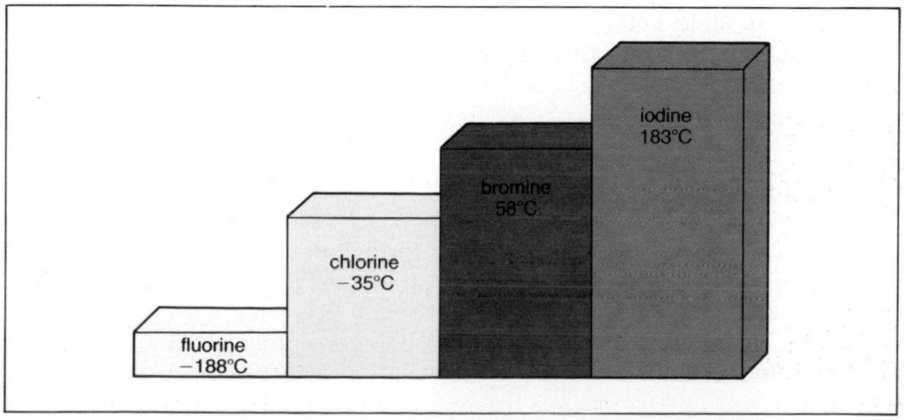

Picture 5 Boiling points of the halogens

Picture 6 When a stream of fluorine is directed onto iron wool, the iron reacts violently and forms iron fluoride

that fluorine, at the top of the group, is a pale yellow gas.

Notice that the trend within a group of *non-metals* is the opposite of that in a group of *metals* (topic F3). With non-metals, the most reactive element is at the top of the group. With metals, the most reactive element is at the *bottom* of the group.

Chemical reactivity of the halogens

The halogens are pretty reactive — in fact, fluorine is the most reactive of all the non-metals (picture 6). But once again, *there is a gradual change as you go down the group: the halogens become steadily less reactive*. Table 1 shows some examples of this. Notice the reaction with iron, for example. Chlorine reacts vigorously, but iodine hardly reacts at all.

Table 1 Some reactions of halogens

Reaction	Chlorine	Bromine	Iodine
With coloured dyes	bleaches quickly	bleaches slowly	bleaches very slowly
With iron	iron wool reacts vigorously with chlorine after heating to start it off. Iron chloride is formed. $2Fe + 3Cl_2 \rightarrow 2FeCl_3$	iron wool reacts steadily with bromine, but needs heating all the time. Iron bromide is formed. $2Fe + 3Br_2 \rightarrow 2FeBr_3$	iron wool reacts very slowly with iodine, even when heated. Iron iodide is formed. $2Fe + 3I_2 \rightarrow 2FeI_3$
With chlorides	no reaction	no reaction	no reaction
With bromides	displaces bromine e.g. $Cl_2 + 2NaBr \rightarrow Br_2 + 2NaCl$	no reaction	no reaction
With iodides	displaces iodine e.g. $Cl_2 + 2NaI \rightarrow I_2 + 2NaCl$	displaces iodine e.g. $Br_2 + 2NaI \rightarrow I_2 + 2NaBr$	no reaction

Displacement reactions of halogens

Table 1 shows how halogens react with compounds of other halogens. Look at the reactions of the three halogens with bromides, for example. If you add chlorine to a solution of sodium bromide, the chlorine **displaces** bromine. Chlorine is more reactive than bromine, so it takes its place and forms sodium chloride.

$$\text{chlorine} + \text{sodium bromide} \rightarrow \text{bromine} + \text{sodium chloride}$$
$$Cl_2(aq) + 2NaBr(aq) \rightarrow Br_2(aq) + 2NaCl(aq)$$

The results in table 1 show the general rule that **a more reactive halogen will displace a less reactive one from its compounds**. You can try some of these reactions in activity D.

Using halogens

Because halogens are so reactive, they form lots of compounds. Many of these compounds are useful for making all sorts of things we need. Picture 7 shows some of them.

Chlorine is the most useful of all the halogens, and is manufactured in large amounts by the electrolysis of salt solution. There is more about this in topic D5.

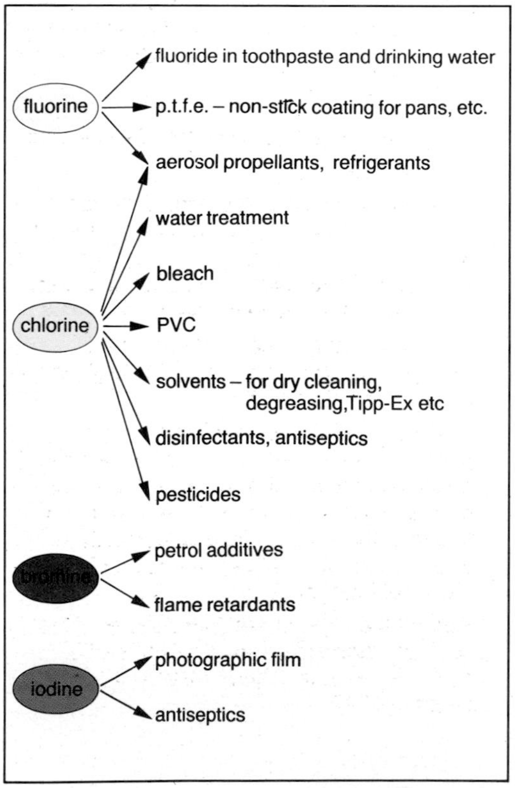

Picture 7 Some of the important uses of the halogens

Picture 8 "Halon" fire extinguishers use an unreactive compound, containing flouorine, chlorine and bromine

Activities

A Comparing halogens as bleaches

You will need a solution of a vegetable dye such as litmus, and solutions of chlorine, bromine and iodine in water.
(**CARE** Corrosive. Eye protection must be worn.)

Plan an experiment to compare the bleaching action of chlorine, bromine and iodine. Your results should enable you to put the halogens in order of their power as bleaches. Show your plan to your teacher before you carry out the experiment.

You will have to bear in mind that the halogens are coloured, and this may make it difficult to see if bleaching has happened. How will you get over this problem?

B Chlorine in swimming pools

Try to find out about chlorine in swimming pools by talking to the people who look after them. For a school swimming pool, this will probably be the school caretaker. Ask these questions:

1. In what form is chlorine added to the pool? Is chlorine gas used? If not, why not?
2. How do you test to see if the right amount of chlorine is present?
3. Is the same amount of chlorine always used? Or is more needed at some times than at others?

C Testing for chlorine in swimming pools

It is important to make sure that the concentration of chlorine in a pool is right. Too much, and the swimmers suffer. Too little, and the germs won't be killed. There are several different ways of testing for chlorine. The one here uses the fact that chlorine bleaches a dye called methyl orange — but only if there is a high enough concentration of chlorine.

You will need a test solution of methyl orange which has been specially made. (**CARE:** Corrosive. Eye protection must be worn.) The solution contains:

0.05 g methyl orange
2.0 g sodium chloride
350 cm^3 dilute (2M) hydrochloric acid
750 cm^3 water.

You will also need a sample of swimming pool water. If you can get several samples you can make interesting comparisons. Your samples could be from different pools, or from the same pool on different days. But the samples must be tested straight after taking them from the pool. (Why do you think this is?)

1 Is there enough chlorine?
Put 0.25 cm^3 of your test solution in a test tube. Add 10 cm^3 of the sample of pool water. If the test solution is bleached at once, this means there is at least 0.001 g of chlorine in each litre of water. This is enough to kill germs. If the solution is not bleached at once it means there is too little chlorine.

2 Is there too much chlorine?
Repeat the test, but this time use 0.75 cm^3 of test solution. If it is bleached at once, there is at least 0.00175 g of chlorine in each litre of water. This is too high.

Looking at your results
Compare your results with other groups. Do you all agree? If not, what might be the reason? Will your results necessarily agree with those of the school caretaker? If not, what might be the reason? Who is more likely to be right?

D Displacement reactions of halogens

You will need:

solutions of chlorine, bromine and iodine (**CARE**: Corrosive. Eye protection must be worn.)
solutions of potassium chloride, potassium bromide and potassium iodide.

Before you start, read the experiment through. Then draw up a suitable table to put your results in.

Put about 2 cm^3 of potassium chloride, potassium bromide and potassium iodide solution in each of three test tubes. Add a roughly equal amount of chlorine solution to each tube in turn. Observe carefully what happens. Has the chlorine displaced the other halogen?

Repeat the experiment using first bromine solution, then iodine solution, instead of chlorine. Do your results agree with table 1 on page 134?

Questions

1 List the halogens in order of reactivity, with the most reactive first.

2 How do each of the following properties of the halogens change as you go down the group?
a Boiling point
b Melting point
c Intensity of colour
d Relative atomic mass

3 Fluorine (F_2), at the top of group 7, is the most reactive halogen. Make predictions about the following reactions involving fluorine. In each case, say what will happen, and write equations for the reactions in (b) and (c).
a A red dye is exposed to fluorine.
b Iron wool is put in a jar of fluorine.
c Fluorine is added to a solution of potassium chloride.

4 Astatine, At, is the last element in Group 7. Very little is known about its properties, because it is radioactive and unstable. Predict the following properties of astatine, using the information about other halogens given in this topic.
a The formula of astatine molecules.
b The appearance of astatine.
c The boiling point of astatine.
d The reaction, if any, of astatine with iron.

5 The name 'halogen' comes from Greek words meaning 'salt maker'. Why do you think this name was chosen?

Chlorine in the First World War

GAS! GAS! Quick, boys! — An ecstasy of fumbling,
Fitting the clumsy helmets just in time;
But someone still was yelling out and stumbling,
And flound'ring like a man in fire or lime...
Dim, through the misty panes and thick green light,
As under a green sea, I saw him drowning.

From *Dulce et Decorum est* by Wilfred Owen, 1917

Chlorine was used as a poison gas in the First World War by both sides. Chlorine affects the cells which line the lungs, and makes them produce a lot of fluid. This fills the lungs, and the victim literally drowns. Those who were not killed by the gas attacks often suffered permanent damage to their lungs which made them invalids for the rest of their lives.

The first chlorine attack was in the Battle of Ypres in 1915. The Germans released 170 tonnes of chlorine from cylinders. The dense gas stayed close to the ground and rolled towards the Allied trenches, blown by a gentle breeze. There were 15 000 casualties, of whom 5000 died.

1 Apart from being poisonous, which other property of chlorine makes it suitable for gas warfare? Could other halogens be used in the same way? Explain.

2 Many other poison gases, even nastier than chlorine, were invented during the First World War. When the Second World War came, everyone expected poison gas attacks, but none came. Why do you think poison gas never became a major weapon?

3 Most countries have now signed an agreement not to use chemical weapons. Why do you think poison gases have been outlawed, but bullets have not?

Picture 1 In the second world war, gas attacks were feared, and everyone was issued with gas masks, but the attacks never came

How the noble gases were found

Some people stand out in a crowd — they are active and colourful, and you can't help noticing them. Other people are quieter and you hardly notice them at all. Just imagine if those people were *invisible* as well as quiet. Picking them out would be a real problem.

Discovering the noble gases was rather like discovering a silent, motionless, invisible person in a crowded room. In 1894, there was no reason to suspect they existed at all.

In that year, Sir William Ramsay did an interesting experiment. He wanted to see what happened when you remove all the gases from air. He did this by passing air over heated copper and heated magnesium. He *expected* to have nothing left at the end. He reasoned that everything in the air would react, either with the hot copper, or with the hot magnesium. *In fact* he found that from every 100 cm^3 of air, about 1 cm^3 always remained behind.

Picture 2 Sir William Ramsay

William Ramsay was such a good experimenter that he knew he hadn't made an error. No matter how often he repeated the experiment, he always had the same proportion of gas left behind. He did lots of experiments on the left-over gas to try and make it react with something. He tried the most reactive substances he knew, including fluorine, phosphorus and potassium, but it never did anything. So he called this rather boring new gas argon, from a Greek word meaning lazy or inactive.

Discovering a new element is always fun, but argon was a problem as far as the Periodic Table was concerned. There was no gap for it to fit into. William Ramsay made a bold prediction. He said there could be only one explanation — argon must be just one member of a *whole new family*. He predicted that other, similar elements must exist, and he started doing experiments to try and find the missing members of the family.

He soon found the first one. In 1868 astronomers had seen a certain frequency of light from the Sun which didn't correspond to any known element. They suggested there must be a new element on the Sun, and they called it helium after the Greek word for the Sun. In 1895 William Ramsay showed that helium also exists on Earth, and that it is a very unreactive gas — like argon.

He examined liquid air in his hunt for other members of the family, and eventually discovered neon, krypton and xenon. Apart from the radioactive gas radon, this completed the family, which we now call the noble gases (table 1). It was a triumph for William Ramsay — and yet another triumph for Dmitri Mendeléev, whose great idea of the Periodic Table led Ramsay to look for the whole family, not just the commonest member.

Picture 3 Helium is very light and unreactive, which makes it safe for filling airships

Table 1 may help you with some of these questions.

1 Why were the noble gases a particularly difficult group of elements to discover?
2 Why was argon easier to find than the other noble gases?
3 Why was it important that William Ramsay's experiments were very accurate?
4 William Ramsay named the first noble gas that he discoverered *argon*. Was it actually pure argon?
5 What made William Ramsay look for other noble gases as soon as he had discovered the first one?
6 Why are two dates given for the discovery of helium?
7 Although the noble gases are very unreactive, some of them have in fact been made to combine with other elements. Use advanced books to find out about some of the compounds of the noble gases.

Table 1 The noble gases

Name	*Symbol*	*Atomic number*	*Percentage in dry air*	*Chemical reactivity*	*Date of discovery*
helium	He	2	0.0005	extremely unreactive	1868/1895
neon	Ne	10	0.0018	extremely unreactive	1898
argon	Ar	18	0.93	extremely unreactive	1894
krypton	Kr	36	0.0001	extremely unreactive	1898
xenon	Xe	54	0.00001	extremely unreactive	1898
radon	Rn	86	usually too little to detect	extremely unreactive (but radioactive)	1900

G1 Looking at acids

Acids can be nasty, but they are also very useful. In this topic, we see what acids are like.

Picture 1 An ant biting a termite. The ant makes a wound with its jaws, and then sprays on formic acid

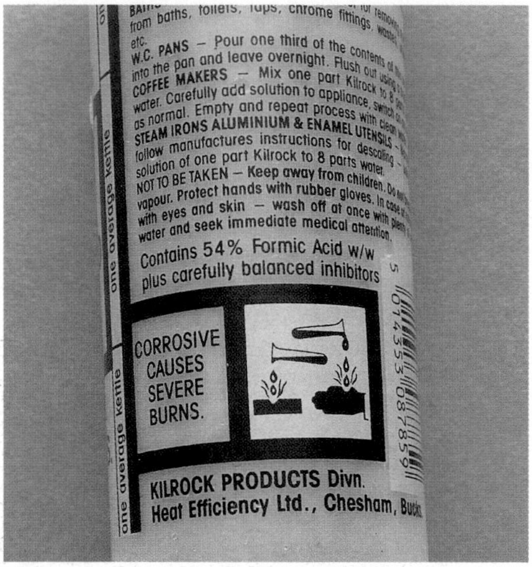

Picture 2 This kettle descaler contains formic acid. The acid is strong enough to react with calcium carbonate, but not strong enough to damage the metal

Picture 1 shows an ant biting its victim. As it bites, it sprays acid onto the open wound. No wonder it stings. The acid it uses is called formic acid, after the Latin word *formica*, meaning an ant. Not long ago, people used to make formic acid by boiling up a saucepanful of ants. Picture 2 shows a more agreeable use of formic acid — to descale kettles. Like all acids, it reacts with carbonates — and kettle scale is calcium carbonate.

Living things are very sensitive to acids, and too much acid can kill (see later). Fortunately, your body is able to use bases (topic G2) to neutralise acid — even if you live off acid drops and salt and vinegar crisps!

What do acids do?

Table 1 summarises some of the most important properties of acids. Let's look at some of them.

Table 1 Typical properties of acids

Acids taste sour
Acids kill cells
Acids react with metals, giving off hydrogen
Acids are neutralised by bases, forming salts
Acids react with carbonates, giving carbon dioxide
Acids change the colour of indicators
Acids have pH less than 7

Acids kill cells, or stop them working properly

This makes acids dangerous to handle. The most vulnerable part of you is your eyes, because they have living cells on the surface. **You should never let acids get on your skin, and you should always wear eye protection when you are handling acids.**

But this property can be useful too, because acids kill undesirable things like bacteria in food. Pickling food in vinegar (acetic acid) is an ancient way of preserving it (picture 3). It makes the food taste sour, but many people like the taste, so we go on pickling food even though we have other ways of preserving it.

Acids react with metals, giving off hydrogen

Metals that are above copper in the reactivity series react with acids, and hydrogen is given off. The metal forms a salt and dissolves. This is why acids are so corrosive to metals (picture 4). For example, magnesium reacts with sulphuric acid:

$$\text{magnesium} + \text{sulphuric acid} \rightarrow \text{magnesium sulphate} + \text{hydrogen}$$
$$Mg(s) + H_2SO_4(aq) \rightarrow MgSO_4(aq) + H_2(g)$$

There is more about the reaction of metals with acids in topic E2.

Picture 4 This tanker is carrying acid. It is made of steel, but inside it is lined with glass. Why?

Picture 3 This cabbage has been pickled, and it will stay edible for years because it is too acidic for bacteria to grow. The cabbage was purple before it was pickled — why has the colour changed?

Acids are neutralised by bases

There is more about neutralisation and bases in topic G2. **Alkalis** are a special type of base. In many ways, alkalis are the opposite of acids.

Acids react with carbonates, giving off carbon dioxide

All carbonates fizz in acid, giving off carbon dioxide. The carbonate forms a salt and usually dissolves. This is why acid rain dissolves buildings made of limestone, which is calcium carbonate.

For example, when copper carbonate reacts with hydrochloric acid:

copper carbonate + hydrochloric acid
→ copper chloride + carbon dioxide + water

$$CuCO_3(s) + 2HCl(aq) \rightarrow CuCl_2(aq) + CO_2(g) + H_2O(l)$$

There is more about this kind of reaction in topic G3.

What's going on?

There are many different acids. Table 2 shows some of them. Clearly they must have something in common, because they have similar properties.

Table 2 Some common acids

Name	Formula	Strong or weak?	Where it's found
hydrochloric acid	HCl	strong	• in the stomach • many important uses
sulphuric acid	H_2SO_4	strong	• in acid rain • many important uses
nitric acid	HNO_3	strong	• in acid rain • many important uses
acetic acid	CH_3COOH	weak	• in vinegar
formic acid	$HCOOH$	weak	• ants, nettles
citric acid	$C_6H_8O_7$	weak	• in lemons, oranges, other citrus fruits

Picture 5 The limestone (calcium carbonate) in this gravestone has slowly reacted with acid in the rain over many years

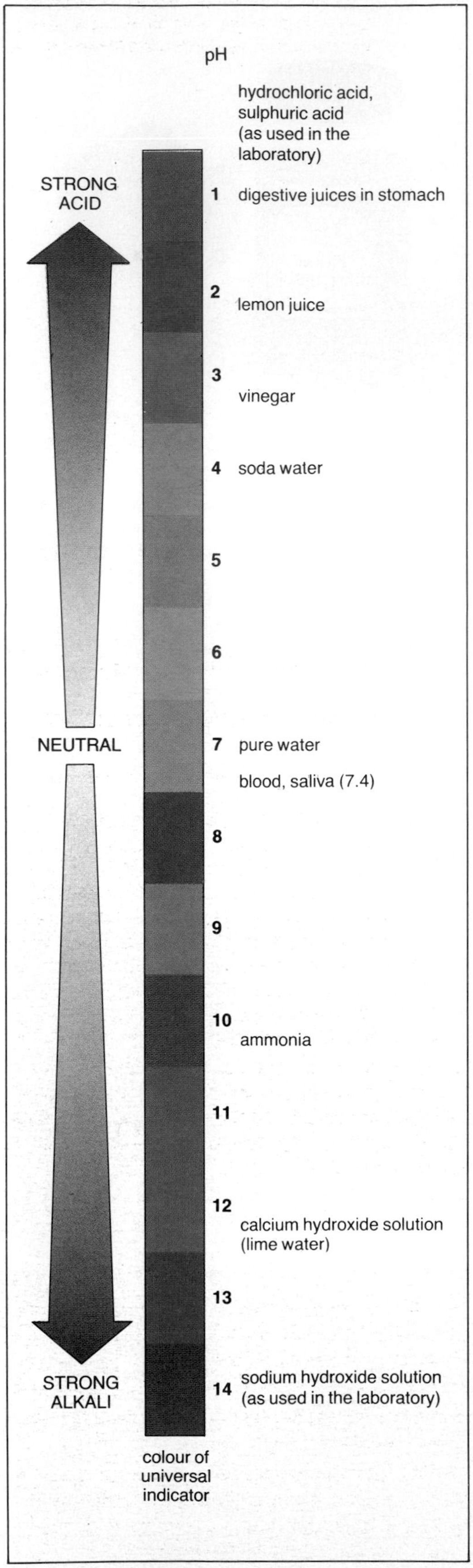

Picture 6 The pH scale. This shows the pH of some common substances. The colours shown are a rough guide only, because they vary according to the brand of indicator used

Look at the formulas of the acids in table 2. You will see that they all contain the element hydrogen, H. But there are plenty of substances that contain hydrogen that are *not* acids — water, to name just one.

To be an acid, a substance must contain hydrogen in the form of hydrogen ions, H^+.

There is more about this idea in topic G3.

When a metal reacts with an acid, the hydrogen in the acid is replaced by the metal. The hydrogen is given off as a gas. So in the reaction of magnesium with sulphuric acid, H_2SO_4, hydrogen gets replaced by magnesium, giving magnesium sulphate, $MgSO_4$.

When a base neutralises an acid, it reacts with the hydrogen ions and turns them into neutral water. More about this in topics G2 and G3.

Indicators — the acid detectors

Indicators are substances that change colour depending on whether they are in acidic or alkaline solution. Litmus is a common indicator. It is red in acid and blue in alkali. Many natural plant colours are indicators — there's an example in picture 3. Some flowers actually change colour because of changes in acidity.

Universal indicator is a mixture of indicators. It can have several different colours, depending on the pH (picture 6).

The pH scale

The pH scale is a measure of acidity. On the pH scale:

Acids have pH less than 7
Neutral substances, like water, have a pH of 7
Alkalis have a pH greater than 7.

The stronger an acid, the lower its pH. Picture 6 shows the pH of some common substances.

Living things can only survive within a narrow range of pH values. Human blood normally has a pH of 7.4, and your body only works within the pH range 7.0 to 7.8. One of the problems with acid rain is that it makes the pH of lakes and rivers too low for many organisms to survive (see *Bringing Trout Back to Loch Fleet* on page 147).

Strong and weak acids

Picture 6 shows that the hydrochloric acid you use in the laboratory has a lower pH than vinegar. This means the hydrochloric acid is more acidic. There are two reasons for this.

Vinegar contains an acid called acetic acid. Like most of the **organic** acids made by living things, acetic acid is a fairly weak acid. Hydrochloric acid is a much stronger acid.

Also, the solution of hydrochloric acid you use in the laboratory is more concentrated than the acetic acid solution in vinegar. Both hydrochloric acid and vinegar are solutions in water, but in vinegar the acid is more dilute (watered down) than in hydrochloric acid. If you added water to the hydrochloric acid, you could dilute it enough to have the same pH as the vinegar.

Often a weak acid is preferable to a strong one. Hydrochloric acid is too strong to put on food, so we use weak acids like acetic acid (vinegar) and citric acid (lemon juice). For de-furring a kettle, a weak acid like formic acid is less likely to corrode the metal than a strong acid like sulphuric acid.

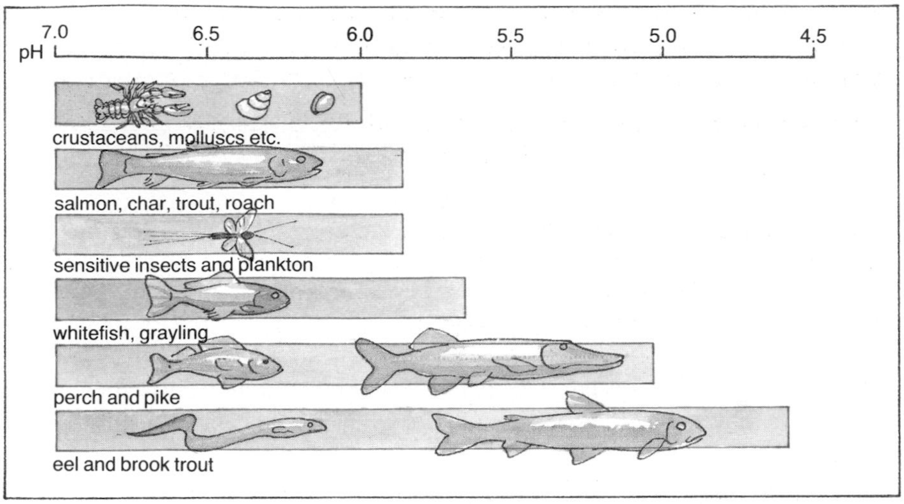

Picture 7 Some organisms can tolerate acid water better than others. This chart shows the pH range in which different organisms can survive

Surprisingly, we all have a strong acid in our stomachs. It is hydrochloric acid, and it helps to digest food (see *The Living World*, topic C8). Fortunately, it is a fairly dilute solution, and the stomach has a special lining to stop it doing much harm. But sometimes your stomach produces too much hydrochloric acid, and then you may suffer from acid indigestion.

Activities

A What do people think acids are?

Everyone has heard of acids, but their ideas are not always very scientific! Try asking people (family, neighbours, friends) what they think acids are. You could ask some of these questions:

1 What do acids do?
2 What different kinds of acids are there?
3 *Why* do acids behave the way they do? (A tricky one, this!)

B Hunt the acid

Many foods and drinks have acids added to them. Look at the ingredients lists of some food and drink items. Find at least 10 that contain acids. Make a list of your results, showing the food or drink item and the acid it contains.

After you have done your survey, answer these questions.

1 How many different acids did you find?
2 Why do you think manufacturers put acids in foods and drinks?
3 Are the acids that are used generally strong or weak?
4 Only certain acids are permitted by the government for use in food and drinks. Why are some acids permitted, but not others?

C Comparing the pH of drinks

Acid causes tooth decay. Decay happens when the pH is lower than 5.5. Are some drinks acidic enough to cause decay?

Plan an experiment to compare the pH of drinks. The drinks you test must include the following: tap water, cola, fizzy lemonade, blackcurrant, orange squash, milk.

You will need to bear the following points in mind.

- The pH of the different drinks will be quite similar. You need to plan a method that will be *as accurate as possible*, so you can detect small differences in pH.
- You must test the drink in the form in which you would actually drink it. For example, when you test orange squash you should dilute it first.
- Some of the drinks are coloured. What problems will this cause? How will you get over them?

Get your plan checked by your teacher before you start work. What do your results suggest? What other factors, apart from pH, might make drinks cause tooth decay?

Questions

1 How do acids react with each of the following?
a Reactive metals
b Bases
c Carbonates

2 What acid would you find in each of the following places?
a A car battery b A grapefruit
c Your stomach d Vinegar

3 For each of the following, say whether you think it would have a pH of
A above 5 **B** about 7 **C** below 9
a vinegar
b rain water
c sulphuric acid used in the laboratory
d sodium hydroxide solution used in the laboratory
e sea water
f sodium hydrogencarbonate solution.

4 Hydrochloric acid and sulphuric acid are both acids.
a Give *three* properties that you would expect *both* these acids to have.
b Give *one* difference between these two acids.

5 Some people like lemon in tea instead of milk. When you put a piece of lemon into tea, the colour of the tea changes slightly. Why do you think this happens?

G2 Neutralising acids

Bases neutralise acids, forming salts.

Acids corrode many things, including teeth (picture 1). Acid forms in your mouth after you have eaten sugary food. Decay starts when the pH is lower than 5.5. (Remember: the stronger the acid, the lower the pH.) Picture 2 shows how the pH in your mouth changes as a result of eating a sweet.

Tooth enamel is the hardest material in your body. It is made from a form of calcium phosphate. This substance is insoluble in water, but it does dissolve in acid. When the pH in your mouth gets lower than 5.5, tooth enamel starts to dissolve — and then you're in trouble.

The best way to avoid tooth decay is to avoid eating sugary food. Cleaning your teeth helps too: for one thing, it clears away at least some of the bacteria which make the acid (see *The Living World*, topic C9). Many toothpastes also help to take away the acidity. This is because they contain a substance which will **neutralise** acids — a **base**. In activity D you can measure the pH of a toothpaste: what do you expect it to be?

People often need to neutralise acids. Picture 3 shows the pH conditions preferred by different vegetables. You can see that many vegetables dislike acid soil. A gardener uses a base such as lime (calcium hydroxide) or limestone (calcium carbonate) to neutralise acid in the soil.

People use bases — also called **anti-acids** — to neutralize stomach acid when they have indigestion. Magnesium hydroxide ('Milk of Magnesia') is often used. We use bases like sodium hydrogencarbonate to treat acid insect bites and stings.

What kind of substances are bases?

Bases are usually oxides, hydroxides or carbonates of metals. Table 1 lists some examples. (By the way, ammonia is a rather unusual base, because it doesn't contain a metal. There is more about ammonia as a base in topic D4.)

You may not have come across the word base in a chemical sense before — in everyday language it has a quite different meaning. But you may well have heard the word **alkali**. An alkali is a special kind of base — a base that dissolves in water (picture 4). Most of the bases in table 1 are also alkalis, because they dissolve in water. When they dissolve, they give a solution whose pH is greater than 7. The stronger the alkali, the higher the pH.

Like acids, strong alkalis are corrosive and dangerous. Sodium hydroxide is often called 'caustic soda' — caustic means burning. In fact, alkalis can do even more damage to your skin and eyes than acids. **Never let alkalis get on your skin, and always wear eye protection when you are using them.**

Picture 1 This tooth is being dissolved by a strong acid. In your mouth the acid is not so strong, but it still attacks your teeth

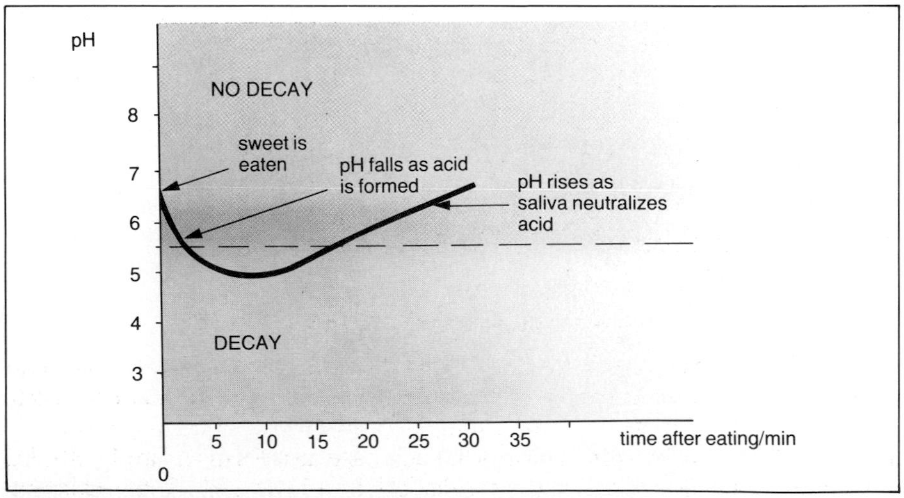

Picture 2 How the pH in your mouth changes after eating a sweet

Table 1 Some important bases. Those marked * are also alkalis

Name	Formula	Where it is used
* sodium hydroxide (caustic soda)	NaOH	in the home, for removing grease many uses in industry
* calcium hydroxide	$Ca(OH)_2$	in farms and gardens, to neutralise soil acidity
magnesium oxide	MgO	in the home, as an 'anti-acid' medicine
calcium carbonate	$CaCO_3$	in farms and gardens, and to neutralise acidified lakes
* sodium hydrogencarbonate (bicarbonate of soda)	$NaHCO_3$	in the home, as an 'anti-acid' medicine and in baking powder
* ammonia	NH_3	in the home, as a cleaning liquid many uses in industry

There are strong and weak alkalis, just as there are strong and weak acids. Sodium hydroxide is a strong alkali, but magnesium hydroxide is weak — which is why it is safe to use it as an anti-acid to treat indigestion.

The pH of *saliva* is just over 7. This means saliva is very slightly alkaline, so it can neutralise acid in your mouth. Chewing-gum manufacturers claim that chewing can help reduce tooth decay, because it makes the saliva flow. (But chewing-gum usually contains sugar. . .)

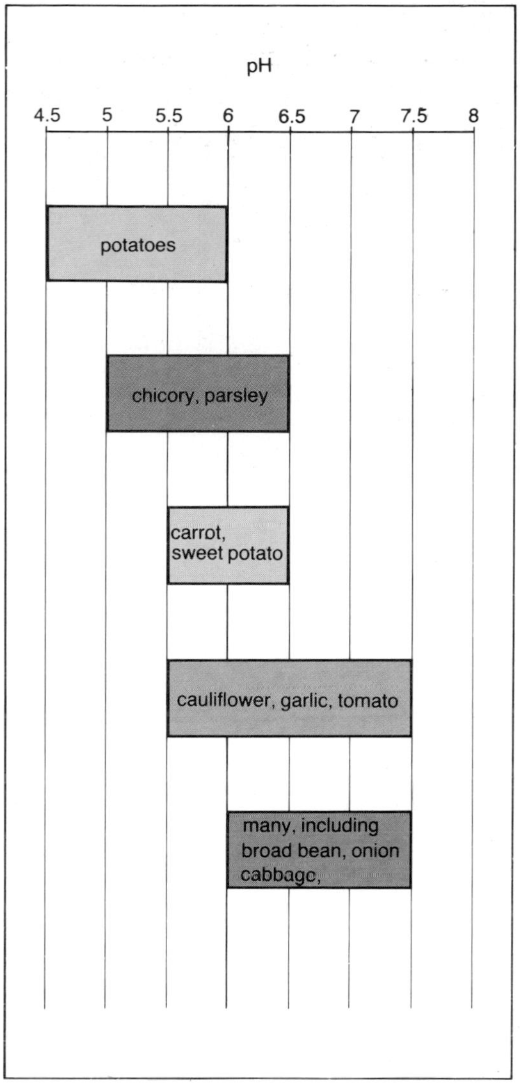

Picture 3 The pH conditions preferred by different vegetables

What happens when a base neutralises an acid?

Acids contain hydrogen ions, H^+. When a base neutralises an acid, it joins with the H^+ and turns it into neutral water (more about this in topic G3). At the same time, the metal in the base takes the place of the hydrogen in the acid, and forms a metal compound called a **salt**.

For example, when hydrochloric acid is neutralized by sodium hydroxide:

hydrochloric acid + sodium hydroxide → sodium chloride + water

$HCl(aq) + NaOH(aq) \rightarrow NaCl(aq) + H_2O(l)$

Notice that the sodium, Na, has taken the place of hydrogen, H, in the acid, forming sodium chloride, NaCl. Sodium chloride is a salt — the common salt we put on our food. But scientists use the word 'salt' to describe *any* compound formed by the reaction between a base and an acid. All salts contain two parts: a metal part which comes from the base, and a non-metal part which comes from the acid. So there are lots of salts, of which sodium chloride is just one.

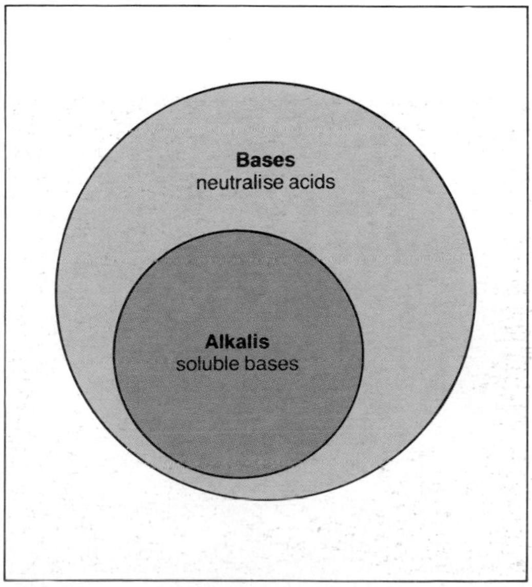

Picture 4 Bases and alkalis

Making salts

The same general reaction happens whenever an acid is neutralised by a base. We can summarise it as

acid + base → salt + water

If the base happens to be a carbonate, then carbon dioxide is formed as well.

Table 2 shows some more examples of making salts. Notice that each acid has its own family of salts — for example, sulphuric acid forms sulphates, and hydrochloric acid forms chlorides. Each base also forms a family of salts — sodium hydroxide forms sodium salts, calcium hydroxide forms calcium salts.

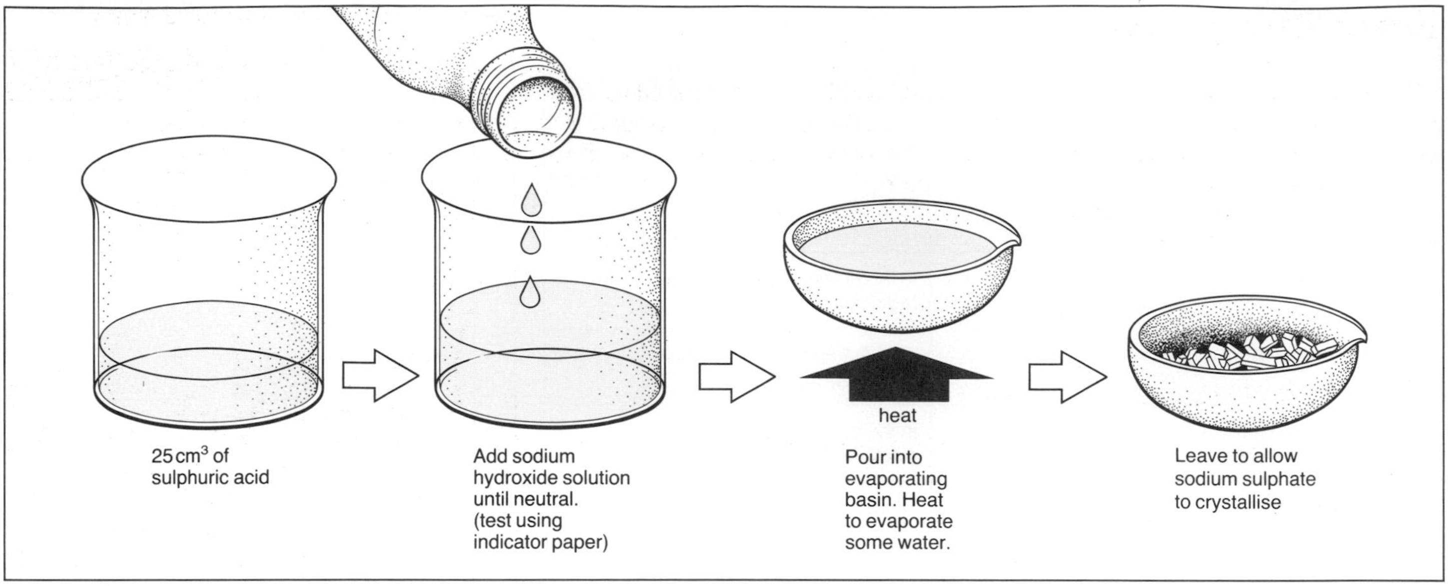

Picture 5 Making sodium sulphate

Table 2 Some examples of making salts

ACIDS / BASES	**Sulphuric acid** forms *sulphates* containing SO_4^{2-}	**nitric acid** forms *nitrates* containing NO_3^-	**hydrochloric acid** forms *chlorides* containing Cl^-
Sodium hydroxide forms *sodium salts* containing Na^+	sodium sulphate Na_2SO_4	sodium nitrate $NaNO_3$	sodium chloride $NaCl$
Calcium hydroxide forms *calcium salts* containing Ca^{2+}	calcium sulphate $CaSO_4$	calcium nitrate $Ca(NO_3)_2$	calcium chloride $CaCl_2$
magnesium oxide forms *magnesium salts* containing Mg^{2+}	magnesium sulphate $MgSO_4$	magnesium nitrate $Mg(NO_3)_2$	magnesium chloride $MgCl_2$

If you want to make a salt, you choose a suitable acid and base and mix them to give a neutral solution of the salt you want. You can then get crystals of the salt by evaporating away the water. Picture 5 shows what you might do if you wanted to make sodium sulphate.

A traditional way of cleaning tarnished copper is by rubbing it with a piece of lemon. Can you see how this works? The tarnish on the metal is a layer of oxide. Metal oxides are bases, and lemons contain citric acid. So when you rub the copper with the lemon, a salt is formed (copper citrate), and this makes the tarnish dissolve away.

Picture 6 Crystals of fluorite, Calcium fluoride. Like many minerals, fluorite is a salt

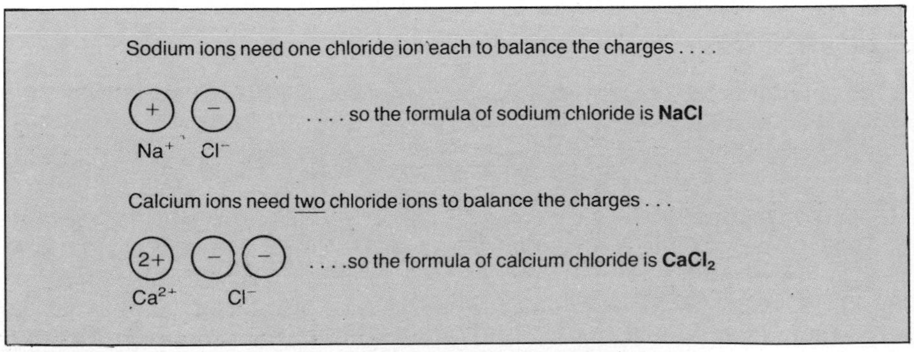

Sodium ions need one chloride ion each to balance the charges . . . .
+ −
Na⁺ Cl⁻
. . . . so the formula of sodium chloride is NaCl
Calcium ions need two chloride ions to balance the charges . . .
2+ − −
Ca²⁺ Cl⁻
. . . .so the formula of calcium chloride is CaCl₂

Picture 7 The formulas of sodium chloride and calcium chloride

More about salts

All salts are ionic compounds — the base provides the positive metal ion and the acid provides the negative non-metal ion (there is more about ionic bonding in topic J5). Like other ionic compounds, salts are crystalline, have high melting points, and often dissolve in water.

Many salts occur in the earth as minerals. Calcium sulphate (gypsum) and calcium fluoride (fluorite) are examples (picture 6). If the salt is soluble in water, it is likely to get washed out of the earth by rain and end up in the sea. That's why the sea is so salty.

Working out the formula of a salt

Salts are ionic, and ions have electrical charges. Yet you don't get an electric shock when you handle a salt. This is because the ionic charges cancel out. There are equal numbers of + and − charges.

Sodium chloride, NaCl, is a simple example. It contains Na^+ and Cl^- in equal numbers, so there are as many + charges as − charges. Overall there is no electrical charge. But suppose we swap the sodium for calcium. Calcium ions are Ca^{2+}, so we need *two* Cl^- ions to balance them. So calcium chloride is $Ca^{2+}(Cl^-)_2$, or $CaCl_2$ (picture 7).

Now think about aluminium nitrate. Aluminium ions have three charges, Al^{3+}. Nitrate ions have one charge, NO_3^-. So Al^{3+} needs three NO_3^- ions to balance its charge, and the formula is $Al^{3+}(NO_3^-)_3$, or $Al(NO_3)_3$. The brackets show that the NO_3 is a single unit, and all of the NO_3 group is multiplied by 3.

Table 3 gives the charges on some ions that are often found in salts. Use the table to answer question 5.

Table 3 Some ions commonly found in salts

Metal ions	Non-metal ions
sodium Na^+	chloride Cl^-
potassium K^+	bromide Br^-
calcium Ca^{2+}	iodide I^-
magnesium Mg^{2+}	sulphate SO_4^{2-}
aluminium Al^{3+}	nitrate NO_3^-
iron (II) Fe^{2+}	phosphate PO_4^{3-}
iron (III) Fe^{3+}	
copper Cu^{2+}	
zinc Zn^{2+}	
ammonium NH_4^+	

Some salts containing these ions:
potassium iodide K^+I^- or KI
iron (II) sulphate $Fe^{2+}SO_4^{2-}$ or $FeSO_4$
zinc chloride $Zn(Cl^-)_2$ or $ZnCl_2$
sodium phosphate $(Na^+)_3\ PO_4^{3-}$ or Na_3PO_4

Activities

CARE: Whenever you are doing experiments involving acids or alkalis, remember to wear eye protection. Do not let acids or alkalis come into contact with your skin.

A Cleaning tarnished copper with acid

Get a piece of tarnished copper and a slice of lemon. Test the idea that the copper can be cleaned by rubbing with the lemon.

When you have tried a lemon, plan experiments to test other acids to see if they work better. You might try the following acids: vinegar, dilute hydrochloric acid, dilute sulphuric acid. Do not try your experiment until you have discussed it with your teacher.

B Testing the dock leaf theory

There is a traditional saying that dock leaves take away the pain of nettle stings.

Suggest a hypothesis that might explain this saying. Then collect some dock leaves and test your hypothesis.

C Testing the pH of toothpaste

For this experiment you will need a range of toothpastes — at least three different brands. Plan and carry out an experiment to compare the pH of the different toothpastes. What can you deduce from the results?

D What is the best pH for a shampoo?

Test the effect of acidic, alkaline and neutral conditions on hair.

1 Get a sample of human hair. Soak the hair in acidic, alkaline and neutral solutions using the method shown in picture 8. Leave it soaking for 30 minutes. Make sure you treat each sample of hair in exactly the same way.

2 Remove each hair sample in turn and rinse it very thoroughly with cold water. Put each sample on a different piece of filter paper and let it dry.

3 Test each sample of hair carefully in the following ways.

a) Look at it under a hand lens or a microscope on low power.

b) Test the strength of a single hair by trying to stretch it.

c) Run your finger up and down the hair. How does it feel?

What do you conclude about the best pH for a shampoo?

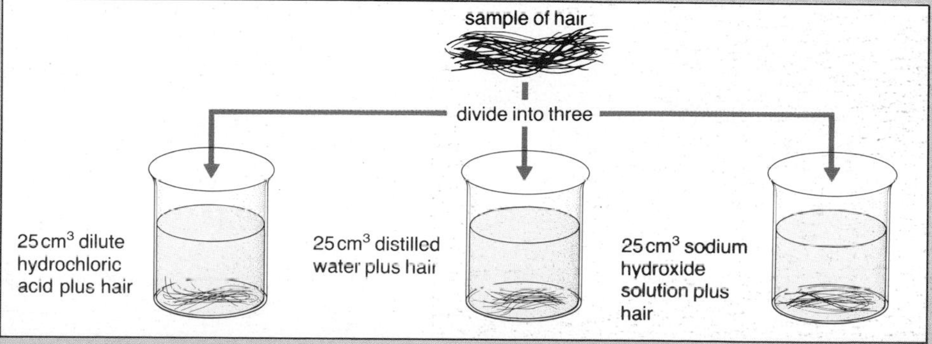

Picture 8 Soaking hair in acidic, alkaline and neutral solution

Questions

1 What is the difference between a base and an alkali?

2 Classify each of the following as an acid, a base or a salt.

a CaO
b HCl
c KCl
d H_2SO_4
e $MgCO_3$
f $FeSO_4$
g $Zn(OH)_2$
h $Al(NO_3)_3$

3a A certain rust remover contains hydrochloric acid. Rust is iron oxide. Name the salt that will be formed when the rust remover reacts with rust.

b Why is sodium hydroxide not used as a cure for acid indigestion, even though it neutralises acids?

c Most oven cleaners contain sodium hydroxide. You have to be careful when you use these cleaners not to let them get in contact with your eyes or skin. Suppose someone in your family has spilt oven cleaner on their skin. What common household substance could you use to treat the spill?

4a Write word equations to show what would be formed in each of the following reactions. The first one has been done for you.

i) nitric acid + sodium hydroxide → sodium nitrate + water
ii) nitric acid + potassium hydroxide →
iii) sulphuric acid + calcium oxide →
iv) hydrochloric acid + magnesium →
v) nitric acid + calcium carbonate →
vi) sulphuric acid + copper carbonate →

b Now try to write balanced equations, using formulas, for as many of these as you can.

5 Use table 3 to work out the formulas of the following salts.

a Potassium bromide
b Zinc iodide
c Iron (III) chloride
d Copper sulphate
e Ammonium chloride
f Ammonium sulphate
g Magnesium nitrate
h Calcium phosphate

Ideas about acids

People have known for centuries what acids *do*. But it has taken longer to build up ideas about *why* acids behave that way. Ideas have changed gradually, and new ideas have built on older ones.

Of course, theories of acids cannot start until you have detailed information about the properties of acids. Nearly a thousand years ago, Arabic chemists were making acids. **Jabir** and **Al-Razi** wrote instructions for how to make sulphuric, nitric and hydrochloric acids. They also investigated alkalis: the word itself comes from Arabic 'al-qali', meaning potassium carbonate. But it was a long time before these early investigations led to a theory of acids.

Picture 1 A representation of the sort of equipment used by the Arabic chemists

Boyle 1675: acids contain special particles Robert Boyle was an Irish nobleman. He tried to explain why acids are corrosive and attack metals and other solids. He suggested that acids contain special kinds of particles, which squeeze into spaces in the solid like tiny wedges and break it apart.

Lavoisier 1777: all acids contain oxygen The Frenchman Antoine Lavoisier did many experiments on burning. He found that when you burn non-metal elements like sulphur and phosphorus, you get acidic gases. He knew that burning always involves oxygen, so he decided that oxygen must be the thing that all acids have in common. It was Lavoisier who invented the name 'oxygen', from Greek words meaning 'acid-maker' (*oxy* means 'sour' in Greek, and the *gen* bit means 'producer').

In fact, Lavoisier's theory was proved wrong by the Englishman Humphry Davy in 1810. Davy showed that *most* acids contain oxygen, but not *all* of them.

Laurent 1854: all acids contain hydrogen The Frenchman Auguste Laurent knew that acids react with metals to give hydrogen. He decided that the hydrogen must be coming from the acid — so all acids must contain hydrogen. He was right, but there are many substances that contain hydrogen and are *not* acids. Laurent's theory needed to go further.

Arrhenius 1887: all acids produce hydrogen ions in solution The Swedish chemist Svante Arrhenius modified Laurent's theory. Acids conduct electricity, which suggests they contain ions. Arrhenius proposed that it must be hydrogen *ions*, $H^+(aq)$, that give acids their special properties.

Arrhenius' theory has been improved a bit, but it is still basically this theory that we use today. It is a good theory because it explains most of the things we know about acids.

1 Look at the acids in table 1 on page 139. Which of them does not fit Lavoisier's theory?

2 Give the formula of two substances that contain hydrogen but are *not* acids.

3 In what way did Arrhenius' theory build on Laurent's?

4 Arabic chemists worked on acids nearly a thousand years ago. Why do you think it took so long before their work was built on?

5 Try to work out what the name 'hydrogen' comes from. (Like 'oxygen', it comes from Greek words.)

6 'If Lavoisier hadn't got the theory of acids wrong, *hydrogen* would be called *oxygen*'. Explain.

Bringing trout back to Loch Fleet

Loch Fleet (picture 1) is a small lake in Galloway, southern Scotland. It was once renowned among anglers for its brown trout, but since 1950 the numbers of trout in the loch have dropped disastrously (picture 2). By the mid-1970s they had disappeared completely.

What happened to the trout? Consider these facts.

- Brown trout are killed by acid. They cannot survive in water whose pH is below 5, and they are only healthy if the pH is above 6.5.
- At the beginning of 1986 the pH of the water in Loch Fleet was about 4.4.
- Brown trout are poisoned by aluminium compounds. They cannot stand a concentration of aluminium ions higher than 40 micrograms per litre.
- At the beginning of 1986 the concentration of aluminium ions in Loch Fleet was about 80 micrograms per litre.
- Loch Fleet is fed by streams draining off the surrounding hills. Water flows out of the loch into a river.
- All soil contains aluminium compounds, but they normally stay in the soil. Acid dissolves these aluminium compounds so they are washed out of the soil by the rain.
- Brown trout need calcium ions in their diet.

Scientists believed that the brown trout were being killed by two things in the water: acid and aluminium ions. They decided that the best way to tackle the problem was to neutralise the acidity with a base.

Picture 1 Loch Fleet

Neutralising the acid

They decided to use limestone (calcium carbonate) as the base. The simplest thing would be to add limestone to the loch itself. However, it would have to be re-treated every six months or so because new water keeps flowing in. So they decided to put the limestone on the surrounding *land* instead.

This was done in 1986 and 1987. Between 5 and 30 tonnes of limestone were added to each hectare (a hectare is about the same area as two football pitches). The graphs in picture 3 show the results.

Putting back the fish

In 1987, 300 brown trout were put into the loch. They didn't just survive — they started breeding. More fish were added in 1988. By 1989, brown trout in excellent condition were once again being caught in the loch.

You will need to use the information above to answer some of these questions.

1 Two things probably killed the brown trout: acid and aluminium.

a Suggest a reason why the loch became acidic.

b How did the aluminium get into the loch?

2 Look at the graphs in picture 3. What happened to each of the following after limestone was added to the land around the loch?

a The pH of water in the loch

b The concentration of calcium ions in the loch

c The concentration of aluminium ions in the loch.

3 Using limestone helped the trout in *three* ways. What are they?

4 Why was it better to add limestone to the surrounding land, rather than adding it to the water in the loch itself?

5 Give *three* reasons why limestone (calcium carbonate) is a particularly good base to use in this situation.

6 Look at graph A in picture 3. What is the earliest date when the acidity would have been low enough to put trout back in the loch?

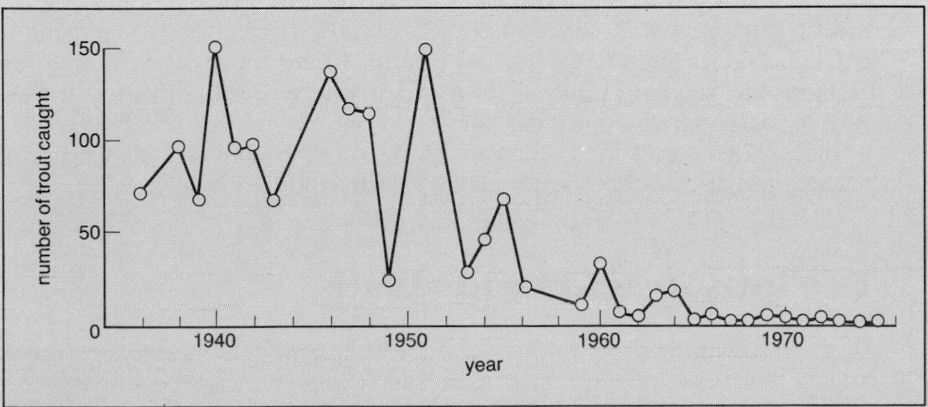

Picture 2 Numbers of brown trout caught in Loch Fleet since 1936

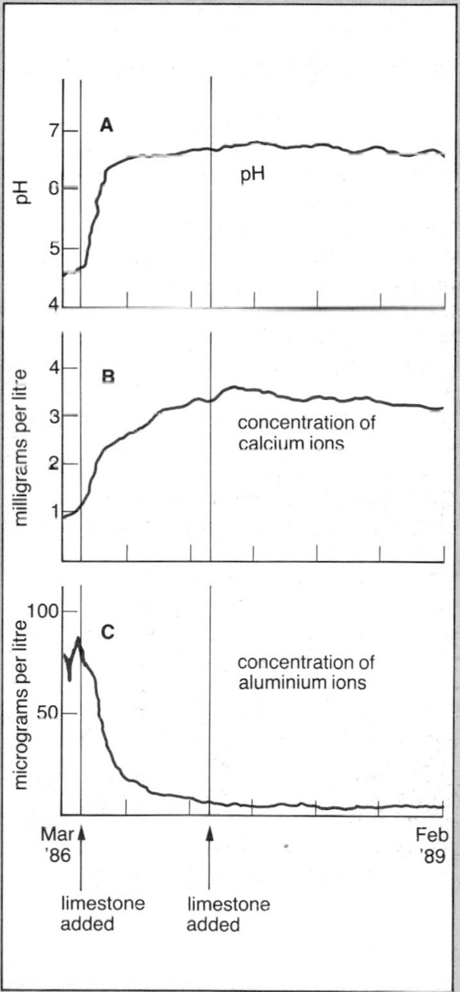

Picture 3 Changes in Loch Fleet from 1986 to 1989

G3 What happens when acids are neutralised?

Neutralisation means getting rid of hydrogen ions.

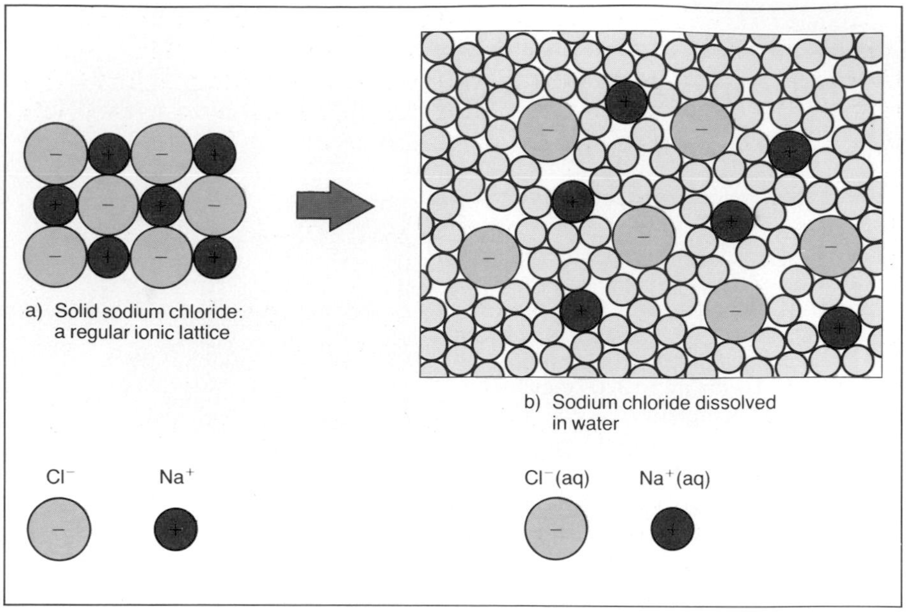

Picture 2 What happens when an ionic substance dissolves (Remember, there are in fact millions of millions of molecules and ions)

The tanker in picture 1 has spilt hydrochloric acid all over the road. The emergency services are treating the spill with an alkali to neutralise the acid. But how does the neutralisation take away the acidity?

There are many different acids, and they all have one thing in common: they contain hydrogen ions, $H^+(aq)$. The (aq) means the hydrogen ions are dissolved in water. Before we go any further, we need to look at the way ions behave when they are in water.

Picture 1 This tanker has spilt hydrochloric acid on the road

What happens when an ionic substance dissolves?

Let's use sodium chloride as an example. (It isn't an acid, of course, but it's a good example of an ionic substance.)

Solid sodium chloride has a giant ionic structure (see topic C6). It contains Na^+ and Cl^- ions arranged closely together in a regular lattice (picture 2a). There are equal numbers of Na^+ and Cl^- ions, so that the electric charges balance.

When you put sodium chloride into water, it dissolves. The Na^+ and Cl^- ions spread out into the water (picture 2b). We describe them as $Na^+(aq)$ and $Cl^-(aq)$. Now the ions are no longer regularly arranged — in fact, they are scattered through the water at random. What's more, now the Na^+ and Cl^- ions are separated they behave independently of each other. It's as if each has forgotten the other exists.

This applies to all ionic substances. As soon as they are dissolved, the positive and negative ions separate and behave independently.

The ions in acids and alkalis

All acids contain hydrogen ions, $H^+(aq)$. They also contain negative ions to balance out these positive hydrogen ions. Different acids contain different negative ions. For example, hydrochloric acid contains chloride ions, Cl^-, and sulphuric acid contains sulphate ions, SO_4^{2-}. Table 1 shows some others.

Table 1 The ions formed by different acids

Acid	Formula	Ions it forms
hydrochloric acid	HCl	H^+ and Cl^-
sulphuric acid	H_2SO_4	$2H^+$ and SO_4^{2-}
nitric acid	HNO_3	H^+ and NO_3^-
acetic acid	CH_3COOH	H^+ and CH_3COO^-
formic acid	$HCOOH$	H^+ and $HCOO^-$
citric acid	$C_6H_8O_7$	H^+ and $C_6H_7O_7^-$

But what about alkalis? Sodium hydroxide, NaOH, is a typical alkali. It contains sodium ions, Na^+ and hydroxide ions, OH^-. When sodium hydroxide dissolves in water, these ions separate as $Na^+(aq)$ and $OH^-(aq)$. **It is the OH^- that gives alkali properties**. Indeed, all alkalis contain OH^- ions, in the same way that all acids contain H^+ ions.

So what happens when an acid is neutralised by an alkali?

Let's take a simple example. When you add hydrochloric acid to sodium hydroxide solution, the acid is neutralised and you get a salt — common salt, sodium chloride.

$$\text{hydrochloric acid} + \text{sodium hydroxide} \rightarrow \text{sodium chloride} + \text{water}$$
$$HCl(aq) + NaOH(aq) \rightarrow NaCl(aq) + H_2O(l)$$

Now, hydrochloric acid contains separate $H^+(aq)$ and $Cl^-(aq)$ ions, and a solution of sodium hydroxide contains separate $Na^+(aq)$ and $OH^-(aq)$ ions. What is more, sodium chloride contains separate $Na^+(aq)$ and $Cl^-(aq)$ ions. So we can show all these ions separately:

$$H^+(aq) + Cl^-(aq) + Na^+(aq) + OH^-(aq) \rightarrow Na^+(aq) + Cl^-(aq) + H_2O(l)$$

If you look closely at this equation, you will see that $Na^+(aq)$ and $Cl^-(aq)$ are on both sides. They are not changed in this reaction — it is as if they are on the sidelines, watching the action going on between $H^+(aq)$ and $OH^-(aq)$ (picture 3). They are described as **spectator ions**.

$Na^+(aq)$ and $Cl^-(aq)$ are there at the beginning of the reaction, and they are there at the end. At the end of the reaction, though, they are the only ions present, because $H^+(aq)$ and $OH^-(aq)$ have got together to make H_2O. Between them, $Na^+(aq)$ and $Cl^-(aq)$ make a solution of sodium chloride — salt. If we leave them out, the equation becomes just

$$H^+(aq) + OH^-(aq) \rightarrow H_2O(l)$$

This equation describes how *any* acid reacts with *any* alkali. It means that, whenever an acid reacts with an alkali, the same simple reaction happens: hydrogen ions react with hydroxide ions to form water. The other ions — negative ions from the acid and positive ions from the alkali — form a salt. That's why all neutralisation reactions amount to

$$\text{acid} + \text{base} \rightarrow \text{salt} + \text{water}$$

This general rule applies to all bases, whether or not they are alkalis. (Remember, alkalis are a special type of base that dissolve in water.) Alkalis contain hydroxide ions; other bases may contain oxide or carbonate ions. But whatever the base, it always contains something that will join up with $H^+(aq)$ ions from acid and turn them to neutral water.

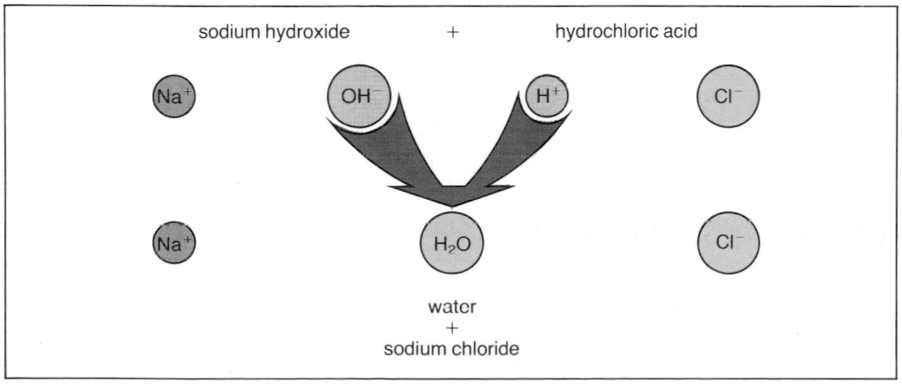

Picture 3 What happens when an ionic substance dissolves (remember there are in fact millions of millions of molecules and ions)

Activity

Does neutralisation involve energy transfers?

CARE Eye protection must be worn.

Put 25 cm^3 of dilute hydrochloric acid in a small beaker. Take its temperature. Add 25 cm^3 of sodium hydroxide solution, and use the thermometer to stir the solution. Read the temperature again. What do you conclude?

Repeat the experiment, but this time use dilute nitric acid instead of dilute hydrochloric acid. The nitric acid should be of the same concentration as the hydrochloric acid was.

Repeat the first experiment, but this time use potassium hydroxide solution instead of sodium hydroxide solution. The potassium hydroxide solution should be of the same concentration as the sodium hydroxide solution was.

Compare the results of the three experiments. What do you conclude?

Questions

1 What ion do all acids contain?

2 What ion do all alkalis contain?

3 Look at table 1. Why does sulphuric acid have two H^+ ions for each SO_4^{2-} ion? Why does hydrochloric acid only have one H^+ for each Cl^-?

4 Here is the equation for the reaction of nitric acid with potassium hydroxide.

nitric acid + potassium hydroxide
→ potassium nitrate + water

$HNO_3(aq) + KOH(aq)$
$\rightarrow KNO_3(aq) + H_2O(l)$

a What ions does nitric acid contain?

b What ions does potassium hydroxide solution contain?

c Rewrite the equation showing all the ions separately (like the equation for the reaction of hydrochloric acid with sodium hydroxide).

d Which ions in the equation in (c) are spectator ions?

e Rewrite the equation, leaving out the spectator ions.

G4
Solids from solutions

You mix two clear solutions and suddenly a cloudy precipitate forms. How does it happen?

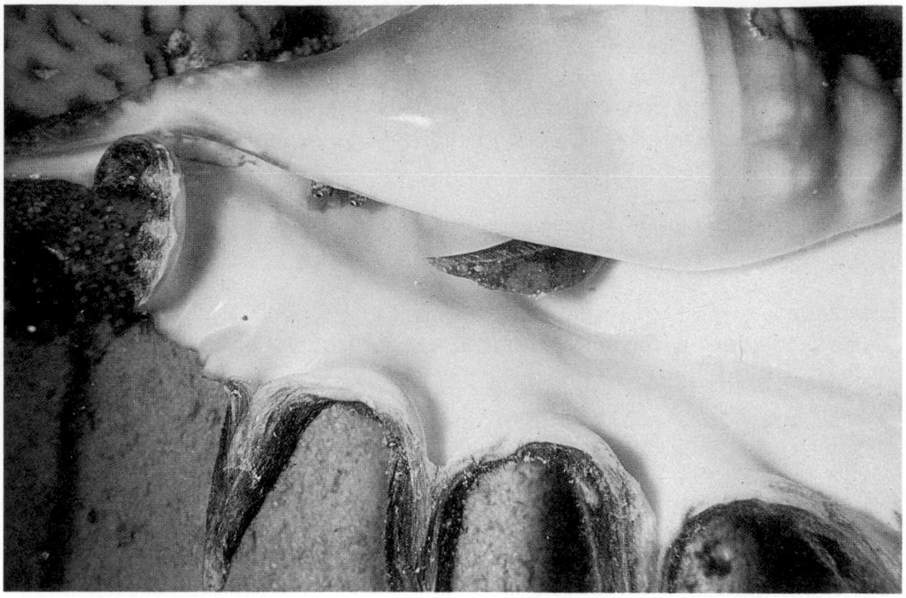

Picture 1 This shell is mainly made from calcium carbonate

Picture 2 Stalactites and stalagmites

The shell in picture 1 is made of calcium carbonate. The mollusc that lives in it made the shell by bringing together calcium ions and carbonate ions from the sea water. Calcium carbonate is insoluble in water, so the shell doesn't dissolve, which is just as well for the mollusc.

The stalactites and stalagmites in picture 2 are also made of calcium carbonate. Like the shell they were formed from calcium ions and carbonate ions.

Forming stalactites and stalagmites can take centuries, and even a mollusc takes several months to build its shell. *You* can form a precipitate much more quickly by mixing solutions of calcium chloride and sodium carbonate in a test tube (activity A). The clear solutions will turn cloudy as a **precipitate** of insoluble calcium carbonate is formed.

What's going on?

Let's look more closely at what happens when calcium chloride and sodium carbonate are mixed. Both these substances are soluble in water. The solution of calcium chloride contains dissolved calcium ions, $Ca^{2+}(aq)$, and chloride ions, $Cl^-(aq)$. The solution of sodium carbonate contains dissolved sodium ions, $Na^+(aq)$ and carbonate ions, $CO_3^{2-}(aq)$. (Look at topic G3 if you are unsure about ions in solutions.)

When you mix the two solutions, all four of these ions — $Ca^{2+}(aq)$, $Cl^-(aq)$, $Na^+(aq)$, $CO_3^{2-}(aq)$ — are together in the same tube (picture 3). But calcium carbonate is insoluble, so $Ca^{2+}(aq)$ and $CO_3^{2-}(aq)$ ions cannot stay in solution together. Billions of these ions join together in a solid lattice which becomes a speck of solid. Between them, these specks make up the powdery precipitate that you see in the test-tube.

While this action is going on between the $Ca^{2+}(aq)$ and $CO_3^{2-}(aq)$ ions, what are the $Na^+(aq)$ and $Cl^-(aq)$ ions doing? *Nothing* — they are not involved in the reaction at all. They stay on the sidelines as **spectator ions** (page 149).

If you filter off the precipitate, you are left with a clear solution containing $Na^+(aq)$ and $Cl^-(aq)$ ions. It's a solution of sodium chloride. So, overall the reaction amounts to:

calcium chloride + sodium carbonate
→ calcium carbonate + sodium chloride

$$CaCl_2(aq) + Na_2CO_3(aq) \rightarrow CaCO_3(s) + 2NaCl(aq)$$

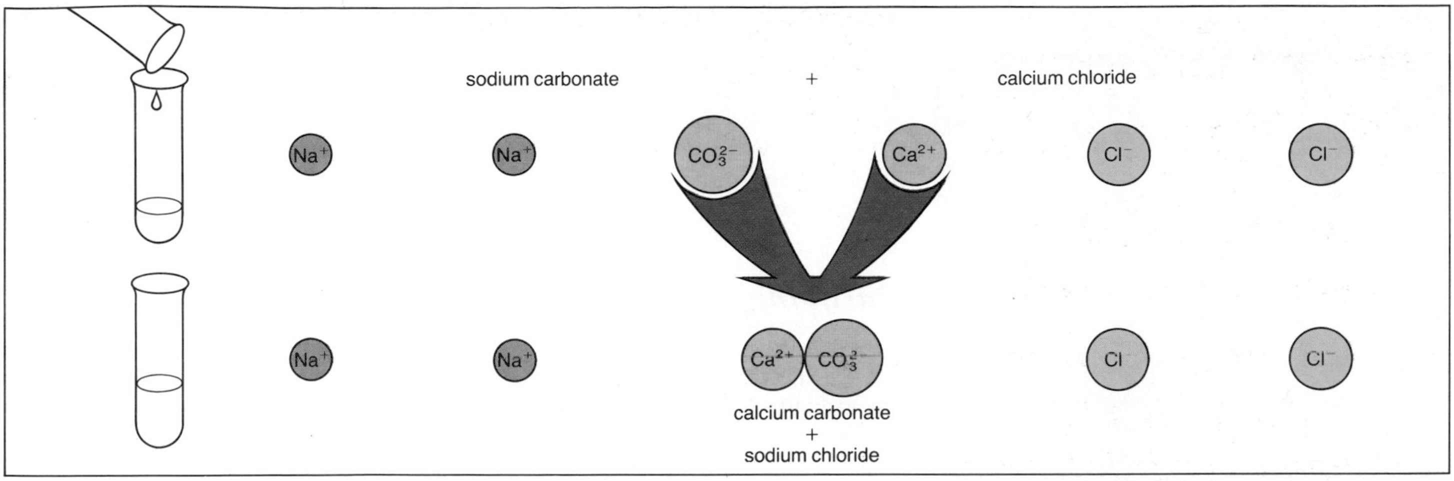

Picture 3 Making a precipitate of calcium carbonate

But the bit that really matters is the $Ca^{2+}(aq)$ and $CO_3^{2-}(aq)$ ions joining together. If we leave out the spectator ions, this amounts to just

$$Ca^{2+}(aq) + CO_3^{2-}(aq) \rightarrow CaCO_3(s)$$

When a mollusc builds its shell, and when stalactites and stalagmites grow, it's this reaction that is going on.

More precipitation

The parking lines painted on roads get their yellow colour from lead chromate, $PbCrO_4$ (picture 4). Lead chromate is insoluble (if it wasn't, the yellow lines would disappear when it rains). You make it by a precipitation reaction — all you have to do is mix solutions containing lead ions and chromate ions, and you get a lovely yellow precipitate of lead chromate. You can try this in activity B.

Picture 4 Lead chromate gives these parking lines their yellow colour

Hard water and precipitation

Do you live in a hard water area? If so, you'll know that hard water makes soap difficult to lather. The soap forms a solid precipitate or 'scum'. Hard water, also leaves a solid deposit called 'fur' in kettles, pipes and shower-heads (picture 5).

Water hardness is caused by dissolved substances, usually compounds of calcium. These calcium compounds get into the water from the rocks, especially in limestone districts. Topic D3 explains how this happens. The calcium compounds contain calcium ions, $Ca^{2+}(aq)$, and these stay dissolved in the water right through the purification process at the water works.

Hard water and soap

Soaps are compounds of sodium or potassium. A common soap is sodium stearate, which we can call Na^+St^- for short. Sodium stearate dissolves in water, as you will know if you have ever left the soap in the bath water for too long. However, *calcium* stearate is insoluble. So when you add sodium stearate (soap) to hard water containing calcium ions, a precipitate of calcium stearate forms. This is the whiteish scum you see around the bath.

calcium ions	+	stearate ions	→	calcium stearate
(from hard water)	+	(from soap)		(scum)
$Ca2^+(aq)$	+	$2St^-(aq)$	→	$CaSt_2(s)$

Picture 5 The scum in this sink came from a precipitation reaction between soap and calcium ions in the hard water

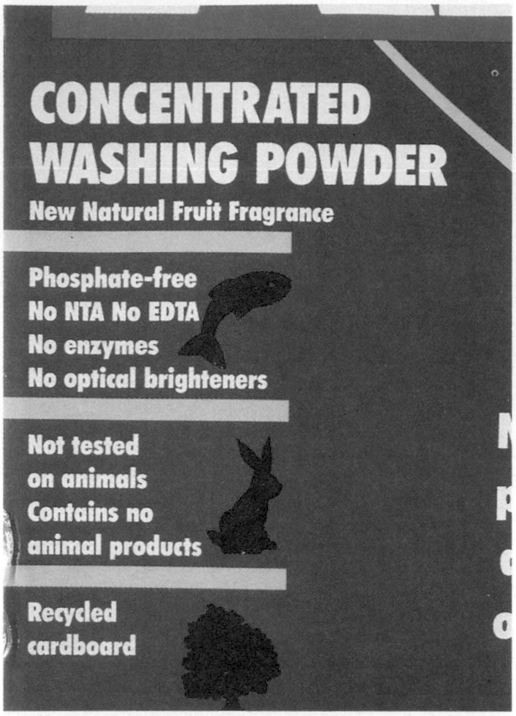

Picture 6 Phosphates are added to washing powder to soften water, but they cause a pollution problem, so makers are replacing them with different softeners

Getting rid of hardness

Hard water has some advantages. Some people feel that it tastes nicer than soft water, and many doctors believe that drinking hard water helps prevent heart disease. But hard water can be a nuisance in homes and a major problem in industry. To **soften** water you need to remove the calcium ions which cause the problem.

Purifying by precipitation

You can use precipitation to remove calcium ions from hard water. One way is to add sodium carbonate to the water. This removes the $Ca^{2+}(aq)$ ions as a precipitate of calcium carbonate. Another name for sodium carbonate is 'washing soda', and it was often used in the days when all the washing was done using soap.

Nowadays, many washing powders have a softener added to them. Phosphates are often used. Calcium phosphate, $Ca_3(PO_4)_2$, is insoluble — it's the main substance in teeth and bones. When the phosphate in the washing powder mixes with the $Ca^{2+}(aq)$ ions in the water, a precipitate of calcium phosphate forms. This takes the $Ca^{2+}(aq)$ ions out of the water.

Unfortunately, phosphates can cause a pollution problem if they get into rivers and streams. They cause the same kind of pollution as fertilisers (see *The Living World*, topic B13). Many washing powder makers are now trying to find ways of softening water without using phosphates (picture 6).

Other ways of softening water

Distillation Your school science department probably has a **still** which makes distilled water. Distillation removes *all* impurities, but it is expensive because it uses a lot of energy. Distilled water is used where purity is particularly important — for cleaning contact lenses, say, or for science experiments.

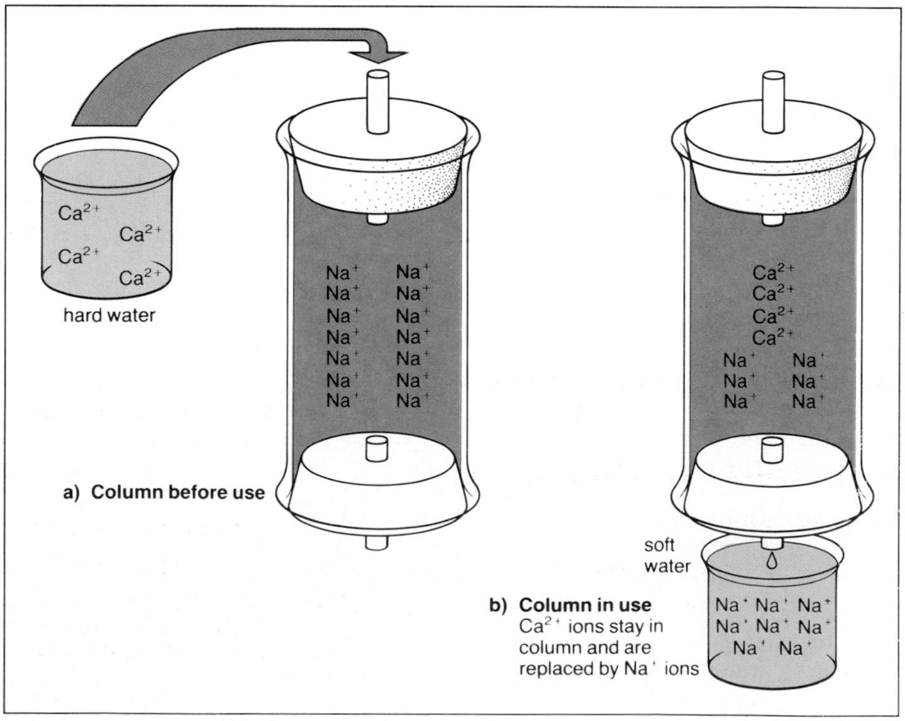

Picture 7 How an ion exchange column works

Ion exchange The most convenient way to soften water is to use an ion exchange column. Many homes in hard water areas have them. The water is run through a column containing a special **ion exchange resin** (picture 7).

The resin has sodium ions in it. When the hard water runs through the resin, calcium ions in the water are exchanged for sodium ions in the column. This removes calcium ions from the water and replaces them with sodium ions, which do not make the water hard.

Every so often, sodium ions have to be put back in the column. This is done by pouring a strong solution of salt through it.

Activities

A Making a precipitate of calcium carbonate

Put 2 cm^3 of calcium chloride solution in a test-tube. Add 2 cm^3 of sodium carbonate solution. You will get a precipitate of calcium carbonate. Note its colour and appearance. You could try filtering off the precipitate and drying it to get calcium carbonate powder.

B More precipitates

Repeat the experiment in activity A to make other precipitates. Some of the solutions or precipitates are toxic. Wear eye protection and avoid getting them on your hands.

Use the solutions listed below. In each case

a) Note the colour and appearance of the precipitate

b) Decide what substance is left in solution (for example, in (l) sodium nitrate is left in solution).

1 Mix silver nitrate solution and sodium chloride solution to get a precipitate of silver chloride.

2 Mix copper sulphate solution and sodium carbonate solution to get a precipitate of copper carbonate.

3 Mix lead nitrate solution (**CARE:** Toxic) and potassium iodide solution to get a precipitate of lead iodide.

4 Mix lead nitrate solution and potassium chromate solution (**CARE:** Toxic) to get a precipitate of lead chromate. After the experiment, wash the precipitate away with plenty of water. Wash your hands.

C Testing water for hardness

You can use the method below to test samples of water to see how hard they are. Plan an investigation using this test to compare the hardness of different samples of water. Read the description of the hardness test first, then make your plan. Bear in mind the following questions.

- How will you make sure that your tests are a fair comparison?
- What information will you record about each sample you test?
- What precautions will you need to take to make your results as accurate as possible?

Use the basic test to compare the hardness of the following samples of water.

(**a**) distilled water (**b**) local tap water (**c**) local tap water that has been boiled (**d**) sea water (if available) (**e**) mineral water (you could try several different brands and see how the hardness depends on the area the water comes from) (**f**) distilled water with a little sodium chloride dissolved in it (**g**) distilled water with a little calcium chloride dissolved in it.

The basic hardness test You will be given a special soap solution (**CARE:** Flammable) to test the water with.

Put 2 cm^3 of a water sample in a test-tube. Use a dropping pipette to add a drop of soap solution to the water. Shake the tube and see if you get a lather that lasts more than a few seconds. If you don't, add two or three more drops of soap solution and shake again, until you get a lasting lather. Then note the total number of drops of soap solution added, and look to see if any white precipitate (scum) has formed.

D Is your water hard?

Try and find the answers to these questions.

1 Is your local water reckoned to be **A** hard **B** moderately hard **C** soft?

2 Where does your local water supply come from? Does that explain your answer to (1)?

3 Do local people use any kind of water softening in their homes? You could try a survey in your class.

4 Try getting in touch with friends or relatives who live in other parts of the country. How hard is their water?

Questions

1 What is a precipitate?

2 Look at this list of solutions.

A calcium nitrate **B** sodium carbonate **C** potassium bromide **D** barium chloride **E** sodium sulphate **F** magnesium chloride **G** silver nitrate **H** zinc nitrate

Which pair of solutions would you mix to get a precipitate of each of the following substances?

(**a**) magnesium carbonate (**b**) barium sulphate (**c**) calcium sulphate (**d**) silver bromide (**e**) zinc carbonate.

3a What is meant by 'hard water'?

b Explain why the amount of hardness in water varies from place to place across the country. (It may help you to look at topic D3.)

c Why does the normal water purification treatment in a water works *not* remove hardness from water? (It may help you to look at topic B4.)

4a i) What is 'washing soda'?

ii) How does washing soda remove hardness from water?

iii) Why is washing soda only rarely used nowadays?

b How does an ion-exchange column remove hardness from water?

H1
Making oil useful

Many of the things we use every day are manufactured from crude oil. Most of the compounds in crude oil belong to a family called the alkanes.

Picture 1 Plastic guttering costs £4 per metre

Picture 2 Cast-iron guttering costs £15 per metre

Oil cuts costs

The guttering in picture 1 is made from a plastic called pvc. It cost £4 per metre, and the householders put it up themselves.

The guttering in picture 2 is made from cast iron. It cost £15 a metre, and it was put up by a builder because it is very heavy.

Apart from price, the plastic guttering has other advantages. It does not rust, so you don't need to paint it, and it does not hurt much if it falls on your head. Aluminium guttering has these advantages too, but it costs £20 a metre.

Like most plastics, pvc is made from crude oil. It is just one of thousands of oil products that we use every day. Many oil products are fuels like petrol and fuel oil. But crude oil can be used to make so many useful things that in a sense it is too precious to burn. Section I of this book looks at fuels: in this section we are mainly looking at the way that useful things like plastics can be made from crude oil.

Counting the environmental cost

One of the advantages of oil products like pvc is that they often cost less than traditional materials. But the *economic cost* of a product is not the only thing we need to consider. Whenever anything is manufactured, there is also an *environmental cost* to take into account (page 89). Some of the environmental costs of a plastic gutter go right back to when the crude oil was first brought out of the ground.

Have you ever got stained with oil on the beach? The chances are the oil came from a tanker carrying crude oil (picture 3). Sometimes tankers have collisions that cause crude oil to leak into the sea. More often, the oil gets there when the tanks are washed out. After the cargo of crude oil has been unloaded, the oil tanks have to be washed out with sea water, and if this is done carelessly, oil can get into the sea. Whichever way it gets there, the spilt oil is a menace to bathers and is often deadly to wildlife.

This kind of pollution is probably the biggest environmental cost associated with crude oil itself. There are also environmental costs when crude oil is turned into products at refineries and factories. Picture 4 shows an example, though fortunately accidents like this are quite rare.

And don't forget, there are environmental costs when oil products are *used*. For example, plastics like pvc are not biodegradable, so they can cause a litter problem. And when fuels like petrol are burned, they can cause air pollution.

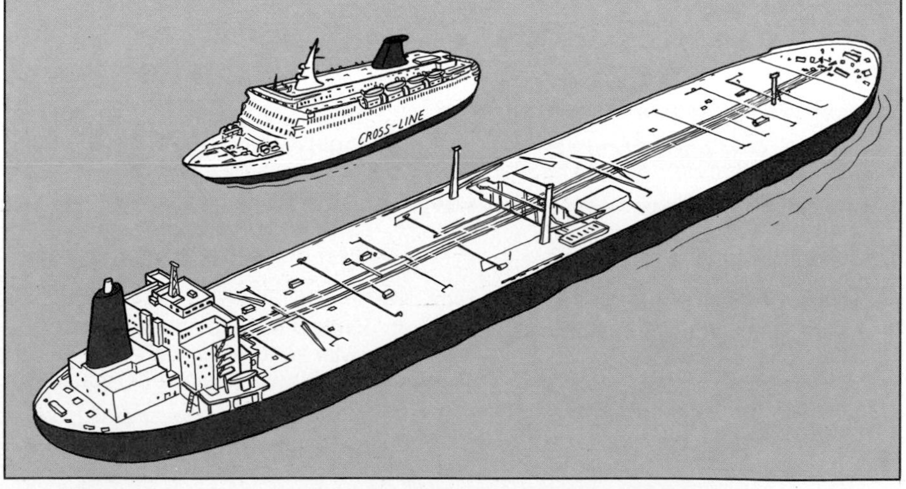

Picture 3 This tanker carries 350 000 cubic metres of crude oil, worth over £70 000 000

Picture 4 A scene following the explosion at the oil refinery at Stanlow in Cheshire, in 1990

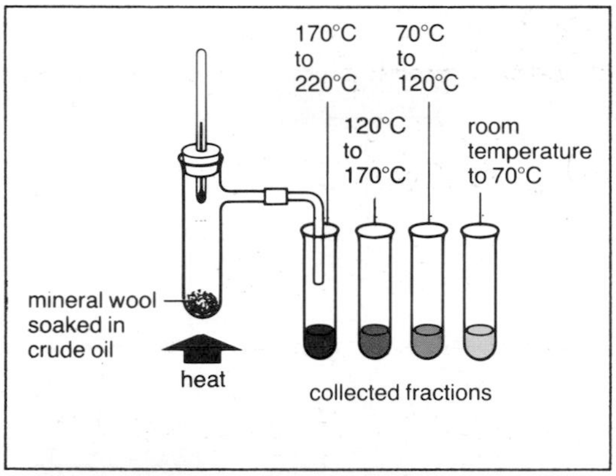

Picture 5 Distilling crude oil in the laboratory

Picture 6 At an oil refinery, fractional distillation is carried out in huge columns like this one. You can see pipes coming off at different levels on the tower: the pipes nearest the top carry the most volatile fractions

Making crude oil useful

Until it has been processed, crude oil is not much use. This is because it is a mixture of many thousands of different compounds with different properties. They are called **hydrocarbons**, because they contain the elements hydrogen and carbon only.

To make crude oil useful, these compounds need to be sorted into batches with similar properties. These batches are called **fractions** and they are separated by **fractional distillation**. The idea behind this technique is that some of the compounds in crude oil are easily vaporised. They are **volatile**, with low boiling points. Others are less volatile and have higher boiling points.

In fractional distillation, the crude oil is heated to make it vaporise. The vapour is then cooled, and the most volatile compounds condense to liquids most easily. Different fractions of the oil are collected at different temperatures. The main fractions are summarised in table 1.

Table 1 Fractions from the distillation of crude oil
Note: In this table we have combined the gasoline fraction with a less volatile fraction called naphtha

Fraction	Colour	Boiling point range/°C	Uses
refinery gas	colourless	below room temperature	gaseous fuel (e.g. bottled gas), making chemicals
gasoline (petrol)	colourless or pale yellow	30–160	motor car fuel, making chemicals
kerosine (paraffin)	colourless or yellow	160–250	heating fuel, jet fuel
diesel oil	brown	220–350	diesel fuel for lorries, trains etc., heating fuel
residue	dark brown	above 350	fuel for power stations, ships etc. Some is distilled further to give lubricating oil, waxes etc.

You can carry out a simple version of fractional distillation of crude oil in the laboratory, using the method summarised in picture 5. On an industrial scale the distillation is carried out in a huge tower. The most volatile fraction comes out at the top and the least volatile at the bottom (picture 6).

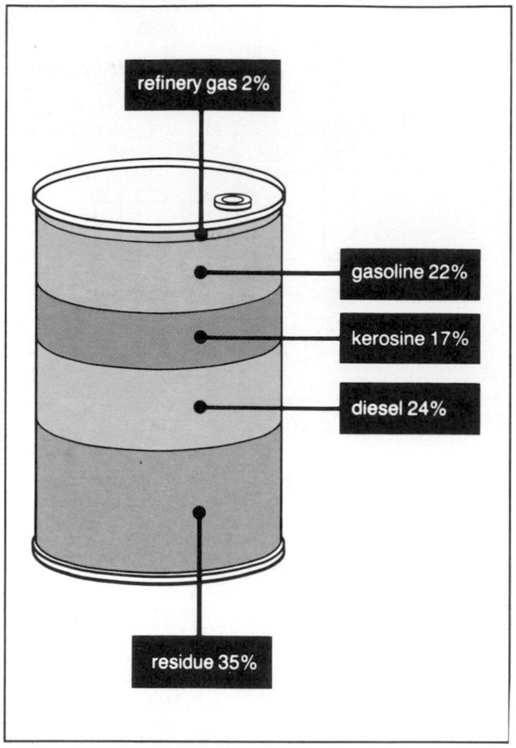

Picture 7 Percentages of different fractions obtained from a barrel of crude oil from the North Sea

Looking at the fractions from crude oil

Table 1 shows the steady change in properties shown by the fractions from crude oil distillation. These different properties lead to different uses, which are also shown in table 1.

The composition of crude oil varies according to where it comes from. Picture 7 shows what you get from North Sea crude.

Fractional distillation is only the first stage in making useful products from crude oil. All the fractions go through further processes before they are used. For example, the gasoline fraction cannot be used for fuel on its own. It must be blended with other compounds to improve its performance. Some of the petrol fraction is not used for fuel at all: it is **cracked** to make chemicals (see topic H2).

What's in crude oil?

Crude oil was formed by the decay of living organisms (see page 186). Organisms contain many thousands of different compounds, and these turn into the thousands of different hydrocarbons you get in crude oil. But all hydrocarbons contain just the same two elements: carbon and hydrogen. How can there be so many of them?

Carbon is an unusual element. Carbon atoms can form four bonds to other atoms. What is more, carbon can also form strong bonds to *other* carbon atoms. This allows it to make **chains** of carbon atoms, with other atoms, particularly hydrogen, attached to the side (picture 8). This gives a huge range of different compounds, all based on the carbon chain. They are called **organic** compounds. Living things are made from organic compounds based on chains of carbon atoms.

The alkanes: a family of hydrocarbons

The simplest type of organic compounds have chains of carbon atoms with only hydrogen atoms in the side positions. Compounds whose molecules contain these simple hydrocarbon chains are called **alkanes**. Most of the hydrocarbons in crude oil are alkanes — table 2 gives some examples. Try making models of alkane molecules in activity B.

The alkanes are a *family* of compounds. Each member of the family has the same general type of molecule: a chain of carbon atoms, with hydrogen atoms attached to the side positions. What makes the members of the family different from one another is the size of the chain. Since carbon can form chains of any length, from very long to very short, you can see that there are many possibilities — so the alkanes are a very big family. Each member has a different name, but the names all end in **-ane**.

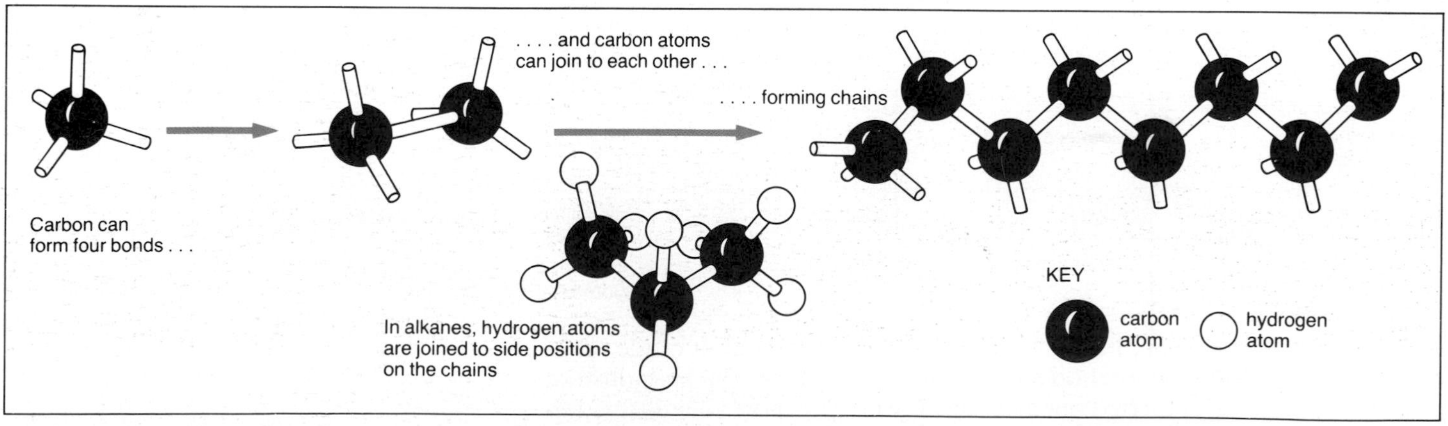

Picture 8 How carbon forms chains

Table 2 Some alkanes
The molecular formula gives the number of each type of atom present.
The structural formula shows how these atoms are joined together.
Carbon atoms are represented by C, hydrogen atoms by H.

Name	Molecular formula	Structural formula
methane	CH_4	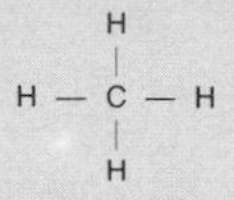
ethane	C_2H_6	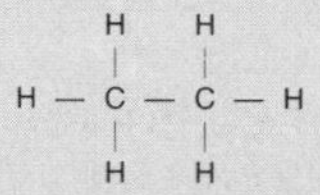
hexane	C_6H_{14}	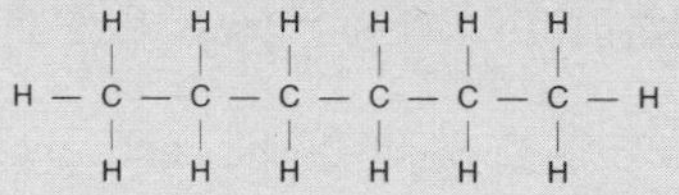
octane	C_8H_{18}	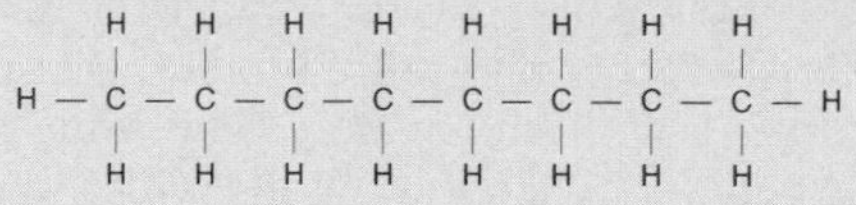

What are alkanes like?

Alkanes are similar

As a family, the alkanes have a lot of similarities. They all burn in air, forming carbon dioxide and water — which is why they are so useful for fuels (section I). They can all be **cracked** by heating so that their molecules break into smaller fragments. More about this in topic H2.

Alkanes are different

Some of the properties of alkanes change as the carbon chain gets longer. For example, as the chain length increases the boiling point increases — the compounds become less volatile. The smallest alkanes — methane, ethane, propane and butane — are actually gases (picture 9). Alkanes with large chains containing more than 20 carbon atoms are solids. Candle wax is made of solid alkanes.

Alkanes also become more sticky, or **viscous**, as the chains become longer. This is because long chains get tangled up together, which makes it more difficult for the liquid to flow.

Table 3 in the Data Section gives more information about alkanes.

Picture 9 Shell's gas separation plant at Mossmorran in Scotland. Gases are separated off from North Sea oil and sent here to be further separated into different alkanes. The big dome-shaped vessels you can see are storage tanks for propane (C_3H_8) and butane (C_4H_{10}). These gases are sold in cylinders as heating fuels

Table 3 The numbers of Carbon atoms in the hydrocarbon chain in different fractions of crude oil

Fraction	Number of carbon atoms in molecules
refinery gas	1 to 4
gasoline	5 to 9
kerosine	10 to 14
diesel oil	14 to 20
residue	over 20

Back to crude oil

We use the differences in properties of the alkanes when we separate crude oil into fractions. The most volatile fractions contain the smallest alkanes. Table 3 shows the approximate numbers of carbon atoms in the molecules in the different fractions. This explains why the fractions become more viscous as they get less volatile: the lowest volatility fractions contain alkanes with large molecules, so they are thick and sticky.

When you come across oil on the beach it is usually thick and sticky — even though crude oil comes out of the ground as a runny black liquid. When crude oil spills into the sea, the more volatile, less viscous hydrocarbons soon evaporate into the air. The thicker, less volatile compounds are left behind as a nasty mess that gets on your skin and clothes and clogs seabirds' feathers.

One thing that all hydrocarbons have in common is that they don't mix with water. What's more, they are less dense than water, so they float on it. Spills of crude oil wouldn't matter so much if the oil just sank to the bottom, or mixed with the water. One way of dealing with oil spills is to use detergents to make the oil mix with the water and disperse.

Activities

A Burning oil fractions

CARE Some oil fractions are highly flammable. Your teacher may prefer to demonstrate this activity.

Use forceps or tongs to put a tuft of glass wool in a hard-glass dish. Put 5 drops *only* of crude oil onto the glass wool. Stopper the bottle of oil and move it well away from the dish. Using a long splint, ignite the oil in the dish and observe carefully.

1 How easy was it to ignite?
2 With what kind of flame did it burn?
3 What residue is left behind after it has stopped burning?

Repeat the experiment using:
- gasoline (petrol) **CARE: highly flammable,**
- kerosine (paraffin),
- lubricating oil.

Answer questions **1** to **3** in each case.

How can you explain the differences between the four samples you burned?

B Making models of alkanes

1 Use a model building kit to make molecular models of each of the following alkanes:
a methane, CH_4
b ethane, C_2H_6
c butane, C_4H_{10}.

2 Build a molecule that has the same numbers and types of atoms as butane, but joined together in a different way.

3 Find as many different ways as you can of joining together 6 carbon atoms and 14 hydrogen atoms.

Questions

1 a Place the following fractions in order of volatility, with the most volatile first.
Diesel oil, kerosine, refinery gas, residue, gasoline.

b Of the fractions in (**a**), which:
i) is the most viscous,
ii) contains ethane,
iii) is used to make jet fuel,
iv) is used to make lubricating oil,
v) is darkest in colour?

2 Look at table 3 in the Data Section showing the properties of alkanes. Which alkane or alkanes:
a contains 10 carbon atoms,
b is a gas at room temperature (25°C),
c is a solid at room temperature,
d burns to form carbon dioxide and water?

3 This question is about an alkane called heptane. To answer it you will need to use the Data Section and tables 1 and 3.
a What is the formula of heptane?
b Is heptane a solid, liquid or gas?
c In what fraction of crude oil would you expect to find heptane?
d What colour is heptane?
e What would you expect to be formed when heptane burns in air?
f Write a balanced equation for the reaction when heptane burns.

4 The environmental costs of a manufacturing process can be considered under the headings:
(i) People's health and safety,
(ii) Pollution of the environment,
(iii) Damage to the landscape,
(iv) Depletion of resources.

a Choose an oil product as an example.
b For your chosen product, give an example of the environmental cost under each of the four headings. (For example, under (ii). you might give the example of spillage of crude oil from tankers.)

The petrol blenders

When you buy clothes, food or a radio you shop around to get the right quality and the right price. Most people don't bother to shop around for petrol — except perhaps to find the cheapest. They assume that the *quality* will always be right, whatever the brand.

Yet getting the right quality isn't easy. At the oil refinery the people who blend petrol work hard to make sure it does the right things. In particular, the petrol needs to

- avoid 'knocking' when the engine is running. 'Knocking' is a rattling sound caused by the petrol igniting too soon in the hot engine,
- ignite easily when cold, so that the car will start even on a cold morning.

To avoid 'knocking', the petrol blenders put special additives in the petrol. Lead compounds were used for a long time, but they are poisonous and cause pollution when they get into the air. Leaded petrol is gradually being replaced by 'unleaded', which uses different additives to prevent knocking.

Petrol for all seasons

A car engine burns a mixture of petrol vapour and air. The petrol is vaporised in the carburettor. Even in Britain, the petrol has to work at many different temperatures. On a cold winter's morning the temperature might be below freezing, but on a hot summer's day it could be 25°C. In Russia or Canada the temperature range could be much greater.

Petrol is a blend of different hydrocarbons with different boiling points. This gives the petrol a **boiling range**, which might be from 25°C to 200°C. To suit the changing weather conditions, the petrol blenders *change* the blend several times a year. In November, for example, they change to a winter blend. With cold weather coming on, the petrol needs to vaporise more readily for colder starting. This means adding more volatile hydrocarbons, with lower boiling points, to the blend.

In April they change to a spring blend. In the warmer weather the volatile hydrocarbons evaporate from the petrol tank, which is wasteful and polluting. So the spring blend contains *less* volatile hydrocarbons.

1 Why does the blend of petrol in the pumps change several times a year?

2 Find table 3 in the Data Section, which gives information about different alkanes. (Remember: most of the hydrocarbons in petrol belong to the alkane family.)

A particular blend of petrol has a boiling range from 25°C to 220°C.

a Which alkanes in the table might be present in this blend?

b Name one alkane from the table which might be added to the blend to make it suitable for warmer weather.

3 Petrol blends differ between countries. How do you think the petrol blend in India differs from that in Britain, for a particular time of year?

4 If you spill some petrol on your hands, it evaporates away very quickly. Yet your hands go on smelling of petrol for a long time. Can you suggest a reason why?

Picture 1 Does he realise all the trouble that goes into getting the petrol blend right?

Making ethene: profit or loss?

Ethene, C_2H_4, is one of the most important industrial chemicals. It is used to make plastics like polythene, solvents like ethanol and much more besides.

Table 1 Costs involved in making one tonne of ethene

Cost of raw materials (naphtha)	£600
Energy cost	£110
Cost of people, buildings, machinery	£200
Selling price of ethene	£400
Selling price of by-products	£550

Ethene is manufactured by cracking larger hydrocarbon molecules (see page 160 for details of cracking). A mixture of hydrocarbons called **naphtha** is used. The process is carried out in huge plants like the one on page 161.

There are three main costs involved in making ethene:

- the cost of the raw material (naphtha),
- the cost of the energy to run the process. Cracking is done at high temperatures, so it uses a lot of energy,
- the cost of the people, buildings and machinery.

Against these costs you can set the money that you get when you sell the ethene. What is more, the process also has useful by-products which can be sold for fuel or as raw materials for other chemical processes.

The details of the costs involved in making one tonne of ethene are shown in table 1.

1 What are the total costs involved in making 1 tonne of ethene?

2 What is the total income from 1 tonne of ethene and by-products?

3 What is the profit from making 1 tonne of ethene?

4 What would happen to your profit in each of the following cases? Explain your answers.

a The price of crude oil rises

b The price of ethene rises.

5 It is cheaper to make ethene in very big plants than in small ones. Suggest why.

H2 Cracking molecules

Cracking is used to break big alkane molecules into smaller ones.

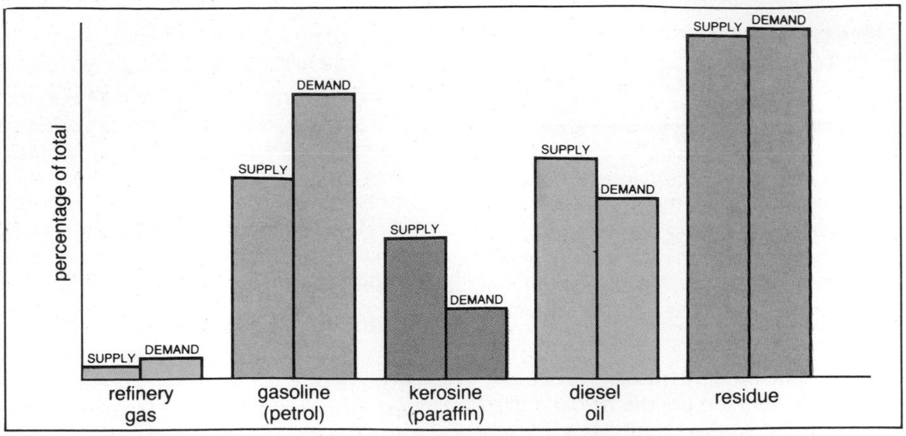
percentage of total
SUPPLY
DEMAND
refinery gas
gasoline (petrol)
kerosine (paraffin)
diesel oil
residue

Picture 1 Supply (what's available) and demand (what's wanted) for fractions from crude oil

A problem of supply and demand

Look at the chart in picture 1. It shows the *supply* and *demand* for the different fractions of crude oil. 'Supply' means the things we get from distilling the oil; 'demand' means what we actually want.

For the more volatile fractions like petrol, demand is greater than supply. Because so many people drive cars, more petrol is needed than we can actually get from distilling oil. On the other hand, for the less volatile fractions like kerosine and diesel, supply is greater than demand. There is more than enough.

Wouldn't it be convenient if you could turn the surplus fractions into fractions there are too little of? Well, you can. The less volatile, less popular fractions like kerosine have larger molecules. By breaking the larger molecules into smaller ones, you can balance supply and demand. This breaking up of molecules is called **cracking**.

Breaking up molecules

Cracking is a chemical reaction, involving breaking bonds and making new ones. It is basically done by heating. When you heat a substance, its molecules move faster. The molecules collide with one another with greater energy as the temperature becomes higher. Eventually the molecules have so much energy that they begin to break up. Picture 2 illustrates this for decane, $C_{10}H_{22}$, which is an alkane found in the kerosine fraction.

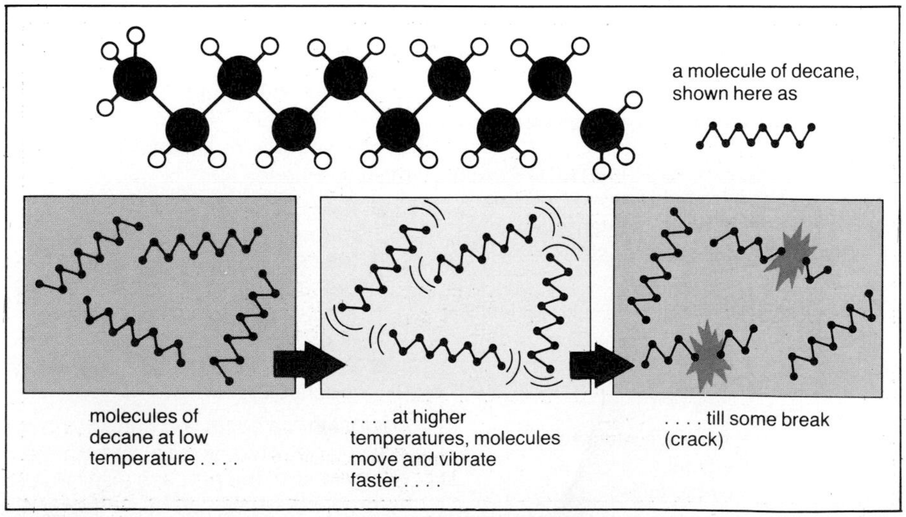
a molecule of decane, shown here as
molecules of decane at low temperature . . . .
. . . . at higher temperatures, molecules move and vibrate faster . . . .
. . . . till some break (crack)

Picture 2 How cracking occurs in a molecule of decane

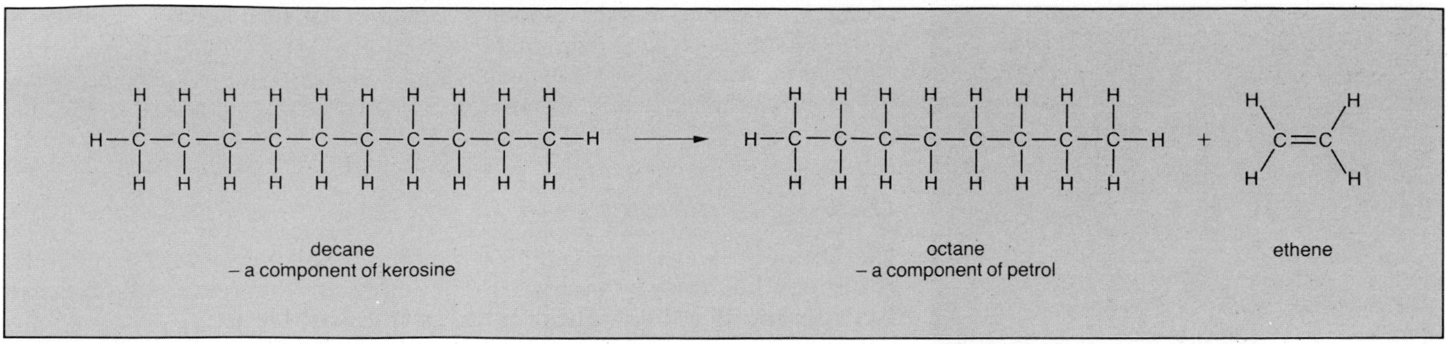

Picture 3 One result of cracking decane

You can try doing this with a model of decane in activity A. One thing you will notice is that, after the molecule has been broken in two, *there isn't enough hydrogen to go around*. There are not enough hydrogen atoms to make two smaller alkane molecules. Because of this, one of the new molecules does not become an alkane at all. Instead, it forms a **double bond** between two carbon atoms, and becomes an **alkene**. More about this below.

One result of cracking decane is shown in picture 3. There are other possible results because the decane molecule can crack apart in several different places. Notice that, like all cracking reactions, it gives two types of product:

- an alkane with a shorter chain than the original,
- a molecule containing a double bond — an alkene.

Both of these products are useful. The shorter chain alkanes can be blended with petrol, to increase the supply. In effect, low demand kerosine is being turned into high demand petrol. What's more, petrol made by cracking is actually higher quality than the petrol you get by straight distillation.

Alkenes are very useful 'building block' substances for making all sorts of useful chemicals, as you will see below.

Cracking in practice

Picture 4 shows a single alkane being cracked. In practice a fraction containing a *mixture* of different alkanes is used. This gives a mixture of smaller alkanes and alkenes.

Heating is essential for cracking molecules. But the reaction can be helped by using a catalyst (see page 199), which reduces the heating required. The

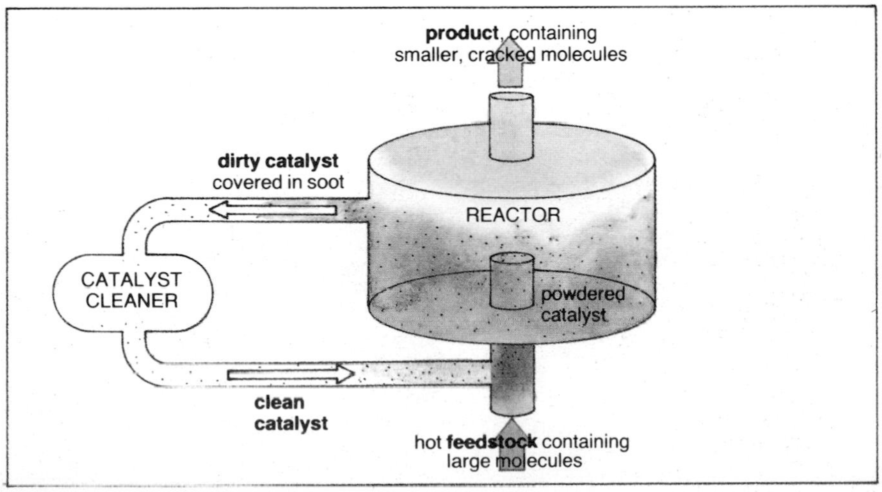

Picture 5 How a Cat Cracker plant works

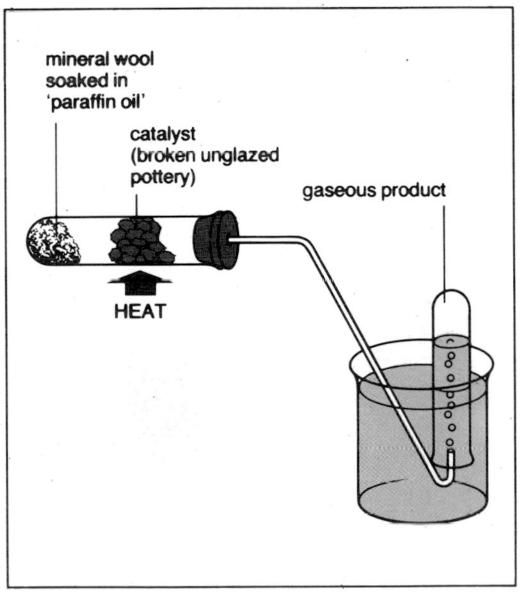

Picture 4 Cracking in the laboratory. In this experiment the fraction being cracked is a purified form of lubricating oil

alkane is vaporised and the vapour passes over the heated catalyst. Picture 4 shows the method that is used in the laboratory — you can try it in activity B.

On an industrial scale, catalytic cracking is done in big 'cat cracker' plants (picture 5). After cracking, the mixture of products is separated by distillation.

Picture 6 A 'Cat Cracker' plant

Looking at alkenes

Like alkanes, alkenes are a family of compounds. Alkenes *sound* very similar to alkanes, but the two families have an important difference. **Alkenes are hydrocarbons with a double bond in their molecule.**

Picture 7 shows what we mean by a double bond. Try building models containing double bonds in Activity C.

You can see from picture 7 that alkenes contain less hydrogen atoms than alkanes do. This is because the carbon atoms have less bonds available to join to hydrogens, having already used two to bond to each other. We say that alkenes are **unsaturated** because they have less than the maximum amount of hydrogen possible. Compounds like alkanes, with the maximum possible amount of hydrogen, are **saturated**.

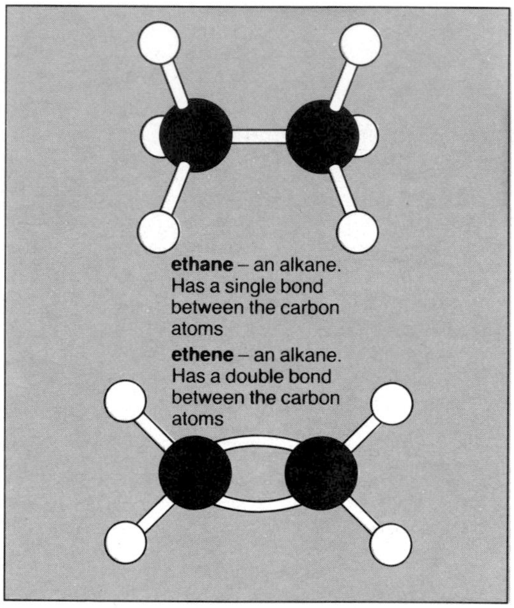

ethane – an alkane. Has a single bond between the carbon atoms
ethene – an alkane. Has a double bond between the carbon atoms

Picture 7 Ethane and ethene

Alkenes: the family

Members of the alkene family all have a double bond in their molecule, but different members have different numbers of carbon atoms. Table 1 gives a few examples of alkenes. All the alkenes have names ending in **-ene.** The first part of the name is the same as for the corresponding alkane.

Table 1 The three simplest alkenes

Name	Structural formula
ethene	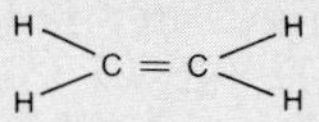
propene	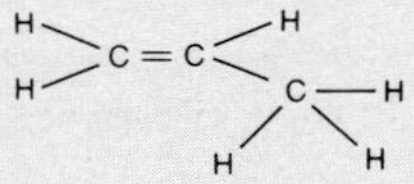
butene	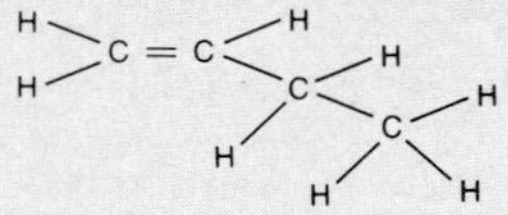

Alkenes as building blocks

Addition reactions

The double bond in alkenes makes them much more reactive than alkanes. Let's look at an example. If you shake up an alkene such as ethene with a

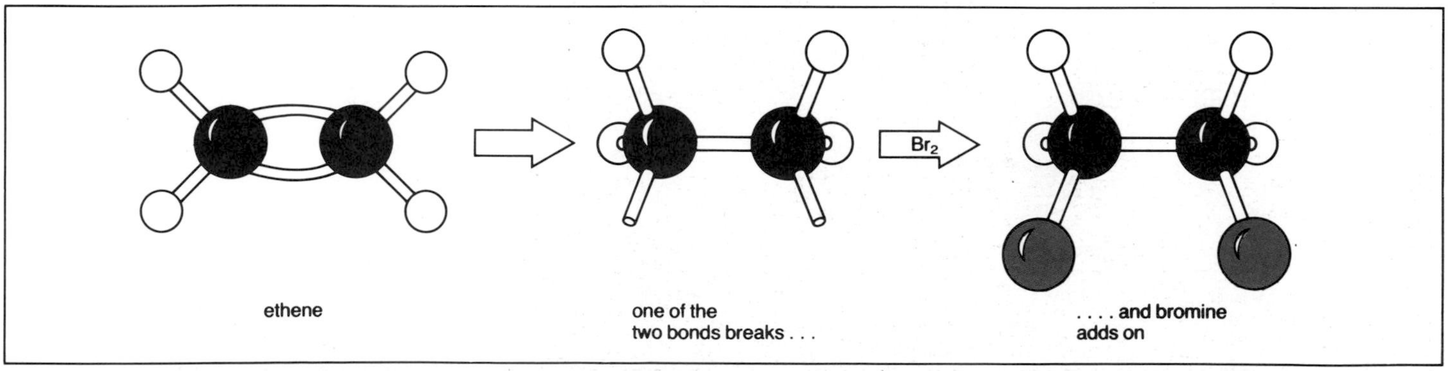

Picture 8 An addition reaction between bromine and ethene

solution of bromine in water, the bromine loses its colour. It has reacted with the ethene. The double bond in ethene breaks open and forms new bonds to bromine atoms (picture 8). This type of reaction, in which a double bond breaks and adds on two new atoms, is called an **addition reaction**.

Alkenes do addition reactions with many other substances. This makes alkenes — especially ethene — very useful building blocks for making other organic chemicals. They are particularly useful for making addition polymers (page 172).

An important addition reaction of alkenes is with hydrogen. Alkenes react with hydrogen to form alkanes: the alkene becomes saturated. In the case of ethene, the reaction is:

$$\text{ethene} + \text{hydrogen} \xrightarrow[\text{nickel catalyst}]{\text{heat,}} \text{ethane}$$

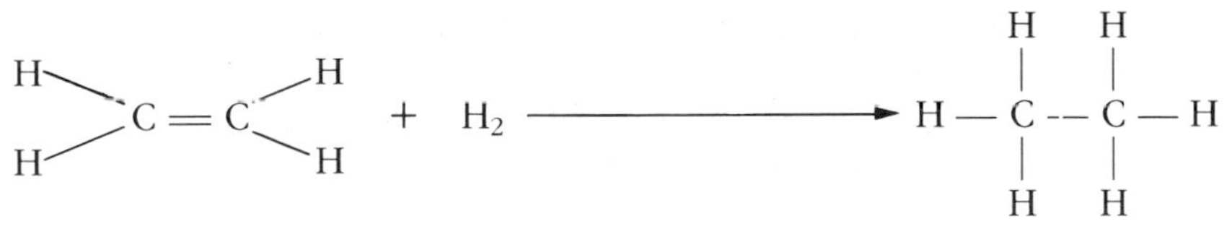

To make the reaction go quickly, a catalyst made of nickel and a temperature of 150°C are used. This reaction is called **hydrogenation**. Hydrogenation reactions are used to manufacture margarine.

Picture 9 Unsaturated and saturated fats

Fats, oils and margarine

Fats and oils are organic compounds with similar chemical structures. Here we are talking about *edible* oils like olive oil and corn oil. They should not be confused with inedible oils like lubricating oil. The molecules of oils and fats are built from substances called **fatty acids**. The main parts of fatty acids are long hydrocarbon chains. In oils, these hydrocarbon chains usually contain one or more double bonds: they are unsaturated. Solid fats, on the other hand, are usually saturated (picture 9). Animal fats tend to be more saturated than vegetable oils and fats.

We can use hydrogenation to change liquid oils to solid fats. This is how margarine is made. An unsaturated oil is reacted with hydrogen using a nickel catalyst. Hydrogen adds across the double bonds and the oil becomes saturated. The more hydrogen you use, the more saturated — and the more solid — the fat becomes. If you want a hard margarine , you use a lot of hydrogen. But if you want a soft, spread-from the-fridge margarine you use less hydrogen.

There is now quite a lot of evidence linking saturated fats with heart disease. So the trend is towards eating more unsaturated vegetable fats and less saturated animal fats. Softer, 'polyunsaturated' margarines are reckoned to be healthier than harder margarines or butter.

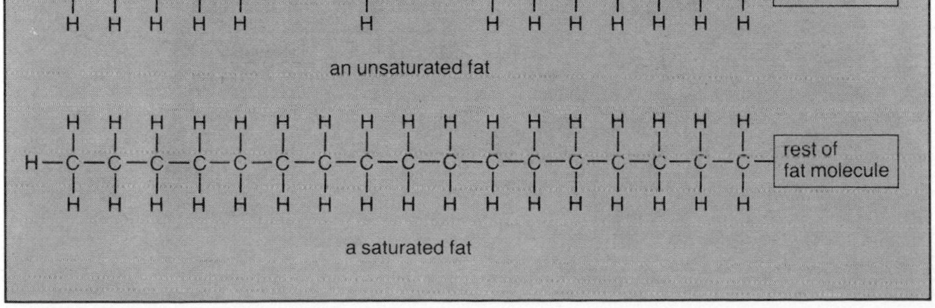

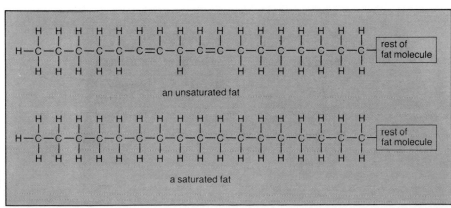

Picture 10

Activities

A Cracking with models

You will need a molecular modelling kit of the 'ball and stick' type. Use it to build a model of a molecule of decane. Its structure is shown in picture 3. Make sure every hole has a stick in it.

Now pull apart one — any one — of the carbon-carbon bonds in the model, so you get two fragments. This represents breaking a bond during cracking.

Rearrange the atoms in the two fragments so that once again every hole has a stick in it.

Try to identify the two molecules that you have formed. (Use table 1 and the Data Section.)

B Cracking in the laboratory

Use the apparatus shown in picture 4 on page 161.
CARE Eye protection must be worn. Beware of 'suck back' (see below).

Set up the apparatus as shown and heat the catalyst strongly. Now heat the paraffin oil more gently so that it vaporises. The vapour will pass over the catalyst where the cracking reaction takes place. Return the flame to the catalyst to keep it hot.

A gaseous product will collect in the second tube. Put a stopper in this tube and keep the gas for testing.

Care There is a danger of the water sucking back into the hot tube. As soon as you stop heating, remove the delivery tube from the water so 'suck back' cannot occur.

Test the gas in the tube by shaking it with bromine water (**CARE** Avoid skin contact). What happens? What does this tell you about the gas?

As well as the gaseous product, there is a liquid product from this experiment. Where does it collect?

C Testing oils and fats for unsaturation

You can use bromine water to test oils and fats to see how unsaturated they are. (**CARE** Avoid skin contact with bromine water.) The more unsaturated the oil, the more bromine it will decolorise.

Put five drops of olive oil or other vegetable oil in a test tube. Add $2 \, cm^3$ of ethanol (this is to help the oil mix with the bromine water).

Add five drops of bromine water to the tube. Stopper the tube and shake. Does the colour of the bromine disappear? If so, add five more drops and shake again. Go on adding bromine water and shaking until it is no longer decolorised. Count the total number of drops of bromine water that get decolourised.

Repeat the experiment for other oils and fats. You will have to plan how to make the results comparable. Place the different oils and fats in order, according to how unsaturated they are.

Questions

1 Explain what is meant by each of these words:

a cracking,

b double bond,

c alkene,

d unsaturated.

2 Cracking reactions are very important in oil refineries. Give *two* reasons why.

3 Dodecane is an alkane found in the kerosine fraction of crude oil. Its structure is:

H H H H H H H H H H H H
| | | | | | | | | | | |
H—C—C—C—C—C—C—C—C—C—C—C—C—H
| | | | | | | | | | | |
H H H H H H H H H H H H

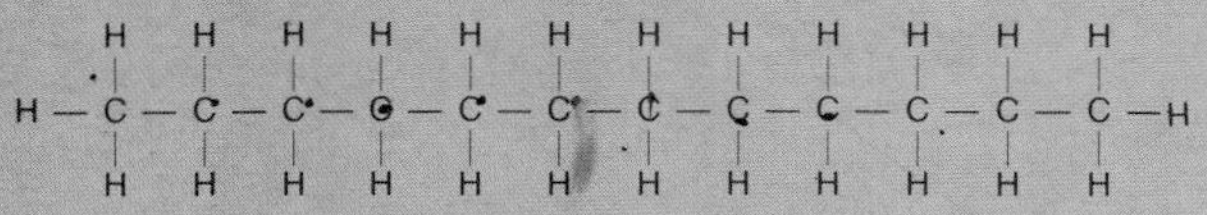

Write equations (similar to the one in picture 3 on page 161) to show two different sets of products that could be formed by cracking dodecane.

4 Table 2 shows the demand for different fractions of North Sea oil in summer and in winter. Use the table to answer questions (a) to (c). You may also need to refer to table 1 on page 155 to remind yourself of the uses of the different fractions.

a Why is the demand for diesel oil and residue greater in winter than in summer?

b Why is the demand for petrol fairly constant in summer and winter?

c What could an oil company do to cope with the changing demand between summer and winter?

5 Look at table 1.

a What do the names of all the alkenes have in common?

b The simplest alk*ane* is methane, CH_4. Why is the simplest alk*ene* ethene, not methene?

c Write an equation to show the reaction that would occur when propene reacts with bromine.

Table 2 Demand for North Sea oil fractions in Summer and Winter

Fraction	Percentage of total demand	
	Summer	Winter
Refinery gas	3.6	3
Gasoline (petrol)	32	29
kerosine (paraffin)	12	6
Diesel oil	17	23
Residue	35.4	39

Sticky stuff

Without adhesives our world would fall apart — literally. This book certainly would, and so would your shoes and probably the chair you're sitting on.

All glues start off runny and sticky, then turn solid. The solid holds the two surfaces together. How is this done? There are two main kinds of glue: solvent glues and polymerising glues.

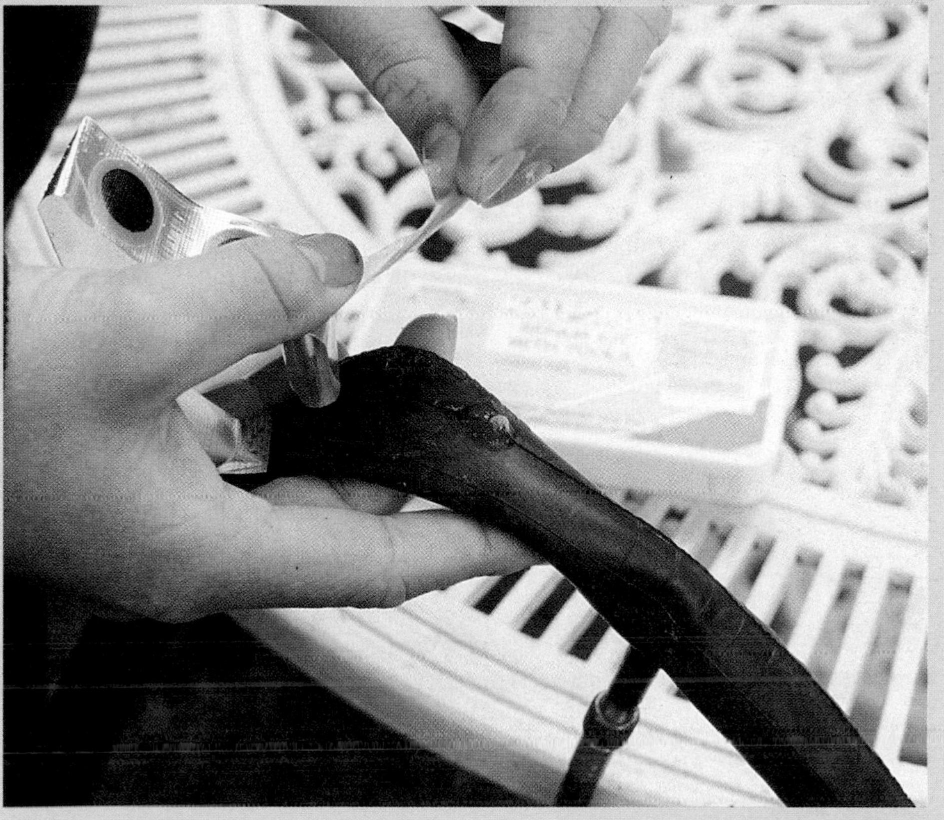

Picture 2 The glue used to mend punctures on bicycle tyres contains rubber dissolved in a volatile solvent

Solvent glues

Solvent glues have a solid dissolved in a solvent that is volatile (easily vaporised). When the solvent evaporates away, the solid is left behind (picture 1). When you stick a stamp on a letter you are using a solvent glue — and you provide the solvent yourself. On the back of the stamp there is a solid gum, similar to starch. When you lick the stamp, the solid gum dissolves in water. When the stamp is stuck on to the letter, the water quickly evaporates and gets absorbed by the paper, leaving the solid to hold letter and stamp together.

Polystyrene cement, used in model making, has polystyrene plastic dissolved in a volatile organic solvent. The solvent quickly evaporates away as the glue sets.

One problem with solvent glues is that the solvent vapour may be toxic. There is more about this in *The Living World*, topic D2.

Polymerising glues

The trouble with solvent glues is that tiny gaps are left where the solvent evaporates. This weakens the join. A polymerising glue has no solvent. It consists of a monomer which polymerises when the glue sets. See topic H3 for more about polymerisation. The polymer holds the surfaces together. The problem is, how do you stop it polymerising in the tube? One way is to have a separate 'hardener' which you mix with the monomer when you're ready to use it. The 'hardener' contains a catalyst which starts the polymerization reaction. Epoxy adhesives like 'Araldite' work in this way

Another way is to use a catalyst that is naturally present in the air. For example, *Superglue* has a monomer which polymerises when it meets water. When you spread the glue on the surface to be joined, it is exposed to water vapour in the air. This starts the polymerisation reaction, which is very quick — as you will know if you've ever got this kind of glue on your skin by accident. In fact, *Superglue* is so good at sticking to skin that doctors use it in skin grafts.

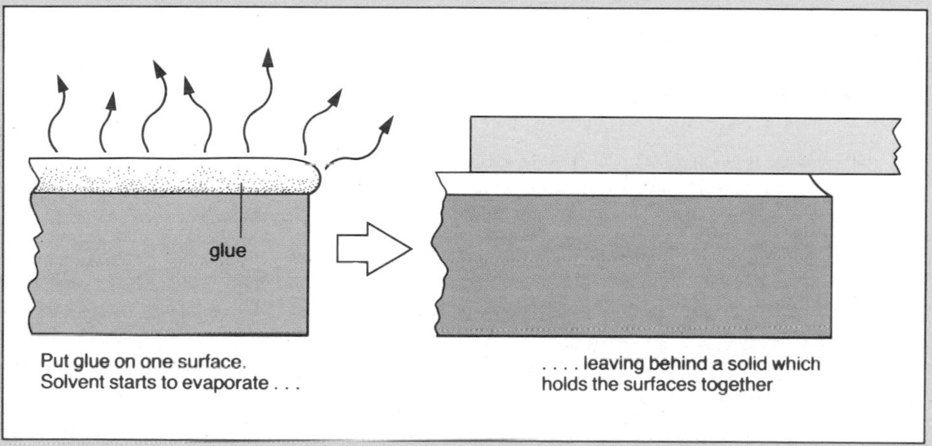

glue
Put glue on one surface.
Solvent starts to evaporate . . .
. . . . leaving behind a solid which
holds the surfaces together

Picture 1 How a solvent glue works

1 Explain why polymerising glues are usually stronger than solvent glues.
2 The instructions on a tube of glue usually say something like: 'Surfaces to be joined must be clean, dry and free from grease'. Why is this important?
3 Wood and paper are easily glued together. Glass and metal are more difficult. Can you suggest why?
4 Why does polystyrene cement not set while it is in the tube?
5 All glues set more quickly at higher temperatures. Why?

H3 Polymers

Polymers have long, thin molecules made by joining together lots of shorter units. In this topic we look at some natural and synthetic polymers.

Picture 1 Both these shirts are made from polymers — one is natural, one is synthetic. Can you tell which is which?

The pages of this book are made from a polymer — cellulose — and the ink contains a polymer to make it stick to the pages. The fingers you use to turn the pages are covered with skin made from a polymer — protein. The eyes you read it with, and the brain you understand it with, are mostly protein too.

All organisms are built from natural polymers like starch, cellulose and protein. We have used naturally occurring polymers like wood, cotton and wool for thousands of years.

Yet the first *synthetic* polymers — synthetic fibres and plastics — were made less than a hundred years ago. Today they are everywhere, but they didn't start being used on a large scale until the 1950s. Your grandparents would have used hardly any synthetic polymers when they were your age — ask them and see.

Why has it taken so long for humans to take advantage of these useful materials? One reason is that most modern polymers are made from oil – and the oil industry only really got going in the 1950s. Another reason is that scientists did not understand what polymers *were* before 1922. Once they understood the kind of molecules that polymers contain, scientists quickly learned how to make polymers to order.

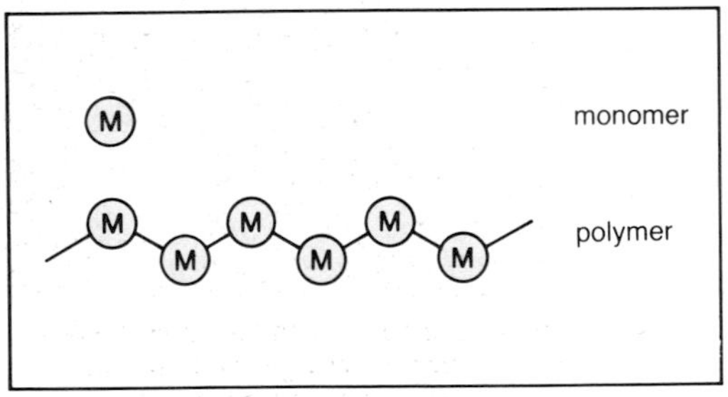

Picture 2 Monomer and polymer

What are polymers?

In 1922, a German chemist called Hermann Staudinger suggested that rubber is made of molecular chains in which identical units are joined together. Many scientists didn't believe him — they thought it just contained clumps of small molecules.

Hermann Staudinger got it right. Like all **polymers**, rubber is made by joining together large numbers of small molecules called **monomers**. Picture 2 gives the general idea. The word 'polymer' comes from Greek words: the *poly* bit means many, and *mer* means part. The process of joining up monomers to form a polymer is called **polymerisation**.

Polymers are named after the monomer unit they contain. Polythene, for example, is made by joining together lots of ethene units — strictly speaking, its name should be poly(ethene). Picture 3 shows the idea another way. Most polymers have hundreds or thousands of monomers in a single chain.

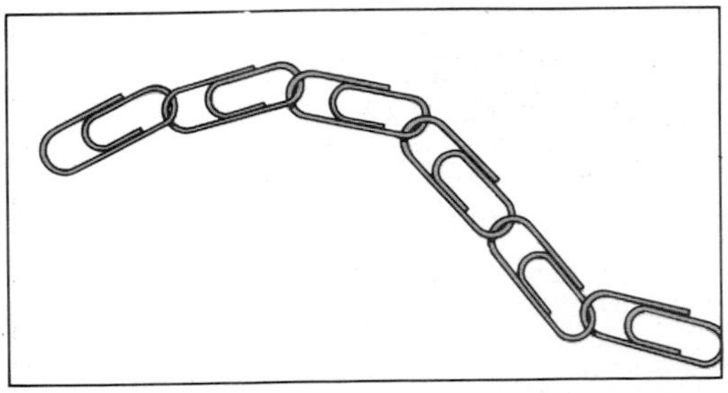

Picture 3 Polypaperclip!

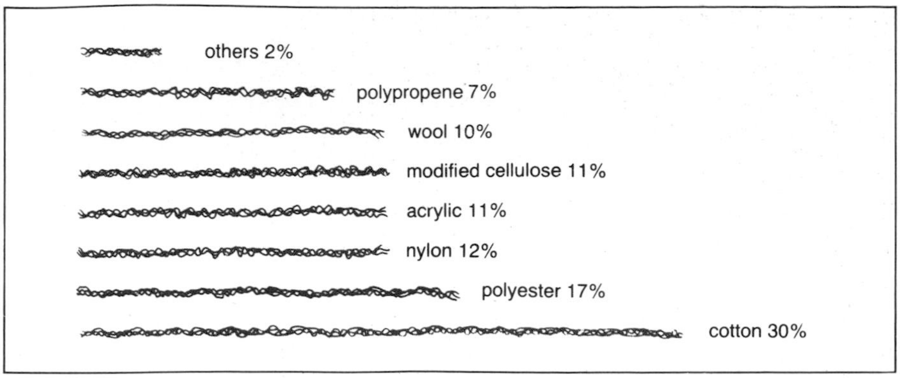

Picture 4 Popularity of clothing fibres in Western Europe. The percentages show the share of the market

Classifying polymers

Topic A2 looks at ways of classifying materials. One classification is as natural and human-made. **Natural polymers**, such as rubber, silk and cotton are made by living things. Human-made or **synthetic polymers** include polythene, nylon and polyester.

Natural polymers come in many different forms (see below). Synthetic polymers are mainly either **plastics** or **fibres** (see A2). Plastics are flexible and easily moulded, whereas fibres form long, thin strands. We'll see the reason for the differences in their properties later in this topic.

Fibres are particularly useful for making clothes, because they can be spun into threads and woven into cloth. Picture 4 shows fibres that are commonly used in clothes. You can see we use both natural and synthetic polymers for clothing fibres.

Another way of classifying polymers is according to the way the monomers are joined together. There are **addition** and **condensation** polymers, and these are explained in topic H4.

Some natural polymers

Carbohydrates: starch and cellulose

Starch and cellulose are polymers of glucose. Starch molecules (picture 5) are just chains of glucose monomers joined together. This type of polymer is called a **polysaccharide** ('many sugars').

You can find out more about how the glucose units are joined together in the next topic. The important thing is that they can be easily joined up and easily separated again. This makes starch a convenient substance for storing glucose — and therefore storing energy. In a grain of wheat or a potato, the starch chains are coiled up so they pack closely together. This way a lot of energy is stored in a small space.

Animals store glucose in a polysaccharide that is very similar to starch, called **glycogen**. Glycogen can be quickly broken down to give a ready supply of glucose when energy is needed (picture 6).

Picture 7 shows the structure of cellulose. You can see that it's very similar to starch, but the glucose units are joined together in a different way. This makes cellulose tougher and more fibrous than starch. Cellulose is the

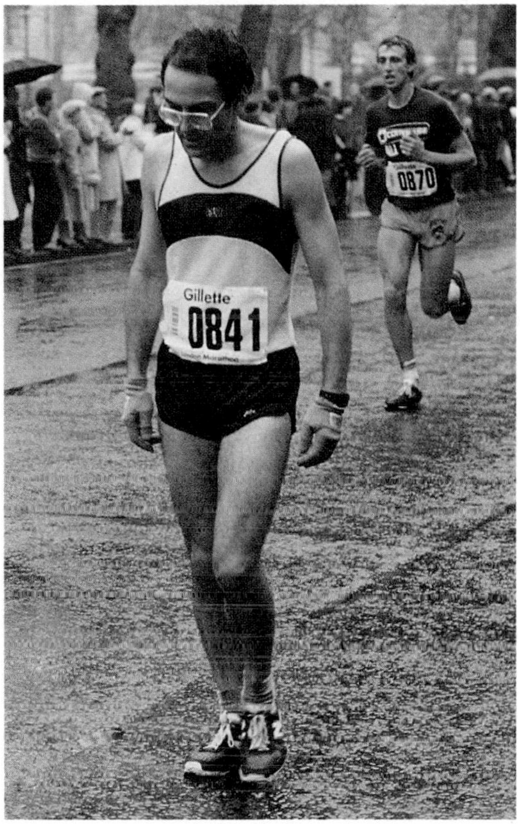

Picture 6 Long-distance runners train their bodies to make lots of glycogen so they can keep going for a long time. When a marathon runner nears the end of the 26 mile race, he or she may run out of glycogen and suddenly feel extremely tired. This often happens after 20 miles and is called 'going through the wall'

Picture 5 The structure of starch

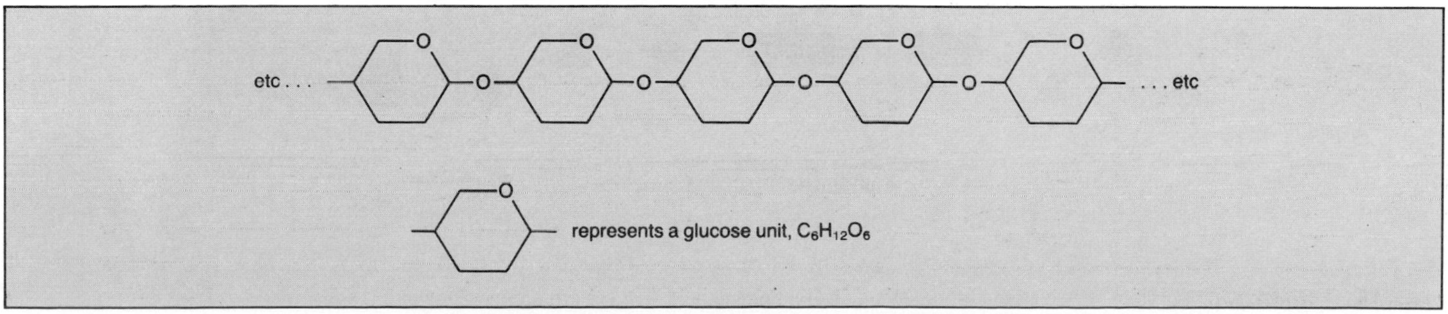

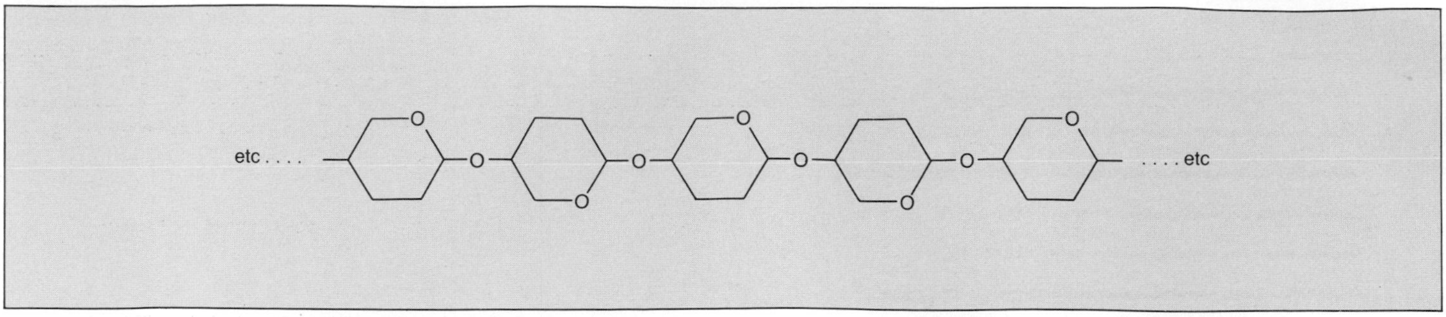
etc....
....etc

Picture 7 The structure of cellulose

structural material that plant cell walls are made of, and it gives plant cells their strength. Many of the materials we use, such as paper, cardboard, cotton and linen, contain mainly cellulose. Cellulose can be modified by treating it with chemicals to make semi-synthetic fibres such as rayon. Picture 8 shows another example.

Picture 8 This fabric is made from a semi-synthetic fibre – a modified form of cellulose

Proteins

Many polymers have only one type of monomer unit. Starch, for example, contains only glucose units. Proteins, on the other hand, use several different monomer units. These units are called **amino acids**, and there are about 20 different ones found in naturally-occurring proteins. Picture 9 shows the idea.

A typical protein molecule may contain thousands of amino acid units joined together. What is more, each amino acid may be one of around 20 different kinds. This means that many different proteins can be made — which is why protein materials are so varied. Hair, skin, muscle, egg white and silk are all made of types of proteins. In fact, there are enough different proteins for every human to have their own, unique set.

After you eat a protein food such as cheese, your digestive enzymes break the protein down into separate amino acids. Later, your cells polymerise the amino acids in a different order to form whatever protein they need. They receive instructions about the right order from another polymer, DNA. This is the substance from which our genes are made. You can learn more about this in *The Living World*, topic F5.

Synthetic polymers

Plastics

Plastics are very useful materials. They are easy to shape by moulding or melting, and they are usually cheap. Chemists can 'design' plastics with all sorts of properties to suit different uses.

The simplest and commonest plastic is polythene, which is made by polymerising ethene. You can see in the next topic how the ethene monomer units are joined together. Table 1 shows some common plastics and their uses.

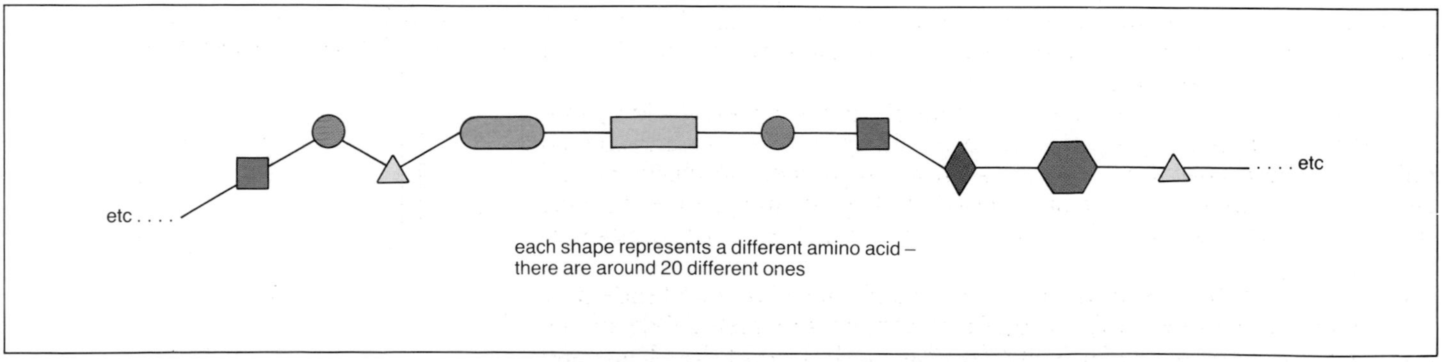
etc....
....etc
each shape represents a different amino acid – there are around 20 different ones

Picture 9 The structure of protein. Each shape represents a different amino acid — there are around 20 different ones

Table 1 Some common synthetic polymers

Polymer	Plastic or fibre	Monomer		Examples of uses
Polythene	plastic	ethene	$\begin{array}{c} H \\ \\ H \end{array}\hspace{-4pt}>C=C<\hspace{-4pt}\begin{array}{c} H \\ \\ H \end{array}$	Plastic bags, squeezy bottles, washing up bowls
Polypropene	plastic, fibre	propene	$\begin{array}{c} CH_3 \\ \\ H \end{array}\hspace{-4pt}>C=C<\hspace{-4pt}\begin{array}{c} H \\ \\ H \end{array}$	Milk bottle crates, carpet, plastic rope
Polystyrene	plastic	styrene	$\begin{array}{c} C_6H_5 \\ \\ H \end{array}\hspace{-4pt}>C=C<\hspace{-4pt}\begin{array}{c} H \\ \\ H \end{array}$	Plastic toys, expanded polystyrene for insulation
Polyvinyl chloride (pvc)	plastic	vinyl chloride (chloroethene)	$\begin{array}{c} Cl \\ \\ H \end{array}\hspace{-4pt}>C=C<\hspace{-4pt}\begin{array}{c} H \\ \\ H \end{array}$	Guttering and pipes, electrical insulation, floor covering
Acrylic fibre	fibre	acrylonitrile (cyanoethene)	$\begin{array}{c} CN \\ \\ H \end{array}\hspace{-4pt}>C=C<\hspace{-4pt}\begin{array}{c} H \\ \\ H \end{array}$	Fibre for clothing (substitute for wool)
Nylon	fibre, plastic	1,6-diaminohexane and hexanedioic acid		Fibre for clothing, carpets, ropes. Plastic for engineering parts.
Polyester	fibre, plastic	ethanediol and benzenedioic acid		Fibre for clothing, boat sails. Plastic for videotape, photo film.

Fibres

Some polymers can be used as both plastics and fibres. For example, polypropene, which is the plastic used to make milk bottle crates, can be made into a fibre for ropes. Nylon is normally used as a fibre, but it can also be moulded as a plastic — it's used where a strong plastic is needed for things like gear wheels. You can read more about this below.

You can see some common synthetic fibres in table 1. Synthetic fibres have replaced natural fibres like cotton and wool for many uses. The synthetic fibres are cheaper, and they are usually harder wearing. What is more, they are often easier to wash and iron: acrylic fibre does not shrink like wool, for example. Polyester does not need ironing as much as cotton.

Even so, many people prefer natural fibres to synthetic ones. Natural fibres feel less 'sweaty' to wear, and they often look more stylish — and expensive.

What gives polymers their special properties?

As with all substances, the properties of polymers are decided by their structures. Polymer molecules are like long, thin chains, and we can think of polymers as one-dimensional giant structures.

A single polymer molecule is like a single piece of spaghetti — long, thin and flexible. Of course, a small piece of plastic or fibre would contain billions of these chains. In a plastic such as polythene, the chains are all tangled up together — rather like a bowlful of spaghetti (picture 10). Like spaghetti, the chains can slide over each other, which is why the plastic is flexible.

When you heat the plastic, the molecular chains move faster and slide over each other even more easily. The plastic softens and melts. One of the reasons plastics are so useful is that you can push around the chains and mould the plastic into any shape you want.

a piece of spaghetti – like a single polymer chain

a bowlful of spaghetti – like polymer chains tangled up together

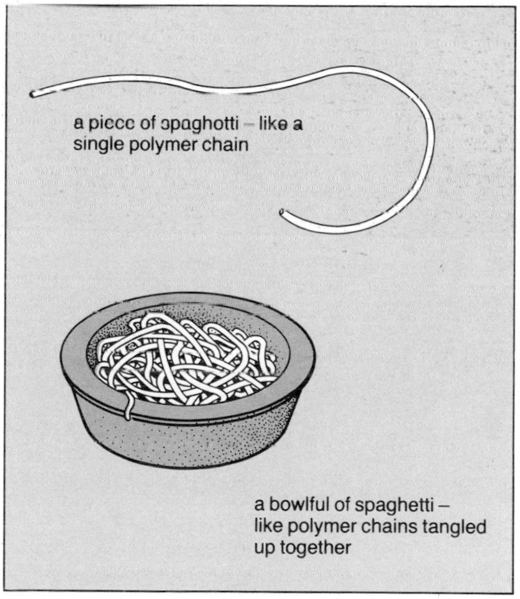

Picture 10 Polymers are like spaghetti

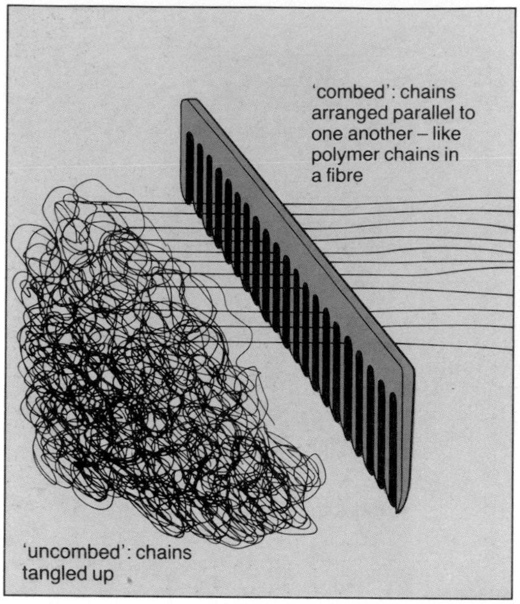

Picture 11 Combing

Picture 12 Splitting a log is easy, because you are splitting separate strands of fibres. But cutting across the grain of the wood is more difficult because you have to break many polymer chains

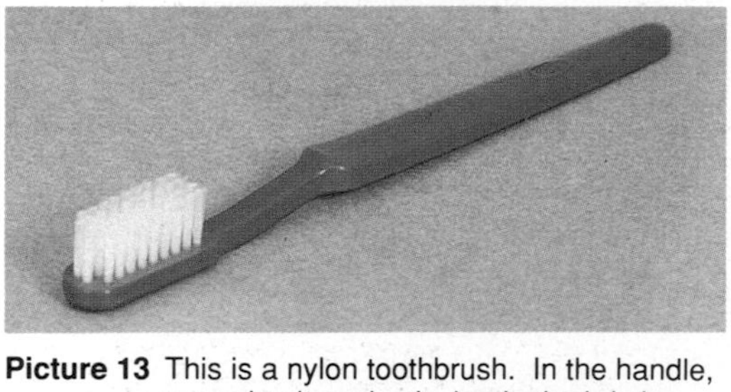

Picture 13 This is a nylon toothbrush. In the handle, the nylon is a plastic, but in the bristles, the nylon is in the form of a fibre

What about fibres?

Imagine combing spaghetti with a large comb so that the spaghetti strands are brought parallel to one another (picture 11). This is the way the polymer chains are arranged in fibres. The strands that you see in a fibre like polyester or cotton contain bunches of parallel polymer chains.

The strands of fibre are difficult to break, because breaking one strand involves breaking many polymer chains all at once. But it is easy to pull the separate strands apart, because that doesn't involve breaking polymer chains. It's much easier to fray a rope than to break it. Picture 12 illustrates the same idea.

How can a plastic become a fibre?

The toothbrush in picture 13 is made of a single polymer — nylon. The handle is flexible and has been moulded: it is a *plastic*. The bristles are *fibres*. To make the nylon behave as a fibre, the polymer chains have to be made parallel, rather like combing the spaghetti in picture 11. This is done by **drawing** the fibres, as shown in picture 14.

Before a synthetic polymer like nylon or polyester can be used as a fibre, it has to be drawn by pulling it so the polymer chains line up. Nylon and polyester make good fibres because, once drawn, the chains stay in their parallel arrangement. Polythene doesn't make a good fibre because, after drawing, the chains tend to go back into the disorganised state of a plastic.

Designing polymers to order

Chemists can make polymers to suit most purposes. There is a plastic that doesn't stick to anything, which is useful for non-stick pans. It's called polytetrafluoroethene or ptfe. There is a fibre called kevlar that, weight for weight, is stronger than steel. It is used to make bullet-proof vests. There are even plastics that conduct electricity. One of the disadvantages of plastics is their low melting point. But there are now plastic roasting bags that you can put in the oven, and there is even the possibility of a plastic car engine.

Suppose a manufacturer wants a polymer to do a particular job. Chemists first decide the type of polymer chain that is needed to give the required properties. Then they make the necessary monomers, usually by breaking down large molecules from crude oil. Finally, they join together the monomers to make the polymer. Polymer chemistry is a matter of breaking down big molecules, then building new ones.

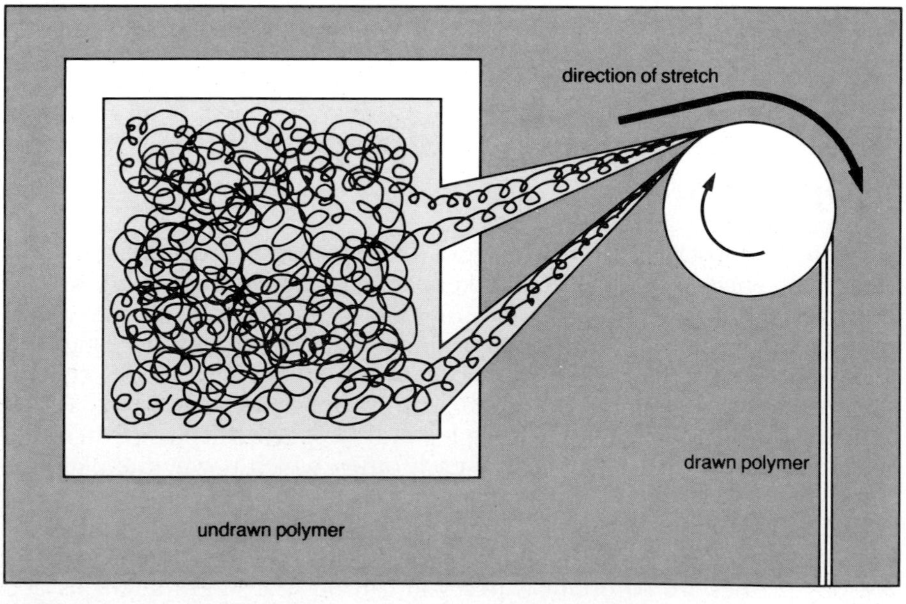

Picture 14 Drawing a polymer

Polymers and the environment

A big problem with synthetic polymers is getting rid of them when they're finished with. Natural polymers, like cellulose in paper and protein in wool, are not too bad. They rot fairly quickly as micro-organisms break them down and use them for food. They are **biodegradable.**

But micro-organisms can't break down synthetic polymers like polythene and nylon. In the 50 years or so that synthetic polymers have been around, micro-organisms have not had time to evolve the ability to use them for food. So plastics can be a serious litter problem — see picture 15 for an example.

One answer to the problem might be to **recycle** waste plastic. Unfortunately, this is not as easy as recycling, say, glass or steel. The trouble is that there are many different types of plastics in use, and it's difficult to tell which is which. To recycle plastics effectively you would need to sort them out first, rather as a bottle bank sorts glass into different colours. But although *you* may be able tell the difference between polythene and polystyrene, many people cannot. At present, recycling plastic is limited to melting down all the different types together. This makes a messy product which is of limited use. Black plastic rubbish bags are made from recycled plastic.

Picture 15 Polythene is not very biodegradable. This means that it stays around long after it has outlived its useful purpose

Activities

A Explaining polymers

A good way to test whether you understand an idea is to try explaining it to someone.

Find a person (a relative or neighbour, perhaps) who does not know much science. Use a simple model, such as 'polypaperclip' on page 166, to explain the following.

1 What is a polymer? (You may have to explain about molecules first.)
2 Why are plastics flexible?
3 Why do fibres form strands?

B Looking for fibres

You can use the label at the back of a garment to find out what fibre it contains. (Often a mixture of fibres is used.)

List at least five different fibres that are used in items of your own clothing. For each fibre, say what kind of clothing items it is used in, and why you think that particular fibre is chosen.

- Which do you wear more: natural or synthetic fibres?
- Why do manufacturers often use a mixture of fibres, rather than a single one?

C Investigating a plastic cup

You will need a plastic cup of the type you get from drink machines — but *not* the insulated type made from expanded polystyrene.

Try tearing the cup in two different directions. First, grasp the cup at the top and bottom and try tearing it apart so the top is separated from the bottom. Can you do it? Now try tearing again, but this time grasp each side of the cup and try tearing it so one side is separated from the other.

What difference do you notice? Can you suggest an explanation? Think about the way the polymer chains are arranged in the cup. It may help you to look at picture 12.

D Packaging for potato crisps

Suppose you are responsible for the packaging department of a big potato crisp manufacturer. You have to decide what material to make your packaging from.

1 Write down the properties that you would want the packaging material to have. Remember that crisps are brittle, and that they must stay crisp and keep their flavour.
2 Can you suggest a natural polymer material that has the properties you wrote down in (1)?
3 Can you suggest a synthetic polymer material that has the properties you wrote down in (1)?
4 What material will you choose for your packaging? What drawbacks, if any, does this material have?
5 Find out what material is actually used by crisp manufacturers. You may have to write and ask them.

Questions

1 Explain what the following words mean: (a) polymer, (b) monomer, (c) plastic, (d) fibre.

2 What is the monomer in each of the following polymers?
(a) Polythene, (b) Starch, (c) Polypropene, (d) Cellulose, (e) Protein, (f) Polyurethane?

3 Each of the following materials contain polymers. For each material, say whether it is (i) natural or synthetic (ii) plastic or fibre.
(a) Wood, (b) Pvc, (c) Linen, (d) Polyester, (e) Rubber, (f) Leather, (g) Raffia, (h) Perspex, (i) Rayon

4 You often hear chemists say 'Crude oil is too valuable to burn'. Why do they say this? If it is true, what can be done about it?

5a Why does plastic cause a particularly bad waste disposal problem?

b Some manufacturers are now making biodegradable plastics. One type, used for making shopping bags, consists of tiny grains of polythene stuck together with cellulose. Why does this make the plastic degradable? Will it degrade completely? Explain.

6 Explain the following:
a There are many types of proteins, but very few types of starch.
b Starch and cellulose are both polymers of glucose. Starch is a good energy food, but cellulose has no food value.

H4 From monomer to polymer

In this topic we look at the different ways monomers can be joined to form polymers.

Picture 1 This paperweight is made from casting resin. When the resin sets hard, a polymerisation reaction takes place

The paperweight in picture 1 was made using casting resin. The clear plastic started off as a liquid monomer. When it was mixed with a special catalyst, the monomer polymerised and turned into a solid plastic.

For plastic or fibre manufacturers, quick polymerisation is important. But they do not want the polymer to break down again (**depolymerise**) quickly, or they might not sell much of their product.

Living things need to be able to join up monomers quickly and easily to form polymers such as starch and protein. They also need to be able to break them down quickly when necessary.

There are two ways of joining monomers in a polymer: they are called addition and condensation polymerisation. Both ways need special conditions, and usually a catalyst, to get them started.

Addition polymerisation

Let's look at polythene as an example. The monomer for polythene is ethene (picture 2). The double bond in ethene makes it rather reactive. It tends to break open, leaving free bonds which can join on to other atoms or molecules in an addition reaction (see page 163). If there's nothing else around, ethene molecules will join on to each other to make a long chain. This is **addition polymerisation**.

Ethene molecules do not polymerise on their own. To make the reaction happen, you need high pressure to squeeze the molecules close together, and a high temperature to give them enough energy to react. A catalyst is used to make the reaction go faster. (There is more about catalysts on page 199.)

The commonest form of polythene is made using a temperature of about 200°C and a pressure of about 2000 atmospheres (20 MPa). It's impossible to get these conditions in the laboratory, so you won't be able to make polythene yourself.

The industrial process uses equipment like that shown in picture 3. Apart from the cost of the ethene, the main cost of this process is the energy needed to produce the high temperature and pressure. Topic D1 looks at some of the costs involved in the whole process of turning crude oil into a polythene article such as a washing-up bowl.

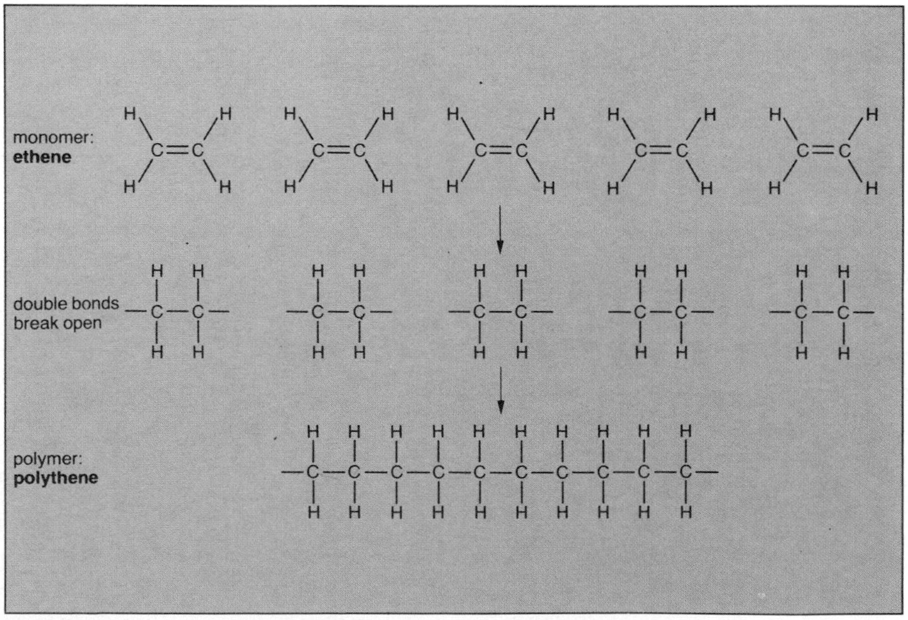

Picture 2 Ethene forms polythene by addition polymerisation

Picture 3 A chemical plant for producing polythene

Other addition polymers

Addition polymerisation needs a double bond in the molecule of the monomer. If you look at table 1 on page 169, you will see that most of the common plastics have this type of monomer. Polystyrene, pvc and polypropene are all addition polymers. Try working out some addition polymers in question 3.

Condensation polymerisation

In a **condensation reaction**, two molecules join together by taking out a small molecule from between them (picture 4). The small molecule is usually water, which is why it is called condensation.

If a condensation reaction happens at *both ends* of the molecules, a polymer chain is formed. This is **condensation polymerisation** (picture 5). In pictures 4 and 5 we have not shown the monomer molecules in detail – we've used boxes to represent part of the molecule, to make it simpler.

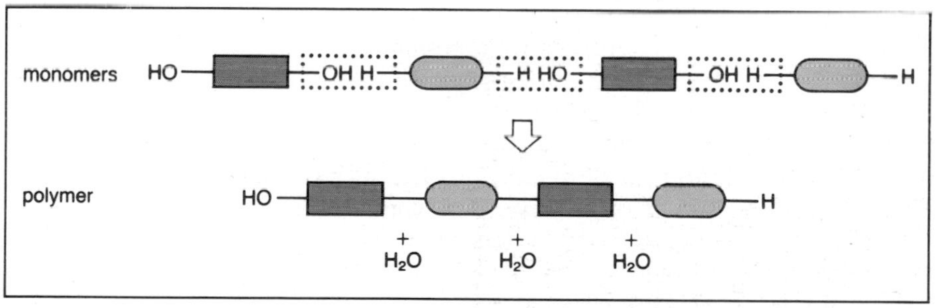

Picture 5 Condensation polymerisation

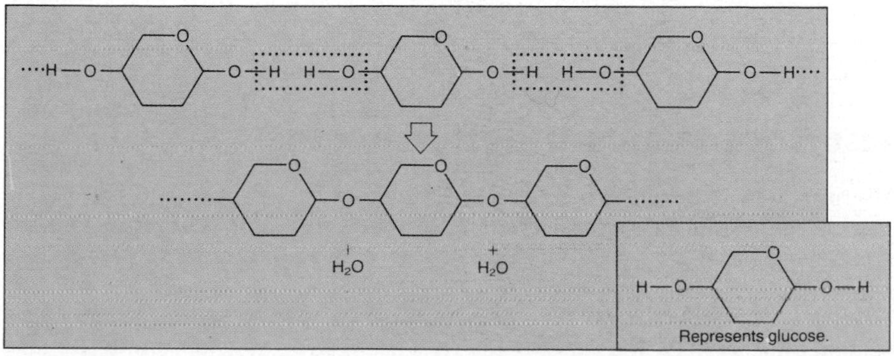

Picture 6 Glucose forms starch by condensation polymerisation

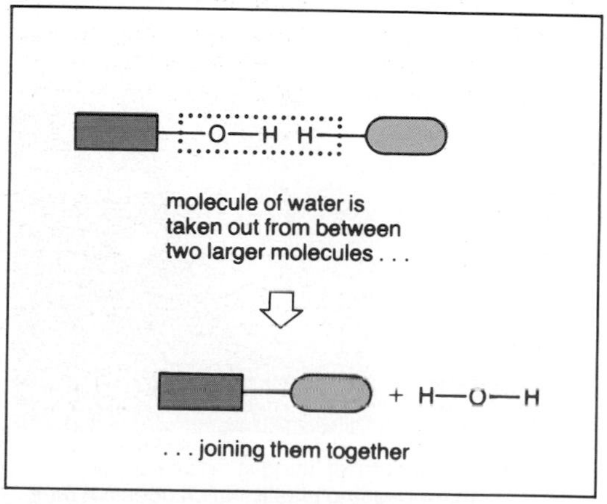

Picture 4 A condensation reaction

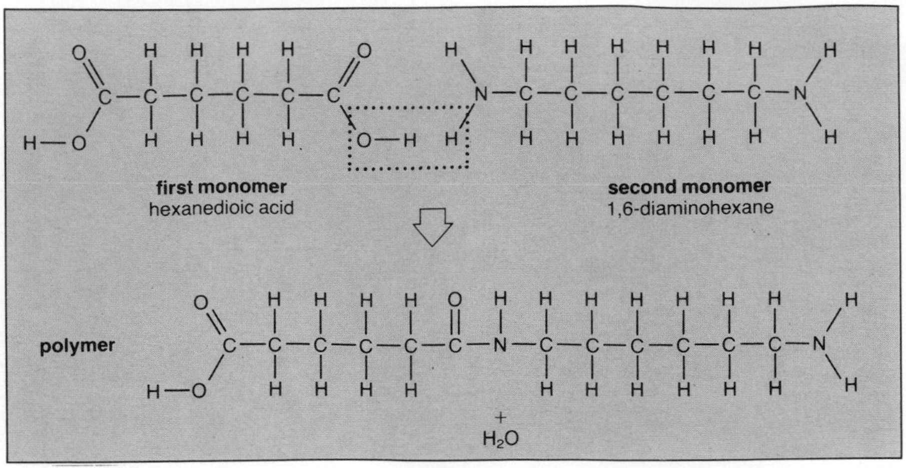

Picture 7 How the monomers join together in nylon

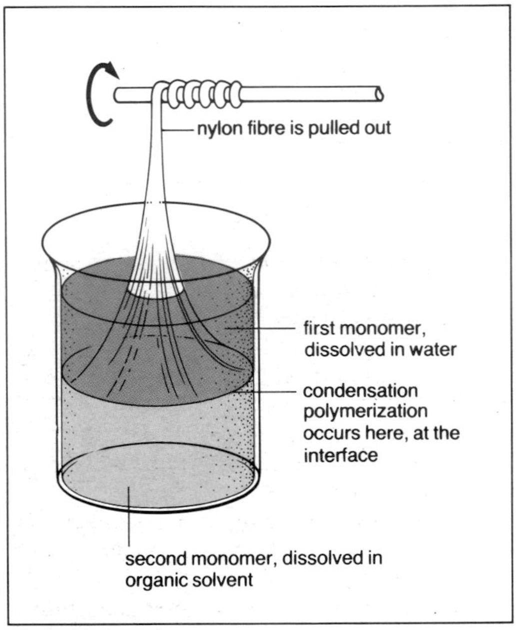

Picture 8 The 'nylon rope trick'

Most natural polymers join up by condensation polymerisation. Picture 6 shows the way glucose molecules join together to form starch. Water molecules are taken out from between glucose molecules. This happens many hundreds of times to form a starch chain. The reaction does not happen on its own — glucose doesn't automatically turn into starch. An enzyme is needed to catalyse the reaction and make it happen.

The starch can be turned back to glucose by putting the water molecules back in. This is called hydrolysis, and it reforms glucose. You can think of it as 'depolymerisation'. On its own, water does not react with starch. A catalyst is needed to make the reaction happen. The catalyst may be dilute acid, or an enzyme called amylase. The hydrolysis of starch is important in digestion: there is more about it in *The Living World*, topic C8.

Proteins are condensation polymers too. The amino acids are joined by condensation and separated by hydrolysis. Once again, enzymes are needed to catalyze the reactions. The link between amino acids is called a **peptide link.**

Nylon and polyester

Nylon and polyester are synthetic condensation polymers.

Nylon is made from two monomers, as shown in picture 7. Unlike starch and proteins, it is difficult to hydrolyse nylon and make it depolymerise. This is just as well for people who buy nylon clothes — you wouldn't want them depolymerising in the washing machine. But it does make nylon, like other synthetic polymers, difficult to dispose of when it's finished with.

Picture 8 shows a version of nylon polymerisation that can be done in the laboratory. It uses slightly different monomers from the industrial process, but the general idea is the same.

Polyester, like nylon, uses two monomers. Have you ever used plastic resin to make a canoe, repair bodywork or make a casting? If so, you probably used a polyester plastic.

Picture 9 This electrical fitting is made from a thermosetting plastic which does not melt when it gets hot

Thermoplastics and thermosets

All the plastic materials we have met so far can be softened and melted by heating, but they set again when cool. We call them **thermoplastics**. Thermoplastics are very useful because they can be moulded into any shape you want.

Some plastics behave rather differently. They do not soften at all when heated, but stay hard and rigid. If you heat them a lot, they just smoulder and char. This type of plastic is called **thermosetting**. You find thermosetting plastics in electrical fittings like plugs and sockets, where it is important that the plastic does not melt when it gets hot. The type shown in picture 9 is called urea-formaldehyde plastic. 'Bakelite', a similar plastic that is brown in colour, was the first synthetic plastic ever made.

Different structures, different properties

As always, we can explain the difference in properties if we look at the different structures. Picture 10 shows the polymer chains in thermoplastic and thermosetting polymers. In thermoplastics the polymer chains are free to slide past each other, so it's easy to change the shape.

In thermosetting polymers the chains are **cross-linked**. Instead of each chain being separate, neighbouring chains are linked together. This makes it difficult for polymer chains to move past each other, so the polymer is hard and rigid. Even when it is heated, the chains are still unable to move, so the polymer does not melt.

When rubber comes out of the rubber tree it is a runny, sticky liquid called latex. It is too sticky and soft to be much use. But if you add sulphur to the rubber, it makes cross-links between the polymer chains, and the rubber gets harder. This is called **vulcanising** the rubber. The more sulphur you add, the more cross-links are formed and the harder it gets. If you want a soft rubber (say for an eraser), you add a little sulphur. If you want a hard rubber for car tyres, you add a lot.

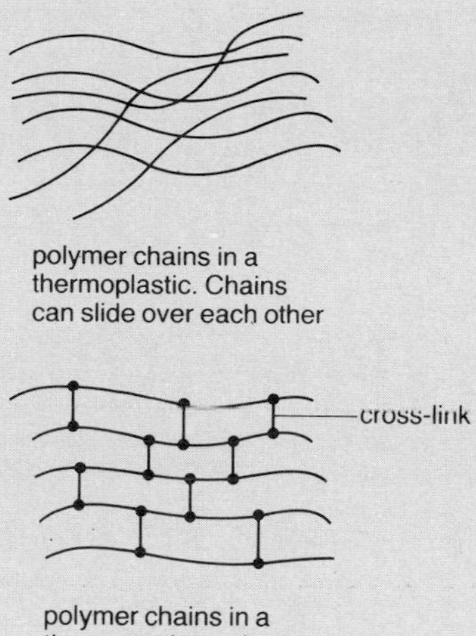
polymer chains in a thermoplastic. Chains can slide over each other
cross-link
polymer chains in a thermosetting polymer. Cross-links stop the chains moving

Picture 10 Polymer chains in a thermoplastic and in a thermoset

Activities

A Modelling addition polymerisation

Use 'ball and stick' models in this activity. Use black 'atoms' for carbon and white for hydrogen.

1 Start by making polythene. Build at least three molecules of ethene, then make them polymerise. If necessary, look at picture 2 to remind yourself what happens when ethene polymerises. Compare your polythene chain with those made by other groups. Are they all the same?

2 Now repeat (a) for a different addition polymer. You could try polyvinyl chloride (pvc) or polypropene. Look at table 1 on page 169 for the structure of the monomers.

3 Try making a **copolymer**. These are addition polymers where two or more monomers are used together in a single polymer.

Are your polymers likely to thermoplastic or thermosetting?

B Breaking down polythene

You can break down polythene into smaller molecules by heating it with a catalyst.

Use the same apparatus as in picture 4, page 161, but use pieces of polythene instead of the mineral wool soaked in paraffin oil. Remember to follow the safety precautions given. Watch especially to make sure the delivery tube does not get blocked.

When you have done the experiment, answer these questions.

1 What evidence was there that polythene was breaking down into smaller molecules?

2 What evidence was there that these smaller molecules contain double bonds?

3 Polythene is a polymer of ethene. Does the experiment prove that polythene turns back to ethene when it is heated with a catalyst?

Compare your answer to (3) with the answers of other students. Discuss any differences.

Questions

1 Explain the difference between addition polymerisation and condensation polymerisation.

2 Explain the difference between a thermosetting polymer and a thermoplastic polymer. How can their differences be explained in terms of their molecular structures?

3 If you know the structure of a monomer, you can work out the structure of the polymer it forms. For each of the following addition polymers, draw a section of the polymer chain containing at least three monomers. Use table 1 on page 169 to find the structures of the monomers.

a Polypropene.

b Polyvinyl chloride (pvc).

c Acrylic fibre.

4 Gloss paint contains a polymer. When the paint is in the tin, the polymer chains are separate, without cross-links. When the paint has been applied, cross-links form between the chains, and the paint hardens.

a Draw pictures to represent paint polymer chains before and after the paint has hardened.

b Why do you think the paint does not harden while it is sealed in the tin?

5 The price of virtually all plastics depends on the price of crude oil. Explain why.

If the cost of oil went up by 20%, would you expect the cost of polythene to go up by:
(a) 20%, (b) less than 20%, (c) more than 20%?

Explain your answer.

I1 Energy and chemical reactions

Whenever a chemical reaction takes place, energy is transferred.

Picture 1 The chemical reactions in fireworks transfer energy as heat, light and sound

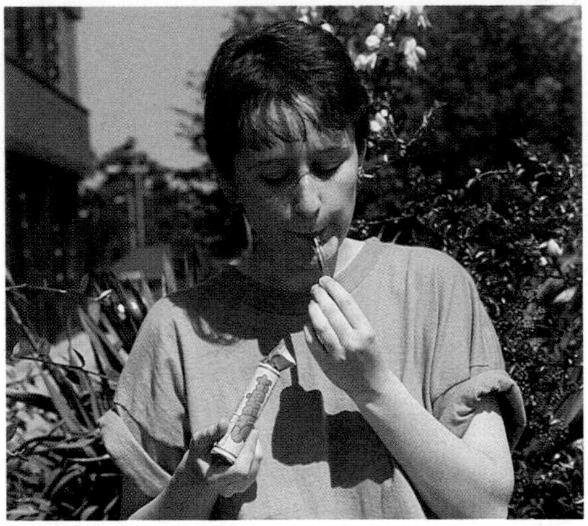

Picture 2 When sherbert mixes with water, an endothermic reaction takes place

Energy out, energy in

Most chemical reactions give out heat. They are called **exothermic reactions.**

We rely on exothermic reactions for the energy we need to keep things going. Most of these exothermic reactions involve fuels.

Fuels are substances that react with oxygen to give out heat. Coal, natural gas, petrol and wood are all fuels. Fuels provide most of the energy needed by society for heating, cooking, transport, industry — and generally keeping everything going. Your own body is kept going by fuel, called food. You can find out more about fuels in topic I2.

Some reactions *take in* heat. We call them **endothermic reactions**. When an endothermic reaction happens you usually notice a fall in temperature. Have you ever noticed that sherbet feels cool in your mouth when you eat it? Sherbet is a mixture of citric acid and sodium hydrogencarbonate. When water is added they react together like this:

citric acid + sodium hydrogencarbonate
→ sodium citrate + carbon dioxide + water

The reaction is endothermic, so heat is taken in from your mouth, making it feel cool.

Many reactions in living things are endothermic. **Photosynthesis** is an important example. In photosynthesis, plants use energy from the sun to make sugars and starch.

Picture 3 illustrates the difference between exothermic and endothermic reactions.

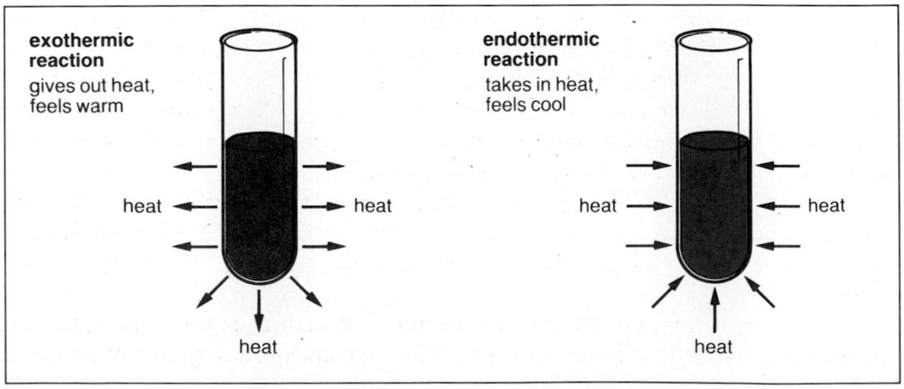

Picture 3 Exothermic and endothermic reactions

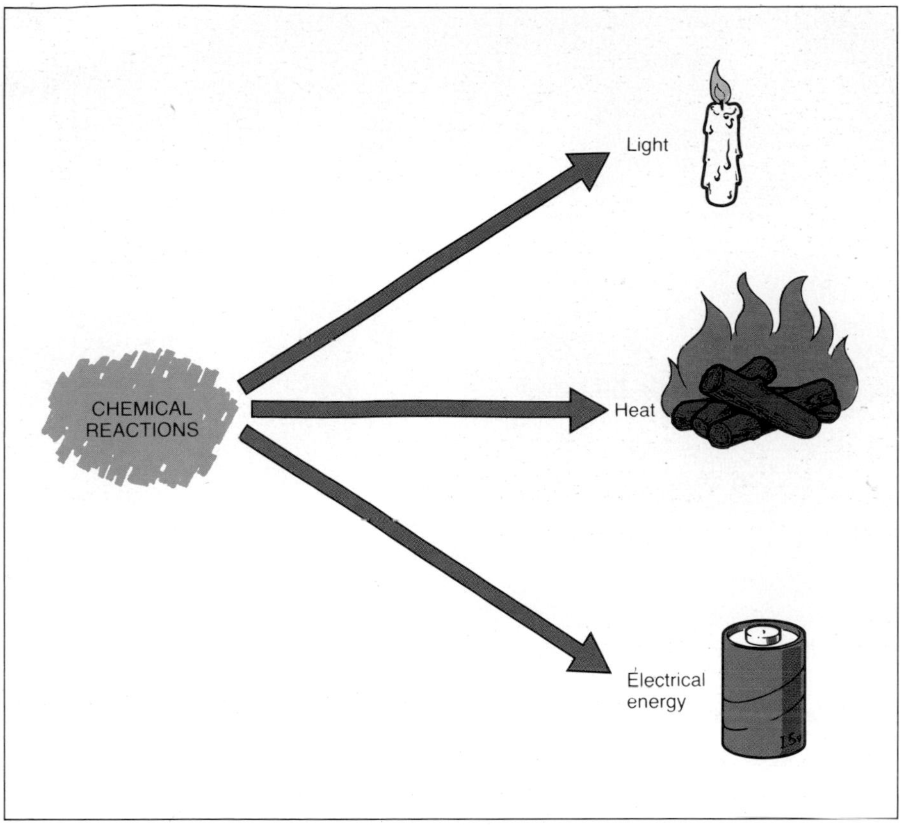

Picture 4 Energy transfers in chemical reactions

Do chemical reactions transfer energy in other ways?

When changes happen, energy is transferred from one thing to another. A common way that energy can be transferred is by heating. When a fuel burns, energy is transferred from the fuel to something else — water in a saucepan for example. The more energy that's transferred to the water, the hotter the water gets.

It is very common for chemicals to transfer energy by heating. But they can transfer energy in other ways too, as you can see from picture 4.

Transferring energy from chemicals by means of electricity is very important in cells and batteries.

Often a chemical reaction transfers energy in more than one way. For example, a burning candle transfers energy by heating *and* as light.

Getting chemical reactions started

Fuels do not start burning until they have been ignited. This is just as well. We do not want fuels bursting into flames until we are ready for them to do so. Burning is a chemical reaction, and like all reactions it goes faster at higher temperatures. At room temperature the reaction is so slow that it is effectively at a standstill. At the ignition temperature, the reaction is much faster. It gives out enough energy to keep itself going.

All reactions need energy to get them started. But some need so little energy that they can start at room temperature without being heated. Rusting is an example of such a reaction, and so is the reaction of carbonates with acid.

The energy needed to get a chemical reaction started is called its **activation energy**. There is more about activation energy in topics I5 and I6.

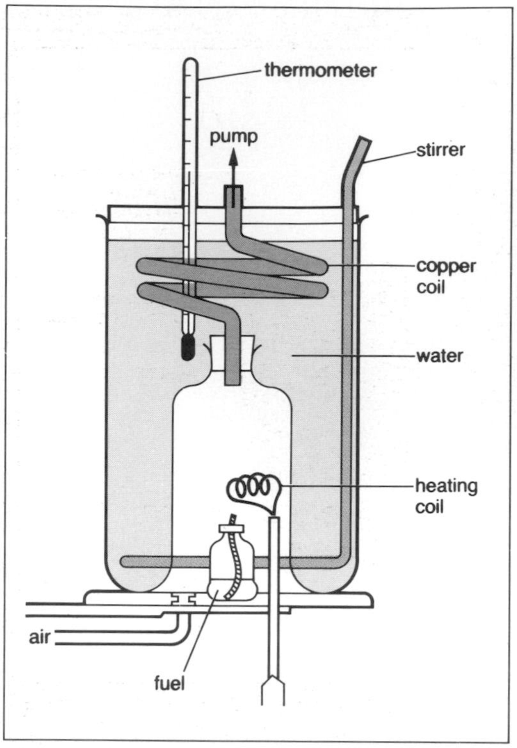

Picture 6 A fuel calorimeter

Picture 5 Providing the activation energy to start chemical reactions in a firework

How do we measure the heat transferred in chemical reactions?

The heat transferred in a chemical reaction can be measured using a calorimeter. Picture 6 shows the type of calorimeter that is often used to measure the heat transferred when a fuel burns. It is particularly useful for measuring the energy value of foods (see *The Living World*, topic C3).

The idea is to burn the fuel so that heat is transferred to water. The experiment is done in two stages.

Stage 1. A measured amount of the fuel is burned in the calorimeter. The pump draws air through the central chamber in which the fuel is burned. The burning fuel produces hot gases. These heat the water as they pass through the copper coil. The temperature rise in the water is noted.

Stage 2. The electrical heater is switched on. It is allowed to heat the water until the temperature has risen by the same amount as it did with the fuel. The amount of energy transferred electrically to the water is measured using a joulemeter.

Since the temperature rise is the same for each stage, the amount of energy transferred must be the same. So the amount of energy transferred by the burning fuel is found by simply reading the joulemeter.

Table 1 shows the results obtained in an experiment using ethanol as a fuel.

Table 1 Results of an experiment to find the energy transferred by heating when ethanol burns

Mass of ethanol used	= 2g
Temperature rise	= 20°C
Energy transferred electrically by heater to produce same temperature rise	= 60kJ
So, energy transferred when 2g of ethanol burns	= 60kJ
So, energy transferred by 1g of ethanol	= 30kJ

This apparatus can be used to compare the energy values of different fuels. Activity B uses a simpler version of the apparatus.

Activities

A Looking at exothermic and endothermic reactions

(**CARE** Eye protection must be worn)

1 Put $2\,cm^3$ of water in a test tube. Record the temperature of the water.

Mix equal quantities of solid citric acid and sodium hydrogencarbonate — about a spatula-full of each.

Add the mixture to the water in the test tube. Stir. Record the new temperature.

2 Put $2\,cm^3$ of dilute hydrochloric acid in a test tube. Record its temperature.

Put $2\,cm^3$ of dilute sodium hydroxide solution in another test tube. Record its temperature.

Pour the contents of one test tube into the other. Record the new temperature.

Classify each reaction as exothermic or endothermic.

B Comparing the energy values of fuel

Picture 7 shows a simple calorimeter that can be used to compare the energy values of different fuels. The idea is to compare the amount of energy transferred when 1 g of each fuel burns.

Plan an experiment which could be used to *compare* the energy transferred when 1 g of different fuels are burned. Your plan should include a note of any safety precautions you will take.

Note: There is no need to measure the *amounts* of energy transferred — you just need to be able to see which fuel transfers a lot, and which a little.

Fuels which might be investigated include ethanol, petrol, candle wax and lighter fuel.

Do not carry out the experiment until you have discussed your method with your teacher.

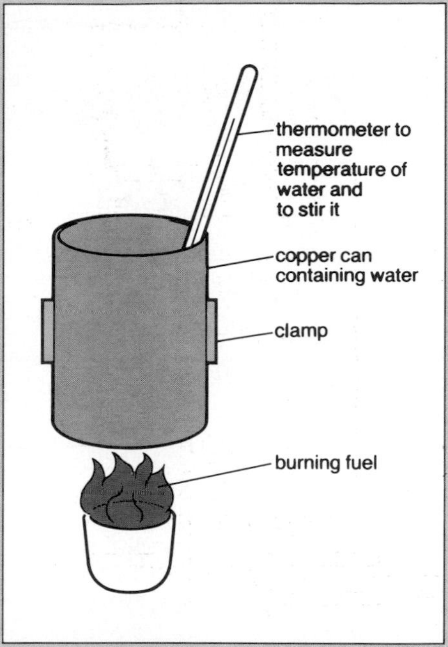

Picture 7 A simple calorimeter for comparing energy values of fuels

Questions

1 Look at the list of reactions below. For each reaction, say whether you think the reaction is exothermic or endothermic.

i) The burning of magnesium in air to form magnesium oxide.

ii) The decomposition of potassium chlorate by heat, forming potassium chloride and oxygen.

iii) The reaction of hydrogen with oxygen to form water.

iv) Respiration:

glucose + oxygen
→ carbon dioxide + water

2 Look at the experiment outlined in activity B.

a Why is this experiment a much less caccurate way of comparing energy values than the method using the apparatus in picture 6?

b What changes could you make to the experiment to make it more accurate?

3 Some camping shops sell 'hand-warmers'. Each hand-warmer consists of a small packet made from porous fabric. The packet contains a dark grey powder. When you buy the hand-warmer, the packet is contained in an outer, airtight plastic bag. The directions in picture 8 are given for using the hand-warmer.

a Try to decide how the hand-warmer works.

b What experiments could you do to check whether your explanation is correct?

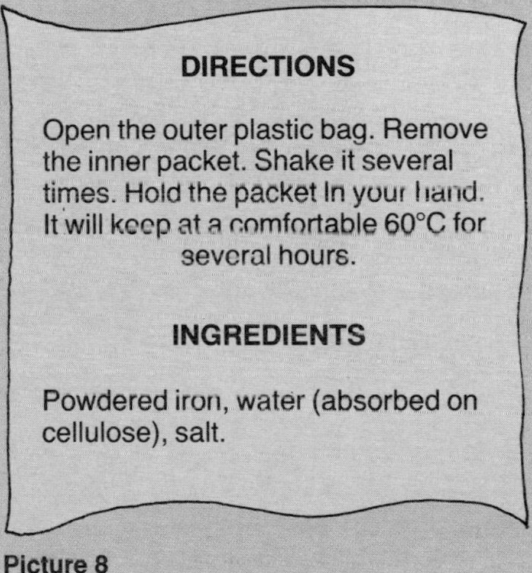

DIRECTIONS

Open the outer plastic bag. Remove the inner packet. Shake it several times. Hold the packet in your hand. It will keep at a comfortable 60°C for several hours.

INGREDIENTS

Powdered iron, water (absorbed on cellulose), salt.

Picture 8

I2 Burning fuels

We get most of our energy from fuels. This topic is about different kinds of fuels and how they give us energy.

Picture 1

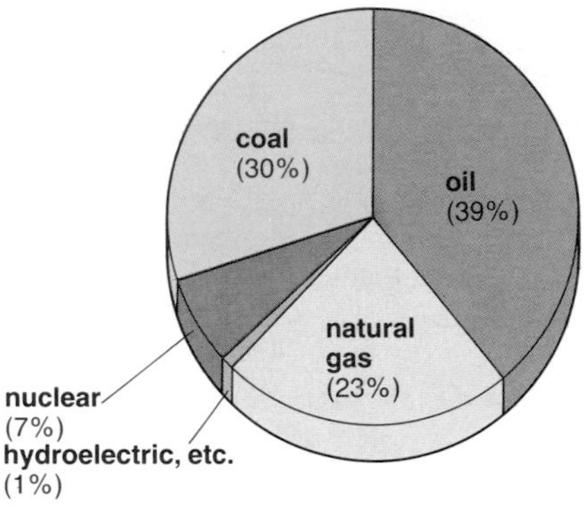

Picture 2 Britain's primary energy sources, 1985. A 'primary' energy source may be used directly, or may be used to generate electricity

How much fuel have you used up today?

Probably more than you think. The food you ate is a fuel, and your home or school is probably heated by gas or oil, which are both fuels. If you used anything electrical, the electricity was generated in a power station probably fuelled by coal. If you have travelled by bus, train or car today, you probably used up some petrol or diesel fuel.

Picture 2 shows Britain's primary energy sources. You can see that the large majority of Britain's energy comes from coal, oil and gas — the fossil fuels. More about fossil fuels in topic I3.

What happens when fuels burn?

Fuels are substances that react with oxygen to give out heat. The fuel is **oxidised**. This reaction is called burning, or **combustion.**

Picture 3 illustrates an experiment that can be used to investigate the substances formed when a fuel burns. When a fuel is tested in this apparatus, it is usually found that the anhydrous copper sulphate turns blue, and the lime water turns cloudy. This suggests that water and carbon dioxide have been formed.

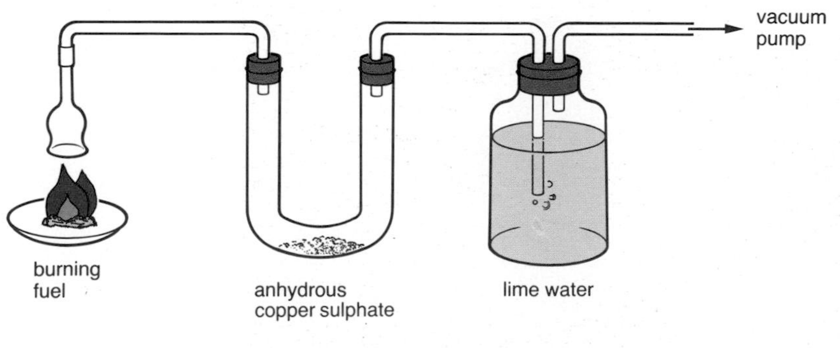

Picture 3 Investigating the products of burning fuels

Most fuels contain carbon and hydrogen, and when the fuel combines with oxygen, the carbon forms carbon dioxide and the hydrogen forms water:

fuel + oxygen → carbon dioxide + water

For example, natural gas is methane, CH_4.

$$\begin{array}{cccccccc} \text{methane} & + & \text{oxygen} & \rightarrow & \text{carbon dioxide} & + & \text{water} \\ CH_4 & + & 2O_2 & \rightarrow & CO_2 & + & 2H_2O \end{array}$$

These combustion products escape into the air as invisible gases. Burning fuels put about 20 thousand million tonnes of carbon dioxide into the Earth's atmosphere each year. This contributes to the 'greenhouse effect', and may change the world's climate (see topic I4).

What if there isn't enough oxygen?

If the air supply is limited when the fuel burns, there may not be enough oxygen available to convert the carbon to carbon dioxide. The carbon may be converted to carbon *monoxide*, CO instead. For example, with methane again:

$$\begin{array}{cccccccc} \text{methane} & + & \text{oxygen} & \rightarrow & \text{carbon monoxide} & + & \text{water} \\ 2CH_4 & + & 3O_2 & \rightarrow & 2CO & + & 4H_2O \end{array}$$

Carbon monoxide is a very poisonous gas. It lowers the ability of the blood to carry oxygen (see *The Living World*, topic C11). To make matters worse it is colourless and odourless, so you cannot tell when it is around. It is therefore very important that in fires and other places where fuel is burned there is a good air supply to make sure the fuel is completely oxidised to carbon dioxide.

If the air supply is *very* poor, there may not even be enough oxygen to oxidise the carbon to carbon monoxide. The carbon is simply given off as small particles which make a sooty smoke.

Car engines burn petrol as a fuel. Petrol is a mixture of hydrocarbons, and if the engine is well maintained there is enough air to oxidise the petrol to carbon dioxide and water. However, if the engine is badly maintained, carbon monoxide is also formed. A certain amount of carbon monoxide is always present in vehicle exhaust gases, which is why they are poisonous.

Carbon monoxide and sooty smoke are just two of the nasty products that may be formed when fuels burn. There are others — for example most solid

Picture 4 Most power stations generate electricity by burning fuels like coal, oil or gas

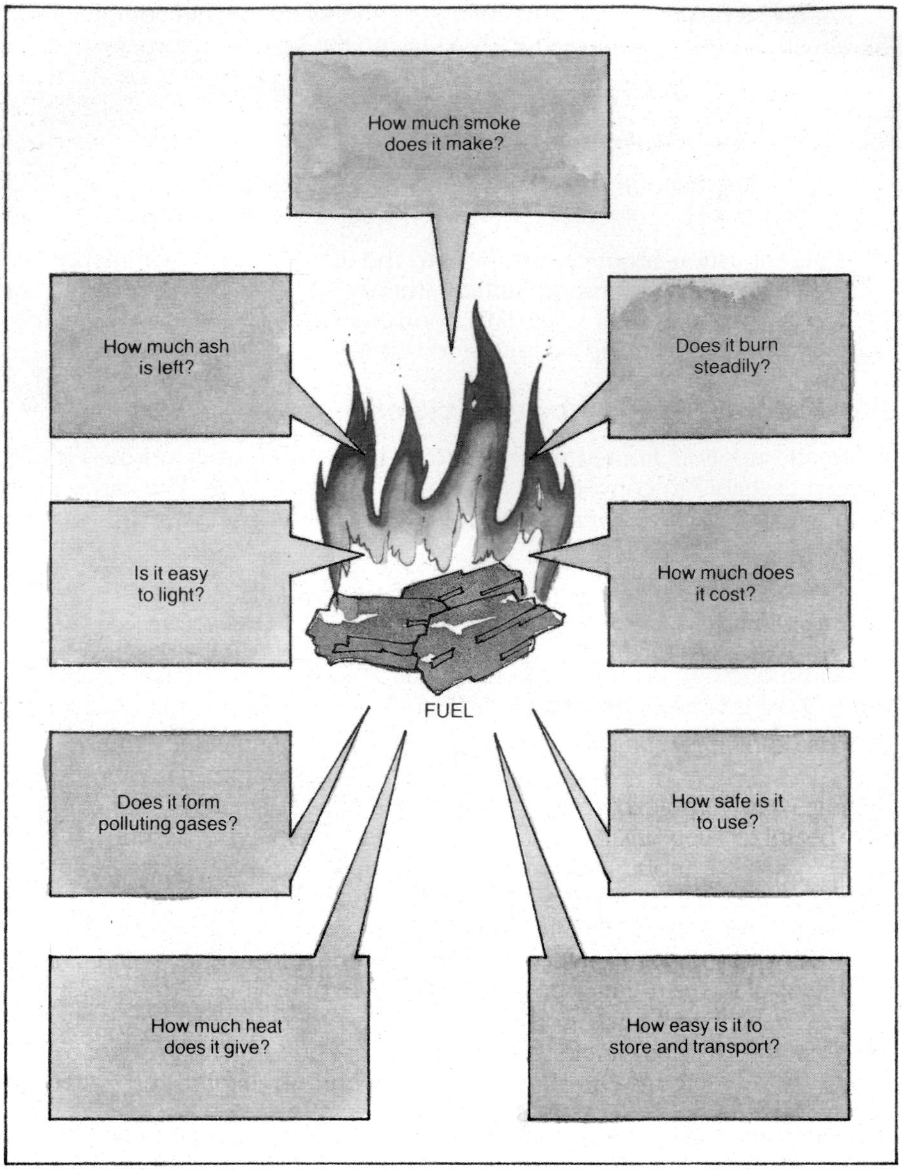

Picture 6 Important properties of a fuel

fuels leave some kind of ash. Many fuels contain sulphur, which is converted to sulphur dioxide when the fuel burns:

$$\text{sulphur} + \text{oxygen} \rightarrow \text{sulphur dioxide}$$
$$S + O_2 \rightarrow SO_2$$

Sulphur dioxide is a serious air pollutant, and a major cause of acid rain. There is more about these and other air pollutants in topic I4.

What makes a good fuel?

Different fuels have different properties. Picture 6 suggests some of the questions we might ask about the properties of a fuel.

No fuel is ideal. Coal is cheap and easy to store, but it is hard to light and it produces smoke and ash. Methylated spirit (ethanol) is easy to light and it produces hardly any smoke, ash or pollution — but it is expensive. When choosing a fuel, you have to balance up the advantages and disadvantages and then decide. You can try doing this in *Choosing the right fuel* on page 187.

Activities

A Comparing fuels

You are going to compare a number of solid fuels, to see which would be most suitable for use on a camping expedition. The fuels may include some of the following: wooden splints, firelighters, 'Meta' fuel, charcoal and candle wax.

1 Design an experiment to compare the following properties:

ease of lighting
how steadily it burns
amount of smoke produced
amount of ash produced
how safe the fuel is to store and use

Describe the experiment you have planned. Explain what you will do. Describe the *safety precautions* you will take. What observations and measurements will you make?

Do not carry out the experiment unless your teacher has seen and approved your plan.

2 The *cost* of the fuels is obviously important. Ask your teacher for information about the cost of each fuel, and decide a fair way of comparing these costs.

B Fuels in the past

Find a person who is over 70 years old — it might be a grandparent, or a neighbour. Ask them about the fuels that were used when they were your age. Try asking them about:

1 The fuels that were used for heating their home. Was every room heated? If not, which rooms were heated?

2 The fuels that were used for cooking their food.

3 The fuels that were used in the commonest forms of transport.

Questions

1 a Name two substances that are *always* formed when a hydrocarbon fuel burns.

b Name two more substances that are *sometimes* formed when a hydrocarbon fuel burns.

c List seven properties that are important in a fuel that is to be used for cooking food.

2 You work for a firm which supplies household fuels. A person comes into your office one day and claims to have developed a new fuel. It is a grey solid.

a What would you want to know about the fuel before deciding whether to order stocks of it?

b You decide to take a sample of the fuel and send it to the laboratory for testing. What tests would you ask to have done on the sample?

3 Look again at picture 3.

a When charcoal is tested as a fuel in this apparatus, the lime water turns milky but the anhydrous copper sulphate stays white. Why?

b When hydrogen is tested as a fuel in this apparatus, the anhydrous copper sulphate turns blue but the lime water stays clear. Why?

c Suppose you wanted to test the fuel to see how much *carbon* was produced when the fuel burned. What changes would you make to the apparatus? Redraw the diagram to show your changes.

4 a Why is it dangerous to leave a car engine running when the car is in a closed garage?

b Car engines are fitted with a choke. When the choke is pulled out, the air supply to the carburettor is cut down. This makes the engine easier to start.

When the engine is running with the choke pulled out, the exhaust is often black and smoky. Why?

c Cigarette smoke contains a considerable amount of carbon monoxide — this is one of the many reasons why smoking is so bad for your health. Why do you think carbon monoxide is in the smoke?

Gas burner design

Picture 1 shows the design of a typical burner on a gas cooker. Look at the picture, then answer the questions.

1 Why is it important that the burner has an efficient way of mixing the gas with air?

2 Explain *how* the burner mixes the gas with air.

3 What would you notice about the appearance of the flame if the air supply became blocked?

4 The design of this burner is similar in some ways to the design of a bunsen burner. What are the similarities? What are the differences?

5 Suppose the gas pressure in the mains has to be permanently reduced. How would you change the design of the burner so it still gives the same rate of heating?

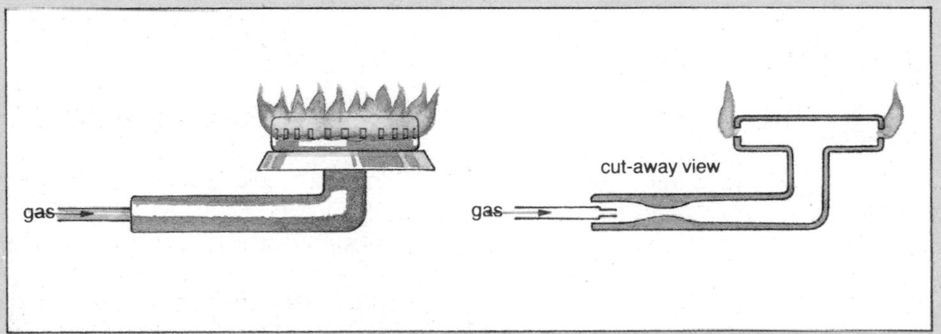

Picture 1 A typical gas burner

13 Fossil fuels

Most of our fuels come from animals and plants that lived millions of years ago.

Picture 1 John Dalton collecting marsh gas. Marsh gas is mainly methane, formed from rotting vegetation. What is his young assistant doing?

Plants make their food by photosynthesis (*The Living World*, topic C12). They use the Sun's energy to turn carbon dioxide and water into carbohydrate foods such as glucose, $C_6H_{12}O_6$.

Normally, the plants then die and decay, or perhaps they get eaten by animals. Either way, the carbohydrate in the plant gets oxidised and converted back to carbon dioxide and water by respiration.

But sometimes, plants die and then get covered up so the air can't get at them. These are called **anaerobic** conditions. It might be because the plants are in a marsh, and get covered by mud. Without air the carbohydrate in the plants cannot be oxidised to carbon dioxide and water. Instead, it slowly gets turned into substances containing carbon and hydrogen, called **hydrocarbons**. These substances make excellent fuels. A similar thing happens when animals die and decay without air present.

Forming fossil fuels

Millions of years ago the climate of Britain was just right for life to flourish. There were tropical forests and warm seas. At that time, the great, slow movements of the continents had placed what was to become the British Isles right on the equator (see *The Physical World*, topic G1). The tropical

Picture 2 How coal is formed

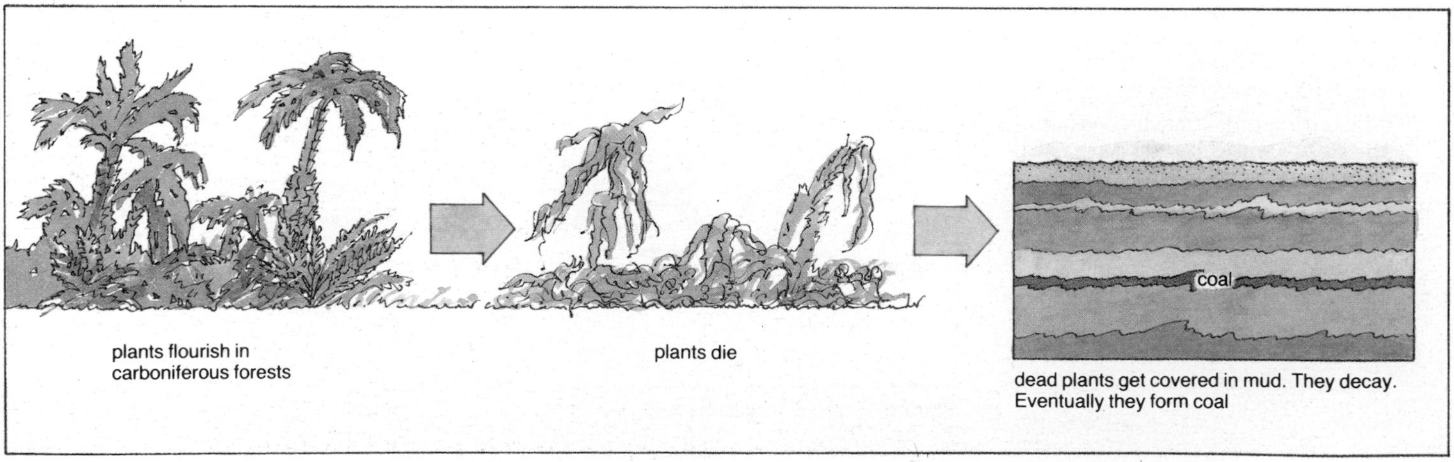
coal
plants flourish in carboniferous forests
plants die
dead plants get covered in mud. They decay. Eventually they form coal

seas were shallow and the low-lying land was covered in fresh-water swamps.

The trees in the swamps grew tall, died and were replaced by their seedlings. The dead trees did not rot away, as they were covered with stagnant water. Layer upon layer of them were built up until they were tens of metres thick. Now and again the sea flooded in and covered the dead trees with sand. This went on happening for millions of years.

The alternating layers of sand and dead trees grew to be hundreds of metres thick. The weight of the new deposits squashed the tree layers into thin seams. In these anaerobic conditions the carbon compounds in the dead material changed chemically, and eventually became coal. Picture 2 summarises the process.

All this happened in the *Carboniferous Era*, which lasted 65 million years and ended 280 million years ago.

Oil and gas were formed in a similar way to coal, but from animals and plants that lived in tropical seas rather than on land.

When fossil fuels are burned, they form carbon dioxide and water and release energy. They are releasing the energy of the Sun that was trapped by plants hundreds of millions of years ago.

Today we are busy getting these fossil fuels out of the ground to use as energy sources. Picture 3 shows how this is done in a coal mine.

Coal

Coal is a hard black solid. It is mainly made of carbon. Most of the coal mined in Britain comes from deep underground. For the miners who work underground it is a dirty and dangerous job to get the coal out. Mining coal also produces a lot of waste rock, which has to be piled up in ugly spoil heaps.

Coal was once very popular for heating people's homes. Nowadays, gas is more popular, and the main use of coal is in generating electricity. Three-quarters of the coal mined in Britain is used to generate electricity. Most of the power stations in Britain are coal-fired. Unfortunately, burning coal can cause serious air pollution (see topic I4).

Picture 3 A coal mine

Picture 4 The scene following the explosion at the oil rig "Piper Alpha". Extracting oil and gas from under the sea has human and environmental costs

Oil

Because it is a liquid, oil is easier to get out of the ground than coal. You just drill a hole and the oil comes out under its own pressure. It comes out of the ground as a black liquid, called **crude oil**, or **petroleum**. It is a mixture of many different substances, all hydrocarbons. It has to be purified and separated into different fractions. This is done at an oil refinery.

Crude oil gives us many important fuels and materials. More is given about them in topic H1.

Gas

Natural gas is formed in a similar way to oil, and the two fuels are often found in the same places. There are large amounts of natural gas under the North Sea off the coast of Britain. To get it out, holes are drilled in the sea bed, and the gas is piped out and brought to shore.

Natural gas is mostly made of methane, CH_4. It burns with a clean flame and is very popular for heating homes and for cooking.

The North Sea isn't the only place where you find methane. Methane is often formed when organic material decomposes anaerobically (without oxygen). For example, it forms inside the gut of cows, where bacteria decompose grass in the absence of oxygen. In fact, an average cow produces about 500 000 cm^3 of methane a day. Three cows could keep an average home supplied with all the gas it needs!

Biogas is a fuel made from waste material such as animal manure and dead plants. Like natural gas, it consists mainly of methane. The waste material is put in a **biogas digestor** where it decomposes anaerobically (picture 5). Biogas digestors are an important source of energy in many developing countries.

How long will fossil fuels last?

It took millions of years for fossil fuels to form, but it will not take long to use them up. There is no place on Earth that is exactly like the old Carboniferous swamps in which coal was laid down. Even if there were such places, it would take millions of years for the coal and oil to be produced.

Picture 6 shows how long fossil fuels may last. Coal supplies are plentiful, but oil is likely to run out before the middle of the next century. And at present we depend on oil more than any other fuel.

Of course, new supplies of fossil fuels are being discovered all the time, but this cannot go on forever. What's more, the new discoveries tend to be in places where the fuel is difficult to get at — like Alaska, or deep under the North Sea. Eventually, supplies of fossil fuels must run out. What will we do then? More about this in *The Physical World*, pages 130 and 131.

Picture 5 An underground biogas digestor. What do you think the various people in the picture are doing?

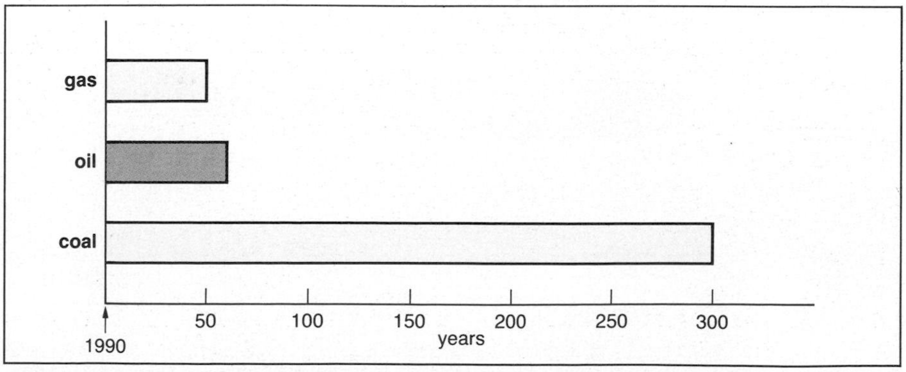

Picture 6 These are estimates of how long world supplies of fossil fuels will last — if we go on using them at the present rate

Questions

1 Coal, oil and gas are called fossil fuels. Why is the word 'fossil' used?

2 When you burn a fossil fuel like oil, you are releasing energy that originally came from the Sun. Explain why.

3 In some places, coal deposits are near to the surface. Instead of mining the coal underground, you can dig it up from above using huge mechanical shovels. This is called **open-cast** mining. Unfortunately, it leaves ugly quarrying scars on the landscape.
What do you think might be the main benefits of open-cast mining compared with underground mining? How do these benefits compare with the possible drawbacks of this method?

Activities

A What can we get from coal?

If you heat coal without air present, the coal cannot burn. Instead, it breaks down into a number of different things.

Design an experiment to investigate what is formed when coal is heated without air. Bear in mind these points:

- The products that are formed may be solid, liquid and/or gas. You will need to think about how you will separate them and collect them.
- You don't need to remove all air from the coal when you heat it. Just make sure it can't get a continuous supply of air to burn in.
- You can crush the coal into small pieces for the experiment.

Draw up a plan for what you will do. Your plan should mention any safety precautions you will take.

Do not carry out the experiment until your teacher has seen and approved your plan.

B Find out about fossil fuels

Ask a relative, use a reference book or a library, but *find out* these things about fossil fuels.

1 Before North Sea Gas was discovered, gas used to be manufactured from coal. Find out how.

2 What other useful substances can be manufactured from coal?

3 Find out about the following fossil fuels:

a peat,

b lignite,

c anthracite.

4 Coal miners dread something called 'fire-damp'. What is it, and why is it dreaded?

Choosing the right fuel

Table 1 gives the properties of various fuels. Use the table to answer the questions.

1 Barbecues are normally heated by charcoal. Suggest a reason why charcoal is used, rather than any other fuel in the table.

2 Ethanol is rarely used as a fuel, even though it is clean and convenient. Suggest a reason for this. Can you think of *any* examples of ethanol being used as a fuel?

3 Decide which fuel you would use for each of the following purposes. In each case, give a reason for your choice.

a Heating a house in a big town.

b Heating a cottage in an isolated part of Scotland.

c Heating the ovens in a large bakery.

4 Which of the fuels would be most suitable for fuelling an electric power station in

a Nottinghamshire, England?

b the Middle East?

Give reasons for your answers.

Table 1 Properties of different fuels

Fuel	Cost in pence per megajoule	Ease of lighting	Cleanliness when burning	Safety in use	Transport
Coal	0.40	Difficult	Dirty	Safe	By road or rail, in bulk
Fuel oil	0.48	Quite easy	Moderate	Fairly Safe	By tanker or pipeline
Natural gas	0.35	Easy	Clean	Leaks can cause explosions	By pipeline direct to user
Ethanol (methylated spirit)	8.0	Easy	Very clean	Highly flammable – can cause accidental fires	By road, in bottles or drums
Charcoal	1.5	Difficult	Fairly clean	Safe	By road, in sacks

14 Air pollution

Human activities release many polluting gases into the atmosphere. In this topic we look at their effects, and how they can be controlled.

Picture 1 Motor vehicles are the most serious source of air pollution

Air pollution isn't new. The earliest humans cooked on wood fires which produced nasty polluting gases. People have been polluting the air ever since humans arrived on earth. It's just that there are many more people on Earth now. More people means more homes, more industries and more motor vehicles — and more air pollution.

The problem is, all gases **diffuse** — that is, they spread out as much as possible. So any gases we release spread all through the atmosphere. Some of the gases released by human activities are fairly harmless, but others can have damaging effects on the environment.

Two effects are particularly serious. Let's look at them in turn.

Acid rain

Some air pollutants are acidic gases, particularly sulphur dioxide and nitrogen dioxide. These gases are formed when fuels are burned, especially in car engines and in power stations. After they have been released into the air, these gases may react with other gases in the air, and with rain water. For example, sulphur dioxide reacts with oxygen to form sulphur trioxide:

$$\text{sulphur dioxide} + \text{oxygen} \rightarrow \text{sulphur trioxide}$$
$$2SO_2 + O_2 \rightarrow 2SO_3$$

The sulphur trioxide then reacts with rainwater to form sulphuric acid:

$$\text{sulphur trioxide} + \text{water} \rightarrow \text{sulphuric acid}$$
$$SO_3 + H_2O \rightarrow H_2SO_4$$

Reactions like this make rain water become acidic. Acid rain has a pH of between 5 and 2. In some extreme cases, the water is as acidic as vinegar. Picture 2 sums up the formation of acid rain.

When acid rain falls into streams and lakes, it makes them acidic and this may kill water life, including fish. Fish are dying in lakes in Scandinavia, probably because of acid rain. The people there believe most of the acid gases come from industries in Britain, carried hundreds of miles on the wind.

Acid rain may also help cause the death of trees in forests in Europe, particularly in Germany.

Acid rain also damages buildings and other structures. It corrodes metals, and wears away the stonework on buildings.

It is not easy to control acid rain. Scientists do not yet understand all the complicated chemical reactions that cause it. Sulphur dioxide is certainly involved. A lot of sulphur dioxide is produced by coal-burning power stations. The sulphur dioxide could be removed from the chimney gases by special equipment, but this is expensive (see *Pollution and power stations* on page 193). Another cause is the nitrogen oxides produced in car exhausts, and this can be controlled by careful engine design.

The greenhouse effect and global warming

A garden greenhouse keeps plants warmer than they would be outside. It does this because the glass traps some of the Sun's radiation energy (*The Physical World*, page 131).

In a similar way, the atmosphere helps keep the Earth warm. It does this by trapping some of the Sun's radiation that would otherwise escape (picture 3). This is just as well. Without this **greenhouse effect** the average surface temperature of the earth would be about 33°C lower than it is, −18°C instead of a nice comfortable 15°C.

Some gases are better than others at keeping the Earth warm. Oxygen and nitrogen are not very effective, but carbon dioxide is very good. So good, in fact, that there may be a problem. Scientists are concerned that human activities are putting so much *extra* carbon dioxide into the atmosphere that the Earth is overheating. The problem is known as **global warming**.

Whenever fossil fuels are burned, carbon dioxide is released into the atmosphere. Altogether, we release about five thousand million tonnes of carbon dioxide into the air every year (picture 4). Scientists believe that by the year 2020 the concentration of carbon dioxide in the atmosphere will have doubled from what it is now.

The average temperature of the Earth is already showing a small increase. In the past 100 years the average temperature in the USA has increased by about 2°C. It is estimated that if the amount of carbon dioxide in the atmosphere doubles, the average temperature of the Earth will rise by about 3°C. This may not sound a lot, but it will make a big difference to the Earth's climate.

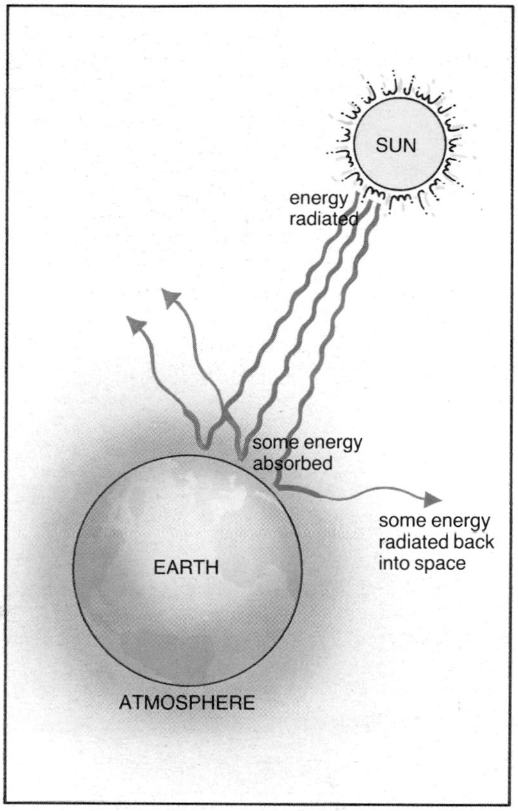

Picture 3 The Earth's atmosphere absorbs some of the Sun's radiation energy before it can escape into space. This helps keep the Earth warm — the 'greenhouse effect'

Picture 2 The formation of acid rain

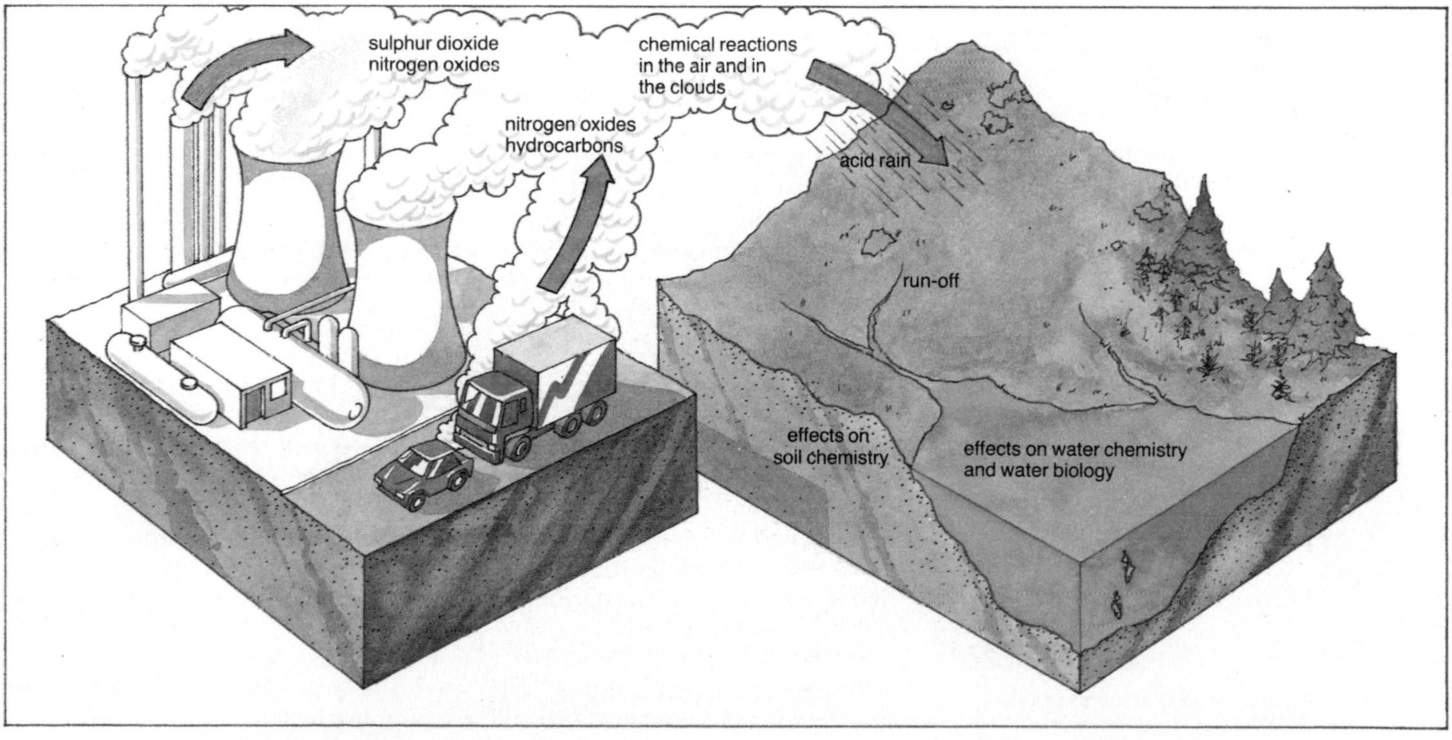

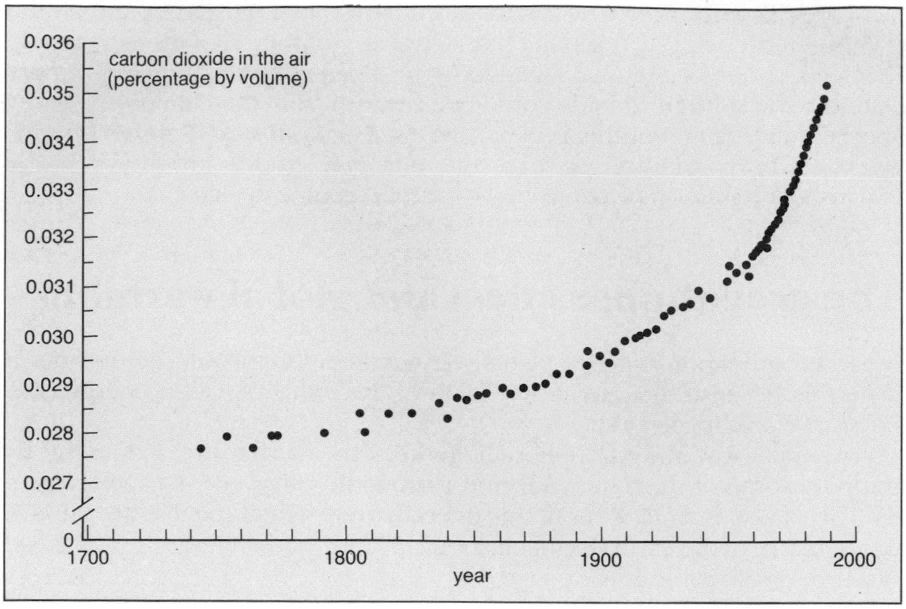

Picture 4 How the concentration of carbon dioxide in the air has changed since 1700

Some of the effects will be good. In places with good rainfall, farmers will be able to grow bigger crops. But there will be more droughts. The level of the sea will rise. This is because water expands when heated, and also because some of the ice at the Poles will bring floods to low-lying countries like Holland and Bangladesh — and also to low-lying parts of Britain.

Carbon dioxide isn't the only 'greenhouse gas'. But it is the most serious one, because there is so much of it. So much that there is no chance of removing it from all the car exhausts, gas boilers and other places it pours from. The only way we can reduce it is to cut down on our use of fossil fuels.

And remember, it takes time to put things right. Even if we cut back on using fossil fuels today, global warming will continue for many years. This is because so much carbon dioxide has already been put in the atmosphere from fossil fuels we have burned in the past.

Picture 5 One result of the greenhouse effect could be more droughts in Britain

Other kinds of air pollution

Table 1 gives some of the substances that are major sources of air pollution. You can see that several of these air pollutants can help cause acid rain and the greenhouse effect. These are *long-range* pollutants: they have effects that are felt over long distances.

In addition, carbon monoxide (CO) and smoke are more *local* pollutants. Their effects are felt mainly near the place where they are produced.

Picture 6 Smoking is a serious source of indoor pollution

Destroying the ozone layer

Ozone, O_3, is an unstable form of oxygen. It is a very reactive gas, and when it is formed near the Earth's surface it can cause nasty pollution problems.

But further up in the atmosphere, ozone does a *useful* job. There is a very thin layer of ozone about 20–40 kilometres above the Earth, in the part of the atmosphere called the stratosphere. This layer acts as a kind of sunscreen. It filters out some of the harmful ultraviolet radiation from the Sun. If this radiation reaches Earth it can cause sunburn and even skin cancer.

In 1984, it was discovered that a large 'hole' had developed in the ozone layer above Antarctica. If this 'hole' spreads to more populated parts of the Earth, there could be serious results for people's health.

Table 1 Major air pollutants

Air pollutant	Source	Effects	Possible methods of control
Sulphur dioxide (SO_2)	Burning fossil fuels	Causes acid rain (see above)	Remove sulphur from fuels before burning. Remove sulphur dioxide from chimney gases of power stations
Nitrogen oxides (NO, NO_2, N_2O)	Vehicle exhausts, burning of fuels	Help cause acid rain and photochemical smog	Fit catalytic converters to vehicle exhausts. Modify engines to run on a weaker mixture of fuel and air
Carbon dioxide (CO_2)	Burning fuels	Causes greenhouse effect, affecting Earth's climate (see above)	Burn less fossil fuels
Carbon monoxide (CO)	Burning fuels, vehicle exhausts, cigarette smoke	Poisonous to animals, including humans	Ensure vehicle engines are well maintained. Prevent cigarette smoking
Hydrocarbons	Vehicle exhausts, burning fuels	Help cause acid rain and photochemical smog	Fit catalytic converters to vehicle exhausts. Modify engines to run on a weaker mixture of fuel and air
Smoke	Burning fuels	Damages lungs; reduces photosynthesis of plants	Use smokeless fuels. Make sure engines and burners have plenty of air to burn fuel efficiently
Lead compounds	Car exhausts	Damage nervous system of humans	Use unleaded petrol
Chlorofluorocarbons (CFCs)	Aerosol propellants, refrigerators	Destroy ozone in the ozone layer which protects Earth from ultra violet radiation Also contribute to the greenhouse effect.	Use different substances as aerosol propellants and refrigerants

Scientists have discovered that the damage to the ozone layer is caused by chemical compounds called chlorofluorocarbons, or CFCs. These compounds are used as refrigerants and as propellants for aerosols. CFCs are very stable and unreactive, and they stay in the atmosphere for a long time. Over the years they slowly diffuse upwards through the atmosphere until they reach the stratosphere. Here they react with ozone, and destroy it.

Many countries have now agreed to stop using the harmful types of CFCs. But even if all use of CFCs is stopped at once, the ozone layer will go on being destroyed for at least 20 years, because of all the CFCs that are already in the atmosphere. It is a problem that will be with us for a long time yet.

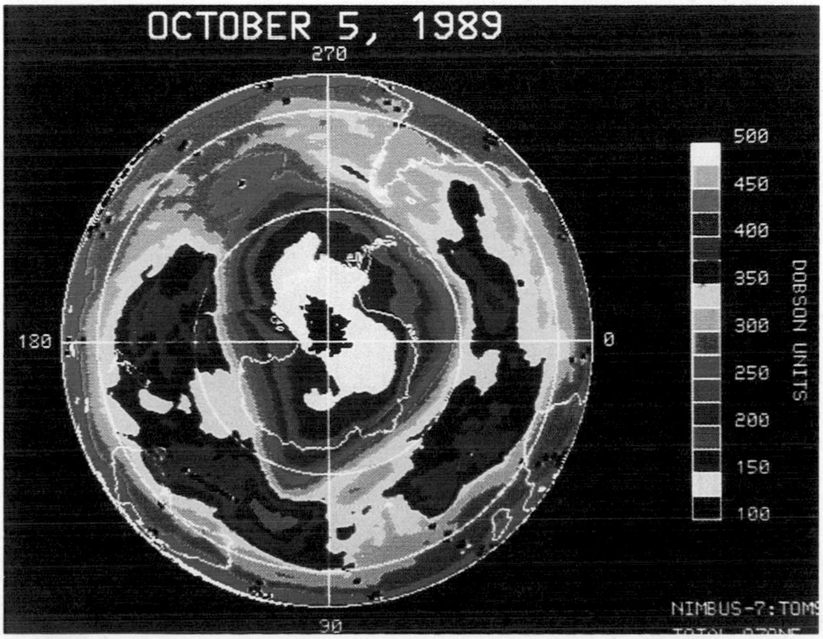

Picture 7 The "hole" in the ozone layer, as photographed by NASA satellites. The white area represents especially low concentrations of ozone

Controlling air pollution

Pollution of the atmosphere is one of the most serious threats to our future. If problems like global warming get out of control, they could have disastrous effects on life on Earth.

Controlling air pollution means controlling the release of pollutant gases. Most of these gases come from the burning of fossil fuels. So there are two important ways to control air pollution:

1. Burn less fossil fuels.
2. Remove the gases before they get into the atmosphere.

In the long run, the best way is the first. But burning less fossil fuels means sacrifices. To put it bluntly: would you be prepared to go without a car of your own to help reduce acid rain?

The second approach, removing pollutant gases before they reach the atmosphere, can be expensive. You can fit a catalytic converter to remove pollutant gases from car exhausts, but each converter costs several hundred pounds. You can fit units to power stations to remove acid gases, but a unit for a large power station costs about £200 million. In the end, it is us, the consumers, who pay these costs. Is it worth it?

Activities

A Investigating the pollution produced by different solid fuels

You can use the apparatus shown in picture 8. Plan how you could carry out the investigation. Decide what you will do, and the observations you will make. Include in your plan a note of any safety precautions you will take.

The fuels that could be tested include coal, coke, wood and charcoal.

Do not carry out any experiment until you have discussed your plan with your teacher. In any case, your teacher may prefer to demonstrate the experiment.

B How aware are the public about air pollution?

Carry out a survey of people's awareness of air pollution. You could ask questions like

- What polluting gases do you think are released by your car, your home and your place of work?
- What harmful effects do you think these gases have on the environment?
- How could you cut down the release of these gases?

You could try asking your family, neighbours or teachers in your school.

C What are your local pollution problems?

Find out the particular air pollution problems in your neighbourhood. What are the major sources of pollution in the area? You could ask your family and neighbours, or use local newspapers.

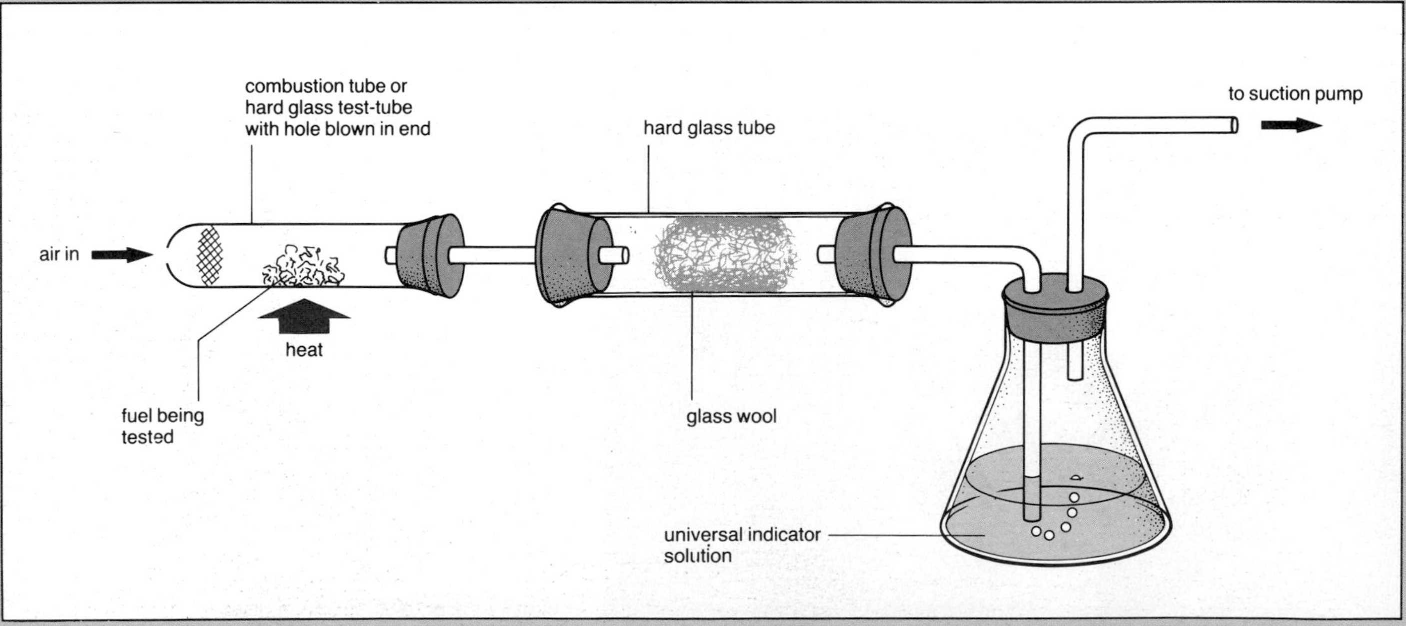

Picture 8 Investigating the pollution caused by different fuels

Questions

1 Consider the various air pollutants mentioned in this topic.

a Which are produced by burning fossil fuels?

b Which are produced by motor vehicles?

c Which are produced by nature as well as by human activities?

d Which do you think could be most easily controlled?

e Which do you think will be most difficult to control?

2 Many important air pollutants are *oxides*.

a List the air pollutants mentioned in this topic that are oxides.

b Suggest a reason why oxides are more common air pollutants than, say, sulphides or chlorides.

c The oxides that pollute the air are non-metal oxides, not metal oxides. Suggest a reason why.

3 Air pollution is a *global* problem. It can only be controlled if *all* the countries of the world agree to do something about it.

a Why is this?

b Some countries cause more air pollution than others. What factors decide how much air pollution a particular country produces?

Name four countries that you think are major polluters of the air.

4 You are Minister for the Environment. You have decided that new laws must be passed to control air pollution. You realise that it is impossible to remove pollution *completely*, but you want to cut it down as much as possible.

What new laws will you make? How will you enforce the laws, and check they are being obeyed?

5 What special air pollution problems would you expect in the following places?

a Near a coal-fired power station.

b Near an airport.

c Near a farm.

d Near a steel works.

Pollution and power stations

Sulphur dioxide is a serious air pollutant which helps cause acid rain.

Fossil fuels like coal and oil contain small amounts of sulphur. When these fuels are burned, the sulphur is oxidised to sulphur dioxide.

Coal-fired power stations are a major source of sulphur dioxide in Britain. They account for nearly half of the sulphur dioxide produced by human activities each year. So cutting down the sulphur dioxide from power stations can do a lot to control acid rain.

There are several possibilities for cutting down the sulphur dioxide from power stations.

- Build nuclear power stations to replace coal-fired ones.
- Use coal with only a small amount of sulphur in it. This low-sulphur coal would have to be imported from abroad, because coal from British mines contains quite a lot of sulphur.
- Remove the sulphur from the coal *before* burning it. This is difficult and expensive.
- Remove the sulphur dioxide from the chimney gases *after* the coal has been burned, but before the gases can escape. The equipment needed to do this is expensive to fit, but it produces calcium sulphate. Calcium sulphate can be used to make plaster for the building industry.

1 For each of the four possibilities, say what you think are the advantages and disadvantages using this method to control sulphur dioxide. Which method would you choose?

2 *All* these different methods cost money. Where should this money come from? Who will pay in the end for removing sulphur dioxide?

15 Energy changes and chemical bonds

The energy changes in reactions come from making and breaking chemical bonds.

Substances are held together by chemical bonds. When a chemical reaction occurs, one substance changes to another. This means that chemical bonds must be broken, then re-made. It is this breaking and making of bonds that causes the energy changes in chemical reactions.

Chemical bonds hold atoms together. Breaking bonds involves pulling these atoms apart — and this needs energy. On the other hand, making new bonds gives out energy.

Breaking bonds takes in energy.
Making new bonds gives out energy.

Picture 1 Igniting methane in a gas cooker

An example — the reaction of methane with oxygen

Methane is the major component of natural gas. When methane burns, it reacts with oxygen, and energy is transferred by heating. The products are carbon dioxide and water. Picture 2 shows the molecules involved in the reaction.

In methane molecules, carbon atoms are bonded to hydrogen. In oxygen molecules, oxygen atoms are bonded to one another. In the reaction between methane and oxygen, all these bonds have to be broken. This takes in energy. New bonds are then formed between carbon and oxygen in carbon dioxide, and between hydrogen and oxygen in water. This gives out energy. This is shown in the energy level diagram in picture 3.

Compare the amount of energy given out with the amount of energy taken in. More energy is given out than taken in. So overall, this reaction gives out energy — it is exothermic. This is just as well, considering how much we rely on the reaction for our household heating.

Putting numbers to the energy transfers

It is quite simple to show the sizes of the energy transfers involved in this bond breaking and bond making.

We can measure the amount of energy transferred by heating when 1 litre of methane burns. It is about 30 kJ.

We can work out where this energy comes from if we know the amount of energy transferred when each bond is broken or made. This is called the **bond energy**. The figures in table 1 show how much energy is involved in each stage.

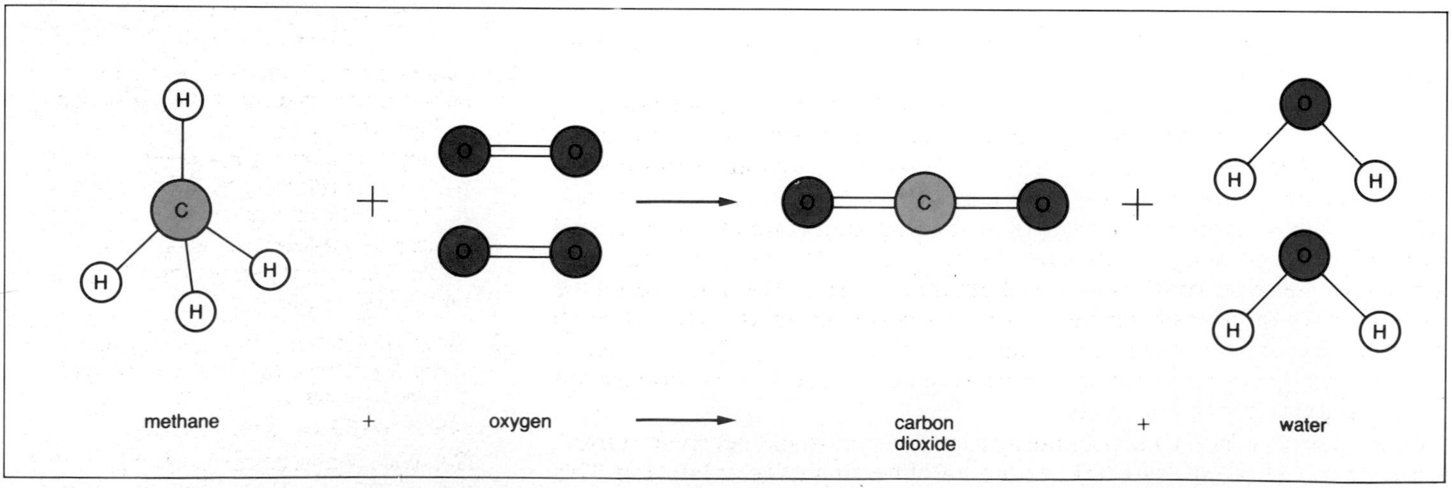

Picture 2 The reaction of methane with oxygen

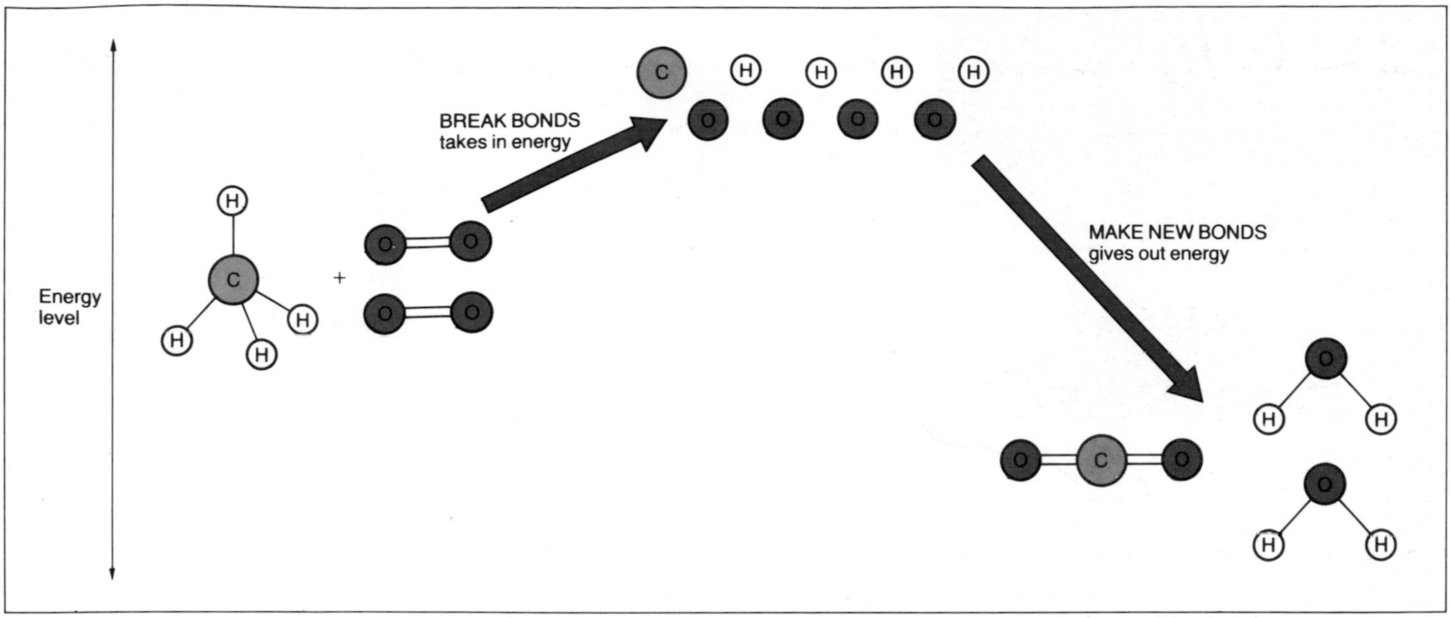

Picture 3 Breaking and making bonds in the reaction between methane and oxygen

Table 1 The energy changes when 1 litre of methane burns

Breaking bonds		
Break four C—H bonds in methane	**takes in**	4 × 18 kJ = 72 kJ
Break two O=O bonds in oxygen	**takes in**	2 × 21 kJ = 42 kJ
Making bonds		
Make two C=O bonds in carbon dioxide	**gives out**	2 × 34 kJ = 68 kJ
Make four O—H bonds in water	**gives out**	4 × 19 kJ = 76 kJ
Total energy given out	=	(68 + 76) − (72 + 42) kJ = **30 kJ**

The total energy given out is equal to the energy given out when bonds are **made**, minus the energy taken in when bonds are **broken.**

Getting reactions started

Fuels need heating before they start burning. They must be supplied with the necessary **activation energy** to start off the reaction between the fuel and oxygen.

If you look again at picture 3 you can see *why* fuels like methane need heating to get them burning.

Before the reaction can start, bonds have to be broken: C—H bonds in methane and O=O bonds in oxygen. This takes in energy — the activation energy needed to get the reaction started. At room temperature, this energy is not available, so the bonds do not break and the reaction does not start.

But if you heat the fuel with a match or spark, enough energy is transferred to break the necessary bonds, and the reaction starts. *All* reactions need activation energy to break bonds and get them started. For some reactions the bonds are quite easily broken so the activation energy is fairly low. Such reactions can start at room temperature, without heating. The reaction of sodium with water is an example of this type of reaction — as soon as you put the sodium in water, it reacts.

Other reactions need a lot of energy to break bonds and get them started. For example, charcoal (carbon) needs a lot of heating to get it burning. This is because the bonds holding the carbon atoms together are very strong.

Questions

1 Using the idea of breaking and making bonds, explain in your own words why fuels need heating before they start to burn.

2 Hydrogen burns in the presence of oxygen to form water. Burning 1 litre of hydrogen gives out about 5 kJ of energy.

hydrogen + oxygen → water

$$2H_2 + O_2 \rightarrow 2H_2O$$

a Draw a diagram similar to picture 3 to show the breaking and making of bonds in this reaction.

b Use the diagram to explain why hydrogen must be heated before it will start burning in oxygen.

c Explain why the diagram shows this reaction *gives out* energy rather than taking it in.

3 'All the energy used by human beings comes from the breaking and making of chemical bonds.'

Is this true? Give some examples.
Can you suggest any exceptions?

16 Controlling chemical changes

In industry and in everyday life, it's important to be able to control how fast a chemical reaction goes.

Picture 1 This food was kept in the freezer so the reactions that make it go off happen slowly. To make cooking reactions happen quickly, it goes in a hot grill

Most kitchens have a machine for speeding up chemical reactions and a machine for slowing them down. They are called a cooker and a fridge. Cooking food involves a lot of complicated chemical reactions, but like all reactions they are speeded up by higher temperatures. When food goes bad, that involves chemical reactions too, and like all reactions they are slowed down by lower temperatures.

Chemical reactions can go at different speeds or **rates**. Some, like explosions, are incredibly fast. Some, like rusting, are much slower. By controlling the conditions, we can vary the rates of reactions to make them as fast or slow as we want. This is useful, not just in cooking but in the chemical industry and in our own bodies.

Picture 2 Chemical reactions involving starch and protein make food go brown on the outside when heated

What affects the rate of a reaction?

Look at these examples:

- It takes less than 10 minutes to fry chips, but 20 minutes to boil potatoes.
- Potatoes cook faster if you cut them up small.
- Badly stained clothes can be cleaned by soaking them in a solution of biological detergent.
- Stained clothes become clean more quickly if you soak them in a more concentrated solution of detergent.

These examples show some of the factors that affect the rate of a chemical reaction. The factors that we will be looking at in this topic are:

- temperature,
- surface area,
- catalysts,
- concentration.

Temperature

All reactions go faster at a higher temperature. Temperature has a very noticeable effect. The rate of many reactions is *doubled* by a temperature rise of just 10°C. Temperature is one of the reasons why chips cook faster than boiled potatoes. The fat is much hotter than boiling water.

Lots of chemical reactions happen when food is cooked. An important one involves starch, the main component of foods like bread and potatoes.

Starch is a polymer containing many glucose molecules joined together. At high temperatures these chains break down into shorter chains called dextrins. Some of the dextrins combine with proteins in the food to form brown compounds. This is why many foods go brown on the outside (where the temperature is highest) when they are cooked (picture 2). The higher the temperature, the faster the reaction and the faster the food browns. (However, just because the food is brown on the outside doesn't mean it's cooked right through. The slowest part of cooking is the conduction of heat from the outside to the middle.)

Living things use **biochemical** reactions to keep going. They are catalysed by enzymes (see below). All biochemical reactions go faster at higher temperatures — but only up to a point. Above a certain temperature, the enzymes are destroyed and the biochemical reactions stop. All enzymes have an optimum temperature at which the reaction is at its fastest — more about this in *The Living World* topic A7.

Biochemical reactions are slowed down at low temperatures. The bacteria which cause food to go bad work only slowly at the temperature of a fridge (5°C). They practically stop at the temperature of a freezer (−20°C).

Many industrial processes use high temperatures to make reactions go fast. The faster the reaction, the quicker you get products, which makes the process more profitable. But there are limits. High temperatures are expensive, because they mean using a lot of energy. And sometimes a high temperature means you actually get a smaller yield of the product. This happens with the production of ammonia by the Haber process (page 101). So in practice most industrial processes use moderately high temperatures — hundreds rather than thousands of degrees Celsius.

Picture 4 Burning powdered coal in a power station

Surface area

Surface area is another reason why chips cook fast. The surface area of a solid means the amount of surface that is exposed to the outside. If you cut up a solid into pieces, the surface area gets larger (picture 3). Chips are cut up small, so more surface is exposed to the hot oil.

You use the surface area effect when you light a fire. Chopping up a big log into smaller pieces makes the burning reaction go much faster. Some modern coal-fired power stations use a **fluidised bed** (picture 4) to burn the coal

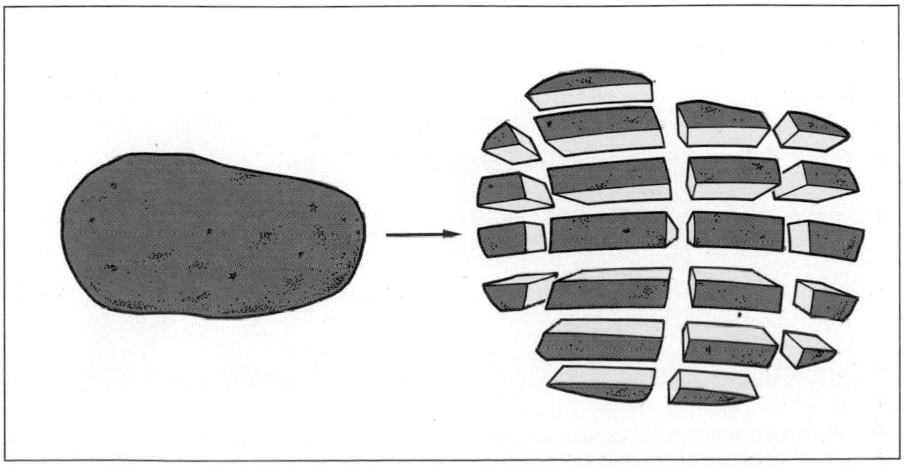

Picture 3 Cutting up a potato into chips. The more finely a solid is divided, the larger is its surface area

Picture 5 When the stonemason made this carving in 1670, the concentration of acid in the rain was much lower than it is today

quickly and efficiently. The coal is powdered into dust to give it a high surface area, and mixed with an unreactive solid like sand. Air is blown through the bed from underneath, so a very high surface area of coal dust is exposed to oxygen. The coal burns very quickly, and there is less pollution than when you burn the coal in lumps.

Surface area effects are important in industry. Chemical engineers make sure that when a solid is involved in a reaction, it has a high surface area — like the catalytic converter in picture 9.

Concentration

The stonemason who made the limestone statue in picture 5 expected it to last for centuries. It might have done, if the air had stayed as unpolluted as it was in 1670. Unfortunately, since the Industrial Revolution, more and more fossil fuels have been burned, making the rain more acidic (page 188). The concentration of acid in the rain has increased, so the rain has reacted faster with the limestone. The statue is now corroding much faster than it would have done in the seventeenth century.

In any reaction involving solutions, a concentrated solution always reacts faster than a dilute one. 'Concentrated' means the solution has a lot of solute dissolved in a particular volume. If you want to clean badly stained clothes, you soak them in a solution of detergent. If you use lots of detergent, the solution is concentrated and the stains are shifted quickly.

We normally use the word 'concentration' for solutions. But gases can have their concentration changed too, by changing the pressure. A gas at high pressure is more concentrated than a gas at low pressure. The same amount of gas is squeezed into a smaller volume (picture 6). Gases react faster at higher pressure, and this is made use of in the petrol engine. The mixture of petrol vapour and air is compressed so that it reacts very quickly — explosively, in fact — when it is ignited by the sparking plug.

Picture 7 shows another example of the effect of increasing the concentration of a gas.

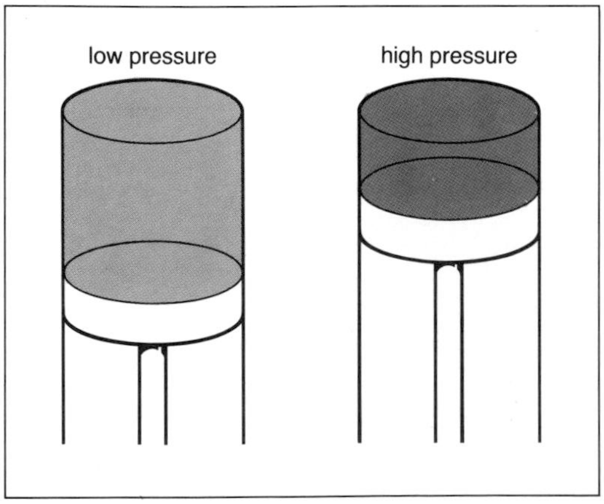

Picture 6 A gas at high pressure is more concentrated than a gas at low pressure

Picture 7 This premature baby is breathing air that is enriched with oxygen. The concentration of oxygen is greater than in normal air, so the baby does not have to breathe so hard to keep its body going at the necessary rate

Catalysts

The adhesive in picture 8 uses a catalyst. There are two tubes: one contains a monomer (see page 166) and the other contains a catalyst. When the two are mixed, the catalyst starts a polymerisation reaction in the monomer. It forms a strong thermosetting polymer, and the glue sets hard. The catalyst itself does not get used up in the reaction.

Catalysts are substances that alter the rate of a chemical reaction without getting used up.

When the reaction has finished, the catalyst is still there. This makes catalysts particularly useful, because they can be used again and again.

Catalytic converters like the one in picture 9 are being fitted to many modern cars. Car exhaust contains polluting gases like carbon monoxide (CO) and nitrogen oxide (NO). These pollutants can react together to make less harmful gases. For example:

$$\text{carbon monoxide} + \text{nitrogen oxide} \rightarrow \text{carbon dioxide} + \text{nitrogen}$$
$$CO(g) + NO(g) \rightarrow CO_2(g) + N_2(g)$$

Unfortunately, this reaction is very slow. But a catalyst made of platinum can speed it up so that 90% of the polluting gases are removed from the exhaust. The catalyst does not get used up, so it does not have to be replaced for years. The only problem is cost: the converter costs several hundred pounds. But several countries are beginning to make catalytic converters compulsory on all new cars.

Catalysts are very important in industrial processes. Most industrial chemistry uses some kind of catalyst — the faster you can make your product, the better. Examples are the manufacture of ammonia (page 101), the cracking of oil (page 161) and the manufacture of plastics (page 172).

Enzymes are biological catalysts. They are superb at their job. One molecule of hydrogen peroxide per minute. Enzymes are being used more and more in industrial processes — see *The Living World,* topic A7 for more about this, and about enzymes in general.

The only problem with enzymes is that they work in a narrow temperature range. Biological washing powders use enzymes to speed the removal of biological stains. But the water must not be too hot, or too cold.

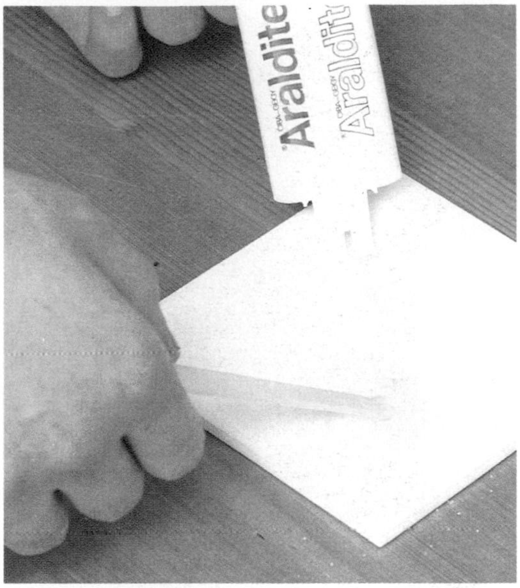

Picture 8 Mixing epoxy resin. One tube contains the monomer, the other contains the catalyst

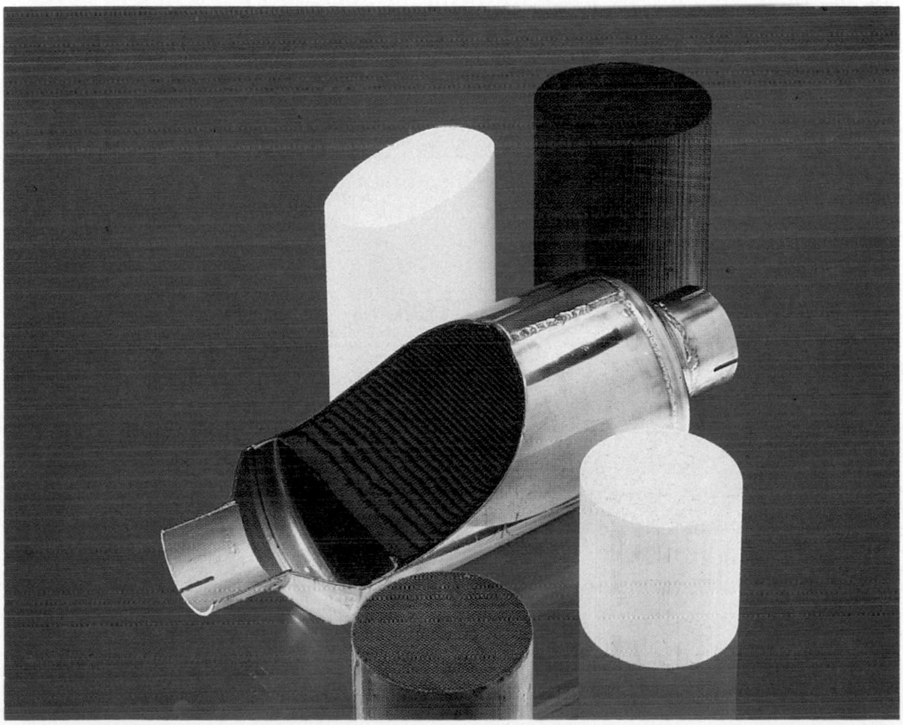

Picture 9 A catalytic converter in a car exhaust. Notice how the catalyst is arranged to give a high surface area

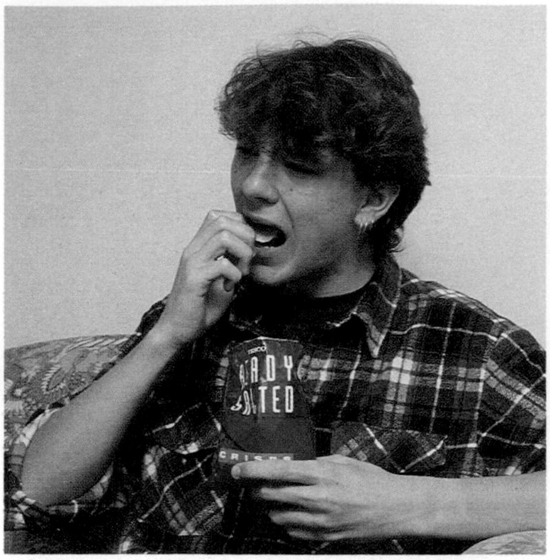

Picture 10 Eat them quickly, before they turn rancid

Our bodies have to be maintained at a precise temperature. You are a finely-tuned biochemical machine, with thousands of enzyme-catalysed reactions running in harmony. If any of these reactions runs too slow, or too fast, the whole machine gets out of control — as you will know if you've ever had a fever.

Slowing reactions down

Sometimes we want to slow reactions down, rather than speed them up. It's particularly important to slow down the reactions that make food go bad. The usual way to do this is to lower the temperature, using a fridge or freezer.

Another way is to get at the enzymes that make the food go bad. This can be done by cooking the food to destroy the enzymes. You can also **inhibit** the enzymes so they work less well. When you cut up an apple, it starts to go brown because of an enzyme-catalysed reaction with the air. Cooks sprinkle lemon juice over cut-up apple to stop this happening. The acid in the lemon juice makes the pH too low for the enzyme to work.

Fats are slowly oxidised by air, forming nasty, rancid-smelling products. Potato crisps are particularly likely to turn rancid, because they are very fatty and have a high surface area. To prevent oxidation, crisp packets are filled with nitrogen. Another way to stop oxidation is to use substances called antioxidants — you will see them mentioned in the ingredients list on a crisp packet (picture 10). Antioxidants slow down the oxidation reaction: they are called **inhibitors**.

Some paints contain corrosion inhibitors. They slow down rusting by slowing down the reaction of iron with oxygen.

Reaction rates and the environment

Plastic bags have advantages and disadvantages. Plastic does not break down (degrade) easily, which means you can use a plastic bag again and again. But it still does not degrade when you throw it away, so it's a nasty litter problem. How convenient it would be if we could make plastics that react quickly with air or water — but only when thrown away. Scientist are trying to develop this kind of **biodegradable** plastic.

There is a similar problem with CFCs, the chemicals used in aerosols. They are very unreactive, and break down very slowly after they've been released into the air. So slowly that they stay in the atmosphere long enough to reach the ozone layer, where they do serious damage (page 191). Chemists are trying to develop replacements for CFCs that react more quickly with the air so they never reach the ozone layer.

Explaining reaction rates

We can use the kinetic theory (topic C1) to try and explain the factors affecting the rates of reactions. This extension of the kinetic theory is called the **collision theory**.

For example, take the reaction between methane (natural gas) and oxygen. Methane molecules have to collide with oxygen molecules before a reaction can happen. What's more, the molecules must collide with enough energy — the activation energy — otherwise they just bounce off each other harmlessly. The activation energy is needed to break the bonds in the molecules and get the reaction started (see page 195).

This is why methane and oxygen do not react at room temperature. To make them react, they need heating to provide the activation energy. In other words, they need to be ignited.

The collision theory says that:

Chemical reactions occur when particles of the reactants collide. They must collide with a certain minimum energy, called the activation energy.

Picture 11 uses the collision theory to explain the effect of surface area, concentration and temperature on the reaction between zinc and hydrochloric acid. You can investigate this reaction yourself in activity A.

Picture 11 Using the collision theory to explain the factors affecting the rate of the reaction between zinc and hydrochloric acid

zinc + hydrochloric acid → zinc chloride + hydrogen

SURFACE AREA
surface area of zinc **low**

surface area **higher** – more zinc exposed to collisions

CONCENTRATION
concentration of acid **low**

concentration **higher** – more chance of particles colliding

TEMPERATURE
temperature **low**

temperature **higher** – particles collide with more energy

Key ● zinc atom ○ hydrogen ion from acid

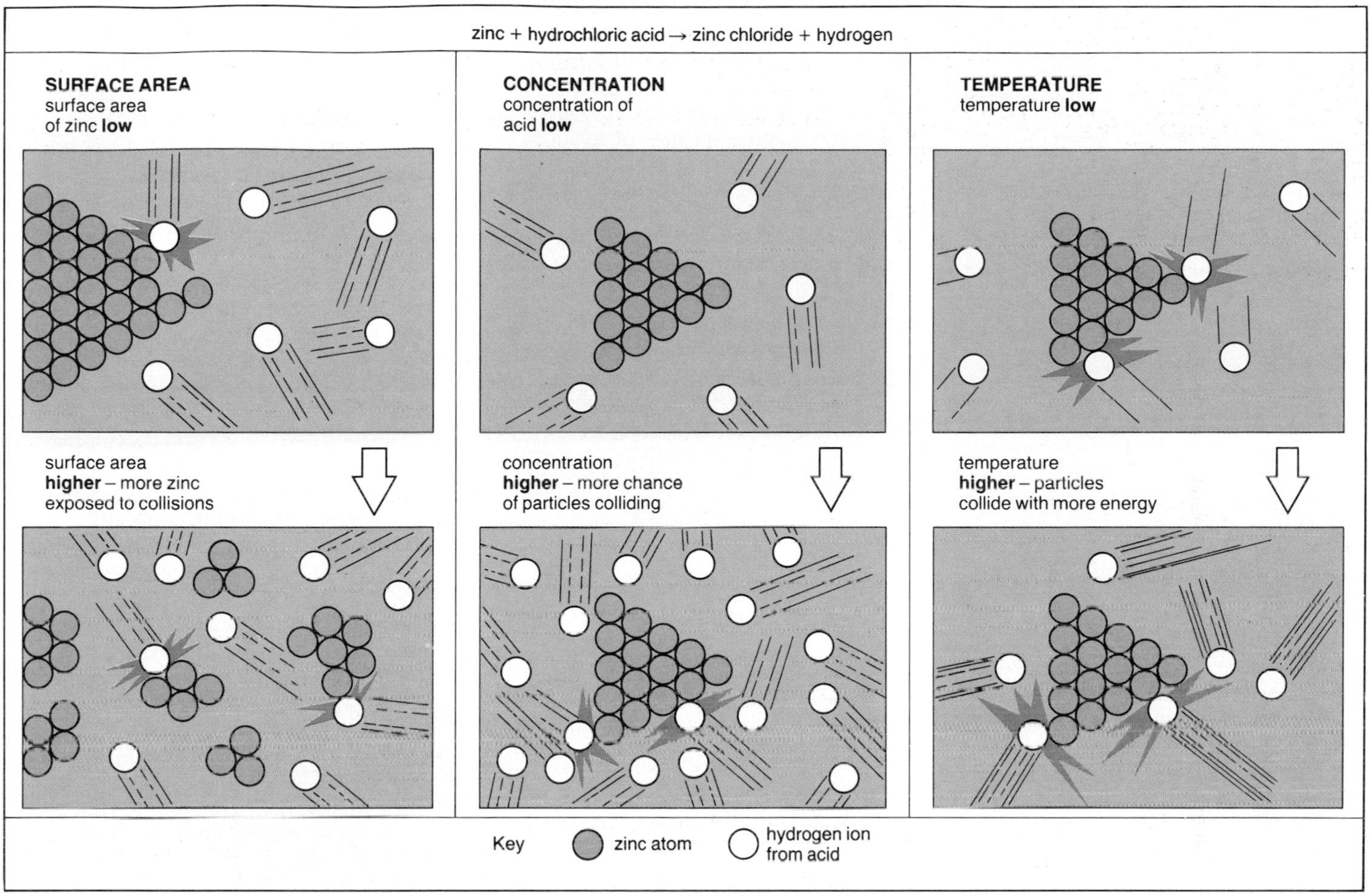

Activities

A Looking at factors affecting the rate of a reaction

This activity is about the rate of the reaction between zinc and hydrochloric acid forming zinc chloride and hydrogen:

$$Zn(s) + 2HCl(aq) \rightarrow ZnCl_2(aq) + H_2(g)$$

In this simple investigation you will not make any measurements. You can estimate the rate of the reaction by just looking at how fast the bubbles of hydrogen come off from the zinc.

CARE Hydrochloric acid is corrosive. Wear eye protection.

1 First, do this basic experiment using dilute hydrochloric acid. ('Dilute' hydrochloric acid has two moles of HCl dissolved in each litre of acid.)
 Put a piece of granulated zinc in a test tube. The piece should be as large as you can fit in the tube. Add dilute hydrochloric acid so the tube is a quarter full. Stand it in a test tube rack. After a minute or two, observe carefully to see how fast it is bubbling.

2 Repeat the basic experiment using hydrochloric acid that is half as concentrated. You will have to make this by diluting the original acid.

3 Repeat the basic experiment, but after adding the hydrochloric acid warm the tube to raise the temperature by 10°C (use a thermometer to check).

4 Repeat the basic experiment, but add two drops of copper sulphate solution. This acts as a catalyst for the reaction.

5 Repeat the basic experiment, but in place of the large piece of zinc use several small pieces.

 Compare how fast hydrogen came off in the different experiments. Explain the differences.

B Measuring the rate of a reaction: (1) The effect of concentration

You can develop the simple experiment in activity A to make some *measurements* of reaction rate. You can use the apparatus in picture 12 on the next page, though you may measure the gas volume in an upside-down burette instead of a gas syringe.

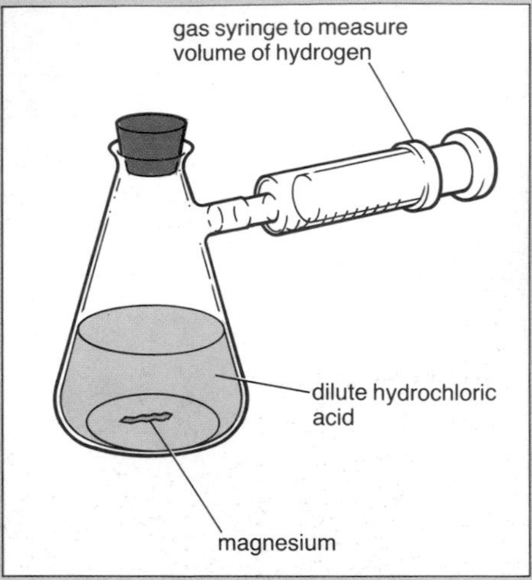

Picture 12 An experiment to investigate the rate of reaction between magnesium and hydrochloric acid

CARE Hydrochloric acid is corrosive. Wear eye protection.

1 Weigh 0.05g of magnesium ribbon. Put it in the conical flask. (Don't add any acid yet.)
2 Put 50cm^3 of dilute hydrochloric acid (concentration 2 moles per litre) in a measuring cylinder.
3 When you are ready to start, take the stopper off the flask. Set the gas syringe to read zero.
4 Now quickly pour in the acid. Replace the stopper *immediately* so no gas escapes, and immediately start timing with a stop-watch.
5 Read the volume from the gas syringe every minute.
6 Plot a graph of volume of hydrogen given off (vertical axis) against time (horizontal axis).
7 Repeat the experiment using hydrochloric acid that is half as concentrated (1 mole per litre). Plot the new graph on the same axes as the first.
8 Compare your graphs. What do they tell you about the rates of the reaction with different concentrations of acid?

The next topic deals with interpreting graphs of this kind.

C Measuring the rate of a reaction: (2) The effect of temperature

In this experiment you will be measuring the rate of the reaction between sodium thiosulphate and hydrochloric acid. In this reaction, a fine precipitate of sulphur slowly forms. You can measure the rate by timing how long the precipitate takes to form.

CARE Hydrochloric acid is corrosive. Eye protection must be worn.

1 Using a ball-pen, draw a cross on a piece of white paper.
2 Use a measuring cylinder to put 50cm^3 of sodium thiosulphate solution (concentration 0.03 moles per litre) in a conical flask. Measure the temperature of the solution, and warm if necessary until its temperature is 20°C.
3 Stand the flask on the paper so the cross is right underneath (picture 13).
4 Add 5 cm^3 of dilute hydrochloric acid and swirl the flask to mix the solutions. Immediately start timing using a stop-clock. Take the temperature of the mixture and record it.
5 Look down at the cross from above. The solution will turn cloudy and the cross will gradually disappear from sight. Stop the clock when you can no longer see the cross.
6 Repeat the experiment, but in stage 1. warm the solution to different temperatures. Do experiments at 30°C, 40°C, 50°C and 60°C. For each temperature, record the time it takes for the cross to disappear.
7 Plot a graph of your results, with time for the cross to disappear on the vertical axis, and temperature on the horizontal axis. What does your graph tell you?

The next topic deals with interpreting graphs of this kind.

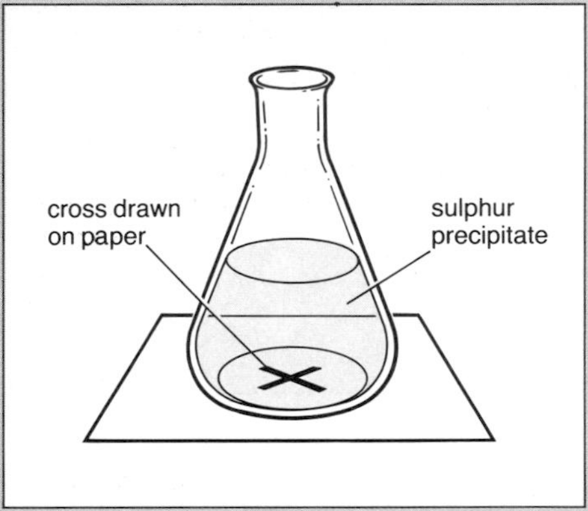

Picture 13 Following the reaction between sodium thiosulphate and dilute hydrochloric acid

D The apple browning problem

Apples go brown when they are cut up. This is a nuisance if you are making fruit salad — no-one likes brown apple. Investigate different ways of slowing down apple browning, using the ideas in this topic. Check your plan with your teacher before doing any experimental work.

E The best temperature for biological washing powders

Plan an experiment to investigate the best temperature for a biological washing powder to work at. You will have to think carefully about how you will measure the effectiveness of the powder. Check your plan with your teacher before doing any experimental work.

Questions

1 Give examples of chemical reactions that go:
a very fast,
b very slowly,
c at a moderate rate.

2 List the factors that affect the rate of a chemical reaction. For each factor, give one example to illustrate it.

3a What is a catalyst?
b In what ways are enzymes similar to a non-living catalyst like platinum? In what ways are they different?
c Pineapple contains an enzyme which breaks down proteins. If you want to make a fruit jelly with chunks of pineapple in, the jelly will not set if you use fresh pineapple, but it works with tinned pineapple.

4 Explain the following.
a Carrots cook more quickly if they are sliced.
b When beer is being brewed, the temperature in the fermentation tank must not be allowed to go above 21°C or below 14°C.

5 Look at picture 5 on page 198. The protruding parts of the statue, like the nose and ears, get worn away first. Why do you think this is?

Making sulphuric acid — quickly

Sulphuric acid is the world's most popular chemical (table 1). More of it is manufactured than any other. Sulphuric acid is needed to make many things, from paints and plastics to fibres and fertilisers.

Table 1 The top ten industrial chemicals (The ten chemicals manufactured in the largest quantities in the USA, 1986)

1	Sulphuric acid
2	Nitrogen
3	Oxygen
4	Ethene
5	Calcium oxide
6	Ammonia
7	Sodium hydroxide
8	Chlorine
9	Phosphoric acid
10	Propene

Picture 1 One of ICI's plants for making sulphuric acid. Why do you think it's made by the Agricultural Division

Such an important chemical has to be manufactured cheaply, and that means quickly. So reaction rates are very important in sulphuric acid manufacture.

How's it done?

Sulphur is the starting material for manufacturing sulphuric acid. There are three stages in the process, summarised in picture 2.

1 Sulphur, S, is burned in air, to give sulphur dioxide, SO_2:

sulphur + oxygen → sulphur dioxide

This reaction is fast.

2 The sulphur dioxide is cooled, then reacted with oxygen to convert it to sulphur trioxide, SO_3:

sulphur dioxide + oxygen → sulphur trioxide

This is the most difficult part of the process, because it is a slow reaction. To speed it up, it is carried out under these special conditions:

- With a catalyst. The catalyst is vanadium pentoxide, V_2O_5. At one time platinum was used, but V_2O_5 is cheaper.
- At a high temperature. However, there is a problem with the temperature, because the reaction is reversible. At *very* high temperatures (above 500°C), the sulphur trioxide breaks down to give sulphur dioxide again. So an intermediate temperature of 450°C is used as a compromise.

3 Finally, the sulphur trioxide made in stage **2** is reacted with water to give sulphuric acid, H_2SO_4.

sulphur trioxide + water → sulphuric acid

This reaction is fast – too fast, in fact. The sulphur dioxide reacts with water so readily that a fine mist of sulphuric acid droplets is formed. To avoid this, the sulphur trioxide is first absorbed in 98 per cent sulphuric acid. This gives 99.5 per cent sulphuric acid, which is then watered down.

This process is called the **Contact Process**, and it is used all over the world to make sulphuric acid.

1 There are three raw materials for making sulphuric acid. What are they?

2 In the second stage of the Contact Process, a temperature of 450°C is used. Why is the temperature not: (a) higher, (b) lower than this?

3 What else, apart from a high temperature, is used to make the second stage of the process go quickly?

4 Write balanced equations for the reactions in each of the three stages of the process.

5 What mass of sulphuric acid could be manufactured from 32 tonnes of sulphur? (S = 32, O = 16, H = 1)

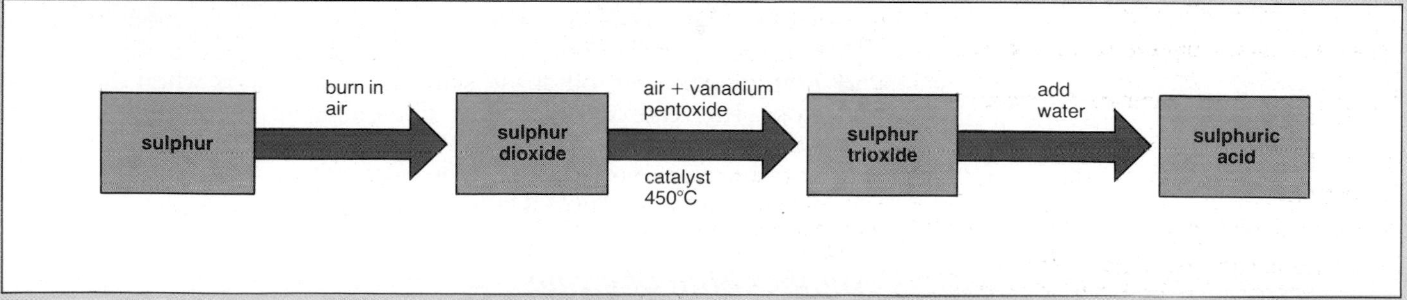

Picture 2 An outline of the Contact process for making sulphuric acid

17 Measuring reaction rates

In this topic we look at ways of finding the speed of chemical reactions.

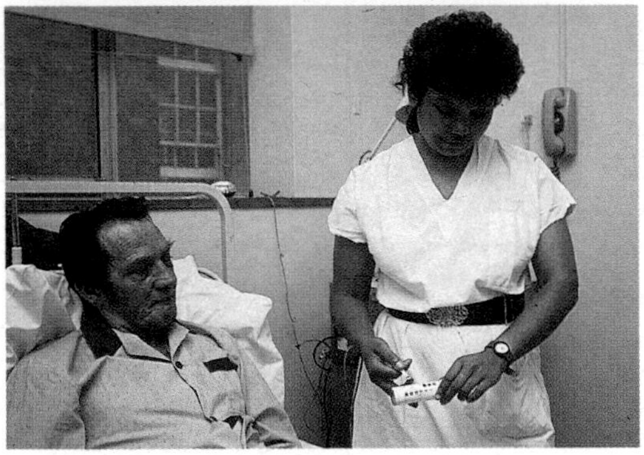

Picture 1 Testing a blood sample

Using graphs to measure rates

The nurse in picture 1 is testing a blood sample from a diabetic person. She needs to know how much glucose the blood contains. She leaves the sample on the test strip for a fixed time, then looks to see what colour it has gone.

We measure the rates of chemical reactions in a similar way. To investigate the rate of a reaction, we need to measure something that changes during the reaction. We choose some property that is easy to detect, such as the colour, or the volume of gas given off, and measure it at fixed times. It's like checking how far a runner has gone each minute. We can use these measurements to find how the amounts of the chemicals change with time. Then we can say:

$$\text{reaction rate} = \frac{\text{change in amount of substance}}{\text{time}}$$

Let's look at an example — the reaction of magnesium with hydrochloric acid. Activity B in the last topic describes an experiment to measure the rate of this reaction — it's on page 201–202.

We measure the volume of hydrogen given off at different times, and plot a graph like the one in picture 2.

If you look at the graph for Experiment X, you will see that in the first minute, 30 cm^3 of hydrogen were given off. Now,

$$\text{reaction rate} = \frac{\text{change in amount of substance}}{\text{time}}$$

$$= \frac{30\,\text{cm}^3\ \text{hydrogen}}{1\,\text{min}} = 30\,\text{cm}^3\ \text{hydrogen per minute}$$

This is the *average* rate of reaction over the first minute.

Fortunately, we don't have to do this kind of calculation all the time. We can tell how fast the reaction is going from the gradient of the graph. The steeper the graph, the faster the reaction.

Interpreting the graph

The graph in picture 2 shows the results of two experiments. In Experiment X the concentration of acid is 2 moles per litre. In Experiment Y its concentration is 1 mole per litre. Look carefully at the graph and notice these points.

- In both experiments the graph starts off steep. This is because the reaction starts off fast. The reaction then slows down and the graph becomes less steep. This is because the hydrochloric acid and magnesium are getting used up. In fact the magnesium runs out first, because there is more than enough hydrochloric acid in this experiment.
- The graph in Experiment X starts off twice as steep as the graph in Experiment Y. This means that the reaction in experiment X starts off twice as fast. So doubling the concentration of the acid doubles the rate.
- Both graphs level off at the same volume. This is when the reaction stops. The reaction stops when all the magnesium is used up, and the same amount of magnesium (0.05g) was used in both experiments. So both reactions produce the same *total* volume of hydrogen — though Experiment X produces it faster.

Another kind of graph

Another way of measuring the rate of a reaction is to time how long it takes for the reaction to reach a particular stage. It's like timing a runner over a

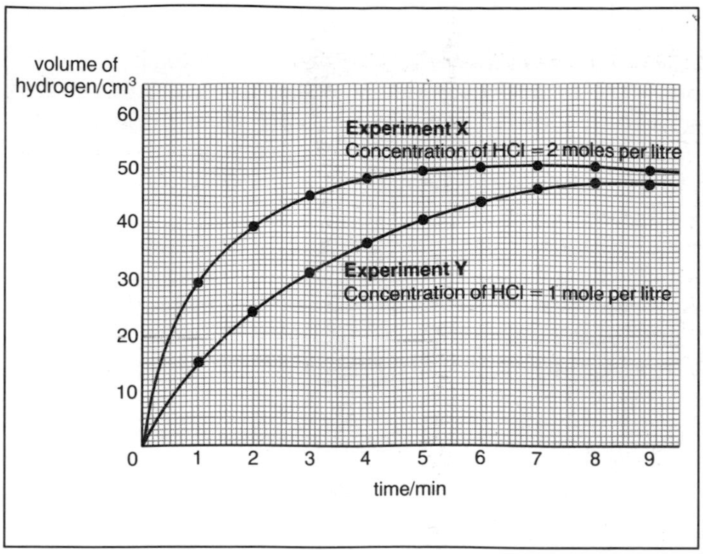

Picture 2 Results of an investigation into the effect of concentration on the rate of the reaction between magnesium and hydrochloric acid

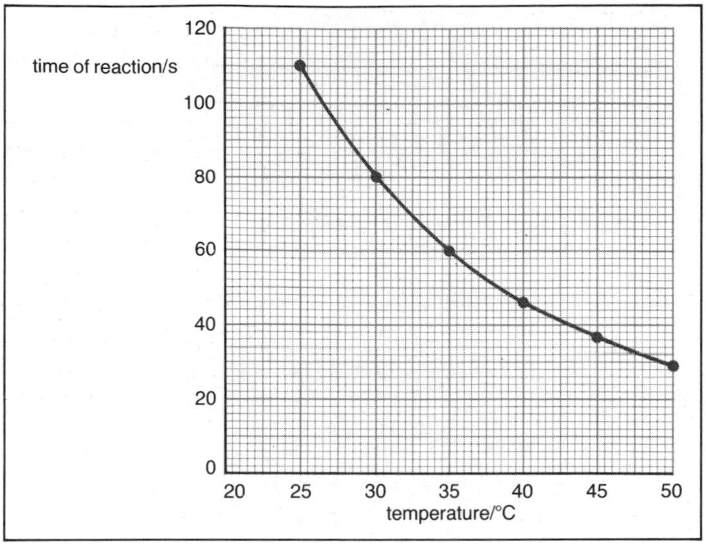

Picture 3 Results of an investigation into the effect of temperature on the rate of the reaction between sodium thiosulphate and hydrochloric acid

fixed distance. The *faster* the runner, the *less* time it takes to cover the distance.

Let's look at an example of this second approach — the reaction between sodium thiosulphate and hydrochloric acid. Activity C in the last topic describes an experiment to measure the rate of this reaction.

We time how long it takes for the reaction to produce enough sulphur to make the cross disappear. The reaction is repeated at different temperatures. It's the same cross each time, so we are timing how long it takes the reaction to reach a particular stage. The *faster* the reaction, the *less* time it takes for the cross to disappear. Picture 3 shows one student's results in this experiment. Look at the graph and notice these points.

- At *higher* temperatures, it takes *less* time for the cross to disappear. In other words, the rate is faster.
- For a 10°C temperature rise (for example, from 30°C to 40°C), the time for the cross to disappear is roughly halved. In other words, the rate of the reaction is roughly doubled for a 10°C rise.

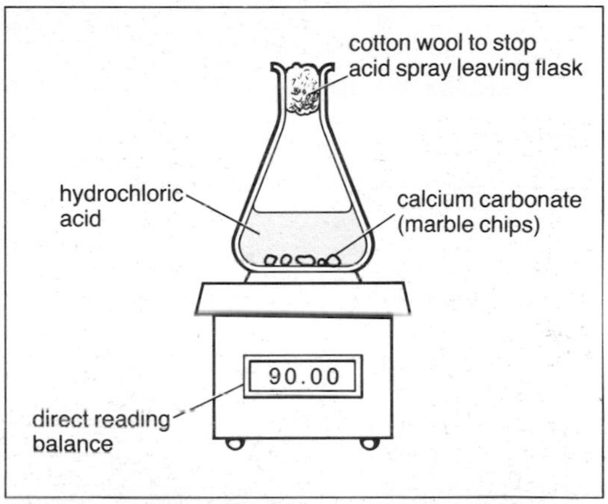

Picture 4 Investigating the rate of the reaction between calcium carbonate and hydrochloric acid

Questions

1 Look at the graph for experiment Y in picture 2. What is the average rate of the reaction, measured in cm³ of hydrogen per minute, over the first minute?

2 Make a sketch copy of the graph for experiment X in picture 2. Now sketch the graph you would expect if the experiment was repeated with the temperature 10°C higher.

3 A student carried out an experiment to measure the rate of the reaction between calcium carbonate (marble chips) and hydrochloric acid. He used the apparatus shown in picture 4. He weighed the flask to find the mass of carbon dioxide given off at different times. His results are shown in table 1.

Table 1

Time/min	Mass of CO_2 given off/g
2.0	1.5
4.0	2.5
6.0	3.1
8.0	3.4
10.0	3.6
16.0	3.8

a Plot a graph of the results, with time on the horizontal axis.

b Compare the gradient of the graph at the start of the experiment and at the end. What does this tell you?

c On the same axes, sketch the graph you would expect if the experiment was done at a temperature of 30°C instead of 20°C.

d On the same axes, sketch the graph you would expect if the marble chips were ground into a powder before the start of the experiment.

J1 Using electrolysis

Electrolysis means using electricity to split up compounds.

On October 6 1807, Humphry Davy was beside himself with excitement. He had just melted some potassium hydroxide (he called it potash) and passed electricity through it. To his delight, tiny globules of a silvery molten metal floated to the surface and burst into lilac flames. He danced around the room in glee, and it was half an hour before he had calmed down enough to write his results in his notebook (picture 2).

Humphry Davy had just discovered the element potassium, by using electrolysis to decompose potassium hydroxide. His experiment opened the way for the discovery of more new elements — he discovered sodium using a similar method just three days later. He had already investigated the electrolysis of water, and found that it gives two parts of hydrogen to one part of oxygen.

Humphry Davy's work with electrolysis led the way to many other things. Today, electrolysis is used to make aluminium, chlorine and many other useful chemicals, as well as for electroplating metals.

Picture 1 Humphrey Davy (1778-1829), aged 23. He made many chemical discoveries, including 'laughing gas' (dinitrogen oxide) and six elements. He also invented a safety lamp which prevented explosions in mines

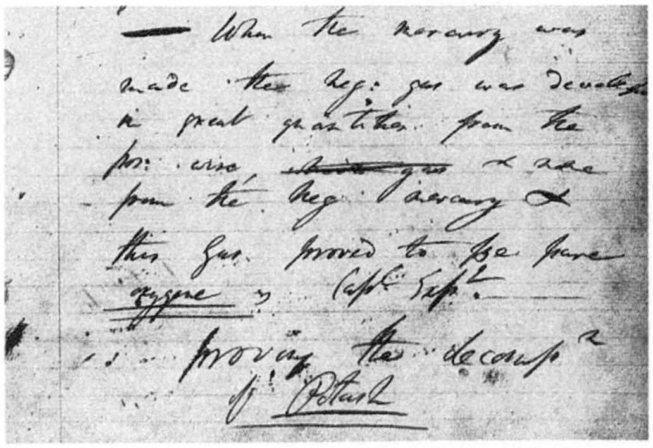

Picture 2 Part of Humphrey Davy's notebook recording his electrolysis of potash. He called it a 'capital experiment'

What is electrolysis?

Some basic words

Humphry Davy's work on electrolysis made him world famous. His assistant in much of his work was a younger man called Michael Faraday. He continued Humphry Davy's work and made some even greater discoveries (see Topic E8 in *The Physical World*).

Michael Faraday was a brilliant scientist, but he didn't have much of an education. He had a friend who was a Greek scholar, and he asked him to invent some new words to describe the basics of electrolysis. We still use these words today. Table 1 gives some of the Greek words that were used.

Electrolysis means using electricity to split up (decompose) substances. The substance that is decomposed is called the **electrolyte**. Two **electrodes** are used to make electrical contact with the solution. They are usually made of an unreactive metal like carbon or platinum. The positive electrode is called the **anode** and the negative one is the **cathode.** Electricity is carried through the electrolyte by **ions** (picture 3).

Conductors and insulators

You can't electrolyse something unless it conducts electricity. But not *all* conductors are electrolytes. You can pass electricity through a metal for years and it doesn't decompose. This isn't surprising, because metals are usually elements, so you couldn't split them into anything simpler.

All electrolytes are ionic compounds. However, ionic compounds don't conduct electricity when they are solid. To conduct, they have to be in a liquid state, either molten or dissolved in water. This makes the ions free to move and carry electricity: more about this in topic J3. So electrolysis always involves ionic compounds, either molten or dissolved in water.

What is formed during electrolysis?

You can try some electrolysis experiments for yourself in the activities at the end of this topic and topic J2. You will find that you get one product at the cathode and one at the anode. Usually the products are elements. For example, when Humphry Davy electrolysed potassium hydroxide, he got potassium at the cathode and oxygen at the anode. The general rule is that:

At the cathode, a metal or hydrogen is formed.
At the anode, a non-metal is formed.

Electrolysis pulls the electrolyte apart, with one part going to each electrode. Just why this happens is explained in the next topic.

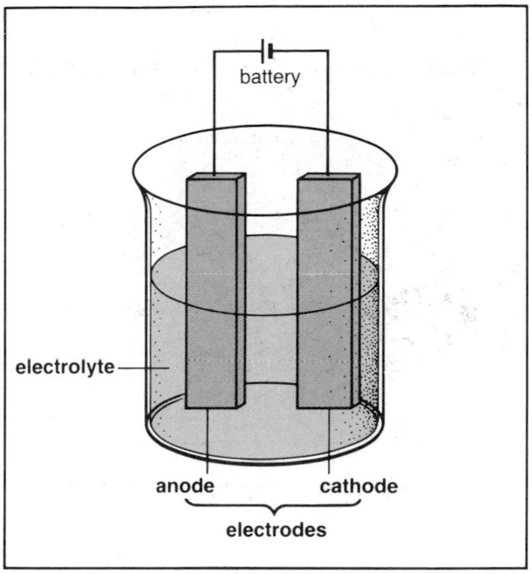

Picture 3 The basic words in electrolysis

Table 1

Greek word	English spelling	English translation
ΕΛΕΚΤΡΟΝ	electro-	amber
ΚΑΤ	cat-	down
ΑΝ	an-	up
ΙΟΝ	ion	going
ΟΔΟΣ	-ode	way
ΛΥΣΙΣ	-lysis	splitting

Using electrolysis

In 1852, the price of aluminium was £250 a kilogram — 30 times the price of silver. Aluminium was an expensive oddity. The Emperor Napoleon III used aluminium plates when he really wanted to impress his guests.

By 1890, the price of aluminium had fallen to less than £1 a kilogram, a fraction of the price of silver.

What had happened? Aluminium is extracted from an ore called bauxite, which is mainly aluminium oxide. Aluminium is a reactive metal, which makes it difficult to extract from the ore. Before 1886, the only way to make it was by heating aluminium chloride with sodium. Sodium itself was expensive, which made aluminium cost even more. Then in 1886, a new process was developed. It used Humphry Davy's method of electrolysing a molten compound. The price of aluminium quickly fell, and the metal became widely available. The same basic method is still used. Today, aluminium is so cheap that if you eat a meal off an aluminium plate, it will probably be a disposable one that you throw away afterwards.

Extracting aluminium

Picture 5 shows the equipment that is used to manufacture aluminium today. The electrolyte is molten aluminium oxide, mixed with another aluminium compound called cryolite to make the melting point lower. The electrolysis cell is lined with carbon, and this lining becomes the negative electrode (the cathode). Molten aluminium collects at the bottom and is tapped off. The anodes are blocks of carbon. Oxygen is given off at the anode.

The voltage used is only 5V, but a plant producing 100 tonnes of aluminium a day needs a current of about 30 million amps. The heating effect of the electric current keeps the electrolyte molten. The cost of electricity is a major part of the total cost of aluminium (picture 6). Because of this, aluminium plants are usually built near to sources of cheap electricity, such as hydro-electric plants.

Other metals are extracted by electrolysis

All the more reactive metals are extracted using electrolysis (see topic E3 for details of metal extraction in general). Usually the chloride of the metal is used, because these have lower melting points. There are more details in the next topic.

Picture 4 The statue of Eros in Piccadilly Circus is made from aluminium. When it was made in 1884, aluminium was an expensive novelty

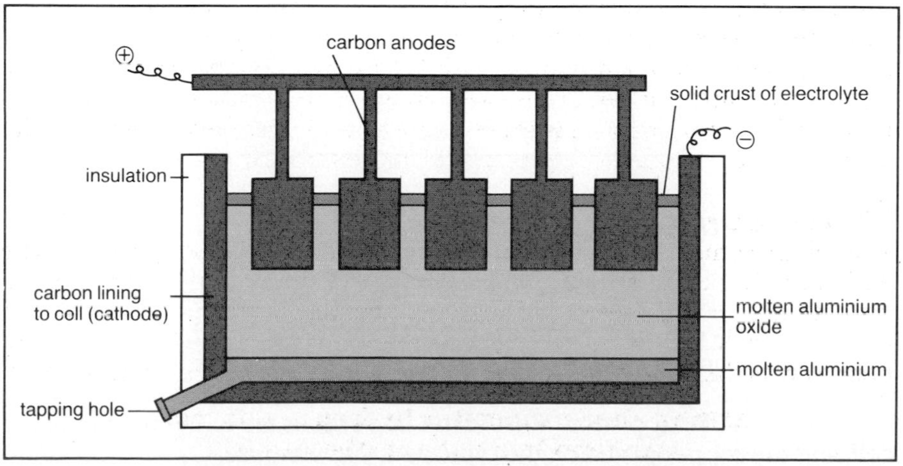

Picture 5 How aluminium is manufactured by electrolysis

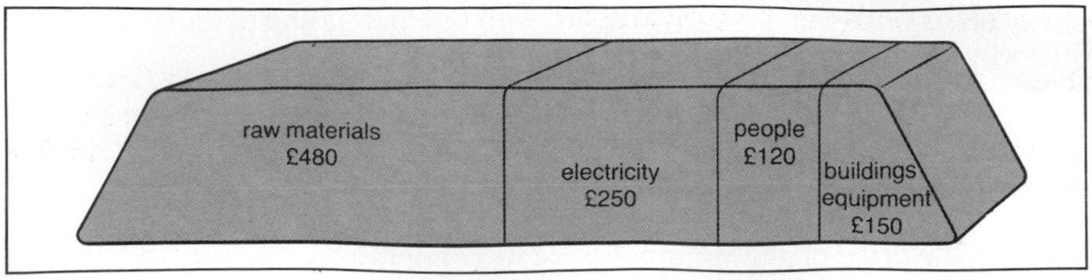

Picture 6 The main costs involved in making £1000 worth of aluminium

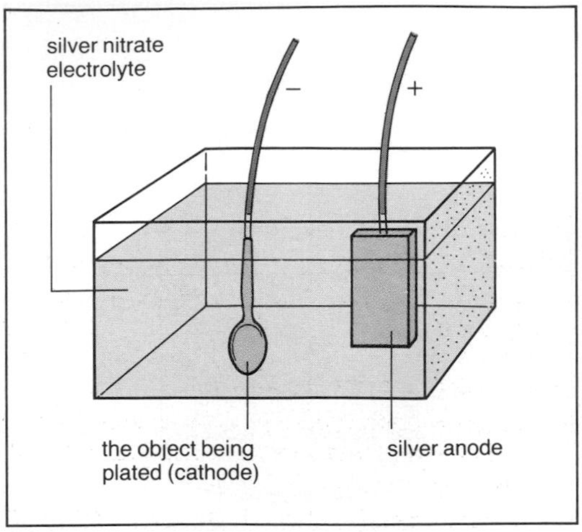

Picture 7 Electroplating

Picture 8 This teapot has been electroplated with silver

Electroplating

You've probably seen silver in a shop. It might have been solid silver, but it's more likely to have been silver *plate*. Look for the letters EPNS: they stand for Electro-Plated Nickel Silver, which is nickel with a thin layer of silver plated on top.

Electroplating is one of the useful applications of electrolysis. It's used to plate a thin layer of a valuable metal on top of a less valuable one. This may be to make the metal look more attractive, or to protect it from corrosion. Steel is often protected in this way. Table 2 gives some examples of the uses of electroplating.

How it's done

Picture 7 shows the basic method. The object that has to be electroplated is connected to the negative terminal of the electrical supply, so that it is the cathode. The anode is a pure piece of the plating metal — silver in this example. The electrolyte is a solution of a compound of the plating metal — silver nitrate in this example. During electroplating, metal dissolves from the anode and gets plated onto the cathode as a thin layer. In effect, metal is transferred from the anode to the cathode.

The metal layer only forms on the cathode where it is facing the anode. So the cathode has to be rotated so that it gets plated evenly all over. This means the equipment needs to be rather more complicated than the simple version in picture 7. It's also important that the object being plated is very clean, otherwise the plating metal does not stick to it properly.

Table 2 Some ways that electroplating is used

What's plated on top?	What's underneath?	Uses
silver	nickel	cutlery
chromium	steel	shiny metal trimmings for cars, bikes, kettles.
zinc	steel	protecting steel from corrosion in dustbins, wheelbarrows
tin	steel	'tin' cans for food

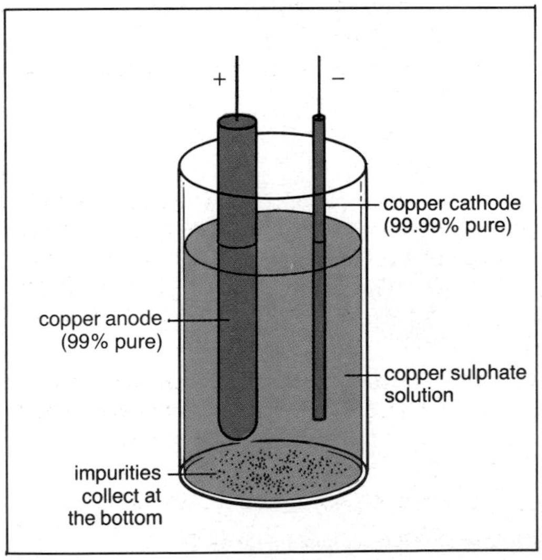

Picture 9 Purifying copper by electrolysis

Purifying copper by electrolysis

Copper that is used for making electrical equipment has to be very pure. Electrolysis is used to purify the copper. The impure copper is the anode in the electrolysis cell shown in picture 9. The cathode is a thin sheet of very pure copper, and the electrolyte is a solution of copper sulphate. When a current passes through the cell, copper moves from the anode to the cathode, as in electroplating. Most of the impuritites fall to the bottom of the cell, and the copper plated on the cathode is 99.99% pure.

Electricity from chemicals

Electrolysis uses electrical energy to produce chemical reactions. The opposite process uses chemical reactions to produce electricity, and it's what happens in an electric cell or battery. You can find out about it in *The Physical World*, topic E9.

Activities

A Electroplating

Use the simple apparatus in picture 10 to do some nickel plating in the laboratory. To be successful you will need to be particularly careful to (i) make sure the object you are plating is clean (ii) control the current. If it is too high your plating won't stick.

CARE Eye protection must be worn.

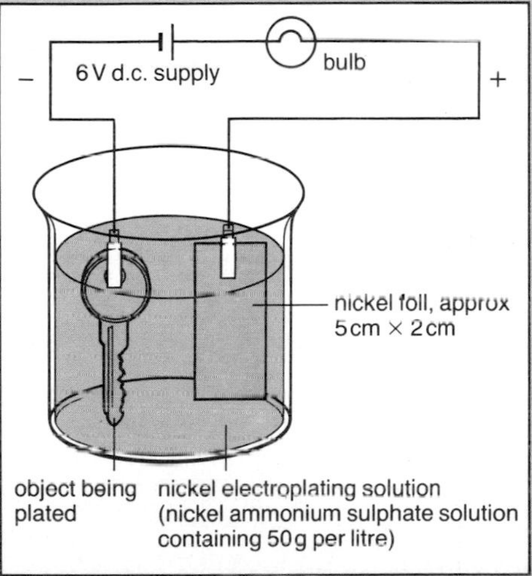

Picture 10 Electroplating in the laboratory

1 Decide on the object you will electroplate — it might be a coin, a knife blade, a key. Clean it *very thoroughly* using steel wool.

2 Set up the electroplating bath as shown in picture 10. The bulb does two things: it tells you when current is flowing, and it limits the current so it is not too big.

3 Let the current flow for three minutes, then have a look to see how well the object is plated. If it looks good, turn it round to plate the other side for three minutes. If the coating looks too thin, give it a few more minutes. If the coating looks powdery, it's probably because the current was too high. Clean it off and start again, but this time have less of the anode dipping into the solution. This will reduce the current.

4 When the object is plated, take it out of the bath and wash it off. Test the plating to see how well it has stuck.

You can try varying this basic experiment to get better results. You could try:

a rotating the cathode during plating.

b varying the distance between anode and cathode,

c varying the current as described in **3** above,

d varying the temperature of the plating solution.

How would you change this experiment if you wanted to do silver plating instead of nickel plating?

B Looking for electroplate

Look around in your home for articles that are electroplated. Decide, as far as you can:

1 what metal is plated on top,

2 what metal is underneath,

3 what the purpose of the plating is.

Choose one of the items and look very closely at it. Are there any places where the plating is less good? Can you see any sign of where the electrical connnection was made?

C 'I owe it all to Volta'

Sir Humphry Davy discovered six new elements in two years using electrolysis. But he could not have made his discoveries without electricity — and remember, there was no mains electricity in 1807. Humphry Davy said: 'Nothing tends so much to the advancement of new knowledge as a new instrument'. What was the 'instrument' that helped him so much? (page 206 may help you).

Questions

1 Give the words that fit in the blanks in the following.

Electrolysis means _(a)_ a substance using _(b)_. The substance being electrolysed is called an _(c)_. Two _(d)_ are used, one positive and called the _(e)_, one negative and called the _(f)_. Normally, a metal or hydrogen is formed at the _(g)_ and a non-metal is formed at the _(h)_.

2 Look at the elctroplating bath in picture 7. What changes would you have to make if you wanted to gold-plate the spoon instead of silver-plating it?

3 Look at the electrolysis cell for the manufacture of aluminium shown in picture 5.

a The electrolyte does not need heating to keep it molten. Why?

b What would happen if you reversed the connections of the cathode and anode?

c The graphite anodes gradually disappear during the electrolysis. What are they turning to? (Think about the product that is given off at the anode.)

4 You can buy plastic items that look metallic. They have been electroplated to coat them with a metal such as chromium.

a What is the difficulty with electroplating plastic?

b How do you think this difficulty is overcome?

5 In an electroplating bath, you have to rotate the cathode so that it gets plated all over. Suggest a design for a cell that would plate the cathode all over *without rotating it.* Use a sketch to illustrate your design.

6 Look at table 1. Use it to explain how the following words were derived. You may have to do some inspired guesswork!

a Electrolysis b Cathode

c Anode d Ion

J2 Explaining electrolysis

We can use ideas about ions to explain what goes on in electrolysis — and to predict the products.

Picture 1 These cells are used by ICI, for the electrolysis of brine. ICI's plant at Runcorn uses 1% of all Britain's electricity

Useful things from salt

Salt — sodium chloride — is an excellent source of chemicals, and most of them are made by electrolysis.

Solid sodium chloride does not conduct electricity. To make it conduct, you can either melt it or dissolve it in water to give an aqueous solution. So there are two ways of doing electrolysis on sodium chloride: on the molten compound or on the aqueous solution. Pictures 2 and 3 show how these experiments could be done in the laboratory — in industry, of course, they use different equipment.

Table 1 shows what you get when you electrolyse sodium chloride in the two different ways. We'll look at the two ways in turn.

Table 1 The products of electrolysing sodium chloride

	At the anode (+)	At the cathode (−)	Left behind
molten sodium chloride, NaCl(l)	chlorine	sodium	nothing
sodium chloride in solution, NaCl(aq)	chlorine	hydrogen	sodium hydroxide

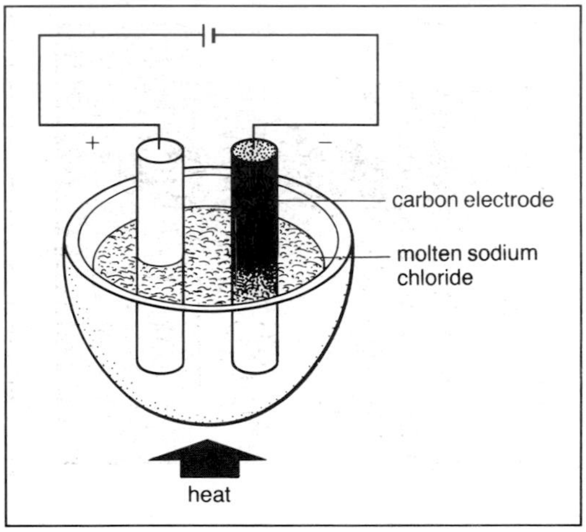

Picture 2 Electrolysing molten sodium chloride in the laboratory

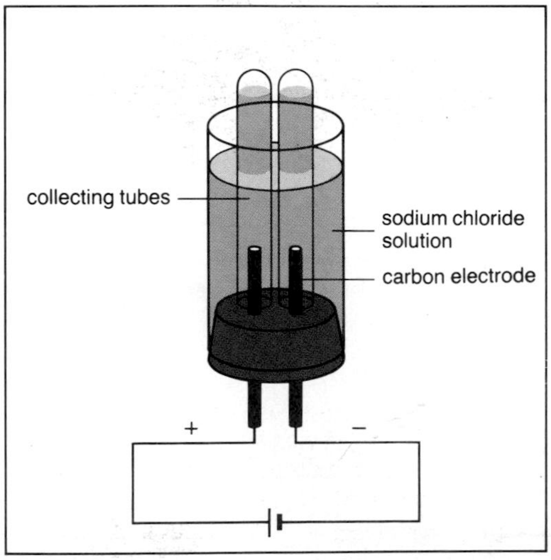

Picture 3 Electrolysing sodium chloride solution in the laboratory

Electrolysis of molten electrolytes

Sodium chloride melts at 800°C, which is too high for ordinary laboratory equipment. However, your teacher may show you the electrolysis of another molten electrolyte, such as lead bromide which melts at 373°C (see activity A).

It's easy to predict the result of electrolysing a molten electrolyte. The compound just gets split into two parts, a metal and a non-metal. The metal is formed at the cathode and the non-metal at the anode.

What's going on?

To explain what happens in electrolysis, you need to remember that all electrolytes contain ions (charged particles). In sodium chloride, the ions are Na^+ and Cl^-. You'll need to remember too that an electric current is a flow of electrons, and that electrons are negatively charged.

When the sodium chloride is solid, the ions are held tightly in a regular lattice (page 64). They cannot move. But when the sodium chloride is melted, the ions are freed from their lattice and they can move.

Picture 4 shows what happens. Opposite charges attract, and the positive ions are attracted to the negative electrode, the cathode. Because of this, positive ions are sometimes called **cations**. In the same way, the negative ions are attracted to the anode. They are sometimes called **anions**.

This explains how the ions get separated, but what happens when they reach the electrodes? The second part of picture 4 shows it.

At the cathode

Let's look at the sodium ions first. Na^+ ions are positively charged because they are short of one electron. The cathode, on the other hand, has an *excess* of electrons — that's where it gets its negative charge from. The electrons are pushed onto the cathode by the battery in the circuit.

When the Na^+ ions arrive at the cathode, they attract electrons from it. The electron cancels out the positive charge on the Na^+, leaving it as a neutral Na atom. The Na^+ has been **discharged**, and it forms molten sodium metal.

We can represent the happenings at the cathode like this:

$$\text{sodium ion} + \text{electron} \rightarrow \text{sodium atom}$$
$$Na^+(l) + e^- \rightarrow Na(l)$$

At the anode

Now let's see what happens to the Cl^- ions when they arrive at the anode. It's the opposite to the situation at the cathode. This time the Cl^- ions have one electron too many. The anode, on the other hand, has a *shortage* of electrons — that's why it's positively charged. The electrons have been pulled off the anode by the battery. The battery is a kind of electron pump, pulling electrons off the anode and pumping them round to the cathode.

When the Cl^- ions arrive at the anode, the anode attracts their electrons. The Cl^- ions lose their extra electron, leaving them as neutral Cl atoms. Like all Cl atoms, they prefer to go around in pairs, so they join up and form Cl_2 molecules. The Cl^- has been **discharged**, and it becomes chlorine gas.

We can represent these events at the anode like this:

$$\text{chloride ion} - \text{electron} \rightarrow \text{chlorine atom}$$
$$Cl^-(l) - e^- \rightarrow Cl(g)$$

Then:

$$2Cl(g) \rightarrow Cl_2(g)$$

Overall, it amounts to:

$$2Cl^-(l) - 2e^- \rightarrow Cl_2(g)$$

Another example

We can apply these ideas to the electrolysis of molten aluminium oxide. This is used in the manufacture of aluminium, described in the previous topic. Aluminium is formed at the cathode and oxygen at the anode.

Aluminium oxide contains Al^{3+} and O^{2-} ions. At the cathode, molten aluminium is formed.

$$Al^{3+}(l) + 3e^- \rightarrow Al(l)$$

Notice that *three* electrons are involved for each aluminium ion. That is because there are *three* positive charges on each ion.

At the anode, oxygen is given off.

$$O^{2-}(l) - 2e^- \rightarrow O(g)$$

Then:

$$2O(g) \rightarrow O_2(g)$$

This time *two* electrons are involved per oxygen ion, because of the two negative charges on the O^{2-} ion.

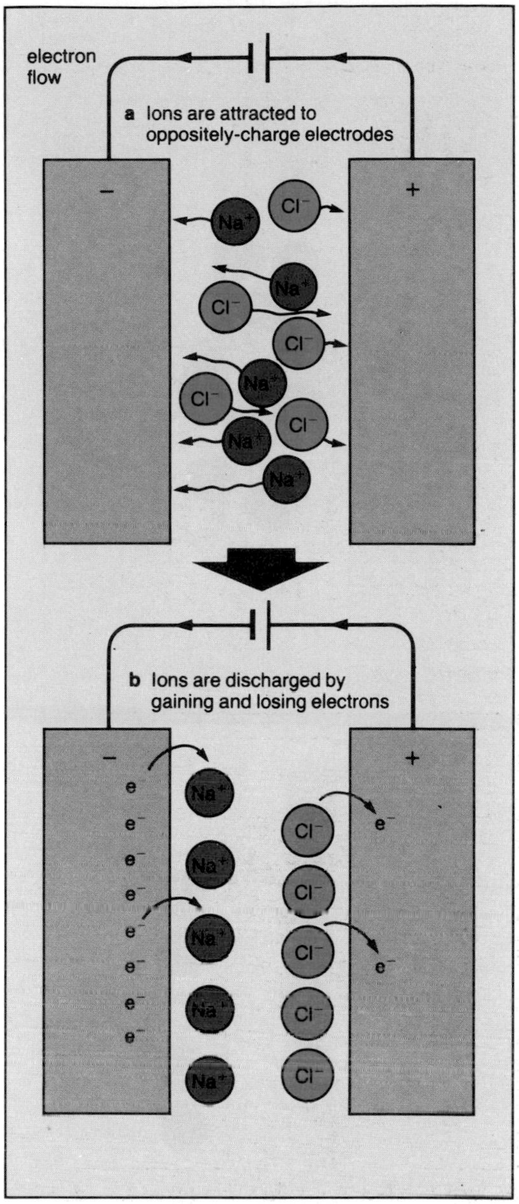

Picture 4 What happens when molten sodium chloride is electrolysed

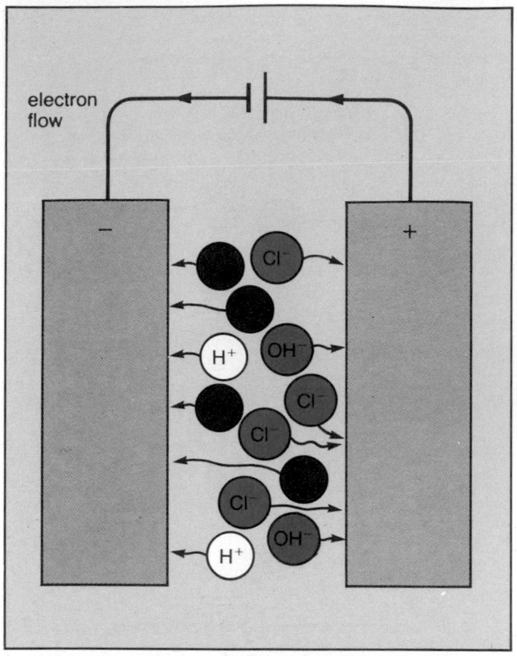

Picture 5 What happens when aqueous sodium chloride is electrolysed

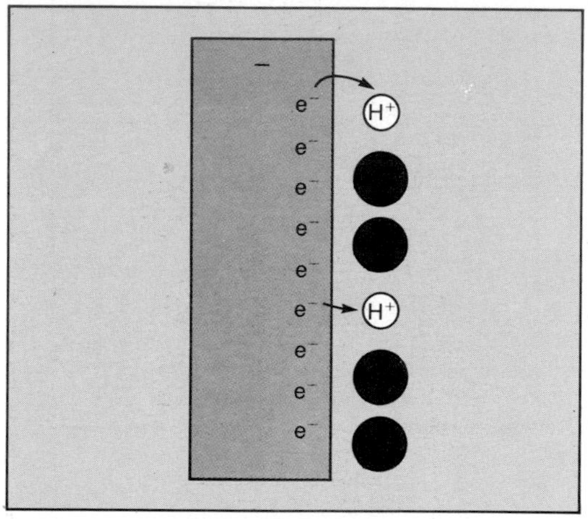

Picture 6 At the cathode H^+ ions are discharged and Na^+ ions stay in solution

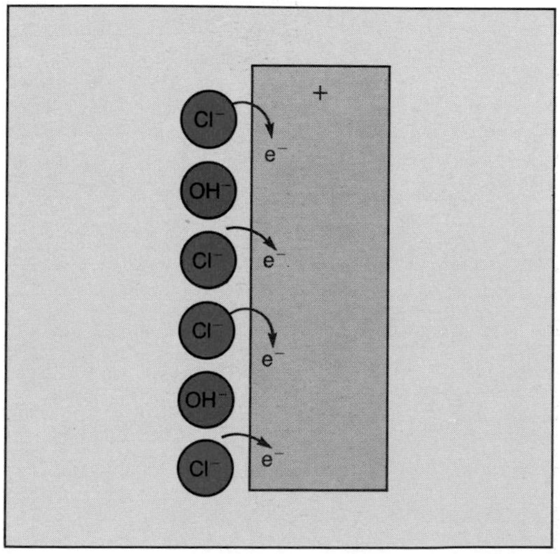

Picture 7 At the anode C1⁻ ions are discharged and 0H⁻ ions stay in solution

Electrolysis of aqueous solutions

You can try electrolysing some aqueous solutions in activity B. You will find that at the cathode you always get either a metal or hydrogen. At the anode you always get a non-metal. For example, in the electrolysis of sodium chloride solution, *hydrogen* is formed at the cathode, and chlorine at the anode. Left behind is a solution of sodium hydroxide.

Behind the scenes

Aqueous electrolytes are more complicated than molten ones, because we have to think about the water as well as the electrolyte itself. But we can use the same basic idea of ions being attracted to the electrodes and then getting discharged.

First, a word or two about water. One of the odd things about water is that, although it's a molecular substance, it does contain a few ions. A few water molecules split up to give hydrogen ions and hydroxide ions:

$$\text{water} \rightarrow \text{hydrogen ions} + \text{hydroxide ions}$$
$$H_2O(l) \rightarrow H^+(aq) + OH^-(aq)$$

Only about one water molecule in a billion does this, so there aren't enough ions to make water conduct electricity very well on its own. But we do have to bear these H^+ and OH^- ions in mind when it comes to the products of electrolysis.

A solution of sodium chloride contains four different ions: Na^+ and Cl^-, and H^+ and OH^- from the water. Picture 5 shows what happens. The positive ions, Na^+ and H^+, travel to the cathode, attracted by its negative charge. The Cl^- and OH^- ions travel to the anode. So we have two ions at each electrode. Pictures 6 and 7 show what happens next.

At the cathode

We have both Na^+ and H^+ ions at the cathode, but only one type of ion gets discharged. We know it's the hydrogen ion, because hydrogen is the product at the cathode. But why not the sodium? Well, sodium is a very reactive metal. Like all reactive metals it tends to stay in the combined form, as a compound, rather than become an element. Another way of saying this is that sodium 'prefers' to be an ion than an atom. So the less reactive hydrogen is discharged in preference to the sodium.

Hydrogen ions gain an electron from the cathode and become hydrogen atoms. The atoms pair up to form H_2 molecules. We can show all this as:

$$H^+(aq) + e^- \rightarrow H(g), \text{ then: } 2H(g) \rightarrow H_2(g).$$

The Na^+ ions are left behind in the solution.

At the anode

Two types of ion arrive at the anode: Cl^- and OH^- (picture 8). Only the Cl^- gets discharged. Overall, it amounts to:

$$2Cl^-(l) - 2e^- \rightarrow Cl_2(g).$$

The OH^- ions are left behind in solution.

So, to summarise, we have H^+ ions discharged as hydrogen gas at the cathode, and Cl^- ions discharged as chlorine gas at the anode. Left behind in solution are Na^+ and OH^- ions, in other words a solution of sodium hydroxide. All these products — hydrogen, chlorine and sodium hydroxide — are very useful, so this is a very important manufacturing process. There is more about this 'chlor-alkali' process in topic D5.

Another example: extracting zinc

One way of extracting zinc is by reducing zinc oxide with carbon. This method is described in topic E3. But zinc can also be extracted by electrolysis. The zinc oxide is first converted to zinc sulphate by dissolving it in sulphuric acid. Then the zinc sulphate is dissolved in water, and the aqueous solution is electrolysed. Zinc is formed at the cathode and oxygen comes off at the anode.

Let's look at what happens at the electrodes. The solution contains Zn^{2+} and SO_4^{2-} ions from the zinc sulphate, and also H^+ and OH^- ions from the water. At the cathode, Zn^{2+} and H^+ ions arrive. Unlike sodium, zinc is a fairly unreactive metal, so it is discharged in preference to hydrogen.

$$Zn^{2+}(aq) + 2e^- \rightarrow Zn(s)$$

At the anode, SO_4^{2-} and OH^- ions arrive. OH^- ions are discharged in prefence to SO_4^{2-}. When they are discharged, these OH^- ions form oxygen gas and water:

$$4\,OH^-(aq) - 4e^- \rightarrow 2\,H_2O(l) + O_2(g)$$

So oxygen bubbles off at the anode, leaving the H_2O behind.

The general rules

There are some general rules that you can use to predict the products of electrolysis of *any* aqueous solution.

1. Decide what metal and non-metal ions are in the electrolyte. Remember that it will also contain H^+ and OH^- from the water.
2. For the cathode product, decide how reactive the metal is. (Look at the reactivity series in the Data Section if you are not sure.) If the metal is in roughly the upper half of the series, then hydrogen will be the product at the cathode. If the metal is in the lower half, then the metal itself will be the product.
3. For the anode product, you can assume it will be oxygen unless the compound contains a halogen (chlorine, bromine or iodine).
4. Decide what ions are left behind in solution after the others have been discharged. There will be a positive ion and a negative one, and between them they make the product that is left behind.

Try using these rules to predict electrolysis products in question 4.

Explaining electroplating

We can explain electroplating using the idea of ions.

Usually in electrolysis the electrodes are made of an unreactive substance like carbon or platinum. They don't play any part in the reactions. In electroplating, though, the anode actually takes part.

Look at the electroplating cell in picture 7 on page 208 in the last topic. When the cell is switched on, silver ions (Ag^+) are attracted to the cathode, which is the object being plated. They gain electrons from the cathode and are discharged. This forms silver, which plates the cathode (picture 8).

$$Ag^+(aq) + e^- \rightarrow Ag(s)$$

Exactly the opposite happens at the anode. Silver atoms in the anode turn to silver ions. These go into solution and replace the Ag^+ ions that are being discharged at the cathode.

$$Ag(s) \rightarrow Ag^+(aq) + e^-$$

The electrolysis of water

On its own, water hardly conducts electricity at all, because it has so few ions in it. But a small amount of an ionic substance dissolved in the water makes it conduct, and then the water can be electrolysed. The products are hydrogen at the cathode and oxygen at the anode. You get two volumes of hydrogen for each volume of oxygen. For the scientists, like Humphry Davy, who first did the electrolysis of water this confirmed that the formula of water is H_2O.

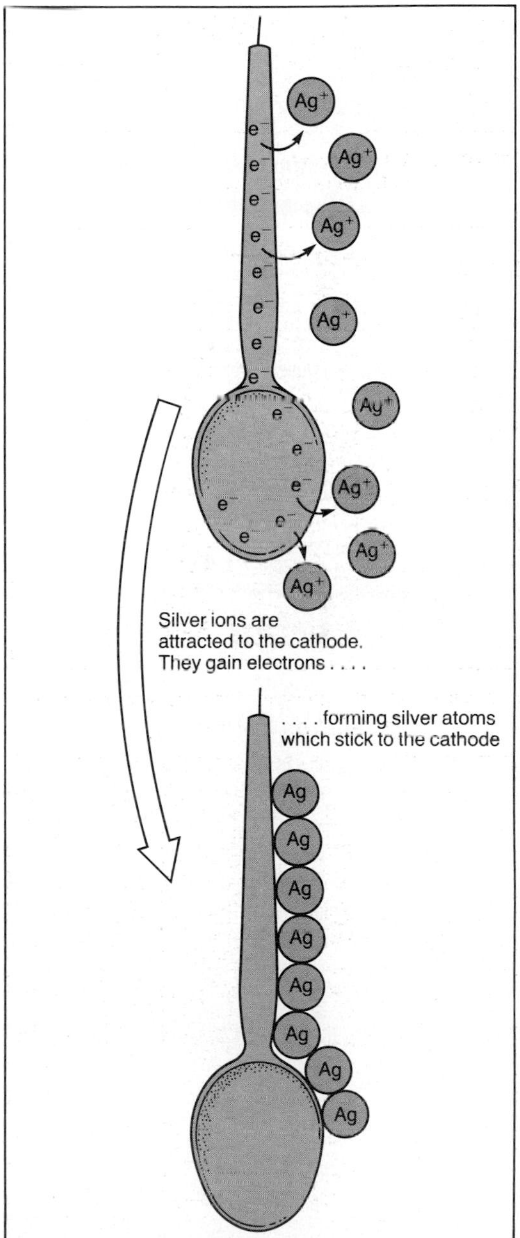

Ag+
e−
Silver ions are attracted to the cathode. They gain electrons . . . .
. . . . forming silver atoms which stick to the cathode
Ag

Picture 8 Explaining electroplating

Activities

A Electrolysing lead bromide

This experiment must be done in a fume cupboard because bromine is given off. It must be demonstrated by a teacher.

Use the apparatus shown in picture 2 (page 210). Include a bulb in the circuit so you can tell when current is flowing. Use a 6V d.c. supply.

1 Switch on the electrical supply while the lead bromide is still solid. Heat it so it melts and note what happens to the bulb. Once the lead bromide is melted you will only need to heat it gently.

2 Examine the electrodes carefully to see if a gas is given off at either of them. Note the appearance of any gas.

3 Continue the electrolysis for about 15 minutes, then stop heating and turn off the current. While the residue is still molten, carefully tip it out onto a metal tray. Look carefully to see if you can see a small bead of lead.

When you have finished, try to answer the following questions.

1 Explain what happened to the bulb in part 1.

2 What was formed at each electrode?

3 Write equations for the discharge of ions at each electrode. The formulas of the ions are Pb^{2+} (lead ion) and Br^- (bromide ion).

B Investigating the electrolysis of aqueous solutions

Use the electrolysis cell shown in picture 3 (page 210) to investigate the products formed when aqueous solutions are electrolyed. Use a 6V d.c. supply, and include a bulb in the circuit so you can see when current is flowing.

Here is the basic method.

CARE Eye protection must be worn.

1 Fill the apparatus with the solution you are going to test. Make sure the collecting tubes are full.

2 Fix the collecting tubes so they are raised a little off the bottom of the cell. This allows the ions to move freely between the electrodes.

3 Switch on the electricity supply and watch the electrodes carefully. Is a gas given off? Is anything formed around the electrode?

4 If a gas is given off, you will have to wait some time before enough has collected for you to test. When you have enough, remove the collecting tube and stopper it. Try to identify the gas. If it is from the cathode, it is likely to be hydrogen. See if it burns with a pop. If it came from the anode, it is likely to be oxygen or chlorine. Note its colour and see if it relights a glowing splint.

5 If the product is not a gas, look carefully at the electrode and see if you can identify the product by its appearance.

6 Finally, try to decide what is left behind in solution in the electrolysis cell. Test the solution with indicator paper.

Try testing the following solutions. You could share them around the class and pool your results at the end.

Sodium chloride, zinc sulphate, potassium iodide, copper bromide, copper sulphate, sulphuric acid.

For each solution, try to answer the following questions.

1 What was formed at the anode?

2 What was formed at the cathode?

3 What was left behind?

C Electrolysing sodium chloride solutions of different concentrations

Design an experiment to see what products you get when you electrolyse sodium chloride solutions of different concentrations. You should aim to start off with a solution containing about 50 g of NaCl per litre, then see what happens when you dilute it. You can use the same apparatus as for activity B.

Do not try the experiment until you have discussed your plan with your teacher.

Questions

1 When molten sodium chloride is electrolysed, sodium is formed at the cathode. But when aqueous sodium chloride is used, the cathode product is hydrogen. Why the difference?

2 Predict what would be formed: (i) at the anode, and (ii) at the cathode when each of the following molten substances are electrolysed using carbon electrodes.

a Magnesium bromide, $MgBr_2(l)$,
b Calcium chloride, $CaCl_2(l)$,
c Lithium oxide, $Li_2O(l)$,
d Sodium hydroxide, $NaOH(l)$.

3 Write equations for the discharge reactions at each electrode for the reactions in question 2. You will need to use the Data Section to find the charges on the ions concerned.

4 Predict what would be formed (i) at the anode and (ii) at the cathode when each of the following aqueous solutions are electrolysed using carbon electrodes.

a Sodium bromide solution, $NaBr(aq)$,
b Copper iodide solution, $CuI_2(aq)$,
c Zinc chloride solution, $ZnCl(aq)$,
d Silver nitrate solution, $AgNO_3(aq)$,
e Dilute hydrochloric acid, $HCl(aq)$.

5 Write equations for the discharge reactions at each electrode for the reactions in question 4. You will need to use the Data Section to find the charges on the ions concerned.

6 Look at the electroplating cell in picture 8 on page 208. What would happen if the anode was replaced by carbon instead of silver?

Hamilton Castner and electrolysis

Picture 1 Hamilton Young Castner, inventor of the mercury cell

Electrolysis made a fortune for Hamilton Castner, but it nearly lost him one too.

Hamilton Y Castner was born in New York, but came to Britain in 1886. He invented a method for making sodium metal from sodium hydroxide. The main use of the sodium was to extract another metal, aluminium, by heating aluminium chloride with sodium.

aluminium chloride + sodium →
aluminium + sodium chloride

A new company was set up in 1888 to run the process, with Hamilton Castner as managing director. But just as they opened their factory in Birmingham, disaster struck — in the shape of electrolysis.

Aluminium by electricity

At just that time, a new process was patented for making aluminium by electrolysis. It's basically the same method that we use today. It was such a success that the price of aluminium fell rapidly. Hamilton Castner's process for making aluminium was no longer economic. The new electrolytic process made aluminium much more cheaply.

Fortunately he was an adaptable sort of person. He gave up trying to make aluminium and concentrated on improving his process for making sodium.

A problem of purity

To make sodium, he needed very pure sodium hydroxide. The sodium hydroxide he used at first wasn't pure enough — so he decided to make his own. He knew he could make it by electrolysing sodium chloride solution, but the problem was that the chlorine and sodium hydroxide tended to mix. Hamilton Castner's great invention was an electrolysis cell with a flowing mercury cathode. This cell produced the sodium hydroxide well away from the anode, so it couldn't mix with chlorine.

Hamilton Castner's cell did more than make sodium hydroxide. It also produced chlorine and hydrogen. Eventually it turned out to be by far his most important invention. A company was set up in Runcorn to run the process. It is now part of ICI, and the chlor-alkali process still operates there. Today, though, mercury cells are being replaced by membrane cells for environmental reasons (see *A better way to electrolyse salt* below).

1 Write a balanced equation for the reaction of sodium with aluminium chloride, $AlCl_3$.

2 Why did the extraction of aluminium need sodium, and not another more abundant metal such as iron?

3 Why was the development of the electrolytic process for making aluminium a disaster for Hamilton Castner?

4 What was Hamilton Castner's original reason for developing the mercury cell?

A better way to electrolyse salt

The electrolysis of salt is a major industry, producing chlorine, sodium hydroxide and hydrogen. The right design of electrolysis cell is crucial. Two things are especially important for a successful cell design.

1 It must give pure products. If you've done the electrolysis of sodium chloride yourself, you'll know that it is difficult to stop the chlorine at the anode mixing with the sodium hydroxide that's formed around the cathode.

2 There must be as little damage to the environment as possible.

The mercury cell

The first commercial cells solved the purity problem by using a flowing mercury cathode. Mercury cells make very pure products, and they are still used today. But there are environmental problems because mercury is very toxic.

Chemical engineers have now developed safer methods for electrolysing salt. The latest is the membrane cell.

The membrane cell

The basic design of the membrane cell is shown in picture 1. It works continuously, with sodium chloride solution flowing in one side and sodium hydroxide flowing out of the other. Hydrogen comes off continuously from the cathode, and chlorine from the anode.

The key to the working of the cell is a cleverly-designed membrane between the anode and cathode compartments. It is an 'ion-selective' membrane which only lets Na^+ ions and water through. This means that sodium hydroxide solution forms *only* in the cathode compartment, so the products can't mix.

1 The mercury cell and the membrane cell both make very pure sodium hydroxide. Why are membrane cells now preferred to mercury cells?

2 Look at picture 1.

a What ions are present in the anode compartment? (Remember there are ions from the water as well as from the sodium chloride.)

b What ions are present in the cathode compartment? (Remember the effect of the membrane.)

c Which ion is discharged at the cathode?

d Explain why the sodium hydroxide flowing out of the cathode compartment is pure and uncontaminated with chlorine.

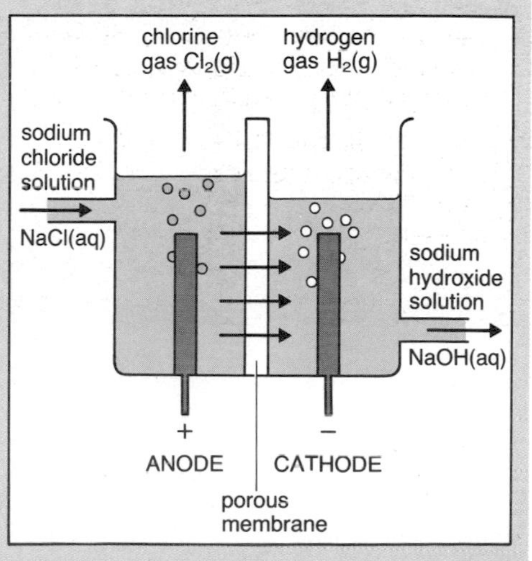

Picture 1

J3 Inside atoms

The word 'atom' means 'indivisible', but we know now that atoms can be split into smaller parts — a nucleus and electrons.

'Thou knowest no man can split the atom'.

So said John Dalton, the man who gave us the Atomic Theory, about 200 years ago. He would have been surprised 100 years later, when scientists began to break up atoms. First they chipped off little bits, like the electrons discovered by J J Thomson in 1897. Then in 1919 Ernest Rutherford split nitrogen atoms by firing alpha particles at them, and after that no atom was safe.

In 1932 the neutron was discovered, and it made a very handy 'bullet' for shooting at atoms to make them split. In 1939, two Germans, Otto Hahn and Fritz Strassmann, published a paper saying they had split uranium atoms by firing neutrons at them. By the end of the year over 100 more papers had been published about this **atomic fission**, as it was called. Then suddenly all publications ceased. The Second World War had started, and governments realised that splitting the atom was more than a scientific curiosity.

For more about nuclear fission and nuclear energy, and the way that ideas about the nucleus developed, see *The Physical World*, topic D7.

What's in an atom?

Over 70 sub-atomic particles have now been discovered. Fortunately, only three of them are really important in deciding how materials behave. They are protons, neutrons and electrons.

You can find out more about these particles in *The Physical World* topic 5. Table 1 just summarises the important properties that we need to know here.

Picture 4 represents the structure of the atom. The nucleus at the centre is made of protons and neutrons. It is tiny, but very dense. The electrons move around outside the nucleus. They move in a random and chaotic way, but to make the picture simpler we've shown them as if they travel in 'orbits' around the nucleus.

Protons and electrons are electrically charged. Yet atoms themselves do not have an overall electrical charge. This is because *the numbers of protons and electrons are equal*, so their charges cancel out. If we add an electron, the atom gets an overall negative charge: it becomes a negative ion, like Cl^-. If we take away an electron, the atom becomes a positive ion, like Na^+.

Picture 1 Ernest Rutherford and JJ Thomson, the men who started taking atoms apart

"I'M NOT SURE, SIR, BUT I *BELIEVE* I'VE SPLIT THE ATOM."

Picture 2 This cartoon appeared in Punch in 1939, when the idea of splitting atoms was quite a novelty

Table 1 The three most important sub-atomic particles

Particle	Charge (relative to a proton)	Mass (relative to a proton)	Where found
proton	+1	1	in the nucleus
neutron	0	1	in the nucleus
electron	−1	1/1840	moving around outside the nucleus

Numbering atoms

The numbers of protons, neutrons and electrons in an atom decide its properties. As far as chemists are concerned, the most important thing is the number of *electrons*. Because they are on the outside, the electrons decide how a particular atom behaves in a chemical reaction. In the next two topics we will look more closely at the way the electrons are arranged.

The number of electrons in an atom is equal to its number of protons, and this is called the **atomic number**, symbol **Z**. Each element has its own unique atomic number. For example, the simplest atom, hydrogen, has just one proton and one electron, so $Z = 1$. The largest naturally-occurring atom, uranium, has $Z = 92$: in other words, it has 92 protons and 92 electrons.

If you split an atom in two, you get two new atoms. They have different atomic numbers from the original atom, *so they are new elements*. For example, when a uranium atom splits, you get one fragment with 56 protons and another with 36. These are barium ($Z = 56$) and krypton ($Z = 36$).

If you look at a copy of the Periodic Table, you will see that the elements are arranged in order of increasing atomic number. You can read more about this in the next topic.

Picture 3 The blue glow from this underwater nuclear reactor is caused by the neutrons it is emitting. Neutrons make excellent 'bullets' for splitting the atom

But what about the neutrons?

Isotopes

Neutrons don't have any electrical charge, so they don't have to be balanced out by a particle with an opposite charge. This means you can add neutrons to an atom without altering its number of protons or electrons. So an element can have different 'versions' of its atoms. Each version has the same numbers of protons and electrons as all the other versions, but a different number of neutrons. These different versions, or **isotopes**, vary in mass, but they are all atoms of the same element.

Isotopes are atoms of a particular element with the same number of protons and electrons but different numbers of neutrons.

Let's look at an example — the simplest example of all, in fact. Picture 5 shows two isotopes of hydrogen. Both of them have one proton and one

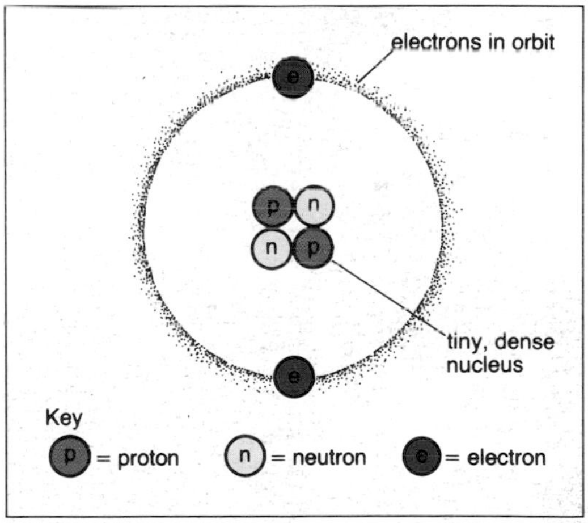

Picture 4 The structure of the atom. The atom shown here is helium

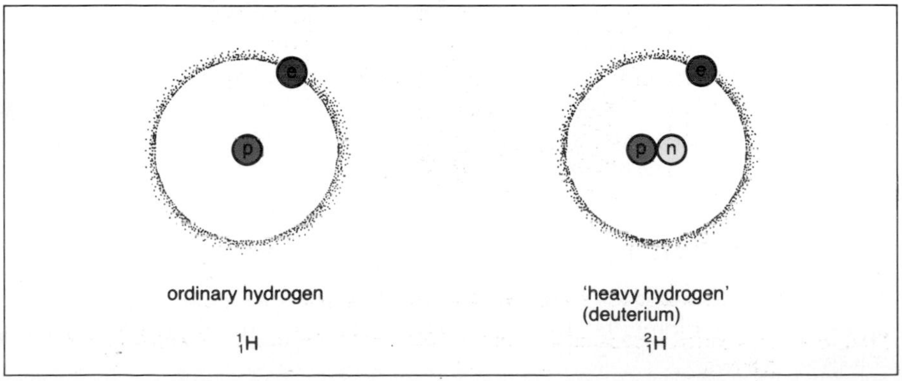

Picture 5 Two isotopes of hydrogen

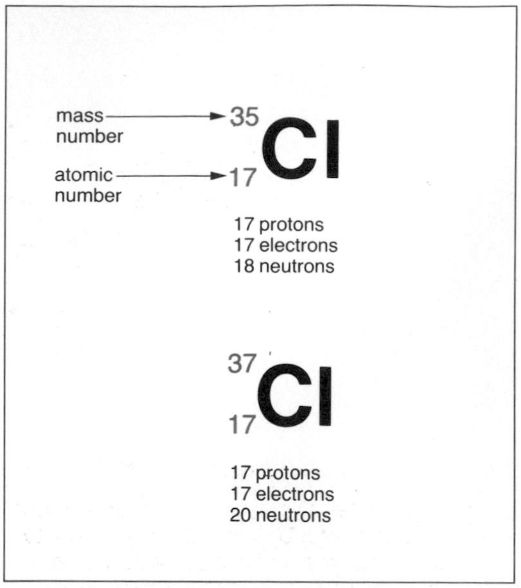

Picture 6 The atomic number and the mass number of chlorine isotopes

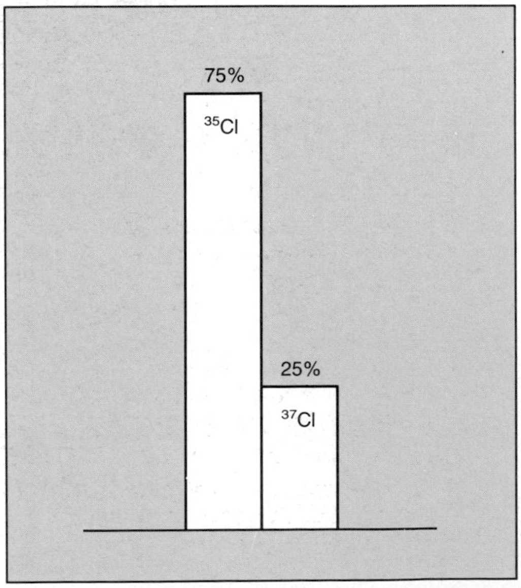

Picture 7 The abundance of two isotopes of chlorine

electron, so they both have the same chemical properties. But the second isotope has one neutron as well as the one proton in its nucleus. This makes the atom almost twice as heavy. In fact this isotope is sometimes called 'heavy hydrogen'. It is also known as deuterium.

Although it's heavier, deuterium has the same chemical properties as hydrogen. It reacts the same way, and it forms the same kind of compounds. For example, 'heavy water' contains deuterium in place of hydrogen. It has the same chemical properties as ordinary water, and you wouldn't notice the difference if you drank it. It's just a little denser.

Isotopes of an element have the same chemical properties. They differ in a few physical properties such as density.

Mass number

To make it easy to tell isotopes apart, each atom is given a **mass number**, as well as its atomic number.

The mass number (symbol *A*) is the number of neutrons plus the number of protons.

The protons and neutrons give the atom most of its mass, because electrons weigh very little. So the mass number tells you the relative mass of the atom.

The mass number of ordinary hydrogen atoms is 1, and the mass number of 'heavy hydrogen' is 2. Picture 6 illustrates this idea for another element. It also shows how the symbol of an element can be written with the atomic number and mass number included.

Table 2 sums up the difference between atomic number and mass number.

Table 2 Atomic number and mass number

Atomic number, Z	Mass number, A
• **Z** = number of protons = number of electrons • Fixed for a particular element	• **A** = number of protons + number of neutrons • Varies depending on which isotope of the element it is

If we know the atomic number and mass number of an atom, we can work out the number of protons, neutrons and electrons it must contain. For example, uranium has several isotopes. The isotope that is used in nuclear reactors is uranium-235, or $^{235}_{92}U$. Like all uranium atoms, it has an atomic number of 92, so it must have 92 protons and 92 electrons. It has a mass number of 235, which means its number of protons and neutrons together is 235. So its number of neutrons must be $(235 - 92) = 143$.

Isotopes everywhere

How do we know the mass number of atoms? They are much too small to weigh directly. Fortunately, a clever invention called the mass spectrometer makes it possible to find the mass of atoms indirectly.

The mass spectrometer shows that most elements have more than one isotope, and some have as many as 20. Not all of these isotopes are stable. Some are radioactive, and decay into other isotopes by giving out ionising radiations (see *The Physical World*, topic D5). Much of the early work on radioactive isotopes was done by Marie Curie and her daughter Irene: see *Marie Curie's search for radium,* page 227 for more about this.

Relative atomic mass

The relative atomic mass of an element is the mass of its atoms relative to atoms of other elements. Table 1 in the Data Section lists relative atomic masses.

But which atoms are we talking about? Most elements have more than one isotope, and different isotopes have different masses. Relative atomic mass is actually an *average* mass for all the different isotopes. It is adjusted (weighted) to take account of the proportions of the different isotopes. If a particular isotope is present in larger amounts, it makes a bigger contribution to the average.

For example, chlorine has two stable isotopes. In natural chlorine, 75% of the atoms have mass number 35, and 25% have mass number 37 (picture 7). In other words, for every 100 atoms, 75 have mass 35 and 25 have mass 37. The weighted average of these mass numbers is:

$$\frac{75 \times 35 + 25 \times 37}{100} = 35.5.$$

This is the relative atomic mass of chlorine.

Activity

Convincing John Dalton

Explaining an idea to another person is an excellent way of improving your own understanding, as well as theirs.

John Dalton, who produced the Atomic Theory, said 'Thou knowest no man can split the atom'. Imagine he were brought by time travel to the present. Could he be convinced he was wrong?

Work in pairs for this activity. One person will play John Dalton, the other will play themselves trying to persuade him. He would need some convincing, and would be likely to want some proof.

You will need to prepare your cases before you start. 'John Dalton' will find it useful to read *Ideas about atoms* on page 67. The other person will find it useful to read this topic and also topic D7 in *The Physical World*.

After the activity, discuss how it went. Was 'John Dalton' convinced?

Questions

1 Give the words that fit in the blanks in the following. The missing words are: negative, positive, nucleus, isotopes, equal, mass number, atomic number, electrons.

Atoms are made of three kinds of sub-atomic particles. Protons and neutrons are found in the small central part of the atom, called the _(a)_. Moving around outside are the _(b)_. Protons have one unit of _(c)_ charge, and electrons have an equal _(d)_ charge. In a neutral atom, the number of protons and electrons is _(e)_. This number is called the _(f)_. The number of protons added to the number of neutrons in an atom is called the _(g)_. Atoms with the same atomic number but different mass numbers are called _(h)_.

2 An atom of a particular element contains 13 protons, 14 neutrons and 13 electrons.

a What is its atomic number?

b What is its mass number?

c Name the element (you will need to look in the Data Section) and write its symbol, including atomic and mass numbers.

Table 3

Symbol	number of protons	number of neutrons	number of electrons	atomic number	mass number
$^{1}_{1}H$	1	0		1	
$^{2}_{1}H$		1		1	
$^{4}_{2}He$					
	6	6			12
$^{63}_{29}Cu$	29				
	29	36			
$^{56}_{26}Fe$					
		12	12		

3 Make a copy of table 3. Fill in all the blank spaces.

4 Which of the atoms in table 3 are isotopes of the same element?

5a All atoms of a particular element have the same atomic number. Explain why.

b Atoms of the same element can have different mass numbers. Explain why.

6a Bromine, Br, has two isotopes, with mass numbers 79 and 81. Naturally-occurring bromine contains the two isotopes in equal amounts. What is the relative atomic mass of bromine?

b Boron, B, has two stable isotopes, with mass numbers 10 and 11. Naturally-occurring boron contains 20% boron-10 and 80% boron-11. What is the relative atomic mass of boron?

7 Picture 5 shows two isotopes of hydrogen. There is a third isotope, called tritium, which is unstable and radioactive. Tritium atoms contain two neutrons.

a How many: (i) protons, and (ii) electrons do tritium atoms contain?

b What is: (i) the atomic number, and (ii) the mass number of tritium?

c What similarities and differences would you expect between tritium and ordinary hydrogen?

J4 Arranging electrons

The chemical properties of an atom are decided by the way its electrons are arranged.

Picture 2 Filling electron shells is like filling a rack. You fill the lowest shells first

Electrons in orbit

Niels Bohr was a Danish scientist. He was interested in the way electrons are arranged in atoms. In 1913 he suggested a model for the electronic structure of atoms which we still use today.

Neils Bohr suggested that electrons move around the nucleus in orbits, rather like the orbits of planets around the Sun. We know now that the orbits aren't as precise and predictable as that, but the model is still a good one. It helps explain many of the properties of atoms.

Picture 1 Niels Bohr (right) in conversation with Albert Einstein. Perhaps Bohr is explaining the electronic structure of atoms. Einstein certainly looks pleased

Filling up the shells

The electron orbits are called **shells** — and they work a bit like a series of shelves in a rack (picture 2). Each shell can only hold a limited number of electrons. The first shell is nearest to the nucleus, and it is the first to get filled up with electrons. When it's full, the second shell starts filling. This shell is a little further away from the nucleus, and the electrons in it have more energy. When this second shell is full, the third shell starts filling, and so on. Each shell is further away from the nucleus than theą previous one, and the electrons in it have more energy.

The first shell can hold just two electrons, and the second can hold eight. Let's see what happens with the three simplest elements, hydrogen (atomic number, $Z = 1$), helium ($Z = 2$) and lithium ($Z = 3$). Hydrogen has just one electron, and that goes into the first shell. Helium has two electrons, and they both go into the first shell, which is now filled. Lithium has three electrons. Two of these fill the first shell, then the third electron starts the second shell (picture 2).

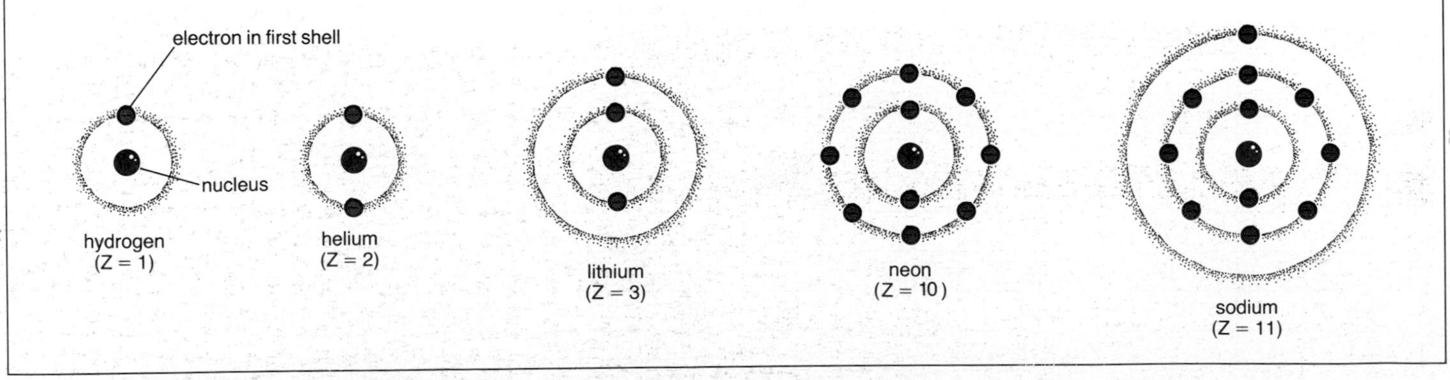

Picture 3 The arrangement of electrons in shells

Table 1 The electronic structures of the first 20 elements

Element	Atomic number, Z	First shell	Second shell	Third shell	Fourth shell	Summary of structure
hydrogen, H	1	•				1
helium, He	2	••				2
lithium, Li	3	••	•			2,1
beryllium, Be	4	••	••			2,2
boron, B	5	••	•••			2,3
carbon, C	6	••	••••			2,4
nitrogen, N	7	••	•••••			2,5
oxygen, O	8	••	••••••			2,6
fluorine, F	9	••	•••••••			2,7
neon, Ne	10	••	••••••••			2,8
sodium, Na	11	••	••••••••	•		2,8,1
magnesium, Mg	12	••	••••••••	••		2,8,2
aluminium, Al	13	••	••••••••	•••		2,8,3
silicon, Si	14	••	••••••••	••••		2,8,4
phosphorus, P	15	••	••••••••	•••••		2,8,5
sulphur, S	16	••	••••••••	••••••		2,8,6
chlorine, Cl	17	••	••••••••	•••••••		2,8,7
argon, Ar	18	••	••••••••	••••••••		2,8,8
potassium, K	19	••	••••••••	••••••••	•	2,8,8,1
calcium, Ca	20	••	••••••••	••••••••	••	2,8,8,2

And so it goes on. By the time you get to neon (Z = 10), the second shell has also been filled up. After the second shell, the third shell starts filling, so sodium (Z = 11) has one electron in the third shell. When this has eight in it the fourth shell begins. After that the numbers get a bit more complicated.

Table 1 shows the electronic structures of the first 20 elements. Notice that there is a short way of summarising the electronic structure by showing the numbers of electrons in each shell. Thus sodium's structure is shown as 2,8,1. This means there are 2 in the first shell, 8 in the second and 1 in the third.

How do we know?

Of course, we can't see directly how electrons are arranged. Niels Bohr had the idea of looking at the light that atoms give out, called **atomic spectra**. Picture 4 shows the atomic spectrum of hydrogen. You can see it consists of lines of light of different colours. Niels Bohr measured the frequencies of these lines, and used them to work out the energy levels of the electron shells. There is more about this in *The Physical World*, topic C8.

Electronic structure and the Periodic Table

If you look closely at the electronic structures in table 1, you will notice some interesting patterns. *Elements in the same group of the Periodic Table have the same number of electrons in their outer shell.* As far as chemical

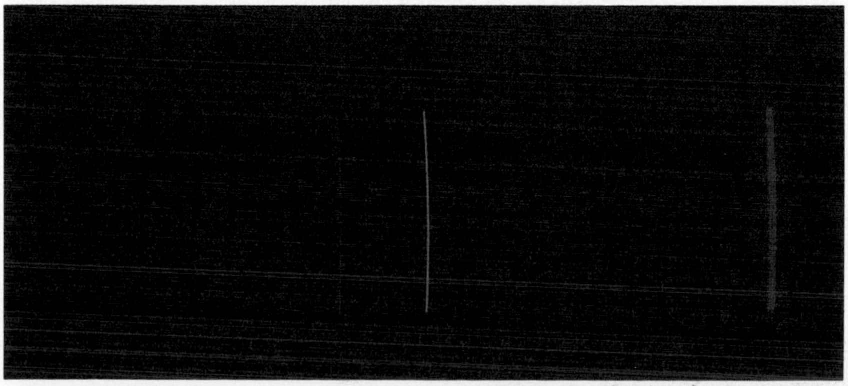

Picture 4 The visible spectrum of the hydrogen atom

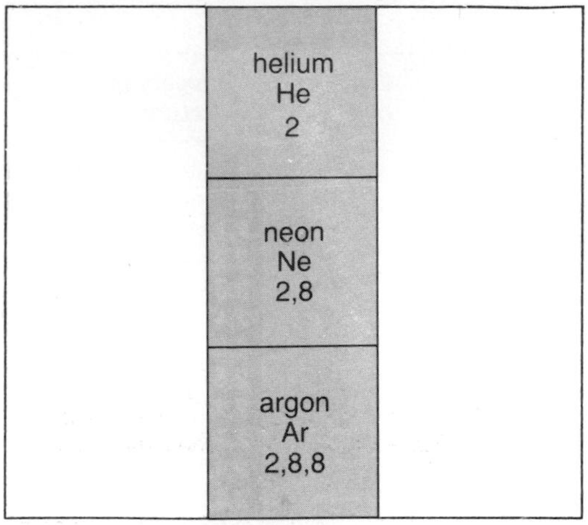

Picture 5 The first elements in Group O, showing their electronic structures

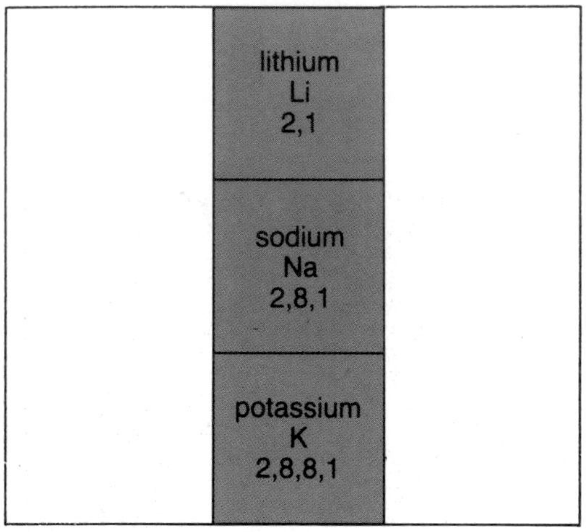

Picture 6 The first elements in Group 1

properties are concerned, the outer shell is the most important one. Chemical reactions involve changes to the numbers of outer shell electrons.

Let's look at some examples.

Group 0: The noble gases

There are three noble gases in table 1: helium, neon and argon. We've shown them and their electronic structures in picture 5. *They all have filled outer shells of electrons.* The other members of group 0 have this structure too. Now, noble gases are very stable and unreactive — that's why they are called noble. Scientists believe that their stability comes from having a filled outer shell.

The electronic structure of a noble gas is very stable.

In fact, other atoms try to get this stable arrangement of electrons when they take part in chemical reactions. More about this later.

Group 1: The alkali metals

There are three alkali metals in table 1: lithium, sodium and potassium. We've shown them in picture 6. Notice the similarity: *they all have just one electron in their outer shell* — as do the other members of this group. This single electron is quite easily removed from the atom, because it is the furthest away from the nucleus.

Removing the outer electron leaves the atom with a filled outer shell. It has a stable electronic structure like the noble gas neon. Alkali metals all tend to lose an electron very easily, which makes them very reactive. They give the electron to a non-metal such as a halogen (see below). Having lost the electron, the atom has become a positive ion. For example, sodium forms Na^+.

Group 7: the halogens

There are two halogens in table 1: fluorine and chlorine. Both have 7 electrons in their outer shell. This is the pattern for all members of group 7. They only need one more electron to get the stable electronic structure of a noble gas. So halogens all tend to gain an electron easily, which makes them reactive. They can gain the electron from a metal such as an alkali metal — which as we've seen tend to give them away rather easily. Having gained the extra electron, the halogen atom now has a negative charge: it has become an ion. For example, chlorine forms Cl^-

Why the periodic table works the way it does

When Dmitri Mendeléev made the first Periodic Table, he had no idea about electrons — they were not discovered until 1897. When he arranged the elements in groups, all he had to go on was relative atomic mass. The modern Periodic Table arranges elements in order of atomic number, but Mendeléev arranged them in order of mass. Fortunately this gives the right order, with one or two exceptions.

Now we know about the electronic structure of atoms, we can see how the Periodic Table works. *The pattern of the Periodic Table corresponds to the pattern of electron shells.* Each period corresponds to a particular electron shell. As you go across a period, the shell is being filled. At the start of each period there is an alkali metal with one electron in its outer shell. At the end there is a noble gas with a filled shell. Picture 7 illustrates the idea.

The elements in a particular group all have the same number of electrons in their outer shell. That's why they all have similar properties. They are not *identical*, though, because they have different numbers of electrons in their *inner* shells.

The number of the group tells you the number of outer shell electrons. For example, the elements in group 6 all have 6 electrons in their outer shell.

How do the elements change as you move across a period?

The elements in groups 1, 2 and 3 at the beginning of the period have a small number of outer shell electrons. They tend to lose these to form positive ions (e.g. Na^+, Mg^{2+}, Al^{3+}).

The elements in groups 4 and 5 in the middle of the period have outer shells that are half full. They don't tend to form ions; instead they *share* electrons and form covalent bonds. More about this in the next topic.

The elements in groups 6 and 7 near the end of the period have outer shells that are nearly full. They tend to gain electrons and form negative ions (e.g. S^{2-}, Cl^-).

The elements in group 0 at the end of the period have stable electronic structures. They do not form compounds at all.

Picture 7 Electronic structure and the Periodic Table. Only the first three periods are shown

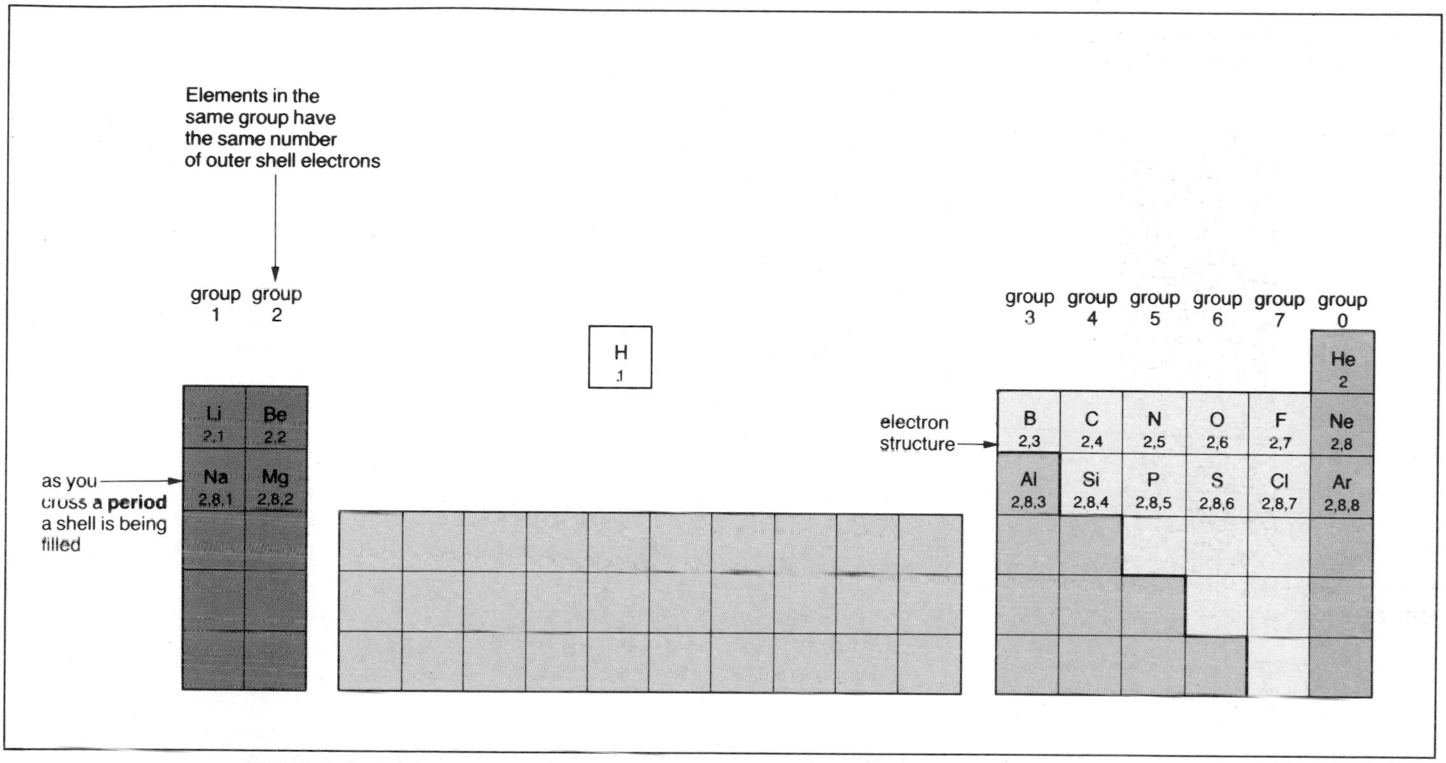

Questions

1 Explain what the following statements mean.

a 'The electrons in an atom are arranged in shells.'

b 'The electronic structure of a sodium atom is 2,8,1.'

2 Look at table 1 on page 221.

a Find the elements beryllium, magnesium and calcium in the table. Write down the electronic structure of each.

b What do the electronic structures of all three elements have in common?

c What group of the Periodic Table are they in?

d What kind of ion will they all form when they react?

3 Draw diagrams, similar to the ones in picture 3, to show the arrangement of electrons in the following atoms.

a carbon, C　b oxygen, O

c aluminium, Al　d chlorine, Cl

4 Look at the copy of the Periodic Table on page 126. How many electrons do each of the following elements have in their outer shell?

a Germanium, Ge　b Strontium, Sr

c Selenium, Se　d Iodine, I

e Caesium, Cs?

5 How many (i) protons and (ii) electrons are there in the following ions? Use table 1 to help you.

a Na^+　b Cl^-　c Mg^{2+}

d S^{2-}　e Al^{3+}　f O^{2-}

6a i) Write down the electronic structure of magnesium.

ii) Explain why magnesium forms ions with formula Mg^{2+}, not Mg^+ or Mg^-.

b i) Write down the electronic structure of chlorine.

ii) Explain why chlorine forms ions with formula Cl^-, not Cl^{2-} or Cl^+.

7 The noble gases form group 0 of the Periodic Table. What other number could this group be given? Why do you think 0 is used instead?

J5 Bonds and electrons

Forming chemical bonds involves rearranging electrons.

Picture 1 In this ball-and-stick model of a water molecule, the sticks represent bonds. But what are the bonds in a real molecule?

In a molecular model like the one in picture 1, the bonds between atoms are represented by 'sticks'. But what makes the bonds in a real molecule?

For a long time chemists wondered about the answer to this question. Electrolysis provided the clue. If electricity could be used to pull atoms apart, it seems likely that electricity is holding them together in the first place.

Electron shells and bonding

Today, we believe that bonds are formed by rearranging the outer shell electrons of atoms. In this topic we will look at a simplified version of what may happen.

When atoms form bonds, they try to get the stable electronic structure of a noble gas.

In practice, this usually means getting eight electrons in the outer shell.

There are two types of bond. **Ionic bonds** (sometimes called electrovalent bonds) involve ions, and are formed between metals and non-metals. **Covalent bonds** involve molecules, and are formed between non-metals.

Ionic bonding

Ionic bonding involves transferring electrons from a metal atom to a non-metal, producing positive and negative ions.

Picture 2 shows how ionic bonding happens in sodium chloride. Sodium has one electron in its outer shell, and chlorine has seven. Sodium gives its electron to chlorine. This leaves the sodium with eight electrons in its outer shell, the same electronic structure as the noble gas neon. The chlorine has eight electrons too, which gives it the electronic structure of the noble gas argon.

So both sodium and chlorine now have stable electronic structures. Having lost an electron, sodium has become a positive ion, Na^+. Having gained an electron, chlorine has become a negative ion, Cl^-. These oppositely-charged ions attract each other, and this electrical attraction is what makes an ionic bond. Many billions of ions together form a regular lattice. You can read more about ionic lattices on page 86.

The lower part of picture 2 shows all this in a simplified way, with only the outer shells drawn. This is called a 'dot-cross' diagram, because we show the electrons from different atoms as dots and crosses. Of course, all the electrons are really identical.

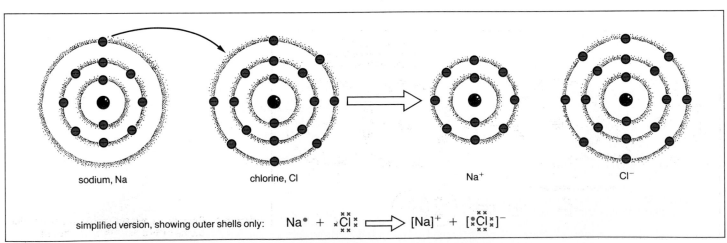

Picture 2 Forming an ionic bond between sodium and chlorine

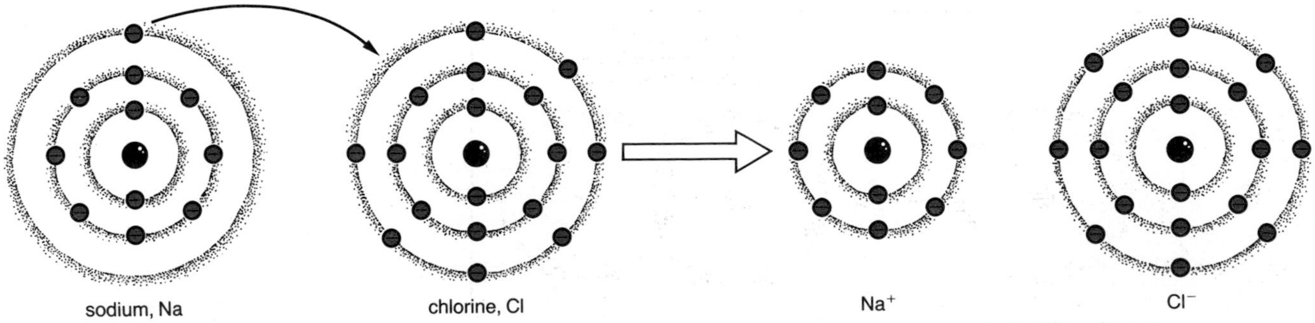

simplified version, showing outer shells only: Na• + Cl (with 7 ×) ⟹ $[Na]^+$ + $[Cl]^-$ (with 7 × and 1 •)

Calcium chloride:

$$Ca + Cl + Cl \longrightarrow [Ca]^{2+} + [Cl]^- + [Cl]^-$$

Magnesium oxide:

$$Mg + O \longrightarrow [Mg]^{2+} + [O]^{2-}$$

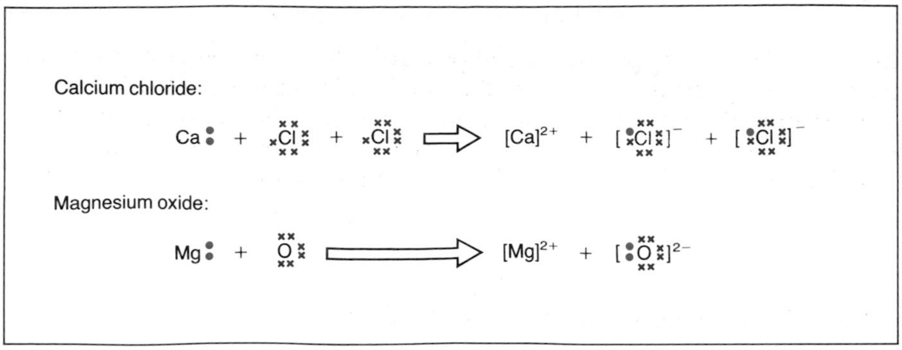

Picture 3 Two examples of ionic bonding

Picture 3 shows two more examples of ionic bonding. Notice these points.

- All the atoms form ions with eight electrons in the outer shell. This makes them stable like noble gases.
- The metals form positive ions, and the non-metals form negative ions.
- Calcium and magnesium have two electrons in their outer shell: two electrons to give away. In the case of calcium chloride, this means that two chlorines are needed. In magnesium oxide, only one oxygen is involved, because each oxygen needs two electrons to fill the outer shell. It gets both these electrons from the one magnesium atom.

Covalent bonding

Covalent bonding involves sharing pairs of electrons between non-metal atoms.

Non-metal atoms need only one or two electrons to get noble gas structures. When two non-metals form a bond, they can't transfer electrons from one to another, because *both* need to gain electrons. Instead, they *share* electrons.

Picture 4 shows how this works when chlorine atoms bond together to make a chlorine molecule, Cl_2. Each chlorine atom has seven electrons in its outer shell. Each shares one electron with the other atom. This way, both atoms get a stable outer shell of eight electrons.

The shared electrons attract the nuclei of both Cl atoms at the same time, and this is what bonds the atoms together. It's called a covalent bond. There are no ions: the atoms are bonded together as an uncharged molecule.

A covalent bond consists of a shared pair of electrons. Each of the atoms that are bonded together contribute one electron to the pair. When we show a 'stick' in a molecular model, it represents a covalent bond. When we draw a picture of a molecule, we use a line to show the bond.

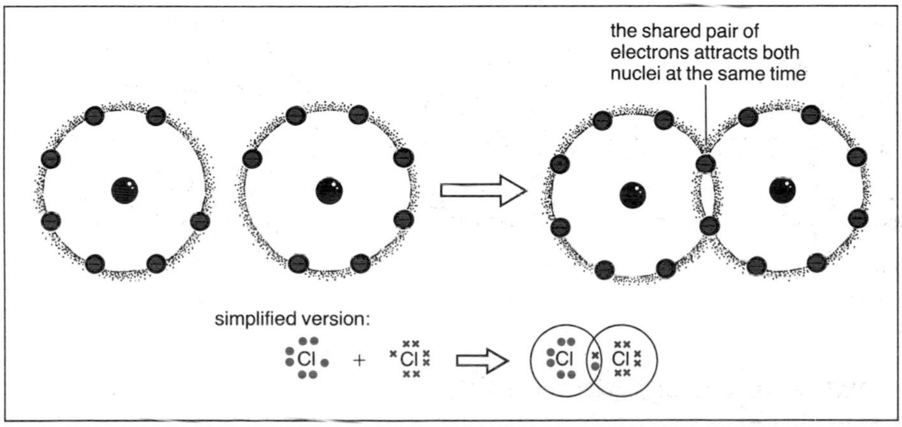

Picture 4 Forming a covalent bond between chlorine atoms (only outer shells are shown)

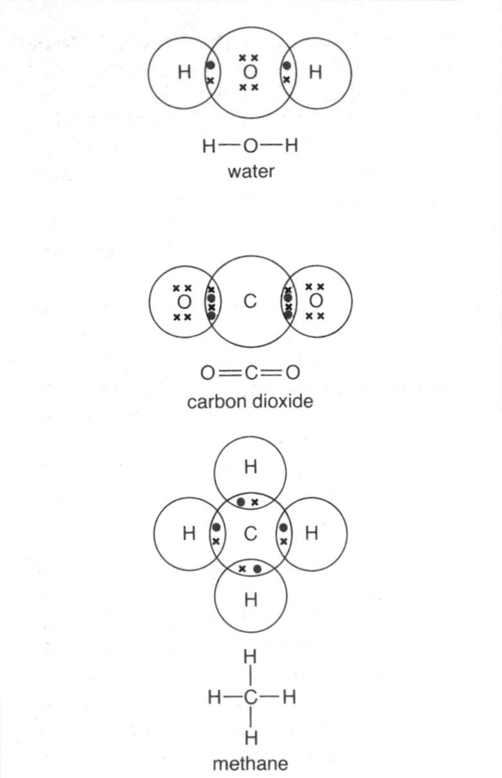

Picture 5 Examples of covalent bonding

Substances with covalent bonding form simple molecular or giant covalent structures. You can read more about these structures in topic C6.

Picture 5 shows covalent bonding in some familiar molecules. Once again all the atoms have stable arrangements of outer-shell electrons. Notice that in carbon dioxide, the carbon shares *two* pairs of electrons with each oxygen. In other words, it is a double bond.

Drawing dot-cross diagrams

These are the steps you need to follow when you draw a dot-cross diagram to show ionic or covalent bonds. You can practise using them in Questions 4 and 5.

1. Decide how many electrons are in the outer shells of each of the atoms involved. The easiest way to tell this is from their group number in the Periodic Table.
2. Decide whether ionic or covalent bonding is involved. If the bond is between a metal and a non-metal, it will be ionic. Between two non-metals, it will be covalent.
3. If it's an ionic bond, transfer electrons from the metal to the non-metal so they both get noble gas arrangements. This usually means eight electrons in the outer shell. Draw a diagram as in picture 3.
4. If it's a covalent bond, share pairs of electrons between the non-metal atoms so they both get noble gas arrangements. Draw a diagram as in picture 5.

A word of warning. Dot-cross diagrams work for many compounds, but by no means all of them. If you take your study of chemistry further — and I hope you will — you'll discover many exceptions.

Questions

1 'Sodium chloride is held together by strong ionic bonds'. What are the bonds, and why are they strong?

2 Look at picture 1. The atoms in the model are held together by 'sticks'. What holds the atoms together in a real water molecule?

3 Humphry Davy, who did the first work on electrolysis, said '*Chemical and electrical attractions are produced by the same cause*'. What did he mean? What name do we use today for 'chemical attractions'?

4 Look at the diagram for the bonding in a molecule of water in picture 5.

a Why are two H atoms needed for each O atom?

b What noble gas structure do (i) the H atoms, (ii) the O atoms have?

c Atoms usually end up with eight outer shell electrons when they form bonds. Why does the H atom only end up with two?

5 Draw dot-cross diagrams to show the bonding in each of the following ionic compounds.

a Potassium fluoride, KF,

b Lithium oxide, Li_2O,

c Magnesium sulphide, MgS,

d Sodium sulphide, Na_2S,

e Aluminium fluoride, AlF_3.

6 Draw dot-cross diagrams to show the bonding in each of the following covalent substances.

a Hydrogen chloride, HCl,

b Ammonia, NH_3,

c Carbon tetrachloride, CCl_4,

d Phosphorus trifluoride, PF_3,

e Nitrogen, N_2.

Ernest Rutherford's big surprise

'It was quite the most incredible event that has ever happened to me in my life. It was almost as incredible as if you fired a 15-inch shell at a piece of tissue and it came back and hit you.'

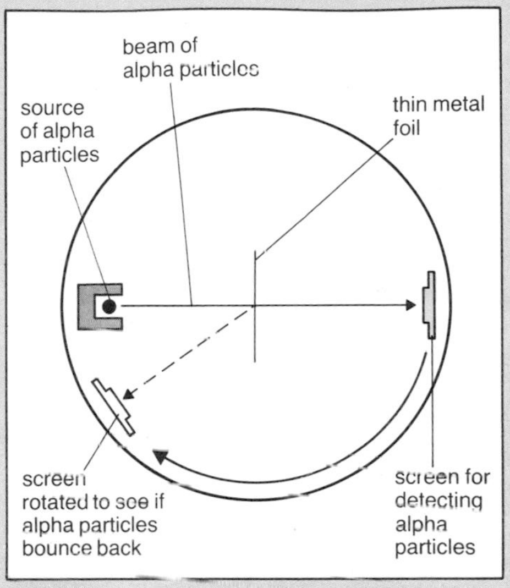

Picture 1 The alpha particle and foil experiment

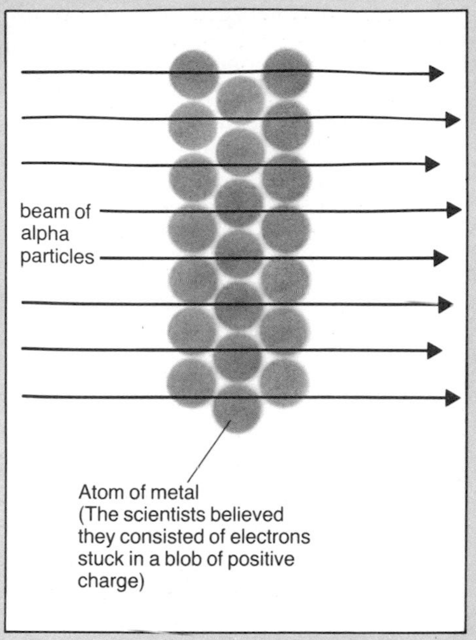

Picture 2 What they expected to happen. Alpha particles pass straight through the atoms

So said Ernest Rutherford in 1909. He had just heard the results of an experiment done by two of his colleagues at Manchester University. They had fired alpha particles at a thin metal foil, using the apparatus shown in picture 1. Alpha particles are tiny, positively charged particles (see *The Physical World*, page 119), and they were using them as minute bullets.

They had *expected* all the alpha particles to go straight through the very thin foil. Picture 2 shows why they expected this. At that time, scientists believed that atoms consisted of tiny electrons stuck into a kind of blob of positive charge. The electrons are too tiny to deflect the alpha particles, which should shoot straight through the blob-like atom.

Ernest Rutherford's big surprise was that some of the alpha particles bounced back from the foil! Most of them went straight through, but about 1 in 10 000 bounced back. They must have collided with something inside the atoms. Rutherford, and all the other scientists, had to rethink their ideas about the structure of atoms.

1. Why did most of the alpha particles go straight through the foil, but some of them bounce back? You may need to look at picture 4 on page 217 to remind yourself of our modern idea of the structure of the atom.
2. Draw a picture, similar to picture 2 on this page, to explain what happened.

Marie Curie's search for radium

Marie Curie's interest was aroused when Henri Becquerel discovered radioactivity in uranium. She studied an ore of uranium called pitchblende, and she noticed something very interesting. *It was more radioactive than uranium itself.* She decided that there was only one explanation: there must be something in the pitchblende that was *more radioactive than uranium.*

So, with her husband Pierre, she set about looking for this highly radioactive substance. It was like searching for a needle in a haystack, and it took four years. They began work in 1898, when the Austrian government donated a tonne of pitchblende. They worked in a dilapidated shack with a leaking roof, patiently purifying the pitchblende to isolate the mystery substance. In 1902 the work was complete. All that was left of the tonne of pitchblende was a fraction of a gramme of a highly radioactive element which they named **radium**.

Marie Curie continued her work with radioactive elements, and was awarded two Nobel prizes. Her old shack was demolished, and a palatial laboratory, the Radium Institute, was built in Paris for her to work in. Her daughter Irene continued the work, and discovered many new radioactive isotopes. She too received the Nobel prize.

1. What made Marie Curie start searching for radium in pitchblende?
2. Why did it take so long to get pure radium from pitchblende?
3. Find radium, Ra, on the Periodic Table on page 126. Which other element do you think it would be most similar to?
4. During the First World War, Marie Curie developed mobile radiography units to help treat the wounded. What is radiography, and what has it to do with Marie Curie's scientific work?

Picture 1 Marie Curie and her daughter Irene in 1925

Data section

Contents

Table 1 The elements

In this table, we have left out elements 58 to 71, which are very rare. We have given structures only for the most important elements.

Atomic number	Element	Symbol of element	Relative atomic mass	Melting point/ °C	Boiling point/ °C	Type of structure	Date of discovery
1	hydrogen	H	1	−259	−253	simple molecular (H_2)	1766
2	helium	He	4	−270	−269	simple molecular (He)	1868/1895
3	lithium	Li	7	181	1331	giant metallic	1818
4	beryllium	Be	9	1283	2487	giant metallic	1798
5	boron	B	11	2027	3927		1808
6	carbon	C	12				
	-diamond			3550	4827	giant covalent	ancient
	-graphite			3650 (sublimes)		giant covalent	ancient
7	nitrogen	N	14	−210	−196	simple molecular (N_2)	1772
8	oxygen	O	16	−219	−183	simple molecular (O_2)	1774
9	fluorine	F	19	−220	−188	simple molecular(F_2)	1887
10	neon	Ne	20	−248	−246	simple molecular (Ne)	1898
11	sodium	Na	23	98	890	giant metallic	1807
12	magnesium	Mg	24	650	1117	giant metallic	1808
13	aluminium	Al	27	659	2447	giant metallic	1827
14	silicon	Si	28	1410	2677	giant covalent	1824
15	phosphorus (white)	P	31	44	281	simple molecular (P_4)	1669
16	sulphur (monoclinic)	S	32	119	445	simple molecular (S_8)	ancient
17	chlorine	Cl	35.5	−101	−34	simple molecular (Cl_2)	1774
18	argon	Ar	40	−189	−186	simple molecular (Ar)	1894
19	potassium	K	39	63	766	giant metallic	1807
20	calcium	Ca	40	850	1492	giant metallic	1808
21	scandium	Sc	45	1400	2477	giant metallic	1879
22	titanium	Ti	48	1677	3277	giant metallic	1825
23	vanadium	V	51	1917	3377	giant metallic	1830
24	chromium	Cr	52	1903	2642	giant metallic	1797
25	manganese	Mn	55	1244	2041	giant metallic	1774
26	iron	Fe	56	1539	2887	giant metallic	ancient
27	cobalt	Co	59	1495	2877	giant metallic	1735
28	nickel	Ni	59	1455	2837	giant metallic	1751
29	copper	Cu	64	1083	2582	giant metallic	ancient
30	zinc	Zn	65	419	908	giant metallic	1746
31	gallium	Ga	70	30	2237		1875

Atomic number	Element	Symbol of element	Relative atomic mass	Melting point/ °C	Boiling point/ °C	Type of structure	Date of discovery
32	germanium	Ge	73	937	2827		1886
33	arsenic	As	75	613			1250
34	selenium	Se	79	217	685		1817
35	bromine	Br	80	−7	58	simple molecular (Br_2)	1826
36	krypton	Kr	84	−157	−153	simple molecular (K)	1898
37	rubidium	Rb	86	39	686	giant metallic	1861
38	strontium	Sr	88	769	1384	giant metallic	1808
39	yttrium	Y	89	1522	3338	giant metallic	1843
40	zirconium	Zr	91	1852	4377	giant metallic	1824
41	niobium	Nb	93	2467	4742	giant metallic	1802
42	molybdenum	Mo	96	2610	5560	giant metallic	1778
43	technetium	Tc	99	2172	4877	giant metallic	1937
44	ruthenium	Ru	101	2310	3900	giant metallic	1844
45	rhodium	Rh	103	1966	3727	giant metallic	1803
46	palladium	Pd	106	1554	2970	giant metallic	1803
47	silver	Ag	108	962	2212	giant metallic	ancient
48	cadmium	Cd	112	321	765	giant metallic	1817
49	indium	In	115	156	2080	giant metallic	1863
50	tin	Sn	119	232	2260	giant metallic	ancient
51	antimony	Sb	122	631	1750		ancient
52	tellurium	Te	128	450	990		1783
53	iodine	I	127	114	184	simple molecular (I_2)	1811
54	xenon	Xe	131	−112	-107	simple molecular (Xe)	1898
55	caesium	Cs	133	29	669		1860
56	barium	Ba	137	725	1640		1808
57	lanthanum	La	139	921	3457		1839
72	hafnium	Hf	179	2227	4602		1923
73	tantalum	Ta	181	2996	5427		1802
74	tungsten	W	184	3410	5660		1783
75	rhenium	Re	186	3180	5627		1925
76	osmium	Os	190	2700	>5297		1803
77	iridium	Ir	192	2410	4130		1803
78	platinum	Pt	195	1772	3827		1735
79	gold	Au	197	1064	3080		ancient
80	mercury	Hg	201	−39	357		ancient
81	thallium	Tl	204	304	1457		1861
82	lead	Pb	207	328	1740		ancient
83	bismuth	Bi	209	271	1560		1753
84	polonium	Po	210	254	962		1898
85	astatine	At	210	302	337		1940
86	radon	Rn	222	−71	−62		1900
87	francium	Fr	223	27	677		1939
88	radium	Ra	226	700	<1137		1898
89	actinium	Ac	227	1050	3200		1899
90	thorium	Th	232	1750	4787		1828
91	protoactinium	Pa	231	<1597	4027		1917
92	uranium	U	238	1132	3818		1841

Table 2 The reactivity series of metals

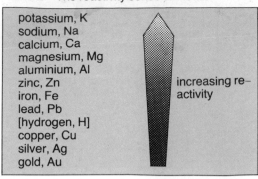

potassium, K
sodium, Na
calcium, Ca
magnesium, Mg
aluminium, Al
zinc, Zn
iron, Fe
lead, Pb
[hydrogen, H]
copper, Cu
silver, Ag
gold, Au

increasing re-activity

Table 3 The alkanes

Name	Formula	Melting point/°C	Boiling point/°C
methane	CH_4	−182	−161
ethane	C_2H_6	−183	−88
propane	C_3H_8	−188	−42
butane	C_4H_{10}	−138	−1
pentane	C_5H_{12}	−130	36
hexane	C_6H_{14}	−95	69
heptane	C_7H_{16}	−91	99
octane	C_8H_{18}	−57	126
nonane	C_9H_{20}	−51	151
decane	$C_{10}H_{22}$	−30	174
dodecane	$C_{12}H_{26}$	−10	216
eicosane	$C_{20}H_{42}$	37	344

Table 4 Charges on some ions

Positive ions (cations) Usually metals		**Negative ions (anions) Usually non-metals**	
ammonium	NH_4^+	bromide	Br^-
hydrogen	H^+	chloride	Cl^-
copper (I)	Cu^+	iodide	I^-
potassium	K^+	hydroxide	OH^-
sodium	Na^+	nitrate	NO_3^-
silver	Ag^+	carbonate	CO_3^{2-}
calcium	Ca^{2+}	oxide	O^{2-}
magnesium	Mg^{2+}	sulphate	SO_4^{2-}
copper (II)	Cu^{2+}	sulphite	SO_3^{2-}
iron (II)	Fe^{2+}	sulphide	S^{2-}
zinc	Zn^{2+}	phosphate	PO_4^{3-}
aluminium	Al^{3+}		
iron (III)	Fe^{3+}		

Table 5 The formulas of some inorganic compounds

This table shows the formulas of some of the compounds you are likely to meet quite frequently in your study of chemistry. It gives the proper chemical names, and also other names that are sometimes used.

Name	Other name	Formula
aluminium oxide	alumina	Al_2O_3
ammonia		NH_3
ammonium chloride		NH_4Cl
ammonium nitrate	'NITRAM'	NH_4NO_3
calcium carbonate	limestone, chalk	$CaCO_3$
calcium chloride		$CaCl_2$
calcium hydroxide	slaked lime	$Ca(OH)_2$
calcium oxide	quicklime	CaO
carbon monoxide		CO
carbon dioxide		CO_2
cobalt (II) chloride	cobalt chloride	$CoCl_2$
copper (II) chloride	copper chloride	$CuCl_2$
copper (II) oxide	copper oxide	CuO
copper (II) sulphate	copper sulphate	$CuSO_4$
hydrogen chloride		$HCl(g)$
hydrochloric acid		$HCl(aq)$
hydrogen fluoride		$HF(g)$
hydrogen peroxide		H_2O_2
hydrogen sulphide		H_2S
iron (II) chloride		$FeCl_2$
iron (III) chloride		$FeCl_3$
magnesium carbonate		$MgCO_3$
magnesium chloride		$MgCl_2$
magnesium oxide	magnesia	MgO
manganese (IV) oxide	manganese dioxide	MnO_2
nitric acid		HNO_3
nitrogen monoxide		NO
nitrogen dioxide		NO_2
potassium chloride		KCl
potassium hydroxide	caustic potash	KOH
potassium manganate (VII)	potassium permanganate	$KMnO_4$
potassium nitrate	saltpetre	KNO_3
silicon (IV) oxide	silicon dioxide, silica	SiO_2
sodium carbonate	soda ash, washing soda	Na_2CO_3
sodium chloride	salt	$NaCl$
sodium hydrogencarbonate	sodium bicarbonate	$NaHCO_3$
sodium hydroxide	caustic soda	$NaOH$
sodium nitrate		$NaNO_3$
sodium sulphate		Na_2SO_4
sulphur dioxide		SO_2
sulphur trioxide		SO_3
sulphuric acid		H_2SO_4
zinc oxide		ZnO
water		H_2O

Index

[Page numbers followed by 'a' refer to activities; those followed by 'c' refer to information given in case studies.]

Acknowledgements

AFRC: 20.7
Allsport: 11.5/Dave Cannon, 26.1
J Allan Cash: 3.5, 32.1, 33.4b, 93.8, 150.2, 167.6, 190.4
Heather Angel: 99.1
Associated Press: 186.4
Atomic Energy Research Establishment, Harwell: 216.1
Didier Barrault: 150.1
Bridgeman Art Library: 56.1 118.1
British Coal: 197.4
British Gas: 68.1
British Geological Survey: 121.6
British Museum: 16.1
BOC: 27.4
British Steel: 35.2
Brunswick Organic Nursery, York: 105.2/Sue Reeves
CEGB: 114.7
Cheshire Fire Brigade 155.4
Courtaulds: 168.8
Bruce Coleman Ltd: 120.5/M P Kahl
Desoto Titanine: 33.4a
Ecoscene: 90.1/Sally Morgan, 100.1/Sally Morgan
ESB, Eire: 181.5
Greg Evans: 112.1
Friends Of The Earth: 46.7
GSF Picture Library: 15.7/W Higgs, 91.2, 91.3, 91.4, 91.5, 91.6, 94.1, 95.3, 99.2, 121.7, 144.6
Dr L F Haber: 105.1
Robert Harding Picture Library: 161.5, 173.3, 180.1
Heikiparthenon: 10.4
ICI: 95.5, 103.9, 203.1, 210.1
The Image Bank: 137.2
The Hulton-Deuttsh Collection: 136.1
Kittery: 27.4
London Fire Brigade: 148.1
Manchester City Council: 184.1
NHPA: 138.1/Anthony Bannister
OPIE: 5.5, 42.6, 50.1
Photo Co-op: 132.1/Gina Glover
Punch: 216.2
Rhone Poulenc: 139.4
Chris Ridgers: 2.1, 2.2, 2.3, 4.1, 5.4, 6.6, 7.7, 12.1, 12.2, 18.1, 19.3, 20.6, 22.1, 24.8a, 24.8b, 29.4, 36.3, 40.1, 44.1, 47.8, 48.3, 51.3, 52.7, 53.9, 54.11, 57.6, 62.4, 69.3, 70.1, 72.4, 72.5, 76.2, 84.6, 85.8, 85.9, 93.11, 93.12, 94.2, 109.5, 109.6, 110.7, 113.6, 115.10, 122.11, 126.1, 130.2, 131.3, 132.2, 138.2, 139.3, 142.1, 150.4, 150.5, 152.6, 154.1, 154.2, 159.1, 163.10, 166.1, 172.1, 174.9, 176.2, 188.1, 190.6, 194.1, 196.1, 196.2, 199.8, 200.10, 204.1
Ann Ronan Picture Library: 71.3, 128.1, 137.1
Royal Holloway and Bedford College, London University, 81.1/Dr Martin Moore
Science Photo Library: 20.8, 17.2/J-L Charmet, 22.3/Biophoto Associates, 45.5/Michael Marten, 46.6/Sam Pierson, 53.8/Andrew Mcclenaghan, 61.4, 78.6/Roberto De Gugliemo, 79.8/Sinclair Stammers, 82.1/Roberto De Gugliemo, 86.13/John Walsh, 176.1/Vaughan Fleming, 191.7/NASA, 193.2, 198.7/David Guyon BOC, 217.3/US Dept of Energy, 221.4/Dept of Physics Imperial College
Scottish Power: 147.1
Shell Photographic Library: 155.6, 157.9
Shuttleworth Collection: 9.2, 109.4
Sporting Pictures: 8.1
SNV: 95.4
Thames Water: 3.4, 36.1, 38.6
Thomas Photos: 198.5
Peter Thorne Photography Ltd: 199.9
Roger Tidman: 40.3
John Topham Picture Library: 81.2
Tony Stone: 28.1, 44.2/Francois Puyplat, 62.1, 122.9/Janet Gill
John Urling Clark: 35.3, 45.4, 61.3, 67.1, 67.2, 68.2, 74.8, 76.1, 77.3a, 77.3b, 82.2a, 82.2b, 93.9, 93.10, 99.3, 108.1, 108.3, 135.8, 139.5, 146.1, 165.1, 170.12, 170.13, 171.15, 178.5, 206.1, 206.2, 207.4, 208.8, 220.1, 227.1
Bob Watkins: 42.7, 79.7
Ray Williams: 112.3
University of Leicester: 134.6/Prof J Holloway
Drawing 186.5: Courtesy of Third World Science Project, University College of North Wales
Cover photographs supplied by Image Bank and Science Photo Library.